Digest of United States Practice in International Law

Cumulative Index

1989–2008

Digest of United States Practice in International Law

Cumulative Index

1989–2008

Elizabeth R. Wilcox
Editor

Office of the Legal Adviser
United States Department of State

OXFORD
UNIVERSITY PRESS

INTERNATIONAL LAW INSTITUTE

The *Digest of United States Practice in International Law* is co-published by Oxford University Press and the International Law Institute under agreement with the United States Department of State, Office of the Legal Adviser. The contents of the *Digest*, including selection of documents and preparation of editorial commentary, are entirely under the auspices of the Office of the Legal Adviser.

INTERNATIONAL LAW INSTITUTE
For fifty-five years the International Law Institute has addressed issues of interest to the international legal community through research, publishing, training, and technical assistance. For information on the activities of the Institute:

Publishing Office
International Law Institute
The Foundry Building
1055 Thomas Jefferson St., NW
Washington, DC 20007

202-247-6006
202-247-6010 (fax)
e-mail: pub@ili.org
Internet: www.ili.org

If you would like to be placed on Standing Order status for the *Digest of United States Practice in International Law*, whereby you will automatically receive and be billed for new annual volumes as they publish, please contact a Customer Service Representative.

In the United States, Canada, Mexico, Central and South America, contact:

Customer Service
Oxford University Press USA
2001 Evans Road
Cary, NC 27513
Email: custserv.us@oup.com
Phone (toll free in US): 1-866-445-8685
Phone (international customers): 1-919-677-0977
Fax: 1-919-677-1303

In the United Kingdom, Europe, and Rest of World, contact:

Customer Service
Oxford University Press
Saxon Way West, Corby
Northants, NN18 9ES
United Kingdom
Email: bookorders.uk@oup.com
Phone: +44 1536 741017
Fax: +44 1536 454518

ISBN: 978-0-19-973856-4 (2008, Hardback)

Table of Contents

Table of Cases (1989–2008)

** An asterisk denotes cases in courts and fora, including the International Court of Justice, other than U.S. Federal and state courts. Alphabetization is letter-by-letter (e.g., "Yang" precedes "Yan Long Xiong"). The bold years indicate the volume and are followed by page numbers in that volume (e.g.,* **2004:** *472, 476–78 refers to the volume for the year 2004 and pages 472 and 476 through 478 in that volume).*

A

A., In re (1988), **1991-99:** 369
Aaran Money Wire Serv.; Inc. v. United States (2002), **2002:** 101
Aaran Money Wire Serv.; Inc. v. United States (2003), **2003:** 180
AAR Int'l, Inc. v. Nimelias Enters. S.A. (2001), **2002:** 860, 861
Abankwah v. INS (1999), **1991-99:** 211–15
ABC Info. Inc. v. Loyd (2001), **2001:** 536–37
Abdah v. Bush (2005), **2005:** 1017
Abdulaziz v. Metropolitan Dade County (1984), **1991-99:** 1239, 1251, 1287–88, 1291; **2002:** 553, 561; **2006:** 654, 659
Abdullahi v. Pfizer, Inc. (2002), **2002:** 345–46; **2004:** 357
Abdullahi v. Pfizer, Inc. (2003), **2003:** 386–87
Abebe-Jira v. Negewo (1996), **1991-99:** 979, 1264
Abiola v. Abubakar (2003), **2003:** 559, 560, 563, 569–70
Abiola v. Abubakar (2006), **2006:** 482
Abourezk v. New York Airlines, Inc. (1990), **2006:** 586
Abourezk v. Reagan (1986), **2006:** 25; **2007:** 21
Abrahim-Youri v. United States (1996), **1991-99:** 1097–98
Abrams v. Société Nationale des Chemins de Fer Francais (2001), **2003:** 521
Abrams v. Société Nationale des Chemins de Fer Francais (2003), **2003:** 520–22

Abrams v. Société Nationale des Chemins de Fer Francais (2004), **2004:** 472, 476–78; **2006:** 78, 85
Abrams v. United States (1919), **2007:** 310–11
Abu Ali v. Ashcroft (2004), **2006:** 1211, 1212*n*
Abu Ali v. Gonzales (2004), **2005:** 582; **2006:** 1198*n,* 1207
Abur v. Republic of Sudan (2006), **2007:** 3
*Access to Info. under Article 9 of the OSPAR Convention (Ireland v. U.K.) (2003), **2003:** 620–21
Achenbach v. United States (2003), **2003:** 475–76
Ackermann v. Levine (1986), **2005:** 850–52, 856
Acosta, Matter of (1985), **1991-99:** 201–2, 209–10; **2000:** 130
Acree v. Republic of Iraq (2003), **2003:** 543–47, 556–57
Acree v. Republic of Iraq (2004), **2004:** 489–93, 507–8; **2008:** 465, 466, 467, 468, 469
Acree v. Republic of Iraq (2005), **2005:** 507, 509, 544
Acree v. Snow (2003), **2003:** 557
Adams v. Baker (1989), **1989-90:** 22, 23–26
Adams v. Commissioner of Internal Revenue (1999), **2003:** 185
Adams v. Howerton (1981), **2004:** 9
Adams v. Vance (1977), **1989-90:** 251–53, 258, 262
Adams v. Vance (1978), **2000:** 496, 552; **2002:** 590
Adams Fruit Co. v. Barrett (1990), **2001:** 82
Adarand Constructors, Inc. v. Mineta (2001), **2001:** 257
Adarand Constructors, Inc. v. Pena (1995), **2005:** 289; **2007:** 299
Ademaj; United States v. (1999), **1991-99:** 260; **2000:** 42
*ADF Group, Inc. v. United States (2003), **2001:** 611–23; **2002:** 641–61; **2003:** 607–10, 624–25*n,* 629; **2004:** 582*n;* **2006:** 700
Adler v. Federal Republic of Nigeria (1997), **2001:** 404; **2006:** 575
Adras v. Nelson (1990), **2000:** 132
Advanced Micro Devices v. Intel Corp. (2002), **2002:** 875–76; **2003:** 873
*Aegean Sea Continental Shelf Case (1978), **1991-99:** 685–86
*Aerial Incident at Lockerbie (Libyan Arab Jahahiriya v. United Kingdom) (Libyan Arab Jahahiriya v. United States) (1992), **2001:** 98; **2003:** 160, 166
*Aerial Incident of 3 July 1988 (Iran v. United States) (1996), **1991-99:** 1092
Aerolineas Argentinas, In the Matter of (2004), **2004:** 568–71
Af-Cap, Inc. v. Chevron (2007), **2007:** 485, 489–94
Af-Cap, Inc. v. Republic of Congo (2004), **2005:** 558
Af-Cap, Inc. v. Republic of Congo (2006), **2006:** 562, 563, 603–11
AFL-CIO v. Kahn (1979), **2000:** 327*n*
Afroyim v. Rusk (1967), **1991-99:** 21; **2000:** 19; **2003:** 9; **2008:** 2
Afshari; United States v. (2005), **2005:** 116–23

Afshari; United States v. (2006), **2006:** 180
Agee v. Baker (1990), **1989-90:** 15, 16
Agee v. Bush (1996), **2005:** 512
"Agent Orange" Prod. Liab. Litig., In re (2005), **2005:** 491–97; **2008:** 429
"Agent Orange" Prod. Liab. Litig., In re (2006), **2006:** 522–26
Agostini v. De Antueno (1950), **1991-99:** 1301
Aguinda v. Texaco, Inc. (1997), **2001:** 486*n*
Aguinda v. Texaco, Inc. (2000), **2000:** 412–14
Aguinda v. Texaco, Inc. (2001), **2001:** 336–37
Aguinda v. Texaco, Inc. (2002), **2002:** 355–57; **2004:** 877
Aguirre-Aguirre; INS v. (1999), **1991-99:** 232–39, 799; **2005:** 144; **2007:** 7
*Ahani v. Canada (2002), **2002:** 267*n*
Ahmad v. Wigen (1989), **1989-90:** 82, 86, 88
Ahmad v. Wigen (1990), **1991-99:** 950; **2001:** 77, 82; **2005:** 80–81; **2008:** 69
Ahmed v. Bush (2005), **2005:** 1017
Ahmed v. Hoque (2002), **2002:** 552–67
Ahmed v. Morton (1996), **2008:** 66
Ahrens v. Clark (1948), **2004:** 999
Aidi v. Yaron (1987), **2001:** 533; **2002:** 551*n*, 563
Air Canada v. U.S. Dep't of Transp. (1988), **2000:** 491*n*; **2006:** 661
Air Courier Conference of Am. v. American Postal Workers' Union (1991), **2000:** 315
Air Crash at Agana, Guam, In re (1997), **2000:** 152–60
Air Crash Disaster Near Roselawn, Ind. on Oct. 31, 1994, In re (1996), **2001:** 494; **2004:** 864–65
Aircrash in Bali, Indonesia, In re (1982), **2000:** 529*n*, 537*n*
Air Crash Off Long Island, N.Y., on July 17, 1996, In re (1999), **2008:** 517
Air Disaster at Lockerbie, Scotland on Dec. 21, 1988, In re (1991), **1991-99:** 1329; **2000:** 597
Air Force, Department of v. Rose (1976), **2002:** 234
Air France v. Saks (1985), **1991-99:** 1346–48, 1350, 1353; **2000:** 529*n*, 537*n*; **2003:** 591–95; **2004:** 60, 200, 564–65
*Air Servs. Agreement of Mar. 27, 1946 Between the United States and France (United States v. France) (1978), **1991-99:** 1110–11, 1113, 1114; **2001:** 369–71
*Akayesu; Prosecutor v. (1998), **2002:** 350
*Akayesu; Prosecutor v. (2000), **2000:** 252–53
Akins v. United States (1977), **2008:** 173
*Akkoc v. Turkey (2000), **2004:** 312*n*
*Aktas v. Turkey (2003), **2004:** 312*n*

Aktepe v. United States (1997), **2001:** 446, 453; **2006:** 525
Alabama v. Shelton (2002), **2005:** 281–82
Alabama and Miss. Boundary Case (1985), **2005:** 699
*Al-Adsani v. The United Kingdom (2001), **2002:** 474
Alahmad; United States v. (1998), **1991-99:** 380
Alameda v. Secretary of Health, Ed. and Welfare (1980), **2003:** 506
Al-Anazi v. Bush (2005), **2005:** 1018; **2007:** 954
Alaska v. United States (2005), **2002:** 738–56; **2005:** 696–705
Alaska (Arctic Coast); United States v. (1997), **2005:** 697–99
Alaska (Cook Inlet); United States v. (1975), **2005:** 699
Alaska Fish & Wildlife Fed'n & Outdoor Council, Inc. v. Dunkle (1987), **1991-99:** 1775
Alberti v. Empresa Nicaraquense De La Carne (1983), **2000:** 593
Alcozer v. State (1999), **1991-99:** 263
Aldana v. Del Monte Fresh Produce, N.A., Inc. (2003), **2007:** 414
Aldana v. Del Monte Fresh Produce, N.A., Inc. (2005), **2007:** 177
Aldrich v. Mitsui & Co. (1988), **2000:** 510, 523, 538; **2001:** 452; **2002:** 437*n;* **2005:** 480
Aldunate, In re (1997), **2003:** 878
Alejandre v. Cuba, Republic of (1997), **1991-99:** 1224, 1228
Alejandre v. Cuba, Republic of (1999), **1991-99:** 1229
Alejandre v. Florida (1997), **2000:** 542
Alejandre v. Telefonica Larga Distancia de Puerto Rico, Inc. (1999), **1991-99:** 1228–34; **2001:** 493
*Aleksovski; Prosecutor v. (2000), **2002:** 350
Alesayi Beverage Corp. v. Canada Dry Corp. (1996), **2001:** 43*n*
Alexander v. Pan Am. World Airways, Inc. (1985), **2001:** 564
Alexander v. Sandoval (2001), **2002:** 223; **2003:** 263, 361; **2004:** 347; **2005:** 62, 1037
Alexis Holyweek Sarei v. Rio Tinto plc (2002), **2001:** 337–39
Alfadda v. Fenn (1998), **2005:** 842
Al Fassi v. King Fahd Bin Abdulaziz (2003), **2003:** 571–72
*Alfonso Martín Del Campo Dodd Case (2004), **2004:** 224
Alfred Dunhill of London, Inc. v. Republic of Cuba (1976), **1991-99:** 647*n,* 1136, 1183–84, 1202, 1203; **2000:** 475, 477, 527; **2002:** 466, 504–5, 509, 510; **2003:** 504; **2004:** 459, 668; **2005:** 501, 582; **2006:** 549, 596, 632; **2007:** 450, 459, 500, 743–44; **2008:** 455
Al-Hamdi; United States v. (2003), **2003:** 573–74
Al-Hamdi; United States v. (2004), **2004:** 533–39; **2006:** 654, 657
Al-Haramain Islamic Found., Inc. v. Bush (2007), **2007:** 246–53
Ali v. Ashcroft (2003), **2004:** 20
Alicog v. Kingdom of Saudi Arabia (1994), **1991-99:** 1289–90; **2001:** 513
Alien Children Educ. Litig., In re (1980), **2001:** 291

Alkhuzai v. Ali Hasan Al-Majid Al-Tikriti (2004), **2004:** 558–59
Allen-Bradley Local No. 1111 v. Wisconsin Employment Relations Bd. (1942), **2000:** 334; **2001:** 194*n,* 196*n;* **2002:** 443
Allendale Mut. Ins. Co. v. Bull Data Sys., Inc. (1993), **2002:** 866*n*
Allende v. Shultz (1985), **1989-90:** 21–22
Alliance of Descendants of Tex. Land Grants v. United States (1994), **2002:** 511
Allied Bank Int'l v. Banco Credito Agricola de Cartago (1985), **2005:** 581
Allied-Bruce Terminix Cos. v. Dobson (1995), **1991-99:** 1848
Allied Local & Reg'l Mfrs. Caucus v. EPA (2000), **2006:** 868
Allstate Ins. Co. v. Hague (1981), **2002:** 454, 456
Al-Marri v. Bush (2005), **2007:** 955
Al-Marri v. Pucciarelli (2007), **2008:** 917
Al-Marri v. Pucciarelli (2008), **2008:** 917–18
Al-Marri v. Rumsfeld (2003), **2003:** 1029–30
Al-Marri v. Spagone (2009), **2008:** 918*n*
Al-Marri v. Wright (2007), **2007:** 968–75
Almendarez-Torres v. United States (1998), **2006:** 869
Al Najjar v. Ashcroft (2001), **2006:** 50
Al Odah v. Bush (2007), **2007:** 955
Al Odah v. United States (2002), **2002:** 980–86
Al Odah v. United States (2003), **2003:** 357, 362, 366, 369, 384–85, 1028
Al Odah v. United States (2004), **2004:** 979, 981, 995, 1000, 1029–35; **2005:** 996, 999, 1006
Alonso v. Saudi Arabian Airlines Corp. (1999), **2000:** 585
Al-Owhali v. Ashcroft (2003), **2004:** 1033
Alperin v. Vatican Bank (2005), **2005:** 420, 421*n,* 481–82; **2006:** 434; **2007:** 122
ALS Scan, Inc. v. Digital Serv. Consultants, Inc. (2002), **2003:** 902–4
Altadis USA, Inc. v. Sea Star Line (2006), **2006:** 919
Altmann v. Austria (2001), **2001:** 457–58; **2002:** 514
Altmann v. Austria (2002), **2002:** 507–9; **2003:** 515–20, 523; **2004:** 494, 496–97
Altmann v. Austria (2004), **2004:** 494–95
Aluminum Co. of Am.; United States v. (1945), **1991-99:** 1531
Alvarado-Torres; United States v. (1999), **1991-99:** 261
Alvarez-Machain v. Sosa (2001), **2000:** 398–412
Alvarez-Machain v. United States (1992), **2000:** 399, 401*n,* 403, 404, 411; **2002:** 77–78
Alvarez-Machain v. United States (1996), **2002:** 335
Alvarez-Machain v. United States (1997), **1991-99:** 1264

Alvarez-Machain v. United States (2001), **2001:** 326–34; **2002:** 346; **2003:** 357, 362–64, 366, 381
Alvarez-Machain v. United States (2002), **2002:** 346; **2003:** 381
Alvarez-Machain v. United States (2003), **2003:** 380–83
Alvarez-Machain; United States v. (1992), **1991-99:** 435–45; **2001:** 326, 420; **2004:** 341, 536; **2005:** 50*n;* **2008:** 156
Alvarez-Machain; United States v. (1993), **2004:** 341, 536
Alvarez-Machain; United States v. (2003), **2003:** 381, 383; **2004:** 341
*Alves v. Hodgson (1797), **2005:** 239
Amanullah v. Nelson (1987), **1989-90:** 24
Amax Coal Co.; NLRB v. (1981), **1991-99:** 1202
*Ambatielos case (1953), **2000:** 657
A-M-E- & J-G-U-, Matter of (2007), **2008:** 306
*Amekrane v. United Kingdom (1987), **2000:** 406*n*
Amer; United States v. (1997), **1991-99:** 380; **2002:** 59
American Acad. of Religion v. Chertoff (2006), **2006:** 19–29; **2007:** 23
American Acad. of Religion v. Chertoff (2007), **2007:** 19–26
American-Arab Anti-Discrimination Comm. v. Reno (1995), **2006:** 190
American-Arab Anti-Discrimination Comm.; Reno v. (1999), **2004:** 16
American Banana Co. v. United Fruit Co. (1909), **1991-99:** 1531
American Baptist Churches v. Thornburgh (1991), **1989-90:** 40–41; **1991-99:** 250
American Bell Int'l Inc. v. Iran (1979), **1989-90:** 216
American Civil Liberties Union v. Department of Def. (2005), **2005:** 1020; **2006:** 1213–18
American Civil Liberties Union; Reno v. (1997), **2007:** 303
American Coalition for Competitive Trade v. Clinton (1997), **2006:** 727, 728
American Dredging Co. v. Miller (1994), **2006:** 965; **2007:** 797–98
*American Indep. Oil Co. (AMINOIL) v. Kuwait (1982), **2003:** 627*n*
American Ins. Ass'n v. Garamendi (2003), **1991-99:** 1133; **2003:** 462–68, 473–74, 497, 500, 541; **2004:** 371, 438, 441–45, 471, 510, 512; **2005:** 38, 42–45, 47, 59, 405, 421–22, 473, 478, 480, 532, 534–35; **2006:** 454, 520, 732; **2007:** 203, 204, 235, 236; **2008:** 192, 417, 418, 419, 421–23, 779
American Ins. Ass'n v. Low (2002), **2002:** 415–29
American Ins. Co. v. 356 Bales of Cotton (1828), **2003:** 367
American Inst. in Taiwan v. United States ex rel. Wood (2002), **2002:** 245–46, 538
American Int'l Group, Inc. v. Iran (1981), **2006:** 1015; **2008:** 449
American Isuzu Motors, Inc. v. Lungisile Ntsebeza (2008), **2008:** 236–38
American Pelagic Fishing Co. v. United States (2004), **2004:** 724–30
American Road Serv. Co. v. Consolidated Rail (2003), **2006:** 919

Americans United for Separation of Church and State v. Reagan (1986), **2003:** 494; **2004:** 454
America W. Airlines, Inc. v. GPA Group, Ltd. (1989), **1991-99:** 1205–6
The Amiable Isabella (1821), **2000:** 492*n;* **2001:** 559; **2006:** 66
Amlon Metals, Inc. v. FMC Corp. (1991), **1991-99:** 990; **2002:** 335, 336
Amstar Corp. v. S/S Alexandros T. (1981), **2006:** 830
Amtsgericht Ingolstadt, In re (1996), **2003:** 881
Anderman v. Austria (2001), **2001:** 396
Anderson v. Creighton (1987), **2000:** 410
Anderson v. Evans (2004), **2007:** 723
Anderson v. Watt (1891), **2002:** 489
Andonian; United States v. (1994), **2007:** 120–21
Andrade v. Gonzales (2006), **2006:** 48
Ange v. Bush (1990), **2001:** 453
*Anglo-Iranian Oil Co. (U.K. v. Iran), **2003:** 624*n;* **2008:** 214
Anonymous v. Anonymous (1992), **2001:** 514
Antares Aircraft, L.P. v. Federal Republic of Nigeria (1993), **2007:** 468
The Antelope (1825), **2005:** 236
Antolok v. United States (1989), **2001:** 386, 446, 455; **2007:** 439
Aoun v. Baker (1990), **1989-90:** 243, 246, 251, 252, 258, 264
The Apollon (1824), **2004:** 366; **2005:** 402; **2006:** 469
Appeal of. *See name of party*
Application of. *See name of applicant*
Apprendi v. New Jersey (2000), **2005:** 278
Aptheker v. Secretary of State (1964), **2001:** 11*n,* 116; **2002:** 14
Aquamar, S.A. v. Del Monte Fresh Produce N.A., Inc. (1999), **2003:** 376, 377; **2005:** 527, 531; **2006:** 607, 611
Aquinda v. Texaco, Inc. (1996), **1991-99:** 990
Arabian Am. Oil Co.; EEOC v. (1991), **1991-99:** 167, 1535; **2000:** 465; **2001:** 328*n;* **2002:** 422; **2003:** 370; **2004:** 366, 512, 999; **2005:** 402; **2006:** 439–40, 455, 469; **2008:** 126
Arango v. Guzman Travel Advisors Corp. (1980), **1991-99:** 1213; **2001:** 445
Arar v. Ashcroft (2004), **2004:** 23
Arar v. Ashcroft (2006), **2006:** 484
Arbelo; United States v. (2002), **2002:** 8
Arcaya v. Paez (1956), **2002:** 553, 560; **2006:** 632
ARC Ecology v. U.S. Dep't of the Air Force (2005), **2006:** 858; **2007:** 689
Arce Gonzalez v. Gutierrez (2002), **2002:** 54–56
*Archer Daniels Midland Co. & Tate & Lyle Ingredients Ams., Inc. v. United Mexican States (2004), **2005:** 600*n*
Ardestani v. INS (1991), **2000:** 193, 196

Argentina v. Amerada Hess Shipping Corp. (1989), **1989-90:** 281, 283–85, 312–14; **1991-99:** 167, 180, 1183, 1196, 1210, 1261, 1280; **2000:** 475, 478, 479, 579, 591; **2001:** 429, 434, 435, 442, 477, 480*n,* 502; **2002:** 218, 222, 465, 467, 469, 473, 578; **2003:** 261, 503, 524; **2004:** 458, 469, 479, 499; **2005:** 49, 406*n,* 501; **2006:** 549, 639*n,* 646; **2007:** 450; **2008:** 157, 455
Argentina v. New York City (1969), **2004:** 545; **2006:** 596; **2007:** 459
Argentina v. Weltover, Inc. (1992), **1991-99:** 1184, 1213, 1220, 1243; **2000:** 555, 579, 580; **2001:** 402, 430, 444, 496, 497; **2002:** 466, 487–88, 502, 521–22; **2003:** 504; **2004:** 459, 486; **2006:** 595, 625; **2007:** 459, 467–68, 489*n,* 499–500, 502
Argersinger v. Hamlin (1972), **2005:** 281
*Argoud, Re (1964), **2000:** 404
Arizona v. Bowsher (1991), **2000:** 547; **2001:** 492
Arizona v. California (1934), **2004:** 200
Arizona; United States v. (1997), **2005:** 275
Arizonans for Official English v. Arizona (1997), **2000:** 762
Arjona; United States v. (1887), **2007:** 179
Arlington, County of Va.; United States v. (1982), **1989-90:** 301, 384; **2000:** 597, 599; **2004:** 454; **2006:** 661
Arlington, County of Va.; United States v. (1983), **1989-90:** 384; **2001:** 500; **2002:** 580; **2004:** 545; **2006:** 661
Arlington, County of Va.; United States v. (2000), **2000:** 597, 599
Armco, Inc. v. Hardesty (1984), **2000:** 326
Armstrong v. Manzo (1965), **2005:** 130
Army, Dep't of v. Blue Fox, Inc. (1999), **2000:** 498, 499, 547; **2001:** 492; **2006:** 601; **2008:** 413–15
Arnbjornsdottir-Mendler v. United States (1983), **1989-90:** 86; **1991-99:** 416, 430, 705; **2004:** 89
Arnett v. Kennedy (1974), **2000:** 201
Aronson v. IRS (1992), **2006:** 1219
*Arrest Warrant of 11 Apr. 2000 (Democratic Republic of the Congo v. Belgium) (2001), **2006:** 672*n*
*Arrest Warrant of 11 Apr. 2000 (Democratic Republic of the Congo v. Belgium) (2002), **2002:** 474
Arteaga v. INS (1988), **1991-99:** 196
Artt, Matter of (1997), **2006:** 115–17
Artt, Matter of (1998), **2006:** 115–17
Artt; United States v. (1998), **1991-99:** 427
Asakura v. Seattle (1924), **2002:** 223; **2003:** 261–62
Asani v. INS (1998), **2000:** 128
Ashcroft v. *See name of opposing party*
Ashwander v. TVA (1936), **2001:** 83
*Asian Agric. Prods. v. Sri Lanka (1991), **2001:** 633–36

Asociacion de Empleados del Area Canalera v. The Panama Canal Comm'n (2003), **2004:** 199
Asociacion de Empleados del Area Canalera v. The Panama Canal Comm'n (2004), **2004:** 198–201
Asociacion de Reclamantes v. United Mexican States (1984), **2000:** 516*n;* **2006:** 595, 596; **2007:** 459, 460
Assicurazioni Generali, In re (2001), **2008:** 418–24
Associated Press v. Department of Def. (2005), **2005:** 1018–20
Associated Press v. Department of Def. (2006), **2006:** 1218–23
Asta Medica, S.A., In re Application of (1992), **1991-99:** 386
*Asylum Case (Colombia v. Peru) (1950), **2003:** 625*n;* **2007:** 68
A-T-, Matter of (2007), **2008:** 306
Atkins v. Virginia (2002), **2005:** 270, 381–84, 386; **2006:** 366; **2007:** 304
Atkinson v. Inter-American Dev. Bank (1998), **1991-99:** 1317–19; **2003:** 576
Atlanta Gas Light Co. v. Federal Energy Regulatory Comm'n (1998), **2000:** 137
Atlantic Tele-Network Inc. v. Inter-American Dev. Bank (2003), **2003:** 523–24, 575–76, **2007:** 222
Atlas Corp. v. United States (1990), **2006:** 325
Atta, In re Extradition of (1988), **1989-90:** 79
Atta, In re Extradition of (1989), **1989-90:** 79–80
Attorney Gen. v. *See name of opposing party*
Attwell v. LaSalle Nat'l Bank (1979), **2000:** 435
Atuar, In re Extradition of (2003), **2005:** 80, 83
Atwood Turnkey Drilling, Inc. v. Petroleo Brasileiro (1989), **1989-90:** 301
Auguste v. Ridge (2005), **2005:** 91
Austin v. Healey (1993), **2000:** 191, 192; **2005:** 99
Australian Govt. Aircraft Factories v. Lynne (1984), **2001:** 404
Austria v. Altmann (2003), **2003:** 516
Austria v. Altmann (2004), **2003:** 515*n;* **2004:** 352*n,* 377, 436, 438*n,* 459, 463–78, 475*n,* 529, 796, 796*n;* **2005:** 423*n,* 470–72, 475, 542, 579, 777; **2006:** 444, 573, 604; **2007:** 225, 234, 506*n,* **2008:** 225–27
Austria v. Whiteman (2004), **2003:** 515*n;* **2004:** 472–75
Austria, Dorotheum GMBH & CO KG, and Osterreischische Industrieholding, AG, In re (2002), **2002:** 503–11
Austrian and German Holocaust Litig., In re (2001), **1991-99:** 1132, 1133; **2000:** 460; **2001:** 391, 392–93*n,* 393; **2004:** 436*n*
Automatic Sprinkler Corp. v. Darla Envtl. Specialists (1995), **2000:** 547
Automotive Refinishing Paint Antitrust Litig., In re (2004), **2004:** 858–63

*Avco Corp. v. Iran Aircraft Indus. (1988), **1991-99:** 1090; **2008:** 416
*Avena and Other Mexican Nationals (Mexico v. United States) (2003), **2003:** 43–103*Avena and Other Mexican Nationals (Mexico v. United States) (2004), **1991-99:** 272, 274, 282, 340; **2004:** 37–48; **2005:** 29–41, 41*n,* 45–48, 54–55, 57, 59, 216–17, 270, 337; **2006:** 70–73, 1023, 1026; **2007:** 73–77, 365*n,* 836; **2008:** 35, 153, 175–215, 339, 339*n*
Avipro Fin. Ltd. v. Cameroon Airlines (2005), **2005:** 829–31
Ayuda, Inc. v. Thornburgh (1992), **1989-90:** 28, 30
*Azinian v. United Mexican States (1999), **1991-99:** 1436; **2000:** 694–95; **2001:** 625, 632, 641–42

B

*B. v. B. (1993), **2004:** 61
Baez; United States v. (2003), **2005:** 82; **2007:** 116, 125
Bagot v. Ashcroft (2005), **2008:** 12
Bailey v. United States (1995), **2002:** 484
Bailey; United States v. (1980), **2004:** 327, 328
Bailey v. Varian Assocs. (1990), **1989-90:** 217
Baiz, In re (1890), **1991-99:** 1251; **2002:** 553; **2004:** 538; **2006:** 654, 669
Baker v. Aoun (1990), **1989-90:** 256–60
Baker v. Carr (1962), **1989-90:** 212, 214; **1991-99:** 665–66, 985–87; **2000:** 214*n,* 402*n,* 496, 528, 569–70; **2001:** 83*n,* 204–6, 386, 445, 446, 452, 455, 457; **2002:** 200–201, 340–43, 475; **2003:** 400, 492, 497*n;* **2004:** 208, 209, 434, 453, 454; **2005:** 416, 419–20, 421*n,* 471, 473–74, 476, 480, 484; **2006:** 322–23, 432, 456, 457, 474, 509, 515–17, 520*n,* 523, 524, 524*n,* 526, 543, 544, 674; **2007:** 220–23, 225, 261, 439–43; **2008:** 444, 445, 449, 453
Baker v. McCollan (1979), **2006:** 84
Balsys; United States v. (1997), **1991-99:** 571
Balsys; United States v. (1998), **1991-99:** 571–78
B. Altman & Co. v. United States (1912), **1991-99:** 661; **2000:** 212*n*
Balzac v. Porto Rico (1922), **1991-99:** 810; **2008:** 896
*Bamaca Valasquez Case (2000), **2002:** 1014
Banco Do Brasil, S. A. v. A. C. Israel Commodity Co. (1963), **2005:** 238
Banco Nacional de Cuba v. Chemical Bank N.Y. Trust Co. (1986), **2001:** 495, 526
Banco Nacional de Cuba v. Sabbatino (1964), **1989-90:** 244, 247, 263; **1991-99:** 656, 758, 971n–972*n,* 983, 987, 988, 1137, 1186, 1237, 1269; **2000:** 335*n,* 529; **2001:** 455; **2002:** 342, 442, 475, 493, 574; **2003:** 367; **2004:** 347, 348, 470, 668; **2005:** 241, 576, 579–83; **2006:** 455, 632*n,* 671*n;* **2007:** 435; **2008:** 234, 449, 474
Bancoult v. McNamara (2004), **2004:** 364–65; **2005:** 415–17

Bancoult v. McNamara (2006), **2006:** 455–59, 541; **2008:** 452
Bancroft & Masters v. Augusta Nat'l, Inc. (2000), **2004:** 879–81
Bank Melli Iran v. Pahlavi (1995), **2000:** 442, 491*n*
Bank Melli Iran v. Pahlavi (1999), **1991-99:** 1833–36
Bank of Credit and Commerce Int'l (BCCI Overseas) Ltd. v. State Bank of Pakistan (2001), **2005:** 842
Bank of Haw. v. Balos (1988), **2008:** 474
Bank of N.Y. v. Rubin (2007), **2007:** 485–86
Bank of the U.S. v. Deveaux (1809), **2001:** 234*n*
Bank of the U.S. v. Planters' Bank of Ga. (1824), **1991-99:** 1202
Bankston v. Toyota Motor Corp. (1989), **2004:** 868–69, 868*n*
Bannerman v. Snyder (2003), **2006:** 84*n*
Bano v. Union Carbide Corp. (2001), **2001:** 335–37
Banyan Licensing v. Orthosupport Int'l (2002), **2002:** 864
Barapind v. Amador (2005), **2005:** 95–96
Barapind v. Enomoto (2004), **2005:** 95
Barapind v. Enomoto (2005), **2005:** 83*n*, 94–97
Barapind v. Reno (2000), **2001:** 76*n*
*Barayagwiza v. Prosecutor (2000), **2000:** 264
*Barbera, Messegue and Jabardo v. Spain (1994), **2000:** 395
*Barcelona Traction, Light and Power Co. (Belgium v. Spain) (1970), **2001:** 584; **2004:** 598*n*, 599*n*; **2006:** 501; **2007:** 284*n*, 418–20
Barclays Bank PLC v. Franchise Tax Bd. (1994), **1991-99:** 647*n*; **2000:** 321–22, 324*n*, 326*n*, 465*n*; **2002:** 453
Barnhart v. Peabody Coal (2003), **2004:** 322*n*
Barrueto v. Larios (2003), **2003:** 385
Bartkus v. Illinois (1959), **1991-99:** 576
Barzilay v. Barzilay (2008), **2008:** 782–89
Barzilay v. Barzilay (2009), **2008:** 783*n*
Base Metal Trading v. Russian Aluminum (2003), **2003:** 895–901
*Bates, In re (1989), **1991-99:** 351
Bayer AG, In re (1998), **1991-99:** 386
Bayer AG v. Betachem, Inc. (1999), **2003:** 874
*Bayview Irrigation Dist. v. United Mexican States (2007), **2006:** 697; **2007:** 551–53
*B. d. B. v. The Netherlands (1989), **2000:** 394
Beacon Prods. Corp. v. Reagan (1986), **2002:** 202
Beanal v. Freeport-McMoRan, Inc. (1997), **2003:** 378
Beanal v. Freeport-McMoRan, Inc. (1999), **1991-99:** 990–91; **2002:** 335, 336; **2005:** 251
Bechtel Enters. Int'l (Bermuda) Ltd. v. Overseas Private Inv. Corp. (2003), **2004:** 427
B.E.E. Int'l v. Hawes (2003), **2003:** 901–4
Beg v. Islamic Republic of Pakistan (2003), **2004:** 497

Beggerly; United States v. (1998), **2008:** 763
Begum v. Saleh (2000), **2000:** 602–16
Behring Int'l v. Imperial Iranian Air Force (1979), **1991-99:** 1221
*Behring Int'l v. Iran (1985), **2004:** 577*n*
*Beilos Case (1989), **1989-90:** 148–49
Belfast, Jr. (a.k.a. Charles Taylor, Jr.); United States v. (2008), **2008:** 123–25
*Belgium v. Spain (1970), **2001:** 584, 602–5, 631, 640–41
Belgrade v. Sidex Int'l Furniture Trading, Inc. (1998), **2001:** 494
Belize Telecom, Ltd. v. Belize (2005), **2005:** 522–23; **2006:** 610
Belk v. United States (1988), **2000:** 515–16*n;* **2001:** 468
Belmont; United States v. (1937), **1989-90:** 245, 247; **1991-99:** 655–56, 672–73, 677, 677*n,* 678, 784, 785; **2001:** 205, 452, 454; **2002:** 442; **2004:** 435*n,* 444; **2005:** 41, 41*n,* 43, 59; **2008:** 192
Beltran-Zavala v. INS (1990), **1991-99:** 226
Benitez v. Garcia (2007), **2007:** 117–24
Benitez v. Rozos (2005), **2005:** 18
Benitez; United States v. (1984), **1991-99:** 504
Benitez v. Wallis (2003), **2005:** 19
Benner; United States v. (1830), **2006:** 668, 674
*Bennett v. Horseferry Rd. Magistrate's Ct. (1993), **2000:** 404*n*
Bensmiller v. E.I. Dupont (1995), **1991-99:** 1244
Benson v. McMahon (1888), **2000:** 212; **2005:** 100
Benz v. Compania Naviera Hidalgo, S.A. (1957), **1989-90:** 447–48; **2000:** 465; **2005:** 710
Beogradska Banka v. Interenergo, Inc. (1998), **1991-99:** 1168–69; **2000:** 569*n,* 570
Berdakin v. Consulado de la Republica de El Sal. (1995), **1991-99:** 1312–13; **2002:** 540
Berenguer v. Vance (1979), **1989-90:** 78
Berman v. Schweiker (1983), **2002:** 588
Bernstein v. N.V. Nederlandsche-Amerikaansche (1954), **2000:** 477*n;* **2001:** 525; **2002:** 508
Bertrand v. Sava (1982), **1991-99:** 161
Bestfoods; United States v. (1998), **2002:** 483
Bethlehem Steel Corp. v. Board of Comm'rs of Dep't of Water & Power (1969), **1991-99:** 657*n;* **2000:** 330*n,* 539
Betteroads Asphalt v. United States (2000), **2003:** 481*n*
Bettis v. Iran (2003), **2003:** 538, 549; **2004:** 508, 513*n;* **2006:** 591
Bevc v. INS (1995), **2000:** 130
Beveridge v. Lewis (1991), **2000:** 530, 539
Bi v. Union Carbide Chems. and Plastics Co. Inc. (1993), **2008:** 233
Bichage v. United States (2002), **2001:** 417*n*
*Biens Britanniques au Maroc Espagno (1924), **2003:** 438*n,* 439*n*

Bigio v. Coca-Cola Co. (2000), **2002:** 334; **2003:** 378
Bigio v. Coca-Cola Co. (2001), **2005:** 414
Bikini v. United States (2007), **2006:** 316–25; **2007:** 256–63; **2008:** 245
Bikini v. United States (2009), **2008:** 245–47, 247*n*
Birch Shipping Corp. v. Embassy of the United Republic of Tanzania (1980), **2000:** 556; **2002:** 541; **2005:** 559
Bird v. United States (1996), **2002:** 985
*Bischoff (Italy) v. Venezuela, **2003:** 633
Bismullah v. Gates (2007), **2007:** 943–44, **2008:** 905*n*
Bismullah v. Gates (2008), **2008:** 905–6, 905*n*
Bitterman v. Ashcroft (2004), **2008:** 12
Bivens v. Six Unnamed Known Agents of Fed. Bureau of Narcotics (1971), **2000:** 410–11; **2002:** 233–34; **2004:** 352; **2005:** 294; **2007:** 239
Black and White Taxicab & Transfer Co. v. Brown and Yellow Taxicab & Transfer Co. (1928), **2004:** 346
Blackburn v. Alabama (1960), **2005:** 1004
Blais v. Iran (2006), **2006:** 581*n*
Blakely v. Washington (2004), **2005:** 278
Blanco v. United States (1985), **2008:** 156
Blankenship v. McDonald (1999), **2003:** 363
*Blaskic; Prosecutor v. (1997), **2006:** 641
*Blaskic; Prosecutor v. (2000), **2002:** 350
Blaxland v. Commonwealth Dir. of Pub. Prosecutions (2001), **2001:** 475–85
Blaxland v. Commonwealth Dir. of Pub. Prosecutions (2003), **2003:** 526–30, 533; **2005:** 82
Bloch v. Powell (2003), **2006:** 1011
Block v. North Dakota (1983), **2002:** 588
Blondin v. Dubois (1999), **1991-99:** 366; **2000:** 97*n*, 99, 102, 104, 105–15; **2001:** 46
Blum v. Yaretsky (1982), **2004:** 357
BMW of N. Am., Inc. v. Gore (1996), **2002:** 421, 424, 453
Board of Regents v. Roth (1972), **1991-99:** 191; **2006:** 1011
Board of Trs. v. Mayor & City Council (1989), **2000:** 331
Boddie v. Connecticut (1971), **2005:** 280
Bodner v. Banque Paribas (2000), **2001:** 407–13
Boimah v. United Nations Gen. Assembly (1987), **2002:** 571
Boim v. Holy Land Found. for Relief and Dev. (2007), **2007:** 150–54
Boim v. Quranic Literacy Inst. (2002), **2007:** 151
Bolchos v. Darrel (1795), **2003:** 370
Bollman, Ex parte (1807), **2005:** 282
Bolton; Doe v. (1973), **2001:** 12

Boos v. Barry (1988), **2000:** 615; **2002:** 561, 566; **2004:** 534; **2006:** 643
Boots; United States v. (1996), **2005:** 234
Boras, In re (1994), **2003:** 881
*Border and Transborder Armed Actions (Nicaragua v. Honduras) (1988), **2001:** 573
Borja v. Goodman (1990), **2000:** 484*n;* **2001:** 441*n*
Borodin v. Ashcroft (2001), **2001:** 62–70
Boshnjaku v. Federal Republic of Yugoslavia (2002), **2002:** 466–67, 491–92
*Boucher v. Lawson (1734), **2005:** 238
Boumediene v. Bush (2005), **2005:** 1008
Boumediene v. Bush (2007), **2007:** 889, 938–44, 950–51, 955–56; **2008:** 914–15
Boumediene v. Bush (2008), **2007:** 939*n;* **2008:** 891–903, 904, 905, 905*n*, 907, 909, 912, 914–15, 915*n*
Boumediene v. United States (2006), **2006:** 1179–83
Bousley v. United States (1998), **2001:** 298; **2006:** 69
Bovio v. United States (1993), **2000:** 212
Bowen v. Georgetown Hosp. (1988), **1991-99:** 1264
Bowen v. Massachusetts (1988), **2000:** 499
Bowers v. Transportes Navieros Ecuadorianpa (1989), **1989-90:** 302
Bowes v. Ashcroft (2001), **2001:** 10
Bowman v. Chicago N.W. Ry. Co. (1885), **2006:** 84
Bowman; United States v. (1922), **2001:** 329*n*
Bowoon Sangsa Co., Matter of (1983), **1991-99:** 815
Bowoto v. Chevron Corp. (2007), **2007:** 231–35
Bowoto v. Chevron Texaco Corp. (pending), **2007:** 232
Bowsher v. Synar (1986), **1991-99:** 754; **2006:** 733
*Bow Street Metro. Stipendiary Magistrate ex parte Pinochet Ugarte; Regina v. (2000), **2004:** 204*n*
*Bo Xilai, Re (2005), **2006:** 672
Boyle v. United Techs. Corp. (1988), **2000:** 334; **2001:** 194*n;* **2002:** 443
Bozilov v. Seiffert (1993), **2006:** 132
BP Chems. Ltd. v. Jiangsu Sopo Corp. (2002), **2002:** 517–18
*BP Exploration Co. (Libya) Ltd. v. Libyan Arab Republic (1979), **2003:** 627*n*
BP Prods. N. Am., Inc. v. Dagra (2005), **2005:** 856, 858–59
BP Prods. N. Am., Inc. v. Dagra (2006), **2006:** 970–73
Braden v. 30th Judicial Circuit Court of Ky. (1973), **2004:** 1000; **2006:** 1206
Bradford Elec. Light Co. v. Clapper (1932), **1991-99:** 1840
Brady v. Maryland (1963), **2000:** 394*n*, 396

Brandenburg v. Ohio (1969), **2006:** 201, 202, 204; **2007:** 330, 332
*Brasserie du pêcheur (1996), **2003:** 693
Braunfeld v. Brown (1961), **2002:** 15
Breard v. Greene (1998), **1991-99:** 257, 258, 313–21; **2001:** 298, 302; **2002:** 47; **2004:** 46, 48; **2005:** 41, 47, 48, 52, 54; **2006:** 69, 71, 78, 81, 801, 1023; **2008:** 183*n*, 185, 515
Breard v. Netherland (1996), **1991-99:** 292
Breard v. Pruett (1998), **1991-99:** 292
The Bremen v. Zapata Off-Shore Co. (1972), **1991-99:** 1268, 1847; **2001:** 231
Brennan v. Cibault (1996), **1991-99:** 355
Brenner v. Shore (1973), **2006:** 625
Brewer v. Williams (1977), **2005:** 281
Breyer v. Ashcroft (2003), **2003:** 8–11
Breyer v. Meissner (2000), **2003:** 8–9
Breyer; United States v. (1994), **1991-99:** 29
The Brig Amy Warwick (1863), **2006:** 458
*Briggs v. Baptiste (1999), **2002:** 267*n*
Briscoe; United States v. (1999), **1991-99:** 262
British Caledonian Airways Ltd. v. Bond (1981), **1991-99:** 160; **2000:** 649–50
British Columbia, Her Majesty the Queen in Right of v. Gilbertson (1979), **2001:** 488*n*
Broad v. Mannesmann Anlagenbau, A.G. (2000), **2004:** 872
Broadbent v. Organization of Am. States (1980), **2000:** 581, 584, 585
Broadfoot v. Diaz (2000), **2005:** 863–64
Brockmeyer v. May (2004), **2004:** 866–70; **2005:** 848–50, 852
Bromley v. Bromley (1998), **1991-99:** 356
Brower v. Evans (2001), **1991-99:** 1754; **2001:** 749, 750; **2004:** 759, 760
Brown v. Duchesne (1857), **2008:** 489
Brown v. Gardner (1994), **2002:** 484
Brown v. Mississippi (1936), **2005:** 282
Brown v. Secretary of the Army (1996), **2001:** 241
Brown; United States v. (1965), **1991-99:** 1241
Bruno; United States v. (2004), **2006:** 461
Bryks v. Canadian Broad. Corp. (1995), **2002:** 477
Brzak v. United Nations (2008), **2008:** 501–4
Buchanan v. Alexander (1846), **2000:** 547, 555; **2008:** 415
Buckley v. Valeo (1976), **2001:** 288*n*
Buell v. Mitchell (2001), **2003:** 363
Building & Constr. Trades Council v. Associated Builders (1993), **2000:** 329, 332
Buong Van Ho v. United States (2002), **2002:** 413

Burda Media, Inc. v. Viertel (2005), **2005:** 853
Burger-Fischer v. Degussa (1999), **2004:** 436*n*
Burger King Corp. v. Rudzewicz (1985), **1991-99:** 1207, 1245, 1246; **2003:** 534–35
Buries Markes Ltd.; United States v. (1998), **1991-99:** 1620–21
Burlington Indus. v. Ellerth (1998), **2005:** 263
Burnet v. Clark (1932), **2002:** 483
Burnett v. Al Baraka Inv. and Dev. Corp. (2003), **2003:** 385–86, 508–9, 533–36
Burnham v. Superior Court of Cal. (1990), **1991-99:** 1336
Burns v. Wilson (1953), **2006:** 1197
Burrafato v. Department of State (1975), **1989-90:** 23
Burt, In re (1984), **1991-99:** 943; **2005:** 244
Burton v. Baker (1989), **1989-90:** 158
Bush v. Gherebi (2004), **2003:** 1027*n;* **2004:** 1017*n*
Bustillo v. Johnson (2005), **2005:** 61
Bustillo v. Johnson (2006), **2006:** 63–75
Butler; United States v. (1936), **1991-99:** 1138
B-West Imports, Inc. v. United States (1996), **1991-99:** 2254–56
Byrd v. Corporacion Forestal y Industrial de Olancho SA (1999), **1991-99:** 1189–90, 1216–18; **2002:** 472; **2006:** 636*n;* **2007:** 513

C
*C. v. C. (1989), **2004:** 60
*C. v. S. (1990), **2004:** 63
*Caballero Delgado and Santana Case (1995), **2002:** 268*n*
Caballo, Estate of v. Fernandez-Larios (2001), **2001:** 340
Caban v. Mohammed (1979), **2000:** 12, 14
Cabebe v. Acheson (1950), **1991-99:** 12
Cabello v. Fernández Larios (2005), **2006:** 477
Cabello Barrueto v. Fernández Larios (2002), **2002:** 351, 474
Cabiri v. Assasie-Gyimah (1996), **1991-99:** 1264, 1265; **2007:** 506
Cabiri v. Republic of Ghana (1999), **1991-99:** 1198–99; **2000:** 481*n*
Cadet v. Bulger (2004), **2004:** 307, 312
Cafeteria and Rest. Workers Union v. McElroy (1961), **1991-99:** 1244
Caicedo; United States v. (1995), **2008:** 128
Calandra; United States v. (1974), **2006:** 67
Calder v. Jones (1984), **1991-99:** 1246; **2003:** 534; **2004:** 879–80
Calero-Toledo v. Pearson Yacht Leasing Co. (1974), **2001:** 113; **2005:** 130–31
Califano v. Aznavorian (1978), **1991-99:** 57; **2001:** 11
Califano v. Sanders (1977), **2001:** 80*n*
California v. ARC Am. Corp. (1989), **2000:** 528–29, 537
California v. Arizona (1979), **2007:** 472

California v. NRG Energy, Inc. (2004), **2006:** 552
California; United States v. (1947), **1991-99:** 656, 839, 1615; **2002:** 248, 255; **2005:** 253
California Bankers Ass'n v. Shultz (1974), **1991-99:** 647*n;* **2001:** 204
Callejo v. Bancomer, S.A. (1985), **1991-99:** 1211, 1212; **2005:** 577
C-A-, Matter of (2006), **2008:** 306
*Cameroon v. Nigeria (1998), **2001:** 573
*Cameroon v. United Kingdom (1963), **2001:** 586
Campbell v. Buckley (2000), **2001:** 136
Campbell v. Clinton (1999), **1991-99:** 2157–58
Campbell v. Clinton (2000), **2000:** 758; **2002:** 199
Campbell v. Office of Pers. Mgmt. (1982), **2000:** 498*n*
Campos-Guardado v. INS (1987), **1991-99:** 220–21
Camps Newfound/Owatonna, Inc. v. Town of Harrison (1997), **2000:** 322*n,* 327
Campuzano v. Iran (2003), **2006:** 570
Can v. United States (1994), **1991-99:** 986; **2000:** 201, 214*n,* 570, 574
Canada v. RJ Reynolds Tobacco Holdings, Inc. (2000), **2002:** 838
Canada v. RJ Reynolds Tobacco Holdings, Inc. (2002), **2002:** 837–41
*Canada; United States v. (1938), **2001:** 577
*Canada; United States v. (2008) (LCIA Case No. 7941), **2007:** 593; **2008:** 583–89
*Canada; United States v. (LCIA Case No. 81010), **2008:** 589–93
*Canada v. United States (Gulf of Maine) (1984), **2008:** 205
Canadian Filters, Ltd. v. Lear-Siegler, Inc. (1969), **2003:** 869
Canadian Overseas Ores Ltd. v. Compania de Acero del Pacifico, S.A. (1982), **2004:** 498
Canadian Overseas Ores Ltd. v. Compania de Acero del Pacifico, S.A. (1984), **2001:** 437
Canadian Transp. Co. v. United States (1980), **1991-99:** 1127; **2000:** 492; **2002:** 218
Canadian Transp. Co. v. United States (1985), **1989-90:** 311–14
Canas-Segovia v. INS (1990), **1991-99:** 214
Canas-Segovia v. INS (1992), **1991-99:** 220
*Canfor Corp. v. United States (2002), **2003:** 636–42
*Canfor Corp. v. United States (2005), **2005:** 596–97; **2007:** 549
*Canfor Corp. v. United States (2006), **2006:** 702, 703*n*
Canon Latin Am., Inc. v. Lantech (CR), S.A. (2007), **2007:** 792–95
*Cantos v. Argentina (2001), **2004:** 225
Capital Cities/ABC, Inc. v. Brady (1990), **2008:** 812
Capitol Converting Equip. v. LEP Transp. (1992), **2006:** 920
Capitol Vending Co. v. Baker (1964), **2005:** 564–65
Cardan v. United States (2000), **2000:** 312–17
Cardona v. State (1998), **1991-99:** 263

Cardoza-Fonseca; INS v. (1987), **1991-99:** 195, 196, 205, 235, 237; **2000:** 129–30; **2004:** 471
Carey v. Piphus (1978), **2004:** 1008; **2005:** 130
Cargill Int'l S.A. v. M/T Pavel Dybenko (1993), **2001:** 437
Cariolan v. INS (1977), **2000:** 130
Carl Marks & Co. v. Union of Soviet Socialist Republics (1988), **1989-90:** 301; **2000:** 476; **2001:** 432, 433, 457; **2002:** 498, 504–7, 509, 513, 514; **2003:** 519
Carl Zeiss Stiftung v. VEB Carl Zeiss Jena (1970), **1991-99:** 984
Carnival Cruise Lines, Inc. v. Shute (1991), **1991-99:** 1848; **2001:** 231
Caro-Quintero; United States v. (1990), **1991-99:** 436
Carpa v. Smith (1998), **2001:** 291
Carrato v. United States (1983), **2002:** 498
Carrera v. Carrera (1949), **1991-99:** 1288, 1291; **2002:** 553; **2006:** 654, 659*n,* 680; **2007:** 518, 520
Carrillo; United States v. (1999), **1991-99:** 262
Carrion-Caliz; United States v. (1991), **2006:** 586
Carter v. Greenhow (1885), **2006:** 84
Carter v. United States (2000), **2002:** 526–27; **2004:** 326
*Casablanca case (France v. Germany) (1916), **2000:** 404*n*
Casanova v. United States ex rel. Fitzpatrick (1963), **2002:** 554
*Case Concerning the Aerial Incident of July 3, 1988 (1996) (Iran v. United States), **1991-99:** 1091
*Case Concerning Avena and Other Mexican Nationals (Mexico v. U.S.) (2003), **2003:** 43–103
*Case Concerning Avena and Other Mexican Nationals (Mexico v. U.S.) (2004), **1991-99:** 272, 274, 282, 340; **2004:** 37–48; **2005:** 29–41, 41*n,* 45–48, 54–55, 57, 59, 216–17, 270, 337; **2006:** 70–73, 1023, 1026; **2007:** 73–77, 365*n,* 836; **2008:** 35, 153, 175–215, 339, 339*n*
*Case Concerning Delimitation of the Continental Shelf (1970), **1991-99:** 718, 723–24
*Case Concerning the Gabcikovo-Nagymaros Project (Hungary v. Slovakia) (1997), **1991-99:** 1109, 1110; **2000:** 663–65; **2001:** 367–69
*Case Concerning Legality of Use of Force (Yugoslavia v. U.S.) (1999), **1991-99:** 2151–54
*Case Concerning Oil Platforms (Iran v. United States) (1992), **1991-99:** 2182–86; **2003:** 1036–66
* Case Concerning Oil Platforms (Iran v. United States) (1996), **2001:** 608–11
* Case Concerning Oil Platforms (Iran v. United States) (2003), **2004:** 974–76; **2006:** 703, 704–5, 1023, 1025
*Case Concerning Temple of Preah Vihar (Cambodia v. Thailand) (1962), **1991-99:** 723, 1117

*Case Concerning the Interpretation of the Air Transp. Servs. Agreement (1963), **1991-99:** 723
*Case Concerning U.S. Diplomatic and Consular Staff in Tehran (1980), **1991-99:** 1086; **2000:** 553, 658*n*
Castaneda-Gonzalez v. INS (1977), **1991-99:** 70
Castillo-Arias v. U.S. Att'y Gen. (2006), **2008:** 306
Catholic Social Serv., Inc.; Reno v. (1993), **2005:** 94
Cedric Kushner Promotions, Ltd. v. King (2001), **2002:** 482
Center for Reproductive Law & Policy v. Bush (2001), **2001:** 283–93
Central Bank of Denver v. First Interstate Bank of Denver (1994), **2004:** 358, 361, 368, 370, 373; **2005:** 405, 409–10; **2006:** 446–48
Chabal v. Reagan (1987), **2000:** 498*n*
Chadha; INS v. (1983), **1991-99:** 2155; **2001:** 206; **2002:** 590; **2006:** 509
Chadha; INS v. (1986), **1991-99:** 647*n*
Chae Chan Ping v. United States (1889), **2000:** 10
Chamber of Commerce v. Reich (1996), **2000:** 327*n;* **2008:** 467
Chan v. Korean Air Lines, Ltd. (1989), **1991-99:** 1346; **2000:** 516*n,* 518, 519*n;* **2001:** 559; **2002:** 436, 440; **2004:** 544, 546
Chang, Matter of (1989), **1991-99:** 202
Chang v. United States (1988), **2006:** 1014
Chaparro-Alcantara; United States v. (1999), **1991-99:** 261
Chaparro-Alcantara; United States v. (2000), **2000:** 42; **2005:** 42*n;* **2006:** 85
Chaplinsky v. New Hampshire (1942), **2007:** 329
Charlton v. Kelly (1913), **1991-99:** 727, 728; **2000:** 212, 492; **2005:** 49
Chase Manhattan Bank v. Traffic Stream (BVI) Infrastructure Ltd. (2000), **2002:** 228
Chase Manhattan Bank v. Traffic Stream (BVI) Infrastructure Ltd. (2001), **2001:** 227–35
Chateau Lafayette Apartments, Inc. v. Meadow Brook Nat'l Bank (1969), **2007:** 461
*Chattin v. United Mexican States (1927), **2001:** 632
Chee Fan Chen, In the Matter of the Extradition of (1998), **1991-99:** 939–43
Cheek v. United States (1991), **2004:** 328
Chen v. INS (1996), **1991-99:** 202
Chen v. INS (1999), **2000:** 130
Chen; United States v. (1993), **2001:** 328, 330
Chen v. United States Marshal (1998), **1991-99:** 942–43
Chenoweth v. Clinton (1999), **2000:** 763*n;* **2002:** 199
Chen Zhou Chai v. Carrol (1995), **1991-99:** 186, 202
Cheung, In re Extradition of (1997), **2000:** 190
Cheung v. United States (2000), **2000:** 190–203; **2001:** 65–66

Chevron U.S.A., Inc. v. Natural Res. Def. Council, Inc. (1984), **1991-99:** 235; **2001:** 82; **2005:** 86; **2006:** 182; **2008:** 467
Chew Heong v. United States (1884), **2001:** 472
Chicago & S. Air Lines, Inc. v. Waterman S.S. Corp. (1948), **1989-90:** 159; **1991-99:** 797; **2001:** 445, 452–54; **2002:** 200, 589; **2003:** 366, 492, 496; **2004:** 18; **2005:** 240, 484, 496; **2006:** 457, 545; **2007:** 122
Chick Kam Choo v. Exxon (1988), **2007:** 798
China Oil and Gas Pipeline Bureau, In re (2002), **2002:** 516–17
China Trade & Dev. Corp. v. M.V. Choong Yong (1987), **2002:** 866*n;* **2004:** 843, 847, 848; **2005:** 832; **2007:** 782–84, 787–93; **2008:** 772–76
Chindawongse; United States v. (1985), **1989-90:** 346, 348, 350–51
Chinese Exclusion Case, The (1889), **1991-99:** 656
Cho v. Republic of Korea (2003), **2003:** 531
Choctaw Nation of Indians v. United States (1943), **1991-99:** 1346; **2004:** 200
Chong Boon Kim v. Yim Young Shik (1963), **1989-90:** 321; **2006:** 670
*Chorzow Factory Case (1928), **1991-99:** 1073, 1117, 1118
Christian Sci. Bd. of Dirs. of the First Church of Christ, Scientist v. Nolan (2001), **2003:** 903
Christopher v. Harbury (2002), **2002:** 231–36
Chubb & Son, Inc. v. Asiana Airlines (2000), **2001:** 555–65; **2003:** 588
Chuen v. Esperdy (1960), **2000:** 200
Chuidian v. Philippine Nat'l Bank (1990), **1989-90:** 302–11; **1991-99:** 1189, 1253, 1274, 1281; **2001:** 405–6, 494, 521; **2002:** 467, 472, 473, 477; **2003:** 509; **2006:** 630, 636, 636*n,* 637*n,* 638, 646, 652; **2007:** 446, 505, 506*n*
*Church of Scientology v. Commissioner of the Metro. Police (1978), **2006:** 641
Chy Lung v. Freeman (1875), **1991-99:** 656; **2002:** 427, 428, 447; **2007:** 204
Chytil v. Powell (2001), **2001:** 385–86
Cicippio v. Iran (1994), **1991-99:** 1218–19; **2001:** 403, 445, 499; **2002:** 503
Cicippio v. Iran (1998), **1991-99:** 1218, 1224, 1264; **2000:** 542, 543, 548–60; **2002:** 534; **2004:** 317
Cicippio-Puleo v. Iran (2002), **2004:** 503
Cicippio-Puleo v. Iran (2004), **1991-99:** 1335; **2003:** 538, 544; **2004:** 483, 488, 501–9, 511, 513–14; **2005:** 509–10, 514–15, 517–18, 544; **2006:** 589, 590, 592
*Cie Air France v. Teichner (1984), **1991-99:** 1349, 1350
City of. *See name of specific city*
Ciurinskas; United States v. (1998), **1991-99:** 27

Civil v. INS (1998), **1991-99:** 230, 231; **2000:** 130
Clancy v. OFAC (2007), **2008:** 812
Clanton v. Cooper (1997), **2005:** 1004
Clark v. Allen (1947), **1991-99:** 727, 972*n;* **2007:** 236
Clark v. Jeter (1988), **2000:** 15
Clark v. Martinez (2005), **2005:** 17–23, 291; **2006:** 1189, 1190; **2008:** 345, 908, 909
Clark v. Propper (1948), **2000:** 619
Clark v. United States (1985), **2001:** 293
*Clegg v. Levy (1812), **2005:** 239
Clerici, In re (2007), **2007:** 800–804
Cleveland Indians Baseball Co.; United States v. (2001), **2004:** 314*n*
Clinton v. Jones (1997), **2001:** 523
Clinton v. New York, City of (1998), **1991-99:** 967, 968; **2003:** 379; **2005:** 424
Coalition for Fair Lumber Exports v. United States (2006), **2006:** 726–37
Coalition for Fair Lumber Imports Executive Comm. v. United States (2005), **2005:** 605
Coalition of Clergy v. Bush (2002), **2002:** 981
*Coard v. United States (1999), **2002:** 1016–17
Coffield, In re (1994), **1991-99:** 361, 367
Cohen v. California (1971), **1991-99:** 892
Cohen v. Cohen (1993), **1991-99:** 355
Coker v. Georgia (1977), **2005:** 387
Cole; United States v. (1989), **1989-90:** 339–52
Coleman v. Burnett (1973), **2005:** 99
Coleman v. Espy (1993), **2006:** 611
Coleman v. Miller (1939), **2000:** 764; **2001:** 445; **2002:** 201
Coleman v. Thompson (1991), **2005:** 283; **2006:** 69
College Savs. Bank v. Florida Prepaid Postsecondary Educ. Expense Bd. (1999), **2006:** 1011
*Colombia v. Peru (Asylum) (1950), **2007:** 68
Colonial Bank v. Compagnie Generale Maritime (1986), **1989-90:** 285
Colorado v. Connelly (1986), **2005:** 282
Colorado River Water Conservation Dist. v. United States (1976), **2002:** 860, 861; **2005:** 816
Columbian Enameling & Stamping Co.; NLRB v. (1939), **1991-99:** 195
Columbus-America Discovery Group v. Atlantic Mut. Ins. Co. (1992), **2006:** 831
Cominotto v. United States (1986), **2001:** 332
Commercial Bank of Kuwait v. Rafidain Bank (1994), **2000:** 591–93
Commissioner's Subpoenas, In re (2003), **2003:** 145–49
*Commission v. Ireland (2006), **2007:** 656

Committee of U.S. Citizens Living in Nicaragua v. Reagan (1988), **2000:** 407; **2001:** 290, 419–20, 441*n*, 470; **2002:** 216; **2005:** 56; **2007:** 76; **2008:** 181
Commodity Futures Trading Comm'n v. Nahas (1984), **2001:** 139
Commodity Futures Trading Comm'n v. Schor (1986), **1991-99:** 754
Commonwealth Edison Co. v. Montana (1981), **2000:** 333*n*
Commonwealth of. *See name of commonwealth*
Community Fed. Sav. & Loan Ass'n v. Federal Home Loan Bank Bd. (1983), **2005:** 564–65
Compagnie des Bauxites de Guinea v. Insurance Co. of N. Am. (1981), **2002:** 866
Compangie Noga D'Importation et D'Exportation, S.A. v. Russian Fed'n (2004), **2005:** 557; **2007:** 414
Compania Espanola de Navegacion Maritima v. The Navemar (1938), **2005:** 42*n*
Compania Interamericana Export-Import, S.A. v. Compania Dominicana de Aviacion (1996), **1991-99:** 1225*n*
Complete Auto Transit, Inc. v. Brady (1977), **2000:** 321*n*
Concerned Jewish Youth v. McGuire (1980), **1991-99:** 1329
Condon; Reno v. (2000), **2007:** 203
Congo, Republic of v. Af-Cap, Inc. (2005), **2006:** 607
Connally v. General Constr. Co. (1926), **2005:** 126
Connecticut Bank of Commerce v. Republic of Congo (2002), **2005:** 550, 568; **2006:** 569, 620, 621, 628; **2007:** 490
Connecticut Nat'l Bank v. Germain (1992), **2007:** 453
Conners; United States v. (1979), **2000:** 597
Conolly v. Taylor (1829), **2002:** 489
Consarc Corp. v. Iraq Ministry (1994), **2000:** 624
Consarc Corp. v. Iraq Ministry (1995), **2000:** 623
Consolidated Edison Co. v. NLRB (1938), **2006:** 193
Constant; Doe v. (2006), **2006:** 478
Consulate Gen. of Mex. v. Phillips (1998), **1991-99:** 260
Container Corp. v. Franchise Tax Bd. (1983), **2000:** 324, 465; **2002:** 454; **2006:** 474
Continental Ore Co. v. Union Carbide & Carbon Corp. (1962), **1991-99:** 1532, 1533
Contractors Ass'n v. Secretary of Labor (1971), **2000:** 327*n*
Cook v. United States (1933), **1991-99:** 957; **2001:** 132
Cooley v. Board of Wardens (1851), **2000:** 324
Copelco Capital v. Brazilian Consulate Gen. (2005), **2005:** 504, 506, 555–56, 567–70
Coplin v. United States (1984), **2004:** 200
Coplon; United States v. (1949), **1989-90:** 351; **2002:** 553
Cordoba-Mosquera; United States v. (2000), **2005:** 42*n*

Corey; United States v. (2000), **2001:** 328–29*n*
*Corfu Channel (U.K. v. Albania) (1949), **2000:** 661; **2003:** 624*n*
Cornejo v. San Diego (2006), **2006:** 86; **2007:** 79–80
Cornejo v. San Diego (2007), **2008:** 43, 44
Cornejo-Barreto v. Seifert (1998), **1991-99:** 959; **2001:** 70–87; **2004:** 83–90
Cornejo-Barreto v. Seifert (2000), **2004:** 92; **2005:** 87*n*, 88*n*, 93, 352–53; **2006:** 150, 152–54
Cornejo-Barreto v. Seifert (2004), **2004:** 92; **2005:** 88*n*, 353; **2006:** 150, 152
Cornell v. Assicurazioni Generali S.p.A. (2000), **2000:** 460*n*; **2001:** 387
Cornfeld v. Investors Overseas Servs., Ltd. (1979), **2005:** 829
*Corn Prods. Int'l, Inc. v. United Mexican States (2005), **2005:** 600–601
Corporacion Mexicana de Servicios Maritimos, S.A. v. M/T Respect (1996), **2001:** 480–82, 482*n*
Correctional Servs. Corp. v. Malesko (2001), **2002:** 223, 234; **2003:** 263; **2004:** 347
Corrie v. Caterpillar, Inc. (2005), **2006:** 438*n*, 446*n*, 472
Corrie v. Caterpillar, Inc. (2007), **2006:** 438*n*; **2007:** 219–24; **2008:** 218, 218*n*, 219
Corzo v. Banco Central de Reserva del Peru (2001), **2001:** 402; **2003:** 524, 526
Costello v. United States (1961), **1991-99:** 29
*Cotesworth & Powell (1875), **2001:** 628
Cotten; United States v. (1973), **2001:** 328*n*
County of. *See name of county*
County Sovereignty Comm. v. Department of State (2002), **2002:** 91; **2005:** 1013
Covington; United States v. (1985), **1991-99:** 816
Cowart, Estate of v. Nicklos Drilling Co. (1992), **1991-99:** 1536
Crawford v. Washington (2004), **2004:** 1027; **2005:** 281
Crawford Enters.; Inc.; United States v. (1986), **2005:** 530; **2006:** 610
Credit Suisse v. United States Dist. Court for the Cent. Dist. of Cal. (1997), **2002:** 342; **2005:** 577–78
Creighton Ltd. v. Government of the State of Qatar (1999), **1991-99:** 1258–59; **2000:** 592; **2003:** 525
Creppel v. United States (1994), **2002:** 511
Crews; United States v. (1980), **1991-99:** 505
Crockett v. Reagan (1983), **2007:** 222
Croesus EMTR Master Fund L.P. v. The Federative Republic of Brazil (2002), **2002:** 519
Croll v. Croll (1999), **1991-99:** 356; **2000:** 110

Croll v. Croll (2000), **1991-99:** 356; **2002:** 56; **2004:** 61
Cronin v. Iran (2002), **2002:** 529–34; **2003:** 537–43
Crosby v. National Foreign Trade Council (2000), **1991-99:** 786; **2000:** 319–40, 342, 465–66*n,* 466, 527–30, 536, 551; **2001:** 193–96, 454; **2002:** 200, 428, 444, 446, 447, 449, 451; **2003:** 466, 467; **2004:** 370; **2005:** 44, 406, 534; **2006:** 454, 474; **2007:** 235, 236, 954
Crowell v. Benson (1932), **2001:** 83, 84
Cruz v. United States (2002), **2002:** 212–18, 498, 500, 511–13
Cruz v. Zapata Ocean Res., Inc. (1982), **2003:** 435–36
*Cruz Varas and Others, In the Case of (1991), **2002:** 267*n*
Cuban Am. Bar Ass'n, Inc. v. Christopher (1995), **1991-99:** 188–94; **2000:** 132*n;* **2002:** 985
Cuevas; United States v. (2007), **2007:** 124–26
Cummings; United States v. (2002), **2002:** 57–58
Cunard S.S. Co. v. Mellon (1923), **2008:** 134, 135
Currier v. Currier (1994), **1991-99:** 363
Curtiss-Wright Exp. Corp.; United States v. (1936), **1991-99:** 56, 172, 415, 646*n,* 671*n,* 725, 796, 813, 993, 1187, 1250, 2256; **2000:** 466, 527, 529; **2001:** 83, 205, 211, 289, 452, 456, 752, 760; **2002:** 442; **2003:** 366, 492, 500; **2004:** 21, 371, 544; **2005:** 38, 42, 240, 405, 1012–13; **2006:** 458, 1179; **2007:** 122, 204, 205; **2008:** 445, 473, 902
Custer County Action Ass'n v. Garvey (2001), **2002:** 340
*Cyprus v. Turkey (1976), **2002:** 1015

D

Daberkow v. United States (1978), **2004:** 481
*Dabhol Arbitration (2005), **2005:** 469, 648, 653
Dabone v. Thornburgh (1990), **2006:** 28
Da Costa v. Laird (1973), **2006:** 473, 523, 524, 526
Dailide; United States v. (2000), **2004:** 4
Dailide; United States v. (2003), **2003:** 6–8; **2004:** 3
Daliberti v. Iraq (2000), **2005:** 521, 580
Daliberti v. Iraq (2001), **2001:** 475; **2002:** 534; **2004:** 317
Dalton v. Specter (1994), **2000:** 560
D'Amato v. Deutsche Bank (2001), **1991-99:** 1132
Dames & Moore v. Regan (1981), **1989-90:** 215; **1991-99:** 646, 672*n,* 673, 1250, 1835; **2000:** 212, 335, 516*n,* 551, 617, 619; **2001:** 116, 210, 470, 471, 474; **2002:** 214*n,* 414, 426, 545; **2003:** 465, 466, 541, 542; **2004:** 435*n,* 438; **2005:** 39, 43–44, 473, 478, 533, 1011; **2006:** 733; **2008:** 188, 192, 233, 468, 488
Dammarell v. Iran (2005), **2005:** 508–9, 512, 517–20, 579; **2006:** 583, 584, 589, 590, 592

*Dann, Petition of (2002), **2002:** 367–82
Dare v. Secretary of Air Force (1985), **1991-99:** 353
Dataphase Sys, Inc. v. C Sys., Inc. (1981), **2006:** 959, 960
Daulton; United States v. (1996), **2004:** 1028
Daventree Ltd. v. Republic of Azerbaijan (2004), **2003:** 571; **2004:** 483
David B. v. Helen O. (1995), **1991-99:** 355
David S., In re Matter of (1991), **2001:** 41
David S. v. Zamira S. (1991), **1991-99:** 356, 363
Davis v. Monroe County Bd. of Educ. (1999), **2005:** 264
Davis v. Passman (1979), **2000:** 401*n*
Davis; United States v. (1985), **2000:** 492; **2003:** 869; **2004:** 845; **2008:** 772, 773
Davis; United States v. (1990), **2008:** 126, 128
Dayton v. Czechoslovak Socialist Republic (1987), **2001:** 386
Dean Witter Reynolds, Inc. v. Fernandez (1984), **2006:** 1009
Debab v. INS (1998), **2000:** 130
DeBartolo Corp. v. Florida Gulf Coast Building and Trades Council (1988), **2001:** 760
De Canas v. Bica (1976), **1991-99:** 787, 789
*Decision of February 27, 1984 (Tabatabai) (1989), **2006:** 676
*Deep Vein Thrombosis & Air Travel Group Litig., Re (2003), **2003:** 595
Defenders of Wildlife v. Hogarth (2001), **2001:** 750–52
Defense Dep't, Dep't of Military Affairs v. FLRA (1992), **2005:** 1024
Degen v. United States (1996), **2005:** 279
De Giacomo, In re (1874), **2000:** 211
*Delalic; Prosecutor v. (1998), **2004:** 312*n*
*Delalic; Prosecutor v. (2001), **2002:** 350, 351
De La Pava; United States v. (2001), **2002:** 215; **2005:** 42*n*, 49, 51, 52
Delaware & Hudson Co.; Attorney Gen. v. (1909), **2001:** 552
Del Conte, Matter of (1964), **1989-90:** 72
De Leon-Reynoso v. Ashcroft (2002), **2005:** 260
DeLetelier v. Republic of Chile (1984), **2001:** 403, 445, 493, 499; **2005:** 523–24, 558–59; **2006:** 569, 605, 639; **2007:** 515
De Lima v. Bidwell (1901), **2005:** 243
Delocque-Fourcaud v. The Los Angeles County Museum of Art (2003), **2003:** 825–30
De Luca v. United Nations Org. (1994), **2002:** 571, 572; **2008:** 504
Demjanjuk v. Petrovsky (1985), **1989-90:** 81; **1991-99:** 1297; **2000:** 597
Demjanjuk v. Petrovsky (2004), **2004:** 1–2
Demjanjuk; United States v. (2002), **2002:** 5–8; **2004:** 1–4
Demore v. Kim (2003), **2004:** 16
Denegri v. Republic of Chile (1992), **2001:** 442*n*

Denlinger v. Chinadotcom Corp. (2003), **2003:** 887–92
Department of. *See specific title of department*
Dependable Highway Express v. Navigators Ins. Co. (2007), **2007:** 772–76
Deportation Proceedings for Doherty (1989), **1991-99:** 235, 239
De Sanchez v. Banco Central de Nicaragua (1985), **1989-90:** 310; **1991-99:** 1205; **2001:** 405, 502; **2004:** 497
DeSilva v. DiLeonardi (1996), **1991-99:** 417–20, 427
Desir v. Ilchert (1988), **2000:** 129
Deutsch v. Turner (2003), **1991-99:** 1134; **2003:** 468–71
*Deutsche Amerikanische Petroleum Gesellschaft Oil Tankers (1926), **2001:** 603
Dexter & Carpenter, Inc. v. Kunglig Jarnvagsstyrelsen (1930), **2002:** 562
Dia Navigation Co. v. Pomeroy (1994), **2000:** 499
Diaz, Matter of (1963), **1991-99:** 209
Diaz v. Trust Territory (1989), **2000:** 456
Dickerson; United States v. (1940), **1991-99:** 2160
Dickerson v. United States (2000), **2005:** 282; **2006:** 66, 74
Dickson v. Ford (1975), **2007:** 222
*Dickson Car Wheel Co. (U.S. v. Mexico) (1931), **2001:** 577
Diekelman; United States v. (1875), **2000:** 491–92; **2008:** 240–41
Dietzsch v. Huidekoper (1880), **2008:** 761, 762
Diggs v. Richardson (1976), **1991-99:** 160, 1128; **2002:** 215; **2005:** 1007; **2008:** 181
Dillman v. Mitsubishi Material Corp. (2003), **2002:** 438
Dion; United States v. (1986), **2001:** 132; **2005:** 140
Diorinou v. Mezitis (2000), **2001:** 40–47
Disconto Gesellschaft v. Umbreit (1908), **2004:** 1001
Discovery Group v. Atlantic Mut. Ins. Co. (1992), **1991-99:** 1613
District of Columbia v. Gandy (1982), **2006:** 586
Djordjevich v. Bundesminister Der Finanzen, Fed. Republic of Germany (1997), **2001:** 432–33
DKT Int'l Inc. v. USAID (2007), **2007:** 254–56
DKT Mem'l Fund v. AID (1986), **2001:** 285*n*
DKT Mem'l Fund v. AID (1987), **2001:** 285*n*
DKT Mem'l Fund v. AID (1988), **2001:** 285*n*
DKT Mem'l Fund v. AID (1989), **1991-99:** 117; **2000:** 497; **2001:** 285*n*, 287*n*, 288*n*, 289–90, 456
Dluhos v. Floating & Abandoned Vessel (1998), **2006:** 831
Doe, In re (1988), **1991-99:** 1285; **2001:** 512, 513, 516, 518; **2003:** 563, 570
Doe v. *See name of opposing party*
Doe; United States v. (1999), **1991-99:** 260

Doherty, In re (1984), **1991-99:** 428
Doherty v. INS (1990), **1991-99:** 235
Dolan v. USPS (2006), **2008:** 485
Dole v. United Steelworkers of Am. (1990), **2002:** 424
Dole Food Co. v. Patrickson (2003), **2002:** 480–91; **2003:** 512, 521; **2004:** 468, 477; **2005:** 552; **2006:** 554, 555, 557
*Dombo Beheer B. V. v. The Netherlands (1993), **2000:** 393
Domingo, Estate of v. Marcos (1982), **1989-90:** 315–16, 321; **2001:** 514, 515
Domingo, Estate of v. Republic of the Philippines (1988), **1989-90:** 321–23; **1991-99:** 1276
*Domingues, In re (2001), **2001:** 303–15; **2007:** 388
Domingues v. Nevada (1996), **1991-99:** 965; **2001:** 304
Domingues v. Nevada (1998), **1991-99:** 739, 965; **2001:** 304
Domingues v. Nevada (1999), **1991-99:** 739, 965–78; **2001:** 304, 311
Donald v. Orfila (1986), **2008:** 504
Dorr v. United States (1904), **1989-90:** 102
Dorsey v. Government of China (2008), **2008:** 481–83
Dorsey v. Government of China (2009), **2008:** 482*n*
Dow Jones v. Harrods (2002), **2002:** 868–71
Downes v. Bidwell (1901), **1991-99:** 12, 13, 647*n,* 810
Dowty Woodville Polymer, Ltd.; United States v. (1997), **2000:** 194
DRC, Inc., United States ex rel. v. Custer Battles, LLC (2005), **2005:** 225; **2006:** 302
DRC, Inc., United States ex rel. v. Custer Battles, LLC (2006), **2006:** 301–5
Drexel Burnham Lambert v. Committee of Receivers for Galadari (1993), **1991-99:** 1192, 1289; **2000:** 480–81; **2001:** 436, 437, 481; **2006:** 575
Dreyfus v. von Finck (1976), **1989-90:** 347; **2001:** 290, 405
Drummond Co.; Doe v. (2004), **2006:** 476
Duarte-Acero; United States v. (2000), **2001:** 301*n;* **2003:** 377
Duarte-Acero; United States v. (2002), **2004:** 447; **2005:** 42*n*
Duchow v. United States (1995), **2006:** 1207
DuMont v. Saskatchewan Government Ins. (2001), **2004:** 512
Duncan v. Kahanamoku (1946), **2002:** 990
Duncan v. Louisiana (1968), **2005:** 278
Duncan v. Navassa Phosphate Co. (1891), **1991-99:** 845–46
Duncan v. Walker (2001), **2004:** 318
Dunhill of London, Inc. v. Cuba (1976), **2006:** 508–9
Dupont Circle Citizens Ass'n v. District of Columbia Bd. of Zoning Adjustment (1987), **1991-99:** 664; **2002:** 538
Dupree v. United States (1977), **2000:** 597
Dynalectron Corp. v. United States (1984), **1991-99:** 660

E
EAL Corp. v. European Org. for the Safety of Air Navigation (1994), **2002:** 469
E & J Gallo Winery v. Andina Licores, S.A. (2006), **2006:** 953–58
Earth Island Institute v. Albright (1998), **1991-99:** 1717–18
Earth Island Institute v. Christopher (1993), **2001:** 752
Earth Island Institute v. Christopher (1995), **1991-99:** 1716
Earth Island Institute v. Evans (2004), **1991-99:** 1754; **2004:** 757–62; **2006:** 883
Earth Island Institute v. Gutierrez (2006), **2006:** 885
Earth Island Institute v. Hogarth (2007), **2007:** 718–20
Eastern Airlines, Inc. v. Floyd (1989), **1991-99:** 1345
Eastern Airlines, Inc. v. Floyd (1991), **1991-99:** 1344, 1345–51, 1353, 1354; **2003:** 598, 601
Eastern Airlines, Inc., Engine Failure, Miami Int'l Airport, In re (1986), **1991-99:** 1345
Eastman Kodak v. Kalvin and Carballo (1997), **1991-99:** 989
East River S.S. Corp. v. Transamerica Delaval, Inc. (1986), **2006:** 928
EAW Group, Inc. v. Gambia (2004), **2005:** 563
Edgar v. MITE Corp. (1982), **2002:** 453
Ediale; United States v. (1999), **1991-99:** 260
Edlow Int'l Co. v. Nuklearna Elektrarna Krsko (1997), **2001:** 494
Edmonson v. Leesville Concerete Co. (1991), **2005:** 278
*E.D. Srl. v. Italo Fenocchio (2000), **2004:** 867
Edward J. DeBartolo Corp. v. Florida Gulf Coast Building and Constr. Trades Council (1988), **2001:** 83, 552
Edwards v. Carter (1978), **1991-99:** 650
Edye v. Robertson. *See* Head Money Cases (1884)
EEOC v. *See name of opposing party*
Egorov; United States v. (1963), **1991-99:** 1239
Ehrenfeld v. Mahfouz (2005), **2005:** 865
Ehrlich v. American Airlines (2002), **2003:** 597–602
*Eichmann; Attorney Gen. v. (1962), **2000:** 406*n*
Eid v. Alaska Airlines (2008), **2008:** 519–25
*Einhorn v. France (2001), **2001:** 87–89
Eisentrager v. Forrestal (1949), **2002:** 982; **2004:** 997–1001
Eisentrager v. Johnson (1950), **2006:** 1178, 1179, 1181, 1182
Elahi v. Iran (2000), **2001:** 464–65, 469; **2004:** 516; **2006:** 612; **2007:** 479
Elahi v. Iran (2003), **2003:** 554
El Al Israel Airlines, Ltd. v. Tseng (1997), **2001:** 528, 563
El Al Israel Airlines, Ltd. v. Tsui Yuan Tseng (1999), **1991-99:** 709–14, 973, 1344, 1345; **2000:** 493; **2003:** 591, 596, 601; **2008:** 183, 514, 524–25

El-Banna v. Bush (2005), **2005:** 1005
*Electricity Co. of Sofia & Bulgaria (Belgium v. Bulgaria) (1939), **2001:** 601
Electronic Broking Servs., Ltd. v. E-Business Solutions & Servs. (2003), **2003:** 904–5
*Elettronica Sicula S.p.A. (ELSI) (U.S. v. Italy) (1989), **1989-90:** 418; **2000:** 657, 660, 662; **2001:** 633–35; **2003:** 645; **2006:** 501, 723
El-Fadl v. Central Bank of Jordan (1996), **1991-99:** 1188–89; **2002:** 472; **2006:** 636*n,* 637, 645; **2007:** 446, 513
El-Hadad v. Embassy of the United Arab Emirates (1999), **2003:** 570
El-Hadad v. United Arab Emirates (2000), **2000:** 583–86
Elias-Zacarias; INS v. (1992), **1991-99:** 194–97, 200; **2000:** 129, 131, 141; **2008:** 307
Elixir Shipping, Ltd. v. Perusahaan Pertambangan Minyak Dan Gas Bumi Negara (2003), **2003:** 524–26
El-Jassem v. United States (1996), **2006:** 657
Elliott v. British Tourist Authority (1997), **2000:** 585
El Mashad v. Bush (2005), **2005:** 1017
El-Masri v. Tenet (2006), **2006:** 163
El-Masri v. United States (2007), **2007:** 238–46, 250–51
El-Shifa Pharm. Indus. Co. v. United States (2004), **2004:** 206–14; **2006:** 525
Emami v. U.S. Dist. Court (1987), **2001:** 484
Embassy of the People's Republic of Benin v. District of Columbia Bd. of Zoning Adjustment (1987), **2001:** 541
Emergency Coal. to Defend Educ. Travel v. U.S. Dep't of the Treasury (2008), **2008:** 810–13
EM Ltd. v. Republic of Argentina (2007), **2007:** 494–504
Emmanuel; United States v. (2007), **2007:** 173–80
Emmanuel Constant, In re (1995), **1991-99:** 118–21
Employment Div., Dep't of Human Res. v. Smith (1990), **2001:** 134, 136
Empresa Cubana del Tabaco v. Culbro Corp. (2005), **2004:** 663–70; **2005:** 663–71
Empresa Cubana del Tabaco v. General Cigar Co. (2005), **2006:** 796–801
Empresa Cubana Exportadora de Alimentos y Productos Varios d/b/a Cubaexport v. Department of Treasury, Office of Foreign Assets Control (2006), **2006:** 1006–15
Empresa Cubana Exportadora de Alimentos y Productos Varios d/b/a Cubaexport v. Department of Treasury, Office of Foreign Assets Control (2007), **2007:** 828–30
Emuegbunam; United States v. (2001), **2005:** 49, 52; **2008:** 38
Enahoro v. Abubakar (2005), **2005:** 425, 504–5, 580–81; **2006:** 443, 482, 571, 636; **2007:** 513

Enahoro v. Abubakar (2006), **2006:** 482
Encuentro del Canto Popular v. Christopher (1996), **1991-99:** 71
Encyclopaedia Universalis S.A. v. Encyclopaedia Britannica, Inc. (2005), **2007:** 788
Enewetak, People of v. United States (1988), **2006:** 321
Enger; United States v. (1978), **2001:** 531; **2002:** 553
Engle v. Isaac (1982), **2006:** 72
Englewood, City of v. Socialist People's Libyan Arab Jamahiriya (1985), **2001:** 500; **2002:** 542, 579; **2006:** 602
Enmund v. Florida (1982), **2005:** 386
Enterprise Mgmt. Consultants, Inc. v. United States (1989), **2007:** 472–73
Entertainment A-Float v. Connecticut (1993), **1991-99:** 1626–29
Erie R.R. Co. v. Tompkins (1938), **2004:** 347, 349
Erie R.R. Co.; United States v. (1929), **2006:** 923, 924
Erika, Inc.; United States v. (1982), **2001:** 559
Erlenbaugh v. United States (1972), **2000:** 195
Escobar v. Gonzales (2005), **2008:** 306
Escobedo v. United States (1980), **2000:** 212; **2001:** 82, 83*n*
Esparza-Ponce; United States v. (1999), **1991-99:** 260
Espinoza v. Reagan (1983), **1989-90:** 213
Estate of. *See name of party*
Estrada-Posadas v. INS (1991), **1991-99:** 224; **2000:** 130
*E-Systems, Inc. and Islamic Republic of Iran (1983), **2004:** 418
Ethiopia v. Nemariam (2003), **2003:** 479
*Ethyl Corp. v. Government of Canada (1998), **1991-99:** 1436; **2004:** 585
Et Ve Balik Kurumu v. B.N.S. Int'l Sales Corp. (1960), **1989-90:** 318
Eunique v. Albright (1999), **2001:** 11, 12
Eunique v. Powell (2002), **2002:** 13–15
Eurodif, S.A.; United States v. (2008), **2008:** 953–60
Eurodif, S.A.; United States v. (2009), **2008:** 953*n*
Euromepa, In re (1995), **2004:** 857
Euromepa, S.A. v. R. Esmerian, Inc. (1995), **2003:** 878, 879
*European Parliament v. Commission of the European Communities (2006), **2006:** 168
*European Parliament v. Council of the European Union (2006), **2006:** 168
Examining Bd. of Eng'rs, Architects and Surveyors v. Flores de Otero (1976), **1991-99:** 13, 810
*Exors. of F. Lederer v. German Government (1923), **2003:** 439*n*
Ex parte. *See name of party*
Export Group v. Reef Indus., Inc. (1995), **2001:** 76
Extradition of. *See name of party*

Exxon Mobil Corp.; Doe v. (2005), **2002:** 357–63, 575; **2003:** 393*n,* 396, 400; **2005:** 411–12, 424
Exxon Mobil Corp.; Doe v. (2007), **2008:** 223
Exxon Mobil Corp. v. Doe (2008), **2008:** 222–27

F

Factor v. Laubenheimer (1933), **1989-90:** 81; **2000:** 199, 597–98
Faculty Senate of Fla. Int'l Univ. v. Winn (2007), **2007:** 235–38
Faddoul v. INS (1994), **2000:** 129
Fairfax's Devisee v. Hunter's Lessee (1813), **2000:** 497*n*
Falcoal, Inc. v. Turkiye Komur Isletmeleri Kurumu (1987), **1989-90:** 286
Fallini v. United States (1995), **2002:** 511
Falls v. Downie (1994), **1991-99:** 354
Faniel v. Chesapeake & Potomac Tel. Co. (1979), **2006:** 586
Faragher v. City of Boca Raton (1998), **2005:** 263
Farmer v. Brennan (1994), **2005:** 292
Fatin v. INS (1993), **1991-99:** 209, 218–23, 221*n*
Faulder v. Johnson (1996), **1991-99:** 255, 272–80
Fauziya Kasinga, In re (1996), **1991-99:** 200, 201
Favour Mind Ltd. v. Pacific Shores, Inc. (1999), **1991-99:** 774–75, 1142
Faysound Ltd. v. Walter Fuller Aircraft Sales, Inc. (1990), **1991-99:** 1333
FBI v. Abramson (1982), **1991-99:** 792
FCC v. League of Women Voters of California (1984), **2007:** 255
FDIC v. Mallen (1988), **2001:** 113; **2002:** 98
FDIC v. Meyer (1994), **2000:** 548; **2002:** 564; **2003:** 365; **2004:** 309, 504, 515; **2008:** 413
Feder v. Evans-Feder (1995), **1991-99:** 353; **2000:** 107*n;* **2004:** 63
Federal Housing Admin. v. Burr (1940), **2000:** 547
Federal Housing Admin. v. Darlington, Inc. (1958), **2000:** 197
Federal Mogul Corp. v. United States (1995), **2001:** 760
Federal Republic of. *See name of country*
Fedorenko v. United States (1981), **1991-99:** 29, 30–31; **2004:** 2–4
*Feldman v. Mexico (2002), **2004:** 579*n,* 582
Felix-Felix; United States v. (2001), **2005:** 42*n*
Felker v. Turpin (1996), **2004:** 997
Feng Suo Zhou v. Li Peng (2000), **2002:** 581–85
Feng Suo Zhou v. Li Peng (2001), **2001:** 549–53
Ferdinand E. Marcos Human Rights Litig., In re Estate of (1992), **1991-99:** 980, 1280–81; **2000:** 400, 401*n,* 403, 408
Ferdinand E. Marcos Human Rights Litig., In re Estate of (1994), **1991-99:** 978, 979; **2001:** 319, 334; **2002:** 324; **2003:** 354; **2004:** 350; **2006:** 434

Ferdinand E. Marcos Human Rights Litig., In re Estate of (1996), **2005:** 526, 576
Feres v. United States (1950), **2004:** 513, 515
Fernandez v. Phillips (1925), **1989-90:** 84; **2000:** 212; **2005:** 99
Fernandez; United States v. (2006), **2008:** 40
Fernandez-Vargas v. Ashcroft (2005), **2006:** 30
Fernandez-Vargas v. Gonzales (2006), **2006:** 29–33, 38
Ferrara; United States v. (1995), **2003:** 534
Ferreira; United States v. (1852), **1991-99:** 423–25
Ferreira; United States v. (2001), **2007:** 176
Ferreiro v. United States (2002), **2002:** 236–42
Ferrostaal Metals Corp. v. S.S. Lash Pacifico (1987), **1989-90:** 301
FG Hemisphere Assocs., LLC v. Democratic Republic of Congo (2006), **2006:** 562, 572, 621–26, 658
Fiallo v. Bell (1977), **1991-99:** 4, 8; **2004:** 17; **2008:** 911
Fidelity Constr. Co. v. United States (1983), **1991-99:** 660
Fidelity Int'l Currency Adviser A Fund, L.L.C. v. United States (2007), **2007:** 98–99
Field v. Clark (1892), **2000:** 212*n;* **2001:** 204*n,* 211; **2006:** 732
*Fierro, Cesar (2003), **1991-99:** 289–90
Filartiga v. Pena-Irala (1980), **1991-99:** 978, 981, 985–88, 990, 1264, 1279, 1281; **2000:** 382, 400; **2001:** 319, 323, 442*n;* **2002:** 323, 328–29, 334, 336, 340, 474, 563; **2003:** 354, 359, 368, 369, 377, 385, 389, 392; **2004:** 340, 346, 350, 353*n;* **2006:** 430, 480, 650, 652; **2007:** 178, 218; **2008:** 216
Filtech S.A. v. France Telecom S.A. (2002), **2002:** 517
Filus v. LOT Polish Airlines (1993), **2002:** 516
Finamar Investors Inc. v. Republic of Tadjikistan (1995), **2000:** 592
Finanz AG Zurich v. Banco Economico S.A. (1999), **2001:** 43; **2006:** 449, 520; **2007:** 229
Finland v. Town of Pelham (1966), **2000:** 598–99; **2001:** 548
*Finnish Ships Arbitration (1934), **2000:** 662
Fireman's Fund Co. v. Fuji Elec. Sys. Co. (2005), **2005:** 847–50
Fireman's Ins. Co. v. Onwualia (1994), **2000:** 613; **2002:** 560
First Am. Corp. v. Al-Nahyan (1996), **1991-99:** 1286–89, 1333; **2001:** 513, 519, 521; **2002:** 548, 549*n;* **2006:** 637
First Am. Corp. v. Al-Nahyan (2000), **2003:** 570
First City, N.A. v. Rafidain Bank (2002), **2006:** 609, 610
First English Evangelical Lutheran Church v. Los Angeles County (1987), **2002:** 224*n*
First Fid. Bank, N.A. v. Government of Antigua & Barbuda—Permanent Mission (1989), **2004:** 462
First Nat'l City Bank v. Banco Nacional de Cuba (1972), **1991-99:** 709, 985, 1268; **2000:** 201; **2005:** 38, 535; **2007:** 744; **2008:** 454

First Nat'l City Bank v. Banco Para El Comercio Exterior de Cuba (1972), **2005:** 519, 552, 554
First Nat'l City Bank v. Banco Para El Comercio Exterior de Cuba (1983) (Bancec), **1989-90:** 306–7; **1991-99:** 1230–31, 1233–34; **2001:** 493, 525, 526; **2002:** 483, 512, 546; **2004:** 505, 517, 668; **2006:** 619, 1009; **2007:** 484, 497–99
Fisher v. INS (1996), **1991-99:** 201; **2000:** 129
Fisher v. Texas (1999), **2004:** 45
*Fisheries Case (U.K. v. Norway), **2002:** 751–52
*Fisheries Jurisdiction Case (Spain v. Canada) (1998), **2006:** 704
Fitzpatrick; United States v. (1963), **1991-99:** 1239
Flatow v. Islamic Republic of Iran (1998), **1991-99:** 1224, 1227, 1243, 1247, 1263–65, 1335; **2000:** 542–48, 554–57, 560; **2001:** 336, 469, 495; **2002:** 545–47; **2003:** 537; **2006:** 582
Flatow v. Islamic Republic of Iran (1999), **2001:** 500; **2002:** 542; **2008:** 413, 414
Flatow v. Islamic Republic of Iran (2000), **1991-99:** 1227–28
Fleming v. Mohawk Wrecking & Lumber Co. (1947), **1991-99:** 2159
Fleming v. Page (1850), **2005:** 1011
Flemming v. Nestor (1960), **1991-99:** 1241
Flick v. Johnson (1949), **2006:** 1208, 1209
Flick v. Johnson (1950), **2007:** 958
Flores v. Arizona (2005), **2007:** 301
Flores v. Contreras (1998), **1991-99:** 355
Flores v. Johnson (2000), **2004:** 48
Flores v. Southern Peru Copper Corp. (2002), **2002:** 344–45; **2003:** 371
Flores v. Southern Peru Copper Corp. (2003), **2003:** 372–74, 389; **2004:** 356–58; **2005:** 57*n,* 251, 396; **2008:** 42
Flores v. State (1999), **1991-99:** 264
Flores; United States v. (1933), **1991-99:** 1256; **2003:** 368
Flores; United States v. (1995), **2001:** 294
Flores-Montano; United States v. (2004), **2005:** 291
Florida v. Van Den Borre (1989), **1989-90:** 339
Florida v. White (1999), **2001:** 114
Florida Power and Light Co. v. Lorion (1985), **2000:** 136
Floyd v. District of Columbia (1997), **2001:** 464
Fluent v. Salamanca Indian Lease Auth. (1991), **2007:** 472
Flynn v. Shultz (1984), **2002:** 589
FMAC Loan Receivables v. Dagra (2005), **2005:** 856–58, 862–63
Fogade v. ENB Revocable Trust (2001), **2004:** 498
Fok Yung Yo v. United States (1902), **2006:** 1192
Foley Bros., Inc. v. Filardo (1949), **1989-90:** 448; **1991-99:** 167; **2000:** 465; **2003:** 370; **2004:** 999

Fong Yue Ting v. United States (1893), **1991-99:** 422*n;* **2000:** 9, 10, 192; **2003:** 365; **2004:** 371; **2005:** 405; **2006:** 1192
Footwear Distributors and Retailers of Am. v. United States (1995), **2001:** 760
Ford v. Clement (1993), **1991-99:** 1311–12
Ford v. Garcia (2002), **2002:** 348–51; **2003:** 377
Ford v. Surget (1878), **1991-99:** 983
Ford v. United States (1927), **2003:** 260
Foreign Ministry of the Kingdom of Denmark v. Los Angeles (2004), **2004:** 542–47
Foremost-McKesson, Inc. v. Islamic Republic of Iran (1990), **1991-99:** 1192, 1231; **2000:** 480; **2001:** 436, 437, 463, 479, 493; **2003:** 504–5
*Forets du Rhodope Central (Greece v. Bulgaria) (1933), **2004:** 598*n*
Forti v. Suarez-Mason (1987), **1991-99:** 985, 1281
Foster v. Florida (2002), **2005:** 270; **2007:** 304
Foster v. Neilson (1829), **1989-90:** 347; **1991-99:** 117, 160, 1128; **2001:** 334; **2002:** 221; **2003:** 259, 261, 363; **2005:** 49, 245; **2008:** 156, 178, 184
Foti v. City of Menlo Park (1998), **2005:** 126; **2006:** 181
Foucha v. Louisiana (1992), **2004:** 1008
Foxman v. Foxman (1992), **2004:** 61
Foxworth v. Permanent Mission of the Republic of Uganda to the United Nations (1992), **2000:** 553, 624
FPC v. Tuscarora Indian Nation (1960), **1991-99:** 801
*Fraenkel (U.S. v. Yugoslavia) (1954), **2001:** 578–79
*France; United States v. (Change-of-Gauge arbitration) (1978), **2000:** 657–61, 665
*Francovich (1991), **2003:** 693
Frank v. Herter (1959), **2003:** 493*n*
Franklin v. Gwinnett County Pub. Sch. (1992), **2005:** 264
Franklin v. Massachusetts (1992), **2001:** 208, 751
Frazee v. Illinois Dep't of Employment (1989), **2007:** 328
FRC Int'l, Inc. v. Taifun Feuerloschgeratebau und Vertriebs GmbH (2002), **2004:** 71
Freedom to Travel Campaign v. Newcomb (1996), **1991-99:** 53–54; **2001:** 83; **2004:** 480; **2008:** 812
Freeport-McMoRan Inc. v. K N Energy, Inc. (1991), **2002:** 489
Free Speech Coalition; Ashcroft v. (2002), **2003:** 199
Freier v. Freier (1996), **1991-99:** 363, 366, 370–71
Frelinghuysen v. Key (1884), **1989-90:** 214; **2006:** 736
French, In re (2006), **2008:** 232
*Frenkel (U.S. v. Austria) (1929), **2001:** 603
Freund v. France (2008), **2006:** 504–7

Friedar v. Israel (1985), **2000:** 586*n*
Friedrich v. Friedrich (1993), **1991-99:** 350–53, 369; **2004:** 63
Friedrich v. Friedrich (1996), **1991-99:** 357–60, 363–65, 367–70; **2000:** 98–101, 103, 104, 111, 112*n*, 137*n*
Friend v. Reno (1999), **1991-99:** 10
Friends of Earth v. Consolidated Rail Corp. (1985), **2000:** 193
Frisbie v. Collins (1952), **1991-99:** 505; **2008:** 130
Fritz v. Salii (1988), **1991-99:** 822
Frolova v. Union of Soviet Socialist Republics (1985), **1989-90:** 283, 285; **1991-99:** 161, 1192, 1193; **2000:** 480; **2001:** 290, 297, 434*n*, 436, 437, 479–81; **2003:** 525; **2005:** 57*n*
Frumkin v. JA Jones, Inc. (2001), **2001:** 387; **2004:** 436*n*
FTC v. Travelers Health Ass'n (1960), **2000:** 469–70
Fuentes v. Shevin (1972), **2005:** 279
Fujitsu Ltd. v. Federal Express Corp. (2001), **2001:** 558*n*; **2002:** 437*n*
Fuller, In the Matter of the Claim of (1971), **2002:** 241*n*
Furman v. Georgia (1972), **2005:** 382
Furnes v. Reeves (2004), **2004:** 54–62
*Futura Trading v. National Iranian Oil Co. (Iran–U.S.) (1986), **2008:** 489
FW/PBS, Inc. v. City of Dallas (1990), **2001:** 464

G

G-A-, Matter of (2002), **2005:** 349–50
*Gabcikovo-Nagymaros Case (Hungary v. Slovakia) (1997), **1991-99:** 1109, 1110; **2000:** 663–65; **2001:** 367–69
Gadsby & Hann v. Socialist Republic of Romania (1988), **1989-90:** 301
Gallina v. Fraser (1960), **1989-90:** 81, 84–85; **1991-99:** 942; **2001:** 77*n*; **2006:** 158*n*
Gallo Winery v. Andina Licores S.A. (2006), **2007:** 774–75, 794
Galvan v. Press (1954), **1991-99:** 9; **2000:** 11
Galvan v. Press (1965), **2008:** 911
Gambell, Vill. of v. Hodel (1989), **2002:** 250–51
Gamez; United States v. (2002), **2005:** 42*n*
*GAMI Invs. v. Mexico (2004), **2003:** 642–48
Gandara v. Bennett (2008), **2007:** 80–81; **2008:** 42–44
Ganjour v. INS (1986), **2000:** 130
Garb v. Republic of Poland (2002), **2002:** 492–94, 497, 509, 513–16; **2003:** 521–22; **2006:** 573, 574, 576
Garb v. Republic of Poland (2004), **2004:** 432, 496–500
Garb v. Republic of Poland (2006), **2006:** 558–61, 572; **2007:** 465–66
Garcia v. INS (1993), **2000:** 132
Garcia v. Lee (1838), **1991-99:** 117
Garcia; United States ex rel. Saroop v. (1997), **2002:** 215–16

Garcia-Mir v. Meese (1986), **2001:** 443; **2005:** 496
Garcia-Mir v. Smith (1985), **1991-99:** 192
Gardiner Stone Hunter Int'l v. Iberia Lineas Aereas de Espana (1995), **2002:** 469
*Garrison's Case (U.S. v. Mexico), **2001:** 631
Garza, In re (2001), **2001:** 294–96
Garza v. Lappin (2001), **2001:** 291–302
Garza; United States v. (1995), **2000:** 389, 396; **2001:** 294
Garza v. United States (1996), **2000:** 389; **2001:** 294
Garza; United States v. (1999), **2000:** 389, 396
Gates v. Bismullah (2008), **2007:** 944*n*; **2008:** 905
Gates v. Victor Fine Foods (1995), **1991-99:** 1188
Gatlin; United States v. (2000), **2004:** 168
Gau Shan Co. v. Bankers Trust Co. (1992), **2002:** 866*n,* 867; **2004:** 842, 844, 848; **2006:** 961
Gebremichael v. INS (1993), **1991-99:** 223–24
Gebser v. Lago Vista Indep. Sch. Dist. (1998), **2005:** 264
Gecas; United States v. (1997), **1991-99:** 571
General Dynamics Corp. v. United States (1998), **2001:** 479
General Elec. Capital Corp. v. Grossman (1993), **2001:** 497
General Elec. Co. v. Deutz AG (2001), **2002:** 866*n,* 867; **2004:** 842; **2006:** 521
General Universal Trading Corp. v. Morgan Guar. Trust Co. (1991), **1991-99:** 385
*Genie Lacayo Case (1997), **2002:** 268*n*
*Genin v. Republic of Estonia (2001), **2007:** 545
Geofroy v. Riggs (1890), **1991-99:** 678
Geren v. Omar (2007), **2007:** 957–68
Gerling Global Reinsurance Corp. v. Gallagher (2001), **1991-99:** 1134; **2001:** 414*n;* **2002:** 417, 421, 425, 451–52*n,* 454, 456*n*
Gerling Global Reinsurance Corp. v. Low (Low I) (2001), **2001:** 414*n,* 470; **2002:** 416
Gerling Global Reinsurance Corp. v. Low (Low II) (2002), **2002:** 416; **2003:** 462, 469
Gerling Global Reinsurance Corp. v. Nelson (2000), **2000:** 461*n*
Gerling Global Reinsurance Corp. v. Quackenbush (2000), **2000:** 460–73, 695
*Germany v. Poland (1932), **2001:** 587
Germany v. United States. *See* LaGrand
*Germany; United States v. (1924), **2001:** 577
*Germany; United States v. (1926), **2001:** 579
*Germany, Federal Republic of v. Denmark (1969), **2001:** 596–98
*Germany, Federal Republic of v. Netherlands (1969), **2001:** 596–98
Germany, Federal Republic of v. United States (1999), **1991-99:** 258

Gerritsen v. Consulado Gen. de Mexico (1993), **1991-99:** 1309–12
Gerritsen v. de la Madrid (1986), **1989-90:** 315; **2001:** 514, 519
Gerritsen v. de la Madrid Hurtado (1987), **2002:** 540; **2003:** 510
Gerritsen v. Escobar y Cordova (1988), **1989-90:** 349–50; **2002:** 562
Gerstein v. Pugh (1975), **2000:** 212
Ghaly v. INS (1995), **2000:** 130
Gherebi v. Bush (2003), **2003:** 1028; **2004:** 980, 1017–18, 1017*n*
Gherebi v. Bush (2004), **2004:** 1017*n*, 1018*n*
Gianoli Aldunate, In re Application of (1993), **1991-99:** 386
Gibbons v. Etpison (1992), **1991-99:** 822
Gibbons v. Etpison (1993), **1991-99:** 822
Gibbons v. Salii (1986), **1991-99:** 822
Gibson v. Babbitt (2000), **2001:** 131
Gibson v. Matthews (1991), **2001:** 12
Gideon v. Wainwright (1963), **2005:** 281
Gilbert v. Homar (1997), **2001:** 113; **2002:** 98
Gill v. Imundi (1990), **1989-90:** 88, 91
Ginsberg; United States v. (1917), **1991-99:** 9, 15; **2000:** 9, 17–18
Giordano; United States v. (1974), **2006:** 66
Gisbert v. U.S. Att'y Gen. (1993), **2001:** 441*n;* **2005:** 496
*Glamis Gold, Ltd. v. United States, **2006:** 709–26; **2007:** 535–48
Glencore Grain Rotterdam B.V. v. Shivnath Rai Harnarain Co. (2002), **2002:** 874
Glen Cove, City of; United States v. (1971), **1989-90:** 384; **2002:** 581; **2006:** 596, 597, 661
Glenore Denrees Paris v. Department of Nat'l Store Branch 1 (Vietnam) (2000), **2000:** 590–93, 616–26
Global Index, Inc. v. Mkapa (2003), **2003:** 507–8
Global Relief Found., Inc. v. O'Neill (2002), **2002:** 94–98; **2006:** 1014
Global Servs. Int'l, Inc. v. United States (2002), **2002:** 101
Globe Nuclear Servs. and Supply GNSS, Ltd. v. AO Technsnaabexport (2004), **2004:** 483
Glucksman v. Henkel (1911), **1989-90:** 81; **2000:** 212; **2005:** 99
Goldberg v. Kelly (1970), **2005:** 279
Goldstar (Panama) S.A. v. United States (1991), **1991-99:** 1126
Goldstar (Panama) S.A. v. United States (1992), **1991-99:** 1126–28; **2000:** 316, 491; **2002:** 215, 216, 992; **2003:** 260, 263; **2005:** 83
Goldwater v. Carter (1979), **1989-90:** 245; **1991-99:** 651, 656, 756; **2001:** 205, 207, 446; **2002:** 199, 201–2; **2004:** 454; **2005:** 484; **2006:** 540; **2007:** 442
Gomez v. INS (1991), **1991-99:** 221, 230
Gomez-Diaz v. Ashcroft (2003), **2003:** 1–2; **2008:** 12
Gonzaga Univ. v. Doe (2002), **2006:** 77–78, 80, 85; **2007:** 79

Gonzales v. O Centro Espirita Beneficente Uniao Do Vegetal (2005), **2005:** 137–44, 137*n*
Gonzales v. O Centro Espirita Beneficente Uniao Do Vegetal (2006), **2006:** 221–25
Gonzales v. Oregon (1992), **2005:** 268*n*
Gonzalez v. Reno (2000), **2000:** 115–41
Gonzalez v. Vila (2007), **2007:** 516–21
Gorshkow; United States v. (2002), **2002:** 5–6
Gospel Missions of Am. v. City of Los Angeles (2005), **2006:** 185
Goss Int'l Corp. v. Man Roland Druckmaschinen AG (2006), **2006:** 959
Goss Int'l Corp. v. Man Roland Druckmaschinen AG (2007), **2007:** 776–80
Goss Int'l Corp. v. Tokyo Kikai Seisakusho, Ltd. (2006), **2006:** 958–63; **2008:** 761, 764–71
*Gould Mktg. Inc. v. Ministry of Def. of the Islamic Republic of Iran (1984), **1991-99:** 1090
Government of. *See name of specific country*
Granados de la Paz, In re (2007), **2008:** 73
Grand Jury Proceedings, In re (1980), **2006:** 649
Grand Jury Proceedings, In re (1987), **1991-99:** 1270; **2003:** 563
Grand Jury Proceedings, In re John Doe #700 (1987), **1991-99:** 1278
*Grand River Enters. Six Nations, Ltd. v. United States, **2006:** 688–93; **2008:** 170–74, 351–57, 528–42
Grannis v. Ordean (1918), **2005:** 279
*Grant v. Jamaica (1988), **2000:** 392*n*
Gratz v. Bollinger (2003), **2007:** 299–300
Gray v. Permanent Mission of People's Republic of Congo to the UN (1973), **2005:** 557
Gray v. Permanent Mission of People's Republic of Congo to the UN (1978), **2000:** 592; **2002:** 540; **2003:** 510; **2004:** 555
Grayned v. City of Rockford (1972), **2005:** 126; **2006:** 181
Great N. Ry. Co. v. O'Connor (1914), **2004:** 833
Great N. Ry. Co. v. Thompson (1963), **2006:** 923
Great W. Ins. Co. v. United States (1884), **1991-99:** 661
Greenbaum v. Islamic Republic of Iran (2006), **2008:** 410–18
Greene v. Le Dorze (1998), **2005:** 855
Greene v. United States (1996), **2000:** 192, 196
Greenspan v. Crosbie (1976), **2001:** 533, 534; **2002:** 552*n*; **2006:** 633, 634, 638; **2007:** 512, 514
Gregoire v. Biddle (1949), **1989-90:** 319; **2006:** 644
Gregorian v. Izvestia (1989), **1989-90:** 301; **2001:** 404
Gregory v. Ashcroft (1991), **2003:** 477
Grin v. Shine (1902), **1991-99:** 602; **2000:** 210, 211
Groh v. Ramirez (2004), **2004:** 353

Gross v. British Broad. Corp. (2004), **2004:** 875–78
Gross v. German Found. Indus. Initiative (2006), **2006:** 507–17, 524*n*
Gross v. German Found. Indus. Initiative (2007), **2007:** 421–26; **2008:** 424, 425
Gross v. German Found. Indus. Initiative (2008), **2008:** 424–27
Gross v. German Found. Indus. Initiative (2009), **2008:** 424
Gross v. Volkswagen (2006), **2000:** 504, 505
Gruenburg v. Kavanagh (1976), **2005:** 277
*Gruslin v. Malaysia (2000), **2006:** 698
Grutter v. Bollinger (2003), **2007:** 299–300
Guam v. Ignacio (1993), **2007:** 180
Guantanamo Bay Detainee Litig., In re (2005), **2005:** 995–1008, 1017–18
Guantanamo Bay Detainee Litig., In re (2008), **2008:** 906–14
Guaranty Trust Co. of N.Y. v. United States (1938), **1989-90:** 245, 247, 255; **2000:** 477; **2001:** 433; **2002:** 497, 507
Guardian F. v. Archdiocese of San Antonio (1994), **1991-99:** 1290–91; **2001:** 514
Guaylupo-Moya v. Gonzales (2005), **2006:** 640
Guinand; United States v. (1988), **2000:** 597
Guinto v. Marcos (1986), **2002:** 336
Gulf Oil Corp. v. Gilbert (1947), **2001:** 336; **2003:** 896–97, 900–901; **2005:** 835; **2007:** 798–99
Gustafson v. Alloyd Co. (1995), **2001:** 586, 587
Gutter v. Bollinger (2003), **2005:** 289

H

H–, Matter of (1996), **1991-99:** 209
Hababou v. Albright (2000), **2001:** 68, 69*n*
Habib v. Bush (2002), **2002:** 981; **2004:** 995
Hafer v. Melo (1991), **2003:** 542
Hagan, In re (1986), **2004:** 546
Hagenbuch v. 3B6 Sistemi Elettronici (2005), **2005:** 843–46
Haig v. Agee (1981), **1989-90:** 14, 16, 213, 261; **1991-99:** 52–53, 56, 647*n*, 794, 801, 1136; **2000:** 400, 411, 527; **2001:** 116, 452; **2002:** 14, 100, 200, 589; **2003:** 468, 492; **2005:** 535; **2006:** 457; **2008:** 13–14, 450, 813
Hair v. United States (2002), **2002:** 460–61
Hair v. United States (2003), **2003:** 475–76
Haitian Ctrs. Council v. Sale (1993), **1991-99:** 188–90
Haitian Refugee Ctr. v. Baker (1995), **1991-99:** 176, 189–90, 193
Haitian Refugee Ctr. v. Gracey (1985), **1991-99:** 161, 170, 172, 178; **2001:** 291
Haitian Refugee Ctr. v. Gracey (1987), **1989-90:** 51; **1991-99:** 159

Hallock v. Bonner (2004), **2006:** 573
Hallowell v. Commons (1916), **1991-99:** 1262; **2002:** 514
Hallstrom v. Tillamook County (1989), **2002:** 482
Hamdan v. Gates (2008), **2008:** 916–17
Hamdan v. Rumsfeld (2004), **2004:** 981, 1017–29; **2005:** 969, 1008
Hamdan v. Rumsfeld (2005), **2005:** 994; **2006:** 84*n*
Hamdan v. Rumsfeld (2006) (Supreme Ct.), **2006:** 369, 462, 1115, 1138–55, 1160, 1185*n*, 1210; **2007:** 883–84, 909, 916, 918, 920–21, 938–39, 956, 973, 975–76; **2008:** 190
Hamdan v. Rumsfeld (2006) (D.D.C.), **2006:** 1177–79
Hamdi v. Rumsfeld (2002), **2002:** 986–97
Hamdi v. Rumsfeld (2003), **2003:** 1028–30
Hamdi v. Rumsfeld (2004), **2003:** 1027*n*; **2004:** 204, 210, 211, 213, 979, 1001–15, 1029; **2005:** 265–66, 963, 1000–1002, 1004–6, 1011, 1016; **2006:** 523, 1183, 1198, 1210; **2007:** 948, 952, 958, 972, 974; **2008:** 309
Hamdi; United States v. (2003), **2003:** 573–74
Hamdi; United States v. (2004), **2004:** 533, 534–39; **2006:** 654, 657
Hamid v. Gonzales (2005), **2006:** 154
Hamid v. INS (1976), **1989-90:** 24, 26
Hamid v. Price Waterhouse (1995), **1991-99:** 979
Hammell v. Banque Paribas (1991), **1991-99:** 1308–9
Hammer v. INS (1999), **1991-99:** 27, 31–34
Hammond; United States v. (2004), **2005:** 117*n*
Hammontree v. NLRB (1991), **2005:** 413
Hammoud; United States v. (2004), **2004:** 127–28
Hanil Bank v. Pt. Bank Negara Indonesia (Persero) (1998), **2006:** 575
Hanover Ins. Co. v. United States (1989), **1991-99:** 1535
Hanson v. Denckla (1958), **1991-99:** 1207, 1245; **2003:** 568
Harbor Gateway Comm'l Prop. v. EPA (1999), **2001:** 469
Harisiades v. Shaughnessy (1952), **1989-90:** 213; **1991-99:** 57; **2000:** 10, 497, 527–28; **2001:** 83*n*, 453, 454; **2002:** 200, 590, 595; **2003:** 492; **2005:** 141
Harkness v. Harkness (1998), **1991-99:** 355
Harlow v. Fitzgerald (1982), **2000:** 410; **2002:** 234
Harris v. McRae (1980), **2001:** 287, 288*n*
Harris v. Polskie Linie (1987), **2004:** 512
Harris Corp. v. National Iranian Radio and Television (1982), **1989-90:** 216
Harriss; United States v. (1954), **2005:** 126
Harsacky v. Harsacky (1996), **1991-99:** 355
Hartford Fire Ins. Co. v. California (1993), **1991-99:** 1529–33, 1535, 1536, 1538; **2000:** 470; **2006:** 948; **2008:** 231, 232

Hartford Underwriters Ins. Co. v. Union Planters Bank, N.A. (2000), **2001:** 469
Hartmann v. Sheikh Zayed Bin Sultan Al-Nahyan (1994), **1991-99:** 1285–89
Hartooni v. INS (1994), **2000:** 130
Harvey; United States v. (1993), **2007:** 179–80
*Harrington & Assoc., Inc. v. Islamic Republic of Iran (1987), **2003:** 453*n*
*Harza v. Islamic Republic of Iran (1986), **2003:** 453*n*
Hashemite Kingdom of Jordan v. Layale Enters., S.A. (In re B-727 Aircraft Serial No. 21010) (2001), **2006:** 563
Haskins Bros. & Co. v. Morgenthau (1936), **2001:** 492; **2008:** 413
Hauenstein v. Lynham (1880), **2006:** 66
Havana Club Holding, S.A. v. Galleon, S.A. (2000), **2004:** 667; **2005:** 667, 670; **2006:** 1009
Haven v. Polska (2000), **2003:** 263
Hawkins Bros. & Co. v. Morgenthau (1936), **2000:** 547
*Haya de la Torre (Colombia v. Peru) (1951), **2003:** 73–74
Hayburn's Case (1792), **1991-99:** 424–25, 427
Head Money Cases (Edye v. Robertson) (1884), **1989-90:** 347; **1991-99:** 161, 665, 667, 729, 969, 978, 1128; **2000:** 492; **2001:** 211, 297; **2002:** 215; **2003:** 260–61; **2005:** 49, 1007; **2006:** 65, 85, 468*n;* **2008:** 37, 179, 181, 186
Healy v. Beer Inst. (1989), **2002:** 421–23, 453, 455
Healy v. James (1972), **2006:** 190
Heaney v. Government of Spain (1971), **1991-99:** 1312*n;* **2006:** 633; **2007:** 512
Heckler v. Chaney (1985), **2001:** 85
Heckler v. Matthews (1984), **2000:** 17, 18
Hegna v. Islamic Republic of Iran (2002), **2004:** 517
Hegna v. Islamic Republic of Iran (2003), **2003:** 552–53; **2004:** 521; **2006:** 660; **2007:** 487–89
Hegna v. Islamic Republic of Iran (2004), **2004:** 517–24; **2005:** 548; **2006:** 617
Hegna v. Islamic Republic of Iran (2005), **2006:** 615
Heimbuch v. Ishihara Sangyo Kaisha, Ltd. (2000), **2000:** 500, 504, 505, 506*n,* 515, 517, 529
Heiser v. Iran (2006), **2006:** 581–84
Helicopteros Nacionales de Colombia, S.A. v. Hall (1984), **2003:** 567, 568
Hellenic Lines, Ltd. v. Moore (1965), **2001:** 533, 534; **2002:** 551; **2004:** 555–57
Heller v. Caberta (2002), **2005:** 813–14
Helvering v. Stockholms Enskilada Bank (1934), **2000:** 195

Hener v. United States (1981), **2006:** 831*n*
The Henry Ewbank (1833), **2006:** 833
Hensley v. Municipal Ct. San Jose Milpitas Judicial Dist., Santa Clara County (1973), **2006:** 1197
Herbage v. Meese (1990), **1991-99:** 1213, 1288; **2001:** 479, 518, 521; **2002:** 469; **2006:** 636, 637, 644, 647
Hercaire Int'l, Inc. v. Argentina (1987), **1989-90:** 301; **2001:** 492, 494, 495
Hernandez v. Commissioner (1989), **2005:** 144
Hernandez-Castillo v. Gonzales (2006), **2006:** 36–39
Hester Int'l Corp. v. Federal Republic of Nigeria (1989), **2001:** 493
Hibi; INS v. (1973), **1989-90:** 13
Hickman v. Taylor (1947), **2004:** 1032
Hicks v. Bush (2004), **2004:** 1021
Higgins v. Islamic Republic of Iran (2000), **2002:** 534
Hilao v. Estate of Marcos (1994), **1991-99:** 979; **2003:** 359, 362
Hilao v. Estate of Marcos (1995), **1991-99:** 1265–66
Hilao v. Estate of Marcos (1996), **1991-99:** 989, 1264; **2000:** 411; **2001:** 482; **2002:** 474; **2004:** 316; **2008:** 241, 476
Hilario v. United States (1994), **1991-99:** 603
Hill v. McDonough (2006), **2007:** 304
Hill v. Republic of Iran (2001), **2001:** 475; **2006:** 587
Hillsborough County v. Automated Med. Labs., Inc. (1985), **2002:** 443; **2004:** 510
*Hilson v. Germany (1922), **2003:** 435
Hilton v. Braunskill (1987), **2001:** 87
Hilton v. Guyot (1895), **1989-90:** 322; **1991-99:** 1268, 1829, 1833, 1836–37; **2000:** 737; **2001:** 43, 44, 139; **2004:** 437, 843; **2005:** 46; **2006:** 449, 521, 947, 957, 960; **2007:** 229, 475*n,* 773; **2008:** 230
Hines v. Davidowitz (1941), **1991-99:** 656, 657*n,* 783; **2000:** 471, 529, 530, 536, 539; **2002:** 426, 442–44, 446, 447; **2004:** 510; **2006:** 454; **2007:** 202–3; **2008:** 418
Hirota v. General of the Army MacArthur (1948), **2006:** 1196–98, 1198*n,* 1201, 1202, 1204, 1207–9; **2007:** 957, 958, 965–66, 967*n;* **2008:** 899, 919
Hirsh v. Israel (1997), **2001:** 442*n*
Hitai v. INS (1965), **2005:** 57*n*
Hitz, Ex parte (1884), **2004:** 538
H-M-V, Matter of (1998), **1991-99:** 240
*Hoffland Honey (1983), **2001:** 580, 581
Hogan, In re (1986), **2004:** 544
Holden v. Canadian Consulate (1996), **1991-99:** 1215–16; **2000:** 582, 583, 586
Holder v. Holder (2004), **2004:** 62–65

Holloway v. Arkansas (1978), **2004:** 71, 840
Holloway v. United States (1999), **2004:** 329
*Holman v. Johnson (1775), **2001:** 488*n*
*Holmes v. Bangladesh Bimani Corp. (1989), **2001:** 561*n*
Holmes v. Jennison (1840), **1991-99:** 656; **2001:** 181–83, 187*n*, 206*n*
Holmes v. Laird (1972), **1989-90:** 81; **2000:** 497; **2002:** 201
Holocaust Victim Assets Litig., In re (2000), **1991-99:** 1132; **2000:** 445–46, 457*n*, 458–59
Holocaust Victim Assets Litig., In re (2001), **2001:** 412, 413
Holtzman v. Schlesinger (1973), **2006:** 473, 523
Holy Land Found. for Relief and Dev. v. Ashcroft (2002), **2002:** 98–101; **2003:** 179–80; **2005:** 131–32; **2006:** 1014
Holy Land Found. for Relief and Dev. v. Ashcroft (2003), **2006:** 1012, 1013; **2007:** 151–52; **2008:** 97–98
Home Ins. Co. v. Dick (1930), **2002:** 422, 423, 454, 455
Honduras v. Philip Morris Cos. (2003), **2003:** 855–56
*Honeker, Re (1984), **2001:** 524*n*
Hongla-Yamche; United States v. (1999), **1991-99:** 257
Hooper v. California (1895), **2001:** 552
Hopland Band of Pomo Indians v. United States (1988), **2002:** 510–11
Houck, In re (1997), **2003:** 881
House v. Bell (2006), **2007:** 305
Howard; United States v. (1993), **1991-99:** 428
Howard-Arias; United States v. (1982), **2000:** 402*n*
Howland v. Resteiner (2007), **2007:** 522–26
Hoxha v. Levi (2005), **2005:** 89–94
Hoxha v. Levi (2006), **2008:** 55, 66, 67, 68
Hrisiades v. Shaughnessy (1952), **2004:** 17
Hualpai Indians v. United States ex rel. Santa Fe Pac. R.R. (1941), **2001:** 260
Huaman-Cornelio v. Board (1992), **1991-99:** 206; **2000:** 130
Hue Thi Nguyen v. United States (2002), **2002:** 413–15
Hughes v. Alexandria Scrap Corp. (1976), **2000:** 327–30, 330*n*
Hughes v. Ashcroft (2001), **2002:** 8
Hughes Aircraft Co. v. United States (1976), **1991-99:** 661; **2000:** 498*n*
Hughes Aircraft Co. v. United States ex rel. Schumer (1997), **2001:** 466; **2002:** 496, 497, 499, 501, 506, 507; **2003:** 518
Humane Soc'y of the U.S. v. Brown (1996), **1991-99:** 1733–35
Humane Soc'y of the U.S. v. Clinton (1998), **1991-99:** 1733–35
Humane Soc'y of the U.S. v. Clinton (1999), **1991-99:** 1734
Humane Soc'y of the U.S. v. Clinton (2001), **1991-99:** 1734; **2001:** 760
Humanitarian Law Project v. Ashcroft (2004), **2004:** 126; **2005:** 124
Humanitarian Law Project v. Department of Justice (2003), **2003:** 175; **2004:** 126

Humanitarian Law Project v. Department of State (2004), **2004:** 126
Humanitarian Law Project v. Department of Treasury (2006), **2006:** 183–91
Humanitarian Law Project v. Gonzales (2005), **2005:** 124–28; **2006:** 180–82
Humanitarian Law Project v. Mukasey (2007), **2007:** 143–50
Humanitarian Law Project v. Reno (1998), **1991-99:** 483
Humanitarian Law Project v. Reno (2000), **2000:** 409; **2001:** 115, 290; **2002:** 93–94; **2004:** 125, 126; **2005:** 121, 123; **2006:** 182, 198
Human Rights in China v. Bank of China (2003), **2003:** 531–32
*Hungary v. Slovakia (1997), **2001:** 367
Hunt v. Washington State Apple Advertising Comm'n (1977), **2000:** 322*n*
Husain v. Olympic Airways (2000), **2003:** 590
Husserl v. Swiss Air Transp. Co. (1975), **1991-99:** 1349
Hutchins v. District of Columbia (1999), **2001:** 11
Hutyrczyk; United States v. (1992), **1991-99:** 28
Hu Yau-Leung v. Soscia (1980), **2001:** 67
Hwang Geum Joo v. Japan (2001), **2001:** 396, 430–57, 476; **2002:** 494–503; **2004:** 472, 475–76, 483
Hwang Geum Joo v. Japan (2003), **2003:** 514–15, 522–24
Hwang Geum Joo v. Japan (2004), **2003:** 515*n*
Hwang Geum Joo v. Japan (2005), **2005:** 472, 475–81; **2006:** 456
*Hyundai Marine & Fire Ins. v. Korean Air Lines (1986), **2001:** 562

I

Ibarra v. State (2000), **1991-99:** 263
Ibeh v. Ibeh (2001), **2001:** 537–38
Ibeto Petrochemical Indus., Ltd. v. M/T Beffen (2005), **2005:** 831–32
Ibeto Petrochemical Indus., Ltd. v. M/T Beffen (2007), **2007:** 783, 789–92
Iceland S.S. Co. v. United States Dep't of the Army (2000), **2004:** 537
Igartúa de la Rosa v. United States (1994), **2001:** 290
Igartúa de la Rosa v. United States (2005), **2005:** 242–44; **2008:** 179
Igloo Prods. Corp. v. Thai Welltex Int'l Co. (2005), **2005:** 859
Illinois v. Gates (1983), **2000:** 212
*Illinois Cent. R.R. Co. v. United Mexican States (1926), **1991-99:** 1118
Imbler v. Pachtman (1976), **2002:** 564; **2006:** 651
Inarco Int'l Bank, N.V. v. Lazard Freres & Co. (1998), **2001:** 232*n*
*India; United States v. (2004), **2004:** 424–30
Indiana v. Strom, **1989-90:** 351
Indussa Corp. v. S.S. Ranborg (1967), **1991-99:** 1844–47
Ingenio Porvenir C. Por A. v. United States (1930), **2004:** 210

Inglis v. Trustees of Sailor's Snug Harbor (1830), **2001:** 234*n*
In re. *See name of party*
INS v. *See name of opposing party*
Institute of Aeronautical Archaeological Research, Inc. v. Wreck of Type A "Midget" Japanese Submarine (1993), **1991-99:** 1619–20
Insular Cases (1901–1922), **1989-90:** 102, 103; **1991-99:** 12, 809–11; **2008:** 895–98
Insurance Antitrust Litig., In re (1989), **1991-99:** 1530
Insurance Antitrust Litig., In re (1991), **1991-99:** 1530; **2000:** 470
Insurance Cos.; United States v. (1875), **1991-99:** 984
*Integral Energy & Envtl. Eng'g Ltd. v. Schenker of Canada Ltd. (2001), **2004:** 867
Intel Corp. v. Advanced Micro Devices, Inc. (1993), **2005:** 819
Intel Corp. v. Advanced Micro Devices, Inc. (2003), **2003:** 873–76
Intel Corp. v. Advanced Micro Devices, Inc. (2004), **1991-99:** 386; **2004:** 851–56, 858; **2006:** 966–69
*Interhandel Case (Switz. v. U.S.) (1959), **2008:** 240, 244
International Aircraft Recovery, L.L.C. v. Unidentified, Wrecked and Abandoned Aircraft (2000), **2003:** 755–58; **2004:** 714
International Aircraft Recovery, L.L.C. v. Unidentified, Wrecked and Abandoned Aircraft (2004), **2004:** 714–15
International Ass'n of Indep. Tanker Owners v. Locke (1996), **1991-99:** 775
International Bank for Reconstruction and Dev. v. District of Columbia (1999), **1991-99:** 1332
International Equity Invs., Inc. v. Opportunity Equity Partners, Ltd. (2006), **2008:** 775
International Ins. Co. v. Caja Nacional de Ahorro y Seguro (2002), **2006:** 571
International Ins. Co. v. Caja Nacional de Ahorro y Seguro (2004), **2004:** 863–65
International Road Fed'n v. Embassy of the Dem. Republic of the Congo (2001), **2005:** 503
International Shoe Co. v. Washington (1945), **1991-99:** 1207, 1244; **2001:** 404; **2003:** 567
International Soc'y of Krishna Consciousness, Inc. v. City of N.Y. (1980), **2003:** 579
*International Tech. Prods. Corp. v. Iran (1985), **2001:** 600
*International Thunderbird Gaming Corp. v. United Mexican States (2006), **2004:** 596–601; **2006:** 713, 714, 723, 724
International Union, UAW v. Johnson Controls (1989), **1989-90:** 171
*Interpretation of the Am. Declaration of the Rights and Duties of Man within the framework of Am. Convention on Human Rights (1989), **1989-90:** 166

*Intpro Properties (U.K.) Ltd. v. Sauvel (1983), **2007:** 461
Intrac Arms Int'l v. Albright (1998), **1991-99:** 2256–62
Ipitrade Int'l v. Federal Republic of Nigeria (1978), **1989-90:** 286; **2003:** 525
Iragorri v. United Techs. Corp. (1999), **2005:** 835–36
Iran v. Boeing Co. (1985), **1991-99:** 1835; **2002:** 216*n*
Iran v. McKesson HBOC, Inc. (2001) (2002), **2002:** 219–26, 502–3, 519–22
Iran v. Pahlavi (1981), **2000:** 437–38
Iran v. Pahlavi (1984), **1991-99:** 678; **2000:** 437*n*
Iran v. Pahlavi (1994), **2000:** 438, 441
*Iran v. United States; *ICJ litigation, see "Case Concerning" and case name.*
*Iran v. United States, Cases Nos. A/4, A/7, A/5 (1:F & III) (1997), **2000:** 556*n*
*Iran v. United States, Case No. A/11, **2000:** 429–44
*Iran v. United States, Case No. A/15 (I:G) (1986), **2000:** 432*n*
*Iran v. United States, Case No. A/15 (II:A), **1991-99:** 1089; **2003:** 441–45; **2008:** 410–11*n*, 489
*Iran v. United States, Case No. A/15 (II:B), **1991-99:** 1089
*Iran v. United States, Case No. A/15 (IV)/A/24, **2003:** 446–48
*Iran v. United States, Case No. A/15 (Claim C) (1996), **1991-99:** 1091–94
*Iran; United States v., Case No. A/17 (1985), **2000:** 432*n,* 433
*Iran v. United States, Case No. A/18 (1984), **1991-99:** 1095–96; **2000:** 432*n;* **2001:** 644–46
*Iran v. United States, Case No. A/27 (1998), **1991-99:** 1090–91; **2008:** 417
*Iran; United States v., Case No. A/28 (1998), **2003:** 450–51; **2004:** 416–20; **2008:** 417
*Iran v. United States, Case A/30, **1991-99:** 1094–95; **2003:** 445–46
*Iran; United States v., Case No. A/33 (2004), **2003:** 450–51; **2004:** 416–20
*Iran v. United States, Case No. B/1 (Claims 2 & 3), **1991–99:** 1089, **2008:** 410–11*n*, 489
*Iran v. United States, Case No. B/1 (Claim 4), **1991–99:** 1087–90; **2000:** 432*n*
*Iran v. United States, Case No. B/1 (Claim 6), **1991–99:** 1089
*Iran v. United States, Case No. B/1 (Counterclaim), **2003:** 448–50; **2004:** 420–24
*Iran v. United States, Case No. B/7, **2008,** 410–11*n*
Iran v. United States, Case No. B/61, **1991–99:** 1089; **2003:** 441–45; **2006:** 617–18, **2008:** 485, 485*n*, 486–89
Iran Aircraft Indus. v. Avco Corp. (1992), **2008:** 416

*Iranian Customs Admin. v. United States (1985), **2000:** 432*n*
Iraq v. Beaty (2007), **2008:** 463, 463*n*, 464–71
Iraq v. Beaty (2009), **2008:** 463, 463*n*
Iraq v. Simon (2009), **2008:** 463*n*
*Ireland v. United Kingdom (1978), **2002:** 370*n;* **2004:** 312*n*
Irwin v. Department of Veterans Affairs (1990), **2002:** 588
Isaac v. Rice (1998), **1991-99:** 355
Isamu Carlos Shibayama, In re (2004), **2004:** 223–32
Isbrandtsen Tankers, Inc. v. President of India (1971), **2002:** 510
Islamic Am. Relief Agency v. Unidentified FBI Agents (2005), **2005:** 128–32; **2006:** 187, 1013, 1014
Islamic Salvation Front; Doe v. (2003), **2003:** 384
Islamic Salvation Front; Jane Doe I v. (1998), **2001:** 420; **2002:** 337
Ismael John v. United States (2006), **2006:** 316–25
Israel; Doe v. (2003), **2003:** 571
Israel; Doe v. (2005), **2005:** 566–67, 581–83; **2006:** 636, 645, 646, 681; **2007:** 441, 505, 506
*Israel, Public Committee Against Torture in Israel v. (2006), **2007:** 915
*Italy; United States v. (1989), **2001:** 634–35
Ivancevic v. Artukovic (1954), **2003:** 247
Iwanowa v. Ford Motor Co. (1999), **1991-99:** 979, 980, 989, 990, 992–93; **2002:** 337; **2004:** 436*n*

J

Jackson v. Denno (1964), **2005:** 1003–4
Jackson v. People's Republic of China (1986), **1989-90:** 300; **2000:** 476; **2001:** 432, 433, 457; **2002:** 498, 500, 506; **2003:** 519
Jaeger v. Mitsubishi Materials Corp., **2002:** 438*n*
Jae Won Jeong v. Taiheiyo Cement Corp. (2005), **2004:** 441
*Jaffe v. Miller (1993), **2006:** 641
Jalbuena v. Dulles (1958), **1991-99:** 40
Jama v. Immigration and Customs Enforcement (2005), **2005:** 14–18; **2008:** 467
Jama v. INS (1998), **1991-99:** 991
Jama v. INS (2003), **2004:** 19
Jama v. INS (2004), **2004:** 361
James Daniel Good Real Prop.; United States v. (1993), **2001:** 114; **2005:** 279
Jamison v. Collins (2000), **2001:** 291
Janakakis-Kostun v. Janakakis (1999), **1991-99:** 356, 367
Janakakis-Kostun v. Janakakis (2000), **2000:** 93–105, 111
Jane Doe v. *See name of opposing party*
Janini v. Kuwait Univ. (1995), **2001:** 499
Jankowski-Burczyk v. INS (2002), **2005:** 260

Japanese Immigrant Case (1903), **2008:** 911
Japanese WWII POW Slave/Forced Labor Litig., In re (2000), **2000:** *500n, 505*
Japan Line, Ltd. v. County of Los Angeles (1979), **2000:** 465; **2002:** 422*n,* 426, 427, 453; **2004:** 512; **2005:** 535; **2006:** 454; **2007:** 235
Japan Whaling Ass'n v. American Cetacean Soc'y (1986), **1991-99:** 987; **2000:** 572; **2004:** 436*n;* **2005:** 417, 480; **2006:** 322, 456, 508, 540; **2007:** 221
J-E-, Matter of (2002), **2005:** 350
Jean v. Nelson (1984), **1991-99:** 192–93; **2000:** 131, 132
J.E.B. v. Alabama (1994), **2005:** 278
Jenco v. Islamic Republic of Iran (2001), **2001:** 459; **2002:** 528
Jenco v. Islamic Republic of Iran (2003), **2003:** 549
Jerome B. Grubart, Inc. v. Great Lakes Dredge & Dock Co. (1995), **2004:** 486
*Jespers v. Belgium (1981), **2000:** 396
Jhirad v. Ferrandina (1976), **1989-90:** 81, 83, 84, 87
Jia-Ging Dong v. Slattery (1996), **1991-99:** 202
Jibreel v. U.S. Department of State (2007), **2007:** 18–19
Jifry v. FAA (2004), **2005:** 1013; **2006:** 1010
Jimenez v. United States Dist. Ct. (1963), **2005:** 81; **2007:** 116
Jimenez-Nava; United States v. (2001), **2003:** 260; **2004:** 46–47; **2005:** 36, 49–52; **2008:** 38
Jin v. Ministry of State Sec. (2003), **2002:** 475; **2003:** 394*n*
Jogi v. Piland (2001), **2001:** 335
Jogi v. Voges (2005), **2005:** 60–64; **2006:** 75–86
Jogi v. Voges (2007), **2007:** 78–79
John v. United States (2007), **2007:** 256; **2008:** 245
John v. United States (2009), **2007:** 256; **2008:** 245–47, 247*n*
John Hancock Mutual Life Ins. Co. v. Yates (1936), **2002:** 456
Johns Hopkins Health Sys. Corp. v. Al Reem Gen. Trading & Co. Rep. Est. (2005), **2005:** 815–18
Johnson v. Browne (1907), **2007:** 120–21
Johnson v. Eisentrager (1950), **1989-90:** 103, 106; **1991-99:** 194, 2166; **2002:** 982–84, 991, 1004*n;* **2004:** 214, 997, 998; **2005:** 49, 997–99, 1011–14; **2006:** 1150, 1151, 1180, 1181, 1196, 1209, 1210, 1212; **2007:** 942, 944; **2008:** 897–900
Johnson v. McIntosh (1823), **2001:** 260
Joint Anti-Fascist Refugee Comm. v. McGrath (1951), **2005:** 280
*Jolis, In re (1933-34), **2000:** 404*n*
Jolley v. INS (1971), **1991-99:** 26
*Jones v. Ministry of Interior (2006), **2006:** 641, 649
Jones v. United States (1890), **1989-90:** 245; **1991-99:** 842–43, 1250; **2000:** 201; **2008:** 473

Jones v. United States (1983), **2004:** 1008
Jones; United States v. (2000), **2000:** 160–62, 216
Joo v. Japan (2003), **2003:** 394*n,* 396, 519
Joo v. Japan (2005), **2006:** 516, 733; **2007:** 952
Joseph v. Office of the Consulate Gen. of Nigeria (1987), **1989-90:** 285, 286; **1991-99:** 1192–93, 1298*n,* 1303; **2000:** 480; **2001:** 436, 479–82
Jota v. Texaco, Inc. (1998), **2001:** 44, 336, 486*n;* **2004:** 877
Jota v. Texaco, Inc. (2000), **2000:** 412–14
JPMorgan Chase Bank v. Traffic Stream (BVI) Infrastructure Ltd. (2002), **1991-99:** 771; **2002:** 227–31
*Juan Raul Garza v. United States (2001), **2002:** 265*n*
Juarez-Yepez; United States v. (1999), **1991-99:** 260
Juda v. United States (1988), **2006:** 321
*Judgments of the Admin. Tribunal of the ILO upon Complaints Made against Unesco (1956), **1989-90:** 359
Jugobanka v. U.C.F. Int'l and Slovenijales (1998), **1991-99:** 1168–69
Jugobanka A.D. Belgrade v. Sidex Int'l Furniture Corp. (1998), **2000:** 570
Jungquist v. Nahyan (1996), **1991-99:** 1239
Jungquist v. Sheikh Sultan Bin Khalifa al Nahyan (1997), **2003:** 508, 509, 543
Jung Tang v. Chinese Cultural Ctr. (2002), **2002:** 535–45
Juragua Iron Co. v. United States (1909), **2002:** 988
Justice, Dep't of v. Reporters Comm. for Freedom of the Press (1989), **2005:** 1023; **2006:** 1215
J.W. Hampton, Jr. & Co. v. United States (1928), **1991-99:** 56, 669

K

Kadic v. Karadzic (1995), **1991-99:** 1281–82, 1284, 1335–39; **2001:** 420, 442*n,* 551; **2004:** 351*n,* 1023; **2005:** 425, 472; **2006:** 445, 485, 516, 650, 652; **2007:** 221; **2008:** 239, 243
Kadic v. Karadzic (1996), **1991-99:** 978, 980–89, 993, 994, 1251, 1264; **2001:** 319, 323, 325, 340; **2002:** 324, 334–35, 337, 340–41, 343, 353, 563–64, 583; **2003:** 354
Kaepa, Inc. v. Achilles Corp. (1996), **2002:** 866*n,* 872; **2007:** 778
Kagama; United States v. (1886), **1991-99:** 651
Kahane v. Baker (1991), **1991-99:** 24
Kahane v. Shultz (1987), **1991-99:** 20
Kahane Chai v. Department of State (2006), **2006:** 191–99
Kahn Lucas Lancaster, Inc. v. Lark Int'l, Ltd. (1999), **2000:** 191
Kaine, In re (1852), **1991-99:** 428; **2007:** 111
Kairys v. INS (1992), **1991-99:** 28, 32–33

Kaiser Aluminum & Chem. Corp. v. Bonjorno (1990), **1991-99:** 1263–64
*Kajelijeli; Prosecutor v. (2003), **2004:** 375
Kalejs v. INS (1993), **1991-99:** 27
Kalorama Rd., Inc. v. District of Columbia Foreign Missions Act–Bd. of Zoning Adjustment and the U.S. (2002), **2000:** 634
Kamla Prasad v. INS (1995), **2000:** 130
Kamya v. United Nations (2002), **2002:** 570–72
Kansas v. Colorado (1907), **1991-99:** 972*n*
Kansas v. Marsh (2006), **2007:** 304
Kanth v. Kanth (1999), **1991-99:** 355
Kao Hwa Shipping Co. v. China Steel Corp. (1993), **2002:** 515–16
Karadzic; Doe v. (1994), **1991-99:** 981, 983, 987, 1282; **2001:** 516
Karadzic; Doe v. (2001), **2001:** 340–41
Karaha Bodas Co. v. Bank of Indon. (2006), **2007:** 781
Karaha Bodas Co. v. Pertamina (2003), **2004:** 511
Karaha Bodas Co. v. Perusahaan Pertambangan Minyak Dan Gas Bumi Negara (2006), **2007:** 778, 780, 795
Karaha Bodas Co. v. Perusahaan Pertambangan Minyak Dan Gas Bumi Negara (2007), **2007:** 780; **2008:** 766, 773
Karpova v. Snow (2005), **2006:** 1017
Karsten v. Kaiser Found. Health Plan (1994), **2005:** 88*n*
Kashin v. Kent (2006), **2006:** 308–11
Kasi v. Angelone (2000), **2002:** 77
Kasi v. Angelone (2002), **2002:** 77–78
Kasi v. Commonwealth (1998), **1991-99:** 263; **2002:** 77
Kasi v. Virginia (1999), **2002:** 77
Kasinga, In re (1996), **1991-99:** 207–11, 213
Kasinga, Matter of (1996), **1991-99:** 229
Kasravi v. I.N.S. (1968), **1989-90:** 26
Kato v. Ishihara (2002), **2002:** 477–78
Katz v. United States (1967), **1991-99:** 2350
Kawakita v. United States (1952), **1991-99:** 40
Kawato, Ex parte (1942), **2006:** 1178
*Kaya v. Turkey (2000), **2004:** 312*n*
*Kayishema; Prosecutor v. (1999), **2002:** 350
Kazakhstan v. Biedermann Int'l (1999), **2003:** 862
Kear v. Hilton (1983), **2000:** 405*n*
Keefe v. Dulles (1954), **2003:** 493, 497–98
Keeton v. Hustler Magazine, Inc. (1984), **2003:** 535
Kelberine v. Societe Int'le, Etc. (1965), **2001:** 455
Keller v. Central Bank of Nigeria (2002), **2006:** 636*n*, 637; **2007:** 446, 513
Kelly v. Syria Shell Petroleum Dev. (2000), **2006:** 556; **2007:** 454

Kelso v. United States Dep't of State (1998), **1991-99:** 52–53
Kemp v. Rice (2007), **2007:** 3–8
Kendall v. Saudi Arabia (1965), **1991-99:** 1267
Kennedy v. Mendoza-Martinez (1963), **2004:** 1010
Kennedy v. Mendoza-Martinez (2004), **2005:** 551, 557
Kensington Int'l Ltd. v. Itoua and Société Nationale des Pétroles du Congo (2007), **2007:** 463–70, 508–16
Kensington Int'l Ltd. v. Republic of Congo (2006), **2007:** 468–69
Kent v. Dulles (1958), **1989-90:** 16; **1991-99:** 56; **2001:** 11, 12; **2002:** 14, 15; **2008:** 813
Kentucky v. Graham (1985), **2004:** 506
Ker v. Illinois (1886), **1991-99:** 437, 440, 505; **2008:** 130
Khadr; United States v. (2007), **2007:** 976–82
Khalid v. Bush (2005), **2005:** 1008–18; **2007:** 938
Khan; United States v. (1993), **2008:** 66
Khattak; United States v. (2001), **2008:** 66
Khulumani v. Barclay Nat'l Bank, Ltd. (2007), **2006:** 476, 477; **2007:** 226–27; **2008:** 236, 237
*K.H.W. v. Germany (2001), **2004:** 235
Kilburn v. Islamic Republic of Iran (2004), **2004:** 508–16
Kilburn v. Socialist People's Libyan Arab Jamahiriya (2004), **2004:** 484–89
Kilroy v. Windsor (1978), **1991-99:** 1267, 1270; **2001:** 515; **2006:** 670, 677, 678; **2007:** 448
Kim v. Kim Yong Shik (1963), **2001:** 515
Kimbell Foods, Inc.; United States v. (1979), **2004:** 347
Kim Ho Ma; Ashcroft v. (2000), **2003:** 30
Kim Ho Ma v. Reno (2000), **1991-99:** 93
*King v. Cowle (1759), **2006:** 1198
King; United States v. (1969), **1991-99:** 660
Kin-Hong; United States v. (1997), **2001:** 76–77; **2005:** 80–82; **2007:** 102, 116, 963
Kinsella v. Krueger (1956), **2008:** 75
Kinsey v. United States (1988), **2002:** 511
Kirby, Extradition of (1995), **2001:** 67
Kircher v. Putnam Funds Trust (2006), **2007:** 453
Kiyemba v. Bush (2005), **2008:** 904*n,* 915
Kiyemba v. Bush (2008), **2008:** 912–14, 915–16
Kiyemba v. Obama (2009), **2008:** 912*n*
Klawitter v. INS (1992), **1991-99:** 225, 225*n*
Klein v. The Unidentified, Wrecked & Abandoned Sailing Vessel (1985), **2003:** 757
Kleindienst v. Mandel (1972), **1989-90:** 21, 23; **1991-99:** 9; **2000:** 10; **2006:** 19*n,* 23, 26; **2007:** 19–20, 22, 23, 25

Kline v. Cordero De La Madrid (1989), **1989-90:** 315
Kline v. Kaneko (1988), **1989-90:** 315; **1991-99:** 1275; **2001:** 515, 519; **2006:** 644
Klinghoffer v. S.N.C. Achille Lauro (1991), **2006:** 588, 589
Klinghoffer v. S.N.C. Achille Lauro Ed Al Tri-Gestione Motonave Achille Lauro In Amministrazione Straordinaria (1991), **1991-99:** 986, 1185–86, 1337, 1338–39; **2002:** 341
Klock v. Cain (1993), **2000:** 484*n;* **2001:** 441*n*
Kluge v. Raiffeisen Zentral (2001), **2001:** 396
KMW Int'l v. Chase Manhattan Bank, N.A. (1979), **2000:** 571
Knab v. Republic of Georgia (1998), **1991-99:** 1292–95
Knapp v. Schweitzer (1958), **2001:** 313*n*
Knauer v. United States (1946), **1991-99:** 14
Knauff, United States ex rel. v. Shaughnessy (1950), **2000:** 132; **2004:** 17; **2005:** 291; **2008:** 911
Knight v. Florida (1999), **2001:** 301*n;* **2005:** 270; **2007:** 304
Koehler v. Bank of Bermuda (2000), **2001:** 229, 232–35
Kokkonen v. Guardian Life Ins. Co. (1998), **2008:** 763
Kolender; United States v. (1983), **2005:** 126
Kolovrat v. Oregon (1961), **1991-99:** 783; **2000:** 493, 497*n,* 526, 537, 554*n,* 587, 597, 607; **2001:** 456*n,* 530, 532; **2002:** 440; **2005:** 1024; **2006:** 72, 661, 1217*n;* **2007:** 487*n;* **2008:** 518
Komet, Inc. v. Republic of Finland (2001), **2001:** 485–88; **2002:** 534–35
Koohi v. U.S. (1990), **1989-90:** 217
Koos v. Hom (2002), **2007:** 5, 7
Korean Air Lines Disaster of Sept. 1, 1983, In re (1992), **1991-99:** 1351; **2001:** 561, 562*n,* 563
Koreh; United States v. (1995), **1991-99:** 27–30
Korematsu v. United States (1944), **2004:** 1012
Kossick v. United Fruit Co. (1961), **2004:** 831
Kostadinov; United States v. (1984), **2006:** 657
Kowalchuk; United States v. (1985), **1991-99:** 29
Kozorowski v. Russian Fed'n (1997), **1991-99:** 1258
Kraft Gen. Foods v. Iowa Dep't of Revenue (1992), **2000:** 322
Krishna v. Krishna (1997), **1991-99:** 366; **2000:** 111
Krome, Matter of (1993), **1991-99:** 218
Kruman v. Christie's Int'l PLC (2001), **2001:** 334–35
K.S.B. Tech Sales Corp. v. North Jersey Dist. Water Supply Comm'n (1977), **2000:** 329*n*
Kucinich v. Bush (2002), **2002:** 198–202
*Kügele v. Polish State (Germany v. Poland) (1932), **2001:** 587
Kulekowskis, In re Extradition of (1995), **1991-99:** 418
Kulekowskis v. DiLeonardi (1996), **1991-99:** 419

Kulko v. Superior Court (1978), **2008:** 755
Kulle, Matter of (1985), **1991-99:** 209
Kulle v. INS (1987), **1991-99:** 32, 33
Kungys v. United States (1988), **2004:** 3, 4
Kun Yun Jho; United States v. (2008), **2008:** 131–36
Kurnaz v. Bush (2005), **2005:** 1005
Kuznetsov; United States v. (2006), **2006:** 653–57
Kwan v. United States (2000), **2000:** 489–99
Kwan v. United States (2001), **2006:** 323
Kwong Hai Chew v. Colding (1953), **1991-99:** 573
Kyle Eng'g Co. v. Kleppe (1979), **2005:** 565

L
*L. v. The Crown (1977), **1989-90:** 350
Labs. of Va.; United States v. (2003), **2003:** 579–82
Lacap v. INS (1998), **1991-99:** 10
La Eugenie; United States v. (1822), **2004:** 367; **2005:** 402
LaFontaine v. INS (1998), **2001:** 466
Lafontant v. Aristide (1994), **1991-99:** 1251, 1266–81, 1287, 1289, 1290; **2000:** 613; **2001:** 513, 519, 522–23, 533; **2002:** 474, 548, 551*n,* 563; **2006:** 652; **2007:** 523–24
*LaGrand (Germany v. United States) (1999), **2002:** 40, 42, 46, 47; **2003:** 41–43, 45, 61–64, 66, 72, 73, 77, 78–79, 82, 85–91, 99, 100–102; **2004:** 37–38, 45–48
*LaGrand (Germany v. United States) (2000), **2000:** 26, 33, 41, 43–93
*LaGrand (Germany v. United States) (2001), **1991-99:** 320; **2001:** 21–24, 26–29; **2005:** 54, 216, 270; **2006:** 70–73, 1023
LAIF X SPRL v. Axtel, S.A. de C.V. (2004), **2004:** 849–50; **2007:** 791
Laipenieks, Matter of (1993), **2000:** 129
Laker Airways Ltd. v. Sabena, Belgian World Airlines (1984), **2001:** 46; **2002:** 866*n,* 867–68; **2003:** 869; **2004:** 842–45, 848; **2006:** 961; **2007:** 690, 691, 773, 775, 776; **2008:** 770, 772, 775
Lam v. Kelchner (2002), **2005:** 1004
Lamont v. Woods (1991), **1991-99:** 986
*Land and Maritime Boundary (Cameroon v. Nigeria) (1988), **2001:** 573
Landgraf v. USI Film Prods. (1994), **1991-99:** 115–18, 1262, 1264, 1265; **2001:** 457, 466; **2002:** 496, 499, 514–15; **2003:** 518; **2004:** 467, 470, 471; **2006:** 31, 33
*Land, Island and Maritime Frontier Dispute (1992), **2000:** 52
Landon v. Plasencia (1982), **1991-99:** 8, 175, 176, 193; **2000:** 132; **2005:** 291
Lane v. Pena (1996), **2000:** 547; **2002:** 588
Langhammer v. Hamilton (1961), **1989-90:** 24

Langley; United States v. (1995), **2005:** 85
Lanza; United States v. (1922), **2001:** 313*n*
Lara; United States v. (2004), **2005:** 143*n;* **2007:** 176
Lara-Ruiz v. INS (2001), **2005:** 260
LaShawn A. v. Barry (1996), **2000:** 547
*Las Palmeras Case (2000), **2002:** 1014
Lathrop v. Unidentified, Wrecked & Abandoned Vessel (1993), **2003:** 757
Latvian State Cargo Lines & Passenger S.S. Line v. McGrath (1951), **1989-90:** 246
Lau v. Nichols (1974), **2007:** 301
*Lauder (U.S.) v. Czech Republic (2002), **2003:** 632*n*
Lauritzen v. Larson (1953), **2002:** 328
Lawton v. The Republic of Iraq (2003), **2003:** 572
Layton; United States v. (1988), **2007:** 180
Lazaro Gonzalez, Matter of (2000), **2000:** 136
Lazo-Majano v. INS (1987), **1991-99:** 218, 224–25
Le v. United States Dep't of State (1996), **1991-99:** 114, 115
Leaf v. United States (1978), **2001:** 332
League of United Latin Am. Citizens v. Perry (2006), **2007:** 307
League of United Latin Am. Citizens v. Wilson (1995), **1991-99:** 786–89
Leatherman v. Tarrant County Narcotics Intelligence & Coordination Unit (1993), **2004:** 322*n*
Leavitt; State v. (1909), **2004:** 729
Lebron v. Nat'l R.R. Passenger Corp. (1995), **2005:** 415
Ledgerwood v. Iran (1983), **2001:** 461
Lee v. Dulles (1957), **2008:** 14
Lee; United States v. (1882), **1989-90:** 316, 317; **2002:** 549; **2003:** 561; **2006:** 671; **2007:** 525
Lee; United States v. (1982), **2001:** 139, 512, 513, 520; **2005:** 144, 562
Legal Assistance for Vietnamese Asylum Seekers v. United States Dep't of State (1995), **1991-99:** 114–15
Legal Assistance for Vietnamese Asylum Seekers; United States Dep't of State v. (1996), **1991-99:** 114
*Legality of the Threat or Use of Nuclear Weapons, Advisory Opinion re (1996), **1991-99:** 2180–82
Legal Servs. Corp. v. Velazquez (2001), **2007:** 255
Legal Tender Cases (Knox v. Lee) (1870), **2006:** 1014
Lehigh Valley Ry. Co. v. Russia (1927), **1989-90:** 256
Lehman Bros. Commercial Corp. v. MinMetals Int'l Non-Ferrous Metals Trading Co. (2001), **2001:** 430
Lehmann v. Acheson (1953), **2003:** 10–11
Lehr v. Robertson (1982), **2000:** 4, 12, 14–16

Lei Shi; United States v. (2008), **2002:** 133–34; **2008:** 125–30
Leith v. Lufthansa German Airlines (1992), **1991-99:** 1288
Leitner; United States v. (1986), **2001:** 67–68
Lem Moon Sing v. United States (1895), **2006:** 1193
Leng May Ma v. Barber (1958), **1991-99:** 169, 175; **2000:** 132, 133
Leon; United States v. (1984), **2006:** 67
Lernout & Hauspie Sec. Litig., In re (2003), **2003:** 868–70, 885–87
Lernout & Hauspie Speech Prods. v. Stonington Partners (2001), **2002:** 865–68
Letelier v. Republic of Chile (1984), **1989-90:** 301; **1991-99:** 1231; **2002:** 503; **2007:** 498, 503
Letter of Request from the Crown Prosecution Serv. of the United Kingdom, In re (1989), **1991-99:** 385
Letter Rogatory from First Court of First Instance in Civil Matters, In re (1995), **1991-99:** 386
Letter Rogatory from the Nedenes Dist. Court, Norway, In re (2003), **2003:** 880–81
Leutwyler v. Office of Her Majesty Queen Rania al-Abdullah (2001), **2001:** 536; **2002:** 548, 549*n*
Levesque v. Levesque (1993), **1991-99:** 354
Lewis v. United States (1980), **2005:** 120
Li; United States v. (2000), **2000:** 491, 527; **2001:** 456; **2002:** 215, 216; **2004:** 513*n,* 536, 537; **2005:** 42*n,* 49, 51, 52, 63*n,* 64; **2008:** 37, 40, 44, 156, 518
Liberia v. Bickford (1992), **1991-99:** 1140
Liberia and the Nat'l Patriotic Reconstruction Assembly Gov't of Liberia v. Liberian Servs. (1992), **1991-99:** 1140
Liberian E. Timber Corp. v. Liberia (1987), **1989-90:** 301; **2000:** 553; **2001:** 497, 500; **2002:** 541; **2005:** 558
Liberian Nat'l Petroleum Co. v. Government of the Republic of Liberia (1992), **1991-99:** 1140
Libra Bank Ltd. v. Banco Nacional de Costa Rica (1982), **1989-90:** 301; **1991-99:** 1271
Library of Congress v. Shaw (1986), **1991-99:** 660
*Libya v. Libyan Am. Oil Co. (1981), **2003:** 627*n*
Libyan Arab Jamahiriya v. Rein (1999), **1991-99:** 1248–52
*Libyan Arab Jamahiriya v. United Kingdom (1992), **1991-99:** 460; **2001:** 98
*Libyan Arab Jamahiriya v. United States (1992), **1991-99:** 460–77; **2001:** 98
*Liechtenstein v. Guatemala (1955), **1989-90:** 214; **1991-99:** 35*n;* **2001:** 586, 646
Lileikis; United States v. (1996), **1991-99:** 28
Lin v. Government of Japan (1994), **2001:** 432

Lin v. United States (2008), **2007:** 1–3; **2008:** 1, 443–47
Lin v. United States (2009), **2008:** 1*n*, 447*n*
Lincoln v. Vigil (1993), **2001:** 85
Linder v. Calero Portocarrero (1990), **1991-99:** 161
Linder v. Portocarrero (1992), **2005:** 484
Lindert; United States v. (1995), **1991-99:** 28
Lindh; United States v. (2002), **2002:** 94, 1001–8; **2005:** 962
Linear Prods. v. Marotech (2002), **2002:** 862–63
Linnas, Matter of (1987), **2004:** 20
Liu v. Republic of China (1989), **1991-99:** 1257; **2004:** 511–12; **2005:** 576
Liu Qi; Doe v. (2002), **2002:** 469–76, 575
Liu Qi; Doe I v. (2004), **2003:** 394*n*, 509–10; **2004:** 363–64, 380–82; **2005:** 579
Li Weixum v. Bo Xilai (2006), **2006:** 662–81
Li Weixum v. Bo Xilai (2008), **2007:** 448; **2008:** 490–91
L.L.M. v. A.J.J.M., Matter of (1987), **2000:** 626
Lloyd v. American Airlines (2002), **2003:** 599, 600
LNC Invs., Inc. v. Banco Central de Nicaragua (2000), **2007:** 498, 503
LNC Invs., Inc. v. Republic of Nicaragua (2000), **2007:** 498, 503
*Loayza Tamayo Case (1997), **2002:** 268*n*
LoBue v. Christopher (1995), **1991-99:** 417–20
LoBue v. DiLeonardi (1999), **1991-99:** 420
Local Loan Co. v. Hunt (1934), **2008:** 762
Locke v. Davey (2004), **2007:** 295
Locke; United States v. (1999), **1991-99:** 775
Locke; United States v. (2000), **1991-99:** 775–85; **2000:** 529, 537
Lo Duca v. United States (1996), **1991-99:** 418–27; **2000:** 192
Loewen v. United States (2005), **2005:** 602; **2006:** 724
*Loewen Group, Inc. v. United States (1998), **1991-99:** 1434–35; **2006:** 501; **2007:** 417, 554
*Loewen Group, Inc. & Raymond L. Loewen v. United States (2003), **2001:** 623–42; **2002:** 623–41; **2003:** 610–15, 645; **2005:** 602
*Loewen Group, Inc. & Raymond L. Loewen v. United States (2004), **2004:** 573
Logan v. Dupuis (1997), **1991-99:** 1293*n*, 1297–1305
Lombera-Camorlinga; United States v. (2000), **1991-99:** 257; **2000:** 23, 24–25, 42–43, 56*n*; **2003:** 148; **2004:** 869; **2005:** 42*n*; **2007:** 80
Longstreath; United States v. (1996), **2004:** 1028
Loos v. Manuel (1994), **1991-99:** 356
Lopes v. Lopes (2006), **2006:** 966–69
Lopez v. Aran (1988), **2005:** 248
Lopez v. Gonzales (2006), **2006:** 33–36

Lopez; United States v. (1995), **2002:** 57–58
Lopez; United States v. (2006), **2006:** 1135
Lopez-Galarza v. INS (1996), **1991-99:** 200
Lopez-Mendoza; INS v. (1984), **1991-99:** 505
Lopez-Smith v. Hood (1997), **2000:** 212; **2001:** 76, 77; **2004:** 85–86, 88; **2005:** 92; **2007:** 963
Lops v. Lops (1998), **1991-99:** 361
Lops v. Lops (2001), **2004:** 57
Lorisme v. INS (1997), **2000:** 129
Louisiana; United States v. (1950), **2002:** 249*n*, 253
Louisiana; United States v. (1960), **1991-99:** 647*n*, 725, 1136; **2000:** 527
Louisiana; United States v. (1969), **2005:** 699, 703
Louisiana; United States v. (Ala. and Miss. Boundary Case) (1985), **2005:** 699
Loving v. United States (1996), **1991-99:** 754
Lowry v. Reagan (1987), **2006:** 544, 545
Loza; State v. (1997), **1991-99:** 263
Loza-Bedoya v. M (1969), **1989-90:** 23
L.P. Consulting Group, Inc. v. United States (2005), **2006:** 325
Lucas v. South Carolina Coastal Council (1992), **1991-99:** 1098; **2004:** 729
Ludecke v. Watkins (1948), **1991-99:** 669; **2001:** 452*n*; **2002:** 988
Lue; United States v. (1998), **2007:** 176
Lugar v. Edmonson Oil Co. (1982), **1991-99:** 893, 985
Lui Kin-Hong, In re Extradition of (1996), **1991-99:** 411–17
Lui Kin-Hong; United States v. (1997), **1991-99:** 411–17, 427–28; **2000:** 206, 215; **2003:** 528–29
Lujan v. Defenders of Wildlife (1992), **1991-99:** 167; **2000:** 495, 763; **2001:** 207, 208; **2006:** 877
Lujan v. National Wildlife Fed'n (1990), **2000:** 315
Lujan v. National Wildlife Fed'n (1992), **2000:** 315
Lujan v. National Wildlife Fed'n (2000), **2001:** 209
Lujan, United States ex rel. v. Gengler (1975), **1989-90:** 347; **1991-99:** 505
Lukwago v. Ashcroft (2003), **2008:** 306
Lumen Constr., Inc. v. Brant Constr. Co. (1985), **2002:** 861
Lummi Indian Tribe v. Washington (1993), **1991-99:** 58
Lumumba; United States v. (1984), **1991-99:** 1186
Luna; United States v. (1999), **1991-99:** 599–600
Luria v. United States (1913), **1991-99:** 14
Lyders v. Lund (1929), **2006:** 632
Lyon v. Augusta (2001), **2001:** 404

M

M.A. v. INS (1990), **2000:** 130
Maalouf v. the Swiss Confederation (2002), **2002:** 522
MacArthur Area Citizens Ass'n v. Republic of Peru (1987), **2002:** 542
Machado; United States v. (1999), **2001:** 265
Macharia v. United States (2002), **2001:** 417–21; **2002:** 461–62
Mackin, In re Extradition of (1981), **1991-99:** 428; **2000:** 208
Mackin; United States v. (1981), **2000:** 196*n*
Macphail v. Oceaneering Int'l (2002), **2002:** 871–72
Madden v. Hofmann (1994), **2005:** 66*n*
Made in the USA Found. v. United States (2001), **2001:** 200–211; **2002:** 199, 201
Madness v. Madness (2001), **2004:** 865
Madsen v. Kinsella (1952), **2002:** 988*n;* **2004:** 1020; **2006:** 1209
Magness v. Russian Fed'n (2000), **2003:** 828
Magness v. Russian Fed'n (2001), **2001:** 501–10; **2002:** 515; **2005:** 557; **2006:** 559, 639*n*
*Maharani Woollen Mills Co. v. Anchor Line (1927), **1991-99:** 1846
Maine; United States v. (1975), **2002:** 249*n*
Maine; United States v. (1985), **2005:** 703–4
Mainero v. Gregg (1999), **2001:** 482, 484
Maiorano v. Baltimore & Ohio R.R. Co. (1909), **1991-99:** 667
Malaysia Int'l Shipping Corp. v. Sinochem Int'l Co. (2006), **2006:** 963, 964
Maldonado-Vences; United States v. (1998), **1991-99:** 259
*Malek v. Iran (1992), **2001:** 599
Malewicz v. City of Amsterdam (2004), **2004:** 792–96
Malewicz v. City of Amsterdam (2005), **2005:** 776
Malewicz v. City of Amsterdam (2007), **2007:** 742–44; **2008:** 732–34
Mali v. Keeper of the Common Jail (1887), **2008:** 134
Malley v. Briggs (1986), **2006:** 651
Malloy v. Hogan (1964), **1991-99:** 573–74
Malm v. INS (2001), **2005:** 83–84, 83*n*, 84–85
Mamet v. Bush (2008), **2008:** 915–16, 915*n*
Mandowsky v. Dresdner Bank AG (2006), **2006:** 517–21
Mandowsky v. Dresdner Bank AG (2008), **2007:** 426
Mangste W. El v. New York Passport Agency (2006), **2006:** 307
Manguerra v. INS (1968), **1991-99:** 12
Mann; United States v. (1987), **2002:** 215
Mannington Mills, Inc. v. Congoleum Corp. (1979), **1991-99:** 161
Manzi, In re Extradition of (1989), **2000:** 216
Marbury v. Madison (1803), **1991-99:** 425, 797; **2001:** 386, 445; **2002:** 340; **2005:** 244; **2006:** 71, 322, 543, 544; **2007:** 220; **2008:** 444
Marchetti; United States v. (1972), **2007:** 242

Marcos, In re Matter of (1989), **1989-90:** 62
Marcos, Estate of v. Hilao (1995), **1991-99:** 978, 979; **2001:** 319; **2002:** 324, 336; **2003:** 354
Marcos, Human Rights Litig., In re Estate of (1996), **2006:** 605
The Maret (1944), **1989-90:** 245–46, 263
Marik v. Powell (2001), **2001:** 385
*Mariposa (U.S. v. Panama) (1933), **2001:** 600–601
*Maritime Boundary in the Gulf of Maine, **2007:** 640
Maritime Ins. Co. v. Emery Air Freight Corp. (1993), **2002:** 436
Maritime Int'l Nominees Establishment (1983), **1989-90:** 286
Maritime Int'l Nominees Establishment v. Republic of Guinea (1982), **1991-99:** 1206, 1222
Maritime Ventures Int'l v. Caribbean Trading & Fidelity (1988), **1989-90:** 286
Marlowe v. Argentine Naval Comm'n (1985), **1989-90:** 287; **1991-99:** 1187
Marquez-Almanzar v. INS (2005), **2007:** 2
Marshalls 201; United States v. (2008), **2007:** 644; **2008:** 642–44
Marshalls 201; United States v. (2009), **2008:** 643*n*
Marshhauser v. The Travelers Indemnity Co. (1992), **2004:** 71
Martin v. Warden, Atlanta Penitentiary (1993), **2005:** 81
Martinez v. City of Los Angeles (1998), **2000:** 400, 401*n,* 411; **2001:** 334; **2003:** 362, 363
Martinez v. State (1999), **1991-99:** 263
Martinez-Villalva; United States v. (1999), **1991-99:** 262
*Marvin Ray Feldman Karpa (CEMSA) v. United Mexican States (2001), **2001:** 642–46; **2006:** 713, 714, 717, 718
Maryland v. Craig (1990), **2004:** 1027–28
Maryland v. Pringle (2003), **2006:** 364
Mashayekhi v. Iran (1981), **1991-99:** 1321
Massaro v. United States (2003), **2006:** 69, 73
Massieu v. Reno (1996), **1991-99:** 124
Matar v. Dichter (2006), **2006:** 465–76, 479–82, 629–52
Matar v. Dichter (2007), **2007:** 224–26, 446, 504–8, 510, 511
Mateo v. Perez (1999), **1991-99:** 1312
Mathews v. Diaz (1976), **1991-99:** 8–9; **2005:** 17
Mathews v. Eldridge (1976), **1989-90:** 16; **2004:** 1007, 1008, 1010, 1011; **2005:** 130, 279, 1000, 1001; **2006:** 197
Matimak Trading Co. v. Khalily (1996), **1991-99:** 769–74
Matimak Trading Co. v. Khalily (1997), **1991-99:** 1142, 1239, 1251; **2002:** 228
Matimak Trading Co. v. Khalily (1998), **2001:** 228–29, 231–33
Matsushita Elec. Indus. Co. v. Zenith Radio Corp. (1986), **1991-99:** 1531

Matta-Ballesteros v. Henman (1990), **2000:** 316; **2002:** 215, 216
Matta-Ballesteros; United States v. (1995), **2001:** 441*n*
Matter of. *See name of party*
Maul v. United States (1927), **1991-99:** 2166
*Mavrommatis Palestine Concessions (1924), **2000:** 656
Maximov v. United States (1962), **2000:** 607
Maximov v. United States (1963), **1991-99:** 1346; **2000:** 519
Maxwell Commc'n Corp., In re (1996), **2004:** 437; **2008:** 231, 232
Mayer v. Banque Paribas (2001), **2001:** 408
McBride v. Shawnee County, Kansas Court Servs. (1999), **2001:** 137, 138
*McCann v. United Kingdom (1995), **2004:** 234–35
McCarthy, In the Matter of the Claim of (1971), **2002:** 241*n*
McCarthy v. Madigan (1992), **2001:** 752
McClain v. United States (1977), **1991-99:** 1804*n*
McCleskey v. Zant (1991), **2005:** 283
*McCollough & Co. v. Ministry of Post, Telegraph & Telephone (1987), **2003:** 453*n*
McCready v. Virginia (1876), **2004:** 729
McCulloch v. Maryland (1819), **1991-99:** 781
McCulloch v. Sociedad Nacional de Marineros de Honduras (1963), **1989-90:** 447; **2000:** 465; **2001:** 473, 474
McDermott Int'l, Inc. v. Wilander (1991), **1991-99:** 1202
McDonnell Douglas Corp. v. Islamic Republic of Iran (1984), **1989-90:** 216
McDonnell Douglas Corp. v. Islamic Republic of Iran (1985), **1991-99:** 1221; **2001:** 499
McGee v. International Life Ins. Co. (1957), **1991-99:** 1264
McGraw-Hill Co. v. Ingenium (2005), **2005:** 826–27
McHenry County v. Brady (1917), **2001:** 183, 191
McKeel v. Islamic Republic of Iran (1983), **1991-99:** 1257; **2001:** 461
McKeeve; United States v. (1997), **2000:** 334
McKesson Corp. v. Iran (1995), **2001:** 493
McKesson Corp. v. Iran (2008), **2008:** 155
McKesson HBOC, Inc. v. Iran (2003), **2003:** 258–67
McMillan v. Pennsylvania (1986), **2004:** 127
McMullen, Matter of (1984), **1991-99:** 234, 235
McMullen v. INS (1986), **1989-90:** 24, 26; **1991-99:** 235, 239; **2005:** 83*n*
McMullin, In re (1979), **1991-99:** 428
McNary v. Haitian Regugee Ctr. (1991), **2001:** 239
McNeil v. Wisconsin (1991), **2006:** 73
McNinch; United States v. (1958), **2005:** 228, 233
*McReady v. Mexico (1868), **2003:** 434–35

Meadows v. Dominican Republic (1986), **1989-90:** 283
Medellín, Ex parte (2005), **2005:** 34–59
Medellín, Ex parte (2006), **2006:** 87–88; **2007:** 73–74; **2008:** 176
Medellín, Ex parte (2008), **2007:** 74–77; **2008:** 196, 198, 199, 208, 212
Medellín v. Dretke (2004), **2004:** 44–47; **2005:** 32–33, 46, 52;
2006: 72, 81, 86–87
Medellín v. Dretke (2005), **2007:** 74*n*
Medellín v. Texas (2008), **2007:** 74*n;* **2008:** 35, 39, 41, 153, 154, 156–58, 175–93
*Megrahi v. Her Majesty's Advocate (2002), **2002:** 111–12;
2003: 160–61
Mehinovic v. Vuckovic (2002), **2002:** 347–48; **2004:** 317, 325, 1023
Melekh; United States v. (1961), **1991-99:** 1239
Melendez v. State (1999), **1991-99:** 214, 215, 263–64
Melkonyan v. Sullivan (1991), **1991-99:** 1212
Mendaro v. World Bank (1983), **2002:** 571
Mendoza; United States v. (1984), **1989-90:** 13
Menominee Indian Tribe v. Thompson (1998), **2004:** 199
Merck & Co., In re Application of (2000), **2003:** 875
Meredith v. Jefferson County Board of Education (2007), **2007:** 300
Meredith v. Meredith (1991), **1991-99:** 354, 356
*Mergé v. Italian Republic (1955), **2001:** 644–46
Meridien Int'l Bank v. Government of the Republic of Liberia (1991),
1991-99: 1140
Meridien Int'l Bank v. Government of the Republic of Liberia (1996),
1991-99: 1138–41
Meritor Sav. Bank, FSB v. Vinson (1998), **2005:** 263
*Merrill & Ring Forestry L.P. v. Canada (2008), **2008:** 526–27
Messenger v. Building Contractors Ass'n Inc. (1989), **2000:** 574
*Metalclad Corp. v. United Mexican States (1999),
2000: 676, 679–83, 694
*Metalclad Corp. v. United Mexican States (2000), **1991-99:** 1436;
2004: 585–86; **2006:** 696, 717, 723
Metallgesellschaft, In re (1997), **2003:** 878–81
*Methanex Corp. v. United States (1999), **1991-99:** 1435–36
*Methanex Corp. v. United States (2001), **2001:** 570–608;
2004: 590*n*
*Methanex Corp. v. United States (2002), **2002:** 626–23; **2003:** 605, 615–36; **2006:** 703, 704, 716
*Methanex Corp. v. United States (2004), **2004:** 574–94
*Methanex Corp. v. United States (2005), **2005:** 593–96; **2006:** 694;
2008: 535, 537, 541
Metropolitan Life Ins. Co. v. Robertson-Ceco Corp. (1996),
1991-99: 1244–45

Metropolitan Washington Airports Auth. v. Citizens for the Abatement of Aircraft Noise, Inc. (1991), **1991-99:** 48, 1237–38; **2002:** 989
Mexico v. Hoffman (1945), **1989-90:** 315; **2001:** 512; **2002:** 548, 549; **2005:** 42*n,* 562, 569; **2006:** 604*n,* 631, 669; **2007:** 524–25; **2008:** 478
Mexico v. Schmuck (1944), **1989-90:** 318, 319
*Mexico; United States v. (1871), **2001:** 631
*Mexico; United States v. (1931), **2001:** 577
Mexico v. United States (2004). *See* Avena and Other Mexican Nationals v. United States
Mexico City Aircrash of October 31, 1979, In re (1983), **2003:** 265*n*
Meyers v. United States (1926), **1991-99:** 47
Mezitis Diorinou v. Mezitis (2001), **2004:** 848
Miami Light Project v. Miami-Dade County (2000), **2002:** 450, 451; **2007:** 236
Michel v. INS (2000), **2006:** 681
Michelin Tire Corp. v. Wages (1976), **2000:** 321, 465; **2002:** 453
Michie v. Great Lakes Steel Div., Nat'l Steel Corp. (1974), **2007:** 689
Michigan; United States v. (1997), **2005:** 275
Microsoft Corp., In re Application of (2006), **2006:** 969, 970
Midwater Trawlers Coop. v. Department of Commerce (2002), **2004:** 760
*Mighell v. Sultan of Johore (1894), **2001:** 516
Mikhael v. INS (1997), **2000:** 130
Mikhailevitch v. INS (1998), **2000:** 129
Milena Ship Mgmt. Co. v. Newcomb (1992), **2002:** 99
Miles v. Apex Marine Corp. (1990), **2005:** 85
*Military and Paramilitary Activities in and against Nicaragua (1986), **2001:** 368; **2003:** 1058, 1060–61; **2007:** 60
Milius; United States v. (1998), **1991-99:** 28
Millen Indus., Inc. v. Coordination Council for N. Am. Affairs (1988), **1991-99:** 1211; **2001:** 403, 445, 496, 497; **2002:** 540
Miller v. Albright (1998), **1991-99:** 1–9; **2000:** 2*n,* 5, 11–12, 15*n,* 16, 17; **2007:** 3
Miller v. United States (1871), **2007:** 942
Milligan, Ex parte (1866), **2006:** 1141, 1142; **2007:** 972, 974; **2008:** 190
Milliken v. Bradley (1977), **1991-99:** 317
Milliken v. Meyer (1940), **2003:** 567
Mills v. Alabama (1966), **2006:** 26
Mims v. Mims (1993), **2005:** 512
Mine Safety Appliances Co. v. Forrestal (1945), **2007:** 472
Mingtai Fire & Marine Ins. Co. v. UPS (1997), **1991-99:** 706–9; **2001:** 237

Mingtai Fire & Marine Ins. Co. v. UPS (1999), **2007:** 222
*Ministry of Def. & Support for the Armed Forces of the Islamic Republic of Iran ("MOD") v. Cubic Def. Sys., Inc. (2004), **2004:** 516–17; **2005:** 549, 559; **2006:** 612, 613, 615, 616, 628; **2008:** 484, 486–87*n*
Ministry of Def. & Support for the Armed Forces of the Islamic Republic of Iran ("MOD") v. Cubic Def. Sys., Inc. (2007), **2007:** 477–85, 490
Ministry of Def. & Support for the Armed Forces of the Islamic Republic of Iran ("MOD") v. Elahi (2005), **2005:** 549
Ministry of Def. & Support for the Armed Forces of the Islamic Republic of Iran ("MOD") v. Elahi (2006), **2006:** 612–21
Ministry of Def. & Support for the Armed Forces of the Islamic Republic of Iran ("MOD") v. Elahi (2009), **2008:** 484, 484*n*, 485–89
Ministry of Defense v. Elahi (2006), **2007:** 477
Minjares-Alvarez; United States v. (2001), **2005:** 42*n*
Minnesota v. Block (1981), **2000:** 597
Minnesota v. United States (1939), **2007:** 472
Miracle Recreation Equip. Co.; United States v. (1987), **2005:** 565
Miranda v. Arizona (1966), **2005:** 282; **2006:** 74
Miranda; United States v. (1999), **1991-99:** 261
Mironescu v. Costner (2003), **2004:** 91
Mironescu v. Costner (2004), **2004:** 91–93; **2005:** 353
Mironescu v. Costner (2007), **2007:** 101–8; **2008:** 68*n*
Mironescu v. Rice (2005), **2005:** 79–89
Mironescu v. Rice (2006), **2006:** 148–55
Mission of Saudi Arabia to the United Nations v. Kirkwood (2003), **2003:** 573
Mississippi v. Johnson (1866), **2001:** 208
Mississippi Band of Choctaw Indians v. Holyfield (1989), **2000:** 13*n*
Mississippi Univ. for Women v. Hogan (1982), **2005:** 261
Missouri v. Holland (1920), **1991-99:** 678, 678*n*, 972*n*, 2255; **2000:** 529*n*, 537*n*; **2001:** 204, 210; **2004:** 444; **2005:** 62; **2007:** 176, 205; **2008:** 127, 780, 781
Mistretta v. United States (1989), **1991-99:** 55–56, 426–27, 1239; **2005:** 1016; **2006:** 732, 870
Mitchell v. Laird (1973), **1989-90:** 253
Mitchell; United States v. (1883), **1991-99:** 2160
Mitchell; United States v. (1980), **2002:** 588, 589
Mitchell; United States v. (1983), **2000:** 498
Mitev v. INS (1995), **2000:** 130
Mitsubishi Materials Corp. v. Superior Court (2000), **2002:** 435–40

Mitsubishi Materials Corp. v. Superior Court of Orange County (2003), **1991-99:** 1134; **2003:** 471–72
Mitsubishi Motors Corp. v. Soler Chrysler-Plymouth, Inc. (1985), **1991-99:** 1268, 1847; **2004:** 848; **2007:** 775, 787; **2008:** 781
M.L.B. v. S.L.J. (1996), **2005:** 280
Mochizuki v. United States (1999), **2004:** 223, 230
Mogharrabi, Matter of (1987), **1991-99:** 201–2, 209; **2000:** 130
Mohammed v. Harvey (2006), **2006:** 1194, 1205–13; **2007:** 949
*Mohsen Asgari Nazhri (1994), **2001:** 581
MOL, Inc. v. People's Republic of Bangladesh (1983), **2003:** 580
MOL, Inc. v. People's Republic of Bangladesh (1984), **1989-90:** 283; **2001:** 498
Mollan v. Torrance (1824), **2002:** 489
Monaco, Principality of v. Mississippi (1934), **1991-99:** 317
*Mondev Int'l Ltd. v. United States (1999), **1991-99:** 1435
*Mondev Int'l Ltd. v. United States (2002), **2002:** 607–16; **2006:** 724
Monegasque de Reassurances S.A.M. v. NAK Naftogaz of Ukraine (2001), **2001:** 458
Monell v. Department of Social Servs. (1978), **1991-99:** 1281
Montana v. United States (1981), **1991-99:** 839
Montecino v. INS (1990), **1991-99:** 205
Montoya v. United States (1901), **1991-99:** 1006
Moore v. Mitchell (1929), **2005:** 240
Moore v. United Kingdom (2004), **2004:** 478
Mora v. New York (2008), **2007:** 77, 80–81, 200–206; **2008:** 36–42, 518
Morales, Extradition of (1995), **2001:** 67, 68
Moran v. Kingdom of Saudi Arabia (1994), **1991-99:** 1257–58
More v. Intelcom Support Servs., Inc. (1992), **2000:** 317, 493, 527; **2001:** 454
Moreno-Morillo; United States v. (2003), **2008:** 128
Morgan Guar. Trust Co. v. Republic of Palau (1986), **1991-99:** 812
Morgan Guar. Trust Co. v. Republic of Palau (1991), **1991-99:** 811–25
Morissette v. United States (1952), **1991-99:** 1202; **2004:** 310*n*
Morongo Band of Mission Indians v. California State Bd. of Equalization (1988), **1991-99:** 1281
Morris, In re (1999), **1991-99:** 355
Morris; United States v. (1996), **1991-99:** 386
Morrisey v. Brewer (1972), **2001:** 113; **2005:** 130
Morrison v. Olson (1988), **1991-99:** 754, 1237; **2001:** 206
Morton v. Mancari (1974), **2001:** 137–38
Morton v. Morton (1997), **1991-99:** 356; **2001:** 41
Mother Doe v. Sheikh Hamdan (2007), **2008:** 227
Mother Doe v. Sheikh Hamdan (2008), **2008:** 227–36

Mother Doe I ex rel. R.M. v. Al Maktoum (2007), **2008:** 227*n*
Motorola Credit Corp. v. Uzan (2003), **2008:** 774
Motorola Credit Corp. v. Uzan (2004), **2007:** 788
Mousa v. Islamic Republic of Iran (2003), **2003:** 554
Mousa Mohammed Abu Marzook, In re (1996), **1991-99:** 126–28
Moussaoui; United States v. (2004), **2007:** 246*n*
Moxon v. The Fanny (1793), **2003:** 370; **2006:** 1180
*MOX Plant (Ireland v. U.K.) (2001), **2003:** 621*n*
Mozes v. Mozes (2001), **2004:** 63, 65; **2008:** 783, 785, 787
Mr. and Mrs. Doe v. United States (1988), **1991-99:** 1270, 1272, 1273, 1277, 1279
Mueller v. Diggelman (1981), **1991-99:** 1275
Mujica v. Occidental Petroleum Corp. (2004), **2004:** 376–80
Mujica v. Occidental Petroleum Corp. (2005), **2005:** 418–20, 424, 819, 839–41; **2006:** 450–55, 944–46
Mujica v. Occidental Petroleum Corp. (2009), **2006:** 438*n,* 446
Mukaddam v. Permanent Mission of Saudi Arabia to the United Nations (2000), **2002:** 477
Mullane v. Central Hanover Bank & Trust Co. (1950), **2000:** 435; **2001:** 551; **2005:** 856, 858, 865
Mullaney v. Wilbur (1975), **2002:** 1006*n*
Mulligan v. Schultz (1988), **2006:** 25
Mumtaz v. Ershad (1989), **1989-90:** 314–19
Munaf v. Geren (2008), **2007:** 957*n;* **2008:** 68–69, 73–78, 916, 918–20
Murphy v. Netherland (1997), **1991-99:** 255–56, 285
Murphy v. Waterfront Comm'n of N.Y. Harbor (1964), **1991-99:** 573–74
Murray v. Schooner Charming Betsy (1804), **2001:** 760; **2005:** 130; **2006:** 640, 1216*n;* **2007:** 979
Mustanich v. Mukasey (2008), **2008:** 13
*M/V "Saiaa" (No. 2) Case (Saint Vincent and the Grenadines v. Guinea), **2003:** 436
Mwani v. United States (2004), **2001:** 418–19
Mwenya, Ex parte (1960), **2006:** 1207
Myers v. United States (1926), **1991-99:** 675; **2006:** 732
Myers v. United States (1963), **1989-90:** 309

N

NAACP v. New York (1973), **2001:** 464
Naartex Consulting Corp. v. Watt (1983), **1991-99:** 1338
*NAFTA Chapter 11/UNCITRAL Cattle Cases, In re (2006), **2006:** 693–701
*NAFTA Chapter 11/UNCITRAL Cattle Cases, In re (2008), **2007:** 553–56; **2008:** 527–29

Nagrampa v. MailCoups, Inc. (2006), **2007:** 776
*Nahimana; Prosecutor v. (2003), **2006:** 461
Nai Fook Li; United States v. (2000), **2000:** 23–43, *56n;* **2006:** 67, 81*n*
Nasseri v. Moschorak (1994), **1991-99:** 200
National Am. Corp. v. Federal Republic of Nigeria (1978), **1991-99:** 1221
National Archives & Records Admin. v. Favish (2004), **2005:** 1023, 1024, 1026
National Bank v. County of Yankton (1880), **1991-99:** 809
National City Bank of N.Y. v. Republic of China (1955), **1991-99:** 1251; **2000:** 575; **2002:** 493; **2006:** 631; **2008:** 477
National Coalition Gov't of the Union of Burma v. Unocal (1997), **1991-99:** 1333; **2002:** 335
National Council of La Raza v. DOJ (2005), **2005:** 1025
National Council of Resistance of Iran (NCRI) v. Department of State (NCRI I) (2001), **2001:** 109–17; **2002:** 91; **2003:** 176, 506; **2005:** 131; **2006:** 195, 197, 198, 1013
National Council of Resistance of Iran (NCRI) v. Department of State (NCRI II) (2004), **2006:** 196
Nationale Industrielle Aerospatiale v. United States Dist. Ct. for the S. Dist. of Iowa (1987), **2006:** 947
National Foreign Trade Council v. Baker (1998), **1991-99:** 785; **2000:** 318
National Foreign Trade Council v. Natsios (1999), **1991-99:** 785; **2000:** 318, 471; **2001:** 197*n;* **2002:** 447, 450, 451
National Oil Corp. v. Libyan Sun Oil Co. (1990), **1991-99:** 1140; **2004:** 668
National Park Hosp. Ass'n v. Department of Interior (2003), **2005:** 94
National Petrochemical Co. of Iran v. M/T Stolt Sheaf (1988), **1991-99:** 813, 983, 1140, 1141, 1186
National S.S. Co. v. Tugman (1882), **1991-99:** 772
National Transp. Safety Bd. v. Carnival Cruise Lines, Inc. (1989), **1989-90:** 447
National Trust for Historic Preservation v. Blanck (1996), **2003:** 758
National Union Fire Ins. Co. v. Republic of China (1958), **1989-90:** 255
National Wildlife Fed'n v. Goldschmidt (1982), **1991-99:** 1239
Native Vill. of Eyak v. Trawler Diane Marie, Inc. (1998), **2002:** 251, 255; **2005:** 253–54
Naturalization of 68 Filipino War Vets, Matter of (1975), **1989-90:** 13
Natural Res. Def. Council v. EPA (2006), **2006:** 868
Natural Res. Def. Council v. Patterson (1998), **2000:** 315
Naukirchen v. Wood County Head Start, Inc. (1995), **2000:** 547
*Naulilaa Case (Portugal v. Germany) (1928), **1991-99:** 1113, 1114
Navarro Sav. Ass'n v. Lee (1980), **2002:** 96

Navy, Dep't of v. Egan (1988), **1991-99:** 647*n*, 794, 798, 1136; **2000:** 527; **2001:** 456; **2002:** 589; **2003:** 541; **2004:** 18, 213, 1009; **2005:** 535–36; **2007:** 242
Nazi Era Cases Against German Defendants Litig., In re (2000), **1991-99:** 1133; **2000:** 450–60; **2001:** 387–93, 413; **2005:** 821
Nazi Era Cases Against German Defendants Litig., In re (2001), **2002:** 342–43; **2004:** 436*n;* **2008:** 234
Nazi Era Cases Against German Defendants Litig., In re (2006), **2006:** 517–21
Nebenzal v. Re (1968), **2000:** 530*n*
Neder v. United States (1999), **2005:** 236
Neely v. Henkel (1901), **1989-90:** 82; **1991-99:** 943; **2000:** 215; **2006:** 1203, 1212; **2008:** 75, 76
Nehme v. INS (2001), **2002:** 8
Neidecker, United States ex rel. (1936), **2008:** 78
Neifert-White Co.; United States v. (1968), **2005:** 228
Neil; United States v. (2002), **2002:** 131–33
*Neira Alegría (1995), **2004:** 234
Neiswender; United States v. (1979), **2004:** 327, 328
Nejad v. United States (1989), **1989-90:** 212, 217; **2001:** 443
Nelson v. Saudi Arabia (1989), **1991-99:** 1208–15, 1264
Nemariam v. Federated Democratic Republic of Ethiopia and The Commercial Bank of Ethiopia (2003), **2003:** 478–80
Nemitz v. United States (2004), **2004:** 741–42
Neptune Orient Lines v. Burlington N. and Santa Fe (2000), **2006:** 920
Neri v. United States (1951), **2004:** 447
Neri v. United States (1953), **2004:** 447
Netizke v. Williams (1989), **2005:** 280
Newcomb v. Commissioner (1955), **2008:** 242
New Jersey v. United States (1996), **2000:** 496
New Rochelle, City of v. Republic of Ghana (1964), **2006:** 597
New York v. Gorsuch (1983), **2004:** 760
New York v. United States (1946), **1991-99:** 1202
New York & Cuba Mail S.S. Co. v. Republic of Korea (1955), **1989-90:** 318, 319
New York Chinese TV Programs, Inc. v. U.E. Enters., Inc. (1992), **1991-99:** 663, 700–5
New York City v. Baker (1989), **2006:** 1192
New York City v. Permanent Mission of India (2006), **2006:** 592, 594–603
New York Times Co. v. City of N.Y. Comm'n on Human Rights (1977), **2002:** 450
New York Times Co. v. Sullivan (1964), **2007:** 329

New York Times Co. v. United States (1971), **1991-99:** 797
Nguyen v. INS (2000), **2000:** 1–19
Nguyen v. INS (2001), **2005:** 261
*Nicaragua v. Honduras (1988), **2001:** 573
*Nicaragua v. United States (1984), **1991-99:** 470; **2000:** 52*n*
*Nicaragua v. United States (1986), **2001:** 368; **2004:** 1024; **2005:** 38*n*–39*n*
Nielsen v. Secretary of Treasury (1970), **2000:** 552; **2006:** 1014
Niesel, Matter of (2004), **2004:** 20
Nippon Paper Indus. Co.; United States v. (1997), **1991-99:** 1534–39
Nippon Paper Indus. Co. v. United States (1998), **1991-99:** 1539
Nishikawa v. Dulles (1958), **2003:** 9
Nishimura Ekiu v. United States (1892), **2000:** 10; **2006:** 1193
Nitol v. United States (1988), **2006:** 321
Nixon v. Administrator of Gen. Servs. (1977), **1991-99:** 757, 1241
Nixon; United States v. (1974), **1991-99:** 794; **2002:** 590; **2007:** 241–42
Nixon v. United States (1993), **1991-99:** 987; **2001:** 205–6, 445, 752
NLRB v. *See name of opposing party*
N-M-A-, In re (1998), **2000:** 130
Nordic Vill., Inc.; United States v. (1992), **2000:** 547; **2001:** 239; **2002:** 588
Norex Petroleum Ltd. v. Access Indus., Inc. (2005), **2005:** 833–39
Norfolk S. Ry. Co. v. Kirby (2004), **2004:** 830–34; **2006:** 918, 921, 926–28
Noriega v. Pastrana (2007), **2007:** 108–17
Noriega v. Pastrana (2008), **2008:** 69–70
Noriega v. Pastrana (2009), **2008:** 70*n*
Noriega; United States v. (1988), **1989-90:** 552
Noriega; United States v. (1990), **1991-99:** 1269, 1282–85; **2002:** 1004*n*
Noriega; United States v. (1992), **2007:** 109, 113, 117
Noriega; United States v. (1997), **1991-99:** 1282–85; **2000:** 407; **2001:** 517; **2003:** 554–70; **2004:** 530; **2007:** 524, 525*n*
Noriega; United States v. (2007), **2007:** 109
North Am. Cold Storage Co. v. Chicago (1908), **2001:** 114
North Carolina v. Rice (1971), **2000:** 316
Northeast Bancorp, Inc. v. Board of Governors of the Fed. Reserve Sys. (1985), **2001:** 183*n*, 185–86*n*, 187, 188, 193*n*
*Northern Cameroons (Cameroons v. U.K.) (1963), **2001:** 586
Northern Mariana Islands v. Atalig (1984), **1991-99:** 810, 816
Northern Mariana Islands v. United States (2002), **2002:** 246–59
Northern Mariana Islands v. United States (2003), **2003:** 275–76
Northern Mariana Islands v. United States (2005), **2005:** 251–54; **2006:** 315–16

Northern Mariana Islands v. United States (2006), **2006:** 315–16
*North Sea Continental Shelf Cases (Federal Republic of Germany v. Denmark; Federal Republic of Germany v. Netherlands) (1969), **2006:** 1072; **2007:** 56, 59, 388, 543*n*
*Nottebohm (Liechtenstein v. Guatemala). *See* *Liechtenstein v. Guatemala (1955)
Ntakirutimana v. Reno (1999), **1991-99:** 598; **2005:** 80
Ntakirutimana v. Reno (2000), **2000:** 203–16
Ntzebesa v. Citigroup (2002), **2003:** 393*n*
Nunez-Escudero v. Tice-Menley (1995), **1991-99:** 366, 369; **2000:** 97, 99, 103, 104
Nuovo Pignone, Spa v. Storman Asia (2002), **2002:** 877–79

O

Occidental of Umm al Qaywayn, Inc. v. A Certain Cargo of Petroleum Laden Aboard Tanker Dauntless Colocotronis (1979), **2001:** 455
Oceanic Steam Navigation Co. v. Stranahan (1909), **2000:** 11
O Centro Espirita Beneficente Uniao do Vegetal v. Ashcroft (2002), **2006:** 223
O Centro Espirita Beneficente Uniao do Vegetal v. Ashcroft (2003), **2003:** 184–86; **2005:** 137
O Centro Espirita Beneficente Uniao do Vegetal v. Reno (2001), **2001:** 128–43
O'Connell Mach. Co. v. M.V. Americana (1984), **1989-90:** 301; **2002:** 515
O'Connor v. Donaldson (1975), **2004:** 1008
O'Connor v. United States (1986), **2000:** 597; **2004:** 200
Odenheimer v. U.S. Dep't of State (2004), **2003:** 486; **2004:** 452
Oetjen v. Central Leather Co. (1918), **1989-90:** 245; **2000:** 201, 497; **2001:** 452, 526; **2002:** 340, 589; **2003:** 365–66; **2005:** 246, 582; **2006:** 457, 522; **2007:** 220, 440; **2008:** 39, 183, 444
Ohio v. Wyandotte Chems. Corp (1971), **2007:** 689
Ohntrup v. Firearms Ctr. Inc. (1981), **1989-90:** 286; **1991-99:** 1206
*Oil Platforms (Iran v. U.S.) (1992), **1991-99:** 2182–86; **2003:** 1036–66
*Oil Platforms (Iran v. U.S.) (1996), **2001:** 608–11
*Oil Platforms (Iran v. U.S.) (2003), **2004:** 974–76; **2006:** 703, 704–5, 1023, 1025
*Ojdanic; Prosecutor v. (2002), **2003:** 214–19
*Ojdanic; Prosecutor v. (2006), **2006:** 260–69
O.K. v. Bush (2005), **2005:** 1018
Oklahoma Natural Gas v. Oklahoma (1927), **2000:** 567
Oklahoma Tax Comm'n v. Jefferson Lines, Inc. (1995), **2000:** 330
Olmstead v. L.C. (1999), **2005:** 276
Olympic Airways v. Husain (2003), **2003:** 589–96

Olympic Airways v. Husain (2004), **2004:** 563–65
Omar v. Harvey (2006), **2006:** 1194–1204, 1211*n*
Omar v. Harvey (2007), **2007:** 956, 957–58; **2008:** 69, 73, 77
Omar Abu Ali v. Ashcroft (2004), **2004:** 203–6
Oncale v. Sundowner Offshore Servs., Inc. (1998), **2005:** 263
One Big Six Wheel; United States v. (1999), **1991-99:** 1622–24
Ontario, Her Majesty the Queen in Right of v. United States EPA (1990), **2007:** 689
OPM v. Government Employees (1985), **1989-90:** 262
Orange v. District of Columbia (1995), **2006:** 1011
Ordinola v. Hackman (2007), **2008:** 68
Osagiede v. United States (2008), **2008:** 44–47
O'Shea v. Littleton (1974), **2000:** 762
Oster v. Dominion of Canada (1956), **2004:** 556
*Ottoman Public Debt Case (1925), **2000:** 572
Owens v. Sudan (2005), **2005:** 502, 517, 578–80; **2006:** 578–81
Owens v. Sudan (2006), **2006:** 578–81
Owens v. Sudan (2008), **2008:** 471–75
Owner-Operator Independent Drivers Ass'n v. Federal Motor Carrier Safety Admin. (2007), **2007:** 557–62
Oyster Bay Cove, Ltd. Bankr., In re (1994), **2006:** 601
Ozanic v. United States (1951), **2000:** 516*n;* **2007:** 262–63

P

*P (Minors), Matter of (1998), **1991-99:** 377
Pacific Gas & Elec. Co. v. State Energy Res. Conservation & Dev. Comm'n (1983), **2000:** 530, 539
Padilla v. Bush (2002), **2002:** 986, 998–1000; **2004:** 1033
Padilla v. Hanft (2005), **2005:** 266, 1018
Padilla v. Rumsfeld (2003), **2003:** 1029
Page; United States v. (2000), **2005:** 42*n*
*Pakistan v. India (1971), **2000:** 664
Pakootas v. Teck Cominco Metals, Ltd. (2006), **2006:** 855–59; **2007:** 687–88
Palestine Info. Office v. Shultz (1987), **1991-99:** 1243
Palestine Info. Office v. Shultz (1988), **2001:** 112, 116; **2005:** 535–36
Palma v. Verdeyen (1982), **2005:** 19
Palmer; United States v. (1818), **2003:** 370; **2004:** 366; **2005:** 402; **2006:** 439–40, 469, 857
Panama v. Citizens & S. Int'l Bank (1988), **1989-90:** 245
Panama Canal Comm'n; The Queen v. (2000), **2001:** 219–24
Pangilinan; INS v. (1988), **1989-90:** 13; **1991-99:** 8, 15; **2000:** 18
Papandreou, In re (1998), **1991-99:** 1221; **2005:** 530, 564–65; **2006:** 611; **2007:** 797–99

Papir v. Wurms (2005), **2005:** 850–52
The Paquete Habana (1900), **1991-99:** 971, 972*n;* **2001:** 292; **2003:** 364, 367, 376; **2004:** 345; **2005:** 496
The Paquete Habana (1903), **1989-90:** 92
Paracelsus Healthcare Corp. v. Philips Med. Sys., Nederland, B.V. (2004), **2004:** 870–72
Paradissiotis v. United States (2002), **2006:** 1013–15
Paraguay v. Allen (1996), **1991-99:** 292
Paraguay v. Gilmore (1998), **2006:** 81
*Paraguay v. United States (1998), **1991-99:** 292–312; **2000:** 26, 32, 35, 41; **2005:** 270
Paramedics Electromedicina Comercial, Ltda. v. GE Med. Sys. Info. Techs., Inc. (2003), **2008:** 774–76
Paramedics Electromedicina Comercial, Ltda. v. GE Med. Sys. Info. Techs., Inc. (2004), **2004:** 845–50; **2007:** 783–84, 788, 791, 794; **2008:** 764
Parden v. Terminal R. Co. (1964), **1991-99:** 1202
Parents Involved in Community Schools v. Seattle School Dist. No. 1 (2007), **2007:** 300
Parham v. Hughes (1979), **2000:** 15
Parhat v. Gates (2007), **2007:** 943
Parhat v. Gates (2008), **2008:** 903–5, 907, 909, 910
Park v. Shin (2002), **2002:** 478; **2006:** 646
Park 'N Fly, Inc. v. Dollar Park & Fly, Inc. (1985), **2006:** 799
Parravano v. Babbitt (1994), **2004:** 728
Parson v. Parson (1998), **1991-99:** 371–77
*Parsons v. United States (1897), **2003:** 633
Pasquantino v. United States (2005), **2005:** 234; **2007:** 76
Pasquini v. Morris (1983), **2000:** 139
*Passage through the Great Belt (Finland v. Denmark) (1991), **1991-99:** 1585–86
Pataki; Doe v. (1997), **1991-99:** 1242
Pathfinder Fund v. AID (1990), **2001:** 285*n*
Patrickson v. Dole Food Co. (2001), **2002:** 480–81; **2003:** 512–14; **2007:** 123
Paul v. Avril (1993), **1991-99:** 979, 1270–71
Pauling v. McElroy (1960), **2005:** 1013; **2006:** 458
Pauly v. United States (1961), **2004:** 446
PDK Labs., Inc. v. Friedlander (1997), **1991-99:** 1246, 1247
PDK Labs., Inc. v. United States DEA (2004), **2006:** 197
Peacock v. Thomas (1996), **2008:** 763, 767
Peninsula Asset Mgmt. v. Hankook Tire Co., Ltd. (2007), **2007:** 454–55
Penn Cent. Transp. Co. v. New York City (1978), **2008:** 603
Pennsylvania v. Einhorn (1995), **2001:** 87–89

Pennsylvania v. Labron (1996), **2001:** 114
Pennsylvania Bd. of Probation and Parole v. Scott (1988), **2006:** 67
Penry v. Lynaugh (1989), **2005:** 382–84
Pension Benefit Guar. Corp. v. R.A. Gray & Co. (1984), **1991-99:** 1248
People of. *See name of specific location*
People's Mojahedin Org. of Iran v. Department of State (1999), **1991-99:** 483; **2002:** 91–92; **2005:** 1013; **2006:** 192, 1009, 1010; **2007:** 954
*People's Mojahedin Org. of Iran v. Department of State (2000), **2001:** 111–12
People's Mojahedin Org. of Iran v. Department of State (2003), **2003:** 176–77, 496; **2006:** 192, 198
Peralta v. Heights Med. Ctr., Inc. (1988), **2001:** 551
Percheman; United States v. (1833), **2002:** 222*n,* 225–26; **2003:** 259; **2008:** 178
Perez-Lopez; United States v. (2003), **2007:** 492
Perez-Perez v. Hanberry (1986), **1991-99:** 193
Perkins v. Elg (1939), **1991-99:** 37; **2008:** 14
Permanent Mission of India to the United Nations v. City of New York (2007), **2007:** 455–62
Permanent Mission of India to the United Nations v. City of New York (2008), **2008:** 456, 495–96
Peroff v. Hylton (1977), **2005:** 80–81, 99–100; **2006:** 153; **2007:** 110; **2008:** 68
Perri v. Dulles (1953), **2003:** 10–11
Persinger v. Islamic Republic of Iran (1984), **1991-99:** 1257; **2000:** 157; **2001:** 461, 464
Pertamina v. Karaha Bodas (2008), **2008:** 760–64, 768
Peru, Ex parte Republic of (1943), **1989-90:** 313, 315, 316, 318; **1991-99:** 1284, 1287; **2001:** 512, 520; **2002:** 497, 507, 548–49; **2004:** 530; **2005:** 42*n,* 562; **2006:** 631, 669, 671, 679; **2007:** 523–25; **2008:** 224
Peru v. Johnson (1989), **1991-99:** 1804*n*
Pescatore v. Pan Am. World Airways, Inc. (1996), **2005:** 519
Pesin v. Rodriguez (1999), **1991-99:** 355, 357, 363
Peter v. United States (1988), **2006:** 321
*Peter Buchanan Ltd. v. McVey (1950), **2005:** 237, 239
Peterson v. Iran (2003), **2006:** 582, 583
Petit v. Ding (2003), **2002:** 475
Petition of. *See name of party*
Petkiewytsch v. INS (1991), **1991-99:** 28, 33–34
Petrol Shipping Corp. v. Kingdom of Greece (1966), **1991-99:** 1202
Peyote Way Church of God, Inc. v. Thornburgh (1991), **2001:** 138, 142

Pfizer, Inc. v. Government of India (1978), **1991-99:** 758, 983, 1239
Pforzheim, In re (1989), **2003:** 881
Phaneuf v. Republic of Indonesia (1997), **2004:** 462; **2006:** 571
Philippine Nat'l Bank v. United States Dist. Court for the Dist. of Haw. (2005), **2005:** 575–78
Philippines v. Marcos (1986), **2003:** 563
Philippines v. Marcos (1987), **1991-99:** 1289; **2001:** 514*n;* **2002:** 561; **2003:** 570; **2006:** 670, 672
Philippines v. Pimentel (2007), **2007:** 470–77
Philippines v. Pimentel (2008), **2007:** 471*n;* **2008:** 233, 475–81
Philippines v. Westinghouse Elec. Corp. (1990), **1989-90:** 320–21
Philippines v. Westinghouse Elec. Corp. (1994), **2002:** 866; **2006:** 610
Philippines v. Westinghouse Elec. Corp. (1995), **2007:** 964
Phillips v. Seiter (1999), **2000:** 498–99*n*
Phillips Petroleum Co. v. Shutts (1985), **2002:** 422, 423, 454
Phinpathya; INS v. (1984), **1991-99:** 196
*Phosphates in Morocco (1938), **2002:** 378
Pierce v. United States (1998), **2001:** 488*n*
Pierce; United States v. (2000), **2002:** 840
Pierre, Matter of (1975), **1991-99:** 225
Pierre-Louis v. Newvac Corp. (2009), **2008:** 513–514, 514*n*, 515–19
Pierson v. Ray (1967), **2002:** 564
Pigeon River Improvement, Slide & Boom Co. v. Charles W. Cox, Ltd. (1934), **1991-99:** 668
Pink; United States v. (1937), **1989-90:** 245, 247
Pink; United States v. (1942), **1991-99:** 656, 672–73, 677, 678, 784, 801, 1137, 1269, 1271; **2000:** 212*n,* 471, 529, 539; **2001:** 452, 468; **2002:** 426, 442, 448, 589; **2003:** 492; **2004:** 435*n;* **2005:** 43–45, 59; **2006:** 540; **2007:** 222, 261; **2008:** 192, 449
Pinkerton; United States v. (1946), **2006:** 461, 462
*Pinkerton and Roach, In re (1987), **2001:** 314, 315
*Pinochet, Ex parte (2000), **2001:** 524*n*
Pioneer Inv. Servs. Co. v. Brunswick Assocs. Ltd. P'ship (1993), **2006:** 623
Piper Aircraft Co. v. Reyno (1981), **2003:** 480; **2005:** 835
*Pirocaco v. Republic of Turkey (1923), **2001:** 630
Pitcherskaia v. INS (1997), **1991-99:** 197–202
The Pizarro (1817), **2001:** 234*n*
Place; United States v. (1983), **1991-99:** 2350
Plaintiff A v. Jiang Zemin (2003), **2003:** 394*n,* 396, 400, 558–69
Plaintiff A v. Xia Deren (2002), **2002:** 469–76, 575
Plaintiff A v. Xia Deren (2004), **2003:** 509–10
Plaintiffs A, B, C v. Zemin (2003), **2006:** 670
*Planche v. Fletcher (1779), **2005:** 238

Planned Parenthood v. Casey (1992), **2005:** 268
Planned Parenthood Fed'n of Am. v. AID (1987), **2001:** 285*n*
Planned Parenthood Fed'n of Am. v. AID (1988), **2001:** 285*n*
Planned Parenthood Fed'n of Am. v. AID (1990), **2001:** 285*n,* 286–90
Planned Parenthood of the Columbia/Willamette, Inc. v. American Coalition of Life Activists (2002), **2007:** 303
Plaster v. United States (1983), **1991-99:** 943; **2005:** 244; **2007:** 104–5, 108, 111
Plata v. Dretke (2004), **2004:** 47–49
PLO; United States v. (1988), **1991-99:** 1320, 1331, 1993*n;* **2000:** 603; **2002:** 554; **2005:** 540–41
Plyler v. Doe (1982), **1991-99:** 788; **2000:** 10; **2001:** 263
Pocket Veto Case (1929), **2001:** 211
Poland v. Garb (2004), **2003:** 515*n;* **2004:** 472–75, 496; **2006:** 573
Polovchak v. Meese (1985), **2000:** 126
Ponath v. Ponath (1993), **1991-99:** 354
Ponnapula v. Ashcroft (2004), **2006:** 39
*Pope & Talbot, Inc. v. Canada (2000), **2000:** 674–94
*Pope & Talbot, Inc. v. Canada (2001), **2004:** 576*n,* 580–81
*Pope & Talbot, Inc. v. Canada (2002), **2002:** 642, 651–60, 662; **2006:** 724
Popular Enters., LLC v. Webcom Media Group, Inc. (2004), **2004:** 873–74; **2005:** 864
Porreca; United States v. (2001), **2001:** 55–59
Posada-Carriles v. Campos (2006), **2006:** 45–50
Posadas v. National City Bank of N.Y. (1936), **2002:** 545
Postal; United States v. (1979), **1991-99:** 160; **2001:** 81
Posters N' Things v. United States (1994), **2006:** 181
*Posti and Rahko v. Finland (2002), **2004:** 227
*Povey v. Civil Aviation Safety Auth. (2002), **2003:** 595–96
Powerex Corp. v. California (2006), **2006:** 550–58
Powerex Corp. v. Reliant Energy Servs., Inc. (2006), **2006:** 550–58
Powerex Corp. v. Reliant Energy Servs., Inc. (2007), **2007:** 452–54
*Power of Municipalities to Levy Rates on Foreign Legations and High Comm'rs' Residences, Re (1943), **2006:** 597
Powers v. Ohio (1991), **2000:** 11; **2006:** 566
Powers Integrations, Inc. v. System Gen. Corp. (2004), **2004:** 874–75
Practical Concepts, Inc. v. Republic of Bolivia (1987), **1989-90:** 281–82; **2005:** 503; **2006:** 624, 625, 629; **2008:** 482
Prasoprat v. Benov (2005), **2005:** 80; **2006:** 150; **2007:** 123
Pravin Banker Assocs., Ltd. v. Banco Popular de Peru (1997), **2001:** 44
Pravin Banker Assocs., Ltd. v. Banco Popular de Peru (1998), **2001:** 493

Preiser v. Newkirk (1975), **2000:** 762
Preiser v. Rodriguez (1973), **2005:** 283
Premier S.S. Corp. v. Embassy of Algeria (1971), **2002:** 554
Presbyterian Church of Sudan v. Talisman (2006), **2006:** 460–65
Presbyterian Church of Sudan v. Talisman Energy, Inc. (2003), **2003:** 383–84, 505; **2004:** 357, 358; **2005:** 394–400, 411, 413, 581, 822–26
Prevatt v. Iran (2006), **2006:** 581*n,* 582
Prevot v. Prevot (1994), **1991-99:** 354
Prewitt Enters., Inc. v. Organization of Petroleum Exporting Countries (2003), **2003:** 557–58
Price v. Socialist People's Libyan Arab Jamahiriya (2000), **2003:** 549–50
Price v. Socialist People's Libyan Arab Jamahiriya (2002), **2002:** 530, 534; **2003:** 550; **2004:** 316, 506, 507, 512; **2005:** 521; **2006:** 1008, 1009
Price v. Socialist People's Libyan Arab Jamahiriya (2003), **2003:** 506, 541, 550
Prince v. Massachusetts (1944), **2005:** 144
Principality of. *See name of specific principality*
Princz v. Federal Republic of Germany (1992), **1991-99:** 1191–93, 1193n–1194*n,* 1194
Princz v. Federal Republic of Germany (1994), **1991-99:** 1054, 1260–64; **2000:** 476, 480–82, 485; **2001:** 420, 433, 434*n,* 437, 438, 440, 444, 457, 481; **2002:** 494, 496, 499–501, 514; **2003:** 514; **2004:** 499; **2006:** 625, 648, 681
Printz v. United States (1997), **2001:** 209; **2007:** 205*n*
The Prize Cases (1863), **2004:** 209, 212–13
Propper v. Clark (1949), **2000:** 617, 619; **2006:** 1014
Prosecutor v. *See name of opposing party*
Provident Bank v. Patterson (1968), **2008:** 480
*Provident Mut. Life Ins. (U.S. v. Germany) (1924), **2001:** 577
Prushinowski v. Samples (1984), **2004:** 92; **2005:** 80
Psinakis v. Marcos (1975), **1989-90:** 316; **1991-99:** 1267; **2001:** 514
Public Citizen v. Office of the U.S. Trade Representative (1992), **2001:** 751
Public Citizen v. U.S. Dep't of Justice (1989), **2001:** 83, 84
*Public Comm. Against Torture in Israel v. Israel (2006), **2007:** 915
Pugh v. Socialist People's Libyan Arab Jamahiriya (2003), **2003:** 505–6, 537
Pugh v. Socialist People's Libyan Arab Jamahiriya (2006), **2006:** 590, 591
Purdue Research Found. v. Sano.-Synthelabo, S.A. (2003), **2003:** 568
*Putnam v. United Mexican States (1923), **2001:** 625

Q

Qassim v. Bush (2005), **2006:** 1184; **2008:** 908
*Qatar v. Bahrain (2001), **2004:** 706
Qi; Doe v. (2004), **2005:** 413
Quaak v. Klynveld Peat Marwick Goerdeler Bedriffsrevisoren (2004), **2004:** 840–45; **2007:** 779, 793
Quackenbush v. Allstate Ins. Co. (1996), **2000:** 573; **2006:** 1141; **2007:** 797
*Quadafi, Re (2001), **2001:** 524*n*
Quaestor Invs., Inc. v. State of Chiapas (1997), **2008:** 412
The Queen v. *See name of opposing party*
Quill Corp. v. North Dakota (1992), **2002:** 454
Quilloin v. Wallcott (1978), **2000:** 4
Quinn v. Robinson (1986), **2001:** 484; **2005:** 95–96
Quinn-Moore v. Lambert (1981), **1991-99:** 1841
Quirin, Ex parte (1942), **2002:** 987, 988*n,* 992, 996–97, 1000, 1004*n,* 1005; **2003:** 367, 1022*n;* **2004:** 208–10, 212, 1004, 1020; **2005:** 1010; **2006:** 1140–44, 1183; **2007:** 972, 981
Quon; United States v. (2001), **2001:** 265

R

*R. v. Re Recognition of an Italian Judgment (2002), **2004:** 867
Rabang v. Boyd (1957), **1991-99:** 12
Rabang; INS v. (1994), **1991-99:** 9–13
Radzanower v. Touche Ross (1976), **2002:** 572
Rafii v. Iran (2005), **2005:** 543–44
Rahmani; United States v. (2002), **2002:** 93; **2003:** 179; **2005:** 117
Rahmani v. United States (2007), **2006:** 180
*Rainbow Warrior Arbitration (New Zealand v. France) (1990), **2000:** 667
Raines v. Byrd (1997), **2000:** 495, 761–65; **2001:** 207; **2002:** 199
Rainwater v. United States (1958), **2005:** 228, 233; **2006:** 303–4
Rajaa al Mukaddam v. Permanent Mission of Saudi Arabia to the United Nations (2000), **2000:** 577–93
Ralpho v. Bell (1977), **2002:** 985; **2005:** 997–98, 1000
Ramirez-Osorio v. INS (1984), **2000:** 132
Rankine v. Reno (2003), **2006:** 38–39
*Raphael Ferrer-Mazorra Case (2005), **2005:** 22–23
The Rapid (1814), **2002:** 983*n*
Rare, In re (2003), **2003:** 870–72
RAR, Inc. v. Turner Diesel, Ltd. (1997), **2003:** 567
Rasoulzadeh v. Associated Press (1985), **2005:** 413
Rasul v. Bush (2002), **2002:** 980–86
Rasul v. Bush (2003), **2003:** 1027–28

Rasul v. Bush (2004), **2004:** 204, 979, 980, 982, 995–1001, 1017*n,* 1018, 1030; **2005:** 963, 996–1000, 1012–14; **2006:** 1178, 1179, 1197, 1210, 1212; **2007:** 939, 944–45, 956, 958; **2008:** 892–94
Rasul v. Myers (2008), **2008:** 914
Rauscher; United States v. (1886), **1991-99:** 438–39, 799; **2005:** 50*n;* **2006:** 1151; **2007:** 120–21
R.A.V. v. City of St. Paul (1992), **2007:** 302, 331
Ravindran v. INS (1991), **1991-99:** 232
Ravindran v. INS (1992), **1991-99:** 220, 224
*R.A.V.N. v. Argentina (1990), **2004:** 226
Ray v. Atlantic Richfield Co. (1978), **1991-99:** 776–83, 785
Reagan v. Wald (1984), **1991-99:** 55, 57
Reed; United States v. (1981), **2002:** 216
Reeves, Inc. v. Stake (1980), **2000:** 327, 329, 330*n*
Regan v. Taxation With Representation (1983), **2001:** 286–87
Regan v. Wald (1984), **2000:** 528; **2001:** 454, 468; **2003:** 499; **2004:** 667; **2005:** 141, 536; **2006:** 542; **2008:** 812
Regina v. *See name of opposing party*
Reid v. Covert (1956), **2008:** 896
Reid v. Covert (1957), **1989-90:** 104–5, 184; **1991-99:** 194, 315, 652, 678*n;* **2000:** 613; **2005:** 244, 999; **2006:** 801; **2007:** 961; **2008:** 75, 896, 897, 900
Reider v. Thompson (1950), **2006:** 920, 925
Rein v. Socialist People's Libyan Arab Jamahiriya (1998), **1991-99:** 1234–52, 1257
Reiss v. Societe Centrale du Groupe des Assurances Nationales (2000), **2007:** 465, 466
Renkel v. United States (2006), **2008:** 156
Reno v. *See name of opposing party*
Republican Party v. White (2002), **2005:** 278
Republic Nat'l Bank of Miami v. United States (1992), **1991-99:** 1262
Republic of. *See name of republic*
Request for Assistance from Ministry of Legal Affairs of Trinidad and Tobago, In re (1988), **1991-99:** 385, 386
*Request for Interpretation of the Judgement of 31 March 2004 in the Case Concerning Avena and Other Mexican Nationals (Mexico v. U.S.) (2009), **2008:** 193–215, 197*n*
*Request for Precautionary Measures (Detainees At Guantanamo Bay, Cuba), **2002:** 1008–17
*Reservations to the Convention on the Prevention and Punishment of the Crime of Genocide (1951), **1989-90:** 147, 355
*Resina, In the marriage of (1991), **2004:** 60
Resource Sav. Assoc. v. Neary (1989), **1991-99:** 1840
Respublica v. De Longchamps (1784), **2003:** 359

*Revere Copper & Brass, Inc. v. Overseas Private Invest. Corp. (1978), **2006:** 716
Reyes; State v. (1999), **1991-99:** 258
Reyes-Requena v. United States (2001), **2001:** 299
Reynolds; United States v. (1953), **2007:** 241, 243, 244, 246*n*, 252–53
Reynolds, Inc. v. Fernandez (1984), **2004:** 668
Rezaq; United States v. (1998), **1991-99:** 507–8
R. Griggs Group, Ltd. v. Filanto Spa (1996), **2003:** 890
Rhanime v. Solomon (2002), **2002:** 552
Rhodes v. Chapman (1981), **2005:** 292; **2006:** 83
Ricaud v. American Metal Co. (1918), **2001:** 526
Rice v. Santa Fe Elevator Corp. (1947), **2000:** 529; **2002:** 443
Richards v. United States (1962), **1991-99:** 196
Richmark Corp. v. Timber Falling Consultants (1992), **2006:** 610
Richmond, City of v. J.A. Croson (1989), **2005:** 289
Riegel Textile Corp. v. Celanese Corp. (1981), **2008:** 40
Riegle v. Federal Open Mkt. Comm. (1981), **2001:** 454
Riggs Nat'l Corp. & Subsidiaries v. Comm'r of IRS (1999), **2005:** 578–79, 582
*Rights of Nationals of the U.S. in Morocco (France v. U.S.) (1952), **2003:** 625*n*
*Right to Info. on Consular Assistance in the Framework of the Guarantees of the Due Process of Law, The Advisory Opinion OC-16/99 (1999), **1991-99:** 338–40; **2000:** 26, 32, 35, 41, 42
Ring v. Arizona (2003), **2002:** 317
Rio Props., Inc. v. Rio Int'l Interlink (2002), **2004:** 874; **2005:** 857, 860, 862–67
Rios v. Marshall (1981), **1991-99:** 1275
Rivera de Gomez v. Kissinger (1976), **1989-90:** 23, 25
R.M.S. Titanic v. Haver (Titanic I) (1999), **2003:** 757; **2006:** 830, 833
R.M.S. Titanic v. Haver (2000), **2003:** 367
R.M.S. Titanic, Inc. v. The Wrecked and Abandoned Vessel Believed to be the RMS Titanic (1996), **2006:** 832
R.M.S. Titanic, Inc. v. The Wrecked and Abandoned Vessel Believed to be the RMS Titanic (Titanic II) (2002), **2006:** 830
R.M.S. Titanic, Inc. v. The Wrecked and Abandoned Vessel Believed to be the RMS Titanic (2004), **2006:** 829
R.M.S. Titanic, Inc. v. The Wrecked and Abandoned Vessel Believed to be the RMS Titanic (2006), **2006:** 828–35; **2008:** 660*n*
R.M.S. Titanic, Inc. v. The Wrecked and Abandoned Vessel Believed to be the RMS Titanic (2007), **2008:** 657–65
Roach v. Aiken (1986), **2001:** 302
*Roach, In re (1987), **1991-99:** 974n–975*n*
*Roach, In re (2001), **2001:** 311, 312–13

Roadway Express, Inc. v. Piper (1980), **2000:** 196
Robel; United States v. (1967), **2004:** 1010; **2006:** 190
Robert C. Herd & Co. v. Krawill Mach. Corp. (1959), **1991-99:** 1847; **2004:** 833
Robertson v. Seattle Audubon Soc. (1992), **1991-99:** 2159–60
Robinson, In re (1997), **1991-99:** 361–63; **2000:** 115
Robinson v. Government of Malaysia (2001), **2006:** 625
Robinson v. Shell Oil Co. (1997), **2004:** 314*n*
Rockwell Int'l Sys., Inc. v. Citibank, N.A. (1983), **1989-90:** 216
Rodrigues; United States v. (1999), **1991-99:** 262
Rodriguez v. Cook (1999), **2002:** 15
Rodriguez v. Drummond Co. (2003), **2006:** 476–79
Rodriguez v. Popular Democratic Party (1982), **2005:** 248
Rodriguez v. Republic of Costa Rica (2002), **2006:** 595
Rodriguez v. Rodriguez (1999), **1991-99:** 367; **2000:** 111
Rodriguez v. Transnave, Inc. (1993), **2001:** 481; **2003:** 525, 526; **2006:** 564
Rodriguez v. United States (1987), **2002:** 543
Rodriguez-Coto, Matter of (1985), **1991-99:** 236
Rodriguez de Quijas v. Shearson/American Express (1989), **2004:** 46
Rodriguez-Rivera v. INS (1988), **1991-99:** 226
Rodriguez-Roman v. INS (1996), **1991-99:** 201
Roe v. Unocal Corp. (1999), **2005:** 582
Roeder v. Iran (2001), **2001:** 460, 462–75
Roeder v. Iran (2002), **2002:** 523–27, 534; **2003:** 547–49
Roeder v. Iran (2003), **2003:** 476–78, 506, 537–38, 541, 547; **2004:** 504, 554; **2005:** 519, 543, 551, 557; **2006:** 560, 582
The Rogdai (1920), **1989-90:** 255
Rogers v. Bellei (1970), **2000:** 5, 8–9
Rogers v. Bellei (1971), **1991-99:** 7, 15
Roman Catholic Diocese of Galveston-Houston; Doe v. (2005), **2005:** 560
Romero v. Drummond Co. (2003), **2006:** 476
Romero v. International Terminal Operating Co. (1959), **2006:** 151
Romine v. Compuserve Corp. (1998), **2002:** 860, 861
Ron Pair Enters., Inc.; United States v. (1989), **2005:** 514
Roper v. Simmons (2004), **2004:** 336–37
Roper v. Simmons (2005), **2004:** 336*n;* **2005:** 269–70, 287, 322, 381; **2006:** 354, 366; **2007:** 304
Rosado v. Civiletti (1980), **1989-90:** 84
Rose v. Himely (1807), **2004:** 366; **2005:** 402; **2006:** 469
Rose v. Silver (1978), **1991-99:** 1338
Rosenfeld v. Volkswagen (2000), **2000:** 504, 505
Rosner v. United States (2002), **2004:** 445
Rosner v. United States (2004), **2004:** 445–49

Rosner v. United States (2005), **2005:** 485
Ross, In re (1891), **2003:** 435
Ross v. McIntyre (1891), **2007:** 203
Rossello-Gonzalez v. Calderon-Serra (2004), **2005:** 243
Rossini v. United States (1996), **1991-99:** 1142
Rostenkowski; United States v. (1995), **2001:** 445
Rostker v. Goldberg (1981), **2002:** 989
Roxas v. Pimentel (2008), **2007:** 470
Royal & Sun Alliance Ins. Co. of Canada v. Century Int'l Arms, Inc. (2005), **2005:** 827–29
Royal & Sun Alliance Ins. Co. of Canada v. Century Int'l Arms, Inc. (2006), **2006:** 950–53
Rozenkier v. Schering AG & Bayer AG (2004), **2004:** 439–41
Rubin v. Iran (2005), **2005:** 543*n*
Rubin v. Iran (2006), **2006:** 564–72, 621
Rubin v. Islamic Republic of Iran (2007), **2007:** 486–89
Ruggiero v. Compania Peruana de Vapores "Inca Capac Yupanqui" (1981), **2002:** 563
Ruiz v. Drummond Co. (2004), **2006:** 476
Ruiz-Massieu, In re (1996), **1991-99:** 121–26
Rumsfeld v. Padilla (2004), **2003:** 1027*n;* **2004:** 979, 1017*n*, 1018*n;* **2005:** 88; **2006:** 1197, 1210
Rush; United States v. (1984), **2001:** 137, 138
Rush Presbyterian St. Luke's Med. Ctr. v. Hellenic Republic (1989), **1991-99:** 1203
Russell, In re (1998), **2000:** 499
Russell v. Clark's Executors (1812), **2008:** 480
Russello v. United States (1983), **2003:** 540
Russian Volunteer Fleet v. United States (1931), **2002:** 224*n*
Rust v. Sullivan (1991), **2007:** 255–56
Ruzatullah v. Gates (2007), **2007:** 944–56
Ryan, In re (1973), **1989-90:** 81
Ryan v. Brunswick Corp. (2002), **2005:** 864, 866–67
Rydder v. Rydder (1995), **1991-99:** 353, 365, 369, 373; **2000:** 99

S
*S. v. Ebrahim (1991), **2000:** 404*n*
Saavedra Bruno v. Albright (1999), **1991-99:** 68–71; **2006:** 24, 1192; **2007:** 21
Sabangan v. Powell (2003), **2003:** 273–75
Sabangan v. Powell (2004), **2004:** 218
*SA Biovilac v. European Economic Cmty. (1984), **2001:** 588
Sablan Constr. Co. v. Government of Trust Territory (1981), **1991-99:** 816

Sablan v. Iginoef (1990), **2000:** 484*n;* **2001:** 441*n*
Sablan v. Superior Court of Commonwealth of N. Mariana Islands (1991), **2000:** 484*n;* **2001:** 441*n*
Sacirbegovic, In the Matter of the Extradition of (2003), **2003:** 246–48
Sackie v. Ashcroft (2003), **2004:** 325*n,* 326
Sacks v. Office of Foreign Assets Control (2006), **2006:** 1015–19
Sadat v. Mertes (1980), **1991-99:** 35, 36–37
Safaie v. INS (1994), **1991-99:** 221*n,* 223
Safety Nat'l Casualty Corp. v. Certain Underwriters at Lloyd's London (2008), **2008:** 777–82
Safety Nat'l Casualty Corp. v. Certain Underwriters at Lloyd's London (2009), **2008:** 778*n*
Sagana v. Tenorio (2004), **2005:** 253
Sage Realty Corp. v. Jugobanka, D.D. (1998), **2000:** 572
Sagermark v. INS (1985), **1991-99:** 199, 200
*Saghi v. Iran (1993), **1991-99:** 1096
St. Cyr; INS v. (2001), **2001:** 83, 466; **2002:** 496, 497, 499–501, 506; **2003:** 518; **2004:** 92; **2006:** 37–39, 153–54; **2007:** 106–8
Saipan, People of v. U.S. Dep't of Interior (1973), **1991-99:** 814; **2002:** 216*n*
Salameh; United States v. (1999), **1991-99:** 261; **2000:** 42
Salas; United States v. (1998), **1991-99:** 259
Salazar v. Iran (2005), **2006:** 582
Sale v. Haitian Ctrs. Council, Inc. (1993), **1991-99:** 58, 150, 163, 175, 177, 188; **2004:** 480; **2007:** 43, 44*n;* **2008:** 127, 368*n,* 893
Sales v. Republic of Uganda (1993), **2002:** 541
Salmon Spawning & Recovery Alliance v. U.S. Dep't of Commerce (2006), **2006:** 876
Saltany v. Reagan (1988), **1989-90:** 311–15; **1991-99:** 1267, 1269, 1270, 1290; **2001:** 513, 515; **2002:** 474, 549*n;* **2007:** 523
*Saluka Invs. BV v. Czech Republic (2007), **2007:** 545–46
*Sambaggio (Italy v. Venezuela) (1903), **2001:** 635
Sampson v. Federal Republic of Germany (1997), **2001:** 432, 434*n,* 442*n*
Sampson v. Federal Republic of Germany (2001), **2001:** 432; **2002:** 492, 494, 501, 589; **2003:** 363, 515; **2004:** 530
Sampson v. Federal Republic of Germany and the Conference on Jewish Material Claims Against Germany, Inc. (1997), **1991-99:** 1133; **2000:** 473–85, 593
Sampson v. Murray (1974), **1989-90:** 262
Sanchez and Escobar, Matter of (1985), **1991-99:** 231
Sanchez-Espinoza v. Reagan (1985), **1989-90:** 312; **1991-99:** 980, 1127, 1136; **2005:** 414
Sanchez-Llamas v. Oregon (2005), **2005:** 61

Sanchez-Llamas v. Oregon (2006), **2006:** 63–75, 79, 79*n,* 81; **2007:** 76, 79*n;* **2008:** 180*n,* 181, 183, 183*n,* 184–86, 192, 515, 518
Sanchez-Trujillo v. INS (1986), **1991-99:** 224, 231
S & Davis Int'l, Inc. v. Republic of Yemen (2000), **2002:** 515
Sandhu, Matter of Extradition of (1993), **2001:** 82
Sandhu v. Burke (2000), **2001:** 77
San Diego Building Trades Council v. Garmon (1959), **2000:** 327
San Diego Cty. Gun Rights Comm. v. Reno (1996), **2001:** 12
Sandin v. Conner (1995), **2005:** 275–76
S&S Mach. Co. v. Masinexportimport (1983), **1989-90:** 301
S&S Mach. Co. v. Masinexportimport (1992), **2002:** 542
Sangha v. INS (1997), **1991-99:** 200; **2000:** 131
Sanidad v. INS (1995), **1991-99:** 9
Sanitary Dist. v. United States (1925), **2005:** 39, 42, 53
Santana v. State (1986), **1991-99:** 280–82
*Santiago Marzioni (Argentina) (1996), **2002:** 370
Santos v. Compagnie Nationale Air France (1991), **1991-99:** 1211
Santos; United States v. (2008), **2008:** 485
Santovincenzo v. Egan (1931), **2000:** 494
The Sapphire (1870), **1989-90:** 255
Saravia; Doe v. (2004), **2004:** 362–63, 382–83
Sardino v. Federal Reserve Bank (1966), **1991-99:** 57
Sarei v. Rio Tinto (2002), **2002:** 333–43, 357, 574–75; **2003:** 393*n;* **2005:** 420, 423*n;* **2006:** 444, 948, 949
Sarei v. Rio Tinto (2006), **2006:** 431–50, 946–50; **2007:** 227
Sarei v. Rio Tinto (2007), **2007:** 222–23*n*
Sarei v. Rio Tinto (2008), **2008:** 238–39
Saroop, United States ex rel. v. Garcia (1997), **2000:** 200, 491; **2001:** 46; **2002:** 215–16; **2006:** 156–57, 521
Sattar; United States v. (2003), **2003:** 177–79
Saudi Arabia v. Nelson (1993), **1991-99:** 1183, 1208; **2000:** 475, 478, 479, 579; **2001:** 403–4, 429, 434, 435, 444, 479, 497; **2002:** 465, 473, 502, 505, 520; **2003:** 503, 564; **2004:** 458, 499; **2005:** 501; **2006:** 549, 648, 681; **2007:** 450, 464, 465–66; **2008:** 455
Saudi Arabian Airlines Corp. v. Tamimi (1999), **1991-99:** 1199
Save Our Valley v. Sound Transit (2003), **2006:** 82
Sayne v. Shipley (1969), **2008:** 66
Sayne v. Shipley (1970), **2008:** 66
Scales v. United States (1961), **2005:** 125
S.C. Chimexim S.A. v. Velco Enters. Ltd. (1999), **1991-99:** 1836–38
Scherk v. Alberto-Culver Co. (1974), **1991-99:** 1847, 1848
Schlesinger v. Councilman (1975), **2006:** 1150
Schlesinger v. Reservists Comm. to Stop the War (1974), **2006:** 456; **2007:** 220

Schloendorff v. Society of N.Y. Hosps. (1914), **2005:** 277
Schmidt; United States v. (1991), **1991-99:** 28
Schmitz, In the Matter of Application of (2003), **2003:** 876–81; **2004:** 858
Schmitz v. Bernstein Liebhard & Lifshitz, LLP (2004), **2004:** 856–58
Schneckloth v. Bustamonte (1973), **1991-99:** 2350
Schneider v. Kissinger (2005), **2005:** 406, 416–17; **2006:** 456, 457, 522, 525, 526, 540, 541, 544; **2007:** 439–41, 952; **2008:** 444, 446
Schneider v. Rusk (1964), **1991-99:** 20, 39
The Schooner Exchange v. McFaddon (1812), **1989-90:** 314, 321; **1991-99:** 1261, 1267, 1277, 1283–84; **2000:** 401, 475; **2001:** 515, 517; **2002:** 504, 561; **2003:** 560, 563, 566; **2004:** 465, 529, 550; **2005:** 496, 561; **2006:** 569, 611, 631, 632, 668; **2007:** 448, 460, 476, 523, 961; **2008:** 74–76, 477
The Schooner Peggy; United States v. (1801), **2000:** 516*n;* **2002:** 448
*Schreiber v. Canada (Attorney Gen.) (2002), **2003:** 529–30
Schreiber; United States v. (1999), **2000:** 191
Schweiker v. Chilicky (1988), **2000:** 411
Scott v. Sanford (1857), **2000:** 8*n*
*S.D. Myers, Inc. v. Canada (2000), **2000:** 692–94
*S.D. Myers, Inc. v. Canada (2002), **2001:** 591, 593, 622–23; **2004:** 577*n,* 582, 582*n,* 586; **2006:** 720, 724
Sea Hunt, Inc. v. The Unidentified, Shipwrecked Vessel or Vessels (1999), **1991-99:** 1612–17
Sealed Case No. 98-3077, In re (1998), **2006:** 611
Sealed Case No. 99-3901, In re (1999), **2000:** 548
Seattle Totems Hockey Club, Inc. v. National Hockey League (1981), **2002:** 866*n;* **2006:** 955, 957
*Secretary of State for Health, ex parte Imperial Tobacco Ltd.; The Queen v. (1991), **2000:** 652
*Secretary of State for the Env't, Transp. and Regions, ex parte Omega Air Ltd.; Regina v. (1999), **2000:** 647–48, 651–52
Security Indus. Bank; United States v. (1982), **2007:** 459
Security Pac. Nat'l Bank v. Derderian (1989), **2001:** 404
Sedco, Inc., In re (1982), **2001:** 499
Seetransport Wiking Trader Schiffarhtsgesellschaft MBH & Co. v. Navimpex Centrala Navala (1993), **1991-99:** 1246, 1259; **2001:** 437
Segni v. Commercial Office of Spain (1986), **2002:** 540
Segni v. Commercial Office of Spain (1987), **2000:** 581–83, 585, 586 767
Seguros Commercial Am. v. Hall (2000), **2002:** 216*n*
Sequihua v. Texaco, Inc. (1994), **2008:** 232
767 Third Ave Assocs. v. Consulate Gen. of the Socialist Fed. Republic of Yugoslavia (2000), **2000:** 565–75

767 Third Ave. Assocs. v. Permanent Mission of the Republic of Zaire to the United Nations (1993), **1991-99:** 1292, 1319–31; **2000:** 587, 590, 597, 606, 607, 613, 615, 616; **2001:** 530, 533, 534, 537, 538; **2002:** 560, 565–67; **2004:** 533, 534, 554–57
SG Avipro Fin. Ltd. v. Cameroon Airlines (2005), **2008:** 774
Shalit v. Coppe (1999), **1991-99:** 354; **2008:** 784, 785, 788
Shamsee v. Shamsee (1980), **2000:** 626
Shanghai Power Co. v. United States (1983), **2002:** 414
Shao v. Link Cargo (Taiwan) Ltd. (1993), **2006:** 919
Shapiro v. Republic of Bolivia (1991), **1991-99:** 1204, 1243; **2001:** 436
Shapiro; United States v. (1942), **1991-99:** 14
Shaughnessy v. United States ex rel. Mezei (1953), **1991-99:** 8, 169, 175; **2000:** 10, 132, 133; **2004:** 17; **2005:** 291; **2006:** 1190, 1191; **2008:** 908, 909, 913
Shearer; United States v. (1985), **1991-99:** 1215
*Sheibani v. U.S. (2003), **2003:** 451–54
Sheikh v. Cahill (1989), **2000:** 115
Sherbert v. Verner (1963), **2007:** 328
Sheridan-Kalorama Neighborhood Council, Appeal of (2004), **2004:** 559–60
Sherwood; United States v. (1941), **1991-99:** 660
Shewmaker; United States v. (1991), **2002:** 544
Shibayama v. United States (2002), **2004:** 224–32
Shillitani v. United States (1966), **2005:** 526; **2006:** 605
Sidali v. INS (1997), **2005:** 92, 99; **2006:** 156, 158; **2007:** 102, 111
Siderman de Blake v. Republic of Argentina (1991), **2003:** 362, 363, 376
Siderman de Blake v. Republic of Argentina (1992), **1991-99:** 974, 976, 1190–92, 1194, 1196, 1199, 1252–55, 1333; **2000:** 401*n,* 481; **2001:** 405, 434*n,* 438, 442, 482, 483; **2002:** 335, 473; **2003:** 527–28; **2004:** 304*n,* 497, 530; **2006:** 681
*Sidhu v. British Airways plc (1977), **1991-99:** 713
Sidhu v. Gonzales (2006), **2006:** 36
Sierra Club v. Morton (1972), **2000:** 314
Sierra Club v. U.S. Dep't of Transportation (2007), **2007:** 557–62
Sierra Club v. U.S. Envt'l Protection Agency (2003), **2004:** 761
Si Lu Tian; United States v. (2003), **2006:** 586
Silverman v. Silverman (2003), **2008:** 784, 786–88
*Simic, Simic, Tadic, Todorovic, and Zaric; Prosecutor v. (2000), **2000:** 255–71
Simmons v. Braun (1980), **2005:** 99
Simon, In re (Hong Kong & Shanghai Banking Corp. v. Simon) (1998), **2006:** 947, 948
Simon v. Eastern Ky. Welfare Rights Org. (1976), **2001:** 207
Simon v. Iraq (2008), **2008:** 463–64, 470, 471

Simons v. Lycee Francais de N.Y. (2003), **2003:** 510, 532–33, 557
Simpson v. Socialist People's Libyan Arab Jamahiriya (2003), **2003:** 550–51; **2004:** 316
Sinaltrainal v. The Coca Cola Co. (2003), **2003:** 378–80
Sindona v. Grant (1980), **1989-90:** 83, 85; **2008:** 55
Singh; In re Extradition of (1987), **2008:** 68
Singh, In re Extradition of (2001), **2005:** 95
Singh, In re Extradition of (2005), **2005:** 95–96
Sinochem Int'l Co. v. Malaysia Int'l Shipping Corp. (2007), **2006:** 964*n;* **2007:** 795–800
Sioux Tribe of Indians v. United States (1942), **1991-99:** 839
Sisal Sales Corp.; United States v. (1927), **1991-99:** 1532
$69,530 in United States Currency; United States v. (1998), **1991-99:** 260
Skinner v. Mid-America Pipeline Co. (1989), **1991-99:** 1239
Skiriotes v. Florida (1941), **2004:** 725
Ski Train Fire in Kaprun, Austria, In re (2002), **2002:** 479–80
Ski Train Fire in Kaprun, Austria, In re (2003), **2003:** 893–95
Slade v. United States of Mexico (1985), **2001:** 433
Slagenweit v. Slagenweit (1993), **1991-99:** 354
Small v. United States (2005), **2006:** 857
Smart v. Leeke (1989), **2002:** 1006*n*
Smith, In re (1994), **2003:** 881
Smith v. Islamic Emirate of Afghanistan (2003), **2003:** 506, 551–52, 555
Smith v. Massachusetts (2005), **2005:** 283
Smith v. Socialist People's Libyan Arab Jamahiriya (1996), **1991-99:** 1194–95, 1197, 1198, 1256–57, 1264; **2002:** 493, 494, 501; **2003:** 515; **2004:** 499
Smith v. Socialist People's Libyan Arab Jamahiriya (1997), **2000:** 480, 481; **2001:** 436, 438, 442, 479; **2006:** 648
Smith v. Sperling (1957), **2002:** 489
Smith; United States v. (1820), **2004:** 350; **2008:** 129
Smith v. United States (1991), **1991-99:** 1142
Smith v. United States (1993), **1991-99:** 167; **2001:** 332
Smith; United States v. (2003), **2004:** 47
Smith ex rel. Estate of Smith v. Federal Reserve Bank of N.Y. (2003), **2003:** 555, 557; **2004:** 526
Smith/Enron Cogeneration Ltd. P'ship, Inc. v. Smith Cogeneration Int'l, Inc. (2000), **2004:** 848
Smyth, In re Extradition of (1994), **1991-99:** 428–35; **2001:** 76
Smyth, In re Extradition of (1995), **2005:** 81
Smyth; United States v. (1995), **1991-99:** 416
Sniadach v. Family Fin. Corp. (1969), **2005:** 279

S.N.T. Fratelli Gondrand v. United States (1964), **2002:** 414–15; **2004:** 446
Socialist People's Libyan Arab Jamahiriya. *See* Libyan Arab Jamahiriya
*Société Les Commissaires Réunis/Receveur des douanes (1978), **2003:** 694
Société Nationale des Chemin de Fer Francais v. Abrams (2004), **2003:** 515*n*
Société Nationale Industrielle Aérospatiale v. United States Dist. Ct. for S. Dist. of Iowa (1987), **1989-90:** 320, 322; **1991-99:** 1346, 1533; **2003:** 860; **2004:** 845, 859–65; **2005:** 564, 814, 844–46; **2007:** 176; **2008:** 230, 231, 242
Software AG, Inc. v. Consist Software Solutions, Inc. (2008), **2008:** 771–76
Software AG, Inc. v. Consist Software Solutions, Inc. (2009), **2008:** 772*n*
Sompo Japan Ins. Co. of Am. v. Union Pac. R.R. Co. (2006), **2006:** 922
*Sonderup v. Tondelli (2000), **2004:** 60
Sosa v. Alvarez-Machain (2003), **2003:** 381, 382–83, 389
Sosa v. Alvarez-Machain (2004), **2004:** 340–62, 364, 365–76, 377*n,* 380, 382, 473*n,* 474, 475*n,* 495, 500; **2005:** 83, 245–47, 396, 398–99, 401, 403–4, 408–10, 412–15, 421, 423*n,* 425–27, 471–72, 475–76, 494, 496, 516, 542, 777; **2006:** 76–77, 85, 431, 433, 436–38, 441–45, 447, 451, 452, 462, 464, 468, 468*n,* 469, 470, 474, 475, 478, 591, 650, 673; **2007:** 178, 201, 219, 225, 227–28, 230, 231, 234; **2008:** 40–42, 155, 157, 216, 217*n,* 218, 219, 222, 225, 226, 235, 237, 238, 239, 243, 428
Soudavar v. Islamic Republic of Iran (1999), **1991-99:** 1255–56
Soudavar v. Islamic Republic of Iran (2003), **2003:** 531
South African Apartheid Litig., In re (2002), **2004:** 351*n*
South African Apartheid Litig., In re (2003), **2003:** 387–90
South African Apartheid Litig., In re (2004), **2004:** 354; **2005:** 400, 407, 412; **2006:** 440, 447, 453–54; **2008:** 237
South African Apartheid Litig., In re (2007), **2006:** 446
South Carolina v. Baker (1988), **1991-99:** 657*n*
South Carolina v. Katzenbach (1966), **1991-99:** 1207, 1238, 1241, 1243; **2006:** 1008
South Carolina v. United States (1905), **1991-99:** 1202
South-Central Timber Dev., Inc. v. Wunnicke (1984), **2000:** 329–31
South Dakota v. Yankton Sioux Tribe (1998), **2008:** 469
South-Eastern Underwriters Ass'n; United States v. (1944), **2000:** 470
Southern Cross Overseas Agencies v. Wah Kwong Shipping Group Ltd. (1999), **2001:** 232

Southern Pac. Co. v. Arizona (1945), **2000:** 321; **2002:** 453
Southern Pac. Terminal Co. v. ICC (1911), **2000:** 762
South Norwalk; State v. (1904), **1991-99:** 646
South Puerto Rico Sugar Co. Trading Corp. v. United States (1964), **1991-99:** 2256–57
*South W. Africa Cases (1966), **2000:** 656, 661; **2002:** 379
Southway v. Central Bank of Nigeria (2003), **2006:** 571
Southwest Livestock and Trucking Co. v. Ramon (1999), **1991-99:** 1838–41
S-P-, Matter of (1998), **1991-99:** 230
Spacil v. Crowe (1974), **1989-90:** 315, 316; **1991-99:** 1285, 1287, 1297; **2001:** 513, 520; **2002:** 548, 549; **2004:** 531; **2005:** 562; **2006:** 669, 671, 679; **2007:** 525
Spanjol; United States v. (1992), **1989-90:** 352
Spatola v. United States (1991), **2000:** 192; **2008:** 55
Spector v. Norwegian Cruise Line Ltd. (2005), **2005:** 708
Spelar; United States v. (1949), **2001:** 333
Spiess v. C. Itoh & Co. (Am.), Inc. (1981), **2005:** 57*n*
Springer v. Philippine Islands (1928), **2002:** 525
Springfield Rare Coin Galleries, Inc. v. Johnson (1986), **2002:** 450
*S.S. "I'm Alone" Case (Canada v. U.S.) (1924), **2003:** 435
*S.S. Wimbledon Case (1923), **1991-99:** 1118
Stafford Ordnance Corp. v. United States (1952), **2002:** 511
Stafoff; United States v. (1923), **2000:** 197, 198
*Standard Oil Co. of N.Y. (U.S. v. Germany) (1926), **2001:** 579; **2003:** 628*n*
Stanford v. Kentucky (1989), **1991-99:** 966; **2002:** 291; **2004:** 336; **2005:** 381, 383–84
Stanley; United States v. (1987), **2002:** 235
State Dep't v. Ray (1991), **2006:** 1220
State Establishment for Agric. Prod. Trading v. MV Wesermunde (1988), **1991-99:** 1844
State Farm Fire & Cas. Co. v. Bomke (1988), **2006:** 446
State Farm Fire & Cas. Co. v. Tashire (1967), **2008:** 480
State of. *See name of state*
*Stato di Rumania v. Trutta (1926), **1991-99:** 1203
Steamship Co. v. Tugman (1882), **2001:** 234*n*
Steel Co. v. Citizens for a Better Env't (1998), **2000:** 494*n*; **2001:** 464
Steele v. Bulova Watch Co. (1952), **1991-99:** 1532
Steel Improvement & Forge Co. v. United States (1966), **2002:** 511
Steffen F. v. Severina P. (1997), **1991-99:** 366; **2000:** 112*n*
Steinmetz; United States v. (1992), **1991-99:** 1609–11, 1615
Stelmokas; United States v. (1996), **1991-99:** 27
Stena Rederi AB v. Comision de Contratos (1991), **2006:** 575

Stenberg v. Carhart (2000), **2005:** 268
Stephens v. National Distillers and Chemical Corp. (1996), **2000:** 470
Sterling v. Constantin (1932), **2004:** 1012
Stethem v. Islamic Republic of Iran (2002), **2002:** 528
Stevic; INS v. (1984), **1991-99:** 159, 161, 168, 178, 953
*Stockè v. Germany (1991), **2000:** 265
Stone v. Powell (1976), **2005:** 282
Stonington Partners v. Lernout & Hauspie Speech Prods. (2002), **2002:** 865–68
Stratievsky; United States v. (2006), **2006:** 107, 110
Strickland v. Washington (1984), **2002:** 48; **2008:** 45, 46
Stuart; United States v. (1989), **2000:** 214; **2003:** 149; **2005:** 51–52; **2006:** 81; **2007:** 519; **2008:** 518
Students Challenging Regulatory Agency Procedures; United States v. (1973), **2000:** 314
Suarez v. Drummond Co. (2003), **2006:** 476
Suarez Medina v. Texas (2002), **2003:** 42–43, 86
Subpoena Issued to Mary Erato, In re (1993), **2002:** 84*n*
Suchodolski Assocs., Inc. v. Cardell Fin. Corp. (2006), **2008:** 775, 776
Suerte; United States v. (2002), **2002:** 134–37
Suk Yoon Kim v. Ishikawajima Harima Heavy Indus., Ltd. (2003), **2003:** 468
Sullivan v. Kidd (1921), **1991-99:** 728
Sullivan v. State of San Paulo (1941), **2002:** 553
Sumang v. Republic of Palau (1994), **1991-99:** 823
Sumitomo Shoji Am., Inc. v. Avagliano (1982), **1991-99:** 373, 712, 973, 1297, 1329, 1834; **2000:** 107, 493, 519, 526, 554*n*, 587, 597, 607; **2001:** 457*n*, 530, 532, 561; **2002:** 440; **2003:** 149, 499, 591, 599; **2004:** 536–37, 556; **2005:** 480; **2006:** 661, 1217*n*; **2007:** 487*n*; **2008:** 41, 158, 183
Sun v. Taiwan (2000), **2002:** 538
Sun Refining and Mktg. Co. v. Brennan (1990), **2002:** 860
Superville; United States v. (1999), **2000:** 42
Surette v. Islamic Republic of Iran (2002), **2002:** 533
Surrender of Ntakirutimana, In re (1999), **1991-99:** 597–603
Sutherland v. Islamic Republic of Iran (2001), **2001:** 459
S–V-, Matter of (2000), **2005:** 349
Swain v. Pressley (1977), **2006:** 1182
Swann v. South Health Partners, Inc. (2004), **2008:** 44
Swift Textiles, Inc. v. Watkins Motor Lines, Inc. (1986), **2006:** 920, 923, 924
*Sylvester v. Austria (2003), **2003:** 123–25
Szabo v. CGU Int'l Ins. (2002), **2002:** 859–62

T

*T. v. Secretary of State for the Home Dep't (1996), **1991-99:** 237
Tabacchi v. Harrison (2000), **2000:** 109–10
Tabion v. Mufti (1996), **1991-99:** 373, 1296–97, 1303–4; **2000:** 587, 606*n,* 607, 613; **2004:** 535–37; **2007:** 518, 519, 521
Tachiona v. Mugabe (2001), **2001:** 319–26, 510–36; **2003:** 562, 565, 566, 570; **2006:** 635, 640, 643
Tachiona v. Mugabe (2004), **2004:** 532, 533, 539, 553–58; **2006:** 635, 670, 682
Tachiona v. Mugabe (I–IV) (2001–2002), **2002:** 324–33, 474, 552*n,* 563
Tachiona v. United States (2004), **2006:** 635, 674; **2007:** 514; **2008:** 501
Tachiona v. United States (2006), **2006:** 682
Tadayasu v. Clark, (1951), **2007:** 6
*Tadic; Prosecutor v. (1995), **1991-99:** 472, 587–97, 603
*Tadic; Prosecutor v. (1997), **2006:** 464
*Tadic; Prosecutor v. (1999), **2000:** 393; **2004:** 375
Tahan v. Duquette (1992), **1991-99:** 367; **2000:** 97, 103, 111, 114
Taiheiyo Cement Corp. v. Superior Court (2004), **1991-99:** 1134; **2002:** 440–56; **2004:** 441–45, 476
Taiheiyo Cement Corp. v. Superior Court of Cal., for the County of Los Angeles (Jae Won Jeong, real party in interest) (2003), **2003:** 472–74
Taipei Economic and Cultural Representative Office in the U.S. v. United States (1998), **1991-99:** 659–66
Taitz; United States v. (1990), **2001:** 67, 68
Taiwan v. United States Dist. Ct. for the N. Dist. of Cal. (1997), **1991-99:** 663, 709; **2002:** 538; **2003:** 573
Takahashi v. Fish and Game Commission (1948), **2007:** 202
Talenti v. Clinton (1996), **2003:** 481*n*
Tapia-Mendoza; United States v. (1999), **1991-99:** 261
Tawakkal, In re Extradition of (2008), **2008:** 64–69
Taylor v. Morton (1855), **1991-99:** 727
Taylor v. Standard Gas Co. (1939), **2007:** 498
Tayyari v. New Mexico State Univ. (1980), **2002:** 450
*Tchacosh Co. v. Islamic Republic of Iran (1992), **2003:** 452–53*n*
Tchacosh Co. v. Rockwell Int'l Corp. (1985), **2005:** 577
Teague v. Lane (1989), **1991-99:** 316; **2004:** 47, 48; **2005:** 283
Teague v. Regional Comm'r of Customs (1968), **1991-99:** 57; **2008:** 812
Teck Cominco Metals, Ltd. v. Pakootas (2008), **2007:** 688–91
Tee-Hit-Ton Indians v. United States (1955), **2001:** 261

Tel-Oren v. Libyan Arab Republic (1984), **1989-90:** 347; **1991-99:** 161, 978, 985; **2001:** 420; **2002:** 215, 222*n*, 323–24, 326, 328–29, 340, 342; **2003:** 260*n*, 361, 367, 371, 376; **2004:** 348, 350, 351*n*, 367; **2005:** 403, 410, 413–14; **2006:** 470; **2008:** 157
*Tembec Inc. v. United States (2003), **2004:** 594–96
*Tembec Inc. v. United States (2005), **2005:** 596–97; **2006:** 702; **2007:** 549
Tembec Inc. v. United States (2006), **2006:** 702
*Tembec Inc. v. United States (2007), **2007:** 549–51
Tembec v. United States (2008), **2008:** 525–26
Temengil v. Trust Territory of the Pac. Islands (1989), **2002:** 216
Tenet v. Doe (2005), **2005:** 94
Tenney v. Mitsui & Co. (2000), **2000:** 530, 537; **2001:** 451
Terlinden v. Ames (1902), **1991-99:** 600, 602, 704, 727; **2000:** 199–200, 210, 211, 214; **2006:** 157
*Terminal Forest Prods. Ltd. v. United States (2005), **2005:** 596–97, 599, 601–2; **2006:** 702; **2007:** 549
Terrence K., In the Matter of (1987), **2002:** 553–54, 560
*Territorial Dispute (Libya v. Chad), **2003:** 624*n*
Terrorist Attacks, In re (2005), **2006:** 636; **2007:** 506–7
Testan; United States v. (1976), **1991-99:** 660; **2003:** 538
Texas v. Cobb (2001), **2005:** 281
Texas; United States v. (1950), **1991-99:** 836–37, 839; **2002:** 249, 253
Texas; United States v. (1993), **2005:** 235
Texas v. United States (1998), **2005:** 93; **2006:** 159
Texas v. White (1868), **1991-99:** 983
Texas Trading & Milling Corp. v. Federal Republic of Nigeria (1981), **1991-99:** 1206, 1211, 1221, 1243, 1245; **2001:** 498; **2006:** 593
Textile Workers v. Lincoln Mills of Ala. (1957), **2004:** 347; **2006:** 446
Then v. Melendez (1996), **2000:** 200
32 County Sovereignty Comm. v. Department of State (2002), **2006:** 1181
Thiry v. Carlson (1996), **2001:** 136
Thomas; United States v. (1990), **2001:** 330
Thomas-Lazear v. FBI (1988), **2001:** 478
Thompson v. Carter (2002), **2005:** 367
Thompson v. Oklahoma (1988), **2001:** 311; **2002:** 318*n*; **2005:** 381, 385–86
Thompson v. Thompson (1988), **2005:** 514
Thompson; United States v. (1991), **1991-99:** 1128
*Thomson v. Thomson (1994), **1991-99:** 369
Thorington v. Smith (1868), **1991-99:** 984
Thornton; United States v. (1982), **2000:** 548*n*

Three Affiliated Tribes of Fort Berthold Reservation v. World Eng'g (1984), **2006:** 542
*Tihomir Blaskic; Prosecutor v. (1997), **2000:** 266, 269, 271; **2003:** 215, 217, 218
Timberlane Lumber Co. v. Bank of Am. (1976), **1991-99:** 1530, 1532
TMR Energy Ltd. v. State Prop. Fund of Ukraine (2005), **2006:** 1009, 1010
Toler v. Gonzales (2006), **2007:** 8
Tom Man v. Murff (1959), **2004:** 20
Toren v. Toren (1999), **1991-99:** 354
Torres v. Mullin (2003), **2004:** 44
Torres v. Oklahoma (2004), **2004:** 43–44
Torres v. Puerto Rico (1979), **1991-99:** 810
Torres v. State (2005), **2005:** 59–60
Torres-Del Muro; United States v. (1999), **1991-99:** 261
Toscanino; United States v. (1974), **1991-99:** 505
Toth v. Quarles (1955), **1991-99:** 510
Touche Ross & Co. v. Redington (1979), **2003:** 538; **2004:** 504–5
Townsend v. Little (1883), **2002:** 544
*Tradex Hellas S.A. v. Republic of Albania (1999), **2006:** 713, 714
Trailer Marine Transp. Corp. v. Rivera Vazquez (1992), **2005:** 243, 248
Trajano v. Marcos (1989), **2002:** 342
Trajano v. Marcos (1992), **2003:** 358–59
Tran Qui Than v. Regan (1981), **2006:** 1014
Transaero, Inc. v. La Fuerza Aerea Boliviana (1994), **1991-99:** 1186–88; **2000:** 592; **2005:** 551, 554–55, 557; **2006:** 559, 560
Transamerica Mortgage Advisors, Inc. v. Lewis (1979), **2002:** 223; **2003:** 263
Transamerican S.S. Corp. v. Somali Democratic Republic (1983), **1989-90:** 287
Transamerican S.S. Corp. v. Somali Democratic Republic (1985), **2001:** 496
Transatlantic Shiffahrtskontor GmbH v. Shanghai Foreign Trade Corp. (2000), **2007:** 464–66
Trans Commodities, Inc. v. Kazakhstan Trading House, S.A. (1997), **2002:** 541
Transportation, Dep't of, v. Public Citizen (2004), **2007:** 557–59
Transportes Aereos de Angola v. Ronair, Inc. (1982), **1989-90:** 247
Trans World Airlines, Inc. v. Franklin Mint Corp. (1983), **2001:** 132
Trans World Airlines, Inc. v. Franklin Mint Corp. (1984), **1991-99:** 1320; **2001:** 472–74; **2002:** 215
Traore v. State (1981), **2002:** 554
Trapilo; United States v. (1997), **2001:** 488*n;* **2002:** 840; **2005:** 234

Treasury Employees v. Von Raab (1989), **2001:** 133
Triestman v. United States (1997), **2000:** 201
Trimble v. Gordon (1977), **1991-99:** 4
Trinidad y Garcia v. Benov (2008), **2008:** 57–64
Trojan Techs., Inc. v. Pennsylvania (1990), **2000:** 329*n;* **2002:** 450
Trop v. Dulles (1958), **2000:** 6; **2005:** 382, 386, 388
Tuan Anh Nguyen v. INS (2001), **1991-99:** 2; **2001:** 7–8
Tuck v. Pan Am. Health Org. (1981), **2002:** 563
Tudor City Place Assocs. v. Libyan Arab Republic Misson to the UN (1983), **2002:** 540
Tulip Computers Int'l v. Dell Computer Corp. (2003), **2003:** 881–85; **2005:** 844, 846
Tumey v. Ohio (1927), **2004:** 1013
Turkmani v. Republic of Bolivia (2002), **2002:** 516
Turner v. Frowein (1998), **1991-99:** 367; **2000:** 110
Turner Entm't Co. v. Degeto Film (1994), **2002:** 862; **2004:** 437
Turtle Island Restoration Network v. Minetta (2000), **2001:** 756–60
Tuteur; United States v. (1954), **1991-99:** 14
2120 Kalorama Rd., Inc. v. District of Columbia Foreign Missions Act-Bd. of Zoning Adjustment (2001), **2001:** 540–44; **2002:** 576

U
*Überseeing B.V./NCC Nordic Constr. Co., **2003:** 692*n*
Ucelo-Gomez v. Mukasey (2007), **2008:** 306
Ukranian Nat'l Ass'n of Jewish Former Prisoners of Concentration Camps & Ghettos v. United States (2001), **2001:** 392*n*
Underhill v. Hernandez (1897), **1989-90:** 255; **1991-99:** 987; **2002:** 475; **2004:** 470; **2005:** 576, 582; **2006:** 631
Underwood v. United Republic of Tanzania, (1995), **2002:** 540
Ungar v. Palestine Liberation Org. (2005), **2005:** 503, 531
Ungar v. Islamic Republic of Iran (2002), **2002:** 529; **2003:** 506
Ungaro-Benages v. Dresdner Bank AG (2001), **2003:** 474–75
Ungaro-Benages v. Dresdner Bank AG (2004), **2004:** 431–39, 475; **2005:** 480, 483, 820–21; **2006:** 455, 520; **2008:** 234
United Feature Syndicate v. Miller Features (2002), **2002:** 863–64
United for Peace and Justice v. City of N.Y. (2003), **2003:** 577–79
*United Kingdom v. Belgium (1934), **2003:** 631*n*
*United Kingdom v. Norway (Fisheries Case) (1951), **2005:** 702
*United Kingdom v. United States (2001), **2004:** 855
*United Mexican States v. Metalclad Corp. (2001), **2001:** 572, 593, 595–96, 641, 642
United Mexican States v. Woods (1997), **1991-99:** 256, 290
United Nations v. Parton (2005), **2005:** 876–78

*United Parcel Serv. of Am., Inc. v. Canada (2002), **2002:** 661–65; **2006:** 703, 704
United States, In re (1989), **1989-90:** 86
United States v. *See name of opposing party*
United States Ass'n of Importers of Textiles & Apparel v. United States (2005), **2005:** 642
*United States – Countervailing Duties on Certain Corrosion-Resistant Carbon Steel Flat Prods. from Germany – AB–2002–4 – Report of the Appellate Body, **2002:** 670–72
United States Dep't of State v. Legal Assistance for Vietnamese Asylum Seekers (1996), **1991-99:** 114
*United States Diplomatic and Consular Staff in Tehran (U.S. v. Iran) ("Tehran Hostages") (1981), **2003:** 74, 441
United States ex rel. *See name of related party*
United States R.R. Retirement Bd. v. Fritz (1980), **2001:** 204*n*
*United States – Section 211 Omnibus Appropriations Act of 1998 – AB–2001–7 – Report of the Appellate Body, **2002:** 672–76
United States Steel Corp. v. Multistate Tax Comm'n (1978), **2001:** 183*n,* 186*n,* 187, 189*n,* 190*n,* 191–92
United Steelworkers v. United States (2001), **2001:** 200
United Transp. Union v. State Bar of Mich. (1971), **2005:** 280
Universal Reinsurance Co. v. St. Paul Fire and Marine Ins. Co. (2000), **2001:** 229, 232
Unocal Corp.; Doe v. (1997), **1991-99:** 989, 993–94, 1333, 1335; **2001:** 445
Unocal Corp.; Doe I v. (2000), **2002:** 338, 343–44; **2003:** 355, 382–83; **2004:** 365–76
Unocal Corp.; Doe I v. (2002), **2002:** 344; **2005:** 581; **2006:** 463
Unocal Corp.; Doe I v. (2003), **2002:** 344; **2003:** 393, 395*n,* 396, 400
Unterweser Reederei Gmbh, In re (1970), **2006:** 955–57
Upjohn Co. v. United States (1981), **1991-99:** 792; **2004:** 1032
Urlic v. American Int'l Group (1997), **1991-99:** 1305–9
Urtetiqui v. D'Arcy (1835), **2008:** 450
USA Found. v. United States (2001), **2001:** 200–211
U.S. Ass'n of Importers of Textiles and Apparel v. United States (2004), **2004:** 613–15
USEC Inc. v. Eurodif, S.A. (2008), **2008:** 953–60
Usha (India), Ltd. v. Honeywell Int'l, Inc. (2005), **2005:** 841–43
U.S.-U.K. Arbitration Concerning Heathrow Airport User Charges (Heathrow Arbitration) (1992), **2000:** 660–61
USX Corp. v. Adriatic Ins. Co. (2003), **2003:** 510–12; **2006:** 555–57

V
Vacco v. Quill (1997), **2005:** 268
Valdez v. Oklahoma (2001), **2001:** 24–31; **2002:** 45–48; **2003:** 42, 83, 87–88
Valentine; United States v. (1968), **2002:** 1004*n*
Valentine v. United States ex rel. Neidecker (1936), **1991-99:** 600–603; **2000:** 186, 209, 210–11
Valmonte v. INS (1998), **1991-99:** 9
Valmore Lacarno Rodriguez, Estate of v. Drummond (2003), **2003:** 374–79
Vance v. Terrazas (1980), **2003:** 9; **2008:** 2
Van Den Borre v. State (1992), **1989-90:** 339
Varrin v. Queen's University (2002), **2002:** 872–73
*Vasiljevic; Prosecutor v. (2004), **2004:** 375, 376; **2006:** 463
Vasquez-Velasco; United States v. (1994), **2001:** 329*n;* **2002:** 133, 543
Vega-Rodriguez v. Puerto Rico Tele. Co. (1997), **2001:** 12
Velasco v. Government of Indonesia (2004), **2004:** 460; **2006:** 636, 636*n,* 637; **2007:** 513
*Velásquez Rodríguez v. Honduras (1988), **2004:** 230, 231
Ventura-Escamill v. INS (1981), **1989-90:** 23
Verdugo-Urquidez; United States v. (1987), **1989-90:** 101
Verdugo-Urquidez; United States v. (1988), **1989-90:** 101
Verdugo-Urquidez; United States v. (1990), **1989-90:** 100–107; **1991-99:** 13, 117, 194, 646; **2000:** 9, 411; **2002:** 235; **2005:** 998–1000, 1013; **2006:** 1010, 1179, 1181
Verdugo-Urquidez; United States v. (1991), **1991-99:** 436, 437, 444–45
Verlinden B.V. v. Central Bank of Nigeria (1980), **1989-90:** 286
Verlinden B.V. v. Central Bank of Nigeria (1983), **1989-90:** 313; **1991-99:** 1183, 1201, 1207, 1210, 1235–36, 1251, 1261, 1274, 1284, 1318; **2000:** 475, 477, 579*n,* 580; **2001:** 429–30, 433, 463, 464, 502; **2002:** 465, 488, 497, 505; **2003:** 503, 519, 560, 561; **2004:** 459, 466, 469–71, 529; **2005:** 472, 561; **2006:** 551, 554, 559, 568, 569, 631; **2007:** 523; **2008:** 481
Vermont Agency of Natural Res. v. U.S. ex rel. Stevens (2000), **2003:** 369
Vermont Yankee Nuclear Power Co. v. NRDC (1978), **2000:** 137
Vernonia Sch. Dist. v. Acton (1995), **2006:** 364
Veterans & Reservists for Peace in Vietnam v. Regional Comm'r of Customs (1972), **2008:** 812
Victoria Sales Corp. v. Emery Air Freight (1990), **2000:** 518
Victory Transp., Inc. v. Comisaria Gen. de Abastecimientos y Transportes (1964), **1991-99:** 1202, 1204, 1213; **2002:** 510
Victrix S.S. Co., S.A. v. Salen Dry Cargo A.B. (1987), **2001:** 43

*Vienna Convention on Consular Relations (Paraguay v. United States) (1998), **2005:** 270
Vietnam v. Pfizer (1977), **1989-90:** 247
Vietnam Ass'n for Victims of Agent Orange v. Dow Chem. Co. (2008), **2008:** 41, 427–30
Vietnam Ass'n for Victims of Agent Orange v. Dow Chem. Co. (2009), **2008:** 428*n*
Vigil, Matter of (1988), **1991-99:** 232
Villafuerte v. Stewart (1998), **1991-99:** 259
Village of. *See name of village*
*Villagran Morales Case (1997), **2002:** 370
Villalta, Matter of (1990), **1991-99:** 226
*Villareal, Ramon Martinez (2002), **1991-99:** 290–91
Villeda Aldana v. Fresh Del Monte Produce, Inc. (2003), **2003:** 386; **2004:** 326; **2007:** 414
Vimar Seguros y Reaseguros, S.A. v. M/V Sky Reefer (1995), **1991-99:** 1843–48; **2001:** 133; **2005:** 140–41, 798; **2006:** 911, 913
Vincenti, In re (1920), **2000:** 403
Vine v. Republic of Iraq (2006), **2006:** 584–92
Viragh v. Foldes (1993), **1991-99:** 356, 359
Virginia v. Black (2003), **2007:** 302–3, 311
Virginia v. Hicks (2003), **2006:** 182; **2007:** 149–50
Virginia v. Tennessee (1893), **2001:** 181, 182–83, 185, 189, 190–91, 192*n*
Virginia; United States v. (1996), **2005:** 260–61, 289
Virginia v. West Virginia (1911), **2000:** 572
Virginian Ry. Co. v. System Fed'n (1937), **2005:** 526; **2006:** 605
Virtual Countries, Inc, v. Republic of S. Africa and S. African Tourism Bd. (2001) (2002), **2002:** 518–19; **2007:** 468
Virtual Def. and Dev. Int'l, Inc. v. Republic of Moldova (1999), **1991-99:** 1220–23, 1333; **2001:** 499
Vishranthamma v. Badar Al-Awdi and Halal Muhammad Al-Shaitan (2004), **2004:** 531–34
Vitamins, In re (2000), **2004:** 862, 863
*Viviana Gallardo, Matter of (1981), **2008:** 241
Voest-Alpine Trading USA Corp. v. Bank of China (1998), **1991-99:** 1217–18
Voevodine v. Government of Commander in Chief (1931), **1989-90:** 256
Volkswagenwerk Aktiengesellschaft v. Schlunk (1988), **1991-99:** 1346; **2003:** 888–89; **2005:** 848, 857
Von Dardel v. U.S.S.R. (1990), **1989-90:** 278, 291, 301
Vonn; United States v. (2002), **2004:** 322*n*
Von Neumann; United States v. (1986), **2001:** 114
Vulcan Iron Works v. Polish Am. Mach. Corp. (1979), **1991-99:** 1274; **2001:** 533; **2002:** 551*n*

W

Wagner v. Islamic Republic of Iran (2001), **2001:** 459; **2002:** 528
Wainwright v. Sykes (1977), **2006:** 74
Walczak; United States v. (1986), **1991-99:** 602; **2002:** 214*n*
Waldron v. INS (1994), **1991-99:** 259
Walker v. Pataki (1999), **1991-99:** 264
Wallace v. Herron (1985), **2003:** 535
Walsh, In re (1998), **1991-99:** 366; **2000:** 110, 111
Walsh v. Brady (1991), **1991-99:** 57; **2008:** 812
Walsh v. Ford Motor Co. (1984), **2005:** 412
Walsh v. Walsh (2000), **1991-99:** 367; **2000:** 99, 102
Walter Fuller Aircraft Sales, Inc. v. Republic of Philippines (1992), **2006:** 571
Walters v. People's Republic of China (2001), **2001:** 488–501
Waltier v. Thomson (1960), **2006:** 633, 644, 647; **2007:** 512
Walton v. Walton (1996), **1991-99:** 355
Wang v. Ashcroft (2003), **2006:** 84*n*
Wang v. Reno (1996), **1991-99:** 185*n*
Wanninger v. Wanninger (1994), **1991-99:** 354, 363, 365
Wan Shih Hsie v. INS (1978), **1989-90:** 25
Wan Shih Hsie v. Kiley (1978), **1989-90:** 25
Ward v. Skinner (1991), **1991-99:** 1136
Ware v. Hylton (1796), **2000:** 497*n, 516n;* **2002:** 448; **2004:** 344; **2005:** 479
Warner; United States v. (1984), **2001:** 134, 138
Warren v. United States (2000), **1991-99:** 842–46
Warren Corp. v. Environmental Protection Agency (1998), **2001:** 133
Washington v. Davis (1976), **2008:** 277
Washington v. Glucksberg (1997), **2005:** 268
Washington; United States v. (1992), **1991-99:** 58
Washington Legal Found. v. United States Sentencing Comm'n (1996), **2000:** 499
Wasserstein Perella Emerging Mkts. Fin., LP v. Province of Formosa (2000), **2003:** 524
*Waste Mgmt., Inc. v. United Mexican States (2000), **2000:** 687, 694
Watson v. Employers Liability Assurance Corp. (1954), **2002:** 454
Watts v. United States (1969), **2007:** 302
Weatherhead v. United States (1998), **1991-99:** 789–801
Weatherhead; United States v. (1999), **1991-99:** 789–801
Webster v. Doe (1988), **2001:** 84–85
Webster v. Reproductive Health Servs. (1989), **2001:** 288*n*
Weinberger v. Rossi (1982), **1991-99:** 661, 669, 783; **2000:** 198; **2001:** 205, 210–11, 473, 474; **2002:** 214*n;* **2005:** 140
Weininger v. Castro (2006), **2006:** 1009

Weinstein v. Albright (2000), **2001:** 11, 12
Weinstein v. Islamic Republic of Iran (2002), **2002:** 527, 528; **2003:** 554; **2004:** 524
Weinstein v. Islamic Republic of Iran (2003), **2005:** 543, 546; **2008:** 413
Weinstein v. Islamic Republic of Iran (2004), **2004:** 524–27
Wei Ye v. Jiang Zemin (2002), **2002:** 547–52, 585–95
Wei Ye v. Jiang Zemin (2003), **2003:** 558
Wei Ye v. Jiang Zemin (2004), **2004:** 527–31, 547–53; **2007:** 524–25
Wei Ye v. Swain (2004), **2005:** 569
Weltover, Inc. v. Republic of Argentina (1991), **1991-99:** 1200–1207
Wesson v. U.S. Penitentiary Beaumont, TX (2002), **2005:** 84, 1015–16
West v. Atkins (1988), **1991-99:** 893
West v. Multibanco Comermex, S.A. (1987), **1991-99:** 1254
West Caribbean Airways, S.A., In re (2007), **2008:** 513
Western and S. Life Ins. Co. v. State Bd. of Equalization (1981), **2000:** 468–69
*Western Sahara (1975), **2001:** 628
Wheaton v. Porreca (2001), **2001:** 55–59
Wheeler; United States v. (1978), **2001:** 313*n*
White v. Massachusetts Council of Constr. Employers (1983), **2000:** 328, 329–30, 330*n*
Whiteman v. Austria (2001), **2001:** 396
Whiteman v. Austria (2002), **2003:** 521–22
Whiteman v. Austria (2004), **2004:** 432, 472, 496
Whiteman v. Dorotheum GmbH & Co. KG (2005), **2005:** 469–70, 475, 489, 506
Whitney v. Robertson (1888), **1991-99:** 315, 665, 704, 728; **2001:** 81; **2002:** 221; **2003:** 259–60; **2004:** 88; **2005:** 49, 245; **2008:** 156, 179, 184
Whren v. United States (1996), **2001:** 257
Wichita & Affiliated Tribes of Okla. v. Hodel (1986), **2007:** 472; **2008:** 480
Wiebe; United States v. (1984), **2006:** 132
Wilbur v. United States (1929), **2007:** 5–6
Will v. Hallack (2006), **2008:** 225
Will; United States v. (1980), **1991-99:** 2160; **2002:** 526; **2008:** 225
Williams v. Advertising Sex, LLC (2005), **2005:** 861–62
Williams v. Bankhead (1874), **2008:** 480
Williams v. Insurance Co. (1839), **2000:** 201
Williams v. Lynagh (1987), **2000:** 395*n*
Williams v. Suffolk Ins. Co. (1839), **1991-99:** 117; **2008:** 449, 451
Williams v. Taylor (2000), **2000:** 388
Williams; United States v. (1980), **2002:** 135–36

Williams; United States v. (1993), **2004:** 1028
Williams; United States v. (2006), **2006:** 1135
Wilson v. Girard (1957), **2007:** 961–62; **2008:** 75, 76, 134
Wilson v. Humphreys (Cayman) Ltd. (1990), **2001:** 232
Wiltberger; United States v. (1820), **2000:** 192–93
Wilton v. Seven Falls Co. (1995), **2005:** 816
Windsor v. State Farm Ins. Co. (1981), **1991-99:** 1306
Winship, In re (1970), **2005:** 278
Winstar Corp.; United States v. (1996), **2001:** 83
Winston Cabello, Estate of (2001), **2003:** 376, 377
Winters v. Assicurazioni Generali S.p.A. Consolidated (2000), **2000:** 460; **2001:** 387
Wipronik v. Superior Ct. (1998), **1991-99:** 367
Wirtz v. Local 30, Int'l Union of Operating Eng'rs (1963), **2005:** 565
Wisconsin v. Pelican Ins. Co. (1888), **2005:** 236
Wisconsin v. Yoder (1972), **2001:** 140
Wisconsin Dep't of Indus., Labor and Human Relations v. Gould, Inc. (1986), **2000:** 327–30
Wisniewski v. United States (1957), **2000:** 763*n*
Wiwa v. Anderson (2002), **2002:** 357
Wiwa v. Royal Dutch Petroleum Co. (2000), **2001:** 336; **2003:** 896; **2008:** 243
Wiwa v. Royal Dutch Petroleum Co. and Shell Transp. and Trading Co. (2002), **2002:** 352–55; **2003:** 379; **2004:** 356; **2005:** 581
Wojcik v. Wojcik (1997), **1991-99:** 361
Wolchok v. Statni Bank Cesoslovenska (1961), **1989-90:** 318
Wolf v. Federal Republic of Germany (1996), **2000:** 476*n*
Wong v. Nakamura (1994), **1991-99:** 823
Wong Kim Ark; United States v. (1898), **1991-99:** 7; **2000:** 3, 8, 9; **2002:** 230; **2004:** 5; **2006:** 668*n*
Wong Wing v. United States (1896), **2006:** 68
Wood v. United States ex rel. American Institute in Taiwan (2001), **2001:** 235–41
Wood ex rel. The American Institute in Taiwan; United States v. (2002), **2002:** 245–46
Woods, United Mexican States v. (1997), **1991-99:** 256, 290
Woods-Tucker Leasing Corp. v. Hutcheson-Ingram Dev. Co. (1981), **1991-99:** 1840, 1841
World Commc'ns Corp. v. Micronesian Telecomms. Corp. (1978), **1991-99:** 813
World War II Era Japanese Forced Labor Litig., In re (2000), **2000:** 505–40; **2001:** 340*n*, 448*n*, 451, 452, 456; **2002:** 434–35, 437; **2003:** 468–69; **2005:** 480

World War II Era Japanese Forced Labor Litig., In re (2001), **2001:** 197*n,* 339–40; **2004:** 443
World Wide Minerals v. Republic of Kazakhstan (2000), **1991-99:** 1333
World Wide Minerals v. Republic of Kazakhstan (2002), **2002:** 574; **2005:** 582; **2007:** 952
World-Wide Volkswagen Corp. v. Woodson (1980), **1991-99:** 1244; **2003:** 904
World Wildlife Fund v. Hodel (1998), **2001:** 500
Worth v. Universal Pictures, Inc. (1997), **2000:** 529, 537
Worthy v. Herter (1959), **2003:** 493, 498
Wright v. Henkel (1903), **2001:** 63
W.S. Kirkpatrick & Co. v. Environmental Tectonics Corp., Int'l (1990), **1991-99:** 1289, 1333; **2001:** 526; **2002:** 475, 490, 573; **2003:** 580; **2005:** 576, 579, 582; **2008:** 234
Wulfsohn v. Russian Socialist Federated Soviet Republic (1923), **2002:** 508
Wunsch; United States v. (1996), **2005:** 125

X

Xia (2004), **2004:** 381
Xiao v. Reno (1993), **1991-99:** 185*n*
Xiao Ji Chen v. U.S. Dep't of Justice (2006), **2008:** 40
Xin-Chang Zhang v. Slattery (1995), **1991-99:** 202
Xuncax v. Gramajo (1995), **1991-99:** 979, 989–91, 1264; **2000:** 484*n;* **2001:** 441*n;* **2002:** 336, 474

Y

Yahoo! Inc. v. La Ligue Controle Le Racisme Et L'Antisemetisme (2004), **2004:** 878–82
Yamaha Motor Corp., U.S.A. v. United States (1991), **2001:** 488
Yamashita, In re (1946), **2002:** 349–50, 988*n;* **2004:** 1020; **2005:** 1016; **2006:** 1143, 1144, 1154, 1183, 1208, 1209
Yamashita v. Styer (1946), **2002:** 438*n,* 439
Yancheng Baolong Biochem. Prods. Co. v. United States (2005), **2006:** 611
Yang v. Maugans (1995), **1991-99:** 184*n,* 185
Yang v. Tsui (2005), **2008:** 785, 786, 788
Yan Long Xiong; United States v. (2002), **2002:** 133–34
Yassin v. United States (1948), **1991-99:** 661
Ye v. Zemin (2004), **2005:** 561–62, 566; **2006:** 679
Yerger, Ex parte (1868), **2006:** 1143
Yong Hao Chen v. INS (1999), **1991-99:** 203–7

York River House v. Pakistan Mission to the UN (1991), **2000:** 613; **2002:** 560
Young v. New Haven Advocate (2002), **2003:** 903
Younger v. Harris (1971), **2008:** 786
Youngstown Sheet & Tube Co. v. Sawyer (1952), **1991-99:** 646, 655, 668, 1237, 2164; **2000:** 212; **2004:** 211, 213, 1009, 1012; **2005:** 42, 421, 533; **2006:** 522; **2008:** 188–90, 468
Yousef; United States v. (1996), **1991-99:** 506; **2008:** 66
Yousef; United States v. (2003), **2008:** 127
Yucatan v. Argumendo (1915), **1989-90:** 255, 256
Yucyo, Ltd. v. Republic of Croatia (1997), **2000:** 572
Yucyo, Ltd. v. Republic of Slovenia (1997), **2000:** 571, 572
Yue Yu v. Brown (1999), **2006:** 28
*Yugoslavia v. Belgium (2004), **2000:** 91
Yugoslavia v. Park-71st Corp. (1995), **2000:** 569*n*, 570, 619
*Yugoslavia; United States v. (1954), **2001:** 578–79
Yunis; United States v. (1991), **1991-99:** 502–5, 508

Z
Zabaneh; United States v. (1998), **2002:** 215
Zadvydas v. Davis (2001), **1991-99:** 93; **2001:** 17–20, 83, 346; **2003:** 30–32; **2004:** 17, 18; **2005:** 10, 17–22, 22*n*, 291, 351, 1013; **2006:** 46–50, 1189, 1190; **2008:** 345, 908, 909
Zadvydas v. Underdown (1999), **1991-99:** 93
Z & F Assets Realization Corp. v. Hull (1940), **2001:** 453
Zappia Middle E. Constr. Co. v. Emirate of Abu Dhabi (2000), **2006:** 576
Zarate v. Perez (1996), **1991-99:** 363
Zardui-Quintan v. Richard (1985), **1989-90:** 263
Zassenhaus v. Evening Star Newspaper Co. (1968), **2000:** 158–59; **2001:** 59
Zdravkovich v. Consul Gen. of Yugoslavia (1998), **1991-99:** 1291
Zemel v. Rusk (1965), **1991-99:** 56; **2002:** 14; **2008:** 473, 812
Zenith Radio Corp. v. Hazeltine Research Inc. (1969), **2000:** 435
Zepeda-Melendez v. INS (1984), **2000:** 130
Zernicek v. Brown & Root, Inc. (1987), **1989-90:** 286; **1991-99:** 1206
Zernicek v. Petroleos Mexicanos (1985), **1991-99:** 1193
Zhang v. Slattery (1995), **1991-99:** 185–86
Zicherman v. Korean Air Lines Co. (1994), **1991-99:** 1351–56
Zicherman v. Korean Air Lines Co. (1996), **1991-99:** 1344, 1351–56; **2003:** 464–601; **2004:** 444; **2008:** 185
Zimmermann v. Zimmermann (1991), **2005:** 66*n*
Zippo Mfg. Co. v. Zippo Dot Com, Inc. (1997), **2003:** 902, 903
Zivotofsky v. Secretary of State (2003), **2003:** 485–501

Zivotofsky v. Secretary of State (2004), **2004:** 452; **2006:** 530–47
Zivotofsky v. Secretary of State (2006), **2006:** 530–47
Zivotofsky v. Secretary of State (2007), **2007:** 437; **2008:** 447
Zivotofsky v. Secretary of State (2009), **2008:** 15*n*, 447–54, 447*n*
Zschernig v. Miller (1968), **1991-99:** 656, 677, 678, 783–84, 972*n*; **2000:** 471–73, 529, 539; **2001:** 196–98; **2002:** 426–29, 443, 444, 447, 450–52; **2003:** 464; **2004:** 512; **2006:** 454; **2007:** 236–37; **2008:** 418
Zuker v. Andrews (1999), **1991-99:** 353
Zveiter v. Brazilian Nat'l Superintendency of Merchant Marine (1993), **2000:** 585; **2002:** 477
Zych v. Unidentified, Wrecked & Abandoned Vessel (1992), **2006:** 833

Index (1989–2008)

*The bold years indicate the volume and are followed by page numbers in that volume (e.g., **2004:** 292, 966–97 refers to the volume for the year 2004 and pages 292 and 966 through 997 in that volume).*

A

Abduction
children. *See* Children, *subheading*: international abduction
Transborder Abductions, Treaty to Prohibit, **2000**: 405. *See also* Mexico

Abkhazia
Georgia–Russia conflict over, **2008**: 863–70

ABM Treaty. *See* Anti-Ballistic Missile (ABM) Treaty (1972) (U.S.–USSR)

Abortion, 1991-99: 907–8, 911; **2000**: 353; **2002**: 278, 301, 308–9, 770; **2003**: 321–22; **2004**: 292, 293, 296–97
asylum request by Chinese citizen based on family planning policy as persecution, **1991-99**: 202–7
customary international law and, **2001**: 291–93
denial of U.S. entry to foreign nationals engaged in forced abortion or sterilization, **1991-99**: 112–13
terms in international documents as not including, **2006**: 376, 384; **2007**: 322, 323; **2008**: 324
U.S. foreign assistance linked to, **2001**: 283–93; **2007**: 255–56

Abstentions. *See* Comity

Abu Ghraib. *See* Detainees, military

Act of state doctrine, 1991-99: 972*n*, 1332–33; **2000**: 290, 439–40; **2003**: 506, 510, 579–82; **2004**: 347; **2005**: 535, 567, 574–83; **2006**: 432–35, 444, 508, 632*n*, 667; **2007**: 234, 743–44, 952

Act of state doctrine (continued)
  Alien Tort Statute and, **1991-99**: 980–88, 993–94; **2002**: 334, 339–40, 342, 358; **2003**: 399–401
  Bernstein letter, **2002**: 508
  expropriation of corporate property, **2002**: 573–74
  foreign sovereign immunity and, **1991-99**: 1202, 1223, 1253
  head-of-state immunity and, **1991-99**: 126, 1286, 1288–89; **2001**: 525–26
  Hickenlooper Amendment and, **2004**: 795
  immunity and, **2002**: 471, 474–75, 573–75
    special missions immunity and, **2006**: 680–81
  private right of action, **2008**: 155
  in specific cases, **2004**: 203, 380–82, 463, 470–71
  U.S. foreign policy and, **2002**: 474–75
Administrative Procedure Act (APA), **1989-90**: 15; **1991-99**: 69–70, 114, 1239–40; **2000**: 313–15, 499; **2001**: 71–72, 73, 75–76, 80, 82, 209; **2002**: 99; **2004**: 87, 761, 980, 994, 997; **2005**: 79, 87, 90, 93–94, 128, 279, 995; **2006**: 150–53, 158–59; **2007**: 104, 830; **2008**: 810
Admiralty law, **2003**: 367–68, 757–58; **2006**: 831–32; **2008**: 134
  jurisdiction, **2004**: 485, 830, 832
Adoption
  acquisition of citizenship in, **2002**: 9
  advance determination of orphan status, **2003**: 122–23
  citizenship of adopted child born abroad, **2001**: 3, 4, 5
  consular functions in adoption of foreign child by U.S. citizen, **1989-90**: 66–72; **2006**: 98
  Convention on the Rights of the Child (1989), **1989-90**: 175
  Hague Convention on Adoption (1993), **1991-99**: 380–81, 1858–62; **2000**: 121, 141–50, 738; **2002**: 286, 299; **2003**: 108–18, 121; **2004**: 828; **2005**: 65, 67–68
    Convention on Rights of the Child, Optional Protocols and, **2008**: 300
    entry into force in U.S., **2008**: 48
    implementation and ratification in U.S., **2000**: 141–50, 363; **2003**: 108–18; **2006**: 89–98; **2007**: 82–90
      Intercountry Adoption Act (2000), **2000**: 147; **2003**: 108–10, 114–15, 116–18; **2006**: 89–94, 96, 97
      record retention, **2006**: 96–98
      State Department implementation guidance, **2008**: 48–49
  Intercountry Adoption Act (2000) (IAA)
    regulations implementing, **2007**: 83–90
  intercountry trends, **2003**: 112–13, 114
  Mexican law, **2003**: 121

Adoption (continued)
notarial service for parental consent to, **2003**: 118–22
paternal rights, **2000**: 14, 362–63
resident aliens and intercountry adoptions, **2007**: 87
in Russia, **2007**: 95–97
U.S. immigration law and, **1989-90**: 67–72; **2000**: 148; **2003**: 117, 119, 120, 122–23; **2007**: 85, 87–89
orphan petition, **2003**: 120, 122–23
U.S.–Vietnam agreement on, **2005**: 67–68
AECA. *See* Arms Export Control Act (AECA)
AEDPA. *See* Antiterrorism and Effective Death Penalty Act (AEDPA) (1996)
Aerial counter-narcotics efforts. *See* Drug issues
Afghanistan
Afghan Allies Protection Act of 2009, **2008**: 16*n*
arms trade restrictions, **2002**: 884–85
bilateral trade and investment agreement, **2004**: 652
child soldiers, **2003**: 308; **2008**: 302–4
claim under Foreign Sovereign Immunities Act (1976), **2003**: 551–52
detainees. *See* Detainees, military
diplomatic relations, **1989-90**: 241–42; **2001**: 423–26; **2002**: 463
drug trade, **2001**: 120; **2002**: 123; **2003**: 181; **2004**: 133–34; **2005**: 135; **2006**: 213–14; **2007**: 163; **2008**: 113
sanctions related to, **2001**: 120
Emergency Supplemental Appropriations Act for Defense and for the Reconstruction of Iraq and Afghanistan (2004), **2005**: 229*n*
enemy combatants. *See* Detainees, military
Geneva Conventions, applicability to conflict in, **2002**: 976–80, 1004–8; **2003**: 1016–27; **2004**: 990, 1016, 1038–41; **2005**: 215, 961–62, 994, 995, 1006–8, 1011, 1015
Hamdan, Salim Ahmed, **2005**: 994; **2006**: 1138–55, 1177–79; **2007**: 395, 883–84, 909, 916, 918, 920–21, 938–39, 973–76, 982; **2008**: 916–17
law enforcement institutions, **2003**: 212
litigation in U.S. courts concerning, **2005**: 994–1018
military and civilian efforts, coordination of, **2005**: 454
military operations in, **2005**: 101, 417
legal basis for, **2005**: 372, 949–50; **2006**: 1106–9, 1111, 1139
money laundering, **2006**: 243
religious freedom concerns under Taliban in, **1991-99**: 925
renditions, U.S. policy on, **2005**: 100–5, 1017
special immigrant visas for certain Afghans, **2008**: 16, 16*n*
Taliban. *See* Taliban
terrorism and

Afghanistan (continued)
collection of judgments under Terrorism Risk Insurance Act, **2003:** 555–57
cooperation in antiterrorism actions, **2002:** 890
financial rewards for terrorist apprehension information, **2005:** 134–35
not cooperating fully in counterterrorism efforts (1999 designation), **1991-99:** 508
response to, **2003:** 151–52, 237, 325, 346, 1004
U.S. response to Sept. 11 terrorist attacks, **2001:** 858–59, 867–72
U.S. strikes against terrorist training camps in, **1991-99:** 2133–35
UN peacekeeping efforts in, **2003:** 958–59
U.S. military intervention in, **2004:** 301, 970, 985, 986, 987, 989, 995
waiver of American Servicemembers' Protection Act, **2003:** 238–39
women's rights in, **2002:** 277, 279–80
gender antidiscrimination measures, **2001:** 269
UN resolution on the girl child, **2001:** 275
Africa. *See also specific countries*
Desertification in Countries Experiencing Drought, Particularly in Africa, Convention to Combat, **1991-99:** 1770; **2000:** 728–33
Horn of Africa Recovery and Food Security Act (1992), **1991-99:** 937–38, 2044
African Growth and Opportunity Act (2000), **2001:** 666; **2004:** 618; **2008:** 573
African National Congress
exemption from INA terrorism-related provisions, **2008:** 20
African Union
conflict resolution efforts
in Mauritania, **2008:** 806, 873
in Somalia, **2007:** 863, 1004; **2008:** 645, 646, 847–50
in Sudan/Darfur, **2007:** 183–84, 867–69; **2008:** 837, 838–39, 841, 847–50
in Zimbabwe, **2008:** 804–5
immunity, **2006:** 684; **2007:** 527
Age Discrimination in Employment Act (1967), **2001:** 250
Agent Orange litigation, 2005: 491–97; **2006:** 522–26; **2008:** 427–30
Aggression, crime of, 1991-99: 577–78, 632; **2000:** 286–90; **2001:** 173–78
Code of Crimes Against the Peace and Security of Mankind, Draft, **1991-99:** 576–79
under customary international law, **2001:** 174, 175
definition, **2000:** 286–90
ICJ role in relation to, **2001:** 176–77
under UN Charter, **2001:** 174–75, 176–78

Agreements, generally. *See also* Memoranda of understanding; Treaties, generally
AIT-TECRO agreements, status of, **1991-99:** 658–66
Alaska role in international agreements, **2000:** 294, 295
choice of form: treaty vs. other form of agreement, **1991-99:** 599–601, 644–58; **2001:** 200–211; **2002:** 177–83
Executive Branch authority in relation to, **1991-99:** 648–52, 656–57, 670–76; **2002:** 177–83, 242–43, 525; **2004:** 200–2, 312–13, 869, 1025. *See also* choice of form, *this heading*; Treaties, generally
with Congress, **1991-99:** 599–601, 644–66
states and, **1991-99:** 655–57, 676–79
treaty modification by, **1991-99:** 666–70, 701–5
waivers of subrogated claims, **1991-99:** 676–79
instruments constituting, **2007:** 51–52
international, under Case-Zablocki Act, **1991-99:** 679, 682, 684–85
legal status of memoranda of understanding. *See* Memoranda of understanding
nonlegally binding commitments between governments, **1991-99:** 682–88
Agricultural policy and trade
Agricultural Act (1949), **1989-90:** 546
Agricultural Act (1956), **1991-99:** 679
Agricultural Bioterrorism Protection Act (2002), **2004:** 1105
agricultural sanctions on designated terrorists, Executive Order 13372, **2005:** 132
Agricultural Workers Protection Act (1983), **2001:** 262
Albania, claims against, **1991-99:** 1076–78
assistance to Iraq, **2004:** 649
biotech products, **2003:** 648–51; **2006:** 737–39
Central America Free Trade Agreement, **2003:** 685
commodity exclusion from U.S. trade sanctions programs, **2000:** 748–50
cotton subsidies, **2003:** 663; **2004:** 608–10; **2005:** 633; **2008:** 557–62
environmental review, **2001:** 670
food security, **2004:** 285; **2006:** 389–94
geographic indications of products, **1991-99:** 1504–5
hormones in meat, **1991-99:** 1418–20; **2004:** 645; **2008:** 562–67
International Plant Protection Convention, **1991-99:** 1784–90
Israel, allowing export of agricultural produce from Gaza, **2005:** 916
Japanese restrictions on U.S. products, **2003:** 652–54

Agricultural policy and trade (continued)
methyl bromide production exemption, **2005**: 721
NAFTA and. *See* North American Free Trade Agreement (NAFTA)
plant genetic resources, **2002**: 810–11; **2004**: 789–90; **2008**: 725–27
reform proposal, **2002**: 701–7
sales to Cuba, **2004**: 286, 918; **2005**: 890
sanctions exemptions, **1991-99**: 1971–72
trade negotiations, **2005**: 608, 609–12, 615, 618, 779
Trade Sanctions Reform and Export Enhancement Act (2000), **2001**: 819–22
UN Food and Agriculture Organization, **2004**: 752–53; **2005**: 326, 613; **2006**: 389–94
high seas fishing agreement, **1991-99**: 694, 1739–44
Right to Food Forum, **2008**: 333–35
U.S. Department of Agriculture, **2004**: 933, 1107
U.S.–EU agreements, **2006**: 754–55
U.S.–India Knowledge Initiative on, **2005**: 1079
WTO and. *See* World Trade Organization (WTO)
Ahmadiyya Muslim community, **2005**: 316
Aiding and abetting. *See* Alien Tort Statute (ATS), *subheading*: secondary liability
AIDS/HIV
exclusion of aliens with, **1989-90**: 18–20
funding eligibility conditions for international organizations, **2007**: 254–56
Global Leadership Against HIV/AIDS, Tuberculosis, and Malaria Reauthorization Act of 2008, **2008**: 17
human rights and, **2005**: 329–31, 772
implications for peace and security, **2003**: 816–17; **2006**: 1058
international cooperation to combat, **2005**: 308, 443, 772, 1079; **2006**: 1066–67
Millennium Development Goals, listed in, **2005**: 453
national security and, **2003**: 816–17
temporary admission to U.S. for aliens with, rule authorizing, **2008**: 17–20
proposed rule, **2007**: 26–30
Thai prostitutes and, **1991-99**: 913–15
UN Resolution on Access to Medicine, **2001**: 281–83; **2003**: 319–20
U.S. assistance and, **2002**: 805–7; **2004**: 129, 280
U.S.–EU Declaration on HIV/AIDS, Malaria and Tuberculosis, **2004**: 784–85
women and, **2003**: 281, 292, 310, 318
Air defense systems, man-portable. *See* Man-portable air defense systems (MANPADS)

Air pollution
aviation emissions, **2008:** 507, 684–88
ICAO discussions concerning, **2008:** 507
trading scheme on aircraft at EU airports, **2006:** 871–72; **2007:** 691–92; **2008:** 686–88
UK proposed per-plane duty, **2008:** 684–86
Clean Air Act. *See* Clean Air Act (CAA) (1990)
greenhouse gas emissions, **2007:** 675–78, **2008:** 329, 675, 682
Kyoto protocol, emissions targets, **2000:** 711–25
ozone protection, **2003:** 777–81
hydrochlorofluorocarbons, **2007:** 697–99, **2008:** 688–91
Long-Range Transboundary Air Pollution to Abate Acidification, Eutrophication and Ground-Level Ozone, Convention on (LRTAP, 1979), **1991-99:** 1666, 1668–69; **2004:** 744–45
Gothenburg Protocol to, **2005:** 731
methyl bromide, **1991-99:** 1657–61
U.S. regulations implementing exemption to production of, **2005:** 719–25; **2006:** 866–71
Montreal Protocol on Substances That Deplete the Ozone Layer (1987), amendments to, **1991-99:** 1655–65; **2002:** 777; **2003:** 777–81; **2005:** 719–21; **2006:** 866–71; **2007:** 697–99; **2008:** 688–91
Protection of the Ozone Layer, Vienna Convention for (1985), **1991-99:** 699; **2008:** 688–89
from ships, MARPOL protocol concerning (1997), **2003:** 784–85, 787–88; **2008:** 691–95. *See also* Pollution from Ships, International Convention for Prevention of (MARPOL)
U.S.–Canada air quality agreement, **1991-99:** 1665–67
Air transport. *See* Aviation issues
Aircraft. *See* Aviation issues
Alaska
Agreement on the Conservation and Management of the Alaska-Chukotka Polar Bear Population (2000), **2007:** 728
Alaska and Submerged Lands Act (SLA), **2005:** 696–98
Alaska Native Claims Settlement Act (1971), **2001:** 261
Alaska Natives, funding and training, **2005:** 295
Arctic Council, **2001:** 741–42
Beaufort Sea, maritime boundary dispute, **2005:** 705–7; **2008:** 640–42
boundary arbitration, **2005:** 701–3
ceding of, **1989-90:** 435
market-participant exceptions to Commerce Clause, **2000:** 329
police use of videotape or audiotape of questioning, **2005:** 360

Alaska (continued)
role in international agreements, **2000**: 294, 295
submerged lands lying off Alaskan coast, title to, **2005**: 696–705
Albania
advance notice requirements for innocent passage through territorial waters, **1989-90**: 444–45
air transport agreement, **2003**: 602
alleged failure of consular notification to nationals of, **1991-99**: 260
American Servicemembers' Protection Act waiver, **2003**: 238
chemical weapons stockpiles, elimination of, **2005**: 1059
diplomatic relations with U.S., **1989-90**: 241; **1991-99**: 1142
domestic violence laws, lack of, **2005**: 313
expropriation claims settlement with U.S., **1991-99**: 1076–81; **2006**: 502–3
extradition and mutual legal assistance, **2000**: 185*n*; **2006**: 156–59
Albania–U.S. extradition treaty, **2005**: 89; **2006**: 156–59
torture claims in case under, **2005**: 89–94; **2006**: 157–59
Kosovo, ethnic component in, **2005**: 935–38
Land Law affecting property rights in investment dispute, **2006**: 713
longshore work prohibition on alien crewmen from, **2002**: 757; **2003**: 764
NATO accession, 874*n*
naturalization treaty, **2002**: 202
preservation of American heritage in, **2004**: 797
relief from immigration requirements for certain resident nationals of, **1991-99**: 250
territorial sea baselines, **1989-90**: 461
totalitarian party and admissibility of aliens from, **1989-90**: 38–39
trade and investment issues, **1991-99**: 1455, 1466
transfer of Uighur detainees from Guantanamo to, **2006**: 1116, 1185
U.S.–Adriatic Charter, **2003**: 939
Albatrosses and Petrels, Agreement on the Conservation of, 2008: 153–54, 166–68, 722–25
Alcoholic beverages
liquor smuggling into Canada, **2005**: 234–42
wine-making practices and labeling, **2006**: 757
Algeria
Alien Tort Statute case, **2003**: 384
conflict resolution
Ethiopia-Eritrea, involvement in, **2006**: 1055–58
Western Sahara, actions needed in, **2006**: 1065
Convention on the Elimination of all Forms of Discrimination against Women and, **2002**: 278

Algeria (continued)
Declaration of Republic of Algeria Concerning the Settlement of Claims by U.S. and Islamic Republic of Iran, **1989-90**: 231, 236; **1991-99**: 1086–87. *See also* Algiers Accords
human rights violations in, **1991-99**: 867–68
intellectual property rights Watch List, **2008**: 607
money laundering, **2006**: 243
trafficking in persons, **2008**: 118
Algiers Accords. *See also* Iran–United States Claims Tribunal
Antiterrorism Act of 1996 and, **2001**: 468–75
assessing intent of legislation to abrogate, **2003**: 476–78
claims under. *See* Iran–United States Claims Tribunal
continuous nationality requirement, **2002**: 632
Iran–United States Claims Tribunal, **2008**: 410–18, 485*n*
Iranian awards
standing for Iranian claim for damages arising from 1953 coup d'etat, **2003**: 451–54
U.S. obligations under, **2008**: 411
jurisdiction over counterclaims, **2003**: 448–50
origins of, **2003**: 441; **2008**: 411*n*, 485*n*
Security Account maintenance, **2003**: 450–51; **2004**: 415–20
settlement of "small claims," **1989-90**: 230–37
sovereign immunity of U.S. and, **2000**: 439–40; **2008**: 414, 416
suit by former hostages barred by, **2001**: 460–75; **2002**: 523–27; **2003**: 547–49
U.S. courts and, **1991-99**: 1833–36; **2002**: 219; **2004**: 517–22; **2008**: 410–18, 484–89
Alien Tort Claims Act. *See* Alien Tort Statute (ATS)
Alien Tort Statute (ATS), **1989-90**: 281, 312; **1991-99**: 978–94, 1126–28, 1335–39; **2000**: 374, 375, 382, 398–412; **2001**: 318–41, 510, 522–23; **2002**: 323–63, 470–76, 563–64, 909–10; **2003**: 354–402; **2004**: 340–83, 473–74, 528, 558, 820, 980, 997, 1000, 1030; **2005**: 60*n*, 171, 393–427, 475–77, 492, 494, 792, 819–26, 995, 1014; **2006**: 430–36; **2007**: 218–31; **2008**: 215–44
act of state and, **1991-99**: 987–88, 993–94; **2002**: 334, 342, 358; **2003**: 384; **2004**: 380–82; **2006**: 432; **2007**: 234
aiding and abetting liability. *See* secondary liability, *this heading*
attorney fees awards, **2001**: 340–41
common law causes of action, **2006**: 431, 441–45, 450–51, 465–76; **2007**: 218–19, 228–31, 234; **2008**: 216–19, 231
corporations, liability of, **1991-99**: 989–90; **2003**: 384; **2005**: 395–97; **2007**: 219–24; **2008**: 218, 222–27, 236–38, 238–44
countries

Alien Tort Statute (ATS) (continued)
Algeria. *See Doe v. Islamic Salvation Front* (**2003**: 384)
Bosnia-Herzegovina. *See Mehinovic v. Vuckovic* (**2002**: 347–48; **2004**: 317, 325, 1023)
Burma. *See Doe v. Unocal* (**1991-99**: 989, 993–94, 1333, 1335; **2001**: 445)
Chile. *See Barrueto v. Fernandez Larios* (**2003**: 385)
China. *See Doe v. Liu Qi* (**2002**: 469–76, 575); *Li Weixum v. Bo Xilai* (**2008**: 490–91); *Plaintiff A. v. Zemin* (**2003**: 374*n*, 396, 400, 558–69, 569)
Colombia. *See Bancoult v. McNamara* (**2004**: 364–65; **2005**: 415–17); *Estate of Valmore Lacarno Rodriguez v. Drummond* (**2003**: 374–79); *Mujica v. Occidental Petroleum Corp.* (**2004**: 376–80; **2005**: 418–20, 424, 819, 839–41; **2006**: 450–55); *Rodriguez v. Drummond* (**2006**: 476–78); *Sinaltrainal v. Coca-Cola Co.* (**2003**: 378, 379, 380)
Ecuador. *See Aquinda v. Texaco, Inc.* (**1991–99**: 990)
El Salvador. *See Doe v. Saravia* (**2004**: 362–63, 382–83)
Germany. *See Iwanowa v. Ford Motor Co.* (**1991-99**: 979, 989, 990, 992–93; **2002**: 337; **2004**: 436*n*)
Guatemala. *See Villeda Aldana v. Fresh Del Monte Produce* (**2003**: 386; **2004**: 326); *Xuncax v. Gramajo* (**1991–99**: 979, 989, 990, 991, 1264; **2000**: 484*n*; **2001**: 441*n*; **2002**: 336, 474)
Haiti. *See Doe v. Constant* (**2006**: 478–79)
Indonesia. *See Beanal v. Freeport-McMorran, Inc.* (**1991-99**: 990–91; **2002**: 335, 336; **2005**: 251); *Doe v. Exxon Mobil* (**2002**: 357–63, 575; **2003**: 393*n*, 396, 400; **2005**: 411–12, 424); *Exxon Mobil Corp. v. Doe* (**2008**: 222–27)
Iraq. *See Alkhuzai v. Hasan Al-Majid Al-Tikriti* (**2004**: 558–59)
Japan. *See In re World War II Era Japanese Forced Labor Litig.* (**2000**: 505–40; **2001**: 340*n*; **2001**: 448*n*; **2001**: 451; **2001**: 452; **2001**: 456; **2002**: 434–35; **2002**: 437; **2003**: 468–69; **2005**: 480); *Joo v. Japan* (**2003**: 394*n*, 396, 519)
Mexico. *See Sosa v. Alvarez-Machain* (**2003**: 381, 382–83, 389, 434–35; **2004**: 340–61, 362, 364, 365–76, 377*n*, 380, 382, 473*n*, 474, 475*n*, 495, 500; **2005**: 83, 245–47, 396, 398–99, 401, 403–4, 408–10, 412–15, 421, 423*n*, 425–27, 471–72, 475–76, 494, 496, 516, 542, 777)
Nigeria. *See Abdullahi v. Pfizer, Inc.* (**2002**: 345–46; **2003**: 386–87; **2004**: 357); *Wiwa v. Dutch Petroleum Co.* (**2001**: 336; **2003**: 896)

Alien Tort Statute (ATS) (continued)
Papua New Guinea. *See Sarei v. Rio Tinto* (**2002**: 333–43, 357, 574–75; **2003**: 393*n*; **2005**: 420, 423*n*; **2006**: 431–50; **2008**: 238–44)
Paraguay. *See Filartiga v. Pena-Irala* (**1991-99**: 978, 981, 985, 986, 987, 988, 990, 1264, 1279, 1281; **2000**: 382, 400; **2001**: 319, 323, 442*n*; **2002**: 323, 328–29, 334, 336, 340, 474, 563; **2003**: 354, 359, 368, 369, 377, 385, 389, 392; **2004**: 340, 346, 350, 353*n*)
Peru. *See Flores v. Southern Peru Copper Corp.* (**2005**: 57*n*, 251, 396)
Philippines. *See Hilao v. Estate of Marcos* (**1991-99**: 989, 1264; **2000**: 411; **2001**: 482; **2002**: 474; **2004**: 316)
South Africa. *See American Isuzu Motors v. Lungisile Ntsebeza* (**2008**: 236–38); *In re South African Apartheid Litig.* (**2003**: 387–90; **2004**: 351*n*, 354; **2005**: 400, 407, 412)
Sudan. *See Presbyterian Church of Sudan v. Talisman* (**2003**: 383–84, 505; **2004**: 357, 358; **2005**: 394–400, 411, 413, 581, 822–826; **2006**: 460–65)
United Arab Emirates (UAE). *See Mother Doe v. Sheikh Hamdan* (**2008**: 227–36)
United States. *See Bancoult v. McNamara* (**2005**: 415–17; **2006**: 455–59)
Zimbabwe. *See Tachiona v. Mugabe* (**2002**: 324–33, 474, 552*n*, 563; **2004**: 532, 533, 539, 553–58)
customary international law and, **1991-99**: 990–91; **2003**: 367, 371–78, 385; **2004**: 344–54; **2008**: 41, 42, 219, 220–21
damages, **2008**: 36–42
default judgments, **2003**: 397
exhaustion of remedies requirements, **1991-99**: 991; **2002**: 336–37; **2005**: 412–13; **2006**: 433–35, 436, 448–50; **2007**: 227–31; **2008**: 218, 219, 238–44
extraterritorial application, **2003**: 369–71; **2004**: 366–68; **2006**: 437–41, 451–52; **2007**: 227–31; **2008**: 218, 219
federal common law, **2006**: 431, 441–45, 450–41, 465–76; **2008**: 216–19, 231
foreign policy implications of cases under, **2000**: 402; **2001**: 337–39; **2002**: 357–63; **2003**: 357, 366–67, 371, 387–90, 393–95, 397, 398–99; **2004**: 359–60, 376–82, 473–74; **2006**: 431–33, 450, 456–59, 476–79; **2008**: 221–22, 223–27, 234–36, 237
foreign states and officials as defendants, **2003**: 397; **2005**: 792. *See also* immunity of foreign government officials and states, *this heading*
forum non conveniens doctrine and, **1991-99**: 988–89; **2001**: 336–37; **2002**: 339, 345–46, 352, 355–57; **2003**: 384, 387; **2004**: 376–80; **2005**: 398–400

Alien Tort Statute (ATS) (continued)
Guantanamo detainee claims under, **2003**: 384–85; **2004**: 980, 997, 1000, 1030; **2005**: 995, 1014; **2008**: 914–15
immunity of foreign government officials and states, **2001**: 522–23; **2002**: 471–74, 563–64; **2004**: 528; **2006**: 629; **2007**: 224; **2008**: 237, 490–91
intent of Congress and, **2007**: 229–31
international comity doctrine and, **2003**: 384; **2005**: 819–22, 825–26; **2006**: 450, 944–50; **2008**: 227–36, 242–43
international law violations alleged
Agent Orange, use of. *See In re "Agent Orange" Prod. Liab. Litig.* (**2005**: 491–97); *Vietnam Assoc. for Victims of Agent Orange v. Dow Chem.* (**2008**: 41–42, 427–30)
aircraft hijacking. *See Burnett v. Al Baraka Inv. and Dev. Corp.* (**2003**: 385–86, 508–9, 533–36)
apartheid, **2007**: 226–27. *See also American Isuzu Motors v. Lungisile Ntsebeza* (**2008**: 236–38); *In re South African Apartheid Litig.* (**2004**: 354; **2005**: 400, 407, 412)
arbitrary arrest and detention, **2007**: 239, 240. *See also El Masri v. United States*
arbitrary arrest and/or detention. *See Doe v. Exxon Mobil* (**2002**: 357–63, 575; **2003**: 393*n*, 396, 400; **2005**: 411–12, 424); *Doe v. Liu Qi* (**2003**: 394*n*, 509–10; **2004**: 363–64, 380–82; **2005**: 579); *Hilao v. Estate of Marcos* (**1991-99**: 989, 1264; **2000**: 411; **2001**: 482; **2002**: 474; **2004**: 316); *Sosa v. Alvarez-Machain* (**2004**: 340–61, 362, 364, 365–76, 377*n*, 380, 382, 473*n*, 474, 475*n*, 495, 500; **2005**: 83, 245–47, 396, 398–99, 401, 403–4, 408–10, 412–15, 421, 423*n*, 425–27, 471–72, 475–76, 494, 496, 516, 542, 777)
civilian targets of military attacks. *See Presbyterian Church of Sudan v. Talisman* (**2003**: 383–84, 505; **2004**: 357, 358; **2005**: 394–400, 411, 413, 581, 822–26)
consular notification. *See Jogi v. Piland* (**2001**: 335); *Jogi v. Voges* (**2005**: 60–64; **2006**: 75–77; **2007**: 78–79); *Mora v. New* York (**2008**: 36, 41–42)
corruption, **2005**: 171
crimes against humanity. *See Doe v. Islamic Salvation Front* (**2003**: 384); *Presbyterian Church of Sudan v. Talisman* (**2003**: 383–84, 505; **2004**: 357, 358; **2005**: 394–400, 411, 413, 581, 822–26); *Sarei v. Rio Tinto* (**2002**: 333–43, 357, 574–75; **2003**: 393*n*; **2005**: 420, 423*n*)
cruel, inhuman, or degrading treatment. *See Bancoult v. McNamara* (**2004**: 364–65; **2005**: 415–17); *Doe v. Liu Qi* (**2003**: 394*n*, 509–10; **2004**: 363–64, 380–82; **2005**: 579)

Alien Tort Statute (ATS) (continued)
detention facility conditions. *See Jama v. INS* (**2004**: 361)
disproportionate use of force, **2007**: 224–26. *See also Matar v. Dichter* (**2006**: 465–76)
environmental harms. *See Aguinda v. Texaco, Inc.* (**2002**: 355–57; **2004**: 877); *Bano v. Union Carbide Corp.* (**2001**: 335–37); *Beanal v. Freeport-McMorran, Inc.* (**1991-99**: 990–91; **2002**: 335, 336; **2005**: 251); *Flores v. Southern Peru Copper Corp.* (**2005**: 57*n*, 251, 396); *Sarei v. Rio Tinto* (**2002**: 333–43, 357, 574–75; **2003**: 393*n*; **2005**: 420, 423*n*; **2008**: 238–44)
extrajudicial killing. *See Doe v. Exxon Mobil* (**2002**: 357–63, 575; **2003**: 393*n*, 396, 400; **2005**: 411–12, 424); *Doe v. Saravia* (**2004**: 362–63, 382–83); *Exxon Mobil v. Doe* (**2008**: 222–27); *In re South African Apartheid Litig.* (**2004**: 354; **2005**: 400, 407, 412); *Presbyterian Church of Sudan v. Talisman* (**2003**: 383–84, 505; **2004**: 357, 358; **2005**: 394–400, 411, 413, 581, 822–26); *Tachiona v. Mugabe* (**2002**: 324–33, 474, 552*n*, 563; **2004**: 532, 533, 539, 553–58)
forced displacement or relocation. *See Bancoult v. McNamara* (**2004**: 364–65; **2005**: 415–17); *Presbyterian Church of Sudan v. Talisman* (**2003**: 383–84, 505; **2004**: 357, 358; **2005**: 394–400, 411, 413, 581, 822–26)
forced labor. *See Doe v. Unocal* (**1991-99**: 989, 993–94, 1333, 1335; **2001**: 445); *In re South African Apartheid Litig.* (**2004**: 354; **2005**: 400, 407, 412); *Iwanowa v. Ford Motor Co.* (**1991-99**: 979, 989, 990, 992–93; **2002**: 337; **2004**: 436*n*); *Mother Doe v. Sheikh Hamdan* (**2008**: 227–36)
fraud, breach of fiduciary duty, and misappropriation of funds. *See Hamid v. Price Waterhouse* (**1991-99**: 979)
genocide. *See Bancoult v. McNamara* (**2004**: 364–65; **2005**: 415–17); *Beanal v. Freeport-McMorran, Inc.* (**1991-99**: 990–91; **2002**: 335, 336; **2005**: 251); *Doe v. Exxon Mobil* (**2002**: 357–63, 575; **2003**: 393*n*, 396, 400; **2005**: 411–12, 424); *In re South African Apartheid Litig.* (**2004**: 354; **2005**: 400, 407, 412); *Kadic v. Karadzic* (**1991-99**: 978, 980–89, 993, 994, 1251, 1264; **2001**: 319, 323, 325, 340; **2002**: 324, 334–35, 337, 340–41, 343, 353, 563–64, 583; **2003**: 354); *Presbyterian Church of Sudan v. Talisman* (**2003**: 383–84, 505; **2004**: 357, 358; **2005**: 394–400, 411, 413, 581, 822–26)

Alien Tort Statute (ATS) (continued)
kidnapping. *See Presbyterian Church of Sudan v. Talisman* (**2003**: 383–84, 505; **2004**: 357, 358; **2005**: 394–400, 411, 413, 581, 822–26)
law of the sea. *See Sarei v. Rio Tinto* (**2006**: 433, 444–45)
price-fixing claims under. *See Kruman v. Christie's Int'l PLC* (**2001**: 334–35)
property, confiscation or destruction of. *See Presbyterian Church of Sudan v. Talisman* (**2003**: 383–84, 505; **2004**: 357, 358; **2005**: 394–400, 411, 413, 581, 822–26); *Tachiona v. Mugabe* (**2002**: 324–33, 474, 552*n*, 563; **2004**: 532, 533, 539, 553–58)
racial discrimination. *See American Isuzu Motor Co. v. Lungisile Ntsebeza* (**2008**: 236–38); *Bancoult v. McNamara* (**2004**: 364–65; **2005**: 415–17); *In re South African Apartheid Litig.* (**2004**: 354; **2005**: 400, 407, 412); *Presbyterian Church of Sudan v. Talisman* (**2003**: 383–84, 505; **2004**: 357, 358; **2005**: 394–400, 411, 413, 581, 822–26)
rape or sexual violence. *See Doe v. Exxon Mobil* (**2002**: 357–63, 575; **2003**: 393*n*, 396, 400; **2005**: 411–12, 424); *Doe v. Unocal* (**1991-99**: 989, 993–94, 1333, 1335; **2001**: 445); *Presbyterian Church of Sudan v. Talisman* (**2003**: 383–84, 505; **2004**: 357, 358; **2005**: 394–400, 411, 413, 581, 822–26); *Tachiona v. Mugabe* (**2002**: 324–33, 474, 552*n*, 563; **2004**: 532, 533, 539, 553–58)
right to associate and organize. *See Estate of Valmore Lacarno Rodriguez v. Drummond* (**2003**: 374–79); *Villeda Aldana v. Fresh Del Monte Produce* (**2003**: 386; **2004**: 326)
sale of bulldozers to Israel used in deaths of civilians. *See Corrie v. Caterpillar, Inc.* (**2007**: 219–24; **2008**: 218, 218*n*, 219)
slavery. *See Mother Doe v. Sheikh Hamdan* (**2008**: 227–36); *Presbyterian Church of Sudan v. Talisman* (**2003**: 383–84, 505; **2004**: 357, 358; **2005**: 394–400, 411, 413, 581, 822–26)
torture. *See Bancoult v. McNamara* (**2004**: 364–65; **2005**: 415–17); *Doe v. Exxon Mobil* (**2002**: 357–63, 575; **2003**: 393*n*, 396, 400; **2005**: 411–12, 424); *Doe v. Liu Qi* (**2003**: 394*n*, 509–10; **2004**: 363–64, 380–82; **2005**: 579); *Doe v. Unocal* (**1991-99**: 989, 993–94, 1333, 1335; **2001**: 445); *Exxon Mobil v. Doe* (**2008**: 222–27); *Filartiga v. Pena-Irala* (**1991-99**: 978, 981, 985, 986, 987, 988, 990, 1264, 1279, 1281; **2000**: 382, 400; **2001**: 319, 323, 442*n*; **2002**: 323, 328–29, 334, 336, 340, 474, 563;

Alien Tort Statute (ATS) (continued)
2003: 354, 359, 368, 369, 377, 385, 389, 392; **2004**: 340, 346, 350, 353*n*); *Hilao v. Estate of Marcos* (**1991-99**: 989, 1264; **2000**: 411; **2001**: 482; **2002**: 474; **2004**: 316); *Kadic v. Karadzic* (**1991-99**: 978, 980–89, 993, 994, 1251, 1264; **2001**: 319, 323, 325, 340; **2002**: 324, 334–35, 337, 340–41, 343, 353, 563–64, 583; **2003**: 354); *Tachiona v. Mugabe* (**2002**: 324–33, 474, 552*n*, 563; **2004**: 532, 533, 539, 553–58)
trafficking in persons. *See Mother Doe v. Sheikh Hamdan* (**2008**: 227–36)
war crimes. *See In re South African Apartheid Litig.* (**2004**: 354; **2005**: 400, 407, 412); *Sarei v. Rio Tinto* (**2002**: 333–43, 357, 574–75; **2003**: 393*n*; **2005**: 420, 423*n*)
political question and, **1991-99**: 985–88, 992–93; **2001**: 340–43; **2003**: 384, 399–401; **2004**: 364; **2005**: 415–17, 419–21, 475–77; **2006**: 431–33, 450–59; **2007**: 219–26; **2008**: 218–19, 218*n*, 220–27, 427–30
secondary liability
accomplice liability under, **2002**: 347–48, 351
aiding and abetting, **2002**: 344, 347–48, 351; **2003**: 384, 398; **2004**: 357–58, 368–76; **2005**: 395–96, 401–11, 412; **2006**: 446–48, 452–54, 463–65; **2007**: 219, 226–27; **2008**: 218, 219, 236–38
conspiracy, **2006**: 460–63
vicarious liability, **2001**: 338; **2003**: 393
state action requirement, **1991-99**: 980–85, 989; **2001**: 322–25; **2002**: 344, 346, 352–55; **2003**: 384, 386; **2004**: 356–57; **2005**: 414–15
state law claims, and, **2005**: 411–12, 422–24; **2006**: 454–55; **2008**: 222–27
statute of limitations, **1991-99**: 992; **2001**: 339–40; **2004**: 382–83
Torture Victim Protection Act and, **2003**: 368–69; **2007**: 219; **2008**: 215–27, 238–45
types of claims under, **2007**: 227–28
USG or USG officials as defendants, **1989-90**: 312; **1991-99**: 1126–28; **2004**: 364–65
Alienage diversity statute, 1991-99: 35–36, 769–75, 1141–42; **2001**: 227–35; **2002**: 227–31
Aliens. *See also* Detainees, military; Immigration and visas
access by Vietnamese nationals to U.S. courts, **1989-90**: 242–43
access to U.S. courts in habeas proceedings by aliens held outside U.S., **2002**: 980–86; **2004**: 997–98
"admitted" to U.S., **2002**: 19–20

Aliens (continued)
crewmen of foreign-flagged vessels performing longshore work, **2002**: 756–57
procedures of military commissions for trial of non-U.S. citizens suspected of terrorism, **2002**: 957–76
recognition of foreign driver's license of, **2002**: 18–20
appropriated funds used for employment of foreign nationals by U.S. government, **1989-90**: 151–53
asylum. *See* Asylum
citizenship. *See* Citizenship
claims of inhumane treatment in detention facility, **2004**: 361
collection of information from visitors and immigrants, **2003**: 15–19
congressional authority in U.S., **2000**: 9–11
constitutional rights, **2000**: 131–33; **2005**: 259–60. *See also* Constitution, U.S.
extraterritorial application of U.S. Constitution to, **2005**: 996–1002
in search and seizure outside U.S., **1989-90**: 100–7
consular relations. *See* Consular functions; Consular notification and access; Consular Relations, Vienna Convention on (VCCR)
contagious disease infection as basis for exclusion of, **1989-90**: 18–20
criminal behavior by, **2001**: 344–46; **2008**: 313–14, 341–44, 370*n*. *See also* Removal of aliens from U.S., *subheading*: criminal aliens
definition of (8 U.S.C. § 1101(a)(3)), **2005**: 259
departure control orders, **1989-90**: 60–62
deportation. *See* Removal of aliens from U.S.
detainees. *See* Detainees, military; Detention of aliens, nonmilitary
with disabilities, waiver of oath of allegiance for naturalization, **2003**: 4–5
entry requirements. *See also* Immigration and visas
Intelligence Reform and Terrorism Prevention Act of 2004 (IRTPA) and document requirements, **2005**: 4–5
Lawful Permanent Residents, **2005**: 2*n*
no constitutional right to enter, **2005**: 291, 336
nonimmigrant aliens, **2005**: 3
sovereign right to control, **2005**: 336
exclusion. *See* Immigration and visas
expulsion of, **2007**: 38–39, 44–49, 54, 55; **2008**: 25–28
extradition. *See* Extradition
federal authority to regulate, in U.S., **2000**: 334
Fifth Amendment invoked by resident alien based on fear of prosecution abroad, **1991-99**: 571–76
freedom of movement, **2001**: 344

Aliens (continued)
human rights issues in U.S. border control policy, **2004**: 232–39
illegal smuggling. *See* Trafficking in persons
immigration. *See* Immigration and visas
minimum standard of treatment. *See* State responsibility
PATRIOT Act and, **2005**: 22*n*
presidential authority and, **2005**: 39–40, 45
prevention of terrorist activities by, **2001**: 925, 932
refugees. *See* Refugees
removal. *See* Removal of aliens from U.S.; Rendition; Repatriation
right to habeas corpus petition, **2004**: 997–98
rights of illegal aliens, **2001**: 343, 344, 346
smuggling of. *See* Trafficking in persons
temporary protected status, **1989-90**: 32, 39–40, 41; **1991-99**: 240–48
extension of, **2003**: 33–36
termination of, **2003**: 36–38
transfer of, for law enforcement purposes, **2000**: 184–85
in transit through U.S., requirements for aliens proceeding, **2003**: 13–15
visas. *See* Immigration and visas
Al-Qaida/Qaeda, **2003**: 152, 154, 168, 170, 171, 967, 1009, 1017–19, 1021–24, 1032–33, 1075. *See also* Detainees, military; Law of war; Terrorism
applicability of executive order concerning CIA interrogations, **2007**: 921–24
applicability of Geneva Conventions to, **2002**: 976–80; **2003**: 1016–27; **2004**: 990, 1016, 1038–41; **2005**: 215; **2006**: 1134, 1152–53
armed conflict with, **2005**: 372; **2006**: 1106–10, 1121; **2007**: 267, 875–76, 922, 926–27, 935, 937, 940, 943, 946, 953, 973; **2008**: 309
attack on U.S. embassy in Tanzania, **1991-99**: 2133
detainees captured during actions against, **2005**: 266, 961–75, 990, 1005–7; **2006**: 1106, 1111–12
foreign terrorist organization (FTO), **2001**: 895
Iraq engaged in combat against, **2008**: 462
North Korea, statement of no relations with, **2008**: 92
sanctions against (including persons and entities associated with), **2001**: 801–2; **2002**: 883, 885, 887–88, 889–90; **2003**: 152, 168–73, 174–75, 1082–83; **2004**: 121–22; **2005**: 894–900, 902–3; **2006**: 206, 1000, 1003–6; **2007**: 249; **2008**: 87–88, 99, 100–1
Sudan, protection by, **2005**: 521
Terrorist Surveillance Program, **2007**: 247, 249–50
unlawful combatant status, **2005**: 102; **2006**: 1140*n*

American Convention on Human Rights (1969), 2007: 51, 384; **2008:** 241*n*. *See also* Inter-American Commission on Human Rights; Inter-American Court of Human Rights
death penalty, **1991-99:** 975*n*; **2001:** 309
Inter-American Court of Human Rights
Berenson case, Peru, **2002:** 73
established, jurisdiction of, **1989-90:** 165–68; **1991-99:** 320–40; **2000:** 32*n*; **2004:** 227
U.S. non-party status, **1991-99:** 852
limits applicability in U.S. court, **2000:** 408
limits powers of Inter-American Commission on Human Rights, **2001:** 296, 299–300; **2002:** 263, 1013–15; **2004:** 976
American Declaration of the Rights and Duties of Man, 2007: 383–89. *See also* Inter-American Commission on Human Rights; Inter-American Court of Human Rights
capital punishment and
juvenile offenders, **2001:** 303–15
sentencing, **2001:** 294–302
as violation of, **2000:** 389–92
claim against U.S. by American indigenous people, **2002:** 367–82
claim of legal obligation under, **2001:** 291, 342
claim of privately enforceable rights under, **2001:** 298
consular notification, **1991-99:** 289–90, 330, 337–38
detention of Cuban nationals and, **2001:** 341–46
jurisdiction of Inter-American Commission on Human Rights, **1991-99:** 289–90; **2002:** 1013–17; **2004:** 223–39
juvenile life sentencing without parole as claimed violation of, **2007:** 383–89
legal status of, **1989-90:** 165–68; **2000:** 408–9; **2001:** 291; **2002:** 49
political status of District of Columbia and, **2001:** 352–53
American Institute in Taiwan. *See* Taiwan
American Jobs Creation Act (2004), 2004: 606
American Samoa
claims to submerged lands by, **1991-99:** 843, 847, 852
contiguous zone of U.S. and, **1991-99:** 1570
drift net fishing, **1991-99:** 1725–28
fisheries, regulation of, **2005:** 736
maritime boundary treaty and, **1991-99:** 1577
migratory fish stock in the Pacific and, **2005:** 742–44
nuclear weapons free zone, **1991-99:** 2316
sovereignty of U.S. and, **2003:** 485
U.S. Constitution applicability to, **1991-99:** 820–21, 823

American Servicemembers' Protection Act (2002), 2002: 168–75; **2003:** 226–27, 228–29, 234, 237–40; **2004:** 176, 185, 187, 188. *See also* International Criminal Court (ICC)
military assistance, definition of, **2006:** 279
waivers to prohibition on assistance, **2005:** 202; **2006:** 278
Americans with Disabilities Act of 1990 (ADA), 2001: 250, 254; **2002:** 283–85; **2003:** 301; **2005:** 276, 288, 292
Title III, **2005:** 707–8, 709, 710, 711
Andean Trade Preference Act (1991), 2001: 665, 666; **2003:** 683; **2008:** 577–82
Andean Trade Promotion and Drug Eradication Act (2002), 2008: 577–79
Andorra
diplomatic relations, **1991-99:** 1151–52
visa waiver pilot program and, **1991-99:** 76
Angola
Article 98 agreement with U.S. (nonsurrender of Americans to ICC), **2005:** 201
atrocities prevention in, **1991-99:** 521
child soldiers, **2008:** 304
Democratic Republic of Congo and, **1991-99:** 2012
diplomatic relations with U.S., **1989-90:** 241
money laundering, **2006:** 243
sanctions on UNITA, **1991-99:** 145–46, 1939–45
termination of, **2003:** 934–35
suspension of entry for certain persons from, **2003:** 27
termination of temporary protected status of refugees from, **2003:** 36–38
Termination of the International Mission of the Cuban Military Contingent, Agreement Between Cuba and (1988), **1989-90:** 199, 202–3
U.S. contributions to peacekeeping forces in, **1989-90:** 201–3
U.S. liaison office in, **1991-99:** 1142–46
Antarctica
Antarctic Conservation Act, **2004:** 780, 781, 783
Antarctic Treaty, **2004:** 731, 733, 779–83; **2007:** 392, 728–29; **2008:** 625
claims to territory in, **2004:** 730–33, 779–80, 782; **2008:** 625
conservation, **1991-99:** 1701–2, 1781–84; **2007:** 721
Antarctic Marine Living Resources, Convention on the Conservation of (CCAMLR), **2005:** 738; **2007:** 580, 709–12; **2008:** 712
Environmental Protection, Treaty Protocol on, **2005:** 755
tourism, **2004:** 779–84; **2007:** 729–30

Anti-Ballistic Missile (ABM) Treaty (1972) (U.S.–USSR), **1989-90**: 567–69, 572; **1991-99**: 742–61, 2220, 2244; **2001**: 829–33; **2002**: 198–202, 1027–28; **2005**: 215–17
Antigua and Barbuda
extradition and mutual legal assistance, **1991-99**: 396, 452; **2000**: 179, 186*n*; **2001**: 92*n*
Inter-American Convention Against Terrorism (OAS Terrorism Convention), party to, **2005**: 111
longshore work prohibition on alien crewmen from, **2002**: 757; **2003**: 764
maritime counter-drug trade agreement, **1991-99**: 1605
maritime litigation concerning, **2005**: 1102
money laundering in, **2004**: 135
WTO disputes. *See* World Trade Organization (WTO)
Antigua Convention (Inter-American Tropical Tuna Commission). *See* Fish and marine mammals
Antiquities Act (1906), 2006: 872
Anti-Semitism, 2005: 305
Global Anti-Semitism Review Act (2004), **2004**: 276–77
OSCE anti-Semitism conference, **2003**: 297–98
report on global, **2005**: 317–18
Anti-suit injunctions, 2002: 864–73; **2004**: 840–50; **2005**: 829–32; **2006**: 953–63; **2008**: 760–77
Anti-Terrorism and Arms Export Amendments Act (1989), **1989-90**: 108–9
Antiterrorism and Effective Death Penalty Act (AEDPA) (1996), **2001**: 102; **2003**: 478; **2007**: 106; **2008**: 98
Algiers Accords and, **2001**: 468–75
designation of Foreign Terrorist Organizations. *See also* Terrorism, *subheading*: designation of foreign terrorist organizations (FTOs) by U.S.
criminalizing material support to, **2004**: 123, 126; **2005**: 125; **2006**: 185–86
standard of judicial review, **2006**: 191–92
Foreign Terrorist Organizations Sanctions Regulations, **2006**: 991
habeas corpus, **1991-99**: 315; **2000**: 388; **2005**: 283
INA, exclusion and deportation, **1991-99**: 78–83, 89, 90
retroactivity, **1991-99**: 1263–65; **2001**: 466*n*, 471; **2006**: 37
standard of judicial review, **2007**: 106, 121
summary of provisions, **1991-99**: 78–83, 480–85
terrorism exception to Foreign Sovereign Immunities Act (FSIA) (1976), **1991-99**: 1184, 1223–24, 1235, 1249; **2001**: 464; **2002**: 523–25, 532; **2003**: 536; **2004**: 485, 503; **2005**: 506; **2006**: 577; **2007**: 450–51; **2008**: 456–75

Antitrust law
auction buyers' commissions and premiums, **2001**: 335
bilateral cooperation agreements, **1991-99**: 1550, 1551
comity agreement with Canada, **2004**: 662–63
enforcement guidelines, international, **1991-99**: 1551–53
European Union–U.S. agreements, **1991-99**: 1540–45
extradition and mutual legal assistance, **2004**: 93–95
extraterritorial jurisdiction, **1991-99**: 1529–39
Foreign Trade Antitrust Improvements Act (1982), **1991-99**: 1532
International Antitrust Enforcement Assistance Act, **1991-99**: 1545–50
judicial assistance in litigation, **2004**: 820, 851, 858–59, 863; **2006**: 969–70
ANZUS treaty. *See* Security Treaty between Australia, New Zealand, and the U.S. (ANZUS treaty, 1952)
Apartheid
Comprehensive Anti-Apartheid Act (1986), **1989-90**: 522, 523; **2004**: 360
Crime of Apartheid, International Convention on the Suppression and Punishment of, **2004**: 357–58
South African apartheid-era claims against multinational corporations, **2003**: 387–90; **2004**: 354–61; **2007**: 226–27; **2008**: 236–38
APEC. *See* Asia-Pacific Economic Cooperation (APEC)
Apostille, 2004: 827. *See also* Authentication
in adoption cases in Russia, **2007**: 96–97
extradition-related documents and, **2007**: 95
immunity and, **2004**: 69
and judicial assistance in Ireland, **2007**: 98
language of, **2006**: 105–7
preparation and execution, **2003**: 863–65; **2004**: 66–69
proper use of, **2004**: 69–70
U.S. authorities competent to issue, **2007**: 95
Appropriations Acts
Commerce, Justice, and State Appropriations Acts
(1988), **1989-90**: 264
(1998), **2003**: 23
(2001), **2001**: 462; **2002**: 523; **2003**: 460, 548
(2004), **2004**: 215–16
Consolidated Appropriations Act
(1999), **1991-99**: 345
(2000), **2000**: 421–22
(2004), **2004**: 214–17
(2008), **2007**: 70–72; **2008**: 29, 30, 307, 401, 496

Appropriations Acts (continued)
Department of Defense and Emergency Supplemental Appropriations for Recovery from and Response to the Terrorist Attacks on the United States Act (2002), **2003:** 548
Department of Defense Appropriations Act
(1993), **1991-99:** 2163
(1996), **1991-99:** 114
(1999), **1991-99:** 2303; **2001:** 808–9, 812
(2001), **2002:** 523
(2008), **2008:** 959
Department of Homeland Security Appropriations Act (2007), **2006:** 9
Department of State, Foreign Operations, and Related Programs Appropriations Act (2008) (Division J of the Consolidated Appropriations Act (2008)), **2008:** 29, 72, 401, 407
Departments of Commerce, Justice, and State, the Judiciary, and Related Agencies Appropriation Acts, **1991-99:** 41, 110, 807, 1711, 1720
Dire Emergency Supplemental Appropriations and Transfers, Urgent Supplementals, and Correcting Enrollment Errors Act (1989), **1989-90:** 201, 202
District of Columbia Appropriations Act (1997), **1991-99:** 249
Emergency Supplemental Act (2000), **2001:** 89
Emergency Supplemental Appropriations Act for Defense, the Global War on Terror, and Tsunami Relief (REAL ID Act) (2005), **2006:** 206–7
Emergency Wartime Supplemental Appropriations Act (EWSAA) (2003), **2003:** 544, 545, 555, 913; **2005:** 508; **2008:** 459
Foreign Operations, Export Financing, and Related Programs Appropriations Act
(1989), **1989-90:** 219
(1990), **1989-90:** 205, 544
(1994), **1991-99:** 1493, 1993–94
(1996), **1991-99:** 860, 1334, 1879–80, 1957, 1963; **2001:** 460; **2004:** 501; **2005:** 507; **2006:** 578
(1997), **2008:** 400–401
(1998), **1991-99:** 583
(1999), **1991-99:** 2330–31
(2000), **2001:** 169–71
(2002), **2002:** 123, 124, 146, 308–9; **2004:** 133
(2003), **2003:** 284; **2004:** 251, 252
(2004), **2004:** 186–87, 215, 216
(2006), **2006:** 279
Military Construction Appropriations Act (2000), **2001:** 89
Omnibus Appropriations Act (2009), **2008:** 16*n*

Appropriations Acts (continued)
Omnibus Consolidated and Emergency Supplemental Appropriations Act
(1996), **1991-99**: 83, 203, 860
(1998), **1989-90**: 72–73, 102, 103, 109, 240–41, 250–51, 348–49; **1991-99**: 583, 943, 1225; **2002**: 21; **2004**: 30
Supplemental Appropriations Act (1987), **1989-90**: 18, 219
Treasury, Postal Service and General Government Appropriations Act
(1988), **1989-90**: 151
(1996), **1991-99**: 34
(1998), **1991-99**: 1225
(2004), **2004**: 215
Arbitration, **1991-99**: 498–99, 909, 968, 1017–18, 1487, 1666, 1699, 1823, 1830; **2004**: 495, 620, 657, 775, 846. *See also* Iran–United States Claims Tribunal; North American Free Trade Agreement (NAFTA); Canada, *subheading*: Softwood Lumber Agreement; World Trade Organization (WTO)
agreement as implied waiver of diplomatic immunity, **2002**: 571–72
Alaska Boundary Arbitration of 1903, **2005**: 701, 703
anti-suit injunction and, **2004**: 843–50; **2005**: 829–32
bilateral investment treaty disputes, **1991-99**: 1463, 1465, 1467, 1472–74, 1477–78, 1481, 1489; **2003**: 265–66
Carriage of Goods Wholly or Partly by Sea, UN Convention on (Rotterdam Rules), **2005**: 794, 798
challenge of arbitrator's impartiality, **2001**: 382–85
collection of judgment against arbitral award, **2004**: 516
commercial, **2005**: 807–8
Convention on the Recognition and Enforcement of Foreign Arbitral Awards (New York Convention), **1989-90**: 501–2; **1991-99**: 1259, 1473, 1827, 1848, 1851; **2000**: 592; **2002**: 197, 873–75; **2003**: 841; **2004**: 809, 822–29; **2005**: 788–89; **2008**: 760–64, 777–82
countermeasures, use during, **2001**: 370–71
Dabhol arbitration (Permanent Court of Arbitration), **2005**: 469, 652–53
discovery for use in foreign tribunal, **2002**: 875–77
of disputes involving Convention on Safety of UN and Associated Personnel, **2001**: 360–61
enforceability of foreign arbitration clauses in bill of lading, **1991-99**: 1843–48
enforcement of arbitration clause, **2004**: 846, 848; **2008**: 777–82

Arbitration (continued)
enforcement of awards, **1991-99:** 1131–32, 1268, 1827; **2001:** 458–59; **2004:** 825–26, 827, 829, 863–64. *See also* Convention on the Recognition and Enforcement of Foreign Arbitral Awards (New York Convention), *this heading*
attachment of UN escrow account, **2000:** 621–26
sovereign immunity and, **2000:** 592
exemptions to immunity in Foreign Sovereign Immunities Act, **2001:** 458–59
Federal Arbitration Act, **2005:** 602
fora for arbitration of cargo claims, **2003:** 845–47
FSIA immunity and, **1991-99:** 1184, 1193, 1224, 1258–59; **2005:** 501, 505, 518, 553
attachment of award, **2006:** 612–21
waiver of FSIA immunity by agreement to, **2003:** 525
Hague Evidence Convention and, **2003:** 859–63
Heathrow Airport User Charges, U.S.–U.K., **1991-99:** 1343–44; **2000:** 645, 660–61; **2004:** 194
ICAO disagreement, EU–U.S., **2000:** 641–67
implied waiver of immunity in agreements to, **1989-90:** 286
India–U.S., **2004:** 424–30
insurance policies, preemption of state action by Convention on the Recognition and Enforcement of Foreign Arbitral Awards (New York Convention), **2008:** 777–82
Inter-American convention, **1989-90:** 501–2
Law of the Sea dispute settlement procedures, **1991-99:** 1563–64; **2004:** 676–77, 684, 693, 695
local remedies rule, **2000:** 656–62
Mediation Act, Uniform (UMA), **2005:** 805–7
Moscow embassy, **1991-99:** 1124
New York Arbitration Convention. *See* Convention on the Recognition and Enforcement of Foreign Arbitral Awards, *this heading*
OECD agreement, **1991-99:** 1487
in OPIC agreements, **1991-99:** 1483; **2005:** 650–51
power to grant ex parte interim relief, **2004:** 806–14
scope of authority of international bodies to grant awards, **2000:** 665–67
Softwood Lumber Agreement, U.S. and Canada, **2007:** 591–97; **2008:** 582–93
state responsibility and, **1991-99:** 1111–12, 1120
tax treaties and mandatory arbitration provisions, **2008:** 610–16
UN Convention Against Corruption, **2005:** 175–76
UN Headquarters Agreement, **2005:** 540
UN transnational crime convention dispute resolution mechanism, **2004:** 148

Arbitration (continued)
UNCITRAL arbitration rules. *See* UNCITRAL (UN Commission on International Trade Law)
U.S.–Iran Claims Tribunal. *See* Iran–United States Claims Tribunal
WTO dispute settlement. *See* World Trade Organization (WTO)
Arctic Council, 2001: 741–42; **2008**: 624
Arctic issues, 1991-99: 1777–80; **2001**: 741–42; **2008**: 623–39
Ilulissat Declaration, **2008**: 624–25, 636–38
maritime boundaries, **2008**: 630
Northwest Passage, **2006**: 814–15; **2008**: 631–32
Russian border demarcation, **2008**: 638–39
sources of law, **2008**: 632–34
Argentina
air transport agreement violation, **2004**: 568–71
Air Transport Services Agreement (2007), **2007**: 532
bilateral investment treaty, **1991-99**: 1477–79
discovery in, for use in U.S. court, **2004**: 863–65
Eichmann extradition to Israel from, **1989-90**: 95
extradition and mutual legal assistance, **1991-99**: 392, 396, 399–401, 447, 449–50; **2000**: 165–66, 179, 186*n*; **2001**: 92*n*; **2004**: 81
fisheries negotiations with U.S., **2005**: 613
FSIA immunity, **1991-99**: 1190–91, 1196, 1200–1207, 1213, 1252–55
central bank assets, **2007**: 494–504
Hague Child Abduction Convention, compliance with, **2006**: 100
human rights abuses in, **2002**: 270–71
retroactive application of laws, **2004**: 225–28
intellectual property rights Watch List, **2006**: 768; **2007**: 608, 610; **2008**: 605*n*
Inter-American Convention Against Corruption, **2006**: 238
maritime boundaries, **1991-99**: 1583–84
nonimmigrant visa waiver pilot program, **1991-99**: 76
non-North Atlantic Treaty Organization (NATO) ally, designation as, **2005**: 1044
outer space agreement, **1991-99**: 1641
trade and investment issues, **1991-99**: 1409, 1466
waiver of immunity on tax issue, **2006**: 596–97
whaling regulation, **2001**: 218
Armed conflict, 2004: 252, 533*n*, 972, 985, 988, 989, 1003, 1004, 1005, 1006, 1051, 1062. *See also* Geneva Conventions on law of war (1949); Hague Conventions, *subheading*: on law of war; Law of war; Military activities; War crimes; *specific countries and wars*
with Al-Qaida. *See* Al-Qaida/Qaeda

Armed conflict (continued)
attack on merchant vessels in Persian Gulf during Iran–Iraq war, **2003**: 1036–66
children in, **1991-99**: 227, 930–31; **2000**: 355–60; **2002**: 287–88, 293, 294–97; **2003**: 306–8; **2004**: 105–7, 281–83, 284; **2005**: 323, 996; **2006**: 387–89
claims by U.S. citizens against U.S. for failure to prevent harm during World War II, **2003**: 475–76
consular relations in, **2005**: 547
conventional weapons. *See* Conventional Weapons
conventions. *See specific conventions*
definition, **1991-99**: 497, 2156–57; **2007**: 985
definition of war in U.S. Constitution, **1991-99**: 2166–68
detainees in. *See* Detainees, military
diamond trade in support of, **1991-99**: 522, 1943–45, 2252; **2003**: 704–9
exception in Terrorist Bombing Convention, **1991-99**: 49
explosive remnants of war, **2003**: 1066–68
extrajudicial killing and, **2003**: 344–47
foreign affairs authority of federal government, **2003**: 469–70
ICC jurisdiction and, **1991-99**: 624, 628, 636–37
internal, **1991-99**: 210, 513, 517, 589, 628, 636–37, 2062, 2073, 2193, 2203, 2346
Iraq, intervention in. *See* Iraq
law enforcement vs., in antiterrorism effort, **2002**: 904, 906; **2006**: 1105, 1111–12; **2007**: 878–79
mercenaries, use of, **2004**: 392; **2008**: 876–77
military justice, **2003**: 343–44
missing persons in, **2003**: 334–36; **2004**: 331, 332
Multinational Force in Iraq. *See* Multinational Force in Iraq
nuclear materials and, **2005**: 960
prisoners of war. *See* Prisoners of war
protection of civilians during, **2005**: 303, 393; **2007**: 895, 905–7. *See also* Geneva Convention IV: on Civilians (1949)
protection of cultural property in, **1991-99**: 2072, 2075–76, 2079–80, 2086, 2096, 2197–2207; **2008**: 888–89
protection of humanitarian workers in, **2003**: 993–96; **2006**: 1076–77
riot-control agents in warfare, **1991-99**: 2345–47; **2003**: 1013–14; **2006**: 1223–25
September 11 attacks and, **2003**: 344–47, 1017–19
sexual violence in, **2007**: 906, **2008**: 286–88
temporary protected status and, **1991-99**: 241–46, 247–48; **2004**: 32
as threat to international peace and security, **1991-99**: 588–92

Armed conflict (continued)
treaty obligations, effect on, **2005**: 222–24; **2006**: 295–98; **2008**: 168–70
treaty obligations of successor states, **1991-99**: 746
UN disabilities convention (draft), U.S. comments on, **2006**: 384
Waiver of Claims Arising as a Result of Collisions between Vessels of War, **2001**: 221–24
war on terror, **2005**: 104, 372. *See also* Terrorism
wars of national liberation, **1991-99**: 2189–90
women and, **2002**: 275–76
Armenia
Armenian Christians discrimination against in Iran, **2005**: 350
Armenians qualifying for Torture Convention protection, **2005**: 349–50
aviation agreement, **2008**: 512
democracy promotion programs, **1991-99**: 1011–14
diplomatic relations, **1991-99**: 1173
domestic violence laws, lack of, **2005**: 313
Nagorno-Karabakh conflict, **2008**: 832
preservation of American heritage in, **2004**: 797
sanctions against companies trading with Iran, **2002**: 1069
succession issues, **1991-99**: 742
trade and investment issues, **1991-99**: 1455, 1466
Arms control. *See also* Arms Export Control Act (AECA); Law of war; Nonproliferation; Strategic Arms Reduction Treaty (START)
Afghanistan, restrictions on, **2002**: 884–85
agreements
with Russia. *See* Russia, *subheading*: arms control
air defense systems, man-portable (MANPADS), **2005**: 1066; **2006**: 210–11
Anti-Ballistic Missile Treaty. *See* Anti-Ballistic Missile (ABM) Treaty (1972) (U.S.–USSR)
antiterrorism legislation, **1989-90**: 108–9. *See also* Terrorism
Arms Export Control Act. *See* Arms Export Control Act (AECA)
Arms Trade Treaty, U.S. opposition to draft, **2008**: 1018–20
biological weapons. *See* Biological weapons; Nonproliferation; Weapons of mass destruction (WMDs)
brokering, **1991-99**: 2268–71
chemical weapons. *See* Chemical weapons; Nonproliferation; Weapons of mass destruction (WMDs)
commercial activities exception to FSIA immunity in sale of military aircraft, **1991-99**: 1220–23

Arms control (continued)
Commerce Control List and Export Administration Regulations, **1991-99**: 2301; **2000**: 746–48; **2003**: 174–75, 1084; **2004**: 892–93, 901, 1113–14, 1131–32; **2005**: 1135–37; **2006**: 1300–1; **2008**: 1024–25
Conference on Disarmament, **2003**: 1070–72; **2007**: 664; **2008**: 940
Conventional Armed Forces in Europe, Treaty on, **1989-90**: 578–79
Russian suspension of, **2007**: 1001–2; **2008**: 1011–17
transfer of certain CFE Treaty limited equipment to NATO members, **1991-99**: 2228
conventional weapons, **1991-99**: 2186–97; **2004**: 1050–53. *See also* Conventional weapons
agreements, **2001**: 835–42
determination of countries not cooperating fully with antiterrorism efforts and, **1991-99**: 383, 508; **2003**: 167; **2004**: 107–8; **2006**: 172; **2007**: 131–32; **2008**: 88–89
diamond trade and, **1991-99**: 552, 2252
dual-use technologies, **1991-99**: 2263–66, 2287–88; **2004**: 1111, 1113–14
embargoes, **2004**: 1069–70, 1110; **2007**: 1003–7; **2008**: 1021–22. *See also* Emergency Economic Powers Act, International (IEEPA); Trading with the Enemy Act (1917)
Afghanistan, arms trade restrictions, **2002**: 884–85
Belarus, arms embargo non-licensing policies toward, **2004**: 1070; **2007**: 1003
on Burma, **2004**: 1070; **2007**: 1003
arms embargo non-licensing policies toward, **2004**: 1070; **2007**: 1003
on China, **1991-99**: 1458–60; **2004**: 1070; **2007**: 1003
arms embargo non-licensing policies toward, **2004**: 1070; **2007**: 1003
on Cote d'Ivoire, **2004**: 922–23; **2007**: 1006
on Cuba, **2004**: 1070; **2007**: 1003
on Democratic Republic of Congo, **2004**: 1069–70; **2007**: 1006
arms embargo non-licensing policies toward, **2004**: 1070
on Eritrea, arms embargo non-licensing policies toward, **2008**: 89
on Haiti, **2004**: 1070
arms embargo non-licensing policies toward, **2004**: 1070
on Iran, **2007**: 1003, 1007
arms embargo non-licensing policies toward, **2004**: 1070; **2007**: 1003
on Iraq, **2002**: 894; **2004**: 884, 890–93; **2007**: 1007
on Lebanon, **2006**: 139–40, 1035, 1037; **2007**: 870; **2008**: 826, 828–29
on Liberia, **2004**: 1070; **2007**: 1003, 1007

Arms control (continued)
arms embargo non-licensing policies toward, **2004**: 1070
Libya, arms embargo non-licensing policies toward, **2004:** 929, 932, 934, 1070; **2007:** 1005
North Korea, arms embargo non-licensing policies toward, **2004:** 1070; **2006:** 1269; **2007:** 1003
on Rwanda, **2003**: 1081–82; **2007**: 1007
on Sierra Leone, **2007**: 1007
on Somalia, **2004**: 1070; **2007**: 1007; 1022–23; **2008**: 1022–23
arms embargo non-licensing policies toward, **2004**: 1070, **2007**: 1004
on Sudan, **2004**: 962, 1070; **2005**: 929–30, 935; **2006**: 1047; **2007**: 1003, 1007
arms embargo non-licensing policies toward, **2004**: 1070; **2007**: 1003
on Syria, **2003**: 1084–86; **2004**: 901
arms embargo non-licensing policies toward, **2004**: 1070; **2007**: 1003
on terrorism-associated persons or groups, **2001**: 801–3; **2002**: 881–85; **2003**: 152, 1082–84; **2005**: 894, 899, 903; **2006**: 903, 1003; **2008**: 87–88
by U.S. to implement UN sanctions, **2002**: 882–85; **2003**: 1081–84; **2004**: 890–93, 922–23, 1069–70, 1111; **2006**: 1269; **2007**: 1004, 1006–7
Venezuela, arms embargo non-licensing policies toward, **2007:** 1003, 1005
Vietnam, arms embargo non-licensing policies toward, **2004:** 1070; **2007:** 1005
Executive Branch authority to regulate, **1991-99**: 2254–55, 2256–57, 2260–61
explosive remnants of war, **2001**: 837–39; **2007**: 895–98, 904; **2008**: 878, 884, 886–88
Fissile Material Cutoff Treaty (FMCT), **2003**: 1070–72; **2005**: 1081, 1084, 1088, 1111; **2006**: 1289–91; **2007**: 1060, 1079
highly enriched uranium stocks, **1991-99**: 2303–7; **2001**: 847–48; **2002**: 1041–42; **2003**: 1110–12; **2004**: 1137–38; **2005**: 1090–91; **2008**: 954–60
human rights, **2003**: 25–27; **2005**: 435–36
ICBMs, Joint Compliance and Inspection Commission, **2005**: 1048–49
Immigration Act (1990) provisions on technology transfer, **1989-90**: 33
inspection of Iraqi weapons programs, **1991-99**: 2125–32
Inter-American arms trade convention, **1991-99**: 554–58, 2262–63
International Traffic in Arms Regulations (ITAR), **1989-90**: 109; **1991-99**: 2253–55; **2002**: 884–85; **2004**: 1069–70; **2005**: 1044; **2008**: 89, 1021

Arms control (continued)
Iran Nonproliferation Act of 2000, **2002**: 1067–69; **2003**: 1122–23; **2004**: 1135–36; **2005**: 1132–35; **2006**: 1298–99
Iran and Syria Nonproliferation Act, **2005**: 1131–32
Iran, North Korea, and Syria Nonproliferation Act, **2008**: 1025–27
Iran–Iraq Non-Proliferation Act of 1992 and, **1991-99**: 2362; **2002**: 1070–71; **2003**: 1123–24
landmines. *See* Conventional weapons
Libyan dismantlement program, **2003**: 1068–69; **2004**: 1059, 1073–74, 1143–44, 1154–55, 1158–63
mines. *See* Conventional weapons
missiles. *See* Nonproliferation, *subheading*: sanctions, U.S., missile-related sanctions
Moscow Treaty on Strategic Offensive Reductions, **2002**: 1017–23; **2003**: 1068; **2004**: 1056–59; **2005**: 1054, 1110; **2008**: 950
North Korean Export Administration Regulations, **2000**: 746–48
North Korea, shipment of missiles to Yemen, **2002**: 1052–57
nuclear. *See* Nonproliferation
Organization for Security and Co-operation in Europe, **2004**: 1071
outer space and, **2007**: 664–68; **2008**: 665–71
Chinese anti-satellite weapon test, **2007**: 665–67
Panama Agreement for Support and Assistance from U.S. Coast Guard for National Maritime Service of the Ministry of Government and Justice, **2004**: 1091
preemptive military action and, **2002**: 947–57
privileges and immunities for arms control delegations in Switzerland, **2004**: 1057–59
prohibited exports and sales, **2004**: 1070; **2007**: 1003–7; *see also* embargoes, *this heading*
Rush-Bagot Agreement (1817), **2003**: 252–56
sanctions related to, **1991-99**: 2252, 2352–55, 2359–60, 2362–66; **2001**: 797–801, 802; **2002**: 881–85, 894, 1066–69, 1070–71; **2003**: 152, 1081–86, 1116–1118, 1118–1120, 1120–25; **2004**: 1069–1070, 1132–37; **2005**: 1125–35; **2006**: 210–11, 995–98, 1047, 1265–71, 1298–1301; **2007**: 823, 1003–7, 1041–50, 1082–84; **2008**: 87–88, 1022–23. *See also* Nonproliferation, *subheading*: sanctions, U.S.; Sanctions
small arms and light weapons, **1991-99**: 2250–53; **2007**: 1012; **2008**: 1021–22, 1023–24
Strategic Arms Reduction Treaty. *See* Strategic Arms Reduction Treaty (START)
termination of CSBM agreement, **2004**: 1071–72

Arms control (continued)
treaties vs. other international agreements, **2002**: 177–78, 180–84
treaties with United Kingdom and Australia, **2007**: 996–1001; **2008**: 1021–22
treaty compliance, **2002**: 1032–35
trial verification and stability measures, **1989-90**: 565–66
UN Register of Conventional Arms, **1991-99**: 2267–68
UN resolutions on Iraq disarmament, **2002**: 934, 937–47
U.S.–Chile relations, **1989-90**: 540
Uzbekistan–U.S. threat reduction agreement, **2001**: 848–50
war crimes. *See* War crimes
Wassenaar Arrangement, **1991-99**: 2251, 2265–66; **2001**: 912; **2003**: 1122; **2004**: 893, 1093, 1132; **2005**: 1086, 1133, 1137; **2006**: 1300–1; **2007**: 1030; **2008**: 1024–25, 1026
Wye River agreement and, **1991-99**: 2000–1
Arms Export Control Act (AECA). *See also* Foreign Assistance Act (FAA) (1961); International Traffic in Arms Regulations (ITAR)
brokering, **1991-99**: 2268–71
Cooperative Research and Technology, **2004**: 195
expropriation, waiver of restrictions with respect to Nicaragua, **2003**: 709
extraterritorial application, **2004**: 1090*n*
firearms, Inter-American Convention Against the Illicit Manufacturing of and Trafficking in Firearms, Ammunition, Explosives and other Related Materials, **1991-99**: 557–58
foreign military sales program, **1989-90**: 89–90, 223–24, 236; **1991-99**: 1088, 1227, 2268, 2299, 2300; **2000**: 230, 543–48; **2001**: 810; **2003**: 448, 554; **2004**: 420; **2007**: 221, 999. *See also* Foreign Military Sales
imports
denial where retransfer authority not provided, **1991-99**: 2256–62
president's authority to restrict, **1991-99**: 2253
imposition of arms embargoes pursuant to UNSCRs, **2002**: 884–85; **2003**: 1081–84; **2004**: 890–93, 922–23, 1069–70, 1111; **2007**: 1004, 1006–7
state sponsors of terrorism, **1989-90:** 108; **1991-99:** 483–84, 508–9, 1223; **2001:** 96, 460n, 819–21; **2002:** 413; **2003:** 167–68, 536; **2004:** 103, 658, 891, 912–13, 932, 934; **2005:** 506; **2006:** 173, 577; **2008:** 90, 471–72
International Traffic in Arms Regulations, **1989-90**: 109; **1991-99**: 2253–55; **2002**: 884–85; **2004**: 1069–70; **2005**: 1044; **2008**: 89, 1021

Arms Export Control Act (AECA) (continued)
missile technology proliferation sanctions. *See* Nonproliferation, *subheading*: sanctions, U.S., missile-related sanctions
nuclear-related sanctions. *See* Nonproliferation, *subheading*: sanctions, U.S.
proscribed countries. *See also* Arms control, *subheading*: embargoes; Nonproliferation, *subheading*: sanctions, U.S.; terrorism, *subheading*: sanctions related to
Iran
exports to, **1991-99:** 1088
Foreign Military Sales, **1991-99:** 1088, 1227, 1228; **2000:** 543–48; **2004:** 420
Libya
waiver of prohibitions on transfer of defense articles and services to, **2005:** 1065–66
North Korea
imports from, **2000:** 746
policy of denial of export licenses to, **2000:** 748
sanctions in response to nuclear detonation, **2006:** 1271
Rwanda, exports to, **2003:** 1082–83
sanctions, generally, changes in law, **2004:** 927
terrorism *see also* Terrorism, *subheading*: sanctions related to
Anti-Terrorism and Arms Export Amendment Act of 1989, **1989-90:** 108–9
countries not cooperating fully with U.S. antiterrorism activities, **1991-99:** 484, 508; **2003:** 167–68; **2004:** 107–8; **2006:** 172; **2007:** 131–32; **2008:** 88–89
state sponsors of terrorism, **1989-90:** 108; **1991-99:** 483–84, 508-9, 1223; **2001:** 96, 460*n*, 819–21; **2002:** 413; **2003:** 167–68, 536; **2004:** 103, 658, 891, 912–13, 932, 934; **2005:** 506; **2006:** 173, 577; **2008:** 90, 471–72
Iraq, rescission of determination as, **2004:** 103–4; **2005:** 506; **2006:** 179
Libya, rescission of determination as, **2005:** 506; **2006:** 173
North Korea, rescission of determination as, **2008:** 89–94, 960–66
implementation of UNSCR 1373, **2001:** 900–1
report on implementation of UNSCR 1540, **2004:** 1096–1118
Trade Sanctions Reform and Export Enhancement Act of 2000, **2001:** 819–21
treaties providing exemption to certain export control requirements of, **2007:** 996–1001; **2008:** 1021–22
weapons of mass destruction sanctions. *See* Nonproliferation, *subheading*: sanctions

Arrests
consular notification. *See* Consular notification and access
transborder. *See* Crime
Article 36 of the Vienna Convention on Consular Relations. *See* Consular notification and access; Consular Relations, Vienna Convention on (VCCR)
Article 98 agreement (nonsurrender of Americans to ICC). *See* International Criminal Court (ICC)
Artwork
FSIA and art immune from seizure, **2004:** 792–96; **2006:** 562–72; **2007:** 742–44; **2008:** 732–34
World War II era claims for stolen art, **1991-99:** 1050–51, 1062–66, 1067–69
ASEAN (Association of Southeast Asian Nations), 2002: 118–19; **2006:** 760–61
Asian Development Bank, 2001: 539–40
Asia-Pacific Economic Cooperation (APEC), 2001: 939–40; **2002:** 119–21; **2003:** 154; **2006:** 209
Multilateral Framework for Regional Movement Alert (RMAL) System, **2006:** 17
Asia-Pacific Economic Cooperation (APEC) Business Travel Card (ABTC), 2007: 36–37
Assassination, 2001: 867
Executive Order prohibiting, **1989-90:** 565
Iraq, response to attempted assassination of U.S. president by, **1991-99:** 2124–25
Assignment in Receivables Financing, UN Convention on (2001), 2001: 792; **2003:** 854–55
Assisted suicide, 2005: 267–68
Association of Caribbean States, 1991-99: 830–31; **2001:** 242–43
Association of Southeast Asian Nations (ASEAN), 2002: 118–19; **2006:** 760–61
Asylum, 2004: 31–35, 163; **2005:** 10, 12, 17, 24, 316, 347, 348–49. *See also* Deportation; Refugees
adjustment of status waiver, **2008:** 20
from Angola, **2003:** 38
applicant's return to country of claimed persecution, **1989-90:** 47; **2002:** 29
applications from deportable vs. excludable aliens, **1991-99:** 175–77
asylum-seekers in third countries, **2002:** 30–31
child claimants, **1991-99:** 226–32; **2000:** 125–26, 138–40, 141; **2008:** 304–5, 306–8
child custody claims and, **2000:** 115–41
child's capacity to request, **2000:** 125–26, 138–40, 141

Asylum (continued)
due process rights in, **2000**: 131–33
eligibility for, in U.S., **2000**: 128–31
Immigration and Nationality Act on, **2000**: 133–40
persecution as basis for, **2000**: 128–31, 141
Child Soldiers Accountability Act of 2008, **2008**: 312–14
citizenship status of asylum-seekers, **2001**: 1–3
confidentiality in application process, **1989-90**: 46–47
Declaration on Territorial Asylum, **2007**: 51, 64
denial of
alien terrorists, **1991-99**: 81–82
criminals, **2008**: 344
derivative immigration status for immediate family members, **2008**: 343
detention pending determination, **2008**: 346–47
treatment during, **2002**: 30; **2004**: 361
diplomatic compounds and, **2002**: 36
discrimination against applicants, **1989-90**: 40–42
due process rights, **2000**: 131–33
eligibility for, in U.S., **2000**: 128–31
employment authorization for applicants, **1989-90**: 47
evidentiary materials, **1989-90**: 44–46
Executive Branch authority, **2004**: 16–17
extradition and, **2004**: 82–83, 91*n*
fear of persecution as basis for. *See* Persecution
frivolous applications, **1989-90**: 47
from Haiti, **2003**: 25
Immigration and Nationality Act provisions, **2000**: 133–40
North Koreans in China seeking, **2002**: 35, 36
procedures for determination of, **1989-90**: 42–47
rights of migrants in safe haven in Guantanamo, **1991-99**: 187–94
role of Asylum Officers, **1989-90**: 43–45
Salvadorans and Guatemalans, **1989-90**: 40–42
threat of torture in receiving country and, **1991-99**: 239–40; **2008**: 308
UN Declaration and Draft Convention on Territorial Asylum, **1991-99**: 154–57
U.S. antiterrorist efforts, **2001**: 915–17, **2008**: 307–8
U.S.–Canada agreement on examination of refugee status claims, **2002**: 31–35; **2004**: 33–34
Uzbek asylum seekers returned to Uzbekistan by Ukraine, **2006**: 60–61
Vietnamese Montagnards in Cambodia seeking, **2002**: 24–25
withholding of deportation, **1989-90**: 46

Atlantic Charter, 1991-99: 683
Atomic Energy Act (1954), 1991-99: 1912, 2316, 2336, 2337, 2339; **2004:** 1103–4, 1111, 1112–13; **2006:** 1271; **2008:** 986
Atomic Energy Agency, International (IAEA). *See also* Nonproliferation
Additional Protocol to bilateral Nuclear Safeguards Agreements
with countries other than U.S., **2002:** 1034, 1057–62; **2003:** 1086, 1092; **2004:** 928, 1077, 1142–46, 1156–59; **2005:** 447, 1075–76, 1081, 1084–85, 1087, 1094, 1097, 1109, 1116
with U.S., **2002:** 1034, 1057–62; **2003:** 1091; **2004:** 1077, 1118–28; **2006:** 1296–97; **2008:** 944–48
U.S. support for universal adherence to, **2008:** 933, 939, 985
compliance monitoring, **2004:** 1077, 1116–17
Convention on Nuclear Safety, **1991-99:** 1693–96, 2331–33
Convention on Physical Protection of Nuclear Material, **1991-99:** 746; **2001:** 107–8; **2002:** 1072; **2004:** 1100; **2005:** 109–10, 447, 1121, 1122
amendment to, **2005:** 109–10, 960, 1092, 1095, 1121–23; **2007:** 142–43, 1076–78; **2008:** 94–97, 889–90
Convention on Supplementary Compensation for Nuclear Damage (CSC), **2008:** 993–99
enrichment and reprocessing programs, **2005:** 447
Global Threat Reduction Initiative, **2004:** 1137–38, 1141; **2005:** 1095
hazardous wastes, **1991-99:** 1689, 2333–34
India and, **2005:** 1081, 1084–88; **2006:** 1284; **2007:** 1018; **2008:** 988
Iran and, **2003:** 1088–89, 1105–10; **2004:** 1142–49; **2005:** 1073–77, 1097, 1108; **2006:** 1272–84; **2007:** 839, 857, 1016, 1031–36; **2008:** 939, 969–75
Iraq and, **1991-99:** 2111, 2125–32; **2002:** 945, 957; **2004:** 1119, 1122
Joint Convention on the Safety of Spent Fuel Management and the Safety of Radioactive Waste Management, **1991-99:** 1696–99, 2333–34
joint workshop with UN Committee on Peaceful Uses of Outer Space (COPUOS), **2005:** 712
Libya and, **2004:** 928, 1159–60; **2005:** 1107
North Korea and, **1991-99:** 2325–27; **2002:** 1045–47, 1052; **2003:** 1103–5; **2004:** 1122, 1150, 1151, 1154; **2005:** 1067–73, 1097; **2006:** 1268
NPT
support for, **2008:** 941
withdrawal and, **2007:** 1056–57; **2008:** 937–38
nuclear fuel, reliable access, **2005:** 1124–25; **2006:** 1292–93

Atomic Energy Agency, International (IAEA) (continued)
Nuclear Non-Proliferation Exporters (Zangger) Committee. *See* Nonproliferation
Nuclear Suppliers Group (NSG), **1991-99**: 2287–88; **2003**: 1092, 1113; **2008**: 989
Nuclear Terrorism, Global Initiative to Combat, **2006**: 1293–96
privileges and immunities, **2002**: 572–73
purpose, **2004**: 1076–77
Russian reactor fuel return, **2004**: 1139, 1140
safeguards, **2005**: 1062, 1069–71, 1073–77, 1081, 1084–88, 1094, 1095, 1120, 1124, 1125; **2007**: 1060; **2008**: 933–34, 938–39, 944–48, 961, 969*n*, 971, 985, 988–92
U.S. safeguards agreement, **1991-99**: 2335–36
Serbia and, **2002**: 1041
South Korea and, **2004**: 1156–58
Special Committee on Safeguards and Verification, **2005**: 1109, 1114–17
support for strengthening, **2005**: 1094
Syrian nuclear reactor, investigation of clandestine construction, **2008**: 984–86
Taiwan retransfer agreements, **1991-99**: 2334–35
Trilateral Initiative, **1991-99**: 2339–40
ATS. *See* Alien Tort Statute (ATS)
Attorney–client privilege
national security and, **2004**: 1033–34
Attorney's fees
Alien Tort Statute (ATS), **2001**: 340–41
Attorneys Fees Awards Act, **2005**: 280
award of for nonappearance of defendant at deposition, **2005**: 813–15
NAFTA Chapter 11 disputes, allocation of costs, **2008**: 525–26
Audiovisual Works, Treaty on the International Registration of (1990), **1989-90**: 415–18
Australia
Al-Qaida/Qaeda, support for U.S. use of force against, **2005**: 372
antitrust assistance agreement, **1991-99**: 1550
ANZUS Treaty, **2001**: 862; **2004**: 985; **2005**: 372
aviation agreement, **2008**: 511
compulsory pilotage scheme for Torres Strait, **2005**: 686–87; **2006**: 810–12; **2007**: 640–41
cooperation in antiterrorism actions, **2002**: 890; **2006**: 210
customs agreements, **2004**: 626
defense trade cooperation agreement with U.S., **2007**: 207, 996; **2008**: 1020–21

Australia (continued)
e-mail service of process, **2005**: 861
environmental issues, **1991-99**: 1677, 1678, 1719, 1755, 1782; **2002**: 791; **2004**: 744, 763, 768, 776; **2007**: 692
extradition and mutual legal assistance, **1991-99**: 390, 394, 452–55; **2000**: 179, 186*n*; **2001**: 483–84; **2005**: 97–100
Protocol on amending the 1974 U.S.–Australia Extradition Treaty, **2005**: 98–99
sovereign immunity to claims arising from extradition proceeding, **2001**: 475–85
fisheries negotiations with U.S., **2005**: 613, 752
Foreign States Immunities Act of 1985, **2003**: 526–30; **2005**: 529
free trade agreement, **2004**: 615–16, 618; **2005**: 637, 640, 757
negotiations, **2002**: 722
Guantanamo detainee transferred to, **2005**: 967
Hague Child Abduction Convention, compliance with, **1991-99**: 353, 355; **2003**: 123–25, 526–30; **2004**: 60, 61
immunity, Australian Foreign States Immunities Act, **2006**: 609
indigenous peoples, views concerning UN declaration on, **2006**: 394–401; **2008**: 353*n*, 353–54
intellectual property rights, **2008**: 606
Kyoto Protocol, favoring status change for China and India, **2005**: 219
maintenance obligations
family support enforcement, **1991-99**: 1866
reciprocity in child support enforcement, **2001**: 51; **2008**: 759
maritime boundaries, **1991-99**: 1578–80
memoranda of understanding, **2004**: 195
military detainees from, **2003**: 1028, 1033–36; **2004**: 979–80, 996; **2007**: 976
missile defense and nonproliferation cooperation, **2004**: 1066, 1067, 1074, 1091
money laundering, **2004**: 135
most-favored-nation status, **2006**: 755
nonimmigrant visa waiver pilot program, **1991-99**: 76
non-North Atlantic Treaty Organization (NATO) ally, designation as, **2005**: 1044
Nuclear Terrorism, Global Initiative to Combat, **2006**: 1295–96
parallel judicial proceedings, **2002**: 871–72
Proliferation Security Initiative (PSI), involvement in, **2005**: 1099
Regional Movement Alert List pilot, **2006**: 209
retransfer of nuclear material to Taiwan, **1991-99**: 2335
Securities and Investments Commission (ASIC), mutual recognition arrangement with SEC, **2008**: 603–4

Australia (continued)
South Pacific regional environmental convention, **1989-90**: 491
stolen and lost passport data exchange agreement with U.S., **2005**: 5–6
Sudan human rights abuses, UN vote on, **2004**: 246
territorial claims in Antarctica, **2004**: 730–33
WTO disputes, **1991-99**: 1407, 1409. *See also* World Trade Organization (WTO)
complaint related to Continued Dumping and Subsidy Offset Act of 2000 (CDSOA), **2006**: 707
Australia Group, 1991-99: 2351; **2004**: 89, 1094, 1117, 1130–31; **2005**: 1086, 1133, 1135–36
Austria
continuity of treaty obligations, **1991-99**: 744
extradition and mutual legal assistance, **1991-99**: 396, 450–52, 456; **2000**: 180, 186*n*; **2001**: 92*n*; **2006**: 136, 146
family support obligations, **1991-99**: 1866
Gulf War-related issues, **1991-99**: 2102, 2104, 2106–7
Hague Child Abduction Convention, compliance with, **2003**: 123–25, 127, 129; **2006**: 101
money laundering, **2004**: 135
nonimmigrant visa waiver pilot program, **1991-99**: 76
post-World War II occupation, **2005**: 298
preservation of American heritage in, **2004**: 797
reciprocity in consular relations, **1989-90**: 345–46
sanctions against corporation of, pursuant to Iran Nonproliferation Act of 2000, **2005**: 1134
service of process in, **2003**: 893–95
sovereign immunity claim by company indirectly owned by, **2002**: 479–80
World War II era claims
claims of Nazi era victims and victims' heirs, **2000**: 485–89; **2001**: 388, 394–406, 417; **2004**: 377, 432, 436, 446–48, 463–75, 494–95
Holocaust victims' compensation agreements, **2002**: 417; **2008**: 422, 423
immunity to claims arising from, **2002**: 503–11
Nazi-era property confiscation claims, **2005**: 397, 423*n*, 469–75, 485–90, 505, 542, 579, 777
retroactive application of FSIA to, **2003**: 515–20
World War II-related issues, **1991-99**: 1044, 1064, 1068, 2256–62
Authentication, 2003: 863–65
apostille. *See* Judicial assistance; Legalization of Foreign Public Documents, Hague Convention on (1961), *this heading*

Authentication (continued)
documents related to citizenship or sovereignty, **2004**: 66–70
Legalization of Foreign Public Documents, Hague Convention on (1961), **2003**: 859–63; **2004**: 66–70, 71, 827; **2005**: 810; **2006**: 105–10; **2007**: 94–95
Authorization Acts
Aviation and Transportation Security Act (2001), **2004**: 108–9
Defense Production Reauthorization Act (2003), **2003**: 270–71
Department of State Authorization Act (1983), **1991-99**: 1992
Export-Import Bank Reauthorization Act (2002), **2002**: 726–27
Foreign Operations Authorization Act (2003), **2004**: 252
Foreign Relations Authorization Act
(1978), **1991-99**: 685
(1985), **1991-99**: 1097
(1987), **1989-90**: 35, 64; **1991-99**: 1992; **2005**: 115
(1990), **1989-90**: 64, 205, 209, 236, 331, 332; **1991-99**: 47, 2317
(1994), **1991-99**: 348–49, 817, 1901–2, 1992, 2289, 2290; **2003**: 709; **2008**: 452
(1999, Admiral James W. Nance and Meg Donovan), **1991-99**: 112–13, 345; **2001**: 8, 398; **2004**: 52; **2006**: 88
(2002), **2002**: 27, 29, 124, 242–45, 1042; **2003**: 181, 182, 487–501; **2004**: 52, 133, 222; **2005**: 9, 135–36, 257, 490
(2003), **2006**: 213, 530–45; **2008**: 447
(2008), **2008**: 581
Bill Conference Report, **2002**: 27, 29
Global Leadership Against HIV/AIDS, Tuberculosis, and Malaria Reauthorization Act (2008), **2008**: 17
Intelligence Authorization Act
(1996), **2003**: 445
(1998), **1991-99**: 343
(1999), **1991-99**: 550
Magnuson-Stevens Reauthorization Act (2006), **2008**: 706, 711
National Defense Authorization Act
(1988), **1989-90**: 571, 575
(1990), **1989-90**: 503
(1993), **1991-99**: 2313–14
(1995), **2001**: 125–26; **2008**: 114
(2004), **2004**: 170, 172, 719–23; **2005**: 229*n*, 232, 356
(2006), **2006**: 279, 1224
(2008), **2008**: 15, 31–32, 400, 402, 407, 457, 458
State Department Authorities Act (2006), **2006**: 210–11
William Wilberforce Trafficking Victims Protection Reauthorization Act, **2005**: 159–60, 273; **2006**: 1066; **2008**: 119, 314

Automobiles
Japan, trade agreements with U.S. on autos and auto parts, **1991-99**: 1451–52
stolen vehicle treaties, **2000**: 169–70; **2002**: 68
WTO dispute brought by U.S. against China, **2006**: 741–42; **2008**: 544–45
***Avena* Case Implementation Act (2008, proposed)**, **2008**: 195*n*, 201, 208
Avian influenza, **2005**: 756
international partnership to combat, **2005**: 772–73
Aviation issues. *See also* Space
actions against Libya in connection with explosion of Pan Am Flight 103 over Scotland, **1991-99**: 457–80, 542, 1029–30
FSIA immunity, **1991-99**: 1194–95, 1197–98, 1234–52, 1256–57
sanctions, **1991-99**: 1911–14, 1921–24
advance notice requirements for overflight, **1989-90**: 440–41
air carrier liability, **1991-99**: 707, 710–11, 712–13, 1341–42. *See also* International Carriage by Air, Convention for the Unification of Certain Rules Relating to, *this heading*
Council of the International Civil Aviation Organization, **2000**: 653, 663–67
determination of compensable damages in, **1991-99**: 709–14, 1344–45, 1351–56
air carriers, U.S., control by non-U.S. entities, **2005**: 588–92; **2006**: 685–86; **2008**: 509–10
Air Transportation Safety and System Stabilization Act (2003), **2003**: 457
Aircraft, Convention on International Recognition of Rights (1948), **2003**: 852
Aircraft Sabotage Act, **1991-99**: 538, 541, 542
airport user charges, **1991-99**: 1343–44; **2000**: 645, 660–61
Anti-Hijacking Act (1994), **1991-99**: 501–8
Aviation and Transportation Security Act (2001), **2007**: 158–59; **2008**: 109
Aviation Security Improvement Act (1990), **1989-90**: 65–66
Belarus balloon shootdown incident, **1991-99**: 1125
bilateral agreements, U.S., **2003**: 602–3; **2007**: 531–32; **2008**: 510. *See also specific countries*
Albania, **2003**: 602
Argentina, **2004**: 568–71; **2007**: 532
Armenia, **2008**: 512
Australia, **2008**: 511
Bosnia-Herzegovina, **2005**: 588, 592
Brazil, **2008**: 511

Aviation issues (continued)
Brunei, Chile, New Zealand, and Singapore, **2001**: 565–66
Canada, **1991-99**: 1356–59; **2005**: 588; **2007**: 531
Chile, **2001**: 565–66
China, **2004**: 566–67; **2007**: 532
Colombia, **2007**: 532
Croatia, **2004**: 1068–69; **2008**: 511
Ethiopia, **2005**: 588
European Union and, **2002**: 598–600; **2005**: 586–87; **2007**: 529–31; **2008**: 505–10; 685–87
France, **1991-99**: 1359, 1361–62; **2002**: 597–98
Georgia, **2007**: 531
India, **2005**: 588; **2008**: 509
Indonesia, **2004**: 567–68
Ireland, **2008**: 512–13
Jamaica, **2002**: 597; **2008**: 512
Japan, **1991-99**: 1359–61
Kenya, **2008**: 511
Laos, **2008**: 511
Liberia, **2007**: 532
Maldives, **2005**: 588
Mali, **2005**: 588
Paraguay, **2005**: 588
Netherlands, **2002**: 1029; **2008**: 512–13
Russia, **2005**: 588; **2008**: 510
Switzerland, **2008**: 511
Thailand, **2003**: 602; **2005**: 588
Uganda, **2002**: 597–98
Uruguay, **2004**: 568
Venezuela, **2004**: 568–71
Vietnam, **2003**: 602–3; **2008**: 512
cargo standards, **2000**: 671–72, 673
CAB (Civil Aeronautics Board), **2005**: 589
collision and emergency landing of U.S. military aircraft in China, **2001**: 703–11
compensation for damages, **1991-99**: 709–14, 1344–56
competency of European Union member states to conclude air services agreements, **2002**: 598–600
consular functions
in aviation disaster response, **1989-90**: 64–66
Convention on International Civil Aviation (Chicago Convention, 1944), **1991-99**: 539–41; **2000**: 641–56; **2004**: 701, 834
in disposition of unidentified remains of aviation disaster victims, **1991-99**: 347–48

Aviation issues (continued)
nondiscrimination provisions, **2000:** 641–67
notification of departure from standards, **2000:** 642–43, 646–48, 651
requirements for negotiations, **2000:** 652–56
Convention on International Civil Aviation (Chicago Convention, 1944), **2008:** 104, 106–7, 685, 687, 748
crash investigation, taking of civil depositions abroad in, **2000:** 152–60
crew list visas, **2004:** 30
criminal jurisdiction and, **2004:** 146–47, 150, 158
Cuba, restrictions on, **1991-99:** 1909, 1910
Cuban downing of U.S.-registered planes in international airspace, **1991-99:** 1362–67, 1902–3, 1904, 1906
definition of "accident," **2004:** 563–65
discriminatory user fees, **2004:** 568–71
downing of Iran Air Flight 655, claims related to, **1989-90:** 211–17; **1991-99:** 1091–94
emissions control, **2008:** 507, 684–88
ICAO discussions concerning, **2008:** 507
trading scheme on all aircraft landing at EU airports, **2006:** 871–72; **2007:** 692–97; **2008:** 686–88
UK proposed per-plane duty, **2008:** 684–86
equipment financing, **2001:** 791; **2003:** 848–54; **2005:** 802; **2008:** 747–51. *See also* Mobile Equipment, Cape Town Convention on International Interests in (2001)
flight information region (FIR), excess air space claims, **2007:** 634–38
Heathrow user charges arbitration. *See* Arbitration
hostage-taking and hijacking cases, **1991-99:** 501–8
Immigration Advisory Program at airports, **2006:** 209
interdiction
of aircraft involved in drug trafficking, U.S. assistance in, **1991-99:** 538–47; **2001:** 121–28; **2005:** 145–47; **2006:** 225–26; **2008:** 113–14
shootdown incident in Peru, **1991-99:** 538–46; **2001:** 121–28
Soviet shootdown of Korean Airlines flight, **1991-99:** 539–41, 1351
of weapons of mass destruction, **2003:** 1095–99
International Air Services Transit Agreement (IASTA) (1944), **2008:** 106–7
International Air Transportation Fair Competitive Practices Act (1994), **2004:** 569, 570
International Carriage by Air, Convention for the Unification of Certain Rules Relating to (Montreal Convention) (1999), **1991-99:** 1342–43; **2000:** 668–74; **2001:** 564; **2002:** 602; **2003:** 505, 583–87, **2008:** 127, 513–15, 517–18
forum non conveniens doctrine, **2008:** 513–19

Aviation issues (continued)
International Carriage by Air, Convention for the Unification of Certain Rules Relating to (Warsaw Convention) (1929), **2000:** 669–72; **2001:** 473, 555–65; **2002:** 601, 603–7; **2003:** 583, 588–89, 597–602; **2004:** 563–65; **2008:** 524–25
forum non conveniens doctrine, **2008:** 517–18
Guatemala City Protocol to (1971), **2000:** 671
Hague Protocol to (1955), **2000:** 670; **2001:** 555–65; **2002:** 600–607; **2003:** 583, 588–89, 597–602
Montreal Protocol No. 3 to (1975), **2000:** 671–72; **2003:** 587
Montreal Protocol No. 4 to (1975), **1991-99:** 1341–42; **2001:** 563–64; **2003:** 586–89
International Civil Aviation Organization (ICAO), **1989-90:** 111, 211–12, 214; **1991-99:** 490, 501, 539, 540; **2000:** 641–67; **2002:** 818, 823; **2004:** 802; **2005:** 7–8, 685; **2006:** 14, 208
aircraft finance Protocol to the 2001 Cape Town Convention and, **2008:** 748
Assembly, **2001:** 561*n*, 723, 724, 779, 790, 893, 910–11, 938
authority to provide relief, **2000:** 653, 663–67
aviation emissions and, **2007:** 693–94; **2008:** 507
dues, impermissible imposition of, **2006:** 871
environmental charges and taxes, **2008:** 685–86
forum non-conveniens, **2008:** 515–16
liability regime, **2000:** 673–74
passport standards, **2008:** 21
requirements for negotiations, **2000:** 652–56
Rules of the Air, **2005:** 685
U.S. filing alleging EU discriminatory practice, **2000:** 641–67
jurisdiction
Corruption Convention, **2005:** 172
offenses committed against children aboard aircraft, **2000:** 363–64
Korean Airlines Flight 801 crash, **1991-99:** 347–48
liability for accidents, **2003:** 589–96
Libya, restrictions on, **1991-99:** 1921–23; **2004:** 929–31
local remedies rule, **2000:** 656–62
lost cargo, coverage for, **2001:** 555–65
mental injury/emotional distress claims, **2003:** 597–602
Multilateral Agreement on the Liberalization of International Air Transportation, **2003:** 251–52
noise regulation, **2000:** 641–43, 646–51, 661
nuclear materials, shipment by air of **2001:** 703

Aviation issues (continued)
Offences and Certain Other Acts Committed on Board Aircraft, Convention on (Tokyo Convention) (1963), **2008**: 519–25
Open Skies agreements, **1991-99**: 2238–41; **2001**: 565–66; **2002**: 1028–32; **2004**: 1068–69; **2005**: 588, 592; **2007**: 529; **2008**: 509. *See also* bilateral agreements, *this heading*
U.S. model agreement, **2008**: 106–7
overflight rules, **2001**: 704–11, 713; **2008**: 103–4, 106–8
Pan Am Flight 103 terrorist case. *See* Terrorism
passenger data
ECJ ruling on and negotiation of replacement agreement, **2006**: 168–72
Secure Flight program, **2008**: 103–9
Switzerland agreement, **2008**: 109–10
U.S.-EU agreement on, **2004**: 108–16; **2005**: 586–87; **2007**: 158–59
passengers, liability for, **2000**: 669, 671–73; **2002**: 602, 605
protocol on matters specific to aircraft to Convention on International Interests in Mobile Equipment. *See* Mobile Equipment, Cape Town Convention on International Interests in (2001)
racial discrimination by airlines, **2003**: 289
response of ICAO to September 11 terrorist attacks, **2001**: 938
sabotage, no immunity from FSIA suit for, **2005**: 506
safety of air navigation, **1989-90**: 211
Secure Flight program, **2008**: 103–9
state aircraft
fees applicable to, **2005**: 585–86
right of transit passage, **2005**: 685
salvage of sunken state aircraft, **2001**: 688–93; **2004**: 716–23; **2005**: 763–65
stolen aircraft
return of, **2002**: 61, 62, 64–65
treaties on, **2000**: 170
subsidies on large civil aircraft, WTO disputes. *See* World Trade Organization (WTO)
suppression of acts of violence at international airports, protocol for, **1989-90**: 34, 110–11
Syrian air carrier sanctions, **2004**: 901, 903
termination of landing rights of carriers violating biological/chemical weapons
executive order, **1989-90**: 516
transition agreement for Berlin air service, **1989-90**: 395–96
territorial airspace, **2004**: 701, 710–11
transit rights, **2004**: 700–2, 705, 710–11

Aviation issues (continued)
UNITA of Angola, restrictions on, **1991-99:** 1941–43
Unlawful Acts Against the Safety of Civil Aviation, Convention for the Suppression of (1971), **1989-90:** 34, 110; **1991-99:** 460–77, 541; **2000:** 218; **2001:** 98; **2003:** 160
Unlawful Seizure of Aircraft, Convention for the Suppression of (1970), **1989-90:** 34; **1991-99:** 501, 504, 507–8; **2001:** 357
warning regarding military aircraft wreckage in international waters, **2002:** 737–38
Warsaw Convention. *See* International Carriage by Air, Convention for the Unification of Certain Rules Relating to, *this heading*
Ayahuasca. *See* Drug issues
Azerbaijan
Bilateral Agreement on Diplomatic and Consular Properties with the Government of Azerbaijan, **2000:** 627–28
bilateral investment treaty, **1991-99:** 1466–77
conventional armed forces in Europe treaty, **1991-99:** 2233–34
diplomatic relations, **1991-99:** 1174
domestic violence laws, lack of, **2005:** 313
FSIA immunity and, **2004:** 483
head-of-state immunity, **2003:** 571
import ban on Caspian Sea beluga sturgeon products, **2005:** 754
intellectual property rights, **2006:** 769
location of diplomatic buildings, **2000:** 626–34
most-favored-nation trade status and, **1991-99:** 1455
Nagorno-Karabakh conflict, **2008:** 830–32

B

Bahamas
country of registration of vessels involved in maritime litigation, **2005:** 708
drug trade, **2001:** 120; **2002:** 124; **2003:** 181; **2004:** 133–34 **2005:** 135; **2006:** 213; **2007:** 163; **2008:** 113
maritime counter-drug trade agreement, **1991-99:** 1605
extradition and mutual legal assistance, **1991-99:** 394; **2000:** 186*n*; **2001:** 61–62
Hague Child Abduction Convention, compliance with, **2003:** 129; **2004:** 54; **2006:** 102
Haitian immigrants in, **2002:** 31
intellectual property rights Watch List, **2006:** 768; **2007:** 608–9
Inter-American Convention Against Corruption, **2006:** 238
money laundering in, **2004:** 135
Proliferation Security Initiative ship boarding agreement with U.S., **2008:** 1003–4

Bahrain
free trade agreement with U.S., **2004**: 616, 618; **2005**: 640, 757; **2006**: 765–66; **2008**: 572
Guantanamo detainees from, **2004**: 980
immunity of diplomatic personnel, **2000**: 602–16
non-NATO ally, designation as, **2005**: 1044
trade and investment agreements, **1991-99**: 1466
trade negotiations with U.S., **2003**: 682–83
Bail
presumption against, in extradition case, **2001**: 62–70
Baker Island
U.S. claim to exclusive economic zone, **2007**: 643–46; **2008**: 642–44
under U.S. sovereignty, **2003**: 485
Balkans, peace process in, 2005: 934–35; **2008**: 815–16
final status talks, **2005**: 935
Kosovo Albanian role, **2005**: 937–38
peace settlement elements, **2005**: 936–37
Sarajevo War Crimes Chamber, **2005**: 190
Serbian role, **2005**: 938
U.S. role, **2005**: 938–40
Ballistic missiles
Anti-Ballistic Missile (ABM) Treaty. *See* Anti-Ballistic Missile (ABM) Treaty (1972) (U.S.–USSR)
North Korea's launch of, **2006**: 1265–68
U.S. defense radar site in Czech Republic, **2008**: 1008–9
U.S. ground-based ballistic missile defense interceptors in Poland, **2008**: 1009–11
Baltic states, self-determination of, 1989-90: 271–75
Bangladesh
Alien Tort Statute litigation alleging trafficking from to UAE, **2008**: 227–36
exclusive economic zone, prohibition on military actions within, **2004**: 688
head-of-state immunity in divorce action, **1989-90**: 314–19
immunity of UN diplomat from suit by domestic servant, **2002**: 552–67
religious tolerance toward Ahmadiyya Muslim community, **2005**: 316
tax convention with U.S., **2005**: 671
Trafficking Victims Protection Act of 2000 and, **2004**: 164
Tropical Forest Conservation Act agreement, **2008**: 722
U.S. government employment of dual nationals of, **1991-99**: 34–37

Bank Secrecy Act (2001), 2002: 128; **2006:** 243, 246
Bankruptcy law, 1991-99: 1814–17; **2001:** 781–83; **2003:** 837–38; **2006:** 930
cross-border insolvency reform, **2002:** 821–22, 828
Foreign Investment and National Security Act (2007) (FINSA), **2008:** 598
parallel judicial proceedings, **2002:** 863–64
anti-suit injunction, **2002:** 865–68
R.M.S. Titanic artifacts, **2008:** 662, 663
Banks and bank accounts. *See* Financial transactions
Barbados
extradition and mutual legal assistance, **1991-99:** 396, 452–55; **2000:** 179, 186*n*; **2001:** 92*n*
longshore work by U.S. crews, prohibition on, **2002:** 757; **2003:** 764
maritime counter-drug trade agreement, **1991-99:** 1605
U.S. military assistance, **2006:** 278
Barbuda. *See* Antigua and Barbuda
Basel Convention on the Control of Transboundary Movements of Hazardous Wastes and their Disposal, 1989-90: 445; **1991-99:** 1687–93; **2002:** 775, 783–85; **2004:** 747–49; **2006:** 863–65
Basic Authorities Act (1990), 1989-90: 64, 66
Beaufort Sea, maritime boundary dispute, 2004: 734–35, 1081, 1082, 1084, 1090; **2005:** 705–7; **2008:** 640–42
Belarus
Agreement Concerning U.S. Resupply of Monitors in Votkinsk, Russian Federation, **2005:** 1052
arms control, **1991-99:** 2210–18, 2222, 2239, 2245; **2004:** 1070
Lisbon Protocol to the Strategic Arms Reduction Treaty (START), party to, **2005:** 1045*n*
Memorandum of Understanding Relating to ABM, **1991-99:** 750–61
Open Skies (aerial observation) treaty, **2002:** 1029; **2004:** 1068
strategic offensive arms reduction, **2004:** 1053–55
bail for release during extradition proceeding, **2001:** 64–65
balloon shootdown incident, **1991-99:** 1125
cooperation in World War II-era cases, **2003:** 5–6
criminal charges against financial institution in, **2004:** 139
diplomatic relations, **1991-99:** 1173
human rights, **2002:** 278, 282; **2004:** 260–61; **2005:** 302, 435–36
immigration issues
suspension of entry (Presidential Proclamation 8015), **2006:** 42–44
visa restrictions, for foreign policy reasons, **1991-99:** 135–36; **2003:** 25–27
intellectual property rights Watch List, **2006:** 768; **2007:** 610

Belarus (continued)
money laundering in, **2004**: 139
nonproliferation. *See* Nonproliferation, *subheading*: country-specific issues
religious freedom violations, **2003**: 297
sanctions against individuals and entities undermining democratic processes, **2007**: 823, 864; **2008**: 807
succession issues, **1991-99**: 742, 750–61, 1170–71
trade and investment issues, **1991-99**: 1455, 1466
Belgium
discovery in, for use in U.S. litigation, **2003**: 885–87
drug trade (methamphetamines), **2007**: 164–66
extradition and mutual legal assistance, **1991-99**: 395, 398, 399; **2000**: 186*n*; **2004**: 73, 81; **2006**: 136, 146, 290–92
Guantanamo detainees transferred to, **2005**: 967
Hague Child Abduction Convention, compliance with, **2003**: 127
naturalization convention, termination of, **2002**: 202
nonimmigrant visa waiver pilot program, **1991-99**: 76
Open Skies (aerial observation) treaty, **2002**: 1029
parallel judicial proceedings, **2002**: 865–68
standing issue when shareholders Belgian but Canadian limited liability company, **2004**: 598*n*
territorial application of International Covenant on Civil and Political Rights, position on, **2005**: 299*n*
Terrorist Bombings Convention, reservation to, **2006**: 288–91
universal application of national criminal statutes, **2002**: 909
waiver of diplomatic immunity, **1989-90**: 338–39
Belgrade Agreement, 2005: 939
Belgrade War Crimes Chamber, 2005: 190
Belize
Cooperating Nation Information Exchange System (CNIES), agreement with U.S. concerning, **2005**: 146
debt for nature swaps, **2001**: 737, 738–40
extradition and mutual legal assistance, **2000**: 166, 185*n*, 186*n*; **2001**: 92*n*; **2002**: 61, 62, 66, 68
intellectual property rights Watch List, **2006**: 768; **2007**: 609, 610
removal from, **2008**: 606
maritime counter-drug trade agreement, **1991-99**: 1605–6
monetary contempt sanctions, case concerning, **2005**: 522–31
Proliferation Security Initiative (PSI) ship boarding agreement with U.S., **2005**: 1106
stolen vehicle treaty, **2000**: 169–70
trafficking in persons, **2006**: 229
Tropical Forest Conservation Act agreement, **2008**: 722

Benin
Article 98 agreement with U.S. (nonsurrender of Americans to ICC), **2005**: 202
location of embassy, **2000**: 634–36; **2001**: 540–44
women's justice program, U.S. assistance for, **2005**: 307–8
Bering Sea
fish and marine mammals, **1991-99**: 1705–7; **2006**: 885–86
Berlin Treaty, 2001: 577
Bermuda
new document requirements for entry into U.S. by citizens of, **2006**: 4–9; **2007**: 8–10, 14; **2008**: 7–8
passport cards for pedestrian, vehicular traffic, and/or sea travel by U.S. citizens to and from, **2006**: 11–13; **2008**: 8–9
Berne Copyright Convention for the Protection of Literary and Artistic Works, 1989-90: 417; **1991-99**: 1512, 1513, 1518–19; **2003**: 200
Bernstein letter, defined, 2001: 525*n*. *See also* Act of state doctrine
Bhutan
diplomatic relations with U.S., **1989-90**: 241
Bilateral investment treaties. *See* Investment
Bilingual Education Act (1988), 1991-99: 891
Bills of lading
backdating claim dismissed on *forum non conveniens*, **2006**: 963–65
Brussels Convention for the Unification of Certain Rules Relating to, **1991-99**: 1846
Carmack Amendment or COGSA applicable, claims concerning, **2006**: 918–28
enforceability of foreign arbitration clause in bill of lading, **1991-99**: 1843–48
Hague-Visby Rules. *See* Hague Conventions
international rules for, **2001**: 787–89; **2006**: 904, 910–11. *See also* Carriage of goods by sea
Biochemical weapons, in antiterrorism conventions, 2001: 107–8; **2005**: 112, 1117–20; **2007**: 140–42, 1062–71
Bioethics and Human Rights, UNESCO Universal Declaration on, 2005: 784–85
Biological and Toxin Weapons Convention. *See* Biological weapons
Biological Diversity, Convention on, 1991-99: 1390, 1757–66; **2002**: 769–70; **2003**: 804–7; **2006**: 888
Biological materials, accidental or intentional release of
International Health Regulations on, **2005**: 769–70
Biological weapons, 2002: 1068. *See also* Arms control; Law of war; Nonproliferation; Weapons of mass destruction
accounting for and securing, **2004**: 1104–6, 1107–8

Biological weapons (continued)
Australia Group, **1991-99:** 2351; **2004:** 1094, 1117, 1130–31; **2005:** 1086, 1135–36
Biological and Toxin Weapons Convention (BWC) (1972), **1989-90:** 570–71, 574; **1991-99:** 746, 2073, 2111, 2351; **2002:** 1032–33, 1034, 1035–38, 1065; **2003:** 1078–81; **2004:** 928, 1059–64, 1079, 1093, 1105, 1114, 1116, 1131, 1159; **2005:** 1094, 1118–19; **2008:** 1006–8
joint statement of U.S., United Kingdom and Russian Federation, **2005:** 1054–55
scientist codes of conduct, **2005:** 1055–57
Sixth Review Conference, U.S. statement to, **2006:** 1238–43
Chemical and Biological Weapons Control and Warfare Elimination Act. *See* Chemical and Biological Weapons Control and Warfare Elimination Act (1991)
country-specific issues
Burma, **2007:** 811
Cuba, **2002:** 1065
Iran, **2002:** 1065; **2006:** 1240
Iraq, **2002:** 1065; **2004:** 891, 1164
Libya, **2002:** 1065; **2004:** 1074
dismantlement program, **2003:** 166–67, 1068–69; **2004:** 1059–60, 1074, 1159, 1161–62
North Korea, **2002:** 1065; **2006:** 1240
Syria, **2004:** 902; **2005:** 1084–86; **2006:** 1240
USSR compliance with agreements on, **1989-90:** 567, 570–71, 574
criminal laws, U.S., **2004:** 1089*n*, 1097–1102
Geneva Protocol on (1925), **1991-99:** 2060, 2064–65, 2071, 2073; **2005:** 495; **2008:** 429–30
Nonproliferation and Disarmament Fund, **1991-99:** 2230–31
Proliferation Security Initiative (PSI), **2003:** 1095–99; **2004:** 1074–75, 1077–91; **2005:** 1099
Soviet Scientists Immigration Act of 1992 (SSIA) and visa classification of scientists with expertise in, **2005:** 9
SUA Convention, coverage under, **2002:** 106–7
SUA Convention 2005 Protocols to, provisions on BCNs, **2005:** 112, 1117–20; **2007:** 140–42, 1062–71
UN Security Council Resolution 1540, **2004:** 107, 1092–1118; **2006:** 1267; **2008:** 999, 1007–8
U.S. export controls, **2004:** 1110–11, 1115, 1130–32; **2005:** 1135–36
U.S. sanctions, **2003:** 1124–25; **2004:** 1101–2, 1105–16, 1131–32, 1136–37

Biological weapons (continued)
Executive Order on, **1989-90:** 509–10, 512–16
presidential veto of U.S. legislation to control, **1989-90:** 508–12
as weapons of mass destruction, **2004:** 902, 1080, 1089*n*, 1098
Biometric identification, 2003: 16–19; **2004:** 27–29; **2008:** 24–25
bilateral agreements as part of visa waiver program, **2008:** 81–83
Germany, sharing information with, **2008:** 80–81
Biosafety Protocol to the Convention on Biodiversity, 2000: 222
Bipartisan Trade Promotion Authority Act of 2002 (TPA Act), 2002: 719–22; **2003:** 621, 679, 682–83; **2004:** 621
extension of, **2005:** 638–40
Bolivia
American Servicemembers' Protection Act waiver, **2003:** 238
Andean Trade Promotion and Drug Eradication Act (2002), **2008:** 577–81
bilateral investment treaty, **1991-99:** 1466
cultural property protection agreement, **2001:** 772–74; **2006:** 897, 901
defense ministry, sovereign function of, **2005:** 551, 557
drug trade, **2001:** 120; **2002:** 124; **2003:** 181; **2004:** 133–34; **2005:** 135; **2006:** 213, 214; **2008:** 113; 577–81
extradition and mutual legal assistance, **1991-99:** 391–92, 395, 398, 399, 400; **2000:** 165–66, 178, 179, 186*n*; **2001:** 90–96
immunity under FSIA, **1991-99:** 1186–88; **2002:** 516
intellectual property rights Watch List, **2006:** 768; **2007:** 610
Inter-American Convention Against Corruption, **2006:** 238
persona non grata declarations, **2008:** 492–93
trade negotiations with U.S., **2003:** 682–83
trafficking in persons, **2005:** 162
U.S. military assistance, **2006:** 278
waiver of Article 98 agreement with U.S. (nonsurrender of Americans to ICC), **2006:** 279
Bombardment by Naval Forces in Time of War, Hague Convention Concerning (IX 1907). *See* Hague Conventions, *subheading*: on law of war
Bombings, convention for suppression of terrorist bombings. *See* Terrorism
Bonn Declaration (1978), 1991-99: 687
Border Environmental Cooperation Commission, 1991-99: 1314

Border issues. *See also* Aliens; Canada; Law of the Sea, UN Convention on (UNCLOS), *subheading*: territorial sea and baselines; Maritime issues; Mexico
Border Crossing Cards (BCC), **2007**: 14–15
Border Security Act (2002), **2003**: 18, 19
delimitation of outer space, **2001**: 720–21
electronic commerce, **2001**: 784–86, 792–96
Eritrea-Ethiopian conflict, **2002**: 925–26
expulsion of aliens at border crossings, **2005**: 23–24, 291, 336, 690
geographical limits of U.S., **1991-99**: 178–81, 184*n*
human rights issues in U.S. border control policy, **2004**: 232–39; **2006**: 210
maritime. *See* Maritime issues
Mexico–U.S. water allocation agreement, **2001**: 714–16
presidential permits for U.S.
border crossings, **2005**: 592–93
construction and maintenance of border facilities, **2002**: 607
cross-border fiber optic installation, **2001**: 566–68
prevention of terrorist activities in U.S., **2001**: 908–11
radio and television broadcasts across, **1989-90**: 397–98
regulation of cross-border motor carriers, **2002**: 666–70, 819–20
Secure Fence Act of 2006, **2006**: 50–52
security, **2002**: 121; **2004**: 6–7, 26–27, 108–16, 123, 626
Security and Prosperity Partnership for North America, **2006**: 207
territorial claims to Antarctica, **2004**: 730–33
trucking arbitration with Mexico, NAFTA Chapter 20, **2002**: 666–70
U.S.–USSR maritime boundary treaty, **1989-90**: 434–37
Bosnia and Herzegovina
American Servicemembers' Protection Act waiver, **2003**: 238
authorization for U.S. military participation, **1991-99**: 2029–31, 2168–70
conflict in, **2005**: 454
criminal prosecutions
crimes against humanity prosecutions, U.S. call for, **1991-99**: 522–28
UN International Criminal Tribunal for former Yugoslavia (ICTY), obligations to, **2004**: 172–73, 174; **2005**: 192–93; **2008**: 148
War Crimes Chamber, **2003**: 221; **2005**: 190
Dayton Peace Accords, **1991-99**: 586, 867, 1958, 1979, 1981–82, 2025, 2031; **2008**: 815–16
military intervention in, **1991-99**: 2135–38
peace agreement, **2004**: 1071–72

Bosnia and Herzegovina (continued)
peacekeeping operations, **1991-99**: 1032–33, 1037, 2024–31, 2347; **2002**: 157–61; **2003**: 220–21; **2004**: 967
unification efforts in, **2005**: 939
denial of U.S. visas and suspension of entry to officials, **1991-99**: 132, 134–35, 149
diplomatic relations and recognition, **1991-99**: 1146–48, 1945, 1979
extradition and mutual legal assistance, **2000**: 185*n*
head-of-state immunity, **1991-99**: 1281–82
human rights violations in, **1991-99**: 216, 522–29, 583, 584, 867, 980–89; **2001**: 340–41; **2002**: 346–48
money laundering in, **2004**: 135
Open Skies Agreement with U.S., **2005**: 588, 592
sanctions, **1991-99**: 1945–47, 1949–50, 1953–58, 1961, 1980
succession issues and, **1991-99**: 1162–67; **2003**: 245–48
temporary protected status for nationals of, **1991-99**: 245
Botswana
forest conservation agreement, **2006**: 886–87; **2008**: 722
Tropical Forest Conservation Act agreement, **2006**: 886–88; **2008**: 722
Boundary Waters Treaty, 2001: 191, 193, 195, 197, 200
Bovine spongiform encephalopathy
NAFTA Chapter 11 disputes, **2006**: 693–701; **2007**: 563; **2008**: 527–28
Brazil
aerial interdiction program, **2005**: 145
antitrust assistance agreement, **1991-99**: 1551
aviation agreement, **2008**: 511
consular bank accounts, immunity of, **2005**: 555–60, 567–70
drug trade, **2001**: 120; **2003**: 181; **2004**: 133–34l; **2005**: 135; **2006**: 213; **2007**: 163; **2008**: 113
controlled substance laws, **2005**: 141, 144
interdiction assistance, **2006**: 225–26; **2007**: 166–67
psychotropic substance (hoasca) importation in U.S. litigation, **2001**: 128–43; **2003**: 184–88; **2005**: 137–44
sacramental tea with hallucinogen, **2006**: 221–25
evidence gathering abroad, **2006**: 966–69
extradition and mutual legal assistance, **1991-99**: 452; **2000**: 178; **2001**: 90–96
fisheries regulations, **2005**: 752
Hague Child Abduction Convention, compliance with, **2006**: 101–2; **2008**: 50
immunity to claims arising from bond marketing, **2002**: 519
intellectual property rights Watch List, **2006**: 768; **2007**: 609, 610

Brazil (continued)
Inter-American Convention Against Terrorism (OAS Terrorism Convention), party to, **2005**: 111
judicial assistance rules, **2001**: 55–59
money laundering, **2004**: 135
most-favored-nation status, **2006**: 755
OAS prisoner transfer treaty, **2000**: 171; **2001**: 51
order of departure for U.S. warship, **1989-90**: 476–77
outer space agreement, **1991-99**: 1641
trade claims, **1991-99**: 1407, 1412
U.S. military assistance, **2006**: 278
WTO disputes. *See* World Trade Organization (WTO)
Bretton Woods Agreement Act (1945), 1991-99: 1332, 1498, 1993
Bribery. *See* Corruption
British Virgin Islands
alienage diversity jurisdiction case, **2001**: 227–35; **2002**: 227–31
Brunei
longshore work prohibition on alien crewmen from, **2002**: 757; **2003**: 764
Open Skies agreement, multilateral, **2001**: 565–66
Brussels Convention and Lugano Convention, 1991-99: 1827–28, 1829–30, 1831; **2000**: 737, 738, 740
Brussels Convention on Jurisdiction and Enforcement of Judgments in Civil and Commercial Matters, 2005: 789
Bulgaria
beluga sturgeon, management plan for, **2005**: 754–55
bilateral investment treaty, **2003**: 695
continuous nationality rule, **2002**: 632–33
Convention on Protection of Underwater Cultural Heritage, party to, **2005**: 766
educational exchange program, **1991-99**: 1807–8
extradition and mutual legal assistance, **2000**: 185*n*; **2008**: 54
Hague Child Abduction Convention, compliance with, **2008**: 50
intellectual property rights Watch List, **2006**: 768; **2007**: 609
location of diplomatic offices, **1989-90**: 376
Missile Technology Control Regime membership, **2005**: 1136
NATO membership, **2003**: 424–26; **2004**: 411–12
nonproliferation sanctions, **2004**: 1137
nuclear fuel return program, **2004**: 1139, 1141
relief from immigration requirements for certain resident nationals of, **1991-99**: 250
Soviet missiles in, **1989-90**: 572
trade and investment issues, **1991-99**: 1455–56, 1466; **2003**: 687–94

Burkina Faso
foreign assistance to, **2004**: 187
threshold agreement with Millennium Challenge Corporation (MCC), **2005**: 672
Burma
antiterrorism cooperation, **2002**: 118
Burmese Freedom and Democracy Act (2003), **2003**: 923–28; **2004**: 136; **2005**: 892; **2007**: 808; **2008**: 792, 795–98
child soldiers, **2003**: 308; **2004**: 281–82; **2006**: 387–89; **2007**: 354–56
drug trade, **2003**: 181; **2005**: 135–36; **2006**: 212–13; **2007**: 163
sanctions concerning, **1991-99**: 1880–82; **2001**: 120; **2002**: 123, 124; **2003**: 181; **2004**: 133–34; **2005**: 135–36; **2006**: 213; **2007**: 163; **2008**: 113
excessive air space claims, **2007**: 635
exemptions to entry restrictions, **2007**: 70–72; **2008**: 29–31
extradition and mutual legal assistance, **2000**: 185*n*
Federal Burma Act, **2000**: 334–38
human rights violations in, **2000**: 320–21; **2002**: 278, 282; **2006**: 1058–60; **2007**: 317
religious freedom, **2006**: 377
money laundering, **2004**: 135, 136–38
resettlement of refugees from, **2006**: 52–55
Chin National Front or Chin National Army members, **2006**: 55
Karen National Union or Karen National Liberation Army members, **2006**: 53–55
sanctions
arms embargo, **2004**: 1070; **2007**: 1003
arms embargo non-licensing policies, **2004**: 1070; **2007**: 1003
blocking property of and prohibiting transactions related to Burma for repression of democratic opposition, **2007**: 807–11; **2008**: 791–93
drug trade, **1991-99**: 1880–82; **2001**: 120; **2002**: 123, 124; **2003**: 181; **2004**: 133–34; **2005**: 135–36; **2006**: 213; **2007**: 163; **2008**: 113
restrictions on entry; obstructing transition to democracy, **2003**: 27–29; **2007**: 41; **2008**: 28–29
Tom Lantos Block Burmese JADE (Junta's Anti-Democratic Efforts) Act (2008) (JADE Act), **2008**: 28–29, 793–98
financial sanctions, **2008**: 793, 795
prohibitions on imports of jadeite and rubies, 795–98
travel sanctions, **2008**: 28–29, 793–95
trafficking in persons, **2006**: 228; **2007**: 169–70; **2008**: 118–19

Burma (continued)
suits under Alien Tort Statute, **1991-99**: 993–94, 1333; **2002**: 343–44; **2003**: 355–71, 396; **2004**: 365–76
trafficking in persons, **2006**: 228; **2007**: 169–70; **2008**: 118–19
UN Security Council
placement on agenda of, **2006**: 1058–60
U.S. efforts to obtain action concerning, **2007**: 841–43
Burundi
child soldiers, **2003**: 308
conflict resolution and human rights, **1991-99**: 521, 531
conflict resolution efforts, **2003**: 951–52
crimes against humanity in, **2000**: 246–47
democracy promotion programs, **1991-99**: 1011
personal conduct unit in UN Mission in, **2005**: 946
temporary protected status for nationals of, **1991-99**: 245; **2003**: 36
U.S. assistance tied to agreement not to enforce Rome Statute against U.S personnel, **2004**: 182–83, 187
Bus Regulatory Reform Act (1982), 2002: 666
Byrd Amendment (Continued Dumping and Subsidy Offset Act of 2000), 2003: 655–57; **2004**: 606–7; **2005**: 626–27; **2006**: 703*n*, 706–8

C
CAB (Civil Aeronautics Board), 2005: 589
CAFTA. *See* Central American Free Trade Agreement (CAFTA)
California
effort to assign claims against U.S. to satisfy judgment in U.S. court under state law and procedure, **2008**: 410–12, 416–418
ban on fuel additives, NAFTA arbitration arising from, **2001**: 574–608
claims of World War II soldiers against Japanese corporations in courts of, **2000**: 500–6, 514–31
Desert Protection Act (1994), **2006**: 718
gold mining and NAFTA Chapter 11 dispute, **2006**: 709–26
Holocaust Victim Insurance Relief Act, **2000**: 460–73; **2002**: 415–29; **2003**: 462–68; **2008**: 419, 422, 424
McCarran–Ferguson Act and insurance regulation, **2008**: 779
preemption of state law. *See* States, U.S.
Sacred Sites Act (1976), **2006**: 714
Surface Mining and Reclamation Act (1975) and regulations, **2006**: 714, 715, 722

Cambodia
antiterrorism cooperation, **2002:** 118
Article 98 agreement with U.S. (nonsurrender of Americans to the ICC), **2005:** 202
Cambodian-flagged vessel, owned by North Korea, transporting WMD, **2005:** 1098
conflict resolution in, **1989-90:** 527–37
arms control, **1989-90:** 533–34
Paris Conference, **1989-90:** 526, 535–37
role of "Permanent Five," **1989-90:** 528–31, 532–33, 535
U.S. policy, **1989-90:** 527, 531–32, 533–34
U.S.–Vietnam relations and, **1989-90:** 526, 527
crimes against humanity in, **2000:** 244–45
cultural artifacts, restrictions on trade in, **2003:** 823–25; **2008:** 729–30
democratic processes in, **2003:** 407–8; **2006:** 487
diplomatic relations, **1989-90:** 241; **1991-99:** 1149–50
drug trade, narcotics control efforts, **2001:** 120–21
human rights in, **2004:** 395–96
Khmer Rouge prosecution, **1989-90:** 119–28; **1991-99:** 607–8; **2000:** 244–45; **2001:** 169; **2002:** 148; **2003:** 221–22; **2008:** 141
maritime counterterrorism measures, conditions for failure to take, **2008:** 112
property claims against, **1991-99:** 1081–82
repatriation to, **1991-99:** 93
sanctions on, **1991-99:** 1967–68
textile agreement, **2002:** 725–26
trade and investment agreement with, **2006:** 761
trafficking in persons sanctions, **2005:** 161–62
Vietnamese Montagnard refugees in, **2002:** 24–25
war crimes prosecution in, **2002:** 148
Cameroon
anti-suit injunction, **2005:** 829–31
claim against U.S. for failure of consular notification, **1991-99:** 257–58
maritime counterterrorism measures, conditions for failure to take, **2008:** 112
Canada
agreements with U.S. *See also* arms control; environmental and conservation issues; fish and marine mammals; tax issues, *this heading*
antitrust, **1991-99:** 1549–51; **2004:** 662–63
aviation, **1991-99:** 1356–59, **2005:** 588; **2007:** 531
Boundary Waters Treaty of 1909, **2005:** 688, 718
customs agreements, **2004:** 626
Execution of Penal Sentences Treaty, **2000:** 37

Canada (continued)
Free Trade Agreement, **2004:** 618; **2005:** 605
Free Trade Implementation Agreement (1988), **2006:** 726, 727
prisoner transfer treaty, **2001:** 51
refugee status claims, agreement on examination of, **2002:** 31–35; **2004:** 33–34
Skagit River and Ross Lake in the State of Washington and the Seven Mile Reservoir on the Pend D'Oreille River in British Columbia (1984 treaty), **2000:** 296
Softwood Lumber Agreement (SLA), **2006:** 762–63; **2007:** 549. *See also* North American Free Trade Agreement (NAFTA); World Trade Organization (WTO)
arbitration concerning, **2007:** 591–97; **2008:** 582–93
award on liabilities, **2008:** 582–85
provincial subsidies circumventing, **2008:** 589–93
remedies, **2008:** 585–89
space station agreement, **1989-90:** 482; **1991-99:** 1641–47
Titanic protection agreement, **2004:** 715–16; **2005:** 762; **2006:** 828–35
water pollution, **2006:** 859–60
Apartheid Convention and, **2004:** 358
Arctic region, **2008:** 623, 624, 628
arms control
missile defense cooperation, **2004:** 1066, 1067
Missile Technology Control Regime, **1991-99:** 2356–59
Open Skies (aerial observation) treaty, **2002:** 1029
Proliferation Security Initiative, **2004:** 1074, 1091
retransfer of nuclear material to Taiwan, **1991-99:** 2334–35
border issues, **2007:** 835, 838
air travel and passport requirements, **2006:** 4–9
Alaska, arbitration agreement (1903) regarding land boundary with, **2005:** 701–2
aviation, overflights, **2008:** 108
Canadian Border Boat Landing Program, **2007:** 12
Caroline case, **2007:** 876, 880
counterterrorism cooperation, **2006:** 210
cross-border fiber optic installation, **2001:** 566–68
maritime boundaries and right of passage, **1991-99:** 1593–96; **2004:** 734–35
Beaufort Sea, **2005:** 705–7; **2008:** 640–42
Machias Seal Island, **2005:** 707
new document requirements for entry into U.S. by citizens of, **2007:** 8–10, 13–14, 15; **2008:** 7–8
NEXUS and, **2007:** 13–14

Canada (continued)
Outlying Area Reporting System (OARS), **2007:** 14
passport cards for pedestrian, vehicular traffic, and sea travel by U.S. citizens to and from, **2006:** 11–13; **2008:** 8–9
presidential permits for construction and maintenance of U.S. border facilities, **2002:** 607
smart-border plans, **2002:** 121
third-country asylum claims at U.S. border, agreement covering, **2002:** 31–35
Canadian corporations, litigation concerning ATS claims for activities in Sudan, **2005:** 394–400, 822–29
consular notification issues, **1991-99:** 255, 272–80
Cuba, U.S. broadcasting to, **2004:** 641
cultural property, protection of, **1991-99:** 1797–98, 1801
deportation, understanding concerning, **2004:** 21–23
diplomatic immunity, **1991-99:** 1297–1305
diplomatic mission employees, status of, **2000:** 582–83
drug trade, **2003:** 183; **2005:** 135; **2006:** 214
environmental and conservation issues, **1991-99:** 1665–71, 1692
Arctic environment protection agreement, **1991-99:** 1777–80
CERCLA violations, **2006:** 855–59
migratory bird protection agreement, **1991-99:** 1770–76
Northeastern Interstate Forest Fire Protection Compact, **2000:** 296
transboundary air pollution agreement, **2004:** 744–45
transboundary water pollution litigation, **2007:** 686–91
U.S.–Canada water pollution settlement agreement, **2006:** 859–60
extradition and mutual legal assistance, **1991-99:** 417–21, 443, 445–46; **2000:** 185*n*; **2002:** 61, 62, 64, 69; **2003:** 145–49
request for expansion of extradition, **1989-90:** 78–79
family support enforcement, **2004:** 836–37. *See also* reciprocity, *this heading*
felony murder doctrine, restriction of use, **2005:** 386
fish and marine mammals, **2004:** 751, 753–55, 766
enforcement agreement, **1989-90:** 488–89; **1991-99:** 1703–5, 1721–25
Pacific Coast Albacore Tuna Vessels and Port Privileges, Agreement Amending Treaty between U.S. and Canada on, **2003:** 801–2
Pacific Hake/Whiting, Agreement between U.S. and Canada on, **2004:** 753–55; **2005:** 734; **2008:** 711
Pacific Salmon Agreement, **1991-99:** 1721–25; **2000:** 294, 295; **2006:** 875–78; **2008:** 709–11

Canada (continued)
flood control negotiations between U.S. and Canada concerning Devils Lake, North Dakota, **2005**: 717–19
Great Lakes issues
arming of certain U.S. ships on the Great Lakes and, **2003**: 252–56
Great Lakes Charter Annex, **2001**: 198–200
Great Lakes–St. Lawrence River Basin Water Resources Agreement and Compact, **2005**: 206–7
Hague Child Abduction Convention, compliance with, **1991-99**: 369
Haiti and, **2004**: 938, 940
Head Harbor Passage and right of passage, **2007**: 638–40
Ilulissat Declaration, **2008**: 636–38
immunity
Canadian State Immunity Act, **2003**: 529–30; **2005**: 529; **2006**: 609
of instrumentalities of government, **1991-99**: 1188, 1215–16; **2006**: 550–58
indigenous peoples, views concerning UN declaration on, **2008**: 354
intellectual property rights Watch List, **2006**: 768, 769
Inter-American Convention Against Corruption, party to, **2006**: 238
Inter-American Convention Against Terrorism, party to, **2004**: 97; **2005**: 111
investor right of action, **2004**: *598n*
liquor smuggling into, **2005**: 234–42
marine navigation services fee, **2005**: 688
memorandum of understanding
between Province of Manitoba and Missouri, **2001**: 179–98
status of, **2004**: 195
money laundering, **2004**: 135
most-favored-nation status, **2006**: 755
NAFTA claims. *See* North American Free Trade Agreement (NAFTA)
Northwest Passage, U.S. vessels transiting, **2006**: 814–15
Nuclear Terrorism, Global Initiative to Combat, **2006**: 1295–96
Panama Canal Commission, claims against, **2001**: 219–24
parallel judicial proceedings, **2002**: 862–64, 872–73
private international law, **2007**: 745–49, 765–68
reciprocity
in recovery of family support obligations, **2001**: 51; **2002**: 841–42; **2008**: 759
service of process rules, **2003**: 891
Somali piracy, cooperation with Transitional Federal Government of Somalia (TFG) in fight against, **2008**: 925, 927
tax issues
limitation on cooperation in tax claim enforcement in U.S. court, **2002**: 837–41

Canada (continued)
tax claims in U.S. courts, **2004**: 820, 826
treaties with U.S., **2008**: 612
U.S. government employment of dual nationals of, **1991-99**: 34–37
Waiver of Claims Arising as a Result of Collisions between Vessels of War (1943), **2001**: 221
Western Hemisphere Travel Initiative, **2005**: 1–5; **2008**: 6–8
WTO disputes, **1991-99**: 1384, 1407, 1409–1410, 1504–6. *See also* World Trade Organization (WTO)
Cape Town Convention. *See* Mobile Equipment, Cape Town Convention on International Interests in (2001)
Cape Verde
claims for archipelagic waters, **1989-90**: 475–76
proposed sale of property in U.S., **1989-90**: 377–79
threshold agreement with Millennium Challenge Corporation (MCC), **2005**: 672
warships, restrictions on innocent passage of, **1991-99**: 1596
Capital Post-Conviction Procedure Act (1995), **2002**: 47
Capital punishment, **2004**: 1100
American Declaration of the Rights and Duties of Man
juvenile offenders, **2001**: 303–15
violation of, **2000**: 390–92
Antiterrorism and Effective Death Penalty Act, **2000**: 388; **2005**: 125, 131, 283, 384, 506
applicability considered under International Covenant on Civil and Political Rights, **2005**: 269–70, 289, 390
consular notification. *See* Consular notification and access
Convention against Torture and Other Cruel, Inhuman or Degrading Treatment or Punishment (1987), **1989-90**: 178–79, 189
criticism of, **2005**: 389–90
customary international law, **1989-90**: 178–79; **1991-99**: 256, 739, 965–67, 970–78; **2008**: 303, 376
regarding juvenile offenders, **2001**: 308–12
due process and, **2004**: 337–38
extradition restrictions, **1991-99**: 390, 399, 402–3; **2000**: 166, 180; **2003**: 140–41; **2004**: 74; **2007**: 118–20, 123
EU–U.S. agreement, **2003**: 137; **2006**: 133–34
extrajudicial, summary or arbitrary execution, **2000**: 397–98; **2001**: 316–17
UN General Assembly resolution on, **2002**: 318–20; **2008**: 375–78
as human rights violation, **2000**: 391–92, 396–97
in judicial procedure in case of, **2000**: 389–96
Inter-American Commission on Human Rights and, **1991-99**: 281, 289–91; **2000**: 389–97; **2001**: 294–315

Capital punishment (continued)
International Covenant on Civil and Political Rights and, **1991-99**: 739, 870, 876–77, 881, 965–70
U.S. reservation on, **2006**: 354, 365–66
international practice, **2000**: 391, 392, 396–97
in Iraq, **2006**: 270
jus cogens and, **1991-99**: 739, 965–67, 974*n*, 976–78; **2001**: 312–13
juvenile offenders, **1991-99**: 965–78; **2000**: 384; **2001**: 303–15; **2002**: 291; **2003**: 341; **2004**: 285, 335–37; **2005**: 322, 381–89; **2007**: 304, 385
Geneva Conventions, Additional Protocol I and II provisions, **2008**: 303
Rights of the Child Convention provisions, **2001**: 308n, 309–10; **2003**: 306
legal protections, **1991-99**: 332–34, 963
mentally retarded prisoners, **2003**: 341
moratorium, **2007**: 382–83
mutual legal assistance, refusal in cases of, **2002**: 69–70
racial discrimination in, **2001**: 259–60
sentencing procedure, **2001**: 294–302
UN Commission on Human Rights resolutions, **2001**: 315–17
UN General Assembly resolution on Congo calling for moratorium on, **2003**: 336–37
U.S. policy, **1991-99**: 963–65; **2002**: 316–18; **2003**: 306, 340–42
U.S. response to UN General Assembly resolution on, **1991-99**: 963–65; **2006**: 354, 365–66; **2007**: 303–5; **2008**: 375–78
Vienna Convention on Consular Relations and, **2000**: 63, 64, 73. *See also* Consular notification and access
Caribbean Basin Trade Partnership Act (2000), **2001**: 666
Caribbean region
passport cards for sea travel, **2006**: 11–13
Pollution from Land-Based Sources and Activities, Protocol Concerning, **2007**: 724–28; **2008**: 714–15
Carmack Amendment, 2006: 918–28
Carriage by air. *See* Aviation issues
Carriage of goods by sea
Carriage of Goods by Sea, Draft Convention, UNCITRAL, **2003**: 839, 843–47; **2004**: 815–18; **2005**: 793–99; **2006**: 903–18
adoption as UN Convention on Contracts for the International Carriage of Goods Wholly or Partly by Sea and U.S. support for, **2008**: 743–45
delay, **2006**: 914–16, 916*n*
liability limitations, **2006**: 916–18

Carriage of goods by sea (continued)
scope of coverage, **2006:** 909–13
shipper's liability, **2006:** 916
shipper's obligations, **2006:** 913
transport documents and electronic transport records, **2006:** 913
Carriage of Goods by Sea Act, **1991-99:** 1843–48; **2002:** 830; **2004:** 830–34; **2005:** 794–98, 831–32; **2006:** 918–28; **2008:** 744
Cartagena Declaration on Refugees (1984), 2007: 51
Case–Zablocki Act (1972), 1991-99: 679–82, 684–85, 686
Cayman Islands
money laundering in, **2004:** 135
CBP. *See* Customs and Border Protection Bureau (CBP)
CCW (Convention on Conventional Weapons). *See* Conventional weapons
Census, 2000: 639–40
Central African Republic
Article 98 agreement (nonsurrender of Americans to ICC) and, **2004:** 187
Central American Bipartisan Accord, 1989-90: 156–60
Central American Free Trade Agreement (CAFTA), 2003: 685; **2004:** 616–19; **2005:** 636–37, 640
CERCLA (Comprehensive Environmental Response, Compensation and Liability Act) (1980), 1991-99: 1620; **2006:** 855–60
Chad
peacekeeping operation (MINURCAT), **2008:** 839
Chanceries. *See* Consular offices and personnel; Diplomatic missions and personnel
Chapeau agreement, 2004: 194–95
Charter, UN. *See* United Nations
Chechnya
conflict resolution and human rights in, **2003:** 953–54
Russian–Chechen conflict, **1991-99:** 516–17
Chemical and Biological Weapons Control and Warfare Elimination Act (1991), 1989-90: 512; **1991-99:** 2351–55, 2364; **2002:** 1068
Chemical materials
accidental or intentional release of, **2005:** 769–70; **2007:** 210–11
hydrochlorofluorocarbons, **2007:** 697–99, **2008:** 688–91
mercury contamination, **2007:** 691–92
Chemical weapons, 2002: 1068
Australia Group, **1991-99:** 2351; **2004:** 89, 1094, 1117, 1130–31; **2005:** 1086, 1133, 1135–36

Chemical weapons (continued)
Burma, **2007**: 811
Chemical and Biological Weapons Control and Warfare Elimination Act. *See* Chemical and Biological Weapons Control and Warfare Elimination Act (1991)
Chemical Weapons Convention (CWC) (1993), **1991-99**: 102, 733, 760, 1030, 2340–50, 2351; **2000**: 756–57; **2002**: 1032–33, 1034, 1035–38, 1065; **2003**: 1013–14, 1072–78; **2004**: 928, 1059–61, 1079, 1101, 1105, 1106, 1114, 1116, 1131; **2005**: 1057–66, 1094, 1118–19, 1133, 1136; **2006**: 1243–51
chemical and bacteriological weapons, Geneva protocol on (1925), **1991-99**: 2060, 2064–65, 2073, 2100, 2189; **2005**: 495; **2008**: 429–30
compliance with, **2005**: 1057–65
destruction of existing stocks, **2003**: 1069, 1076, 1077–78; **2005**: 1061, 1064–65
entry into force, **1991-99**: 2345
extension of deadline for destruction of stockpiles, **2006**: 1243–46
goals, **2003**: 1073; **2008**: 1004–6
implementation in U.S., **1991-99**: 102, 2347–49; **2004**: 1105, 1114; **2006**: 1249–51
Chemical Weapons Convention Implementation Act (1998), **1991-99**: 102, 2347, 2349; **2004**: 1105, 1114; **2006**: 1250
incentives to accede to, **2003**: 1073
Iraqi weapons program, **1991-99**: 2100, 2111
key features, **1991-99**: 2340–44
Libya, **2003**: 1068–69, 1074; **2004**: 1059; **2005**: 1059, 1065–66
national implementation, **2003**: 1075–78; **2006**: 1246–49
second CWC review conference, **2008**: 1004–6
use of riot-control agents and, **1991-99**: 2345–47; **2003**: 1013–14; **2006**: 1223–25
verification and compliance, **2003**: 1073–75
Conference on Prohibition of Chemical Weapons, **1989-90**: 576–78
dioxin (Agent Orange) litigation, **2005**: 491–97; **2006**: 522–26; **2008**: 427–30
Executive Order on, **1989-90**: 509–10, 512–16
Export Administration Regulations, **2005**: 1135–36
Maritime Navigation, Convention for the Suppression of Unlawful Acts Against, (SUA) and fixed platforms protocol, coverage under, **2002**: 106–7
2005 protocols to, provisions concerning chemical weapons, **2005**: 112, 1117–20; **2007**: 140–42, 1062–71

Chemical weapons (continued)
Nonproliferation and Disarmament Fund, **1991-99:** 2330–31
presidential veto of U.S. legislation to control, **1989-90:** 508–12
sanctions related to, **1991-99:** 2352–55, 2363–66, **2002:** 1070; **2003:** 1124–25; **2004:** 1136–37
UN Security Council Resolution 1540, **2004:** 107, 1092–1118; **2005:** 1059; **2006:** 1267; **2008:** 999, 1007–8
U.S. export controls, **2004:** 1100–2, 1105–16, 1131, **2005:** 1135–36
U.S. policy on chemical weapons, **1989-90:** 576–78
USSR compliance with agreements on, **1989-90:** 567, 570–71, 574
Chicago Convention. *See* Aviation issues, *subheading*: Convention on International Civil Aviation (Chicago Convention, 1944)
Child abduction. *See* Children
Child Citizenship Act (2000), 2000: 16*n*; **2001:** 3–6; **2002:** 8, 9
age limitations for gaining citizenship, **2003:** 1–2
effect of citizen-grandparent death, **2003:** 2–3
eligibility of children born out of wedlock, **2003:** 3–4
Child labor. *See* Children
Child soldiers. *See* Children, *subheading*: in armed conflicts
Child support. *See* Maintenance obligations
Children
abduction. *See* international abduction, *this heading*
abuse of
as argument against return in international child abduction, **1991-99:** 365–70
immigration status of abused child, **1991-99:** 75
inadmissibility of alien convicted of crime against, **1991-99:** 90
Violence Against Women Act of 2000 (VAWA 2000), **2005:** 264
adoption. *See* Adoption
African Charter on the Rights and Welfare of the Child, **2005:** 387
American Declaration of the Rights and Duties of Man, **2007:** 383–89
armed conflicts and, **1991-99:** 227, 930–31; **2000:** 355–60; **2002:** 287–88, 293, 294–97; **2003:** 306–8; **2004:** 105–7, 281–83, 284, 326; **2005:** 323, 996; **2006:** 340, 387–89, 997, 1065–68
child soldiers, **2003:** 308; **2004:** 281–82; **2007:** 349–51, 354–56. *See also* Rights of the Child, Convention on, *this heading*
Child Soldiers Accountability Act (2008), **2008:** 312–14
Child Soldiers Prevention Act (2008), **2008:** 314–15
conference on, **2007:** 356–58
involvement in hostilities, **2007:** 346–49
asylum claims. *See* Asylum. *See also* immigration issues, *this heading*
Born-Alive Infants Protection Act of 2002, **2005:** 267

Children (continued)
capacity to make legal decisions, **2000**: 112–15, 121–22, 124–26, 135–36, 141
child labor issues, **1991-99**: 227, 847, 866, 928, 929–30, 932–34, 1000, 1399, 1425–26, 1429; **2002**: 286–87, 288, 289; **2004**: 658–59, 924
Convention 182 on the Worst Forms of Child Labor (ILO) (1999), **1991-99**: 929–30, 932–34; **2002**: 286–87, 288, 289; **2005**: 323, 996
child soldiers. *See* armed conflicts and, *this heading*
child support enforcement. *See* Maintenance obligations
Children's Justice Act, **2007**: 342
citizenship. *See also* immigration issues, *this heading*
acquisition of citizenship in adoption, **2002**: 9
blood tests to establish citizenship claims, **1989-90**: 1–2
child born abroad
of unwed U.S. citizen father, **2000**: 1–19, 47; **2001**: 7–8; **2005**: 261
of unwed U.S. citizen mother, **1991-99**: 1–9
of U.S. citizen parents, **2001**: 3–6; **2002**: 8
Child Citizenship Act (2000). *See* Child Citizenship Act (2000)
child conceived in vitro, **2002**: 10–11; **2006**: 2–3
children born of surrogate parentage, **1989-90**: 13
proof of parentage, **1989-90**: 1–3; **1991-99**: 4–5, 128–31
U.S.-born child of foreign diplomat with U.S. citizen mother, **2005**: 1
U.S.-born child of foreign head of state or ministers, **2004**: 4–5; **2006**: 668*n*
consular protection of U.S. citizen children abroad, **2000**: 117–19
in criminal justice system, **1991-99**: 871
capital punishment of juvenile offenders, **1991-99**: 965–78; **2000**: 384; **2001**: 303–15; **2002**: 291; **2003**: 341; **2004**: 285, 335–37; **2005**: 322, 381–89; **2006**: 366; **2007**: 304, 385
sentenced to life without parole, **2006**: 366–69; **2007**: 383–89
diplomatic immunity of dependents. *See* Diplomatic missions and personnel; Diplomatic Relations, Vienna Convention on
disappearance, draft convention on and, **2006**: 428
genocide and, **2004**: 241, 247, 258
Hague Convention on the Protection of Children (1996), **1991-99**: 1859–61; **2000**: 121; **2004**: 63, 830
Health Act of 2001, **2005**: 276
human rights of, **1991-99**: 366, 370–71, 927–34; **2001**: 273–75; **2002**: 285–93; **2004**: 279–85

Children (continued)
Convention on Rights of the Child. *See* Rights of the Child, Convention on, *this heading*
of girl child, **2001**: 275; **2002**: 304; **2003**: 309
immigration issues
asylum claims adjudication, **1991-99**: 226–32
asylum for child soldier, **2008**: 306–8
asylum for unaccompanied child, **2000**: 123–41
consular assistance for, **2002**: 59–60
consular protection of citizen children abroad, **2000**: 117–19
consular protection of foreign nationals, **2001**: 36
custody claim from Cuban father and third-party application for child's asylum, **2000**: 115–41
of dual nationality, custody case involving, **2001**: 40–47
humanitarian resettlement, **2005**: 26
as refugees, **1991-99**: 227
standing to contest passport rules, **2003**: 491
UN Refugee Children Guidelines, **2000**: 135, 138–39
international abduction
child's capacity to testify, **2000**: 112–15, 121–22, 124–25, 138–39, 141
European Court of Human Rights and, **2003**: 123–27
extradition and mutual legal assistance, **1991-99**: 410–11; **2002**: 70–71
Hague Convention on Child Abduction (1980), **1991-99**: 110, 349–80, 410, 1861; **2000**: 93–114, 117–18, 121–22, 137–38*n*; **2001**: 40–48; **2002**: 52–59, 75–76, 286, 289; **2003**: 123–29; **2004**: 52–65, 820, 828; **2005**: 65–67; **2007**: 17, 90–93
judicial abstention, **2008**: 782–89
State Department regulations issued, **2008**: 49–50
U.S. report on compliance by other countries with, **2006**: 98–103; **2008**: 50
human rights as defense to return of abducted child, **1991-99**: 370–71
International Child Abduction Remedies Act (1988), **1991-99**: 372; **2001**: 40–47; **2002**: 55, 56; **2004**: 55–56
International Parental Kidnapping Crime Act (1993), **1991-99**: 377–80; **2002**: 56–59
passports
issuance for abducted child, **2002**: 12–13
runaways, **2007**: 17
two-parent consent for issuance, **2007**: 16–17; **2008**: 10
"special family circumstances" and, **2007**: 17

Children (continued)
two-parent consent for passport issuance, **2001**: 8–9; **2002**: 11–13; **2004**: 7–8
wrongfully stranded abroad, **2007**: 17
reciprocity among nations in matters of, **2000**: 120–21, 137–38
recognition of foreign court determinations, **2001**: 40–47
return of children to non-Hague countries, **2000**: 115–23, 137, 138
visa ineligibility of persons involved in, **1991-99**: 109–10; **2002**: 52–54
international adoption. *See* Adoption
Internet Crimes Against Children Task Forces (ICACs) program, **2008**: 294
juveniles detained by the Department of Defense at Guantanamo Bay, **2004**: 987; **2008**: 308–12
labor issues
Child Labor, ILO Convention (No. 182) for Elimination of the Worst Forms of, **2007**: 349
forced labor, **2007**: 336–37
of multinational families, international law framework for, **2000**: 121
National Organ Transplant Act (1984), **2007**: 335
offenses committed against children aboard ships or aircraft, **2000**: 363–64
parent-child relationship. *See also* Adoption; international abduction, *this heading*
parental access, memoranda of understanding on
Egypt–U.S., **2003**: 129–31
Jordan–U.S., **2006**: 103
parental authority to speak for, **2000**: 124–25
parental responsibility to protect, convention on, **1991-99**: 1859–61
parental rights, **2002**: 286, 291–92; **2003**: 305
passports. *See* Passports, U.S.
pornography, **2003**: 198–99
prevention of crimes against, **2007**: 343–44
protection from illegal trafficking, **1991-99**: 852, 911, 912–17, 928–29, 930; **2000**: 225–30, 355–57, 360–64; **2003**: 189–90; **2004**: 95–96, 101–2, 142, 149–57, 166, 280; **2007**: 341–43; **2008**: 291–96
questioning and detention of juveniles, **2000**: 383–84
right to education, **1991-99**: 788, 933
rights in safe haven in Guantanamo, **1991-99**: 192–94

Children (continued)
Rights of the Child, Convention on, **1989-90**: 171–76; **1991-99**: 852, 855, 927–29, 975; **2000**: 134–35, 355, 356, 361; **2001**: 273–74; **2002**: 285, 287, 289–93, 303; **2003**: 303–6, 307, 342; **2004**: 283–85, 294; **2005**: 322–23; **2006**: 386
abuse and neglect provisions, **1989-90**: 175
on adoption, **1989-90**: 175
Article 37, **2005**: 387
capital punishment provisions, **2001**: 308*n*, 309–10; **2003**: 306
disabled, **1989-90**: 176
family reunification provisions, **1989-90**: 175
financing implementation of, **1989-90**: 174
freedom of religion and thought, **1989-90**: 172–73
Optional Protocols, **2004**: 283–85; **2006**: 385, 386; **2008**: 290–300
detention of children, **2008**: 315–17
Involvement of Children in Armed Conflict, **2000**: 354, 356, 357–60; **2001**: 274–75; **2002**: 184, 287–90, 293, 294–97; **2005**: 323, 996; **2007**: 333–45; **2008**: 300–12
international cooperation and assistance, **2007**: 351–53
Sale of Children, Child Prostitution and Child Pornography, **2000**: 354, 356, 360–64; **2001**: 274–75; **2002**: 184, 287, 288–90, 293, 297–300; **2005**: 323; **2006**: 384–85; **2007**: 345–54; **2008**: 291–300
international cooperation and assistance, **2007**: 343–45
territorial, ship, and aircraft jurisdiction for crimes against, U.S., **2007**: 339–41
U.S. ratification of although not party to Convention, **2007**: 353–54, 358
preambular language, protection, **1989-90**: 172–73
rights of girl child, **2001**: 275; **2002**: 304; **2003**: 309
U.S. decision not to ratify, **2005**: 322–23
U.S. objections, **2002**: 290–93, 303; **2006**: 385–87
Rights of the Child, UN General Assembly resolution on, **2002**: 302–3; **2007**: 358–59; **2008**: 317–18
sanctions applicable to, **2004**: 25, 31, 906, 909
sexual abuse
child sex tourism, **2008**: 293
pornography, **2007**: 334, 338
prostitution, **2007**: 334, 337–38
sexual exploitation of, **2007**: 334–35
support of. *See* Maintenance obligations

Children (continued)
trafficking in. *See* Trafficking in persons
transfer of organs for profit, **2007**: 335–36
UN Special Session on Children, **2002**: 300–302; **2004**: 279–81
U.S. efforts to protect rights of, **1991-99**: 929–32
U.S. jurisdiction, child custody
Uniform Child Custody Jurisdiction Act (1988), **1991-99**: 372, 378
Uniform Child Custody Jurisdiction and Enforcement Act (1997), **1991-99**: 378
U.S. participation in treaties protecting, **2002**: 285–97
victims of war. *See* armed conflict and, *this heading*
Children's Health Insurance Program, 1991-99: 929
Chile
Alien Tort Statute and Torture Victims Protection Act claims, **2002**: 351–52; **2003**: 385
democracy in human rights, statement on role of, **2005**: 431
extradition and mutual legal assistance, **1991-99**: 391, 442–43; **2000**: 185*n*
fisheries negotiations with U.S., **2005**: 613
Free Trade Agreement, **2002**: 723; **2005**: 640, 757
Hague Child Abduction Convention, compliance with, **2006**: 101–2; **2008**: 50
intellectual property rights
Watch List, **2006**: 768, 769; **2007**: 608, 610; **2008**: 605
Inter-American Convention Against Corruption, party to, **2006**: 238
Inter-American Convention Against Terrorism (OAS Terrorism Convention), party to, **2005**: 111
military coup in, U.S. covert involvement allegations, **2005**: 416
murder of former Chilean ambassador in U.S. (Letelier case), ex gratia payment for and claims related to, **1989-90**: 97–98, 537–41; **1991-99**: 1072–73; **2005**: 523, 558–59
Open Skies agreements, **2001**: 565–66
Pinochet prosecution, **1991-99**: 518–19
restrictions on work performed by longshoremen from, **2002**: 757; **2003**: 764
trade agreement with U.S., **2003**: 679–82
transport of nuclear materials through territorial waters of, **2003**: 758–59
Treaty for the Peaceful Settlement of Disputes that May Occur Between U.S. and Chile (1914), **1989-90**: 537–41; **1991-99**: 1072–73
U.S.–Chile environmental cooperation agreement, **2003**: 811, 812–13
whaling regulation, **2001**: 218
WTO disputes. *See* World Trade Organization (WTO)

China, People's Republic of. *See also* Hong Kong; Taiwan
accession to WTO, **1991-99:** 1460; **2001:** 649, 651–53; **2004:** 602
act of state doctrine applicable to court judgment, **2005:** 576
antiterrorism actions, cooperation in, **2002:** 890
applicability to Taiwan of treaty, **1991-99:** 700–709
aviation agreement, **2004:** 566–67; **2007:** 532
bombing of Chinese Embassy in Belgrade, **2000:** 421–29
apology by U.S. for accidental bombing, **2000:** 425
appropriations law and, **2000:** 421, 423–24
compensation issues, **2000:** 428
ex gratia payment by U.S. for deaths and injuries, **2000:** 428–29
payment to China for, **2000:** 421–24
payment to U.S. for damage to property in China, **2000:** 424–25
collision and emergency landing of U.S. military aircraft, **2001:** 703–11
constructive engagement with, **2005:** 405
consular notification. *See* Consular notification and access
customs agreements, **2004:** 626
drug trade, **2001:** 120; **2002:** 124; **2003:** 181; **2004:** 133–34
drug transit and producer list, removal from, **2005:** 136
methamphetamines, **2007:** 164–66
embassy construction agreement, **2003:** 256–58
enforcement of arbitral awards in, **1991-99:** 1131–32
Executive Branch authority and, **2002:** 245; **2004:** 454
Falun Gong movement, repression of, **2002:** 469–76; **2003:** 394, 396, 397, 398–99, 558–69; **2004:** 380–82; **2006:** 662, 663, 664
fisheries, regulation of, **1991-99:** 1705–7, 1738; **2003:** 730–31; **2005:** 736–38, 740
force majeure visit by Chinese ship to Honolulu, **2007:** 650–53
foreign control of U.S. company, prohibition on, **1989-90:** 418–24
forum non conveniens issues, **2006:** 963–65
genocide, cooperation in opposing in Darfur, **2006:** 423, 1051
Hong Kong, role in treaties with
Agreement between U.S. and Hong Kong for the Surrender of Fugitive Offenders, **1991-99:** 403–5, 408, 412–13, 689–93; **2000:** 190–203
Agreement between U.S. and Hong Kong for the Transfer of Sentenced Persons, **1991-99:** 382–83
Hong Kong, transfer to of sovereignty over, **1991-99:** 382, 405, 413, 764, 773–75
continuation in force of treaties, **1991-99:** 764–67, 1175
Hong Kong, **2002:** 384–85; **2004:** 395

China, People's Republic of (continued)
human rights in, **1991-99**: 868–70; **2002**: 278, 282, 384–85; **2004**: 260–61, 270, 272, 363–64, 395, 405, 528
International Covenant on Civil and Political Rights applicable to, **1991-99**: 405
prison labor, **1991-99**: 1000–1003
religious freedom concerns. *See* religious freedom, *this heading*
status of U.S. consulate general, **1991-99**: 1176
terms, **1991-99**: 1175, 1177–78
U.S. policy, **1991-99**: 1179–80
U.S. trade policy and, **1991-99**: 1456–60
Human Rights Council membership, **2006**: 334
illegal logging and associated trade, MOU with U.S. on, **2007**: 734–35
immigration issues
asylum request by citizen of, based on family planning policy as persecution, **1991-99**: 202–7
deferred departure of nationals of, **1989-90**: 54–57
detainee cases and, **2004**: 998
dual nationals, agreement with U.S. addressing, **2001**: 34
relief from immigration requirements for certain Chinese students, **1991-99**: 248–49
totalitarian government and admissibility of aliens from, **1989-90**: 38–39
immunity. *See also* Service of process abroad
of Bank of China under FSIA, **2003**: 531–32
in collection of judgment, **2001**: 488–501
of corporation owned by, **2002**: 516–17
of head-of-state, **2002**: 547–52; **2004**: 527–31, 547–53
of mayor and other government officials for official acts, **2002**: 469–76
of official on special mission, **2006**: 662–81; **2008**: 490–91
intellectual property
agreements, **1991-99**: 1517–23
rights, **2007**: 606–10, **2008**: 604–6, 605–6, 605*n*
Watch List, **2006**: 768, **2007**: 607, 610; **2008**: 605*n*
Internet use, **2004**: 265
ITER International Fusion Energy Organization, **2006**: 893
Joint Communique of 1979, one China policy announced in, **2006**: 545–46
judicial assistance in criminal matter in, **2000**: 160–62
juvenile offenders, execution of, **2005**: 387
Kyoto regime, **2005**: 219
Macau, transfer to of sovereignty over, **1991-99**: 1180
Macau Special Administrative Region

China, People's Republic of (continued)
Financial Crimes Enforcement Network (FinCEN) action concerning money laundering activities of Banco Delta Asia, **2005**: 180–84
North Korean involvement, **2005**: 181–82
maritime boundaries, **1991-99**: 1578
maritime claims, **2004**: 686, 688; **2007**: 647–48
money laundering, **2004**: 135
most-favored-nation status, **1991-99**: 1456–60; **2006**: 755
North Korean refugees in, **2002**: 35–38; **2006**: 57
nonproliferation. *See* Nonproliferation, *subheading*: country-specific issues
nuclear weapons programs and policies. *See* Nonproliferation, *subheading*: country-specific issues
outer space
antisatellite weapons test, **2007**: 663–67
commercial launch service agreement, **1989-90**: 481
outer space, voluntary transparency and confidence-building measures concerning, **2008**: 672
population planning policies, **2002**: 309
religious freedom, **1991-99**: 925, 927; **2001**: 272; **2003**: 295, 296; **2004**: 270, 272, 363, 528; **2005**: 314, 316; **2006**: 377
Falun Gong. *See* Falun Gong movement, repression of, *this heading*
sanctions on, **1991-99**: 1456–60. *See also* Nonproliferation, *subheading*: country-specific issues; Nonproliferation, *subheading*: sanctions check
service of process
on government of, **2008**: 481–83
on Chinese diplomatic official while on special mission in U.S., **2006**: 672–81; **2008**: 490–91
on government official of, for alleged human rights abuses, **2001**: 549–53
on visiting foreign officials of, **2002**: 581–95
Taiwan and, **2007**: 435–36; **2008**: 444–47. *See also* Taiwan
passports and, **2006**: 545–46
PRC treaties not applicable to Taiwan, **1991-99**: 706–9
U.S.–Taiwan relations, **1991-99**: 662, 702–5; **2000**: 533–34, 600; **2001**: 237, 238–39
textiles
agreement on textiles and clothing (U.S.–China), **2005**: 640–45
safeguard provision, **2005**: 642–45
trade with U.S., product quality and food safety issues in, **2007**: 589–90

China, People's Republic of (continued)
Uighurs and, **2006**: 1184–85; **2007**: 893
U.S. consular district, **1991-99**: 1181
World War II war claims against Japan, **2002**: 444–46
"comfort women," **2003**: 522–23
Alien Tort Statute action brought against Japan, **2005**: 475–81
settlement of, **2000**: 532–40; **2001**: 450
WTO disputes. *See* World Trade Organization (WTO)
China, Republic of, 2007: 434–35
Chinese Student Protection Act (1992), 1991-99: 248–49
Choice of forum, 2005: 788, 834–39
Choice of Court Convention, **2005**: 213, 787–89, 791
Cigarettes
duty exemption for cigarettes from Canada and U.S. states' tobacco settlement, **2008**: 170–74
Master Settlement Agreement, **2006**: 690
NAFTA Chapter 11 disputes and, **2006**: 688–93; **2008**: 170–74, 351–57, 528–42
Citizenship, 2004: 15, 20. *See also* Nationality
alienage diversity status of corporate entities, **2001**: 227–35
applicant's awareness of possible claims to, **1989-90**: 7
authentication or notarization of documents related to, **2004**: 69–70
authority to determine, **1991-99**: 8–9; **2001**: 1–3, 7–8; **2007**: 179
Bureau of U.S. Citizenship and Immigration Services, **2004**: 8, 10, 361
Child Citizenship Act. *See* Child Citizenship Act (2000)
children. *See also* Children
adopted child, **2002**: 9
based on intercountry adoption, **2007**: 84–85, 87–88
child born abroad
requirements for retention of, **1989-90**: 6–9
of unwed U.S. citizen father, **2000**: 1–19, 47; **2001**: 7–8; **2005**: 261
of unwed U.S. citizen mother, **1991-99**: 1–9
of U.S. citizen parents, **2001**: 3–6; **2002**: 8
child conceived in vitro, **2002**: 10–11; **2006**: 2–3
proof of parentage, **1989-90**: 1–3; **1991-99**: 4–5, 128–31
surrogate parentage, **1989-90**: 13
U.S.-born child of foreign diplomat with U.S. citizen mother, **2005**: 1
U.S.-born child of foreign head of state or minister of, **2004**: 4–5; **2006**: 668*n*
constitutional definition, **2001**: 234–35
constitutional requirements, **2000**: 8–9; **2003**: 274; **2004**: 5, 218
of corporations, **1991-99**: 771–75; **2002**: 227–31

Citizenship (continued)
airline under control of U.S. citizens, **2006**: 685–86
in overseas territory, **2001**: 227–35
deference to congressional authority in, **2000**: 9–11, 17–18
derivative, **2008**: 11–15
detainees. *See* Detainees, military
documents, **2005**: 2
dual. *See* Nationality
eligibility for, **2005**: 26
espousal of claims and. *See* Nationality, *subheading*: continuous nationality requirement for claims
expatriation. *See* loss of, *this heading*
false claims of, **1991-99**: 89
health care abroad, **2004**: 49–52
held in Saudi Arabia, **2004**: 203–6
"immediate relatives" status, **1989-90**: 10, 11–12
indigenous people and, **2006**: 396
Israeli, extradition and, **2005**: 74–75
jus soli/jus sanguinis principles, **2000**: 5
loss of, **1989-90**: 4–6, 406; **1991-99**: 19–23; **2001**: 599; **2003**: 8–11. *See also* revocation, *this heading*
determination of intent to expatriate, **1989-90**: 4–6; **2003**: 8–11
elements of, **2008**: 2–4
expatriating acts
serving as Prime Minister of foreign country, **1991-99**: 19–21
serving in foreign army, **1991-99**: 21–23; **2003**: 8–11
jurisdiction of review of determinations relating to, **2008**: 4–6
renunciation, **1991-99**: 24–27, 90
outside U.S., **2007**: 7–8
within U.S., **2007**: 3–7
right of expatriation, **2001**: 2
NAFTA and
investor discrimination, **2005**: 595–96
standing to bring Chapter 11 claims, **2001**: 642–46
nationality and, **2001**: 2, 645; **2007**: 2–3
naturalization
denaturalization provisions, **2004**: 3
naturalization in second state, effect on primary citizenship, **1989-90**: 6
naturalization of Philippine veterans, **1989-90**: 12–13
Northern Mariana Islands, **2004**: 218
of persons born in, **2003**: 273–75
status of residents, **1989-90**: 9–12
oath of allegiance requirement

Citizenship (continued)
satisfaction by guardian or proxy, **1991-99**: 16–19
waiver of, **1991-99**: 13–16
for aliens with disability, **2003**: 4–5
passports, requirements for travel, **2005**: 3–5; **2006**: 5–8. *See also* Passports, U.S.
Philippine veterans of World War II, **1989-90**: 12–13
proof of U.S., **2005**: 3; **2006**: 5–8
Puerto Rican citizens, **2000**: 340–41, 344–45
removal to country of. *See* Removal of aliens from U.S.
revocation. *See also* loss of, *this heading*
for participation in Nazi persecution, **1991-99**: 27–34; **2002**: 5–8; **2003**: 5–11; **2004**: 1–4
right of, **2001**: 2
rights in expropriated property and, **2001**: 405–6, 599–600
statelessness, **2006**: 1–2
status of residents of U.S. possessions, **1991-99**: 9–13, 811
statutory authority, **2000**: 8–11, 17–18
U.S. air carriers, relevance to investment in, **2005**: 588–92
USG employment and
in continental U.S., **1991-99**: 34–41
dual nationality of U.S. consular and diplomatic employees, **2002**: 1–4
employment of foreign nationals by U.S. government, prohibitions on use of appropriated funds for, **1989-90**: 151–53
Civil Aeronautics Board (CAB), 2005: 589
Civil and Political Rights, International Covenant on. *See* International Covenant on Civil and Political Rights (ICCPR)
Civil Liberties Act (1988), 2004: 223–24, 231, 232
Civil procedure. *See* Authentication; Evidence; Hague Conventions; Jurisdiction
arbitration. *See* Arbitration
Choice of Court Convention. *See* Choice of forum
Civil rights, U.S. *See also* Constitution, U.S.; Discrimination
Attorneys Fees Awards Act, **2005**: 280
Education Department, U.S., Office for Civil Rights, **2005**: 262, 288
Homeland Security, Department of, Office for Civil Rights and Civil Liberties, **2005**: 260
Justice Department, U.S., Civil Rights Division, **2005**: 274–75, 288; **2006**: 418
Pregnancy Discrimination Act (PDA) of 1978, **2005**: 262
Civil Rights Act (1964), 1991-99: 891, 893, 901; **2001**: 250, 266; **2002**: 477; **2005**: 288; **2007**: 327
Title VI, **2008**: 278
Title VII, **2005**: 262, 263; **2008**: 277

Civil Rights Act (1983), 2001: 324, 326
Civil Rights Act (1991), 2002: 514–15
Civil Rights of Institutionalized Persons Act (CRIPA) (1980), 2000: 378–79; **2001:** 251; **2005:** 275, 276, 370; **2006:** 368–69, 412, 417
Civil service employees
definitional issues in sovereign immunity cases, **2000:** 581–87
Claims. *See specific countries and subjects of claims*
false. *See* False Claims Act (FCA)
Classified information
agreement with European Union on sharing of, **2007:** 128–29; **2008:** 80
Clayton Act (1914), 2003: 557–58
Clean Air Act (CAA) (1990), 1991-99: 1657, 1658, 1661, 1664; **2002:** 670; **2003:** 777; **2005:** 721, 725; **2006:** 866, 868, 869
amendments of 1990 (CAAA of 1990), **2005:** 720, 721
Clean Diamond Trade Act (2003), 2003: 704–9; **2004:** 216, 653–54, 935; **2006:** 1060
Clean Water Act (1982), 2001: 618; **2003:** 749
Climate change, 2001: 730–38; **2002:** 777–82; **2003:** 773–75; **2004:** 743–44; **2005:** 727–30; **2008:** 673–91. *See also* Air pollution; Environmental issues; Kyoto Protocol
Bali conference (2007), **2007:** 678–85; **2008:** 673, 674
human rights and, **2008:** 326–32
Kyoto Protocol, U.S. proposal for framework changes post-2012, **2007:** 673–78
major economies meeting, **2007:** 673–78; **2008:** 676–78
UN Framework Convention on, **1991-99:** 1671–73, 1674, 1680; **2000:** 711–25; **2002:** 781–82; **2003:** 773–75; **2004:** 743; **2006:** 853–55; **2007:** 578, 674–75, 678–85, 694, 696–97; **2008:** 678–84
determining whether issues fall under Framework Convention or Kyoto Protocol, **2005:** 728
Cloning, 2002: 807–9; **2003:** 817–18; **2004:** 787–89
prohibition of human cloning (UN General Assembly Resolution A/RES/59/280), U.S. approval, **2005:** 771–72
CNIES (Cooperating Nation Information Exchange), 2005: 145–46
Coalition Provisional Authority (CPA). *See* Iraq
Coastal Zone Management Act (1972), 1991-99: 1769
Code of Crimes Against the Peace and Security of Mankind, Draft, 1991-99: 576–79
COE. *See* Council of Europe

Coffee
International Coffee Agreement, **2004**: 412–14; **2005**: 467–68; **2007**: 585
International Coffee Organization, **2005**: 467–68; **2006**: 493–94; **2007**: 412, 585–87
Colombia
Air Transport Agreement (2007), **2007**: 532
Alien Tort Statute (ATS) issues, **2005**: 418–24, 819–22; **2006**: 450–55, 476–78
Andean Trade Promotion and Drug Eradication Act (2002), **2008**: 577–79
bombing in Santo Domingo, **2005**: 418
child soldiers, **2003**: 308; **2004**: 281, 282
comity as basis for dismissal of suit in U.S. court, **2006**: 945–46
cultural property protection agreement, **2006**: 897–99
designation of foreign drug traffickers, **2001**: 143
drug trade, **2001**: 120; **2002**: 124; **2003**: 181; **2004**: 133–34, 379; **2005**: 135–36, 145; **2006**: 213; **2007**: 163; **2008**: 113
interdiction assistance, **1991-99**: 538–44, 547–50; **2003**: 187–88; **2006**: 225–26; **2007**: 166–67
maritime counter-drug trade agreement, **1991-99**: 1606
U.S. assistance to fight narcotrafficking, **2001**: 89, 123
extradition and mutual legal assistance, **1991-99**: 392; **2000**: 179, 183–84, 186*n*; **2001**: 90–96
under domestic law, **2003**: 140, 143
foreign affairs implications of lawsuit, **2004**: 376–80; **2006**: 450–55
forum non conveniens issues, **2005**: 840–41
free trade agreement, **2004**: 618; **2006**: 764–65; **2007**: 585
Hague Child Abduction Convention, compliance with, **2003**: 127, 129; **2004**: 54; **2006**: 102
human rights, **2003**: 284; **2004**: 251–54, 376, 378–79
indigenous peoples, views concerning UN declaration on, **2008**: 354
intellectual property rights Watch List, **2006**: 768; **2007**: 610
Inter-American Convention Against Corruption, party to, **2006**: 238
money laundering, **2004**: 135
Panama Canal Treaty and, **2000**: 312–17
political question doctrine, **2006**: 450–55, 945–46
satellite regulation and, **2003**: 430; **2004**: 637, 638; **2008**: 392
trade negotiations with U.S., **2003**: 682–83
treaty issues, **1991-99**: 744
Tropical Forest Conservation Act agreement, **2008**: 722
Colorado
agreement on accreditation of adoption agencies for intercountry adoptions, **2006**: 92–95
Combat Methamphetamine Enforcement Act (CMEA), **2007**: 162, 164

Comfort women. *See* Japan
Comité Maritime Internationale, 2001: 788; **2002**: 831
Comity, 1991-99: 321, 1865; **2001**: 41, 43–47, 459, 512–13, 518, 523, 526; **2002**: 517; **2008**: 69, 343. *See also* Reciprocity
access to U.S. courts and, **1991-99**: 1237
Alien Tort Statute (ATS), application of, **2003**: 384; **2005**: 819–22, 825–26; **2006**: 450, 946–50; **2008**: 227–36, 241–42
anti-suit injunctions, **2002**: 864–73; **2004**: 842–50; **2005**: 829–32; **2007**: 776–80, 783–84, 787–88, 790–91; **2008**: 763–64, 766, 772–73
antitrust agreement, **2004**: 662–63
choice of court agreements between commercial parties, **2005**: 788
claims against foreign governments and officials, **2005**: 526, 564, 582–83; **2007**: 227; **2008**: 478
definition, **2004**: 843; **2008**: 242
discovery and, **2004**: 854, 860–61
enforcement of judgments and, **1991-99**: 1268, 1829–30, 1836–37; **2005**: 838; **2008**: 175
European Communities–U.S. agreement, **1991-99**: 1543–45
exhaustion of remedies and, **2008**: 241, 243
in extradition cases, **1989-90**: 81, 95; **2005**: 80
extraterritoriality and, **2005**: 791
jurisdiction in antitrust case, **1991-99**: 1529, 1530, 1532–33, 1537–39, 1551
foreign court criminal conviction and, **2007**: 967
foreign-flagged ships and, **2008**: 134
forum non conveniens and, **1991-99**: 1831
head-of-state immunity and, **2004**: 529
Holocaust-era victim claims, **2005**: 474, 483; **2006**: 518, 520–21
immunities and, **1991-99**: 1236, 1261, 1268, 1270, 1272, 1277, 1284
immunity of foreign officials from depositions, **1989-90**: 322
in international pollution case, **2007**: 687–91
Japan's Special Measures Law, **2008**: 764–71
judicial abstention on basis of, **2002**: 859–64; **2004**: 432–39; **2005**: 815–29; **2006**: 944–53; **2007**: 229, 772–76; **2008**: 782–89
judicial assistance, **1991-99**: 453
presidential determination requiring states to give effect to ICJ decisions on basis of, **2005**: 30, 32–48; **2007**: 74–75
private international law, **2004**: 825–26
sovereign immunity and, **2004**: 463–64, 467–68, 545, 547; **2008**: 477, 479
treatment of foreign diplomats and representatives, **1989-90**: 30
violation of domestic law not affected by doctrine of, **2001**: 139–43

Commercial law. *See also* Carriage of goods by sea; Contracts; Electronic commerce; Private international law; UNCITRAL (UN Commission on International Trade Law)
arbitration, commercial, **2005**: 807–8. *See also* Arbitration
Choice of Court Convention, **2005**: 787–89
Contracts for the International Sale of Goods, Convention on, **1991-99**: 1817, 1824; **2002**: 824; **2003**: 838–39; **2004**: 805, 823
Cross-Border Insolvency Procedure, UNCITRAL Model Law on, **2005**: 808–9
development policies and, **2006**: 928–31
Direct Guarantees and Standby Letters of Credit, Convention on (UN), **1991-99**: 1812–14
electronic commerce, **2006**: 936–38
extraterritoriality and conflicts of jurisdiction, **2005**: 789–91
Limitation Period in the International Sale of Goods, Convention on (UN), **1991-99**: 1817–20
Limitations, Sales of Goods, Negotiable Instruments, and Guarantees, Conventions on, **2002**: 836
Mediation Act, Uniform (UMA), **2005**: 805–7
private international commercial law, Brussels and Lugano conventions on, **1991-99**: 1827–28, 1829–30, 1831; **2000**: 737, 738, 740
procurement, UN Commission on International Trade Law (UNCITRAL) model laws relating to, **2005**: 808
secured transactions, **2006**: 929–30
securities held through intermediaries, **2006**: 936
Uniform Commercial Code (UCC), Article 8, **2005**: 808
Commercial Space Act (1998), **1991-99**: 1647–48
Committee on Foreign Investment in U.S. (CFIUS), **2006**: 774–80; **2007**: 601–5; **2008**: 593–600
Common law. *See also* Customary international law
admiralty, **2003**: 367–68, 757–58; **2006**: 831–32
Alien Tort Statute cases. *See* Alien Tort Statute (ATS)
countries, **2004**: 60, 823
definition of persecution, **2002**: 26
forum non conveniens, **2004**: 876; **2007**: 797
habeas corpus, **2007**: 889, 940, 955–56; **2008**: 893, 894
immunity under, **2004**: 461–62, 508, 513*n*
of foreign officials, **2006**: 630–43; **2007**: 446, 504, 506*n*
FSIA. *See* Foreign Sovereign Immunities Act (FSIA) (1976)
head-of-state immunity. *See* Head-of-state immunity
special mission, **2007**: 447–48
mens rea, **2004**: 327

Common law (continued)
private international law, **2004:** 824
revenue rule, **2003:** 855–56
right to fish in exclusive economic zone and, **2004:** 729–30
state secrets privilege, **2007:** 241, 247, 253
trademark protection, **2004:** 666
Commonwealth of Independent States, 1991-99: 742, 1170–71, 1173–74
Communications law. *See* Telecommunications
Community of Democracies, 2002: 382–84
Compact Clause, 2001: 180–93, 198; **2005:** 207. *See also* Constitution, U.S.; Treaties, generally
Compact of Free Association, 1989-90: 268–71
between U.S. and Federated States of Micronesia (1986), **2003:** 271–73
between U.S. and Marshall Islands (1986), **2003:** 271–73; **2007:** 256–64; **2008:** 246–47
between U.S. and Palau, **1991-99:** 815, 816–25
Compact of Free Association Amendments Act (2003), 2003: 272–73
Compact of Free Association Approval Act (1989), 1991-99: 820
Competency
alien guardian for helpless alien, **1991-99:** 88
Mexico–U.S. prisoner transfer agreement, **2003:** 131–33
passport issuance and, **2002:** 17–18
punishment of mentally retarded persons, **1991-99:** 256
waiver of oath of allegiance for aliens with disability, **1991-99:** 15–19; **2003:** 4–5
Comprehensive Environmental Response, Compensation and Liability Act (CERCLA) (1980), 1991-99: 1620; **2006:** 855–60
Comprehensive Test Ban Treaty, 1991-99: 2271–79, 2280–81, 2295, 2297
Conference on Disarmament, 2003: 1070–72; **2008:** 940
Conference on Prohibition of Chemical Weapons, 1989-90: 576–78
Confiscation. *See also* Expropriation; Seizure of assets
claims against Albania, **1991-99:** 1077
by Cuba, **2004:** 31, 431
denial of U.S. claims related to, **1991-99:** 94–102, 103–9, 1445
by Iraq, **1991-99:** 2076–77
by Nazi Germany, **1991-99:** 1057, 1064; **2004:** 448, 474
Peru–U.S. agreement on sharing of forfeited assets, **2004:** 140–41
seizing or freezing assets vs., **2004:** 526
Conflict resolution. *See also* Peacekeeping missions
African Great Lakes region, **2004:** 942–43; **2007:** 861–63
agreement on prevention of accidental conflict, **1989-90:** 549–51

Conflict resolution (continued)
in Angola, **1991-99**: 145
in the Balkans. *See* Balkans, peace process in
in Belarus, **2007**: 864
in Burma, **2007**: 840–44
in Burundi, **2003**: 951–52
Cambodian conflict, **1989-90**: 527–37
in Chechnya, **2003**: 953–54
in Congo, Democratic Republic of, **1991-99**: 2012–15; **2003**: 954–55; **2006**: 996–98, 1001; **2007**: 860–63
in Cote d'Ivoire, **2005**: 933–34
Darfur and Comprehensive Peace Agreement (CPA), **2007**: 860, **2008**: 835–36
international courts and tribunals and, **2007**: 834–36
Ethiopia–Eritrea, **1991-99**: 2010–12; **2002**: 925–26; **2004**: 942; **2006**: 1055–58
in former Yugoslavia, **1991-99**: 588–89, 1979–82, 2024–43, 2139, 2168–70; **2004**: 967; **2005**: 934–40. *See also* Yugoslavia, Socialist Federation Republic of
in Georgia, **2008**: 865–68
in Haiti, **2002**: 926–31; **2003**: 942–43; **2004**: 937–42
institutional mechanisms for, **2002**: 902–3
International Atomic Energy Agency role in, **2007**: 837–39
International Court of Justice and, **2007**: 835–36
international law, role of, **2002**: 901–10
Israeli-Palestinian conflict. *See* Middle East Conflict, Israeli-Palestinian
in Lebanon, **2005**: 932–33. *See also* Lebanon
UN Special Tribunal related to murder of Lebanese Prime Minister, **2007**: 835; **2008**: 141–42
Liberian civil war, **1991-99**: 2018
Lusaka Peace Accords, **1991-99**: 145, 1142
Macedonia Framework Agreement, **2001**: 825–28
mechanisms for, **2007**: 836–40
Middle East. *See* Middle East Conflict, Israeli-Palestinian
Mozambique civil war, **1991-99**: 2010
Nagorno-Karabakh conflict, **2008**: 830–32
NATO role, **1991-99**: 1031–32, 1033–34
North Korea nuclear program, **2007**: 839–40
Organization of American States, role of, **2003**: 937–38
Peru–Ecuador border dispute, **1991-99**: 2004–10
reconstruction and stabilization assistance for troubled areas, **2005**: 947–48. *See also* Development
in Sierra Leone, **1991-99**: 2015–18

Conflict resolution (continued)
in Somalia, **2007**: 863–64; **2008**: 832–33
Special envoy for Gaza disengagement, **2005**: 907
in Sudan. *See* Darfur; Sudan
U.S. approach to, **2007**: 834–45
U.S.–Adriatic Charter, **2003**: 939
U.S.–Chile dispute over murder in U.S. (Letelier case), **1989-90**: 537–41; **1991-99**: 1072–73
in Western Sahara, **2003**: 958; **2006**: 1064–65; **2008**: 850–52
Congo, Democratic Republic of
arms embargo, **2004**: 175, 1069–70; **2007**: 1006
child soldiers in, **2003**: 308; **2004**: 281–82; **2006**: 387
conflict resolution efforts, **1991-99**: 2012–15; **2000**: 248; **2004**: 131; **2006**: 996–98
regional peace agreement, **2004**: 942–43
democracy promotion programs, **1991-99**: 1011
human rights in, **2002**: 320; **2003**: 336–37
immunity issues
diplomatic properties, attachment of, **2006**: 621–29, 658–62
International Criminal Tribunal for Rwanda (ICTR), obligations to, **2002**: 140–41; **2005**: 193
juvenile offenders, execution of, **2005**: 387
Rome Statute ratification and, **2002**: 320
sanctions on, **2006**: 996–98
sanctions on individuals who have supplied arms contributing to conflict in, **2007**: 823
transitional government in, **2003**: 954–55
UN personal conduct unit in, **2005**: 946
waiver of American Servicemembers' Protection Act, **2003**: 238
war crimes in, **2002**: 139–42; **2004**: 131
Congo, Republic of
Article 98 agreement (nonsurrender of Americans to ICC), **2004**: 187
bilateral investment agreement with, **1991-99**: 1466
contempt sanctions, contrary to FSIA, **2006**: 603–11
diplomatic immunity and commercial activity, **2007**: 490–504
extradition and mutual legal assistance, **2000**: 185*n*
no waiver of immunity under FSIA, **2006**: 562–64
Conscription
of dual citizens, **2003**: 10–11
resistance to, as "political opinion" for asylum claim, **1991-99**: 194–97
loss of citizenship and, **1991-99**: 22–23
Conservation issues. *See* Environmental issues

Constitution, U.S., **2004**: 24, 78, 298, 301, 303, 824, 912, 914, 920, 991, 1133. *See also* Due process; Equal protection; President, U.S.
Articles:
I, **1991-99**: 7, 12, 14, 55–56, 332, 647, 650, 652, 659, 810, 811, 827, 893, 2166; **2000**: 9, 293–94, 295–96, 342–43, 759; **2001**: 138, 180, 202, 203–4, 210, 269; **2002**: 987–88, 994; **2004**: 980; **2005**: 143*n*, 207; **2006**: 523, 734, 1141, 1142; **2007**: 176, 177, 204, 237, 312, 663*n*; **2008**: 126, 207, 444, 472, 891*n*, 910
II, **1989-90**: 212–13, 244–45, 246, 258, 260, 370–71; **1991-99**: 46, 47, 599–600, 640, 641, 645, 652, 661, 666, 711, 729, 756, 794, 795, 805, 814, 967, 1136, 2191; **2000**: 147, 173, 293, 345, 491*n*; **2001**: 200–211; **2002**: 175, 202, 589–90, 958, 988, 994, 995–96; **2003**: 497–98, 541; **2004**: 538, 1003, 1020; **2005**: 40, 42, 44, 231, 243, 421; **2006**: 66, 522, 661, 664, 665, 668, 674, 677, 678–79, 732, 869, 1141; **2007**: 176, 202, 241, 440; **2008**: 127, 180–81*n*, 444, 7779*n*
III, **1989-90**: 29–30; **1991-99**: 422–26, 1141–42, 1251; **2000**: 192, 316, 762, 763, 765; **2001**: 75–76, 207, 228, 230, 236, 284, 391; **2002**: 198, 228, 229, 341, 988, 993; **2003**: 367; **2004**: 208, 453, 1006; **2005**: 249; **2006**: 71, 83, 456, 523, 532, 729–30, 1141, 1204, 1206; **2007**: 22, 220, 559, 974; **2008**: 464, 472, 916
IV, **1991-99**: 650, 808, 814, 828, 829, 839, 1615; **2000**: 342–43; **2005**: 243, 244; **2008**: 895
V, **2005**: 244
VI, **1989-90**: 384; **1991-99**: 266, 653, 667, 677, 729, 783, 841, 895, 969, 972; **2000**: 294–95, 386, 528; **2001**: 540; **2004**: 444, 1024–25; **2005**: 40, 48, 1007; **2007**: 203
VII, **2007**: 386
anti-discrimination protections. *See* Equal protection
antiterrorism statutes, challenges to as unconstitutional
designation of terrorists and terrorist organizations, **2002**: 93–94, 98–101; **2003**: 176–77, 179–80; **2004**: 126–28; **2006**: 180, 183–99
asset freezing procedures, **2001**: 109–17; **2002**: 94–101
criminal penalty for support of designated entities, **2002**: 93–94; **2003**: 177–79; **2004**: 125–26; **2005**: 124–28; **2006**: 180–82; **2007**: 143–50
exception to FSIA, **1991-99**: 1234–52; **2008**: 471–75
applicability to U.S. constituent entities, **1991-99**: 808–11; **2000**: 345–46

Constitution, U.S. (continued)
Appointments Clause, **2007:** 709
authority for continuing U.S. combat operations in Iraq, **2008:** 857–59
Bill of Attainder Clause, **1991-99:** 1234, 1236, 1238, 1241–42
capital punishment and, **2003:** 341, 342; **2004:** 335–36; **2005:** 287, 289; **2006:** 354, 365
citizenship, acquisition or loss of and, **1991-99:** 7, 8, 11–13, 14; **2000:** 8–9; **2004:** 5, 218
Citizenship Clause of Fourteenth Amendment, **1991-99:** 11–12; **2004:** 125–28
Commerce Clause, **1991-99:** 647, 648, 650–51, 657, 785, 811; **2000:** 319–20, 321–33, 465, 466, 468–69; **2001:** 203–4; **2002:** 56–58, 416, 420, 421–22, 429, 453–54, 455; **2007:** 312
Compact Clause, **2001:** 180–93, 198; **2005:** 207
Confrontation Clause, **2004:** 1027–28; **2005:** 281
on controlled substances, use for religious purposes, **2001:** 129
Convention on Elimination of All Forms of Discrimination Against Women and, **1989-90:** 169
Convention on Elimination of All Forms of Racial Discrimination and, **1991-99:** 885, 886–87, 891–94
cruel and unusual punishment, **2003:** 324, 341; **2006:** 347, 354, 355, 406, 409–12, 419, 1129, 1134, 1173; **2007:** 175–76, 216, 376, 386; **2008:** 358–60
detained or arrested persons, rights of, **1991-99:** 331–32; **2007:** 939–43, 944–48, 971, 973. *See also* Human rights
detention of aliens and, **2001:** 17–19; **2003:** 31. *See also* Detainees, military; Detention of aliens, nonmilitary
diplomatic immunity practices and, **2000:** 613–15; **2002:** 561–65
due process. *See* Due process
Eighth Amendment, **1989-90:** 179, 182, 187; **2000:** 373; **2003:** 324, 341–42; **2004:** 336, 980; **2005:** 270, 276, 277, 289, 360, 366, 381, 382, 385, 386, 995; **2006:** 354; **2007:** 304, 922; **2008:** 914–15
Eleventh Amendment, **1991-99:** 255, 256, 260, 292, 316–17
Equal Protection Clause. *See* Equal Protection
Establishment Clause, **2007:** 325
ex post facto doctrine, **1991-99:** 1234, 1242–48
on exclusion of evidence, **2003:** 75–76; **2006:** 67
Export Clause, **1991-99:** 659
extradition and, **1991-99:** 417–28; **2000:** 208–9, 210–12; **2004:** 75, 78; **2007:** 105

Constitution, U.S. (continued)
extraterritorial application, **1989-90**: 100–107; **1991-99**: 188–94; **2002**: 135, 136; **2006**: 1177–82, 1199, 1212–13; **2008**: 892, 894, 897
Fifteenth Amendment, **2005**: 247
Fifth Amendment, **1989-90**: 16, 17, 102, 103–4, 179, 182, 187; **1991-99**: 1, 52–53, 54, 56, 114, 117–18, 188, 193–94, 251, 331–32, 571–76, 659, 810, 1098, 1207, 2261; **2000**: 1, 373; **2001**: 17–18, 257–59, 260, 261, 283; **2002**: 14, 15, 58–59, 98, 101, 243, 460–61, 986–87; **2003**: 175, 258, 262, 324, 506; **2004**: 125–26, 206, 223, 724, 728, 980, 1006, 1007, 1019; **2005**: 125, 128, 129–30, 260, 276, 277, 282, 289, 360, 366, 995, 999, 1031; **2006**: 67–68, 183, 317, 352, 484, 712, 1006, 1008–15; **2007**: 239, 295, 363, 830, 922, 938; **2008**: 157, 277, 281, 810, 812, 897, 914–15
First Amendment, **1989-90**: 25; **1991-99**: 54, 58, 131, 189, 193–94, 891–92, 906, 924, 1309; **2001**: 129, 136, 248–49, 265, 283, 285–90; **2002**: 14, 98, 292, 869, 870–71; **2003**: 175; **2004**: 75, 125–28, 266, 881–82; **2005**: 122–23, 128, 278, 314, 989; **2006**: 19, 23, 25–26, 79, 117, 183, 184, 189–90, 191, 198, 201, 204, 284, 350, 714; **2007**: 20–24, 147–49, 152, 154, 254–56, 302–3, 310, 325–26, 329, 330–32, 537–38; **2008**: 810, 812
foreign affairs authority, **1989-90**: 158–60; **1991-99**: 41–42, 45–47, 671–73, 725–29, 753–54, 805–6, 1136–38; **2001**: 82–84, 196, 197, 203, 339–40*n*, 414*n*, 452–53, 513, 518, 520, 525, 865, 871; **2002**: 416–17, 447–52, 453, 525; **2003**: 269–71, 364–66, 469–70, 488–98, 541; **2004**: 452, 454, 511–12; **2005**: 30, 41*n*, 42, 64, 207, 231*n*, 246, 417, 476, 480, 532, 607; **2006**: 457, 540, 664, 668, 674, 678; **2007**: 201–6, 236–37, 262–63, 817; **2008**: 39, 89, 183–84, 188–89, 191, 192, 207, 408, 444–45, 452–54, 467–68, 778, 792, 801, 858. *See also* Foreign affairs; President, U.S.; Treaties, generally
Fourteenth Amendment, **1989-90**: 179, 182, 187; **1991-99**: 7, 11–13, 331, 332, 336, 788, 810, 871, 893, 1610–11; **2000**: 5, 8, 9; **2001**: 257, 262; **2002**: 416, 420, 421–25, 986–87; **2003**: 274, 324; **2004**: 5, 218, 980, 1006; **2005**: 260, 270, 278, 281, 284, 289, 360, 366, 382, 995, 1031; **2006**: 115, 668*n*, 712; **2007**: 295, 303, 304, 307, 311–13, 325, 329; **2008**: 277

Constitution, U.S. (continued)
Fourth Amendment, **1989-90**: 100, 101–2, 103, 104, 105–7; **1991-99**: 13, 194, 810, 2349–50; **2000**: 373; **2001**: 114, 414*n*; **2002**: 98, 99, 101; **2003**: 180; **2004**: 352; **2005**: 128, 129, 276, 277; **2006**: 120–21, 364, 365; **2008**: 54–55
Free Exercise Clause, **2007**: 325
Full Faith and Credit Clause, **2000**: 736
human rights and. *See* Human rights
Law of Nations Clause, **2004**: 367–68; **2007**: 177–78
NAFTA compliance with, **2005**: 605; **2006**: 726–37
Necessary and Proper Clause, **2007**: 175–76; **2008**: 127
Nineteenth Amendment, **2005**: 247
Ninth Amendment, **2001**: 12–13
on nonjusticiable political issues, **2003**: 492–93; **2004**: 208–9, 210, 453; **2007**: 122, 202, 215, 220, 222–23, 234, 242, 262–63, 391, 439–40, 487, 525, 709, 805, 952; **2008**: 447, 448, 453
nonresident aliens, **2005**: 1013; **2006**: 27, 1181
obscenity laws, **2003**: 199
Offense Clause, **2008**: 126
paramount rights doctrine, **2002**: 246–59
passport issuance and, **2007**: 19
power of Congress under, **2005**: 123, 221, 246. *See also* Article I, *this heading*
presidential authority to decline to execute unconstitutional statutes, **1991-99**: 802–8
prisoners, treatment of, **2005**: 275–76, 292–93, 359–60, 382, 963, 971, 996, 1030, 1038. *See also* Detainees, military; Human rights
on private right to force disclosure of intelligence information, **2002**: 231–36
procedural default rules, **2004**: 46
Property Clause, **1991-99**: 650; **2004**: 722
Second Amendment, **2005**: 290
Sixth Amendment, **1989-90**: 102, 104; **1991-99**: 332; **2000**: 383; **2004**: 980, 1028; **2005**: 281, 995; **2008**: 45, 46, 897
submerged lands. *See* Submerged lands
Supremacy Clause, **1991-99**: 159–60, 256, 602, 652–53, 655, 661, 667, 677, 785–86, 969, 972; **2000**: 294–95, 319–20, 333, 386, 528–29, 537, 597; **2001**: 193–96, 198, 540; **2002**: 198, 246, 253–54, 1003–4; **2004**: 544–45

Constitution, U.S. (continued)
Suspension Clause, **2006**: 1177, 1180–82; **2007**: 939–40, **2008**: 891, 893, 898, 899–901, 913–14
Takings Clause, **2008**: 247
Tenth Amendment, **1991-99**: 678*n*, 828; **2000**: 386; **2002**: 191; **2007**: 205
Territory Clause, **1991-99**: 808–10, 814, 828
Thirteenth Amendment, **1991-99**: 12, 893; **2002**: 553; **2003**: 735; **2004**: 156; **2005**: 155; **2007**: 337
on travel restrictions, **1991-99**: 55–58; **2001**: 11–13; **2002**: 13–15
treaties, **2000**: 38–39, 201–2; **2006**: 66, 71, 125; **2007**: 105, 176, 202, 209–12, 215, 218, 291, 295, 302, 310. *See also* Treaties, generally
reservations to, **1991-99**: 967–68
termination of, **2002**: 198, 199–200, 201–2
Treaty Clause, **1991-99**: 645–52, 705; **2001**: 200–211, 563
U.S. reservations required by, **2007**: 210–11, 387
Twenty-fourth Amendment, **2005**: 247, 260, 381
Twenty-sixth Amendment, **2005**: 247
Twenty-third Amendment, **2001**: 267; **2005**: 247
Uniformity Clause, **1991-99**: 810–11, 827
unreasonable searches prohibited under, **2005**: 294
U.S. reservations to Genocide Convention and, **1989-90**: 144
war powers, **1991-99**: 2157–62, 2166–68; **2000**: 760; **2002**: 987–89; **2004**: 209–14, 1009; **2005**: 995, 1010, 1012; **2006**: 523; **2007**: 974–75; **2008**: 902
Consular functions, **2006**: 88–89. *See also* Consular notification and access; Consular offices and personnel; Consular Relations, Vienna Convention on (VCCR); Diplomatic missions and personnel
access to citizen detainees, **1991-99**: 268–69
assistance for children, **2002**: 59–60
assistance in aviation disaster response, **1989-90**: 64–66; **1991-99**: 347–48
assistance to imprisoned nationals, **2001**: 36–38
assistance to prisoners, **2004**: 51–52
assistance to victims of crime, **2001**: 38–40
authentication or legalization of documents related to citizenship or sovereignty, **2004**: 66–70
availability of services in Iraq, **2003**: 106–7
civil service employees performing, **1991-99**: 348–49
death and estate of U.S. citizens and foreign nationals abroad, **2006**: 88

Consular functions (continued)
death of foreign national, **2001**: 36
deaths and estates and, **2007**: 81–82
disaster assistance, **1989-90**: 64–66
disposition of unidentified remains, **1991-99**: 347–48
estates of U.S. citizens who die abroad, **1991-99**: 345–47
guardianship for mentally incompetent citizens, **2004**: 51
immunity for, **1989-90**: 348–50; **2006**: 308–11
international adoption, **1989-90**: 66–72; **2006**: 98; **2007**: 89–90
judicial assistance in Ireland, **2007**: 98–99
loans, **2004**: 51
medical care for American citizens living abroad, **2004**: 49–52
nonreviewability of visa decisions, **1989-90**: 22–23, 25; **1991-99**: 68–71, 116; **2006**: 23–25
notarial service for parental consent to adoption, **2003**: 118–22
notification of detention. *See* Consular notification and access
protection of citizen children abroad, **2000**: 117–19
protection of foreign minors, **2001**: 36
protection of foreign nationals lacking full capacity, **2001**: 36
provision of information on crimes abroad to victims and families of victims, **1991-99**: 343–45
review of employment contracts of domestic servants of diplomatic personnel, **1989-90**: 389–90
role of consular agents and agencies, **1989-90**: 63–64
scope of, **1989-90**: 348–50
State Department travel advisory system, **1991-99**: 340–43
taking of depositions in Korea, **2000**: 153–60
temporary emergency refuge for U.S. citizens, **2003**: 104–6
travel risk warnings, **1989-90**: 64–65
treaty obligations of successor states, **1991-99**: 746
Consular notification and access
in absence of consular or diplomatic relations, **2003**: 103–4
bilateral agreements not necessary, **2006**: 88–89
diplomatic communications regarding, **1991-99**: 272–89
dual nationals, **2001**: 1–3, 33–34
failure to afford (VCCR Article 36(1)(b)) by U.S. authorities, issues concerning
Albanian nationals, **1991-99**: 260
Cameroon nationals, **1991-99**: 257–58
Canadian nationals, **1991-99**: 255, 272–80
Chinese nationals on high sea and in U.S., **2000**: 23–42
Cuban national, **1991-99**: 263
Dominican nationals, **1991-99**: 259, 280–82; **2008**: 36–42
Egyptian nationals, **1991-99**: 261, 307

Consular notification and access (continued)
El Salvador nationals, **1991-99**: 263–64
German nationals, **1991-99**: 258; **2000**: 43–93; **2001**: 21–24; **2005**: 270
Guatemalan national, **1991-99**: 258–59
Guyanese national, **1991-99**: 262
human rights and, **1991-99**: 281, 289–91, 320–40; **2000**: 35, 74–80; **2002**: 48–52; **2003**: 66–70, 74–76; **2004**: 43
due process rights and, **1991-99**: 285, 287, 320, 339–40; **2000**: 78–80; **2002**: 50; **2003**: 45, 66–70, 81–82; **2004**: 43
ICJ cases concerning, **1991-99**: 257, 258, 291–320, 322–23; **2000**: 26–27, 32–33, 35, 41–42; **2005**: 270; **2006**: 70–74, 1026. *See also* U.S. litigation concerning, *this heading*
Avena *(Mexico v. U.S.)*, **2001**: 21; **2003**: 43–103; **2004**: 37–43; **2005**: 29–30; **2007**: 73–77; **2008**: 35, 153, 175–215
Avena, Request for Interpretation *(Mexico v. U.S.)*, 193–215
Breard *(Paraguay v. U.S.)*, **1991-99**: 291–313
LaGrand *(Germany v. U.S.)*, **1991-99**: 320; **2000**: 43–93; **2001**: 21–24
Presidential Determination pursuant to *Avena*, **2005**: 30, 32–48; **2006**: 87, 1026
Secretary of State action in response to provisional measures order in *Breard*, **1991-99**: 313–14
Indian national, **2005**: 60–64
Inter-American Commission and Court of Human Rights, **1991-99**: 281, 289–91, 320–40; **2002**: 48–52
Inter-American Court of Human Rights, **1991-99**: 320–40; **2000**: 26–27, 32, 35, 41, 42
Mexican nationals, **1991-99**: 255–56, 259–64, 282–91, 320–40; **2000**: 24–25, 32n; **2001**: 24–31; **2002**: 39–52; **2003**: 42–103; **2004**: 37–49; **2005**: 29–30, 32–60, 270; **2006**: 86–88, 1023; **2008**: 175–215
U.S.–Mexico Memorandum of Understanding, **1991-99**: 269–72
Nigerian national, **1991-99**: 258; **2008**: 44–47
Pakistani national, **1991-99**: 263
Paraguayan nationals, **1991-99**: 257, 291–320, 323; **2000**: 26–27, 32n, 35, 41–42; **2003**: 41; **2005**: 270
international practice, **1991-99**: 296–98, 308; **2000**: 39–41, 57–58; **2003**: 56–60
law enforcement and, **2006**: 75–86
object and purpose, **2003**: 48–52, 89–90
remedies for, **2000**: 58, 65; **2006**: 63–75

Consular notification and access (continued)
clemency, consideration of based on, **1991-99**: 317–20; **2001**: 24–31; **2002**: 39–48; **2003**: 83–88; **2005**: 59–60
suppression of evidence obtained prior to, **2006**: 63–75
State Department communications and guidance to state and local authorities, **1991-99**: 264–69, 303, 313–14; **2001**: 24–27; **2002**: 39–48, 51; **2003**: 39–42; **2004**: 41
State Department guidance to posts for treatment of American nationals abroad, **2001**: 31–36
dual nationality and, **2001**: 33–35
timeliness of, **1991-99**: 263, 324–26, 339; **2000**: 23–42; **2003**: 46, 50–61, 78; **2004**: 41–42
U.S. citizen in North Korea, DPRK disputes nationality, **2001**: 1–3
U.S. litigation concerning
criminal cases, **1991-99**: 254–64, 291–92, 313–17; **2000**: 23–42, 57–58; **2003**: 82–83; **2004**: 43–49; **2005**: 32–60; **2007**: 73–77; **2008**: 35, 44–47, 175–215
damage claims against law enforcement officials, **2005**: 60–64; **2006**: 75–86; **2007**: 78–81; **2008**: 36–44
Medellín v. Texas (2008), **2008**: 35, 175–215
standing of defendant to invoke consular conventions, **1991-99**: 264; **2000**: 30–38; **2004**: 46–47; **2005**: 32–64
Consular offices and personnel. *See also* Consular functions; Consular Relations, Vienna Convention on (VCCR); Diplomatic missions and personnel
Azerbaijan, bilateral agreement on diplomatic and consular properties with, **2000**: 627–28
census compliance, **2000**: 639–40
consular agents, **1989-90**: 63–64
employment contracts for workers in U.S. consular offices, **1989-90**: 390
immunity and inviolability, **1989-90**: 348–50; **1991-99**: 1309–13; **2000**: 601–2; **2002**: 37, 478; **2004**: 537; **2005**: 567–74. *See also* Consular Relations, Vienna Convention on (VCCR), *and subheadings*: Articles 41, 43, *and* 71
bank accounts, **2005**: 544–47, 555–60, 567–70
concept of "grave crime" in, **1989-90**: 339, 351–52
for consular functions, **1989-90**: 348–52
of consular residence, **2007**: 487–89
in criminal cases, **1989-90**: 339–52
of dependents, **2003**: 573–74
exemption from state taxes. *See* taxation, *this heading*
of foreign consul and consulate under FSIA, **2003**: 510, 532–33
inviolability vs. immunity, **1989-90**: 351–52

Consular offices and personnel (continued)
most-favored-nation treatment, **1989-90:** 339, 340–48
of personnel, **2007:** 446–47
reciprocity, **1989-90:** 340–42, 344–46
waiver of, **1989-90:** 338–39
interpretation of consular conventions, **2000:** 39
labor law, applicability of, **1989-90:** 388–90
location in U.S., **2004:** 559
location of buildings, **2000:** 626–37; **2002:** 576
protection from attachment of properties, **2003:** 458; **2004:** 518, 523–24
protection of property, **2003:** 553
Puerto Rican sovereignty, implications of, **2000:** 344–45; **2006:** 312–14
service of process on personnel, **2004:** 555–56
special maritime and territorial jurisdiction, **2004:** 171–72
status of U.S. consulate general in Hong Kong, **1991-99:** 1176, 1181
taxation, **1989-90:** 382–85; **2000:** 594–99; **2001:** 545–49; **2004:** 542–47; **2008:** 498–501. *See also* Consular Relations, Vienna Convention on (VCCR), *subheadings*: Articles 32 *and* 49
London congestion charge, **2005:** 570–74
waiver of attachment and execution under FSIA, **1991-99:** 1226
workers' compensation plans, applicability of, **1989-90:** 390–93
Consular Relations, Vienna Convention on (VCCR), 1989-90: 169; **1991-99:** 316–17, 321, 322, 324, 329–30, 1309–13; **2000:** 549; **2003:** 458; **2004:** 22, 37, 38, 44, 518*n*, 562; **2005:** 35, 270, 337, 545, 556, 568, 569, 952. *See also* Consular functions; Consular notification and access; Consular offices and personnel; United Nations
Articles:
1, **1991-99:** 304; **2007:** 487; **2008:** 500
5, **1989-90:** 348, 349; **1991-99:** 295; **2000:** 59–60, 118, 161, 601–2; **2001:** 56; **2002:** 59–60; **2003:** 44, 49, 130–31; **2006:** 103
14, **2003:** 56
26, **2000:** 34
27, **2000:** 552–53; **2004:** 523–24; **2007:** 487–88
27(1)(a), **2005:** 547
28, **2005:** 568
32, **2004:** 542–47
35, **2002:** 40–42

Consular Relations, Vienna Convention on (VCCR) (continued)
36, **1991-99**: 253–54, 255, 257, 259, 260, 261, 262, 273, 281, 282, 283, 285, 286, 289–90, 292, 293, 304, 305, 306–8, 312, 315, 320, 324–27, 329, 339–40; **2000**: 28, 39, 41, 43, 44–45, 48, 50*n*, 56, 57–58, 59–60, 61–62, 63–64, 72–73, 74, 77, 78, 79–80; **2001**: 21–24, 25, 26, 29, 30–36; **2002**: 39–41, 44, 45, 50–51; **2003**: 43, 44, 46–103; **2004**: 38–43, 45, 46–49; **2005**: 29, 35–36, 37, 41, 41*n*, 48, 50*n*, 51–54, 58, 60, 60*n*, 62; **2006**: 63–70, 72–74, 75, 77–82, 86; **2007**: 73, 78–81, 203, 365; **2008**: 36–47, 208
36(1)(b). *See* Consular notification and access
37, **2000**: 49*n*, 118; **2001**: 36; **2008**: 499
41, **1989-90**: 351–52
43, **1989-90**: 348
49, **1989-90**: 384, 385; **2005**: 572
55, **1989-90**: 391; **2000**: 154
71, **2005**: 572; **2008**: 499
72, **1989-90**: 340, 382
bilateral MFN clause and, **1989-90**: 344, 346
codifying customary international law, **2000**: 118
Compulsory Settlement of Disputes, Optional Protocol Concerning, **2005**: 35, 35*n*, 36, 44, 50, 51, 54, 57; **2007**: 75–76
U.S. withdrawal from, **2005**: 30–31, 55, 216–17, 270; **2006**: 1026
on consular assistance for children, **2002**: 59–60
immunity provisions. *See* Articles 43 and 71, *this subheading*; Consular offices and personnel
intent of drafters, **2008**: 39–40
inviolability provisions. *See* Article 41, *this subheading*; Consular offices and personnel
on judicial assistance, **2001**: 56
Optional Protocol to, **2004**: 543; **2005**: 270
U.S. withdrawal from, **2005**: 30–31, 216
on protection of citizen minors, **2000**: 118
protection of consular property under, **2002**: 410, 411, 412; **2003**: 553
purpose, **2003**: 48
reciprocity, **1989-90**: 340; **2000**: 58, 75–76
rights of individuals under, **2000**: 33, 34
on satisfaction for breach of obligation, **2000**: 63–68, 71–72
sending state, **2003**: 235
tax exemption provisions. *See* Articles 32 and 49, *this subheading*; Consular offices and personnel

Consular Relations, Vienna Convention on (VCCR) (continued)
treaty obligations between countries without diplomatic relations, **2003:** 103–4
U.S. compliance with, **2005:** 31, 341
state and local obligations under, **2007:** 77, 203–5
Consumer protection
APEC Consumer Protection Principles, **2005:** 660
data protection and privacy, **2005:** 660
spam, **2005:** 659, 801
U.S.–EU air transport agreement, **2005:** 587
Container Security Initiative, 2002: 120
Contempt sanctions. *See* Sanctions
Continental Shelf, 2001: 683–84; **2005:** 458
Arctic, **2007:** 613, 617–19, 629, 630
Beaufort Sea Alaska, oil and gas lease dispute over Outer Continental Shelf, **2005:** 705–7; **2008:** 640–42
Canada, continental shelf limits with, **2001:** 676–78
Commission on the Limits of the Continental Shelf, **2005:** 732; **2006:** 806; **2007:** 618–20; **2008:** 620, 629, 639–40
Conventions on the Law of the Sea (1958), **1991-99:** 1563; **2000:** 699; **2004:** 675; **2005:** 678, 759–60
deepwater port in Gulf of Mexico, **2005:** 695
fixed platforms. *See* Maritime issues, *subheading*: Suppression of Unlawful Acts Against the Safety of Maritime Navigation, Convention for (1988) and fixed platforms protocol
Geneva Convention on (1958), **2000:** 699; **2005:** 759–60
Law on the Exclusive Economic Zone and the Continental Shelf (Taiwan), **2005:** 683, 684
marine pollution and, **2007:** 702
Outer Continental Shelf Lands Act (1953), **2002:** 739–40
rights of coastal states, **2000:** 708–9
UNCLOS, **1991-99:** 1573; **2001:** 676–78; **2002:** 732–37; **2003:** 717, 731–32, 741; **2004:** 675, 679, 683, 685, 698, 705, 727, 730–33; **2005:** 678, 682, 759–60, 763, 765; **2007:** 613–14, 617–18, 624, 629–30; **2008:** 620–21, 623–24, 629, 639–40
underwater cultural heritage and, **2005:** 759–61, 763, 765, 766
U.S.–Mexico Treaty on Delimitation of the Continental Shelf in the Western Gulf of Mexico Beyond 2000 Nautical Miles, **2000:** 697–700
Continued Dumping and Subsidy Offset Act of 2000 (Byrd Amendment or CDSOA), 2003: 655–57; **2004:** 606–7; **2005:** 626–27; **2006:** 703*n*, 706–8

Contracts. *See also* Commercial law; Electronic commerce; Private international law; UNCITRAL (UN Commission on International Trade Law)
Carriage of Goods Wholly or Partly by Sea, Draft Convention, UNCITRAL, and contractual freedom, **2005:** 798–99
choice of court agreements between commercial parties, **2005:** 788
Contracts for the International Sale of Goods, Convention on, **1991-99:** 1817, 1824; **2002:** 824; **2003:** 838–39; **2004:** 805, 823
electronic commerce. *See* Electronic commerce
International Contracts, Inter-American Convention on the Law Applicable to, **1991-99:** 1841–43
jurisdiction rules in private international law, **2000:** 738
liability of successor states, **2000:** 570–73
Office of Federal Contract Compliance Programs, **2005:** 288
treaty law and, **2000:** 494
waiver of FSIA immunity in, **2003:** 523–24
Control and seizure of assets. *See* Seizure of assets
Controlled substances. *See* Drug issues; Drug trade
Conventional Armed Forces in Europe, Treaty on (1990), 1989-90: 578–79; **2007:** 1001–2; **2008:** 1011–17
Conventional Forces in Europe Treaty Implementation Act (1991), 1991-99: 2228
Conventional weapons
Convention on (CCW), **1991-99:** 514–15, 2074, 2186–97, 2247–50; **2000:** 755–57; **2001:** 835–41; **2003:** 1066–68; **2004:** 1050–53; **2005:** 1041–42; **2006:** 1085–1100; **2008:** 877–88
Amended Protocol II, land mines, **2001:** 840–42; **2005:** 955–56; **2007:** 898–99
Amendment to Article 1, **2006:** 1094–97; **2007:** 895–96, 904
cluster munitions, **2007:** 899–903, 904–5, 906–7; **2008:** 877–85
explosive remnants of war, **2001:** 837–39; **2007:** 895–98, 904; **2008:** 878, 884, 886–88
incendiary and laser weapons, **1991-99:** 2192–94; **2006:** 1093–94; **2007:** 895–96, 904; **2008:** 885–88
meeting of states parties to, **2007:** 901–5
Protocol III, **2008:** 885–86
Protocol IV, **2008:** 886–88
Protocol V, **2006:** 1097–1100

Conventional weapons (continued)
Prohibitions or Restrictions on the Use and Transfer of Mines Other than Anti-Personnel Mines (MOTAPM), **2001**: 840; **2004**: 105; **2005**: 1041, 1042; **2006**: 1087–89, 1092
Protocol on Prohibitions or Restrictions on the Use of Mines, Booby-Traps and Other Devices (1996), **1991-99**: 511, 2186, 2187
mines
Amended Mines Protocol, **2004**: 1050; **2005**: 956
anti-vehicle mines, **2001**: 840–41; **2007**: 903
declaration on, **2006**: 1089–93
landmines, **1991-99**: 514, 852, 2060, 2071, 2192–94, 2195–97, 2247–50; **2000**: 751–55, 757; **2004**: 1050–53; **2005**: 955–56; **2006**: 1085–94; **2008**: 883
Prohibitions or Restrictions on the Use and Transfer of Mines Other than Anti-Personnel Mines (MOTAPM), **2001**: 840; **2004**: 105; **2005**: 1041, 1042; **2006**: 1087–89, 1092
Protocol on Prohibitions or Restrictions on the Use of Mines, Booby-Traps and Other Devices (1996), **1991-99**: 511, 2186, 2187
UN Register of Conventional Arms, **1991-99**: 2267–68
Conventions. *See specific topics*
Cook Islands
environmental protection agreement, **2002**: 791
maritime boundaries, **1991-99**: 1577
maritime interdiction agreement, **2008**: 650
restrictions on work performed by longshoremen from, **2002**: 757; **2003**: 764
Cooperating Nation Information Exchange (CNIES), 2005: 145–46
Cooperative Threat Reduction Act (1993), 1991-99: 2313–14
Coordination Council for North American Affairs, 2000: 600
COPUOS (UN Committee on Peaceful Uses of Outer Space). *See* Space
Copyright law, 1991-99: 1509–13. *See also* Intellectual property rights; Trade Related Aspects of Intellectual Property Rights (TRIPS Agreement)
Berne Copyright Convention for the Protection of Literary and Artistic Works, **1989-90**: 417; **1991-99**: 1512, 1513, 1518–19; **2003**: 200
computer programs, **1991-99**: 1512–13
Copyright Act (1978), **1991-99**: 701, 703–4
Copyright Act (1998), **2003**: 661–63
Digital Millennium Copyright Act, **1991-99**: 1516–17

Copyright law (continued)
international registration of audio-visual works and, **1989-90:** 416–17
private international law and, **2000:** 740
Protection of Performers, Producers of Phonograms and Broadcasting Organizations, Convention for (1961), **1991-99:** 1509–12, 1514–16, 1526
Russia, **2008:** 606
taxation of royalties, **1989-90:** 412
Watch List, **2006:** 766–69; **2007:** 605–11; **2008:** 604–8
World Intellectual Property Organization (WIPO) treaties, **2008:** 606
Corporate responsibilities and rights
air carrier's ownership structure and citizenship requirements, **2005:** 588–92; **2006:** 685–86
Alien Tort Statute cases. *See* Alien Tort Statute (ATS)
citizenship of, **1991-99:** 769–75
cybercrime, **2003:** 201. *See also* Crime
financing of terrorism and, **2001:** 109
Holocaust victims insurance relief, **2003:** 462–68
human rights abuses, involvement in, **1991-99:** 989–90. *See also* Alien Tort Statute (ATS)
Torture Victim Protection Act and corporate liability, **2003:** 378–79; **2005:** 411, 419, 424–25
UN Commission on Human Rights on, **2004:** 299
as instrumentality of state, **2003:** 512–14, 520–21
Johannesburg Declaration on Sustainable Development, **2002:** 765–71, 782
NAFTA Chapter 11 arbitration. *See* North American Free Trade Agreement (NAFTA)
OECD Guidelines for Multinational Enterprises, **2002:** 727–28
service of process on foreign corporation, **2005:** 860
shell corporations and money laundering, **2005:** 176–80
social responsibility, **2000:** 364–68
conditions in privately managed prisons, **2000:** 387
transnational, U.S. vote against UN Commission on Human Rights (UNCHR) Resolution 2005/69 concerning, **2005:** 328–29
Treaty Establishing the European Community and, **2003:** 691–94
Warsaw Convention liability, **2004:** 563–65
World War II-era claims, **2004:** 476–78. *See also* World War II
forced labor, **1991-99:** 989, 992, 1048–49, 1070–71; **2003:** 468–74
insurance claims, **1991-99:** 1049–50, 1051–52, 1066–67, 1069–70, 1071, 1133

Corruption
Belarus, **2006**: 42–44, 983–84
bribery of officials, **2008**: 121–23. *See also* conventions on, *this heading*
as criminal, extraditable offense, **1991-99**: 561–63
conventions on
Council of Europe convention on corruption, **2002**: 195–96
Inter-American convention against corruption (1996), **1991-99**: 563–71; **2000**: 231–38; **2001**: 159–63; **2002**: 117; **2003**: 938; **2004**: 139–40; **2006**: 237–38
OECD convention on bribery of foreign public officials, **1991-99**: 558–71, 1394; **2000**: 233, 236; **2001**: 161, 163–64; **2002**: 117; **2003**: 207–8, 213, 343; **2004**: 924*n*; **2005**: 165–76; **2006**: 287–88; **2008**: 122
UN Convention Against Corruption, **2003**: 207–8, 213, 343; **2004**: 145; **2005**: 170, 172; **2006**: 229–33; **2007**: 170–71; **2008**: 121, 122, 123, 479
in courts, **2004**: 85–86, 810, 819
extradition request from Pakistan for, **2008**: 64–69
Foreign Corrupt Practices Act, **2005**: 171; **2008**: 122
incompatibility with full enjoyment of human rights, **2005**: 432–34; **2008**: 327
Latvia, **2005**: 178, 179; **2006**: 251
Millennium Challenge Account and anti-corruption measures, **2005**: 429
National Strategy Against High-Level Corruption, **2006**: 234–37
Nigeria, **2006**: 215, 483
organized crime and, **2005**: 165–66, 170–76. *See also* Crime, *subheading*: organized crime
Palestinian government, **2005**: 912; **2006**: 1027
Peru–U.S. asset sharing agreement, **2004**: 140–41
Preventing and Combating Corrupt Practices and Transfer of Assets of Illicit Origin and Returning Such Assets, UN draft resolution, **2005**: 335
rule of law and, **2004**: 388, 389, 394
Russian oil company case, **2005**: 834, 838
Sudan, **2008**: 834, 835
suspension of entry of persons involved in, **2004**: 24–25; **2006**: 42–44
Syria, **2005**: 880; **2006**: 247; **2008**: 798, 799
threat of, **2008**: 121–23
UN Oil-for-Food Program, **2004**: 893–98; **2005**: 871, 873–77
UNCITRAL and procurement activities of developing countries, **2005**: 808
World Bank disqualification for, **2008**: 122
Zimbabwe, **2008**: 801, 802

Costa Rica
child support enforcement, **2005**: 809–10; **2008**: 760
climate change initiatives, **2002**: 781
Environmental Cooperation Agreement with U.S., **2005**: 756–57
expropriation claims against, **2003**: 480–82
extradition and mutual legal assistance, **2001**: 90–96
forest conservation agreements, **2007**: 733–34, **2008**: 722
free trade agreement, **2004**: 617–19
hazardous waste disposal agreement, **2002**: 783–84
human cloning, **2004**: 787–88
intellectual property rights Watch List, **2006**: 768
intellectual property Watch List, **2007**: 610
Inter-American Convention Against Corruption, party to, **2006**: 238
Inter-American Court of Human Rights in, **2002**: 73
maritime issues
counter-drug trade agreement, **1991-99**: 1606
search and rescue memorandum of understanding, **2008**: 656–57
money laundering, **2004**: 135
naturalization convention, **2002**: 203
Pact of San Jose, **2005**: 387
prisoner transfer treaty, **2001**: 51
reciprocity in recovery of family support obligations, **2008**: 760
stolen vehicle treaty, **2000**: 169–70; **2002**: 64–65, 68
territorial sea baselines, **1989-90**: 461–62
trade, **1991-99**: 1413, 1834; **2003**: 683–86
Tropical Forest Conservation Act agreements, **2007**: 733–34; **2008**: 722
tuna conservation agreement, **2000**: 307; **2003**: 800–1; **2005**: 744
U.S. military assistance, **2006**: 278
waiver of Article 98 agreement with U.S. (nonsurrender of Americans to ICC), **2006**: 279
Cote d'Ivoire
Accra III Accord, **2005**: 933–34
agreement concerning crisis in, **2005**: 933–34
arms embargo, **2007**: 1006
child soldiers in, **2004**: 281, 282
Linas-Marcoussis Accord, **2005**: 933–34
sanctions on, **2004**: 922–24; **2006**: 995–96
UN personal conduct unit in, **2005**: 946
Council of Europe, 2001: 52; **2007**: 68
Anti-Doping Convention, **2005**: 782
comments on U.S. war on terror, **2005**: 100–101
Corruption Convention. *See* Corruption
Criminal Law Convention, **2001**: 161

Council of Europe (continued)
Cybercrime Convention, **2001**: 152–59; **2002**: 196–97; **2003**: 191–207; **2004**: 95–96, 97–99; **2005**: 164, 657; **2006**: 239–41
Protocol on Criminalization of Acts of a Racist or Xenophobic Nature, **2001**: 268–69; **2004**: 267
racially threatening communication, **2001**: 264–65, 267–68
Nazi-confiscated art and, **1991-99**: 1069
OECD Convention on Mutual Administrative Assistance in Tax Matters (1988), **1989-90**: 410–11
report on U.S. renditions and detentions, **2007**: 240
Sentenced Persons, Convention on Transfer of, **1989-90**: 72; **1991-99**: 381–83; **2001**: 52; **2005**: 71, 74–75; **2006**: 104–5; **2008**: 51
state immunity, convention, **2006**: 599
Venice Commission on renditions, **2006**: 161–62
Countermeasures, 2000: 665
customary international law and, **1991-99**: 1109–15; **2000**: 417, 665; **2001**: 365–71
ILC Draft articles on State Responsibility and, **1991-99**: 1120, 1122, 1414; **2001**: 365–71
Counternarcotics agreements. *See* Drug trade
Counter-Terrorism Committee, UN (CTC), 2005: 898, 899, 900, 901; **2006**: 199–210, 999–1000
Country code top level domains (ccTLD), 2005: 655, 658
Courts. *See also* International Court of Justice (ICJ)
criminal tribunals. *See* Criminal tribunals, international, hybrid, and other; International Criminal Court (ICC)
evidentiary issues. *See* Evidence
human rights. *See* European Court of Human Rights; Inter-American Court of Human Rights
interpreters in courtroom, **2003**: 82
judicial procedure. *See* Judicial procedure
military commissions. *See* Military commissions for trial of certain non-U.S. enemy combatants[1]
Nuclear Claims Tribunal, Republic of Marshall Islands, **2006**: 316–25
U.S. domestic, international law and, **2007**: 215–18
CPA (Coalition Provisional Authority). *See* Iraq
Crime. *See also* Criminal tribunals, international, hybrid, and other; Law enforcement; Mutual legal assistance
aggression. *See* Aggression, crime of

[1] Editor's note: The Military Commissions Act of 2009, Pub. L. 111-84, uses the term "enemy belligerents" rather than "enemy combatants."

Crime (continued)
bribery. *See* Corruption
Canada, liquor smuggling into, revenue rule considerations, **2005**: 234–42
committed at sea. *See* Maritime issues; Piracy
conspiracy to overthrow government, **2006**: 203–4
corruption. *See* Corruption
Crime Bill of 1994, **2005**: 274, 370
Criminal Justice Act, **2005**: 388
cybercrime
Council of Europe Convention on. *See* Council of Europe
cyberstalking crime, **2005**: 264
in extradition context, **2008**: 53
prosecution, **1991-99**: 453
racially threatening communication, **2001**: 264–65, 267–68
Death Penalty Act, Federal, **2005**: 384
detainees held at Guantanamo Bay. *See* Detainees, military
domestic violence, **2005**: 264, 313
domestic vs. international crimes, **2008**: 141
Draft Code of Crimes Against the Peace and Security of Mankind, **1991-99**: 579
drug trafficking. *See* Drug trade
extradition. *See* Extradition
felony arrest warrant, passport denial for, **2008**: 10–11
genocide. *See* Genocide
hijacking and hostage taking. *See* Hostage-taking and Hijacking
humanity, against. *See* Crimes against humanity
immigration and. *See* Removal of aliens from U.S., *subheading*: criminal aliens
inchoate crimes, **2006**: 203–4
mens rea, **2004**: 327, 375
money laundering. *See* Money laundering
mutual legal assistance. *See* Mutual Legal Assistance
organized crime, **2000**: 151, 221–25
airline passenger name record data, **2004**: 111
corruption and, **2001**: 161; **2005**: 165–66, 170–76
cybercrime, **2001**: 154, 155. *See also* cybercrime, *this heading*
extradition issues, **2004**: 147–48
International Crime Control Strategy, **1991-99**: 396–97
jurisdiction, **2004**: 146–47
migrant smuggling, **2000**: 24, 221–23; **2003**: 142, 213, 736; **2004**: 95–96, 99–100, 102–3, 141–42, 149–63, 201–2; **2005**: 153–56; **2006**: 838–40

Crime (continued)
obstruction of justice, **2004**: 147
Racketeer Influenced and Corrupt Organizations (RICO) Act (1970), **1989-90**: 73; **1991-99**: 1286; **2002**: 837–38, 839–40, 841; **2003**: 355, 855, 895; **2004**: 361, 820, 1102; **2005**: 514
Summit of the Americas declaration, **2004**: 1065
trafficking in persons. *See* Trafficking in persons
UN Convention Against Transnational Organized Crime, **2001**: 151; **2002**: 110; **2003**: 142, 213, 343, 735–36; **2004**: 95, 96, 99–101, 141–63, 191, 201–2; **2005**: 153–55, 156, 165; **2008**: 122–23
Prison Litigation Reform Act of 1996 (PLRA), **2005**: 367
Prison Rape Elimination Act of 2003 (PREA), **2005**: 275
Protocol Against Smuggling of Migrants. *See* Smuggling
sedition, **2006**: 203–4
smuggling of persons. *See* Smuggling; Trafficking in persons
solicitation, **2006**: 202–3
Texas Code of Criminal Procedure, **2005**: 58–59
torture. *See* Torture
trafficking in persons. *See* Trafficking in persons
transborder arrest, **1989-90**: 91–98; **1991-99**: 435–45, 504–5; **2001**: 326–34; **2002**: 346
arrest and transfer of Ante Gotovina to International Criminal Tribunal for Former Yugoslavia (ICTY), **2005**: 192
customary international law and transborder arrest, **2000**: 408–9
human rights and, **2000**: 398–412; **2004**: 352
legality of, **2001**: 326–34
in Mexico (Alvarez Machain), **2000**: 398–412; **2001**: 326–34; **2003**: 380–83; **2004**: 340–54
Treaty to Prohibit Transborder Abductions, **2000**: 405
victims
of international terrorism, **2005**: 272
sexual exploitation of women, **2005**: 162–64
Trafficking and Violence Protection Act of 2000 (TVPA), **2000**: 225–30, 540, 541–42; **2001**: 145, 146–47, 148, 149, 150, 151–52, 264; **2002**: 244–45, 532–33; **2003**: 188–89, 190, 540; **2004**: 101–2, 156; **2005**: 156–57, 159, 160–61, 162, 272–74
Discretionary Grant Program, **2005**: 273
Presidential Determination on. *See* Trafficking in persons, *subheading*: Victims of Trafficking and Violence Protection Act (TVPA) (2000)
Special Watch List, **2005**: 158–60; **2008**; 116

Crime (continued)
tier classification of efforts to comply with, **2001**: 149–50; **2008**: 115–17
Victims of Crime Act of 1984 (VOCA), **1989-90**: 334; **1991-99**: 481; **2005**: 271, 272
Victims Protection Reauthorization Act, **2005**: 159–60
visas, T- and U-, **2005**: 272–73
Violent Crime Control and Law Enforcement Act (1994), **1991-99**: 75, 77–78; **2005**: 264
war crimes. *See* War Crimes
World War II. *See* Holocaust; World War II
Crime of aggression. *See* Aggression, crime of
Crimes against humanity, 1991-99: 515–22; **2001**: 118–19; **2002**: 321; **2004**: 178, 180, 186, 409. *See also* Genocide
accountability mechanisms, **2000**: 239–43
Alien Tort Statute jurisdiction, **2006**: 460–65
apartheid as, **2004**: 355, 360
Bosnian atrocities, **1991-99**: 522–28, 981
Burundi, **2000**: 246–47
Cambodia, **2000**: 244–45
Darfur, **2004**: 239–50
disappearances. *See* Human rights
in Draft Code of Crimes Against the Peace and Security of Mankind, **1991-99**: 576–79
East Timor, **2000**: 245–46
El Salvador, **2004**: 362–63
ICC and, **2007**: 181, 184, 197
Indonesia, **2000**: 245–46
International Criminal Court. *See* International Criminal Court (ICC)
International Criminal Tribunal for Former Yugoslavia. *See* International Criminal Tribunal for Former Yugoslavia (ICTY)
International Criminal Tribunal for Rwanda. *See* International Criminal Tribunal for Rwanda (ICTR)
Iraq, **2000**: 247
actions under Saddam Hussein, **1991-99**: 532–38, 2118–19
Khmer Rouge, prosecution for. *See* Cambodia
Kosovo, **1991-99**: 962, 2147
Pinochet prosecution, **1991-99**: 518–19
prevention, **1991-99**: 520–21; **2000**: 248–49
rape as, **1991-99**: 584; **2000**: 241–42, 251–55
requirement of state action, **1991-99**: 981
Rwanda, **1991-99**: 529–32; **2000**: 203–4, 242
sovereign immunity and, **2002**: 491–92

Crimes against humanity (continued)
Special Court for Sierra Leone, **2008**: 140–41
Statutes of Limitation, Convention on Nonapplicability of (1968), **2001**: 119
UNHRC General Comment 31 and, **2007**: 280–81
use of force to prevent, **2004**: 971
war crimes. *See* War crimes
World War II. *See* Holocaust; World War II
Criminal Justice Act (1964), **2004**: 1030
Criminal tribunals, international, hybrid, and other, **2001**: 164–67; **2005**: 188–90; **2006**: 254–79; **2008**: 136–38. *See also* International Criminal Court (ICC)
Cambodia, for Khmer Rouge, **1989-90**: 119–28; **1991-99**: 607–8; **2000**: 244–45; **2001**: 169; **2002**: 148; **2003**: 221–22; **2008**: 141
European Court of Justice, **2005**: 395
Iraqi High Tribunal, **2005**: 191; **2006**: 259–60, 269–73
Lebanon, **2006**: 257, 272–75; **2007**: 190–93, 835; **2008**: 141–42
Rwanda. *See* International Criminal Tribunal for Rwanda (ICTR)
Sierra Leone, Special Court for, **2000**: 243–44; **2001**: 168; **2002**: 147–48; **2005**: 190–91, 217, 430; **2006**: 275–77; **2008**: 140–41
U.S. support for, **1991-99**: 388, 607–8, 610, 858–60; **2007**: 197, 390, 835–36; **2008**: 136–44
Yugoslavia. *See* International Criminal Tribunal for Former Yugoslavia (ICTY)
Croatia
abortion in, **2002**: 278
aviation agreement, **2004**: 1068–69; **2008**: 511
bilateral investment treaty, **1991-99**: 1466
Bosnia and Herzegovina peace agreement, **2004**: 1072
court system, U.S. support for, **2005**: 190; **2008**: 139
Croatian Liberation Movement, **2005**: 482
diplomatic relations and recognition, **1991-99**: 1146–48, 1945, 1979
extradition and mutual legal assistance, **2000**: 185*n*
intellectual property rights, **2007**: 609
Watch List, **2006**: 768
NATO accession, **2008**: 874*n*
peace process, **1991-99**: 1981–82, 2027, 2029–30
Proliferation Security Initiative (PSI) ship boarding agreement with U.S., **2005**: 1106
sanctions related to, **1991-99**: 1945, 1946–52, 1956

Croatia (continued)
succession issues and UN membership, **1991-99**: 1163, 1167
Underwater Cultural Heritage, Convention on Protection of, **2005**: 766
U.S. military assistance, **2006**: 278
U.S.–Adriatic Charter, **2003**: 939
Ustasha (fascist regime supported by Nazis during World War II), **2005**: 482
Cross-Border Insolvency Procedure, UNCITRAL Model Law on, **2005**: 808–9
Cruel and unusual punishment, 2005: 270, 276, 289, 292–93, 342, 360, 381–82, 386, 388, 1012; **2006**: 355; **2008**: 358–60. *See also* Capital punishment; Constitution, U.S.; Torture
Cruise ships. *See* Maritime issues
CTC. *See* Counter-Terrorism Committee, UN (CTC)
Cuba
allegation of U.S. interference with telecommunications services, **2005**: 663
Alzados Resistance Fighters, **2007**: 70–72; **2008**: 30
biological warfare and, **2002**: 1065
claims by Cuban nationals for U.S. Civil Service benefits, **2002**: 236–42
Commission for Assistance to a Free Cuba, **2004**: 903–12; **2006**: 998
Cuban Assets Control Regulations, **1991-99**: 53–59; **2002**: 674–75
Cuban Democracy Act (1992), **1991-99**: 188, 191, 1899–1902, 1910
diplomatic relations with U.S., **1989-90**: 241
downing of U.S.-registered planes in international airspace, **1991-99**: 1362–67, 1902–3, 1904, 1906
entry of U.S. vessels in Cuban waters, **2004**: 913, 914, 915–17
exception to customary U.S. entry requirements, **2005**: 3
extradition and mutual legal assistance, **2000**: 185*n*
foreign tax credit, **2004**: 659
freedom of navigation, **2004**: 696–99
FSIA exception to sovereign immunity
attachment of assets in execution of judgment, **1991-99**: 1228–34
gifts to, **2004**: 908–10
mobile phones, **2008**: 808–9
Guantanamo Bay. *See also* Detainees, military
habeas statute and, **2005**: 948, 1013–14
lease, **2004**: 996, 999–1000
sovereignty over, **2005**: 997–1000, 1012; **2008**: 892–94, 914–15
human rights and detention of Cuban nationals (“Mariel Cubans”), **2001**: 341–46; **2005**: 18–23
Human Rights Council membership, **2006**: 334

Cuba (continued)
human rights in, **1991-99:** 1908; **2003:** 403, 404–7; **2004:** 261–62, 268, 392, 396–98, 405, 643, 905–7, 913, 918–19; **2005:** 302; **2006:** 343–46
right to return, **2001:** 17–20, 344; **2005:** 937
immigration issues
compliance with Migration Accords, **2004:** 30
Cuban Refugee Adjustment Act, **2005:** 19
denial of U.S. visas
to beneficiaries of uncompensated expropriations, **1991-99:** 94–102, 1445, 1905–6
to traffickers in confiscated property, **2004:** 31
Elian Gonzalez case, **2000:** 115–41
exclusion of aliens from, **1989-90:** 38–39
family reunification policy, **2006:** 40–41
medical personnel from Cuba, ability to apply for parole at U.S. embassy in third country, **2006:** 41–42
relief from immigration requirements for certain nationals of, **1991-99:** 249–50
rights of migrants from, in safe haven on, **1991-99:** 188–94
Guantanamo Bay, status of, **1991-99:** 188–90
U.S. refugee policy, **2003:** 23; **2006:** 40–42, 56
U.S.–Cuba migration arrangements, **1991-99:** 59–68; **2002:** 20–22
LIBERTAD Act. *See* Cuban Liberty and Democratic Solidarity (LIBERTAD) Act (1996)
litigation, **2005:** 38, 241, 501, 519, 535, 576, 579, 582, 663–71
maritime issues
maritime counterterrorism measures, conditions for failure to take, **2008:** 112
traffic separation and ship reporting system, **1989-90:** 470–71
Namibian Independence and, **1989-90:** 197, 199, 202–3
national emergency related to, **2004:** 912–17
private right of action against, **1991-99:** 1128–31; **2003:** 457
regarding Cuban expropriations, **2003:** 712–13; **2004:** 431
remittances to, **2004:** 905, 907, 918
sanctions on, **1991-99:** 1899–1911, 1974, 2260; **2004:** 905–6, 916, 917–19, 924–27, 1070. *See also* trademark litigation, *this heading*
arms embargo non-licensing policy, **2004:** 1070; **2007:** 1003
family visits to, **2004:** 906, 907
humanitarian exceptions, **1991-99:** 1907–11
publishing activities, **2004:** 924–27
terrorism. *See* terrorism and, *this heading*
trafficking in persons, **2005:** 161–62; **2006:** 228

Cuba (continued)
travel restrictions. *See* travel restrictions, *this heading*
U.S. embargo, **2000**: 749–50; **2004**: 286, 667, 917–19, 1070; **2005**: 290, 664–71, 889–91; **2006**: 998
terrorism and, **2004**: 912–15; **2007**: 397
designation as state sponsor of terrorism, **1991-99**: 508–9, 1223; **2001**: 820; **2003**: 168; **2004**: 103, 659; **2005**: 506; **2006**: 173, 577; **2007**: 236; **2008**: 89, 472
maritime counterterrorism measures, conditions for failure to take, **2008**: 112
not cooperating fully with antiterrorism with antiterrorism efforts, **1991-99**: 508; **2003**: 167; **2004**: 108; **2006**: 172; **2008**: 88–89
trademark litigation, **2004**: 663–70; **2006**: 796–801, 1006–15; **2007**: 828–30
trafficking in persons, **2003**: 188; **2004**: 164; **2006**: 228; **2007**: 169; **2008**: 118–19
travel restrictions, **1991-99**: 53–59; **2000**: 749, 750; **2003**: 21–23; **2004**: 906, 907–8, 910–12, 915–17; **2007**: 830–31; **2008**: 810–13
travel rights of Cuban nationals, **2003**: 20–21
U.S. broadcasts to, **1989-90**: 396–99; **2001**: 353–54; **2003**: 429–30, 698; **2004**: 638, 639–44, 905; **2005**: 378; **2008**: 391–92
Cuban objections to, **1989-90**: 399–409; **2008**: 391–92
in U.S. interdiction of Panamanian-flagged ship in international waters, **1989-90**: 452–56
WTO disputes. *See* World Trade Organization (WTO)
Cuban Liberty and Democratic Solidarity (LIBERTAD) Act (1996), **1991-99**: 64, 94–102, 104, 1128–31, 1367, 1445–48, 1902–6, 1909, 1976–77; **2003**: 712–13; **2004**: 31, 431, 667; **2008**: 770. *See also* World Trade Organization (WTO)
European Union–U.S. understanding, **1991-99**: 1445–48, 1976–77
Cuban Refugee Adjustment Act (1966), **1991-99**: 188, 191
Cultural diversity, **2003**: 311, 830–31
draft convention on, **2004**: 798–99
Cultural issues
Antiquities Act (1906), **2006**: 872
archeological and cultural artifacts, protection of, **1991-99**: 1794–1803; **2001**: 769–74; **2002**: 813–15; **2003**: 821–25; **2004**: 791–92, 886; **2005**: 775–76; **2006**: 897–901; **2008**: 729–30
in armed conflict, **1991-99**: 2199; **2008**: 888–89. *See also* Hague Conventions, *subheading*: on law of war
Cambodia, restrictions on trade in cultural artifacts, **2003**: 823–25; **2008**: 729–30

Cultural issues (continued)
Cultural Expressions, Convention on Protection and Promotion of Diversity of, **2007**: 197–98
role of European Community, **2005**: 208–10
U.S. views, **2005**: 778–80
Cultural Property, Convention on Means of Prohibiting and Preventing Illicit Import, Export and Transfer of Ownership of (UNESCO) (1970), **1991-99**: 1794–1801; **2001**: 769–72; **2002**: 813–15; **2003**: 821–25; **2004**: 791–92; **2005**: 775–76; **2006**: 219, 897; **2008**: 729, 731
Cultural Property Implementation Act (1983), **1991-99**: 1795, 1796, 1801; **2001**: 769, 771, 773, 774; **2002**: 813; **2003**: 821, 822, 823–25; **2005**: 775; **2006**: 897; **2007**: 739–40; **2008**: 729, 731–32
definition of "pillage," **1991-99**: 1801
human rights and cultural diversity, UN General Assembly Resolution 60/167, **2005**: 780–81
immunity from seizure of culturally significant objects imported under 22 U.S.C. § 2459, **2003**: 825–30; **2004**: 792–96; **2005**: 776–77; **2008**: 733–34
Intangible Cultural Heritage, Convention on Protection of, **2002**: 311–12; **2003**: 832
Intentional Destruction of Cultural Heritage, Declaration on, **2003**: 832
Iraqi, UNSC Resolution 1783 concerning return of, **2004**: 886; **2008**: 730–32
Native Hawaiian cultural activities, Northwestern Hawaiian Islands Marine National Monument, **2006**: 872–75
preservation of American heritage abroad, **1991-99**: 1793–94; **2004**: 797; **2008**: 734–37
Stolen or Illegally Exported Cultural Objects, Convention on (UNIDROIT, 1995), **1991-99**: 1803–7
underwater cultural heritage
preservation of artifacts from Titanic, **2001**: 696, 697; **2004**: 715–16; **2008**: 658, 660–61
UN Convention on the Law of the Sea (UNCLOS), applicable sections, **2005**: 759–66
Underwater Cultural Heritage, UNESCO Convention on Protection of (2001), **2005**: 758–66
U.S. views, **2001**: 693–95; **2005**: 761–66
World Cultural and Natural Heritage, Convention for the Protection of (1992), **1991-99**: 1802–3; **2002**: 198

Customary international law. *See also specific subject headings*
abortion rights in, **2001:** 292–93
acceptance of repatriated national, **2004:** 156, 162
aggression, crime of. *See* Aggression, crime of
aiding and abetting liability, **2004:** 357–59, 372–76. *See also* Alien Tort Statute (ATS)
arbitrary arrest not covered by, **2005:** 247. *See also* Human Rights
arbitrary detention and, **2004:** 353–54. *See also* Human Rights
assurances and guarantees of nonrepetition. *See* Remedies
breaches of, found by ICJ, **2005:** 38*n*
capital punishment and, **1989-90:** 178–79; **1991-99:** 256, 739, 965–67, 970–78; **2003:** 341; **2008:** 303, 376. *See also* Capital punishment
juvenile offenders, **2001:** 304, 308–15
cause of action, **2002:** 225; **2006:** 433–35
not providing except as allowed under Alien Tort Statute, **2006:** 468*n*
chemical and biological weapons, **1989-90:** 510; **2004:** 1063
civil aircraft and, **1991-99:** 540
common law and, **2006:** 77
consular and diplomatic relations, **2000:** 27, 39, 118, 587, 605–6, 681–83; **2006:** 499
consular notification and, **1991-99:** 266; **2001:** 31; **2008:** 41–42
contiguous zone authority, **1989-90:** 466–67, 468–69
continuous nationality rule. *See* Nationality
controlling executive act as pre-empting, **2005:** 492, 494–97
Convention on the High Seas and, **1989-90:** 48, 292, 455
Convention on the Law of the Sea, **1989-90:** 48, 164, 292, 427, 439, 440, 442, 444, 445, 455, 457, 459, 463, 465, 466, 467, 469, 470, 472, 473, 475, 476; **2001:** 698–99, 700
advantages to becoming party to and, **2007:** 617, 626–27
reflecting, **2005:** 680, 683–84, 695; **2006:** 444, 815–21; **2007:** 617, 638–39; **2008:** 623, 632
exclusive economic zone, **2007:** 647, 649
President Reagan ocean policy statement, **2007:** 626
territorial sea, **2007:** 635
Conventional Armed Forces in Europe and, **2008:** 1013–17
corporate liability for violations of *jus cogens* and other norms. *See* Alien Tort Statute (ATS); *Jus cogens*
countermeasures. *See* Remedies
crimes against humanity. *See* Crimes against humanity
Cultural Property in the Event of Armed Conflict, Hague Convention for Protection of, **2008:** 888
customs and practices of States as, **2005:** 396

Customary international law (continued)
denial of justice. *See* State Responsibility
diplomatic protection, **2002:** 394; **2003:** 433–41; **2006:** 499–502; **2007:** 415–21
discrimination against aliens, **2001:** 592
entry into ports under *force majeure*, **2007:** 650–51
environmental issues and, **1991-99:** 990–91; **2002:** 344–45; **2003:** 374; **2006:** 1077–84
evidence. *See also* Evidence
exclusion of, **2003:** 74–75, 76
national security privilege in, **2003:** 217–18
Executive Branch authority to interpret, **1991-99:** 726; **2004:** 721–22
exhaustion of remedies, **2004:** 351, 978, 981, 994; **2006:** 502; **2007:** 416; **2008:** 240–42
existence of norm, **1989-90:** 53
expropriation and, **2000:** 681–83; **2003:** 631, 632; **2004:** 497, 498, 499–500; **2008:** 155, 601–3
extradite or prosecute obligation and, **2006:** 159–60; **2008:** 71
extrajudicial killing liability, **2004:** 362–63
flag state responsibility for safety of vessels, **1989-90:** 454, 455, 457
forum shopping disputes, **2004:** 821
genocide, war crimes, and crimes against humanity, **1991-99:** 595, 636; **2000:** 246; **2004:** 477. *See also* law of war, *this heading*; War crimes
good faith, **2008:** 534–35
human rights and, **1991-99:** 984, 993; **2001:** 291–92; **2002:** 326–27, 328–31, 336, 347, 351, 353; **2003:** 350. *See also* Human rights
particular forms of government not required by, **2005:** 247
prolonged arbitrary detention, **2000:** 412
remedies for human rights violation, **2003:** 348
right of self-determination, **2003:** 244
right to food, **2004:** 288
right to life and health, **2003:** 371–74
rights of indigenous peoples and, **2002:** 380; **2007:** 370
rights to associate and organize, **2003:** 375–77, 386
torture and, **2002:** 353; **2004:** 304. *See also* Torture
humanitarian law, ICRC study on customary, **2006:** 1069–85
humanitarian relief personnel, treatment of, **2006:** 1076–77
immunity and inviolability, **2004:** 530–31, 532–33. *See also* Consular offices and personnel; Diplomatic missions and personnel; Immunity
diplomatic, **2001:** 538; **2002:** 561–63; **2006:** 671–72, 671*n*, 675–78, 680; **2007:** 447

Customary international law (continued)
foreign minister, **2001**: 515
government officials, **1989-90**: 325
head of state. *See* Head-of-state immunity
inviolability of missions, **1991-99**: 1324–28
sovereign, **1991-99**: 1191; **2002**: 467, 473, 492; **2004**: 457, 475*n*, 717; **2006**: 614, 640–44, 648
special mission, **2007**: 447
of state owned or operated vessels or aircraft, **1989-90**: 496; **1991-99**: 1689, 1765–66; **2008**: 724
UN immunity convention and, **2006**: 641–42
indigenous people's rights, **2008**: 352–57
International Court of Justice and, **2007**: 59–60, 68, 543
international law as basis for, **2007**: 544–45
inter-temporal application of law and, **2002**: 379
investment and. *See also* NAFTA and, *this heading*
bilateral investment treaty, expropriation and minimum standard of treatment, **2006**: 790–96
judicial assistance and, **2000**: 154, 156–58, 161; **2001**: 56; **2006**: 107–8; **2007**: 98
jurisdiction and, **1991-99**: 503–4; **2000**: 282–84
outside jurisdiction of Inter-American Commission on Human Rights, **2007**: 388
jus cogens and, **1991-99**: 976; **2003**: 381–82; **2004**: 530–31; **2005**: 396, 823; **2006**: 646–50. *See also Jus cogens*
juvenile life sentencing and, **2007**: 383, 388–89
law of the sea, **1991-99**: 716, 1566–67, 1568–69, 1579, 1587, 1588–89, 1591, 1597, 1598, 1599, 1617, 1703; **2000**: 699, 704, 707; **2002**: 339; **2003**: 723–24; **2004**: 678, 679, 680, 682, 689, 691, 695, 703, 713, 717, 732, 1079
exclusive economic zone, **1989-90**: 463–65; **2006**: 817–18
freedom of navigation, **2008**: 700, 923
innocent passage rights through territorial waters, **1989-90**: 437–40, 441, 443, 445, 446–47, 468, 471
military survey rights in coastal waters, **2001**: 698–99
patrimonial sea concept, **1989-90**: 451
regulation of sea lanes, **1989-90**: 444
sovereign rights of coastal states, **1989-90**: 164, 451; **2008**: 135
territorial sea limits, **1989-90**: 444, 445, 459, 462, 470
transit through archipelagic waters, **1989-90**: 472–73
wrecks, draft convention on, **2006**: 815–21; **2007**: 654–55. *See also* Convention on the Law of the Sea, *this heading*
law of war, **1991-99**: 2072–73, 2088, 2097, 2171–76, 2187, 2205, 2227; **2000**: 757. *See also* Law of war

Customary international law (continued)
combatant status and, **2007:** 979, 980–81
Geneva Conventions
Additional Protocol I and, **2007:** 884, 885, 915–16
Common Article 3 and, **2007:** 883–85, 920
Guantanamo detainees, alleged breaches of, **2005:** 996
herbicide use during Vietnam War not prohibited by, **2005:** 492; **2006:** 525
ICRC study on. *See* Humanitarian law
use of nuclear weapons not violating, **1991-99:** 2172, 2181–83; **2006:** 1256, 1263
least-restrictive measures principle in trade agreements, **2001:** 596–98
local codification, **2002:** 330–31
marine scientific research, **1989-90:** 478
military commissions, **2002:** 974–75. *See also* Military commissions for trial of certain non-U.S. enemy combatants[2]
minimum standard of treatment of aliens. *See* investment and, *this heading*; NAFTA and, *this heading*; State responsibility
NAFTA and. *See also* North American Free Trade Agreement (NAFTA); State responsibility
Article 1105(1) as incorporating (minimum standard of treatment of aliens), **2001:** 570; **2006:** 710, 720–26; **2007:** 536, 542–49; **2008:** 532–33
economic discrimination against foreigners, **2003:** 625–30; **2008:** 536, 537–38
foreign investors, treatment of, **2003:** 611, 625–30; **2007:** 536
full protection and security standards, **2001:** 633–36
investor right of action, **2004:** 598–99, 600
liability of state for political subdivisions, **2000:** 679
nature and development of, **1991-99:** 990–91, 2172; **2001:** 291–92, 419–20, 572, 596–97; **2002:** 327, 330, 335, 657–58, 659; **2003:** 372–73, 376–77; **2007:** 55–56, 543–46, 885–86
notice of suit against foreign government required by, **1989-90:** 295; **2004:** 457–58
opinio juris, **2006:** 722, 1073–75; **2007:** 56, 61–69, 388; **2008:** 326, 328, 534, 535
preemptive military self-defense, **2002:** 951, 953
price fixing prohibitions, **2001:** 335
protection of sunken government property, **2004:** 721–22
rape as crime, **2000:** 251

[2] Editor's note: The Military Commissions Act of 2009, Pub. L. 111-84, uses the term "enemy belligerents" rather than "enemy combatants."

Customary international law (continued)
refugees, **1989-90:** 47–48, 49*n*
non-refoulement obligations and, **2007:** 42, 55–69
Convention Relating to the Status of Refugees and, **2007:** 42, 55, 61–69
human rights law and, **2007:** 42, 55, 65–70
temporary refuge, **1989-90:** 53
search and rescue, **2008:** 657
self-incrimination, prohibition on, **1991-99:** 574*n*
sharing of transboundary natural resources, **2002:** 396; **2008:** 721
sovereignty
judicial, **2001:** 57
territorial, **2001:** 839
standing of corporations and shareholders, **2001:** 602–5; **2003:** 644–48; **2006:** 501. *See also* Standing
state practice, **2006:** 159, 671, 1071–73; **2007:** 56, 57–61, 370, 388, 544, 547–48
UN General Assembly resolution not establishing, **2007:** 64
state responsibility, **2007:** 536, 546
ILC draft articles on. *See* State responsibility
state-to-state reparations and compensation, **1991-99:** 1115–19
succession of states, **2000:** 563
succession of treaty parties. *See* Treaties, generally
support of states, **2000:** 483
takings of property, **2001:** 405. *See also* Expropriation
torture, prohibition against, **2007:** 178
trade embargoes, **2004:** 286
transborder abductions, **1991-99:** 438; **2000:** 408–9. *See also* Crime, *subheading*: transborder arrest
treaties and, **1991-99:** 438, 714–31, 824, 1302*n*. *See also* Treaties, generally
as reflecting
UN Convention on the Law of the Sea provisions reflecting, **2005:** 680, 683–84, 695; **2006:** 444, 815–21; **2007:** 617, 638–39; **2008:** 623, 632
Vienna Convention on Consular Relations, **2000:** 118
Vienna Convention on Diplomatic Relations, **2000:** 587, 605–6
Vienna Convention on Law of Treaties, **1989-90:** 122, 145; **2000:** 118; **2001:** 212–13, 678; **2003:** 60; **2004:** 544; **2005:** 217–18, 722; **2006:** 287–88, 392; **2007:** 43n
full powers, **1989-90:** 142–43
interpretation of, **2002:** 653; **2004:** 201–2; **2008:** 250, 360
objections to reservations, **1989-90:** 145
obligations of constituent parts of a State, **2002:** 643

Customary international law (continued)
obligations of signatories before ratification, **2001**: 212–13
reservation, **1991-99**: 880–81
use of force, **2004**: 970
violation of, as purported basis of suit against U.S. officials, **1989-90**: 312
wrongful acts done under governmental authority, **2006**: 645*n*
Customs and Border Protection Bureau (CBP)
airline passenger name record data, **2006**: 168–72; **2007**: 158–59; 109–10
confiscation of fraudulent travel documents, **2006**: 208–10
import restrictions, **2008**: 730–32
inspection duties, **2005**: 3, 775; **2008**: 23
Customs Procedures, International Convention on the Simplification and Harmonization of, 2004: 95–96, 624–26
Cybercrime. *See* Council of Europe; Crime
Cyprus
cultural property protection agreement, **2002**: 813–15; **2006**: 897, 899–901
EU accession and trade agreements, **2006**: 754–56
extradition and mutual legal assistance, **1991-99**: 396; **2000**: 166, 180, 186*n*; **2001**: 92*n*; **2006**: 136, 146
forum non conveniens issues, **2005**: 833–39
money laundering in, **2004**: 135; **2008**: 120–21
Proliferation Security Initiative (PSI) ship boarding agreement with U.S., **2005**: 1106
restrictions on trade in cultural artifacts, **2003**: 821–23
waiver of Article 98 agreement with U.S. (nonsurrender of Americans to ICC), **2006**: 279
Czech Republic
bilateral investment treaty, **1991-99**: 1480–82; **2003**: 687, 695; **2004**: 623
chemical weapons precursors, training exercise under Proliferation Security Initiative (PSI), **2005**: 1104–5
diplomatic relations and succession issues, **1991-99**: 764, 1148–49, 1174–75
educational exchange program, **1991-99**: 1807
EU accession and trade agreements, **2006**: 754–56
extradition and mutual legal assistance, **1991-99**: 452; **2000**: 185*n*; **2006**: 136, 146
family support enforcement, **1991-99**: 1866
missile defense cooperation, **2004**: 1066
U.S. ballistic missile defense radar site, **2008**: 1008–9
NATO accession, **1991-99**: 738–39, 1030–40, 2243

Czech Republic (continued)
naturalization treaty, **2002**: 203
Open Skies Treaty, **1991-99**: 2238; **2002**: 1029
preservation of American heritage in, **1991-99**: 1793–94
reactor fuel return, **2004**: 1139, 1140–41
reciprocity in child support enforcement, **2001**: 51; **2008**: 759
service of process rules, **2003**: 891
trade and investment agreements, **1991-99**: 1466, 1480–82
visa waiver program, **2008**: 81–83
Czechoslovakia. *See also* Czech Republic
bilateral investment treaty, **1991-99**: 1480–82
diplomatic relations with successor states, **1991-99**: 1148
educational exchange program, **1991-99**: 1807–8
lifting of sanctions against, **1989-90**: 520–21
naturalization treaty, **2002**: 202–3
relief from immigration requirements for certain resident nationals of, **1991-99**: 250
Soviet missiles to, **1989-90**: 572
U.S. espousal of claims against, **2001**: 385–86

D

Dabhol arbitration, 2005: 469, 652–53
Dakota Waters Resources Act (2000), **2001**: 189–90*n*, 192, 193, 195, 197
Damages. *See* Remedies
Darfur. *See also* Sudan
Comprehensive Peace Agreement for Sudan, effect on, **2005**: 921, 941; **2008**: 833–37
conflict resolution efforts, **2004**: 959, 961–64, 966; **2006**: 1042–54
Addis Ababa high-level meeting on, **2006**: 1050–54
Darfur Peace Agreement, **2006**: 342, 978, 1042–54; **2007**: 860, 867–69
Darfur Peace and Accountability Act (2006), **2006**: 978–83; **2007**: 812
Declaration of Principles on, **2005**: 928–31
N'djamena Ceasefire Agreement, **2005**: 929; **2006**: 1046
peacekeeping forces in, **2006**: 1043–54; **2007**: 867–69; **2008**: 841–43
political solution, U.S. call for, **2005**: 922–27
role of African Union in, **2006**: 340, 1050–51
sanctions concerning imposed by U.S., **2007**: 811–16; **2008**: 807–8
genocide, **2005**: 197–98, 239–50; **2006**: 422–23
UN Commission on Human Rights (UNCHR), U.S. call for action on, **2005**: 376–77

Darfur (continued)
UN Security Council actions, **2005**: 376–77, 928–30, 940–41; **2006**: 975, 1043, 1047, 1053; **2008**: 807, 841–43
referral to ICC, **2005**: 192, 193–96, 198, 952; **2006**: 258; **2007**: 182–84, 197; **2008**: 144, 145, 836–37
U.S. condemnation of violence in, **2006**: 1046; **2008**: 872–73
Death on the High Seas Act (1920), 1991-99: 1351
Death penalty. *See* Capital punishment
Debt relief, 1991-99: 1493–1500
Declaration of Rights of 1689 (England), 2005: 388
Deep Seabed Hard Minerals Resource Act (1980), 2003: 744, 751–52
Deep water port approval for liquefied natural gas facility, 2005: 693–95
Deepwater Port Act of 1974 (DWPA), 2005: 693, 694
Defamation of religion. *See* Religion and religious freedom
Defense of Marriage Act (1996), 2004: 9, 10
Defense Production Act (1992), 1989-90: 418–24; **1991-99**: 1461; **2003**: 271
Defense Production Reauthorization Act (2003), 2003: 270–71
Deficit Reduction Act (2005), 2006: 16, 708, 744
Democracy. *See also* Human rights
in Angola, **1991-99**: 1143–46
attempted military coup in Venezuela and, **2002**: 385–87
in Belarus, **2003**: 26–27
Burmese Freedom and Democracy Act of 2003 (BFDA), **2005**: 892
Cambodian elections, **2003**: 407–8
climate change and, **2008**: 327
in Colombia, **2008**: 571
Community of Democracies, **2002**: 382–84; **2004**: 389–90
in Cuba, **1991-99**: 1129–31, 1445–47, 1899, 1902, 1903, 1904–5, 1907, 1909; **2003**: 403–7; **2004**: 904–5, 906, 910, 913; **2008**: 809
Democracy Caucus, **2004**: 255, 391, 405–6
FOIA, **2005**: 1026
goals of decolonization, **2003**: 408–9
in Haiti, **1991-99**: 1153, 1882–98
human rights and, **2003**: 281–83, 403–4, 414; **2005**: 257
in India, **2005**: 1078–79, 1082
Inter-American Charter, right to, **2005**: 250
international organizations in promoting, **2003**: 413–14
in Iraq, **2008**: 460, 461, 462, 858
in Kosovo, **2008**: 435
in Lebanon and Middle East, generally, **2005**: 133
in Mauritania, **2008**: 806

Democracy (continued)
NATO expansion and, **1991-99**: 1031, 1032, 1033–34, 1037
in Niger, **1991-99**: 1962–64
opposition to, **2005**: 637, 890
in Organization of American States, **1991-99**: 1019–20, 1021–22
Palestinian, **2005**: 909, 912, 914, 935, 975
principles of, **2003**: 414; **2005**: 250, 390
promotion of, **1991-99**: 1011–14; **2005**: 14, 407, 427–40, 443, 446, 457, 884; **2006**: 486–87
protection of human rights through, **2004**: 387
racism and, **2003**: 298
role of international organizations in promoting, **2003**: 419–21
in Russia, **2008**: 875
self-determination and, **2004**: 393–94
socioeconomic development and, **2003**: 311
in Sudan, **2005**: 921
travel restrictions on certain persons impeding Burma's transition to, **2003**: 27–29; **2007**: 41; **2008**: 28–29, 793–95
in UN decision-making, **2003**: 415–17, 419–20, 421
UN Democracy Fund, support for creation of, **2005**: 446
UN Security Council membership and, **2008**: 385
women's rights and, **2003**: 291, 292, 293
Democratic People's Republic of Korea. *See* Korea, North (Democratic People's Republic of Korea (DPRK))
Denmark
Arctic Council, **1991-99**: 1777–80; **2008**: 633
Arctic region, **2008**: 623, 624, 628
bridge across international strait, **1991-99**: 1585–86, 1592
extradition and mutual legal assistance, **2000**: 186*n*; **2006**: 136, 146
Greenland, agreement with U.S. concerning troops in, **1991-99**: 2167
Guantanamo detainees from, **2004**: 987, 989
Ilulissat Declaration, **2008**: 636–38
maritime boundaries, **1991-99**: 1583
missile defense cooperation, **2004**: 1066
naturalization convention, **2002**: 203
nonimmigrant visa waiver pilot program, **1991-99**: 76
Open Skies (aerial observation) treaty, **2002**: 1029
right of innocent passage in, **1991-99**: 1506, 1596–98
Social Security totalization agreement, **2007**: 81
Somali piracy, cooperation with Transitional Federal Government of Somalia (TFG) in fight against, **2008**: 925, 927
taxation of consular properties, **2004**: 542–47
Treaty of Friendship, Commerce and Navigation (FCN), **2007**: 30–32
whaling regulation, **2002**: 210
reservation to Whaling Convention, **2001**: 217

Deportation. *See also* Asylum; Immigration and visas; Refugees; Removal of aliens from U.S.
acceptance by receiving country, **2004**: 20
of A/G visa holders, **1989-90**: 28
Anti-Terrorism and Effective Death Penalty Act of 1996 provisions, **1991-99**: 78–83, 89, 90
Canada–U.S. understanding, **2004**: 21–23
extradition and, **1991-99**: 125–26, 391, 962; **2004**: 91*n*, 92
fear of persecution for serious nonpolitical crime, **1991-99**: 232–39
grounds for, **1991-99**: 87–89. *See also* Immigration and visas, *subheading*: denial of visas; Immigration and visas, *subheading*: exclusion of aliens
criminal acts, **1989-90**: 31; **1991-99**: 82–83, 90, 91
foreign policy reasons, **1991-99**: 118–28
illegal entry, **1991-99**: 84
of naturalized citizens involved in Nazi persecution, **1991-99**: 27–34. *See also* Citizenship, *subheading*: revocation
terrorist-related, **1991-99**: 79. *See also* Immigration and visas, *subheading*: terrorism and; Removal of aliens from U.S., *subheading*: based on terrorism
unlawfully admitted, **1991-99**: 81
for withholding of, **1989-90**: 45–46
Illegal Immigration Reform and Immigrant Responsibility Act provisions, **1991-99**: 84–85
INA protection against, **2004**: 91*n*
from Israel, **1991-99**: 24–25
judicial review, **1991-99**: 91–92; **2004**: 18
for law enforcement purposes, **2000**: 184–85
nonacceptance of return of nationals, **2001**: 17–20, 344
proceedings consolidated with exclusion proceedings, **1991-99**: 84
prohibited if likelihood of torture, **2000**: 379, 380–81, 387–88
repatriation of Mexicans to interior, **2004**: 26–27
from Saudi Arabia, **2004**: 273
of stateless persons, **2006**: 2
withholding and suspension of, **1991-99**: 81
grounds for, **1989-90**: 45–46
Derivative citizenship, 2008: 11–15
Desertification in Countries Experiencing Drought, Particularly in Africa, Convention to Combat, 1991-99: 1770; **2000**: 728–33

Detainees, military. *See also* Military commissions for trial of certain non-U.S. enemy combatants;[3] Multinational Force in Iraq; Prisoners of war; Torture
Civil and Political Rights, International Covenant on (ICCPR), U.S. periodic report on, **2005**: 265–66
Combatant Status Review Tribunals for Guantanamo detainees, **2005**: 963–65, 1019, 1030, 1032–34; **2006**: 1114, 1135, 1140; **2007**: 908, 936, 943–44
establishment of by DOD, **2004**: 982–84, 1015–17
judicial review, **2008**: 903–5
litigation challenging constitutionality of, **2004**: 980–81; **2005**: 995–1008
Commission on Human Rights, UN, response to Special Rapporteurs, **2005**: 987–92; **2006**: 1117–24
Commission on Human Rights, UN, response to Working Group on Arbitrary Detention, **2003**: 1016–17
Committee against Torture, UN
U.S. reports to, **2005**: 961–87; **2006**: 1124–36; **2007**: 374–77, 930–38
U.S. response to conclusions and recommendations (May 2006), **2006**: 1136–37
cruel and unusual punishment, **2005**: 104, 274, 343, 373, 439–40, 983, 1012, 1018, 1030–31, 1038
Detainee Treatment Act (DTA) (2005), **2005**: 242, 1030; **2006**: 402, 406–7, 1114, 1126, 1130, 1136, 1138, 1159, 1162, 1166, 1167, 1174, 1181–83, 1185*n*; **2008**: 891
cruel and unusual punishment, prohibition on, **2005**: 1003
judicial review, **2008**: 903–5, 921–22
nullification of direct review provision, **2008**: 905–6
status review procedures, **2005**: 1032–35; **2007**: 908–9
President Bush comments on signing, **2005**: 1037–39
protection of U.S. personnel engaged in interrogations, **2005**: 1031–32
standards for interrogation, **2005**: 1030
training of Iraqi forces, **2005**: 1036–37
detention, treatment, and trial of, U.S. laws and procedures governing, **2006**: 1113–16, 1126, 1132–33, 1139
updated Department of Defense detention and treatment policies, **2006**: 1130, 1155–56, 1163–68

[3] Editor's note: The Military Commissions Act of 2009, Pub. L. 111-84, uses the term "enemy belligerents" rather than "enemy combatants."

Detainees, military (continued)
documents and photographs, litigation concerning legal protection of, **2005**: 1020–29; **2006**: 1213–23
International Committee of the Red Cross documents, **2005**: 1021–22
photographs of abuse of detainees, **2005**: 1022–29
enemy combatants, unlawful. *See also* Guantanamo, enemy combatants held in,[4] *this heading*
access to counsel or courts, **2006**: 360–61, 1111–12
Afghanistan, held in, **2007**: 890
authority to transfer to Afghan government, **2007**: 950–56
status, **2005**: 961–63, 968
treatment, **2005**: 273–74, 971–74, 975; **2006**: 407, 1108, 1127, 1133, 1157
authority to detain, **2004**: 1003–6; **2005**: 265–66; **2006**: 1106–9; **2007**: 907–8
basis for term in law of war, **2007**: 911–17
definition of, **2005**: 1004–5; **2006**: 1140*n*
determination of status, **2003**: 1021–23
due process, **2006**: 1175–76, 1198
Guantanamo. *See* Guantanamo, Department of Defense detainees held in, *this heading*
habeas availability, litigation concerning, **2007**: 944–56
Bagram Airfield and Guantanamo distinguished, **2007**: 945–47
ICRC access to, **2006**: 1125, 1127, 1161. *See also* Red Cross, International Committee of (ICRC)
interrogations, **2006**: 1123–24, 1130, 1132–33; **2007**: 927–29, 937
coerced statements, inadmissibility of, **2006**: 1135
education and training for personnel conducting, **2006**: 1131
law of war vs. criminal law enforcement and, **2006**: 1105, 1111–12
litigation concerning enemy combatants held in U.S.
non-U.S. citizens, **2003**: 1029–30; **2008**: 917–18
U.S. citizens, **2002**: 986–1008, 1010–17; **2003**: 986, 1028–29; **2004**: 1001–15; **2005**: 266
prisoners of war distinguished, **2002**: 904–6, 976–80, 1004–8; **2005**: 1007–8; **2006**: 1112–16, 1117; **2007**: 912–15, 979–82

[4] Editor's note: On March 13, 2009, in conjunction with a filing in Guantanamo habeas litigation, the U.S. Justice Department declared that it would cease to employ the term "enemy combatant" for detainees in custody of the Defense Department at the Guantanamo Bay Detention Facility.

Detainees, military (continued)
Taliban and al Qaeda detainees as, **2005**: 961–75; **2007**: 887, 889, 908, 911–17, 922, 924, 938, 940–41, 973
President's determination, **2002**: 976–80; **2005**: 961–63, 1008
transfer, repatriation or release, **2007**: 885, 892, 911, 936–37, 954
diplomatic assurances, **2007**: 893, 932–35
torture, policy measures to safeguard against, diplomatic assurances, **2007**: 893, 932–35; **2008**: 366, 373–75, 922
Uighur detainees, **2008**: 906–14
United States, held in
court-ordered release from military custody, **2007**: 968–75
President's authority to detain, **2008**: 917–18
Guantanamo, Department of Defense detainees held in, **2002**: 976, 978–80, 983–86; **2003**: 277–78, 384–85, 1009–10
Administrative Review Boards, **2004**: 987–89; **2005**: 965–67, 1032–33; **2006**: 1114, 1135
arbitrary detention, **2003**: 1016–17
authority to hold, **2005**: 961–63, 1009–12; **2006**: 1184–94
Combatant Status Review Tribunals. *See* Combatant Status Review Tribunals for Guantanamo detainees, *this heading*
FOIA requests for documents related to, **2005**: 1018–20; **2006**: 1218–23
former detainees, civil suit against U.S. officials, **2008**: 914–15
future closure of Guantanamo detention facilities, **2006**: 1116–17; **2007**: 910–11, 935–37
habeas availability. *See* habeas availability, litigation concerning Guantanamo detainees, *this heading*
Inter-American Commission on Human Rights, precautionary measures request by, **2002**: 1008–17; **2004**: 976–94
juveniles held as detainees, **2004**: 987; **2008**: 308–12
law of war and, **2004**: 978, 984–87, 988, 1020–25, 1029; **2006**: 1112–16, 1121, 1125. *See also* Geneva Conventions on law of war (1949); Hague Conventions, *subheading*: on law of war; Law of war
lawfulness of detention, **2007**: 941–43
military commissions. *See* Military commissions for trial of certain non-U.S. enemy combatants5
non-refoulement, **2004**: 992–93
status as no longer enemy combatants, **2006**: 1184–94
thirty days' advance notice of removal, **2008**: 915–16

[5] Editor's note: The Military Commissions Act of 2009, Pub. L. 111-84, uses the term "enemy belligerents" rather than "enemy combatants."

Detainees, military (continued)
transfer or release, **2003**: 1015, 1019, 1023–25; **2005**: 965–69, 983–87, 993–94, 1016–18; **2006**: 1116–17, 1161, 1184–94
failure to meet burden of proof by preponderance of evidence, **2008**: 902–3
torture, policy measures to safeguard against, diplomatic assurances, **2008**: 366, 373–75, 922
Uighur detainees, **2008**: 903–5, 906–14
treatment, **2002**: 976–80; **2003**: 322–26, 1025–27; **2005**: 103, 970–74, 988–92; **2006**: 1132; **2007**: 908, 916–17
abuse, allegations of, **2004**: 989–92; **2005**: 215, 973–74
updated military guidance, **2006**: 1163–68
U.S. response to UN Commission on Human Rights, **2003**: 1016–27; **2006**: 1117–24
habeas availability, litigation concerning Guantanamo detainees, **2002**: 980–86; **2003**: 1027–28; **2004**: 979–82, 984, 994, 995–1001, 1017–29; **2005**: 265–66, 994, 996–97, 1009–16; **2006**: 1138, 1141–42, 1174, 1176, 1177–83; **2007**: 889, 938–43; **2008**: 891–914
access to counsel, **2003**: 1024; **2004**: 1029–35; **2006**: 1121
Geneva Convention protections, **2005**: 961–62, 994, 1006–8, 1015, 1024–25, 1026–29; **2006**: 1133, 1154, 1155–56, 1163–64, 1170. *See also* Geneva Conventions on law of war (1949); *specific Geneva Conventions*
separation of powers, **2008**: 894, 902, 907, 911–14
status of Guantanamo, **2002**: 983–86; **2003**: 1028; **2004**: 999–1000; **2005**: 997–98, 1012; **2008**: 893–901
Uighur detainees, **2008**: 906–14
U.S. constitutional protections, whether applicable, **2004**: 1001–15; **2005**: 995–1006, 1007, 1009–14; **2006**: 1104–17
hostile forces, laborers and others supporting, **2007**: 888, 941
Iraq, prisoners held in, **2005**: 975–76, 977–78
Abu Ghraib, allegations of abuse, **2004**: 300–301, 330, 990, 993–94; **2005**: 104, 373, 431, 978, 980, 981, 1022–23
detention or release, **2005**: 977; **2008**: 73–78, 918–20
FOIA cases, **2005**: 1022–29; **2006**: 1213–18
Geneva Convention protections, **2004**: 1039–41; **2005**: 1024–25, 1026–29
investigations, **2004**: 993–94, 1035–46; **2005**: 980–82
legal framework and policy, **2005**: 978–80
remedies for victims, **2005**: 982–83
civilian security internees, **2007**: 890

Detainees, military (continued)
habeas availability, **2006**: 1206–13
prisoners of war, **2003**: 997–1015; **2004**: 300, 301
status review, **2005**: 976–77, 1032–33
treatment, **2005**: 977–78, 1036–37
training of Iraqi forces in treatment of, **2005**: 1036–37
military commissions. *See* Military commissions for trial of certain non-U.S. enemy combatants[6]
Racial Discrimination, inapplicability of Convention on Elimination of All Forms of, **2008**: 920–21
secret detentions outside U.S., **2006**: 1157–60
torture, policy measures to safeguard against in context of transfer or release of detainees, **2008**: 77, 366, 373–75, 922
transfer of CIA detainees to Guantanamo, **2006**: 1104, 1156–63
Detention of aliens, nonmilitary, 2003: 286, 327–34; **2004**: 361; **2008**: 281, 346–47. *See also* Detainees, military; Human Rights; Immigration and visas
connected with 9/11 investigations, **2005**: 361–64
consular notification, **2005**: 29–64; **2006**: 63–88
for foreign policy reasons, **2005**: 10–14
length of pending removal, **2001**: 17–19, 925; **2005**: 18–23, 290–92, 351, 496; **2006**: 45–50; **2008**: 56
"Mariel Cubans," **2001**: 341–46; **2005**: 18–23
physical and verbal abuse of, **2005**: 363–64
Development
Development Fund for Iraq, **2006**: 1235–38
Coalition Provisional Authority management of, **2005**: 230–31
continuation of national emergency protecting, **2005**: 869
False Claims Act not applicable to, **2005**: 227
legal status, **2005**: 226–27
Millennium Challenge Corporation, **2005**: 671–74
right to. *See* Human rights
transnational corporations, role in, **2005**: 328–29
Devils Lake, North Dakota, U.S.–Canada flood control negotiations, 2005: 717–19
DHS. *See* Homeland Security, Department of (DHS)
Diamond trade. *See* Trade
Digital Millennium Copyright Act (1998), 1991-99: 1516–17
Dioxin (Agent Orange) litigation, 2005: 491–97; **2006**: 522–26; **2008**: 427–30

[6] Editor's note: The Military Commissions Act of 2009, Pub. L. 111-84, uses the term "enemy belligerents" rather than "enemy combatants."

Diplomatic missions and personnel. *See also* Diplomatic Relations, Vienna Convention on; Diplomatic relations and recognition
accreditation in U.S. of foreign representatives, **1989-90**: 248, 323–24, 326, 375–76
ambassadorial functions, **1989-90**: 153–55
attachment of property, **2006**: 626–29, 658–62. *See also* Diplomatic Relations, Vienna Convention on
attachment and execution under FSIA in terrorist cases, waiver of, **1991-99**: 1226; **2000**: 541–60
attachment of assets of foreign state in settlement of foreign judgment, **2004**: 523–24
attacks on embassies. *See also* protection of diplomatic property, *this heading*
Belgrade embassy, **2008**: 493–95
claims against U.S. arising from bombing of U.S. embassy in Kenya, **2001**: 417–21
compensation to U.S. for attack on U.S. embassy in China, **2000**: 424–25
responses to bombing of U.S. embassies in Africa, **1991-99**: 2133–35
U.S. bombing of Chinese Embassy in Belgrade, **2000**: 421–29
Azerbaijan, bilateral agreement with on diplomatic and consular properties, **2000**: 627–28
census, request for cooperation with, **2000**: 639–40
chiefs of mission, authorities and responsibilities of U.S., **1989-90**: 153–55
communications through diplomatic channels, **2004**: 14, 81, 144, 147, 219, 535, 561, 680, 699, 702, 705, 710, 723, 731, 732, 734, 737, 874, 875, 900, 1056, 1057, 1058, 1067
competing claims to diplomatic properties in U.S., **1989-90**: 243–64; **2000**: 562–75
construction of diplomatic property
China–U.S. agreement to provide for embassy construction, **2003**: 256–58
settlement regarding construction of U.S. embassy in Moscow, **1991-99**: 1124
zoning issues, **1989-90**: 377–81
dependents
employment of, **1989-90**: 385–87
immunity of. *See* immunity, *this heading*
diplomatic protection of corporate entities, **2002**: 394
employees

Diplomatic missions and personnel (continued)
claims of U.S. employees in Vietnam, **2002**: 413–15
domestic servants of diplomatic personnel, **1989-90**: 389–90; **2000**: 577–93, 637–39; **2002**: 552–67
employment of dependents of diplomatic personnel in U.S., **1989-90**: 385–87
employment of family of foreign service personnel, **2004**: 560–62
Zimbabwe, attacks on U.S. embassy staff, **2008**: 495
establishment of, **2006**: 527–30. *See also* construction of diplomatic property, *this heading*
limitations on personnel in U.S., **1989-90**: 374–76
location and zoning in U.S., **1989-90**: 377–81; **2000**: 626–37; **2001**: 540–44; **2002**: 576; **2004**: 559–60
U.S. diplomatic posts, **2004**: 451–52
immunity, **1991-99**: 1291–92, 1297–1305; **2000**: 382–83; **2001**: 537–38; **2008**: 492–501. *See also* attachment of property, *this heading*; Diplomatic Relations, Vienna Convention on, *subheadings*: Articles 27, 31, 37-39, 40, 41, 44; inviolability, *this heading*
abuses of, **1989-90**: 324–31
bank accounts, **2000**: 549; **2005**: 556
certification of, by Department of State as to presence or absence of, **2000**: 602, 613; **2004**: 535, 537–39; **2006**: 654, 662–66
courts bound by, **2006**: 666–67, 669–73, 678–80
compensation for victims of crime committed by diplomatic personnel in U.S., **1989-90**: 332–37
compensation for victims of terrorism and, **2000**: 541–60
criminal jurisdiction, **2008**: 491–92
customary international law and, **2000**: 587, 606; **2002**: 561–63, 566
dependents of diplomatic personnel, **1989-90**: 329–30; **2003**: 573–74; **2004**: 534–39, 560–62
of diplomatic personnel, **1989-90**: 77, 324; **1991-99**: 1292–95; **2000**: 603, 605, 606–7, 611–12; **2001**: 511, 537–38; **2002**: 558–59, 561, 564; **2004**: 531–34; **2005**: 572; **2006**: 682; **2007**: 202, 446–47
dual nationality and, **2002**: 4
of embassy construction personnel, **2003**: 257
exceptions, **1991-99**: 1296–1309
extended to representatives to UN, **1991-99**: 603–16; **2004**: 531–34. *See also* United Nations
Hague Child Abduction Convention, applicability of, **1991-99**: 371–77

Diplomatic missions and personnel (continued)
identification of diplomatic personnel, **1989-90**: 323–24, 326
importance of, in international law, **2000**: 615
landlord–tenant dispute, **1991-99**: 1297–1305, 1319–31
protection from enforcement of awards, **2000**: 540–53
reciprocity in, **2002**: 565–67
recognition by receiving state as requirement for, **2006**: 653–57
residual immunity, **1991-99**: 1295
from service of process, **2001**: 531–36; **2004**: 553–58
special missions immunity, **2006**: 662–81; **2008**: 490–91
suit by employee and, **2000**: 541–42, 577–93; **2002**: 477–78, 552–67; **2007**: 516–21
suits against insurers, **1991-99**: 1305–9
from taxes and dues, **1989-90**: 381–85, 388–90; **2000**: 594–99; **2001**: 538–40, 545–49; **2002**: 576–81; **2005**: 570–71; **2006**: 593, 597–98; **2008**: 495–501
U.S. procedures for requests for, **2006**: 659*n*
U.S. workers' compensation plans, applicability of, **1989-90**: 390–93
of U.S. foreign service officer in line of duty abroad, **2006**: 308–11
waiver of, **1989-90**: 77, 324, 338–39; **1991-99**: 1271, 1292–95, 1304
injuries sustained on embassy grounds, **2002**: 522
of missions, **2000**: 577–93
inviolability. *See also* Diplomatic Relations, Vienna Convention on, *subheadings*: Articles 27, 29, 30, 38, 40
of diplomatic and consular pouch, **1989-90**: 330
of documents, **2003**: 573
of foreign dignitaries attending UN conference to service of process, **2006**: 681–82
of missions, **1991-99**: 1322–31; **2006**: 627, 658, 660
of personnel, **2001**: 531–36; **2002**: 37; **2003**: 564–65, 573–74; **2004**: 549, 550, 554–57
of missions, **2007**: 461
opposition to allowing in case of terrorism, U.S. views, **2000**: 542–60
persona non grata status of ambassadors, **2008**: 492–93
of pouch, **2007**: 445–50, 521–22
President's constitutional authority with respect to, **2002**: 244; **2003**: 270
protection of diplomatic property, **1989-90**: 249–50, 254, 264; **2000**: 549, 553–54; **2002**: 410–12, 577; **2003**: 458, 553; **2004**: 521–24; **2005**: 545–48; **2006**: 499–502; **2008**: 493–95. *See also* attacks on embassies, *this heading*

Diplomatic missions and personnel (continued)
Bilateral Agreement on Diplomatic and Consular Properties with the Government of Azerbaijan, **2000:** 627–28
during cessation of diplomatic relations, **2000:** 552–53
request for U.S. protection of Lebanese embassy in U.S., **1989-90:** 243–64
U.S. takes custody by request of Panama Embassy, **1989-90:** 370–74
special maritime and territorial jurisdiction, **2004:** 171–72
status of Kosovo Diplomatic Observer Mission, **1991-99:** 2042–43
status of Taipei Economic and Cultural Representative Office and employees in U.S., **2000:** 599–602; **2002:** 536–39
status of U.S. liaison office in Afghanistan, **2001:** 424–26
status of U.S. liaison office in Angola, **1991-99:** 1142–46
successor states, continue as parties to treaties on diplomatic and consular relations, **1991-99:** 746
taxation. *See* immunity, *this heading*
temporary refuge for U.S. citizens, **2003:** 104–6
U.S. facilities in Israel, Jerusalem, West Bank, **1989-90:** 264–68
U.S. request for extradition of Nicaraguan diplomat from Japan, **1989-90:** 77–78
U.S.–Libya relations, **2006:** 527–28
Vietnam–U.S. diplomatic property agreement, **1991-99:** 1083, 1085–86
visas, issuance and revocation for diplomatic personnel
issuance, **2004:** 29
revocation or denial, **1989-90:** 328–29, 331
waiver of U.S. law allowing attachment for victims of terrorism, **2000:** 541–42, 549–50
Diplomatic Relations, Vienna Convention on. *See also* Consular notification and access; Diplomatic missions and personnel
Articles:
4, **2006:** 653
7, **2000:** 578, 587–90
9, **2008:** 492–93
10, **1989-90:** 248
21, **1989-90:** 269
22, **1989-90:** 249–50; **1991-99:** 1322–24, 1327–29; **2000:** 590, 593; **2004:** 554; **2005:** 571; **2006:** 627, 658; **2008:** 494
23, **2000:** 595; **2001:** 549; **2002:** 580
24, **2000:** 589; **2002:** 569; **2003:** 573
25, **2000:** 553, 590; **2005:** 571
27, **1989-90:** 269; **2002:** 569–70; **2003:** 573
28, **2000:** 595

Diplomatic Relations, Vienna Convention on (continued)
29, **2001**: 532, 533; **2002**: 551; **2003**: 564–65, 574; **2004**: 533, 554–55, 556, 557–58; **2007**: 202
31, **1989-90**: 338; **1991-99**: 1294, 1296–1305; **2000**: 589–90, 606, 612; **2001**: 537; **2003**: 574; **2004**: 532, 535, 554, 556; **2005**: 571–72; **2006**: 598, 653; **2007**: 202, 461, 517; **2008**: 503
32, **1991-99**: 1293, 1304
33, **1989-90**: 388
34, **1989-90**: 382, 384, 385, 388; **2000**: 595; **2005**: 570–71
36, **2000**: 595
37, **1989-90**: 338, 388; **2000**: 589–90, 595, 606–7, 612; **2001**: 537; **2003**: 574; **2004**: 532, 533, 535, 537; **2007**: 517; **2008**: 499
39, **1991-99**: 1293, 1295; **2000**: 598; **2004**: 533*n*; **2006**: 659*n*; **2008**: 502–3
41, **1989-90**: 391; **2000**: 154; **2001**: 58; **2002**: 564
42, **1991-99**: 1296; **2007**: 517
45, **2000**: 552; **2005**: 545–48
47, **1989-90**: 340, 383
applicability
to construction of Embassy, **2003**: 256–58
to Eritrea–U.S. relations, **1991-99**: 1150–51
to Marshall Islands–U.S. relations, **1989-90**: 268–71
to Micronesia–U.S. relations, **1989-90**: 268–721
to nonparties by U.S. statute, **1991-99**: 1291
to Palau–U.S. relations, **1991-99**: 824–25, 1152
to United Nations Permanent Representatives, **2002**: 558–59
to U.S. Liaison Office in Afghanistan, **2001**: 424
to Vietnam–U.S. relations, **1991-99**: 1157
codifying customary international law, **2000**: 587, 606
dual nationality provisions, **2002**: 4
failure by Belarus to comply with, **1991-99**: 135
immunity provided by. *See also* Diplomatic missions and personnel
commercial activity exception, **2007**: 518–21
extended to non-parties in U.S. through Diplomatic Relations Act, **2006**: 676*n*
private immovable property exception, **2007**: 461; **2008**: 456–57
special missions immunity as distinct from immunity of permanent missions under, **2006**: 675–78
interpretation, **2004**: 537
inviolability
of diplomatic premises, **1989-90**: 248–49; **1991-99**: 1322–31; **2003**: 564–65, 573–74

Diplomatic Relations, Vienna Convention on (continued)
of Saudi Arabian embassy documents, **2002**: 567–70
from service of process, **2001**: 511, 532–36; **2006**: 682
London congestion charge on U.S. embassy vehicles as contrary to, **2005**: 570–74
not inconsistent with U.S. Constitution, **2002**: 561–65
obligation to respect local law, **1991-99**: 805
persona non grata, **2008**: 492–93
on personal inviolability, **2002**: 551
protection of diplomatic property under. *See* Diplomatic missions and personnel
reciprocity provisions, **1989-90**: 340
recognition of foreign government representatives, **1989-90**: 248–49; **1991-99**: 1291
self-executing nature of, **1991-99**: 1291
tax exemption. *See* Diplomatic missions and personnel, *subheading*: immunity
as treaty pre-existing FSIA and applicability preserved by, **2006**: 626
Diplomatic Relations Act (1978), **1989-90**: 334; **1991-99**: 1291, 1305, 1306; **2002**: 558, 561–62; **2003**: 574; **2004**: 535
Diplomatic relations and recognition, **2004**: 87, 524, 659. *See also* Consular functions; Consular offices and personnel; Foreign affairs
Afghan Interim Authority, **2001**: 423–26
Afghanistan, **2001**: 424–26; **2002**: 463
Albania, **1991-99**: 1076–77, 1142
Alien Tort Statute and, **1991-99**: 983–85, 1142
alienage diversity jurisdiction and, **1991-99**: 769–70, 1141–42
Andorra, **1991-99**: 1151–52
Angola, **1991-99**: 1142–46
Armenia, **1991-99**: 1173
Azerbaijan, **1991-99**: 1174
Baltic States, non-recognition of Soviet annexation, **1989-90**: 271–75
Belarus, **1991-99**: 1173
Bosnia-Herzegovina, **1991-99**: 1146–48
Cambodia, **1991-99**: 1149–50
China, Taiwan and, **2007**: 434–36; **2008**: 446
Croatia, **1991-99**: 1146–48
Czech Republic, **1991-99**: 1148–49
diplomatic relations
absence of, effect on consular relations under VCCR, **2003**: 103–4
President's constitutional authority with respect to, **2002**: 244; **2003**: 270

Diplomatic relations and recognition (continued)
as relevant to assurances on torture, **2005**: 985; **2008**: 366–75. *See also* Torture, *subheading*: transfers to other countries and likelihood of
status of U.S., overview, **1989-90**: 241–42; **2003**: 485
East Timor, **2002**: 463–64
Eritrea, **1991-99**: 1150–51
Estonia, **1989-90**: 242
nonrecognition of incorporation by USSR, **1989-90**: 272, 274
Georgia, **1991-99**: 1174
Haiti, **1991-99**: 1152–53
ILC draft articles on diplomatic protection, **2007**: 415–21
Iran, **1989-90**: 241; **2003**: 485; **2005**: 13, 545–46, 548
Iraq, **2004**: 451–52
Kazakhstan, **1991-99**: 1173
Kosovo, **2008**: 433–39
Kyrgyzstan, **1991-99**: 1173
Latvia, nonrecognition of incorporation by USSR, **1989-90**: 272, 274
Lebanon, **1989-90**: 243–64
Libya, **2004**: 451
Lithuania, nonrecognition of incorporation by USSR, **1989-90**: 271–75
Marshall Islands–U.S., **1989-90**: 268–71
Micronesia–U.S., **1989-90**: 268–71
Moldova, **1991-99**: 1174
Montenegro, **1991-99**: 1163–67
North Korea, talks concerning, **2007**: 1019, 1022
Palau, **1991-99**: 823–25, 1152
recognition
access to U.S. courts, **1989-90**: 242–43, 247; **1991-99**: 1138–42
effect of nonrecognition, **1989-90**: 247–48
exclusive presidential authority over, **1989-90**: 244–46, 264; **1991-99**: 758–59, 1135–38; **2003**: 488–501; **2004**: 452, 454; **2006**: 542
protection of diplomatic and consular property despite nonrecognition, **2000**: 552–53
statehood and, **1991-99**: 983–85
status of U.S., overview, **1989-90**: 241–42; **2003**: 485
successor states, **1991-99**: 758–59, 1169–74
Slovak Republic, **1991-99**: 1148–49
Slovenia, **1991-99**: 1146–48
Soviet Union, claims settlement and, **2007**: 262
Soviet Union successor states, **1991-99**: 1169–74

Diplomatic relations and recognition (continued)
Taiwan, nonrecognition of, **1991-99**: 662–64, 702–3; **2005**: 740; **2007**: 434–36
Tajikistan, **1991-99**: 1174
Turkmenistan, **1991-99**: 1174
Ukraine, **1991-99**: 1173
Uzbekistan, **1991-99**: 1174
Vietnam, **1989-90**: 241, 526–27; **1991-99**: 241, 1083–86, 1153–62, 1493, 1969–70; **2000**: 570
Yugoslavia (Former Republic of), **1991-99**: 983, 2042; **2000**: 561–64
Diplomatic Security Act (1986), 1989-90: 264–65
Direct Guarantees and Standby Letters of Credit, Convention on (UN), 1991-99: 1812–14
Disabilities, persons with, 1991-99: 951; **2001**: 272–73. *See also* Competency
alien guardian for helpless alien, **1991-99**: 88
Americans with Disabilities Act of 1990 (ADA), **2001**: 250–54; **2002**: 283–85; **2003**: 301; **2005**: 276, 288, 292
Title III, **2005**: 707–11
Civil Rights of Institutionalized Persons Act. *See* Civil Rights of Institutionalized Persons Act (CRIPA) (1980)
criminal law in U.S. and, **1991-99**: 333–34, 964
discrimination against, **2002**: 283
human rights of, **2001**: 272–73
Individuals with Disabilities in Education Act (IDEA), **2005**: 292
Persons with Disabilities, draft Comprehensive and Integral International Convention on the Protection of, **2002**: 283; **2005**: 320–21; **2006**: 382–84
adoption of, **2006**: 383
U.S. not party to, **2006**: 284, 382–83
Rehabilitation Act, **2005**: 292
right of everyone to enjoyment of highest attainable standard of physical and mental health, **2005**: 332–33
U.S. antidiscrimination policy, **2002**: 283–85; **2003**: 299–303
waiver of oath of allegiance for naturalization of, **1991-99**: 15–19; **2003**: 4–5
Disappearances. *See* Human rights
Disarmament, gender equality and, 2000: 354
Disaster relief
consular functions, **1989-90**: 64–66
protection of persons, **2008**: 274–75
telecommunications for disaster mitigation and relief operations, **1991-99**: 1791
U.S.–India initiative, **2005**: 1080
Discovery process. *See* Evidence

Discrimination
anti-Semitism, **2003**: 297–99
disabilities. *See* Disabilities, persons with
Discrimination (Employment and Occupation), Convention Concerning, **1991-99**: 994–95
Equal Employment Opportunity Commission, **2005**: 288
Executive Order 13160, **2005**: 261–62
gender, **1991-99**: 897–911; **2000**: 351–55; **2001**: 269–71; **2002**: 277–80; **2003**: 290–93; **2004**: 269; **2006**: 372–76
Afghanistan, **2001**: 269
Africa, women's justice and empowerment in, U.S. initiative, **2005**: 307–8
antidiscrimination efforts, **2001**: 269; **2002**: 277–80
in citizenship laws, **1991-99**: 1–9
Convention on the Elimination of All Forms of Discrimination Against Women (CEDAW) (1980). *See* Gender issues
economic globalization, **2000**: 354
equal opportunity for women and men, **2005**: 311–13
immunity of UN officials, **2008**: 501–4
reproductive rights. *See* Health issues
Security Council resolutions on, **2008**: 286–88
U.S. report to UN Committee on sex discrimination in education, **2005**: 262
women's ownership rights over land and housing, **2005**: 310–11
persons with disabilities. *See* Disabilities, persons with
Pregnancy Discrimination Act (PDA) of 1978, **2005**: 262
race. *See* Racial discrimination
religion. *See* Religion and religious freedom
Displaced Persons Act (1948), **1991-99**: 28, 29–30; **2002**: 6–7; **2003**: 6–9; **2004**: 2, 3–4
Dispute resolution, **2002**: 392–93. *See also* Arbitration; Canada, *subheading*: Softwood Lumber Agreement (SLA); North American Free Trade Agreement (NAFTA); World Trade Organization (WTO)
District of Columbia
location of diplomatic and consular buildings, **2000**: 626–37; **2001**: 540–44
political status, **2001**: 266–67, 352–53
Divorce. *See also* Children; Head-of-state immunity; Maintenance obligations
evidence taken abroad, **2006**: 966–69
Djibouti
advance notice requirements for passage through territorial waters, **1989-90**: 440–42

Djibouti (continued)
American Servicemembers' Protection Act waiver and, **2003**: 238
exclusive economic zone limits, **1989-90**: 463–64
Horn of Africa Recovery and Food Security Act (1992) and, **1991-99**: 938
territorial sea baselines, **1989-90**: 459–60
DNA databases. *See* Biometric identification
Doha declarations. *See* World Trade Organization (WTO)
Dolphin protection. *See* Marine conservation
Dominica
extradition and mutual legal assistance, **1991-99**: 396, 452; **2000**: 185*n*; **2001**: 92*n*
maritime counter-drug trade agreement, **1991-99**: 1606
party to Inter-American Convention Against Terrorism (OAS Terrorism Convention), **2005**: 111
U.S. assistance tied to agreement not to enforce ICC Statute against U.S personnel, **2004**: 187
Dominican Republic
Article 98 agreement (nonsurrender of Americans to ICC) with U.S., **2005**: 202
claim to be archipelagic state, **2007**: 641–43
consular immunity, **1991-99**: 1312
consular notification and nationals of, **1991-99**: 259, 280–82
damages, **2008**: 36–44
Dominican Republic–Central American Free Trade Agreement (DR-CAFTA), **2004**: 616–19; **2005**: 636–37, 640, 757; **2006**: 606, 764; **2008**: 573, 582
drug trade, **2001**: 120; **2002**: 124; **2003**: 181; **2004**: 133–34; **2005**: 135; **2006**: 213; **2007**: 163; **2008**: 113
maritime counter-drug trade agreement, **1991-99**: 1606
Environmental Cooperation Agreement with U.S., **2005**: 756–57
extradition and mutual legal assistance, **1991-99**: 392, 396; **2000**: 179, 185*n*; **2001**: 93*n*; **2003**: 139–40; **2007**: 124–26
Haiti and, **1991-99**: 1884; **2002**: 31
intellectual property rights
legal reform, **2008**: 606
Watch List, **2006**: 768; **2007**: 610
Inter-American Convention Against Corruption, party to, **2006**: 238
money laundering in, **2004**: 135
stolen vehicle treaty, **2000**: 169–70; **2002**: 68
trade negotiations with U.S., **2003**: 682–83, 684

Doping in sports. *See also* Drug issues
Convention against (UNESCO), **2005:** 774, 781–84; **2008:** 737–42
Council of Europe Anti-Doping Convention, **2005:** 782
Executive Order 13165, **2005:** 782
World Anti-Doping Agency (WADA), **2005:** 781–83; **2008:** 737–42
World Anti-Doping Code, **2005:** 781; **2008:** 737–42
Double jeopardy, 1991-99: 507, 526, 872
DPRK. *See* Korea, North (Democratic People's Republic of Korea (DPRK))
Dromoland Castle Declaration on Combating Terrorism and on Non-Proliferation of Weapons of Mass Destruction, 2005: 1096
Drug issues
Note: This heading does not deal with trafficking and illegal drugs which is covered at the heading Drug trade.
Controlled Substances Act (CSA), **2006:** 223
patents, **1991-99:** 1372, 1374–75, 1506; **2003:** 673–79, 815–16. *See also* Trade Related Aspects of Intellectual Property Rights (TRIPS Agreement)
research and development, **2002:** 718
Drug trade, 2000: 164, 167, 232; **2006:** 212–16. *See also* Crime; Money laundering; specific countries
aerial interdiction assistance
involving non-lethal force, **2005:** 145–47
use of force in, **1991-99:** 538–47; **2001:** 121–28; **2005:** 145; **2006:** 225–26; **2007:** 166–67; **2008:** 113–14
blocking assets of drug traffickers, **1991-99:** 547–51; **2001:** 143–44, **2008:** 114–15
in Burma. *See* Burma, *subheading*: drug trade
Colombia. *See* Colombia, *subheading*: drug trade. *See also* aerial interdiction assistance, *this heading*; law enforcement and, *this heading*
Controlled Substances Act (CSA), **2001:** 128, 130, 131, 133–35; **2003:** 184; **2005:** 137–39, 142, 143, 268; **2006:** 34, 35–36, 223
Cooperating Nation Information Exchange (CNIES), **2005:** 145–46
denial of visa for person suspected of participation in, **1991-99:** 68–71
deportation of aliens based on, **1989-90:** 31
doping. *See* Doping in sports
Ecuador. *See* Ecuador, *subheading*: drug trade
Egypt and, **2005:** 182
Foreign Narcotics Kingpin Designation Act (1999), **1991-99:** 550–51; **2001:** 143, 144–45, 822; **2003:** 186–87; **2006:** 220–21; **2008:** 114–15

Drug trade (continued)
Foreign Narcotics Kingpins Sanctions Regulations, **2000**: 744–45
Inter-American Drug Abuse Control Commission (CICAD), **2006**: 220
International Crime Control Strategy, **1991-99**: 396–97
International Criminal Court jurisdiction and, **1991-99**: 577, 632
International Narcotics Control Board, **2006**: 219
International Narcotics Control Strategy Report. *See* U.S. narcotics report and certification, *this heading*
law enforcement and
counternarcotics assistance, **1991-99**: 860, 916; **2001**: 89–96
extradition and, **1991-99**: 389, 392, 398, 420–21; **2001**: 89–96
extraterritorial arrest, **1989-90**: 95–98; **1991-99**: 442, 444–45
law enforcement needs in developing countries, **2003**: 212
multilateral extradition treaties, **2003**: 142
mutual legal assistance treaties, **1991-99**: 447–58
protecting confidentiality of communications, **1991-99**: 801
Maritime Drug Law Enforcement Act (2002), **2002**: 134–37; **2008**: 128, 129
maritime interdiction, **1989-90**: 449, 450, 452–56; **1991-99**: 1600–8; **2002**: 133–37; **2004**: 691–92, 1078, 1091; **2005**: 147–53; **2008**: 651
methamphetamines, **2007**: 164–66
Combat Methamphetamine Epidemic Act (CMEA) (2006), **2006**: 215–16; **2007**: 162, 164
International Narcotics Control Strategy Report and, **2006**: 216–20
Narcotics Control Trade Act (1974), **2001**: 119; **2002**: 125; **2004**: 133
prohibition on assistance to drug traffickers, **1991-99**: 551–54
Project Prism, **2006**: 219
Psychotropic Substances Act (1978), **2001**: 131; **2005**: 142
religious use of controlled substances, **2001**: 128–43; **2003**: 184–86; **2006**: 221–25
self-defense by country against, **1989-90**: 95–96
treaties and international agreements
Air and Maritime Trafficking in Illicit Drugs, Caribbean Cooperation Agreement on, **2005**: 147–53
Illicit Drug Traffic, UN Convention on (1988), **1989-90**: 128–33, 450, 455; **1991-99**: 449, 557, 1601–2, 1604; **2000**: 407; **2001**: 129–33, 135, 140–41; **2002**: 122, 126, 137; **2003**: 142, 184–86; **2004**: 145; **2005**: 137–44; **2006**: 219, 221–25
maritime interdiction agreements, bilateral, **1991-99**: 1604–8
multilateral extradition treaties, **2003**: 142
mutual legal assistance treaties, **1991-99**: 447–58
Psychotropic Substances, UN Convention on (1971), **2001**: 129–33, 135, 140–41; **2003**: 184–86; **2005**: 137–44

Drug trade (continued)
ship boarding agreements, **2006**: 838–40
Transnational Crime, UN Convention on. *See* Crime, *subheading*: organized crime
treaty obligations of successor states, **1991-99**: 746, 750
UN Office of Drugs and Crime (UNODC), **2008**: 396–97
U.S. military action in Panama and, **1989-90**: 552, 553
U.S. narcotics report and certification
designations and certifications, **1991-99**: 396–97; **2001**: 119–21, 143–45; **2002**: 122–25; **2003**: 181–84; **2004**: 133–34; **2005**: 135–36; **2006**: 212–16; **2007**: 163–64; **2008**: 113
International Narcotics Control Strategy Report, **1991-99**: 396–97; **2001**: 119; **2002**: 125–26; **2003**: 180; **2004**: 133, 135; **2005**: 136; **2006**: 212, 216–20; **2007**: 162; **2008**: 112–13
USA PATRIOT Improvement and Reauthorization Act (2005), **2007**: 162
Dubai
immunity in U.S. courts, **1991-99**: 1285–89
Dubai Declaration on chemicals management, 2006: 865–66
Dubai Ports World, 2006: 774–80
Due process, 1991-99: 408–9, 413, 659, 942, 961, 1134, 1336, 1718, 1829–30, 1831, 1875, 2261. *See also* Constitution, U.S.
alien detainees in U.S. custody, **1991-99**: 93; **2001**: 17–18; **2003**: 330. *See also* Detainees, military
American Declaration of Rights and Duties of Man and, **2007**: 387
applicability to U.S. constituent entities, **1991-99**: 810
asylum application, **2000**: 131–33
capital punishment and, **1991-99**: 963, 964; **2000**: 392–96; **2001**: 294, 313, 316; **2004**: 335, 337–38; **2008**: 377
Civil Liberties Act and, **2004**: 231, 232
claim in IACHR against U.S. by indigenous people, **2002**: 370
clemency request for Mexican national in U.S. prison, **2002**: 49–50
constitutionality of California's Holocaust Victims' Insurance Relief Act, **2002**: 415–29
constitutionality of California's World War II forced labor statute, **2002**: 454, 455
consular notification and, **1991-99**: 260, 285, 287, 310–11, 320, 332, 334, 336, 339–40; **2003**: 45, 66–70, 81–82. *See also* Consular notification and access
designation of terrorist organization as violation of, **2001**: 109–10, 111, 112–17; **2002**: 91–94; **2003**: 175–79; **2006**: 197–98, 1000–1. *See also* Constitution, U.S., *subheading*: antiterrorism statutes, challenges to as unconstitutional

Due process (continued)
individuals detained by the Department of Defense at Guantanamo Bay and, **2004:** 1001–3, 1005–15. *See also* Detainees, military
enforcement of foreign judgments in U.S. courts, **1991-99:** 1832, 1833–41; **2000:** 442
equal protection component. *See* Equal protection
ex parte interim relief in arbitration, **2004:** 810–11
Executive Branch foreign affairs authority and, **2002:** 243, 989–90
expropriation considerations, **1991-99:** 1465, 1470; **2008:** 541, 602
under NAFTA, **2004:** 599–600
extradition considerations, **1991-99:** 413–14, 431; **2004:** 76–77
objection to extradition based on requesting country's lack of, **2000:** 215–16
relevance to extradition request of possible violation of, **1989-90:** 80–88
extraterritorial jurisdiction and, **2002:** 135, 421, 422–23, 454
forcible abduction by law enforcement and, **1991-99:** 505
FSIA and, **1991-99:** 1183, 1207, 1222, 1243–48; **2002:** 465, 500, 534; **2003:** 505–6; **2004:** 459, 494, 512
governmental obligation to provide, **2008:** 350
habeas corpus review under, **2004:** 204–5, 980, 996–97, 998–99, 1011, 1012–13; **2005:** 282, 995, 1003, 1008–18, 1033, 1037–38
claims by individuals detained in U.S. as enemy combatants, **2002:** 986–1000; **2006:** 1175–76, 1198; **2008:** 918
in extradition request, **1989-90:** 82–84, **2008:** 11
ICCPR and, **2008:** 376
immigration issues, **2008:** 281, 311
admission of aliens, **2008:** 911
deportation, **1991-99:** 124
family unity, **2008:** 344
Inter-American Commission on Human Rights and, **2004:** 229, 231
International Criminal Court and, **1991-99:** 614, 628; **2004:** 176–77
International Criminal Tribunal for former Yugoslavia and for Rwanda, **1991-99:** 526, 588, 605
international travel rights and, **2001:** 11–13; **2002:** 14
jurisdiction, basis for, **2008:** 755
maritime laws and, **2008:** 128, 129
migrants in safe haven in Guantanamo, **1991-99:** 188, 191–94
Native Americans
in Indian Claims Commission case, **2002:** 376–77
tribal compensation for treaty abrogation, **2008:** 283
passport revocation, **1989-90:** 16–17; **1991-99:** 52–53

Due process (continued)
personal jurisdiction requirement, **2002**: 534, 875
racial discrimination, **2008**: 277
re-importation of arms cases, **1991-99**: 2261–62
required in U.S. treaties, **1991-99**: 1831–32, 1835, 1874
right to counsel, **2005**: 280
rights of nongovernmental foreign entity, **2001**: 112–13
rule of law and, **2008**: 327
service of process on visiting foreign officials, **2002**: 581–85
in time of war, **2004**: 1009–14
torture and, **2004**: 318–19*n*
trademark denial, Cuban litigation over, **2006**: 1010–13
in U.S. Constitution, **2000**: 1, 738; **2001**: 414*n*; **2003**: 332, 506; **2004**: 204–5, 923*n*; **2005**: 117–22, 124–25, 126, 129–32, 260, 266, 278, 279, 281, 392, 791, 856–58, 861, 863, 865–66, 964, 995, 998–1006, 1012, 1013; **2006**: 67, 729; **2007**: 105, 141, 196, 239, 830, 938, 963, 970, 975. *See also* Constitution, U.S., *subheading*: Fifth Amendment
Due Process Clause, **2007**: 239, 971, 974; **2008**: 128–30, 277, 281, 283
Vienna Convention on Consular Relations and, **2004**: 40, 43
visa processing and, **1991-99**: 114, 117
Dumping. *See also* Continued Dumping and Subsidy Offset Act of 2000 (Byrd Amendment or CDSOA); Trade; World Trade Organization (WTO)
Antidumping Act, **2003**: 636, 655, 656
antidumping measures. *See also* World Trade Organization (WTO)
applicability to low-enriched uranium, **2008**: 953–60
on beef and rice, settlement of dispute, **2005**: 624–25
duty order on oil country tubular goods from Mexico, **2005**: 634
anti-suit injunctions, **2008**: 764–71
NAFTA Chapter 11 and Chapter 19 disputes, **2003**: 636–42; **2006**: 702–9
regulations under Law of the Sea, UN Convention on (UNCLOS), **2003**: 741–42

E

Early Release Scheme
UK policy, **2006**: 123
East African Community
Trade and Investment Framework Agreement (TIFA), **2008**: 573–74
East Timor
American Servicemembers' Protection Act waiver and, **2003**: 238
crimes against humanity in, **2000**: 245–46

East Timor (continued)
peacekeeping and humanitarian effort in, **1991-99**: 519–20, 962, 2047–48; **2002**: 903
treaty affairs, **2002**: 177
UN Mission in Support of, **2002**: 157–58
UN Transition Administration in, **2000**: 308–10; **2001**: 426–27
U.S. diplomatic relations, **2002**: 463–64
Economic, Social and Cultural Rights, International Covenant on. *See* Human rights
Economic assistance. *See* Foreign assistance
Economic sanctions. *See* Sanctions
Ecuador
Andean Trade Promotion and Drug Eradication Act (2002), **2008**: 577–79
Antarctica, environmental protection in, **1991-99**: 1749
anti-suit injunction, **2006**: 953–58
border dispute with Peru, **1991-99**: 2004–10
citizens' claim against U.S. corporation under Alien Tort Statute, **2002**: 355–57
class action claims against U.S. oil company, **2001**: 336–37
cultural objects protection, **1991-99**: 1803
drug trade, **2001**: 120; **2002**: 124; **2003**: 181; **2004**: 133–34; **2005**: 135; **2006**: 213, 214–15; **2007**: 163; **2008**: 113
counter-drug trade agreement, **1991-99**: 1608
ship-boarding agreements, **2006**: 838–40
environmental and conservation issues, **1991-99**: 1782
European Union–U.S. banana trade dispute, **2001**: 650
evaluation of impartiality of court, **2000**: 412–14
extradition and mutual legal assistance, **2000**: 185*n*; **2001**: 90–96
fisheries negotiations with U.S., **2005**: 613
free trade agreement, **2004**: 618
Hague Child Abduction Convention, compliance with, **2003**: 127; **2004**: 54; **2006**: 101; **2008**: 50
intellectual property rights Watch List, **2006**: 768; **2007**: 610
Inter-American Convention Against Corruption, party to, **2006**: 238
Inter-American Tropical Tuna Commission, **2000**: 307
prisoner transfer treaty, **2000**: 171; **2001**: 51
reservation to Whaling Convention, objection to, **1991-99**: 1584
satellite regulation and, **2008**: 392
succession to treaties, Colombian Union, **1991-99**: 744
territorial claims, **1991-99**: 1584; **2004**: 700–703
trade and investment issues, **1991-99**: 1415–16, 1466
trade negotiations with U.S., **2003**: 682–83
trafficking in persons actions, **2004**: 164; **2005**: 162

Ecuador (continued)
U.S. military assistance, **2006**: 278
waiver of Article 98 agreement with U.S. (nonsurrender of Americans to ICC), **2006**: 279
whaling regulation, **2001**: 218
Education, 2003: 322
Cuba, educational travel to, **2008**: 810–13
Education Amendments of 1972, Title IX, **1991-99**: 901; **2005**: 262, 263, 288
equal access for women, **2005**: 312
Higher Education and Vocational Education and Training, Agreement Between U.S. and European Community, **2000**: 310–11
Holocaust Education, Remembrance and Research, Task Force for International Cooperation on, **2005**: 319
on human rights, OAS Inter-American Program for the Promotion and Protection of the Human Rights of Migrants, **2005**: 340
Individuals with Disabilities in Education Act (IDEA), **2005**: 292
religious hatred and, **2005**: 320
right to, **2005**: 333–34
U.S. report to UN Committee on sex discrimination in, **2005**: 262
Education Department, U.S., Office for Civil Rights, 2005: 262, 288
Educational exchange, 1991-99: 1807–8
Iran, **2006**: 989–90
Effective assistance of counsel. *See* Constitution, U.S., *subheading*: Sixth Amendment
Egmont Group, 2002: 892–93
Egypt
agreement concerning parental access, **2003**: 129–31
alienage jurisdiction statute and, **1991-99**: 36–37
assassination attempt on Mubarak, Hosni, **1991-99**: 144
consular notification and, **1991-99**: 261, 307
cultural property protection in armed conflict and, **1991-99**: 2072
drug trade, **2005**: 182
extradition and mutual legal assistance, **2000**: 166, 185*n*
human rights in, **1991-99**: 853
intellectual property rights Watch List, **2006**: 768; **2007**: 608, 610; **2008**: 606
international child abduction case, **1991-99**: 380
maritime issues, **1991-99**: 1580–83, 1596
Middle East Peace Process and, **1991-99**: 1986, 1991, 1995, 2003; **2004**: 951
non-North Atlantic Treaty Organization (NATO) ally, designation as, **2005**: 1044
nuclear fuel return program, **2004**: 1139
Palestinian talks, participation in, **2005**: 905, 907

Egypt (continued)
Protocol between Egypt and Israel, **1989-90**: 206–7
religious freedom violations, **1991-99**: 926; **2003**: 296
Terrorist Bombings Convention, **2006**: 288–91
transfer tax on sale of diplomatic property belonging to, **2002**: 579–81
treaty issues, **1991-99**: 744
El Salvador
boarding of U.S. vessel on high seas, **1991-99**: 1600–1602
citizens of U.S. claim against military commanders under Torture Victims Protection Act, **2002**: 348–51
consular immunity, **1991-99**: 1312–13
consular notification and, **1991-99**: 263–64
debt for nature swaps, **2001**: 737; **2008**: 722
Environmental Cooperation Agreement with U.S., **2005**: 756–57
extension of temporary protected status of refugees from, **2003**: 33–36
extradition and mutual legal assistance, **1991-99**: 392; **2000**: 185*n*; **2001**: 90–96
extrajudicial killing, **2004**: 362–63, 382–83
family support enforcement, **2006**: 942
free trade agreement, **2004**: 617–19
human rights issues, **1991-99**: 220, 851, 962
Inter-American Convention Against Corruption, party to, **2006**: 238
Inter-American Convention Against Terrorism (OAS Terrorism Convention), party to, **2005**: 111
Inter-American Tropical Tuna Commission, **2000**: 307
naturalization convention, **2002**: 203
nonlethal aerial counternarcotics efforts, assistance for, **2005**: 146
protection of cultural property in, **1991-99**: 1795–97
reciprocity in child support enforcement, **2008**: 759
relief from immigration requirements for certain resident nationals of, **1991-99**: 250
sanctuary movement to protect asylum seekers from, **1989-90**: 40–42
trade and investment issues, **1991-99**: 380, 1466, 1749
trade negotiations with U.S., **2003**: 683–86
Tropical Forest Conservation Act agreement, **2008**: 722
Elections
Cambodia, political transition in, **1989-90**: 529–30, 531–32, 533
corruption. *See* Corruption
Cote d'Ivoire, **2005**: 933–34
democracy and, **2005**: 434, 435. *See also* Democracy
Help America Vote Act (HAVA), **2005**: 284, 285, 288
judicial elections in U.S., **2005**: 294
Lebanon, **2005**: 931–33
OSCE observers in 2004 U.S. presidential election, **2005**: 284–86

Elections (continued)
Palestinian Legislative Council elections, **2005**: 914
Palestinian presidential election, **2005**: 905, 912
Puerto Ricans and right to vote in U.S. presidential elections, **2005**: 246–51
Voting Rights Act of 1965, **2005**: 288
Electronic commerce, **2006**: 935–38
electronic contracts convention, **2002**: 820; **2003**: 838–39; **2004**: 804–5, 814–15; **2005**: 214, 799–800, 801
Federal E-Signature and Global E-Commerce Act, **2003**: 838; **2004**: 805
Hague Judgments Convention and, **2000**: 736, 740–41
Internet transactions as basis for personal jurisdiction over foreign entities, **2003**: 901–5
joint statements on electronic commerce
U.S.–European Union, **1991-99**: 1525–27; **2000**: 301–5; **2005**: 801–2
U.S.–Ireland, **1991-99**: 1527–28
OECD Guidelines for Consumer Protection in Electronic Commerce, **2005**: 660
private international law work on, overview of, **2001**: 791–96
tariffs on electronic transmissions across borders, **1991-99**: 1393–94
UNCITRAL work on, **1991-99**: 1809–12, 1854, 1857–58; **2001**: 784–86; **2002**: 820, 834–37. *See also* electronic contracts convention, *this heading*
model laws, **1991-99**: 1809–12; **2001**: 784–85, 791–93; **2006**: 934–36
UNIDROIT Principles for International Commercial Contracts and, **2001**: 786, 793
WTO and, **1991-99**: 1390, 1398, 1503
E-mail. *See* Internet
Embargoes. *See* Sanctions; Trade
Embassies. *See* Consular offices and personnel; Diplomatic missions and personnel
Emergency Economic Powers Act, International (IEEPA). *See also* Trading with the Enemy Act (1917)
amended by International Emergency Economic Powers Enhancement Act (2007), **2007**: 827–28
authority exercised
Belarus, **2006**: 984
Burma, **1991-99**: 180; **2000**: 334–35; **2005**: 891–94; **2007**: 808; **2008**: 792
Haiti, **1991-99**: 189
Iran, **1991-99**: 1913, 1916–18; **2000**: 230, 541, 550, 557, 559–60, 617–19; **2006**: 986–90; **2007**: 482; **2008**: 414, 983

Emergency Economic Powers Act, International (IEEPA) (continued)
Iraq, **2000**: 621, 624; **2003**: 556, 909, 911, 917, 921–25; **2004**: 885, 888; **2005**: 869; **2007**: 818, 819
Kuwait, **1991-99**: 1925
Lebanon, **2007**: 805–7
Liberia, **2004**: 919–22
Libya, **1991-99**: 1913; **2002**: 577; **2004**: 929, 933
narcotics traffickers, **1991-99**: 547–51; **2001**: 143–44
nonproliferation, **1989-90**: 512; **1991-99**: 2363; **2001**: 848; **2002**: 1039; **2003**: 1116–18; **2004**: 1109–12, 1114, 1133–34; **2005**: 1126, 1128; **2007**: 1083
North Korea, **2008**: 965
Panama, **1989-90**: 372
Sierra Leone, **2001**: 797
Sudan, **1991-99**: 1938; **2006**: 975–77, 979
Syria, **2004**: 901; **2005**: 886–88; **2008**: 799
Taliban, **1991-99**: 1964; **2001**: 803; **2002**: 883–84
terrorism, **1991-99**: 1964; **2001**: 803, 881, 883–86, 889, 892, 899; **2002**: 95–98, 100, 412, 883–84; **2003**: 172; **2005**: 128–32, 265, 545; **2007**: 155; **2008**: 99–101
Yugoslavia/Serbia and Western Balkans, **1991-99**: 1950, 1956, 1958–59; **2001**: 803–4, 806; **2003**: 931–33
Zimbabwe, **2003**: 929; **2005**: 889, 921; **2008**: 801
authority to attach blocked assets, **1989-90**: 419, 422; **1991-99**: 55, 1225; **2000**: 230, 541; **2004**: 518*n*, 525–26; **2005**: 265; **2008**: 802
diplomatic property, **2000**: 541–42
protective blocking of Russian property relating to the downblending of Russian uranium stocks, **2002**: 1039–41
Chemical Weapons Convention and, **2006**: 1250
derogations under International Covenant on Civil and Political Rights, relation to, **2005**: 265–66
exemptions
agricultural commodities, medicines and medical devices, **2000**: 748
humanitarian aid, **2005**: 131–32
informational materials, **2004**: 925
and Foreign Investment and National Security Act of 2007 (FINSA), **2007**: 604
UN Participation Act and, **2006**: 1017–19
USA PATRIOT Act amendments, **2001**: 925–28
Emergency Security Assistance Act (1973), **2007**: 222
Emergency Telecommunications Resources for Disaster Mitigation and Relief Operations, Tampere Convention on Provision of, **1991-99**: 1791

Employees of consular and diplomatic missions. *See* Diplomatic missions and personnel
Employment. *See also* Labor issues
American Jobs Creation Act of 2004 (AJCA), **2005:** 626
child labor. *See* Children
Declaration on Fundamental Principles and Rights at Work, **2000:** 369
disabled employees. *See* Americans with Disabilities Act of 1990 (ADA)
discrimination. *See* Discrimination
employment-based immigrants, classification of certain former Soviet and Baltic State scientists as, **2005:** 9
sexual harassment, Title VII actions, **2005:** 263–64
V-11 category—former employees of private U.S. companies or organizations, **2005:** 26
Endangered Species Act (1973), 1991-99: 257, 1717, 1721, 1723, 1767, 1769; **2001:** 685; **2005:** 753
Endangered Species of Wild Fauna and Flora, Convention on International Trade in, **2001:** 489, 490; **2003:** 581, 582, 810; **2004:** 769, 771, 775
Enemy combatants. *See* Detainees, military; Prisoners of war
Energy issues. *See* Nuclear energy; Oil
Energy Reorganization Act (1974), 2004: 1103–4
Enforcement of Foreign Arbitral Awards, New York Convention on, 1989-90: 501, 502; **1991-99:** 1259, 1473, 1827, 1848, 1851; **2000:** 592; **2002:** 197, 873–75; **2003:** 841; **2004:** 809, 822, 823, 825–26, 827, 829; **2005:** 788, 789; **2008:** 760, 764, 777–82. *See also* Arbitration
Enforcement of Judgments, draft Convention on. *See* Hague Conference on Private International Law (HCCH)
England. *See* United Kingdom
Enhanced Border Security and Visa Entry Reform Act (2002), 2003: 17
Enhancement of Trade, Security, and Human Rights through Sanctions Reform Act (1999), 1991-99: 1974
Entry requirements into U.S. *See* Border issues; Immigration and visas; Passports, U.S.
Environmental Cooperation, Commission for, 1991-99: 1314
Environmental issues. *See also* Fish and marine mammals; Marine conservation; Trade; World Trade Organization (WTO)
air pollution. *See* Air pollution
Alien Tort Statute claims concerning, **1991-99:** 990–91; **2001:** 336–37; **2002:** 333–34, 339–40, 344–45, 355–56, 357; **2003:** 371–74; **2008:** 239
Antarctica
Antarctic Treaty Protocol on Environmental Protection, **1991-99:** 1781–84; **2002:** 798–800

Environmental issues (continued)
environmental emergencies, **2005**: 755
tourism measure, **2004**: 779–84
ship-based tourism and, **2007**: 728–29
Arctic issues, **1991-99**: 1777–80; **2001**: 741–42; **2008**: 624, 626
armed conflict and, **2006**: 1077–84
Basel Convention. *See* Basel Convention on the Control of Transboundary Movements of Hazardous Wastes and their Disposal
biological diversity protection, **2002**: 769–70
Convention on, **1991-99**: 1757–66; **2006**: 888
Biosafety Protocol to, **2000**: 222; **2003**: 804–7
chemicals management, strategic approach to, **2006**: 865–66
climate change. *See* Climate change
Comprehensive Environmental Response, Compensation and Liability Act (CERCLA) (1980), **1991-99**: 1620; **2006**: 855–60; **2007**: 687–89
cooperation on in Western Hemisphere
agreement, U.S. and Costa Rica, Dominican Republic, El Salvador, Guatemala, Honduras, Nicaragua, and U.S., **2005**: 756, 757
Border Environment Cooperation Commission, **2005**: 606
border environmental cooperation agreement between U.S. and Mexico, **2005**: 606
Rio Declaration on Environment and Development, **1991-99**: 1649–55; **2002**: 768–69; **2003**: 373
customary international law, **1991-99**: 990–91; **2002**: 344–45; **2003**: 373–74; **2006**: 1077–84
desertification, **1991-99**: 1770; **2000**: 728–33
Federal Insecticide, Fungicide and Rodenticide Act, **1991-99**: 1687; **2002**: 775, 776, 777
fish. *See* Fish and marine mammals
forest conservation, **2003**: 775–77; **2004**: 745
debt-for-nature agreements, **2001**: 667, 737, 738–40; **2003**: 776–77; **2004**: 745; **2006**: 886–88; **2007**: 732–34; **2008**: 721–22
illegal logging, **2007**: 677, 734–36
Indonesia logging initiative, **2006**: 801–3
International Tropical Timber Agreement, **2007**: 736
Northeastern Interstate Forest Fire Protection Compact, **2000**: 296
Tropical Forest Conservation Act (1998), **2001**: 738; **2002**: 780; **2003**: 775, 776; **2004**: 745; **2006**: 887; **2007**: 733; **2008**: 722
Gulf War damage, **1991-99**: 1099, 1102, 1104, 2101–2

Environmental issues (continued)
hazardous activities, transboundary harm arising from, International Law Commission on, **2000**: 420; **2002**: 395–96; **2006**: 861–62; **2007**: 685–91. *See also* Basel Convention on the Control of Transboundary Movements of Hazardous Wastes and their Disposal
hazardous chemicals agreement, **2004**: 777–78
heavy metal pollutants, UN Economic Commission for Europe regional agreement on, **1991-99**: 1668, 1669
intellectual property issues, **1991-99**: 1653–54, 1761–62
law of the sea. *See* Law of the Sea, UN Convention on (UNCLOS)
marine environment. *See* Fish and marine mammals; Marine conservation
mercury contamination, **2007**: 691–92
migratory bird and animal protection agreements, protocols with Canada and Mexico, **1991-99**: 1770–77
Multilateral Agreement on Investment and, **1991-99**: 1490–91
natural resources, shared, **2005**: 767; **2006**: 862–63
oil pollution. *See* Marine conservation
ozone protection. *See* Air pollution
Persistent Organic Pollutants (POPs). *See* Persistent Organic Pollutants (POPS)
polar bears, Russia–U.S. agreement on protection of, **2002**: 800–805
presidential permit, considerations in transfer of for border crossing, **2005**: 592–93
private international law and, **1991-99**: 1856
radioactive waste management agreement, **1991-99**: 1696–99
regulatory enforcement, **2001**: 747
sea. *See* Law of the Sea, UN Convention on (UNCLOS); Maritime issues
sustainable development, **1991-99**: 1649–55; **2001**: 743–48; **2002**: 765–71, 787; **2005**: 462
trade issues, **1991-99**: 1388–90, 1392, 1401, 1412–13, 1651, 1652, 1653; **2003**: 808–13; **2007**: 576–79, 580–81, 585
bilateral environmental cooperation, **2004**: 776
multilateral environmental agreements, **2004**: 618, 767–76
NAFTA side agreement on, **1991-99**: 1424, 1426–28, 1429
Prior Informed Consent Procedure for Certain Hazardous Chemicals and Pesticides in International Trade, Rotterdam Convention on, **1991-99**: 1683–87; **2002**: 783–85; **2004**: 769, 771, 775, 777–78
U.S. trade agreements and, **2001**: 665, 667–72; **2003**: 686
transboundary aquifers, **2008**: 716–21
U.S. state law, preemption by federal laws and treaties, **1991-99**: 775–85

Environmental issues (continued)
water pollution. *See* Marine conservation
wilderness areas, regulation of, **2006:** 718–19
wildlife. *See also* Wildlife
trafficking, **2007:** 730–31
Environmental Modification Techniques, Convention on the Prohibition of Military or Any Other Hostile Use of, 1991-99: 2073
E-passports. *See* Passports, U.S., *subheading*: electronic (e-passports)
Equal Employment Opportunity Commission, 2005: 288
Equal opportunity for women and men. *See* Gender issues
Equal protection, 2007: 199, 217, 295, 313. *See also* Constitution, U.S.
anti-discrimination protections, **1989-90:** 169; **1991-99:** 885–87, 891–97, 901; **2001:** 257, 259, 267; **2005:** 305; **2008:** 277, 279. *See also* Human rights
capital punishment and, **1991-99:** 332
in citizenship determinations, **1991-99:** 1–8; **2000:** 1–19; **2001:** 7–8
controlled substances for religious purposes, **2001:** 129, 136–39
domestic family planning organization claiming harm from U.S. foreign assistance policy, **2001:** 283
Equal Protection Clause, **1991-99:** 8, 788, 810, 897; **2005:** 278, 284; **2007:** 303
immigration law and, **1991-99:** 8, 114, 117–18, 788; **2008:** 281
undocumented immigrants, **2001:** 262
international travel rights, **2001:** 13
migrants in safe haven in Guantanamo, **1991-99:** 188, 192–94
Military Commissions and, **2004:** 1019
Native Americans, **2008:** 282
preemption of claims by federal foreign affairs authority and, **2004:** 444–45
racial discrimination, **2008:** 277
U.S. understanding on International Covenant on Civil and Political Rights, **1991-99:** 871, 876; **2008:** 346
Equality of arms, 2000: 392–96
Equatorial Guinea
government efforts regarding trafficking in persons, **2004:** 164, 165; **2007:** 169–70
maritime counterterrorism measures, conditions for failure to take, **2008:** 112
Eritrea
diplomatic relations, **1991-99:** 1150–51
Ethiopia peace agreement (2000), **2000:** 311–12; **2006:** 1055–58
Ethiopia/Eritrea Claims Commission, **2003:** 478–80
Ethiopian border dispute, **1991-99:** 2010–12; **2002:** 925–26; **2004:** 942

Eritrea (continued)
Ethiopian war, atrocities in, **2000**: 247–48
religious freedom violations, **2003**: 297; **2004**: 270, 272, 273; **2005**: 314, 316; **2006**: 377
terrorism and, noncooperation with antiterrorism efforts, **2008**: 88–89
UN peacekeeping mission in, **2005**: 943–45
Espionage, 1991-99: 86, 2320–22
Espousal of claims, 1989-90: 214–15. *See also* Remedies, *subheading*: exhaustion of remedies, requirement for; State responsibility
continuous nationality requirement, **1991-99**: 1075–76; **2001**: 385–86; **2002**: 395, 626–33; **2003**: 437–41, 610–13
dominant and effective nationality, Iran–United States Claims Tribunal (Case A/18; Case 298), **1991-99**: 1095–96
equitable vs. nominal ownership, **2002**: 634–36
NAFTA Chapter 11 disputes, **2002**: 624–41; **2003**: 610–12
loss of continuous nationality after corporate reorganization, **2002**: 624–41; **2003**: 613–15
transfer of international claims to corporate entity, **2002**: 636–40
expropriation claims, **1991-99**: 1075–76; **2004**: 500, 598*n*. *See also* Expropriation
Holocaust-related claims not espoused, **1991-99**: 1133
political question, **2001**: 385–86
requirements for, **1991-99**: 1075–76
settlement of espoused claim by U.S. not a "taking," **1991-99**: 1097–98
U.S. claims against German Democratic Republic, **1989-90**: 238–40
Esquipulas Accords, 1989-90: 156–60
Estonia
Australia Group membership, **2004**: 1130
bilateral investment treaties, **2003**: 609, 687, 695; **2004**: 623
diplomatic relations with U.S., **1989-90**: 242
nonrecognition of incorporation by USSR, **1989-90**: 272, 274
EU accession and trade agreements, **2006**: 754–56
extradition and mutual legal assistance, **1991-99**: 452; **2000**: 185*n*; **2006**: 127, 137, 138–39, 146; **2008**: 54
longshore work by alien crewmen from, **2002**: 757; **2003**: 764
NATO membership, **2003**: 424–26; **2004**: 411–12
relief from immigration requirements for certain resident nationals of, **1991-99**: 250
trade and investment issues, **1991-99**: 1455, 1466
visa waiver program, **2008**: 81–83
Estoppel, 1991-99: 9, 721–22, 724, 729; **2005**: 818

Ethiopia
border dispute with Eritrea, **1991-99**: 2010–12; **2002**: 925–26; **2004**: 942
Eritrea peace agreement (2000), **2000**: 311–12; **2006**: 1055–58
Eritrean war, atrocities in, **2000**: 247–48
Ethiopia/Eritrea Claims Commission, **2003**: 478–80
family as persecuted social group in asylum application, **1991-99**: 223–24
Horn Act and, **1991-99**: 938
open skies agreement with U.S., **2005**: 588
UN peacekeeping mission in, **2005**: 943–45
Eurojust
DOJ agreement with, **2006**: 163–67
European Atomic Energy Community, 1991-99: 2336–39
European Charter of Fundamental Rights, 2007: 68
European Commission, 1991-99: 1067, 1638; **2004**: 203, 227, 524. *See also* European Community; European Union
access to airline passenger data, **2004**: 108–16; **2005**: 586–87; **2006**: 168–72
administrative antitrust claims before, **2004**: 820, 851–56
antitrust issues, **1991-99**: 1549–50
bilateral investment treaties with U.S., Understanding concerning, **2004**: 624
exhaustion requirements for filing of foreign claims, **2004**: 351*n*
GPS agreement, **2004**: 738–39
regulatory cooperation with, **2004**: 647
suit by in U.S. court, **2004**: 820, 826
trade issues, **1991-99**: 1392, 1416, 1446
U.S.–EURATOM agreement, **1991-99**: 2336
European Commission on Human Rights, 2002: 266–67, 268, 1015
European Community, 1991-99: 1506; **2000**: 301; **2004**: 109, 115. *See also* European Commission; European Union
antitrust agreements with U.S., **1991-99**: 1540–45
customs, administration of, **2006**: 739–40
Diversity of Cultural Expressions Convention, role in negotiations, **2005**: 208–10
Electronic Communications in International Contracts, Convention on the Use of, as party, **2005**: 214
Global Positioning System consultations with, **1991-99**: 1637–39
Hague Conference on Private International Law (HCCH), membership in, **2005**: 210–14
Higher Education and Vocational Education and Training, Agreement Between U.S. and, **2000**: 310–11

European Community (continued)
Inter-American Tropical Tuna Commission (Antigua Convention), participation in, **2005:** 746–47
International Coffee Organization, **2004:** 413–14
and international organization membership, **2007:** 410–12
Kimberley Process, **2004:** 654
nuclear safeguards, **1991-99:** 2339
peace efforts in Former Yugoslavia, **1991-99:** 1951, 1979, 1986
private international commercial law, Brussels and Lugano conventions on, **1991-99:** 1827–28, 1829–30, 1831; **2000:** 737, 738, 740
Processing and Transfer of PNR by Air Carriers to U.S. Department of Homeland Security, Bureau of Customs and Border Protection, Agreement Between U.S. and, **2004:** 108–16
role in UN-sponsored conferences, **2004:** 407–8
shark management, **2004:** 766
steel import duties, **2002:** 697
WTO disputes. *See* World Trade Organization (WTO)
European Convention on Human Rights, 1989-90: 148–49; **1991-99:** 306; **2001:** 88, 142; **2003:** 99, 124; **2004:** 234–35, 311, 312; **2005:** 959; **2007:** 67–68
European Convention on State Immunity, 2001: 509; **2005:** 527–28; **2006:** 599, 603, 607
European Council, 2001: 863
Regulation 925 (1999), **2000:** 641–42, 648, 654, 662
European Court of Human Rights, 1991-99: 306, 877; **2000:** 393–94; **2001:** 88–89; **2002:** 265, 266–67, 268; **2003:** 123–27; **2004:** 227, 234–35, 311–12*n*; **2007:** 53, 68
extradition, **2003:** 142
international child abduction case, **2003:** 123–25
reservations to treaties, **1989-90:** 148–49
European Court of Justice, 2000: 648, 652; **2007:** 218, 656
jurisdiction, **2000:** 662
rulings on airline passenger name record data, **2006:** 168–72
rulings on Open Skies air transport agreements, **2002:** 598–600
European Police Office (Europol), 2002: 80–84, 467–69
European Space Agency, 1989-90: 482; **1991-99:** 1314
European Union. *See also* European Commission; European Community
accountability and, **2003:** 419
actions on Sudanese atrocities, **2004:** 246
air transport agreement with U.S., **2005:** 586–87; **2007:** 529–31; **2008:** 505–10
aviation emissions, **2006:** 871–72; **2007:** 692–96; **2008:** 686–88

European Union (continued)
Belarus, concern about developments in, **2005**: 436
bilateral investment treaties with member countries, **2003**: 687–97; **2004**: 623–24
Bosnia and Herzegovina, role in, **2005**: 939
classified information, agreement on sharing of, **2007**: 128–29; **2008**: 80
communicable disease declaration, **2004**: 784–85
competency
allocation of competence within, **2000**: 301–2, 303–4, 307–8
Cuban Liberty and Democratic Solidarity (LIBERTAD) Act and, **1991-99**: 1445–48, 1976–77. *See also* World Trade Organization (WTO), *subheading*: dispute resolution
of EU to make and join treaties, **1991-99**: 696–99, 1511–12; **2000**: 296–308; **2003**: 241–43, 834; **2004**: 148–49, 191–93, 801–2
Hague Conference on Private International Law (HCCH), membership of EC in, **2005**: 210–14
of member states to conclude air services agreements, **2002**: 598–600
role of EC in UN-sponsored conferences, **2004**: 407–8
to vote in addition to member states, **1991-99**: 695–99
counterterrorism recommendations, **2006**: 210
Darfur, **2004**: 960
death penalty abolition, **2005**: 389. *See also* Capital punishment
driftnet fishing, **1991-99**: 1738
economic cooperation, **2004**: 644–47
electronic commerce, **1991-99**: 1525–27; **2000**: 301–5; **2005**: 801–2
Eurojust, DOJ agreement with, **2006**: 163–67
Europol, U.S. agreement with, **2006**: 164
extradition and mutual legal assistance, **1991-99**: 391; **2003**: 135–43, 241–43; **2004**: 73; **2005**: 78; **2006**: 127–47; **2008**: 53–57, 78
founding instruments, **2003**: 241–42
Global Positioning System, **1991-99**: 1637–39; **2004**: 191, 193, 738–40
intellectual property rights, **2006**: 768; **2007**: 609
Inter-American Tropical Tuna Commission, Convention on the Establishment of, **2000**: 305–8
International Coffee Organization and, **2004**: 414
International Criminal Court and, **2002**: 166; **2004**: 184–85
Iran and Libya Sanctions Act and, **1991-99**: 1448, 1977
ITER International Fusion Energy Organization, **2006**: 893
KEDO role, **2004**: 1155
Kosovo and, **2007**: 429–33

European Union (continued)
European Union Rule of Law Mission in Kosovo (EULEX), **2008:** 439–43
measures affecting import from U.S. of biotech products, **2003:** 648–51
in Middle East conflict resolution, **2002:** 916–19; **2003:** 943–47; **2004:** 945, 953; **2006:** 1031; **2007:** 844–50; **2008:** 816–19. *See also* Middle East Conflict, Israeli-Palestinian, *subheading*: Quartet (EU, Russia, UN, U.S.) peace efforts
passenger data
U.S.–EU agreement on, **2004:** 108–16; **2005:** 586–87; **2007:** 158–59; **2008:** 109, 110
ECJ ruling on and negotiation of replacement agreement, **2006:** 168–72
rules of private international law, **2000:** 736–37
secured finance law, **2003:** 836
Security and Cooperation in Europe, Conference on, **1991-99:** 2228–29, 2241
Security Cooperation in Europe, Commission for, **1991-99:** 852
taxation
challenge to U.S. foreign sales corporation taxation, **2003:** 660–61
challenge to U.S. tax law as export subsidy, **2001:** 653–63
terrorism and
antiterrorism actions, **2003:** 156
Declaration on Combating Terrorism, **2004:** 114–18
September 11 terrorist attacks, response to, **2001:** 935–38
U.S. Terrorist Finance Tracking Program (TFTP), **2007:** 160–61
trade. *See also* World Trade Organization (WTO)
agricultural and industrial trade, **2006:** 754–55
customs, administration of, **2006:** 739–40
wine-making practices and labeling, **2006:** 757
trademark law, **2000:** 297–301
U.S. filing on discriminatory practice in aviation, **2000:** 641–67
WTO cases. *See* World Trade Organization (WTO)
Evidence
access to foreign government information in defense of Alien Tort Statute cases, **2003:** 397–98
admissibility of evidence obtained abroad, **1989-90:** 100–107
antitrust prosecution, international cooperation in obtaining, **1991-99:** 1546, 1548–50
arbitration rules, **2003:** 861–63
authentication of documents. *See* Authentication
authority of U.S. State Department reports on human rights, **2001:** 64–65*n*
child's capacity to testify, **2000:** 112–15

Evidence (continued)
of customary international law, **2004:** 498
discovery
depositions
abroad under U.S. rules, **2000:** 152–60; **2001:** 55–59; **2004:** 863–65
deposition of high-level foreign officials, **2005:** 564. *See also* Head-of-state immunity; Immunity
gathering of evidence abroad, **1991-99:** 385–86; **2003:** 859–63, 881–87; **2004:** 858–65; **2005:** 813, 814, 815, 843–46; **2006:** 966–70
Hague Convention on (1970), **2003:** 859–63, 881–85; **2004:** 822–23, 827–28, 858–65; **2005:** 810, 813–15, 843–46; **2006:** 108
Inter-American Convention on, **2003:** 867–68
letters rogatory to obtain, **1991-99:** 453–54, 455; **2000:** 394*n*; **2006:** 107–10, 966*n*
rules, **1991-99:** 385–86
rules of People's Republic of China, **2000:** 161, 162
Vienna Convention on Consular Relations on, **2000:** 161
in U.S. for use in foreign forum, **2002:** 875–77; **2003:** 872–81; **2004:** 850–58
equality of arms in judicial procedure, **2000:** 393–96, 394*n*
in extradition process, **2003:** 142–43
probable cause standard for extradition, **2000:** 181–82, 212–13
standard of proof, U.S.–EU Extradition Agreement, **2008:** 54–56
Fifth Amendment protections for resident aliens based on fear of prosecution abroad, **1991-99:** 571–76
FOIA to obtain. *See* Freedom of Information Act (FOIA)
illegally obtained, in arbitration, **2004:** 589
immunity and inviolability. *See also* Consular offices and personnel; Diplomatic missions and personnel; Head-of-state immunity
head-of-state immunity from depositions, **1989-90:** 320–23
of UN mission archives, **2003:** 573
mutual legal assistance. *See also* Mutual legal assistance
cooperation with international tribunals, national security and, **1991-99:** 636
judicial assistance in criminal matter in China, **2000:** 161
judicial assistance to foreign and international authorities, **1991-99:** 383–86
authority of International Criminal Tribunal for the Former Yugoslavia to compel evidence from SFOR, **2000:** 255–71

Evidence (continued)
request for production of information to International Criminal Tribunal, **2003**: 214–19
role of mutual legal assistance treaties, **1991-99**: 452, 453–55
telecommunications surveillance in mutual legal assistance, **2004**: 94–95
protection of witnesses 580, **1991-99**: 587
for specific purposes and determinations
for asylum, **1989-90**: 44–45; **1991-99**: 195, 197, 200, 205–6, 213–14, 226
in capital sentencing, **2000**: 392, 395*n*; **2001**: 294–302
certification of diplomatic status as conclusive, **2004**: 533, 538
cybercrime, **2003**: 192, 202; **2004**: 98
genocide, **2004**: 240–41
Holocaust claims and lack of, **1991-99**: 1064
mistreatment of national imprisoned abroad, **2001**: 37, 38
paternity, for citizenship, **1991-99**: 4–5
proof of denial of justice, **2001**: 632
for treaty interpretation, **2004**: 199–200
in visa determinations, **1989-90**: 23–24, 25–26
genetic testing for visa, **1989-90**: 1–3; **1991-99**: 128–29
EWSAA (Emergency Wartime Supplemental Appropriations Act). *See* Appropriations Acts
***Ex gratia* payment.** *See* Remedies
Exclusion of inadmissible aliens. *See* Immigration and visas
Execution of judgment. *See* Foreign Sovereign Immunities Act (FSIA) (1976); Garnishment
diplomatic immunity. *See* Diplomatic missions and personnel, *subheading*: attachment of property
Executions, extrajudicial, summary, and arbitrary. *See* Human rights
Executive Branch. *See also* Executive Orders, Presidential; Foreign affairs; President, U.S.; Presidential Declarations, Determinations, Memoranda, Proclamations, and Directives; States, U.S., *subheading*: preemption of state action by federal foreign affairs authority
act of state doctrine, views on, **2004**: 380–82; **2005**: 580–81
aliens. *See also* Deportation; Removal of aliens from U.S.
authority to exclude on foreign policy grounds, **1989-90**: 35; **1991-99**: 131–36
discretion as to, **1991-99**: 117, 192–93; **2007**: 19–21
no authority for court to order Executive to parole alien into U.S., **2006**: 1191–94
removal authority, **2004**: 14–18; **2005**: 17

Executive Branch (continued)
citizenship, role in renunciation of, **2007**: 5–7
claims
authority to espouse, **1991-99**: 673; **2001**: 386
authority to settle and to waive, **1991-99**: 671–79; **2004**: 476, 500; **2005**: 43; **2007**: 1070; **2008**: 191–93
Coalition Provisional Authority (CPA) and, **2005**: 229*n*, 230, 231*n*, 234
Commander in chief authority. *See* President, U.S., *subheading*: war powers
deep water port approval and, **2005**: 694
deference to, **2001**: 452–53
in designation of extraterritorial enemy property, **2004**: 206–14
in determination of customary international law, **1991-99**: 726, 973
downing of Iran Air Flight 655 and nonjusticiable claims, **1989-90**: 212–15
in foreign affairs. *See* foreign affairs, *this heading*; President, U.S., *subheading*: separation of powers
in FSIA interpretation, **2000**: 599
in interpreting statutes, **2001**: 760; **2008**: 467–68
in relation to claims. *See* claims, *this heading*
in treaty interpretation. *See* Treaties, generally
deposition of high-level officials, precedent against, **2005**: 564
determination of immunities, **1989-90**: 315, 316–19; **2002**: 548–49
art and cultural objects, immunity from judicial seizure, **2005**: 776–77; **2007**: 742–44; **2008**: 732–34
certification of diplomatic status, **2004**: 535, 537–39
foreign officials, **2007**: 445–49, 521, 524–25; **2008**: 490–91
head of state. *See* Head-of-state immunity
sovereign, **1991-99**: 1236, 1240, 1249, 1251
sovereignty reserved to, **2007**: 2, 434, 440, 442
extradition. *See* Extradition
foreign affairs. *See also* Foreign affairs
foreign relations as bearing on denial of visa, deportation or removal of aliens. *See* Deportation, *subheading*: grounds for; Immigration and visas, *subheading*: denial of visas; Immigration and visas, *subheading*: exclusion of aliens; Removal of aliens from U.S.
judicial deference to Executive Branch in relation to, **1989-90**: 243–64, 316–19; **1991-99**: 117, 707, 709; **2001**: 468; **2003**: 474–75, 498–500; **2004**: 204–5, 348, 359–60, 369–82, 436*n*, 471–76; **2005**: 17, 472–75, 534–42, 579–80. *See also* President, U.S., *subheading*: separation of powers

Executive Branch (continued)
not relevant to determination on dolphin-safe tuna, **2004**: 757–62
request to vacate restraining order based on, **1989-90**: 251–64
foreign travel by officials of, **2001**: 57
German reparations claims and, **2005**: 821
Military Commissions Act and, **2007**: 111
nonjusticiable political questions. *See* Foreign affairs
ordering Executive Branch officials to serve process on visiting foreign dignitaries. *See* Service of process abroad
preemption of state action and law. *See* States, U.S., *subheading*: preemption of state action by federal foreign affairs authority
standing, based on foreign affairs interests of, **2004**: 553–54
state secrets and, **2007**: 241–42
treaties and international agreements. *See* Agreements, generally; Treaties, generally
Executive Orders, Presidential. *See also* Presidential Declarations, Determinations, Memoranda, Proclamations, and Directives
African Union Mission, privileges and immunities (No. 13427), **2007**: 527
AIDS/HIV pharmaceuticals, access to (No. 13155), **2001**: 764–67
Angola, blocking property of and prohibiting certain transactions with UNITA (No. 12865; 13069; 13098; 13298), **1991-99**: 1940, 1941–45; **2003**: 934–35
arms-related
arms export controls (No. 12581; 13222), **2002**: 1066
arms sales, certification of eligibility for (No. 12163), **1989-90**: 540
delegation of arms trade control to State Department (No. 11958), **1991-99**: 2257; **2007**: 131, 1003; **2008**: 88
Rwandan arms embargo (No. 12918), **2003**: 1081–82
assassination prohibition (No. 12333), **1989-90**: 565; **2001**: 867
Belarus, blocking property of certain persons undermining democratic processes or institutions (No. 13405), **2006**: 983–84; **2007**: 823, 864; **2008**: 807
blocking assets of and prohibiting transactions with foreign drug traffickers (No. 12978), **1991-99**: 547–50; **2001**: 144, 822
blocking of Panamanian property in U.S. (No. 12635), **1989-90**: 372
border crossing regulation (No. 11423; 13212; 13337), **2004**: 571–72
border facilities, permits for construction and maintenance of (No. 11423), **2002**: 607
Burma, sanctions against (No. 13047; 13310; 13348; 13464), **1991-99**: 1880; **2000**: 334, 335, 336; **2003**: 923–28; **2004**: 136–38; **2005**: 891–92; **2007**: 807–9; **2008**: 791–93

Executive Orders, Presidential (continued)
China trade policy (No. 12850), **1991-99**: 1456–60
classified information, criteria for (No. 12958), **1991-99**: 793, 798, 801; **2006**: 1222
collection of information from visitors and immigrants (No. 13323), **2003**: 15, 17–18
Commission on Aviation Security and Terrorism (No. 12686), **1989-90**: 65
Committee on Foreign Investment in the United States (CFIUS) (No. 11858; 13456), **2008**: 594
conflict diamonds (No. 13194; 13213; 13312), **2001**: 797–801; **2003**: 706–9; **2004**: 653
Congo, blocking property of certain persons contributing to the conflict in (No. 13413), **2006**: 996–98; **2007**: 823
coral reef protection, **1991-99**: 1756–57
Cote d'Ivoire, blocking property of certain persons contributing to the conflict in (No. 13396), **2006**: 995
counterintelligence activities (No. 12333), **2004**: 1098–99
cross-border fiber optics (No. 11423; 12847), **2001**: 566–68
Cuba, sanctions against (No. 12854), **1991-99**: 1899–1902
deferred forced departure of Chinese nationals (No. 12711), **1989-90**: 55–57
delegation of sanctions authority (No. 12163), **1989-90**: 517
detainees, treatment of (No. 13440), **2007**: 921–25
discrimination
equal employment opportunity (No. 11246), **2005**: 288; **2007**: 327
No. 13160, **2005**: 261–62
drug use in sports, White House task force on (No. 13165), **2005**: 782
environmental protection
No. 12916, **2005**: 606
No. 13380, **2005**: 606
environmental review of trade agreements (No. 13141), **2001**: 668–70
establishing Interagency Import Safety Working Group (No. 13439), **2007**: 587
export controls (No. 12730), **1989-90**: 513
Haiti, sanctions against (No. 12775; 12779; 12853; 12872; 12914; 12917; 12920; 12922; 12932), **1991-99**: 1882–83, 1886–98
Holy See, extending privileges and immunities to Permanent Observer Mission to the UN (No. 13444), **2007**: 527
human rights treaties (No. 13107), **1991-99**: 861–64; **2000**: 376; **2005**: 287
immunity of international organizations (No. 10873; 13307), **1991-99**: 1314–15; **2003**: 575

Executive Orders, Presidential (continued)
interdiction of illegal aliens (No. 12342), **1991-99**: 162–66, 171
international emergency economic powers (No. 12924), **2000**: 748. *See also* Emergency Economic Powers Act, International (IEEPA)
International Fusion Energy Organization (ITER), extending privileges and immunities to (No. 13451), **2007**: 527
Iran. *See also* Iran, *subheading*: sanctions against; nonproliferation, *this heading*; Nonproliferation, *subheadings*: country-specific issues *and* sanctions, U.S.
on attempts by Iran to recover assets in U.S. (No. 12284), **2000**: 435, 439*n*, 441*n*
blocking of Iranian assets (No. 12170), **2000**: 435, 550, 551–52, 557; **2003**: 442; **2004**: 525; **2005**: 548; **2007**: 486
oil embargo (No. 12613), **2003**: 1062–63
prohibition on claims against Iran arising from Tehran hostages (No. 12283), **2001**: 468–69
sanctions against (No. 12170; 12613; 12659; 12957; 12959; 13059), **1991-99**: 1916–21; **2006**: 987
Iraq
blocking assets of persons threatening stabilization of (No. 13438), **2007**: 818, 989; **2008**: 805–6
blocking certain assets and providing for vesting and transfer to Development Fund for (No. 13303; 13315; 13350; 13364), **2003**: 920–23; **2007**: 818, 820
Development Fund for (No. 13303), **2003**: 545–46, 916–20; **2005**: 869
restriction on travel to (No. 11259), **1991-99**: 50; **2001**: 13, 14
sanctions against (No. 12722–12725; 13290; 13303; 13315; 13350; 13364), **1991-99**: 1924–28, 1929–30; **2000**: 619, 621; **2004**: 883, 884–89, 890; **2006**: 1016, 1018
settlement of claims against, **2001**: 210
vesting of blocked Iraqi assets (No. 13290), **2003**: 554–55, 909–11
labor practices of U.S. firms in South Africa (No. 12532), **1989-90**: 523
Lebanon, blocking assets of persons undermining sovereignty or democratic processes of (No. 13441), **2007**: 805–7
Liberia (No. 13213; 13324; 13348), **2004**: 919–22, 934–35; **2007**: 820, 821
Libya
sanctions against (No. 12538; 12543; 12544; 12801; 13222; 13357), **1991-99**: 1922–24; **2002**: 577; **2004**: 931–32, 933, 1158; **2006**: 173
settlement of claims against (No. 13477), **2008**: 402, 408–10

Executive Orders, Presidential (continued)
on national security implications of foreign investment in U.S. (Committee on Foreign Investment in the United States (CFIUS)) (No. 11858; 12661; 13456), **1989-90**: 422 **2006**: 774, 777; **2007**: 601; **2008**: 594
nonproliferation of weapons of mass destruction and related issues
Additional Protocol to U.S.–IAEA Safeguards Agreement (No. 13458), **2008**: 945
biological and chemical weapons control (No. 12735), **1989-90**: 509–10, 512–16
revocation and amendment (No. 12938; 13094), **1989-90**: 516
blocking attachment of Russian property relating to the downblending of Russian uranium stocks (No. 13159), **2002**: 1039–41
Chemical Weapons Convention, implementation of (No. 13128), **2006**: 1250
nonproliferation sanctions (No. 12851; 12938; 13094; 13222), **2003**: 1116–19, 1124–25; **2004**: 1111–12, 1132, 1133–34; **2007**: 1082, 1083. *See also* Weapons of mass destruction, *this heading*
weapons of mass destruction (WMDs)
(No. 11850; 12735; 12938; 13904), **1991-99**: 2064–65, 2363–66; **2007**: 1082–83
(No. 13382), **2005**: 1125–31; **2006**: 1297; **2007**: 1041–45, 1083–84; **2008**: 977–80, 983
North Korea, sanctions against (No. 13466), **2008**: 965–66
Office of Homeland Security, establishment of (No. 13228), **2001**: 928–32
procedures of military commissions for trial of non-U.S. citizens suspected of terrorism (No. 12958), **2002**: 958
public international organizations (No. 11059), **2005**: 749
Puerto Rico task force (No. 13183; 13209; 13319), **2006**: 311
riot-control agents in warfare (No. 11850), **1991-99**: 2345–47; **2003**: 1013–14; **2006**: 1223–25
Sierra Leone (No. 13194; 13324), **2004**: 653, 934–35
Sudan, sanctions against (No. 13067; 13400; 13412), **1991-99**: 1937–39; **2006**: 975, 979, 980, 981, 982; **2007**: 812
Syria
sanctions against (No. 13338; 13460), **2004**: 900–903; **2005**: 133–34, 886; **2006**: 985; **2007**: 40; **2008**: 798–800
sanctions against (No. 13399), **2006**: 984–86
sanctions regulations (No. 13372), **2005**: 132–33
Taiwan relations (No. 12143; 13014), **2000**: 600; **2007**: 435
terrorism

Executive Orders, Presidential (continued)
blocking property of and prohibiting transactions with terrorist organizations (No. 12947; 13099; 13224), **1991-99** 127, 485–89; **2001**: 822, 881–93, 895, 896, 899, 918; **2002**: 94–98, 100–1; **2003**: 156–57, 171–75, 180; **2004**: 123; **2005**: 129, 132–33; **2006**: 183–91, 205–6; **2007**: 155–57, 1041–43, 1046, 1049–50; **2008**: 99, 100–1, 806
designation of countries not cooperating fully with antiterrorism efforts (No. 11958), **2004**: 107–8; **2006**: 172; **2007**: 131; **2008**: 88
information sharing (No. 13388), **2006**: 171
Taliban, sanctions against (No. 13129; 13244; 13268), **1991-99**: 1964–66; **2001**: 802–3; **2002**: 882–84
travel restrictions to Iraq and Libya (No. 11295), **2003**: 11–13
Yugoslavia,
sanctions against entities of (No. 12808; 12810; 12831; 12846; 12934; 13088; 13121), **1991-99**: 1946–53, 1958–62, 1980; **2001**: 803–8; **2003**: 930–31
unblocking of blocked assets of (No. 13192), **2002**: 898
Zimbabwe, blocking assets of regime of (No. 13288; 13391; 13469), **2003**: 929–30; **2005**: 889; **2008**: 800–3
Exhaustion of remedies. *See* Remedies
Exon-Florio amendment, 2006: 777–80
Expatriation. *See* Citizenship, *subheading*: loss of
Explosives offenses
extradition treaty and, **2006**: 114–16
Export Administration Act (1979)
chemical and biological weapons control, **1991-99**: 2352; **2002**: 1070; **2003**: 1124–25; **2004**: 1136–37; **2005**: 1134
dual-use export controls, **1989-90**: 511; **2004**: 1111, 1113–1114; **2005**: 1134
missile technology control, **1989-90**: 503; **1991-99**: 2359–60; **2000**: 748; **2001**: 814; **2002**: 1066; **2003**: 1119–24; **2004**: 1132–36
state sponsors of terrorism, **1989-90**: 108; **1991-99**: 483–84, 508-9, 1223; **2001**: 96, 460*n*, 819–21; **2002**: 413; **2003**: 167–68, 536; **2004**: 103, 658, 891, 912–13, 932, 934; **2005**: 506; **2006**: 173, 577; **2008**: 90, 471–72
Iraq, rescission of determination as, **2004**: 103–4; **2005**: 506; **2006**: 179
Libya, rescission of determination as, **2006**: 173
North Korea, rescission of determination as, **2008**: 90

Export Administration Regulations, 2000: 746–48; **2004:** 1111, 1114–15; **2005:** 1135–36; **2006:** 177–80, 989, 990, 1299, 1300–1301; **2007:** 810–11, 1027–31, 1084; **2008:** 808, 809, 1024, 1027
Export-Import Bank Act (1945), **1991-99:** 1124, 1912, 2303; **2001:** 809, 810; **2004:** 648, 650, 1163
Export-Import Bank Reauthorization Act (2002), **2002:** 726–27
Exports. *See* Trade
Expropriation
  act of state doctrine and, **2002:** 574
  of artwork, **2001:** 395; **2005:** 776–77
  bilateral investment treaties and, **1991-99:** 1463, 1465, 1467, 1470; **2000:** 683; **2004:** 620; **2008:** 600–3
  citizenship and, **1991-99:** 1253; **2001:** 405–6, 599–600. *See also* diplomatic protection, *this heading*
  claims agreements
    Albania-U.S., **1991-99:** 1076–81; **2006:** 502–3
    Austria-U.S., **2001:** 394–96
    Cambodia-U.S., **1991-99:** 1081–82
    by Cuba, **1991-99:** 1902–5, 1976; **2002:** 240–41
    denial of visas in connection with, **1991-99:** 94–102, 1445; **2004:** 31
    Germany-U.S., **1991-99:** 1074–75
    Honduras-U.S., settlement of claims against Honduras, **1989-90:** 219–20
    private right of action in case of (LIBERTAD Act), **1991-99:** 1128–31, 1447; **2003:** 712–13; **2004:** 431
    trademark rights in connection with assets confiscated by Cuba, **2002:** 672–76
    Vietnam-U.S., **1991-99:** 1083–85
  claims by U.S.
    against Costa Rica, **2003:** 480–82
    against India over Dabhol energy project, **2004:** 426, 427–28
    against Iran, **2002:** 219–26, 519–22
    against Mexico, **1991-99:** 1075–76
    against Nicaragua, **1989-90:** 237–38; **2003:** 709–12
  customary international law, **2000:** 681–83; **2003:** 631, 632; **2004:** 497, 498, 499–500; **2008:** 601–3
  diplomatic protection
    for citizen shareholders in foreign corporation, **2003:** 436–37
    for dual nationals, **1991-99:** 36
    espousal, **2001:** 385–86; **2004:** 500
  Foreign Sovereign Immunities Act exception to immunity for, **1989-90:** 308–9; **1991-99:** 1190–91, 1252–56; **2001:** 405–6, 501–2; **2002:** 492–94; **2003:** 519; **2004:** 469, 494–500, 795–96; **2006:** 572–77; **2007:** 742–44; **2008:** 732–34
    retroactive application of FSIA, **2002:** 492; **2003:** 521–22

Expropriation (continued)
Helms Amendment restricting assistance based on, **2003**: 480–82, 709–12
indirect, **2007**: 546
Multilateral Agreement on Investment, **1991-99**: 1447, 1487, 1488
under NAFTA. *See* North American Free Trade Agreement (NAFTA)
no private right of action against U.S. under U.S.–Iran Treaty of Amity, **2003**: 258–67
OPIC and, **1991-99**: 1483; **2005**: 652
as sovereign act, **2001**: 403
sovereign immunity and claims arising from, **2002**: 492–93, 508–11, 519–22
taxation and, **2000**: 685
U.S. law restrictions as a consequence of
on aid to Nicaragua, **2003**: 709–12
denial of visas, **1991-99**: 94–109
on GSP benefits, **2004**: 657
on international lending, **1991-99**: 805
U.S.–EU Understanding on Expropriated Properties, **1991-99**: 105
Extradition, **2001**: 181–82; **2004**: 1089. *See also* Mutual legal assistance; Prisoner transfer; Rendition
alternatives to, **1991-99**: 121–28, 391, 435–46, 962; **2000**: 184–85; **2002**: 77–78; **2005**: 102
Antiterrorism and Effective Death Penalty Act (AEDPA) (1996), **2007**: 144–45
asylum and, **2004**: 82–83, 91*n*
in capital punishment cases. *See* denial of, possible bases for, *this heading*
of Chilean head of state, **1991-99**: 518–19
denial of, possible bases for, **1991-99**: 402–3, 406–7; **2001**: 94–95. *See also* extraditable offenses, *this heading*
capital punishment, **1991-99**: 390, 399, 402–3; **2000**: 166, 180; **2002**: 69; **2003**: 137, 140–41; **2006**: 133–34
extraterritorial offenses, **2000**: 182
insufficiency of evidence, **2000**: 181–82
life imprisonment assurances, requests for, **2002**: 70, 73–74
military offenses, **2000**: 182; **2004**: 75–77
nationals of requested state, **1991-99**: 398, 399–401, 402–3; **2000**: 165–66, 177–80, 185–86; **2001**: 92–94; **2002**: 63, 64; **2004**: 91*n*
domestic prosecution vs., **1991-99**: 400
non bis in idem doctrine, **2000**: 182
political offense exception, **1989-90**: 79–80; **1991-99**: 412, 428–35; **2000**: 182; **2002**: 109; **2004**: 75–77; **2005**: 75–77, 94–97; **2006**: 114–16, 122–27

Extradition (continued)
politically motivated requests for, **2000:** 182–83; **2004:** 76–77; **2005:** 70–71, 75–77
possibility of torture in requesting state. *See* U.S. practice, *this heading*
statute of limitations issues, **2000:** 180–81
trial *in absentia* in U.S., **2001:** 87–89
detention of persons pending, **2008:** 56
expulsion, distinguished from, **2007:** 38
extraditable offenses, **2000:** 165, 181
attacks against UN personnel, **2001:** 356–57
bribery of foreign officials, **1991-99:** 562, 563
crimes not listed by treaty, **2000:** 181, 188
cybercrime and, **2003:** 203, 204; **2004:** 98; **2008:** 53
dual criminality issues, **1991-99:** 394, 402, 410, 418–19, 421, 562; **2000:** 165, 181; **2002:** 63; **2003:** 141–42; **2004:** 74–75; **2008:** 53, 79
genocide, **1989-90:** 123
parental child abduction, **1991-99:** 377, 409–11; **2002:** 70–71
extradite or prosecute requirements, **2000:** 178; **2005:** 358; **2007:** 137–38, 140, 986, 1078
Convention for the Suppression of Unlawful Acts Against the Safety of Maritime Navigation, U.S. implementation of requirement in, **2002:** 133–34; **2008:** 126–27
International Law Commission (ILC) on, **2006:** 159–60; **2008:** 70–72
Foreign Affairs Reform and Restructuring Act of 1998 (FARR Act). *See* Foreign affairs
foreign assistance, restriction on, **2008:** 72
Geneva conventions and, **2007:** 108–17; **2008:** 69–70
Hong Kong, **1991-99:** 403–9
extradition to Hong Kong, **2000:** 190–203
issues related to sub-sovereign government status of, **1991-99:** 689–93; **2000:** 190–203
Illicit Traffic in Narcotic Drugs and Psychotropic Substances, Convention Against, **1989-90:** 130
and Intelligence Reform and Terrorism Prevention Act (IRTPA 2004), **2007:** 145–54
Inter-American Convention against Corruption and, **2001:** 160
International Covenant on Civil and Political Rights and, **2004:** 81–83
International Crime Control Act provisions, **2000:** 188–90
International Crime Control Strategy, **1991-99:** 396–97
to International Criminal Court and, **2000:** 172–73

Extradition (continued)
American Servicemembers' Protection Act, prohibition on surrender to in, **1991-99**: 640–41; **2002**: 170
Article 98 agreement (nonsurrender of Americans to the ICC), **2002**: 167–68, 170, 175; **2003**: 224–25, 234–40
to international criminal tribunals for Rwanda and Yugoslavia, **1991-99**: 388, 582, 597–603; **2005**: 358
litigation concerning surrender to ICTR, **1991-99**: 597–603; **2000**: 203–16; **2005**: 358
judicial finding of extraditability. *See* U.S. practice, *this heading*
judicial review, **2006**: 148–59
treaty between U.S. and UK, **2006**: 118–19
judicial reviewability, removal versus extradition, **2007**: 106–8
Libya, requests to in connection with airline bombing, **1991-99**: 457–60, 468–73
Security Council authority to order surrender, **1991-99**: 472–73
Mexico–U.S. relationship, **1991-99**: 392–93, 396, 435–45; **2008**: 72–73
temporary surrender under U.S. –Mexico bilateral extradition agreement, 72–73
narcotics agreements. *See* Drug trade
non-inquiry, rule of, **1989-90**: 79–88; **1991-99**: 411, 416–17, 430, 950, 959; **2000**: 215–16; **2001**: 64–66; **2002**: 72–73; **2004**: 83–93; **2005**: 76, 79–87, 92–94, 352; **2006**: 148–51, 155, 156; **2007**: 104–5, 116, 952, 963; **2008**: 59–60, 64, 68–69
Nuclear Terrorism Convention, **2005**: 108; **2007**: 132, 135, 137–39
Pakistan, requests from in connection with corruption, **2008**: 64–69
Philippines. *See* Philippines
Physical Protection of Nuclear Material, Convention on and, **2007**: 1078; **2008**: 96–97
prisoners held in Iraq, transfer to Iraqi government distinguished, **2007**: 960–61; **2008**: 77–78
provisional arrest, standard of proof for obtaining, U.S.–EU Extradition Agreement, **2008**: 54–56
Safety of Maritime Navigation, Convention for Suppression of Unlawful Acts Against and Protocol on Fixed Platforms, Protocols to and, **2005**: 112–13; **2007**: 140, 986
Sale of Children, Child Prostitution and Child Pornography, Protocol on and, **2007**: 334, 339
seizure of property in connection with, **2004**: 78–79
sovereign immunity to claims arising from, **2001**: 475–85
specialty, rule of, **1989-90**: 78–79; **1991-99**: 406, 439, 640; **2001**: 61–62; **2004**: 79–80; **2005**: 50*n*

Extradition (continued)
waiver of rule, **2006:** 121–22
statute of limitations, **2004:** 77–78, 83–84; **2005:** 70–71
Suppression of Unlawful Acts Against the Safety of Maritime Navigation, Convention for, **1989-90:** 113–14
of terrorists, **1991-99:** 494–95, 496; **2000:** 165; **2001:** 103–4, 105, 108–9; **2002:** 64; **2004:** 105, 106; **2006:** 122–27
torture, transfers to other countries and likelihood of. *See* Torture
Torture Convention, implementation by U.S. in cases alleging violation of. *See* U.S. practice, *this heading*
Transfer of Sentenced Persons, Council of Europe Conventions and, **1989-90:** 72; **1991-99:** 381–83; **2000:** 295; **2001:** 52; **2005:** 71, 74–75
treaties, bilateral, **1991-99:** 393–409; **2000:** 163, 164–66, 173–84; **2002:** 61, 62, 63–64; **2005:** 69–79; **2006:** 111–39
Extradition Treaties Interpretation Act (1998), **1991-99:** 410; **2002:** 71
interpretation, **1991-99:** 410–11, 415–16; **2000:** 199
sanctions for noncompliance, **2000:** 187–88
specific treaties between U.S. and
Albania, **2005:** 89–92
Australia, **2005:** 97–100
Bulgaria, **2008:** 54
Dominican Republic, **2007:** 125–26
Estonia, **2008:** 54
EU, **2004:** 73; **2006:** 127–38; **2008:** 53–57
related bilateral instruments with EU member states, **2002:** 73; **2004:** 127, 129–32, 135–38; **2008:** 54, 57
Finland, **2002:** 73
Hong Kong. *See* Hong Kong, *this heading*
Israel, **1989-90:** 79; **2005:** 71, 74–75
Japan, **1989-90:** 78
Jordan–U.S. treaty, **1991-99:** 401–3
Latvia, **2008** 54
Malta, **2008:** 54
Mexico, **1991-99:** 435–45; **2008:** 72–73
Pakistan, **2008:** 64–69
Romania, **2004:** 91–93; **2008:** 54
Serbia (1901), **2003:** 246–48
United Kingdom, **1991-99:** 428–35; **2004:** 73–83; **2005:** 70–71, 73–77, 94–97; **2006:** 111–27; **2007:** 126–28
Venezuela, **2007:** 118–26
Webster-Ashburton Treaty, **2005:** 50*n*
UN Convention Against Corruption, **2005:** 173–74, 176

Extradition (continued)
UN Convention Against Transnational Organized Crime and, **2004**: 147–49; **2008**: 122–23
unilateral conditions, attempt to impose by surrendering country, **2007**: 117–26
U.S. citizen arrested in U.S. by Canadian law officer, **1991-99**: 445–46
U.S. dispute with Chile related to murder of former Chilean ambassador in U.S., **1989-90**: 537
U.S. practice, **1991-99**: 387–93; **2000**: 174–76
documents related to, authentication of, **2007**: 95
judiciary, finding of extraditability, **1991-99**: 413–14, 419–20, 421–22, 425–27, 950; **2006**: 118–19. *See also* non-inquiry, rule of, *this heading*
presumption against bail in cases of, **2001**: 62–70
probable cause standard for, **2000**: 181–82, 189*n*, 208, 212–13; **2005**: 82, 89, 92, 94, 97–100
procedures, **2000**: 175–76, 189, 191–92
provisional arrest, **1991-99**: 388, 446; **2004**: 78; **2006**: 120
procedures, **2007**: 101–2
Secretary of State role
Department of State procedures, **1989-90**: 88–91; **1991-99**: 939–52; **2008**: 57–63, 371
non-inquiry, rule precluding court consideration of issues reserved for Secretary. *See* non-inquiry, rule of, *this heading*
non-reviewable authority to surrender following court's determination of extraditability, **1991-99**: 389, 411–17, 420, 422, 427, 430, 440–41, 600–601, 949–52, 959; **2000**: 191–92; **2004**: 83–89; **2005**: 79–94, 88*n*; **2006**: 148–59; **2007**: 101–8, 110–11; **2008**: 58, 62–63
statutory regime, **1991-99**: 388–93, 414–17; **2000**: 174*n*, 205–6, 210–12; **2001**: 65–66, 70–87
constitutional challenges to, **1991-99**: 417–28
possible amendments to, **2000**: 188–90
Torture Convention, implementation of, **1991-99**: 390, 518–19, 939–52; **2000**: 176, 379, 380–81; **2001**: 70–87; **2004**: 83–93; **2005**: 79–94, 346, 351–53; **2006**: 157–59; **2007**: 54, 102–4; **2008**: 58, 60–61, 367–75, 922
treaty, requirement for by statute, **1991-99**: 388; **2000**: 175, 188–89, 193–94
exceptions to reliance on bilateral treaty, **1991-99**: 388
no constitutional requirement, **1991-99**: 599–603; **2000**: 208–9, 210–12
U.S. request for extradition of Nicaraguan diplomat from Japan, **1989-90**: 77–78

Extradition (continued)
U.S. requests to countries receiving counternarcotics assistance from U.S., **2001:** 89–96
of U.S. nationals, **2004:** 91*n*
Extrajudicial, summary, or arbitrary killing. *See* Capital punishment; Human rights
Extraordinary Challenge Committee (ECC), NAFTA, 2005: 603–4
Extraterritorial Income Exclusion Act (2000), 2003: 660–61
Extraterritoriality and conflicts of jurisdiction. *See* Jurisdiction

F
FAA. *See* Foreign Assistance Act (FAA) (1961)
Fair Labor Standards Act (FLSA), 1991-99: 1296; **2001:** 262
Fairness in Music Licensing Act (1998), 2003: 661–63
False Claims Act (FCA), 2001: 235, 236, 240; **2002:** 245–46, 496. *See also* Iraq
applicability to Iraq Coalition Provisional Authority (CPA), **2005:** 225, 228, 233–34; **2006:** 301–5
False imprisonment, 2001: 478
Family planning policy, 2001: 283–93
Family structure, 2004: 292
Family support obligations. *See* Maintenance obligations
FAO. *See* Agricultural policy and trade, *subheading*: UN Food and Agriculture Organization
FARR Act (Foreign Affairs Reform and Restructuring Act of 1998). *See* Foreign affairs
FAST (Free and Secure Trade) program, 2005: 4
Fast track legislative procedure, 1991-99: 1453; **2001:** 200–211
Federal Advisory Committees Act (1972), 2002: 234
Federal Arbitration Act (1947), 1991-99: 1473, 1844; **2002:** 874–75
Federal Aviation Act (1958), 1991-99: 1950
Federal Aviation Administration
prohibition of DC-10 aircraft in U.S. airspace, **2000:** 649–50
Federal employees
dual nationals as, **1991-99:** 34–41
electronic passport, pilot program, **2005:** 7
foreign nationals as, **1989-90:** 151–53; **2004:** 1–4
U-11 humanitarian resettlement category for former U.S. government employee, **2005:** 26
Federal E-Signature and Global E-Commerce Act (2000), 2003: 838; **2004:** 805
Federal Insecticide, Fungicide and Rodenticide Act (1947), 1991-99: 1687; **2002:** 775, 776, 777
Federal Noxious Weed Act (1974), 1991-99: 1790

Federal paramountcy doctrine, 2005: 251, 253–54
Federal Plant Pest Act (1957), 1991-99: 1790
Federal Property and Administrative Services Act (1949), 1991-99: 347
Federal Seed Act (1939), 1991-99: 1790
Federal Tort Claims Act (1946), 1989-90: 309; **1991-99:** 189, 1126–28; **2001:** 327, 332–33, 418, 477; **2002:** 461; **2004:** 340, 341–42, 479, 511, 515
  foreign country exception, **1991-99:** 1142
  suit against U.S. foreign service officer for tort committed in line of duty abroad, **2006:** 308–11
Federal Trade Commission Act (1914), 1991-99: 1746
Federalism. *See* States, U.S.; Treaties, generally
Felonies. *See* Crime
Fiji
  environmental protection agreement, **2002:** 791
  extradition and mutual legal assistance, **2000:** 185*n*
  South Pacific regional environmental convention, **1989-90:** 491
  trafficking in persons, **2008:** 118
Financial Action Task Force on Money Laundering (FATF). *See* Money laundering
Financial Crimes Enforcement Network (FinCEN). *See* Money laundering
Financial transactions, 2004: 142, 159, 647; **2005:** 119, 181, 1095, 1105. *See also* Sanctions
  anti-corruption conventions, **1991-99:** 558–71
  assignment of receivables in international trade, **2003:** 854–55
  bilateral investment treaties. *See* Investment
  bribery. *See* Crime
  capital and current account transfers, **1991-99:** 1465, 1471, 1479
  case against Italy for interference with foreign investment, **1989-90:** 418
  commercial arbitration, inter-American convention on, **1989-90:** 501–2
  corruption. *See* Corruption
  cybercrime. *See* Crime
  drug trafficking
    Convention Against Illicit Traffic in Narcotic Drugs and Psychotropic Substances, **1989-90:** 129, 131
    prohibition on transactions with drug traffickers, **1991-99:** 547, 548–49, 550–51
    sanctions against foreign drug traffickers. *See* Sanctions
  electronic commerce. *See* Electronic commerce
  Financial Action Task Force. *See* Money laundering
  financing of international projects, **1991-99:** 1852–53; **2002:** 821

Financial transactions (continued)
foreign control of U.S. company, prohibition on, **1989-90**: 418–24
foreign direct investment, U.S. policy on, **1991-99**: 1461–63
foreign sales corporation tax law. *See* Foreign Sales Corporation (FSC)
fraud, **2004**: 805–6
freezing of assets of terrorist organizations. *See* Terrorism
freezing of assets of weapons of mass destruction proliferators and their supporters. *See* Nonproliferation
government interest and, **1991-99**: 1098
insolvency law, **2003**: 837–38
involving proliferation of weapons of mass destruction. *See* Nonproliferation, **2004**: 1097, 1102
leasing, UNIDROIT model law on, **2008**: 745–47
medallion stamp guarantees, **2001**: 59
mobile equipment financing, with draft space protocol and aircraft protocol. *See* Mobile Equipment, Cape Town Convention on International Interests in (2001)
model law of public procurement, **1991-99**: 1820–22
money laundering. *See* Money laundering
Multilateral Agreement on Investment, **1991-99**: 1447, 1486–93
payment guarantees and credit, **1991-99**: 1812–14
price fixing, **2001**: 334–35
receivables financing, **1991-99**: 1822–24
securities. *See* Investments
secured financing interests, **1991-99**: 1853–56; **2002**: 818–19, 822–29; **2003**: 836–37; **2004**: 803
statute of limitations for transaction-related claims, **1991-99**: 1817–20
terrorism. *See* Terrorism, *subheading*: designation of foreign terrorist organizations (FTOs) by U.S.; Terrorism, *subheading*: financing of
WTO
action brought by U.S. against China on financial information services, **2008**: 543–44
Agreement on Trade in Financial Services, **1991-99**: 1376–78, 1396
Financing of terrorism. *See* Terrorism
FinCEN (Financial Crimes Enforcement Network). *See* Money laundering
Fines. *See* Sanctions
Fingerprinting. *See* Biometric identification
Finland
advance notice requirements for passage through territorial waters, **1989-90**: 442–44
Arctic region, **2008**: 625, 627, 628, 633
environment protection agreement, **1991-99**: 1777–80

Finland (continued)
EU accession and trade agreements, **2006**: 755–56
European Atomic Energy Community (EURATOM) agreements and, **1991-99**: 2338
extradition and mutual legal assistance, **2000**: 186*n*; **2004**: 73; **2006**: 137, 146
family support enforcement, **2006**: 942
maritime navigation claims against Denmark, **1991-99**: 1585–86
nonimmigrant visa waiver pilot program, **1991-99**: 76
objections to U.S. reservations to Genocide Convention, **1989-90**: 144
reciprocity in child support enforcement, **2008**: 759
sovereign immunity from claims related to taxation, **2002**: 534–35
tax agreements with U.S., **1989-90**: 415; **2001**: 485–88, 547–49
treaty issues, **1991-99**: 744
warnings of hazardous navigation by vessels registered in, **1989-90**: 458–59
Firearms. *See* Guns and firearms
First Amendment. *See* Constitution, U.S.
Fish and marine mammals, 1989-90: 487; **1991-99**: 734, 1707–11, 1741; **2001**: 682; **2002**: 786–88; **2003**: 729–31, 739–41, 753–54, 801; **2004**: 724–30, 762, 764. *See also* Marine conservation
Bering Sea pollock resources, **2006**: 885–86
convention on conservation and management of, **1991-99**: 1705–7
U.S.-USSR joint statement on, **1989-90**: 487–88
bottom fishing, **2007**: 709–12; **2008**: 712–13
calculation of optimum yield and allowable catch in EEZ, **2003**: 739–40, 741
Canada fisheries agreements, **1989-90**: 488–89; **2004**: 751
Canada–U.S. Pacific salmon agreement, **1991-99**: 1721–25; **2000**: 294, 295; **2006**: 875–78; **2008**: 709–11
Conservation and Management of Pollock Resources in the Central Bering Sea, Convention on, **2006**: 885–86
Pacific Hake/Whiting agreement, **2004**: 753–55; **2005**: 734; **2008**: 711
Conservation of Antarctic Marine Living Resources, Convention on (CCAMLR), **2007**: 580, 709–12; **2008**: 712
conservation zones, **1989-90**: 162–63
dolphin protection in tuna harvesting, **1989-90**: 485–86; **1991-99**: 1745–54; **2001**: 748–52; **2002**: 794–96; **2004**: 757–62; **2006**: 883–85; **2007**: 718–20
Dolphin Conservation Program (AIDCP), International Agreement on, **2005**: 746
Dolphin Protection Consumer Information Act (1972), **2007**: 719

Fish and marine mammals (continued)
Dolphin Protection Consumer Information Act (1991), **1991-99:** 1746, 1753–54; **2002:** 795; **2004:** 757–62; **2006:** 883
International Dolphin Conservation Act (1992), **1991-99:** 1747–49, 1751–53
International Dolphin Conservation Program Agreement and Act (1997), **1991-99:** 1749–53, 1787*n*; **2001:** 748–52; **2004:** 762; **2006:** 884
driftnet fishing regulation
enforcement and compliance, **1991-99:** 1737–39
global moratorium, UN, **1991-99:** 1729, 1731, 1735
High Seas Driftnet Enforcement Act, **1991-99:** 1730–37; **2007:** 708–9
Long Driftnets in the South Pacific Region, Convention for the Prohibition of Fishing with, **1989-90:** 137, 491–97
in South Pacific, **1989-90:** 137–38; **1991-99:** 1725–29
Ecuador
Inter-American Tropical Tuna Commission, **2000:** 307
negotiations with U.S., **2005:** 613
whaling regulation, **2001:** 218
environmental protection and conservation agreements, **2002:** 785–98
Fisheries Act (1995), **1991-99:** 1732, 1743–44
fisheries subsidies and, **2005:** 612–13
Fishery Conservation and Management Act (1976), **1989-90:** 161–63, 488, 489; **1991-99:** 1575, 1576–77, 1707–8, 1721, 1728, 1739, 1744–45; **2002:** 190; **2003:** 729–30, 731, 739, 800; **2004:** 725, 726, 727–28, 729–30; **2005:** 744; **2008:** 642, 643, 711
fishery conservation zone, U.S., **2004:** 726
Fishing and Conservation of Living Resources of the High Seas, Convention on, **1991-99:** 1563
Food and Agriculture Organization high seas fishing agreement, **1991-99:** 1739–44
Global Fisheries agreement, **2001:** 685–88
Governing International Fisheries Agreements, **1989-90:** 488–89; **2003:** 730–31
High Seas Fishing Compliance Act (1995), **1991-99:** 1743–44; **2004:** 752
highly migratory fish
Conservation and Management of Straddling Fish Stocks and Highly Migratory Fish Stocks (UN Fish Stocks Agreement), **1991-99:** 734, 1708–11; **2002:** 786, 797; **2004:** 762–64; **2005:** 735, 744, 746, 748, 749–50; **2006:** 880; **2007:** 714–16; **2008:** 704, 709, 713

Fish and marine mammals (continued)
Highly Migratory Fish Stocks in the Western and Central Pacific Ocean, Convention for the Conservation and Management of (WCPF Convention), **2000**: 700–2; **2002**: 188; **2004**: 751; **2005**: 219–21, 733–44; **2007**: 712–13; **2008**: 704, 709, 713
tuna, treatment by U.S. in EEZ, **1989-90**: 164; **1991-99**: 1707–11
illegal, unregulated and unreported fishing, **1991-99**: 1700–1702; **2001**: 687–88; **2003**: 792–97; **2004**: 751–53; **2007**: 708, 715, 716; **2008**: 703–9
Inter-American Tropical Tuna Commission, **2000**: 306–8; **2008**: 707, 709
Inter-American Tuna Commission (IATTC), Convention Strengthening ("Antigua Convention"), **1989-90**: 485, 486; **2002**: 792; **2003**: 800–802; **2005**: 733, 738, 744–49; **2008**: 709
specially protected areas and wildlife, protocol on (1990), **2002**: 792–94; **2003**: 789–90
International Conservation and Management Measures by Fishing Vessels, Agreement to Promote Compliance with, **2005**: 746
Law of the Sea. *See* Law of the Sea, UN Convention on (UNCLOS)
Magnuson-Stevens Fishery Conservation and Management Act. *See* Fishery Conservation and Management Act (1976), *this heading*
Magnuson-Stevens Fishery Conservation and Management Reauthorization Act (2006), **2007**: 706–9, 712, 728; **2008**: 706, 711
Marine Mammal Protection Act (1972), **1991-99**: 1746, 1749, 1753, 1768, 1769; **2001**: 685, 748; **2002**: 795, 801, 802; **2006**: 880; **2007**: 709
marine wildlife initiatives, **2003**: 789–803
maritime issues. *See* Maritime issues
no compensable right to fish in exclusive economic zone, **2004**: 724–30
North Pacific Marine Science Organization, **1991-99**: 1315
North Western Pacific regional fisheries management, **2007**: 714
Northern Mariana Islands, limitations on rights of, **1989-90**: 161–64
Northern Pacific Ocean anadromous stocks, **1991-99**: 1315, 1703–5
polar bear protection, **2007**: 728
Russia, fisheries agreements and management, **1991-99**: 1703–7, 1731–32, 1738, 1744–45; **2003**: 730–31; **2005**: 557; **2008**: 711
sea turtle protection, **2001**: 761–62; **2003**: 790–92

Fish and marine mammals (continued)
Inter-American Convention for, **1991-99**: 1719–21
shrimp import restrictions for, **1991-99**: 1412–13, 1711–19; **2001**: 752–60; **2003**: 791–92; **2004**: 765; **2005**: 750–52; **2006**: 882–83; **2007**: 716–17
shark protection, **2003**: 797–99; **2004**: 763–64, 766; **2007**: 732; **2008**: 706–8
shrimp importation. *See* sea turtle protection, *this heading*
South Pacific Regional Fisheries Management Organization (proposed), **2007**: 713–14; **2008**: 713
South Pacific Tuna Act (1988), **2002**: 190; **2003**: 800; **2005**: 753
specially protected areas and wildlife, protocol to Cartagena Convention on (1990), **2002**: 792–94; **2003**: 789–90
straddling fish stocks, **1991-99**: 1709. *See also* highly migratory fish, *this heading*
sturgeon, beluga, ban on importation of caviar from, **2005**: 753–55
sustainable fisheries, **2007**: 714–16
UN Fish Stocks Agreement. *See* highly migratory fish, *this heading*
UN General Assembly resolutions on, **2004**: 762–64; **2005**: 749–50; **2006**: 880–82
trade agreements and, **2007**: 580
tuna. *See also* dolphin protection in tuna harvesting, *this heading*
Inter-American Tropical Tuna Commission, **2000**: 306–8; **2008**: 707, 709
Inter-American Tuna Commission (IATTC), Convention Strengthening ("Antigua Convention"), **1989-90**: 485, 486; **2002**: 792; **2003**: 800–802; **2005**: 733, 738, 744–49; **2008**: 709
International Commission for the Conservation of Atlantic Tunas, **2008**: 707
South Pacific Tuna Act (1988), **2002**: 190; **2003**: 800; **2005**: 753
treatment by U.S. in EEZ, **1989-90**: 164; **1991-99**: 1707–11
UN Convention on Law of the Sea. *See* Law of the Sea, UN Convention on (UNCLOS)
U.S. policy, **1991-99**: 1700–1702
U.S.–Pacific Island States Treaty (1987), **2002**: 186–90; **2003**: 799–800; **2005**: 736
amendments to, **2005**: 752–53
whaling regulation, **1991-99**: 1584; **2001**: 214–18, 684–85; **2002**: 206–12; **2003**: 243–44, 802–3; **2004**: 755–57; **2006**: 878–80

Fish and marine mammals (continued)
Iceland undermining of, **2001**: 214–18; **2002**: 206–12; **2003**: 243–44, 755–77; **2006**: 878–80
International Whaling Commission, **2007**: 720–21; **2008**: 714–15
moratorium, **2007**: 720–21
subsistence whaling by Makah tribe, **2007**: 722–24; **2008**: 714–15
Fishermen's Protective Act (1967), 2001: 685; **2004**: 755; **2006**: 879
Fissile Material Cut Off Treaty (FMCT). *See* Nonproliferation
Fixed Platforms Protocol. *See* Maritime issues; Nonproliferation; Terrorism
Flag Cruise Ship Competitiveness Act (1992), 1991-99: 1625
Flatow Amendment (1996). *See* Foreign Sovereign Immunities Act (FSIA) (1976)
Flood control negotiations between U.S. and Canada concerning Devils Lake, North Dakota, 2005: 717–19
FLSA. *See* Fair Labor Standards Act (FLSA)
FMA. *See* Foreign Missions Act (FMA)
FMCT (Fissile Material Cut Off Treaty). *See* Nonproliferation
FOIA. *See* Freedom of Information Act (FOIA)
Food. *See also* Agricultural policy and trade
Committee on World Food Security, **2006**: 389–94
Food Aid Convention (1999), **1991-99**: 934–37
food security, **2004**: 285; **2006**: 389–94
Horn of Africa Recovery and Food Security Act (1992), **1991-99**: 937–38, 2044
Oil-for-Food Program. *See* Iraq
right to, **2001**: 280; **2004**: 285–88; **2008**: 333–37
U.S. comments on UN Commission on Human Rights (UNCHR) Resolution 2005/18 concerning, **2005**: 325–26
World Food Programme deliveries to Somalia, **2008**: 925, 927
Force, use of. *See* Armed conflict; Conventional weapons; Geneva Conventions on law of war (1949); Law of war
***Force majeure*, 1989-90**: 549–50
Forced labor. *See* Slavery and forced labor
Foreign affairs. *See also* Constitution, U.S.; Diplomatic relations and recognition; Executive Branch; National security, U.S.; President, U.S.; *specific countries*
act of state doctrine and, **2003**: 580; **2005**: 576, 579
admission and departure decisions based on foreign policy reasons
choice of country for removal, **2004**: 16–18
denial of visas, **1991-99**: 131–36; **2007**: 19, 23
deportation, **1991-99**: 118–28
exclusion of aliens, **1989-90**: 34–37; **2008**: 911
prohibition on departure of wife of former president Marcos, **1989-90**: 60–62

Foreign affairs (continued)
prohibition on transport of remains of former president Marcos to Philippines, **1989-90**: 57–59
Alien Tort Statute and. *See* Alien Tort Statute (ATS)
ambassadorial functions, **1989-90**: 153–55
American Servicemembers' Protection Act and, **2003**: 226–27
conduct of as criterion in determining "foreign state" under FSIA, **2005**: 551, 557
contempt sanctions, no enforcement of, **2006**: 603–11
domestic family planning organization claiming harm from U.S. foreign assistance policy, **2001**: 283–93
effect of adjudication in certain cases on, **1989-90**: 251–64; **2002**: 357–63, 474–76; **2004**: 44, 359*n*, 360, 369–71, 373, 376–82, 431–39, 442, 471, 473–74
California Holocaust era victim compensation plan as intrusion upon, **2000**: 465–68, 471–73
Nazi era governments and corporations, **2001**: 391–93, 395–406, 408–11
South African apartheid, **2003**: 387–90
state law claims, **2005**: 422–24
Executive Branch authority. *See* President, U.S., *subheading*: foreign affairs authority
federal government authority
delegation of foreign affairs authority by Congress to Executive Branch, **1991-99**: 54–55; **2007**: 2, 122–23, 234–35, 434–35, 437–43, 440, 442, 487*n*, 708–9, 954, 965–66; **2008**: 68, 119, 192, 207, 246, 446, 451–52, 467, 473, 911
political branches authority, **2001**: 82–83, 116, 288–89, 452–53; **2007**: 1, 3, 19, 22, 77, 202, 221, 439–40, 442, 521, 744, 952; **2008**: 39–40, 66, 68, 74–77, 183, 224, 246, 445, 454, 911–12
preemption
of rights of constituent entities, **1989-90**: 162–64; **2005**: 252–54
of state laws, **1991-99**: 775–89, 1133–34; **2000**: 319–40, 460–63; **2001**: 193–97, 413–17, 451–57; **2002**: 415–29, 434–56; **2003**: 462–74; **2007**: 202, 206, 235–38, 418, 817
Puerto Rican status, **1991-99**: 830–31; **2000**: 340–44, 345–46; **2001**: 242–45
Foreign Affairs Reform and Restructuring Act of 1998 (FARR Act), **1991-99**: 103–4, 105–6, 109, 240, 943–44, 945, 948–50, 956; **2001**: 71, 72, 77, 78–79, 80–85, 337–39; **2004**: 52, 85, 86, 87–88; **2005**: 79, 85–87, 90–91; **2006**: 148–55, 158, 485; **2007**: 54; **2008**: 61, 369, 372
extradition and, **2007**: 101–8

Foreign affairs (continued)
Foreign Relations Authorization Act (2003), **2006**: 213, 217
heads of state, determinations of immunity of. *See* Head-of-state immunity
Hong Kong, conduct of, **1991-99**: 404, 1175–80
human rights and U.S. foreign policy, **1991-99**: 851–53, 856–60
Macau, conduct of, **1991-99**: 1180
Niue, conduct of, **1991-99**: 1577
nonjusticiable questions in litigation, **1989-90**: 158–59, 212–15; **1991-99**: 57, 665–66, 985–89, 992–94, 1250; **2001**: 202–7, 391–92, 451–57, 751–52; **2002**: 199–202, 333, 339–44, 357–63, 495; **2003**: 365–66, 399–401, 486, 491–96; **2004**: 206–14, 351–52*n*, 364, 382, 431–32, 434–36, 439–41, 443–44, 452, 453–54, 471–72, 530–31; **2005**: 418–21, 473–76, 480, 493–96; **2006**: 450–59, 482*n*, 507–26, 588–89; **2007**: 19, 122, 219–26, 256–63, 433–43, 957; **2008**: 222–27, 246, 443–47, 447–54, 893–94
in human rights cases, **2002**: 333, 339–44, 357–63, 495
official U.S. documentary record, **2001**: 227
protection of intelligence and foreign relations information. *See* President, U.S., *subheading*: protection of information
sanctions as instrument of foreign policy, **1991-99**: 1973–78. *See also* Sanctions
signing statements to legislation on President's authority in foreign affairs, **2007**: 438–39, 442–43, 708–9, 817. *See also* President, U.S., *subheading*: separation of powers
U.S. interests in immunity claims of USSR in Wallenberg case, **1989-90**: 281, 288–91
Foreign Assets Control Regulations, 2000: 540, 743, 744, 745–46; **2006**: 1299–1300
Foreign assistance, 2002: 307–8, 770
arms control and, **1991-99**: 2269–70, 2353, 2364
for children's health, **2004**: 280–81
Cuba, **1991-99**: 1130, 1907–11
Darfur crisis in Sudan, **2004**: 244–45
debt restructuring, **1991-99**: 1493–1500
democracy promotion programs, **1991-99**: 1011–14
development assistance, **1991-99**: 1655
Development Fund for Iraq and, **2003**: 914–23
extradition-related restriction on, **2008**: 72
family planning and, **2002**: 308–9
Food Aid Convention, **1991-99**: 934–37
Foreign Assistance Act (FAA) (1961). *See* Foreign Assistance Act (FAA) (1961)

Foreign assistance (continued)
foreign governments' efforts regarding trafficking in persons and, **2004**: 164–65; **2007**: 169; **2008**: 118
to former Communist bloc countries
lifting of sanctions against former Communist bloc countries, **1989-90**: 517–22
Support for East European Democracy Act, **1989-90**: 541–44
U.S. goals, **1989-90**: 544–46
global climate change initiatives and, **2002**: 780–81
to Haiti, **2003**: 938
Horn of Africa Recovery and Food Security Act, **1991-99**: 937–38
human rights violations and, **2004**: 251–52
prohibition on assistance to certain security forces suspected of, **1991-99**: 860–61
International Criminal Court, restrictions on availability to parties to, **2004**: 186–88; **2005**: 202
Millennium Challenge Account, **2004**: 298
narcotics trafficking and, **1991-99**: 551–54
nuclear proliferation activities and, **1991-99**: 2289, 2291–93, 2299–2300
Poland, donation of U.S. agricultural commodities and funds to, **1989-90**: 546–47
reconstruction and stabilization assistance for troubled areas, **2005**: 947–48
rule of law programs, **1991-99**: 853; **2007**: 392–93
Somalia humanitarian relief operation, **1991-99**: 2043–45
telecommunications for disaster mitigation and relief operations, **1991-99**: 1791
U.S. policy, **1991-99**: 1655; **2003**: 309–10
Foreign Assistance Act (FAA) (1961)
arms exports, **1991-99**: 2251, 2257; **2005**: 1044
chemical and biological weapons, **1989-90**: 515; **1991-99**: 2352, 2364
contributions to international organizations, PLO withholding, **1991-99**: 1992
expropriation, **2003**: 709
HIV/AIDS, **2001**: 764
human rights, **2001**: 293
reports, **1989-90**: 511; **1991-99**: 847, 941; **2000**: 347; **2001**: 247; **2002**: 261; **2003**: 277; **2004**: 221; **2005**: 257–58; **2007**: 265; **2008**: 249
humanitarian assistance, **1991-99**: 931
lifting of prohibition on military assistance, **2006**: 278
missile technology control, **1989-90**: 503; **1991-99**: 2359–60

Foreign Assistance Act (FAA) (1961) (continued)
narcotrafficking, **1991-99**: 551–52, 554; **2001**: 119; **2002**: 122, 124–26; **2003**: 182; **2004**: 133; **2005**: 135–36; **2006**: 213, 216–17; **2007**: 162–66; **2008**: 112, 578, 580, 581
nuclear proliferation, **1989-90**: 108; **1991-99**: 483–84, 508, 1223; **2001**: 809–10
India, **1991-99**: 2289, 2299, 2303; **2001**: 809–10
North Korea, **2008**: 90
Pakistan, **1991-99**: 2303; **2001**: 809–10
OPIC, **1991-99**: 2040–41
Palestinian Authority, limitation on assistance to, **2006**: 993–95
sanctions for transfer of MANPADS, **2006**: 211
state sponsors of terrorism, **1989-90**: 108; **1991-99**: 483–84, 508, 1223, 1225; **2001**: 819–20; **2002**: 413; **2003**: 167–68, 536, 555, 913, 919, 1085; **2004**: 103–4, 490–91, 890–91, 912–13, 932, 934, 1137; **2006**: 577; **2008**: 90, 459, 464–465, 467, 471–72
Iraq, rescission of determination as, **2004**: 103–4; **2005**: 506; **2006**: 179
Libya, rescission of determination as, **2005**: 506; **2006**: 173
North Korea, rescission of determination as, **2008**: 89–94, 960–66
West Bank and Gaza, limitation on assistance for, **2006**: 993–95
Foreign Claims Settlement Commission, 1989-90: 236
Foreign Commerce Clause, 2001: 203–4
Foreign Corrupt Practices Act (1977), 1991-99: 559, 563, 568; **2000**: 232–33, 237–38; **2005**: 171
Foreign Corrupt Practices Act (1997), 2000: 232–33, 237–38
Foreign direct investment
Overseas Private Investment Corporation investment incentives, **1991-99**: 1482–86
U.S. policy and practice, **1991-99**: 1461–63, 1464
Foreign Intelligence Surveillance Act (FISA), 2007: 246–53
Foreign Investment and National Security Act (FINSA) (2007), 2007: 601–5; **2008**: 593–600
Foreign Military Sales (FMS), 1989-90: 89–90, 223–24, 236; **1991-99**: 1088, 1227, 2268, 2299, 2300; **2000**: 230, 543–48; **2001**: 810; **2003**: 448, 554; **2004**: 420; **2007**: 221, 999
Foreign Missions Act (FMA), 1989-90: 324, 371, 372–73; **2000**: 550; **2001**: 540–43, 544; **2004**: 560; **2005**: 532, 533, 535, 536, 537
jurisdiction over location and construction of diplomatic missions, **1989-90**: 377–81; **2000**: 628–29, 630–34; **2006**: 659
prohibition on seizure of diplomatic property, **2000**: 557–58
tax exemption provisions, **2000**: 597

Foreign Money-Judgments Act (1967), 1991-99: 1834
Foreign Narcotics Kingpin Designation Act (1999), 1991-99: 550–51; **2001:** 143, 144–45, 822; **2003:** 186–87; **2006:** 220–21; **2008:** 114–15
Foreign Narcotics Kingpins Sanctions Regulations, 2000: 744–45
Foreign Sales Corporation (FSC)
provisions of U.S. tax law, challenge to, **2004:** 606; **2005:** 625–26
Repeal and Extraterritorial Income Exclusion Act of 2000 (ETI Act), **2001:** 653–63; **2002:** 677–93; **2005:** 625, 626
Foreign Service Act (1980), 2000: 155; **2001:** 57
Foreign Sovereign Immunities Act (FSIA) (1976), 1989-90: 115–16; **1991-99:** 1183–84; **2000:** 474–75; **2001:** 230–31, 429–30; **2002:** 465–66; **2003:** 503–4; **2004:** 458–59, 822; **2005:** 429–30; **2006:** 549–629; **2008:** 455–83. *See also* Sovereign immunity
absent party, effect of immunity on jurisdiction over claim, **2007:** 472–76
act of state and, **2000:** 473–85; **2005:** 578–80
Algiers Accords and, **2001:** 468–75; **2002:** 523–27
Alien Tort Statute and, **2004:** 371, 380–82; **2005:** 406
amendments to, **1991-99:** 1184, 1223–26; **2000:** 230, 540–42, 557, 558–60; **2001:** 485; **2002:** 410–13; **2003:** 552; **2008:** 457–63
art immune from seizure and, **2004:** 792–96; **2006:** 562–72; **2008:** 732–34
attempts to satisfy judgments against Iran through assignment of Iran–U.S. Claims Tribunal awards, **2008:** 414–16
cause of action not provided by,[7] **2000:** 593; **2003:** 537–52; **2004:** 501–16; **2005:** 509; **2006:** 578
causes of action in cases brought under terrorism exception
execution of judgments. *See* execution of judgments, *this heading*
federal law, **2005:** 513–16; **2006:** 578, 589–90
civil cause of action under Antiterrorism Act (1990) and, **1989-90:** 115–19
common law, **2005:** 513–14; **2006:** 590–91

[7] Editor's note: Section 1083(b) of the National Defense Authorization Act for Fiscal Year 2008 (NDAA), Pub. L. No. 110-181, 122 Stat. 343, replaced the terrorism exception to immunity under the FSIA and was codified at 28 U.S.C. § 1605A. Section 1605A(c) creates a new private cause of action against designated state sponsors of terrorism, as well as any official, employee, or agent of the state acting in the scope of his or her office, employment, or agency for terrorism-related claims under § 1605A(a).

Foreign Sovereign Immunities Act (FSIA) (1976) (continued)
Flatow Amendment cause of action against officials, employees, and agents of foreign states acting in their personal capacities for conduct described in FSIA terrorist act exception, **1991-99**: 1334–35; **2000**: 540–42; **2002**: 523–24, 530–34; **2003**: 537–43, 551–52; **2004**: 501–16; **2005**: 507, 509–11, 513–15, 517, 544; **2006**: 589–90
none provided by FSIA,[8] **2000**: 593; **2003**: 537–52; **2004**: 501–16; **2005**: 509; **2006**: 578
state law, **2004**: 511–12; **2005**: 511–13, 518; **2006**: 583–84, 591–92
claims of victims of Nazi era and, **1991-99**: 1181–83; **2000**: 473–85; **2003**: 503–11, 513–16; **2004**: 463–75
commercial activity exceptions. *See* exceptions to immunity, *this heading*
common law, **2004**: 461–62, 508; **2005**: 513–14; **2006**: 590–91; **2008**: 478
counterclaims, **1991-99**: 1198–99; **2001**: 482*n*; **2002**: 493
decision as to applicability made by courts, **2000**: 577–79, 591–92; **2004**: 821–22; **2005**: 579–80
default judgments, **1989-90**: 277–91; **1991-99**: 1224; **2000**: 593; **2001**: 459–68; **2003**: 505, 506; **2005**: 502–3; **2006**: 581–84
definition of "foreign state," **1991-99**: 812–13, 1184–85; **2002**: 466–67, 468–69, 479–80, 489, 515–16, 536, 539–40; **2003**: 507–12, 561–62; **2004**: 458, 460–63, 529–30; **2006**: 550–61
agency or instrumentality of, **1991-99**: 1188, 1189, 1228–34, 1254–55, 1275; **2002**: 479–91; **2003**: 512–14, 520–21, 561–62; **2005**: 504–5; **2006**: 558–61, 612–21; **2007**: 451–54
core functions test, **2006**: 558–61
Europol, **2002**: 467–69
foreign consulate, **2003**: 510, 532–33

[8] Editor's note: Section 1083(b) of the National Defense Authorization Act for Fiscal Year 2008 (NDAA), Pub. L. No. 110-181, 122 Stat. 343, replaced the terrorism exception to immunity under the FSIA and was codified at 28 U.S.C. § 1605A. Section 1605A(c) creates a new private cause of action against designated state sponsors of terrorism, as well as any official, employee, or agent of the state acting in the scope of his or her office, employment, or agency for terrorism-related claims under § 1605A(a).

Foreign Sovereign Immunities Act (FSIA) (1976) (continued)
foreign military, **1989-90:** 313; **1991-99:** 1186–88; **2002:** 466–67; **2005:** 549–55; **2006:** 618–19
government officials. *See* government officials and, *this heading*
organ of foreign state, **2003:** 510–12; **2006:** 550–58; **2007:** 454–55
Palau, **1991-99:** 811–16
Palestinian entities, **1991-99:** 1185–86; **2005:** 503–4, 531–42
Taipei Economic and Cultural Representative Office, **2002:** 535–45
United Nations, inapplicable to, **2002:** 571–72
diplomatic and consular property, **2000:** 552–58; **2002:** 542; **2003:** 552–58; **2005:** 543–48, 555–60; **2008:** 456–57, 495–98
emotional distress claims, **2004:** 503
enforcement of contempt sanctions not available under, **2005:** 522–31; **2006:** 603–11
exceptions to immunity, **1991-99:** 1183, 1184; **2000:** 478–81, 548; **2002:** 220, 502–3, 517–22; **2003:** 504; **2004:** 459; **2006:** 572–603; **2008:** 456–57
arbitration agreements and confirmation of arbitral awards, **2000:** 592; **2001:** 458–59; **2002:** 571–72; **2006:** 612–21; **2008:** 484–89
causes of action in cases brought under. *See* causes of action in cases brought under terrorism exception, *this heading*
commercial activity, **1989-90:** 291–94, 297–98, 391; **1991-99:** 1184, 1199–1223, 1254–55, 1303–4; **2000:** 555, 577–89; **2001:** 402–4, 429–30, 443–45, 491, 496–501; **2003:** 503–9, 518–19, 530–32; **2004:** 455–56, 457, 459, 460–63, 482–83; **2005:** 475; **2006:** 572, 573–75, 620–21; **2007:** 463–70, 518*n*
attachment of bank accounts, **2002:** 541–43
civil servants and, **2000:** 577–90; **2002:** 477–78
definition, **2000:** 555, 580
origins of, **2002:** 465–66, 505, 543–44
private company indirectly owned by foreign government, **2002:** 479–91
retroactive application, **2002:** 497–99, 506, 513, 516
expropriation claims, **1989-90:** 308–9; **1991-99:** 1252–56; **2001:** 405–6, 458; **2002:** 497, 508, 509–11, 513–16, 520–22; **2003:** 509–11, 519; **2004:** 463–72, 494–500, 795–96; **2006:** 558–61, 572–77; **2008:** 733
immovable property, rights in, **2007:** 455–62; **2008:** 456–57
international agreements at time FSIA enacted, application preserved by

Foreign Sovereign Immunities Act (FSIA) (1976) (continued)
only where express conflict with FSIA, **1989-90**: 283–84; **1991-99**: 1196–97, 1320–21; **2000**: 587–90; **2004**: 478–82; **2006**: 626
at time FSIA enacted, **1991-99**: 1196–97, 1320–21; **2000**: 587–90; **2004**: 478–82
jus cogens violations, no exception for. *See jus cogens* violations, no exception to immunity for, *this heading*
noncommercial torts, **1989-90**: 288, 309–10, 333; **1991-99**: 1256–58; **2002**: 472, 522; **2003**: 532–36
takings. *See* expropriation claims, *this subheading*
terrorist acts, **1991-99**: 1195; **2000**: 542–43, 547–48; **2001**: 336, 435–36, 459–75; **2002**: 466, 471–72, 522–34; **2003**: 536–43; **2004**: 459, 484–89; **2005**: 506–22; **2006**: 577–92; **2007**: 470; **2008**: 457–75. *See also* causes of action in cases brought under terrorism exception, *this heading*
constitutional challenges to, **1991-99**: 1234–52; **2003**: 505–6; **2005**: 520–21; **2008**: 471–75
execution of judgments. *See* execution of judgments, *this heading*
Iran, suits by U.S. hostages against, **2001**: 459–62; **2002**: 523–27
Iraq-related legislative and executive actions, effect of, **2004**: 489–93; **2008**: 460–71
legislative enactments (1996 and 2008), **1991-99**: 481, 1184, 1223–24; **2008**: 457–63
Libya, legislation restoring Libya's immunity for acts prior to June 30, 2006, **2008**: 399–402, 462–63
state sponsors of terrorism, applicable only to, **2002**: 471–72; **2005**: 506, 509, 511, 518, 520, 579, 580; **2006**: 582
waiver. *See* waiver, *this heading*
execution of judgments, **1989-90**: 296–300; **1991-99**: 1227–34; **2000**: 554–57, 558–60; **2006**: 612–29
amendments providing for certain attachments and presidential waiver thereof (1998 and 2000), **1991-99**: 1224–26; **2000**: 230, 540–42, 554, 557–60
arbitration award, attachment of, **2006**: 612–21 ;**2007**: 477–89; **2008**: 414–16, 484–89
central bank assets immune from, **2007**: 494–504
Chinese pandas and associated funds not available for, **2001**: 488–501
commercial activity exception to immunity under FSIA for, **2007**: 489–94, 495–96, 499–502
diplomatic and consular property and, **2000**: 540–42, 552–54; **2003**: 552–57; **2005**: 545–48, 555–60; **2006**: 626–29

Foreign Sovereign Immunities Act (FSIA) (1976) (continued)
distinction between foreign state and agent or instrumentality in, **2007**: 495
excusable neglect, **2006**: 621–26
immunity of property from attachment as distinct from immunity to jurisdiction, **2004**: 516–27
National Defense Authorization Act for Fiscal Year 2008 provisions concerning; **2008**: 414–15, 458–59
Palestinian observer mission to UN not available for, **2005**: 531–60
Philippines, ownership of assets in, **2008**: 475–81
property in possession of third party, **2006**: 564–72
under Terrorism Risk Insurance Act amendment (2002) providing for attachment of blocked assets in certain cases, **2002**: 410–13; **2003**: 552–57; **2004**: 517–27; **2005**: 543–48; **2007**: 477–89; **2008**: 411, 466, 467, 484–89
exhaustion of remedies, **2004**: 494–95
extradition and, **2001**: 475–85
Flatow Amendment. *See* causes of action in cases brought under terrorism exception, *this heading*
foreign policy interests and, **1989-90**: 288–91; **2004**: 352*n*, 380–82
head-of-state immunity as separate, **1991-99**: 1273–77, 1287–88; **2001**: 511, 516–21; **2004**: 529–30. *See also* Head-of-state immunity
fugitive disentitlement doctrine, **2006**: 562*n*
government officials and, **1989-90**: 302–11; **1991-99**: 1188–90, 1215–16, 1223; **2001**: 322–23; **2002**: 466–67, 472–73, 477–78; **2003**: 507–10, 560, 561–62; **2005**: 504–5; **2007**: 504–16
common law not replaced by FSIA for, **1989-90**: 302; **2006**: 634–39; **2007**: 504, 509–16
special missions immunity and, **2006**: 680–81; **2007**: 447–48; **2008**: 490–91
jus cogens violations, no exception to immunity for, **1991-99**: 1133, 1190–95; **2000**: 478–85; **2001**: 396, 430–43, 481; **2002**: 467, 491–94, 501; **2003**: 514–15, 522, 523, 563–64; **2004**: 499; **2006**: 646–50
monetary contempt sanctions, no enforcement of, **2005**: 522–31
restrictive theory of sovereign immunity and, **2001**: 429, 432, 477, 516; **2004**: 459; **2007**: 445, 459–60
retroactive application, **1991-99**: 1191–92, 1247, 1258, 1260–65; **2001**: 433, 457–58, 466; **2002**: 492–94, 513, 516; **2003**: 515–23; **2004**: 463–78, 796*n*; **2005**: 470, 505–6; **2006**: 573

Foreign Sovereign Immunities Act (FSIA) (1976) (continued)
role of Department of State in cases under, **2007:** 449
sanctions for frivolous filings against foreign government, **1989-90:** 313–14
service of process, **1991-99:** 1141, 1186, 1274; **2000:** 592–93; **2001:** 501–10; **2003:** 557–58; **2004:** 549, 555–56; **2005:** 567; **2008:** 481–83
time requirement as customary international law, **1989-90:** 295; **2004:** 457–58
sovereign as judgment debtor, **2000:** 590–93
tax issues and, **2001:** 485–88; **2002:** 534–35; **2006:** 592–603; **2008:** 456–57
terrorist acts exceptions. *See* exceptions to immunity, *this heading*
third party ability to assert immunity of Iranian art in its possession, **2006:** 562–72
Torture Victim Protection Act and, **2007:** 507–8
waiver, **2002:** 497, 516–17; **2003:** 523–24. *See also jus cogens* violations, no exception to immunity for, *this heading*
implied, **1989-90:** 281–93; **1991-99:** 1133, 1197–99; **2000:** 478–81; **2001:** 435–43, 479–85; **2006:** 562–64
participation in litigation, not constituting, **1989-90:** 306–8; **2003:** 524–25
treaty rights and obligations, undertaking or invoking not constituting, **1989-90:** 285–87; **2001:** 479–85; **2002:** 467; **2003:** 526–30
violation of customary international law and, **2002:** 473, 492
by sovereign, **2000:** 478–81, 548
Foreign terrorist organizations (FTOs). *See* Terrorism, *subheading*: designation of foreign terrorist organizations (FTOs) by U.S.
Foreign Trade Act (1974), 2003: 277
Foreign Trade Antitrust Improvements Act (1982), 1991-99: 1532
Forest conservation. *See* Environmental issues
***Forum non conveniens* doctrine, 1991-99:** 987–88; **2001:** 336–37, 458–59; **2003:** 386–87, 895–901; **2004:** 378, 796*n*, 875–78; **2005:** 418, 474, 519, 819, 822, 827, 833–43; **2006:** 963–65
Alien Tort Statute, Torture Victim Protection Act jurisdiction, **2002:** 339, 345–46, 355–57, 481
Montreal Convention, **2008:** 513–19
Fourth Amendment. *See* Constitution, U.S.
France
air transport agreement with U.S., **1991-99:** 1359, 1361–62
aircraft subsidies and, **2004:** 603–4; **2005:** 622

France (continued)
Andorra independence and, **1991-99:** 1151
Apartheid Convention and, **2004:** 358
arms control and, **1991-99:** 2232
Change of Gauge Arbitration, **2000:** 657, 658, 659–60
compliance with Hague abduction convention, **2006:** 102
consular notification, **1991-99:** 310
coral reef protection, **1991-99:** 1755
customary international law, specially affected state under, **2006:** 1077–81
environmental protection agreements, **1991-99:** 1782; **2002:** 791
extradition and mutual legal assistance, **1991-99:** 396, 600–601; **2000:** 166, 178, 180, 186*n*; **2001:** 87–89, 92*n*; **2004:** 73; **2006:** 137, 146
extradition of Manuel Noriega requested by, **2007:** 108–17; **2008:** 69
extradition to U.S. from, after trial in absentia, **2001:** 87–89
family support enforcement, **1991-99:** 1866
fisheries, regulation of, **2005:** 737, 742
French Central Authority, certificate of service, **2005:** 853–56
French Polynesia, **2005:** 736, 742–43
Gold Train property, return to Hungary, **2005:** 488
Guantanamo detainees transferred to, **2005:** 967
Gulf War and, **1991-99:** 2057, 2072, 2074, 2089, 2116
Haiti and, **2004:** 940
hoasca (hallucinogenic tea), ban on, **2005:** 144
immunity under FSIA, **2002:** 517
immunity of consulate, **2003:** 510, 532–33
Inter-American Tropical Tuna Commission, **2000:** 307, 308
International Covenant on Civil and Political Rights, comments on, **2005:** 298–99, 300*n*
International Space Station Partners Agreement, **1991-99:** 1642
Iran and Libya Sanctions Act (1996) and, **1991-99:** 1915
Libya involvement in UTA 772 and, **1991-99:** 457–58, 459
lost or stolen passports, reporting of, **2004:** 81
money laundering, **2004:** 135
Multilateral Agreement on Investment negotiations, **1991-99:** 1491–93
New Caledonia, **2005:** 736
nonimmigrant visa waiver pilot program, **1989-90:** 27
nonproliferation efforts. *See* Nonproliferation, *subheading*: country-specific issues
Open Skies agreement, **2002:** 597–98
Open Skies (aerial observation) treaty, **2002:** 1029
OSCE Minsk Group co-chair, efforts to settle Nagorno-Karabakh conflict, **2008:** 831–32

France (continued)
outer space framework agreement with U.S., **2007**: 670–72
parental child abduction, **1991-99**: 354, 355; **2000**: 105–15
peace process, involvement in
Darfur, **2006**: 1051
former Yugoslavia and, **1991-99**: 134, 1980, 2031, 2139
Kosovo peace process, role in, **2005**: 935
Lebanon, **2006**: 257, 1036*n*
Middle East peace process and, **1991-99**: 1024; **2005**: 880
religious freedom, actions promoting, **2005**: 315
rendition, use of, **2005**: 102; **2006**: 161–62
service of process issues, **2003**: 557; **2005**: 853–54
Somali piracy, cooperation with Transitional Federal Government of Somalia (TFG) in fight against, **2008**: 925, 927
South Pacific regional environmental convention, **1989-90**: 491
Subsidies and Countervailing Measures, Agreement on, **2005**: 622, 625, 628, 636
sunken ships, issues concerning, **1989-90**: 429–34; **1991-99**: 1614; **2004**: 715–17, 722
recognition of U.S. title to salvaged artifacts, **1991-99**: 1608–11
Titanic protection agreement, **2004**: 715–16; **2006**: 828–35; **2008**: 657–65
tax convention with U.S., protocol amending, **2005**: 671
treaty interpretation, **1991-99**: 152, 722, 723–24, 732, 744, 1353–54
underwater cultural heritage (UCH), position on, **2005**: 762, 766
World War II-era issues, **2004**: 476–78, 881
Austria, French-occupied (World War II), **2005**: 485
Holocaust restitution and compensation issues, **1991-99**: 1043–46, 1053, 1061, 1064, 1065, 1068, 1069–70, 1081
Nazi era victims, claims of, **2001**: 406–13; **2006**: 504–7
retroactive application of FSIA to World War II-era claims, **2003**: 520–21
trials by military commissions after World War II, **2005**: 969
Franchising, **2002**: 820–21
Fraud
banking fraud claims, **1991-99**: 1285–89
cybercrime, **2003**: 198
document fraud in smuggling of migrants, **2004**: 160–61, 162
financial transactions, **2004**: 805–6
immigration documents, **2005**: 156; **2006**: 15, 51, 207–10
securities transactions, SEC enforcement efforts against, **2008**: 603–4
wire fraud statute and, **2005**: 235–42

Free and Secure Trade (FAST) program, 2005: 4
Free speech rights, 1991-99: 148, 189, 961; **2001:** 353–54. *See also* Constitution, U.S. *subheading*: First Amendment
constitutional protection in U.S., **2004:** 266. *See also* Constitution, U.S., *subheading*: First Amendment
Convention on the Elimination of All Forms of Discrimination Against Women and, **1991-99:** 906–7
Convention on the Elimination of All Forms of Racial Discrimination and, **1991-99:** 885, 891–94, 906
criminalization of hate speech on Internet, **2004:** 263–69
customary international law, **2001:** 291–92
democracy and, **2004:** 387, 389, 957
designation of terrorist organization as alleged violation of, **2006:** 198–99
domestic family planning organization claiming harm from U.S. foreign assistance policy, **2001:** 283, 285–90
Holocaust denial and, **2007:** 326, 378–80
incitement to commit terrorist acts, **2006:** 200–210
International Covenant on Civil and Political Rights, **1991-99:** 870, 874, 876
international law obligations and, **2007:** 217–18
racial hate speech, **2001:** 248–49, 256, 264–65, 268–69
UN Special Rapporteur on Freedom of Opinion and Expression, **2006:** 486–87
Free Trade Agreement of the Americas, 1991-99: 1437–41, 1491
Free Trade Area of the Americas, 2001: 350
Freedom for Russia and Emerging Eurasian Democracies and Open Markets Support Act (1992), 1991-99: 1011–14, 2330–31
Freedom of Information Act (FOIA), 1991-99: 789–801, 1014; **2002:** 234; **2004:** 112–13, 114, 1125
litigation concerning, **2005:** 1018–22
Abu Ghraib photos, **2005:** 1022–29; **2006:** 1213–23
Freedom of navigation program. *See* Maritime issues, *subheading*: navigation rights
Freezing of assets of terrorist organizations. *See* Terrorism, *subheading*: freezing or blocking assets of designated terrorist organization or supporters
Friendship, Commerce and Navigation treaties, 2003: 261–62, 265–66, 267; **2007:** 30–32; **2008:** 156
Italy–U.S. (1965), **1989-90:** 418
U.S.–Republic of Korea, **2000:** 497
FSC Repeal and Extraterritorial Income Exclusion Act (2000). *See* Foreign Sales Corporation (FSC)
FSIA. *See* Foreign Sovereign Immunities Act (FSIA) (1976)

FTCA. *See* Federal Tort Claims Act (1946)
FTOs (foreign terrorist organizations). *See* Terrorism, *subheading*: designation of foreign terrorist organizations (FTOs) by U.S.
Fugitive disentitlement doctrine, 2006: 562*n*

G

G-8 countries
Action Plan for Africa, **2002:** 307
counterterrorism recommendations, **2002:** 121–22; **2006:** 210
Global Partnership Against the Spread of Weapons and Materials of Mass Destruction, **2005:** 1095; **2008:** 1000
kleptocracy prevention, **2006:** 234
Gabon, 2003: 238
Gambia
agreements, **2003:** 238
extradition and mutual legal assistance, **2000:** 185*n*
Gambling
Gambling Devices (Johnson) Act, **1991-99:** 1625–29
Gambling Ship Act (1994), **1991-99:** 1621–25
WTO dispute resolution. *See* World Trade Organization (WTO)
Garnishment
Algiers Accords, **2008:** 488
dissolution of writs due to lack of jurisdiction, **2006:** 562–64
Libya Claims Resolution Act, **2008:** 401
sovereign immunity, **2008:** 413–14
Garrison Diversion Reformulation Act (1986), 2001: 189, 193, 195, 197
GATS. *See* General Agreement on Trade in Services (GATS)
GATT. *See* General Agreement on Tariffs and Trade (GATT)
Gender discrimination. *See* Discrimination; Gender issues
Gender issues, 1991-99: 88, 805
abortion. *See* Abortion
access to housing, **2003:** 317
advancement of women, **2006:** 373–74
Afghanistan, women's rights in, **2001:** 269, 275; **2002:** 277, 279–80. *See also* Taliban
Africa, women's justice and empowerment in, U.S. initiative, **2005:** 307–8
asylum adjudications, **1991-99:** 215–26
family planning policy in China, **1991-99:** 202–7
female genital mutilation as basis for, **1991-99:** 207–15
gender as group, **1991-99:** 221–23, 230–31
gender guidelines, **1991-99:** 215–26, 230–31
sexual violence or harassment as persecution, **1991-99:** 218, 225
citizenship and, **1991-99:** 1–9. *See also* Citizenship, *subheading*: children

Gender issues (continued)
naturalization of out-of-wedlock child, **2000:** 4–5, 6, 8, 12–17
transmission of U.S. citizenship to foreign-born child of foreign father, **2001:** 7–8
cloning, **2004:** 788
comfort women. *See* Japan
Convention on the Elimination of All Forms of Discrimination Against Women (CEDAW) (1980), **1989-90:** 168–71; **1991-99:** 852, 855, 897–911; **2001:** 270, 275; **2002:** 277–80; **2003:** 293–94; **2004:** 294; **2005:** 219, 311; **2007:** 276, 322, 361–63; **2008:** 266–67
U.S. reasons for not ratifying, **2007:** 198–99
disarmament issues and, **2000:** 354
discrimination. *See* Discrimination, *subheading*: gender
domestic violence, **2005:** 313
economic globalization and, **2000:** 354
in employment, **1989-90:** 170–71
equal opportunity for women and men, **2005:** 311–13
female military personnel, **1991-99:** 902–3
gender equality, **2000:** 351–55; **2005:** 312, 313
goals, **2003:** 292, 293, 294
health care access, **1991-99:** 907–8
International Criminal Court definition of crimes against women, **1991-99:** 637
international efforts, **2000:** 351–55
in labor, **1991-99:** 903–5
military policies and, **1989-90:** 170
in naturalization of out-of-wedlock child, **2000:** 12–17
and peacekeeping, **1991-99:** 911; **2000:** 227; **2004:** 166–68. *See also* Violence Against Women Act (VAWA) (2000), *this heading*
pregnant women, **1991-99:** 271, 870, 908, 966
property rights, **2001:** 270–71
equal ownership, access to and control over land and equal rights to own property and to adequate housing, **2005:** 310–11
protection from illegal trafficking. *See* Trafficking in persons
rape and sexual violence as war crime or crime against humanity, **1991-99:** 584, 637, 918; **2000:** 41–42, 251–55, 287; **2006:** 420, **2007:** 317–21, 906, **2008:** 287
rights of girl child, **2002:** 304
security during armed conflict, **2002:** 275–76
threats to, **2003:** 290–92
trafficking. *See* Trafficking in persons

Gender issues (continued)
UN Commission on Status of Women (CSW), **2003**: 290; **2005**: 308–9
reproductive rights, U.S. comments regarding to, **2005**: 308–9
UN declarations and programs, **1991-99**: 850, 855–56
Fourth World Conference on Women, **1991-99**: 898, 917–18; **2000**: 351–52; **2007**: 321–22
UN Development Fund for Women (UNIFEM), **2006**: 372–73
UN Special Rapporteur on Violence Against Women, **1991-99**: 850
UN General Assembly resolution on Follow-up to Fourth World Conference on Women, **2007**: 321–22
U.S. foreign policy objectives, **1991-99**: 852, 855
violence against women, **2001**: 269–70; **2004**: 181, 296; **2006**: 374–76; **2008**: 286–88
Violence Against Women Act (VAWA) (2000), **2005**: 264, 271
women in development draft resolution, **2007**: 322–24
in workplace, **1991-99**: 903–4
General Agreement on Tariffs and Trade (GATT), **1991-99**: 662, 1382; **2003**: 618–21, 652, 655
applied in NAFTA, **1991-99**: 1422
constitutional considerations, **1991-99**: 652–54, 655*n*
EU–U.S. tariffs, **2006**: 754–55
fiftieth anniversary of, **1991-99**: 1390–94
Law of the Sea Convention and, **1991-99**: 1561; **2003**: 618, 619–21
NAFTA dispute settlement, **2001**: 593–95
Summit of the Americas, **1991-99**: 1438–39
Uruguay Round Agreements, **1991-99**: 1371–75, 1382, 1500
U.S.-EU Understanding, **1991-99**: 1445
WTO dispute settlement, **1991-99**: 1403–5, 1415–16, 1418, 1420; **2001**: 650, 662; **2003**: 652, 655–56, 663; **2005**: 621–22, 628, 630–31, 636; **2008**: 551–52
General Agreement on Trade in Services (GATS), **1991-99**: 77, 1374, 1376–78, 1397–98, 1415–16, 1445, 1526; **2001**: 650, 669; **2003**: 663–64; **2004**: 602, 604, 610; **2005**: 616, 624, 635; **2006**: 755–56, **2008**: 544
General Assembly, UN. *See also* Human rights; International Law Commission (ILC)
Declarations
on human cloning, **2005**: 771–72
on protection from torture and other cruel, inhuman or degrading treatment or punishment, **2000**: 373
on rights of indigenous people (2007), **2007**: 368–73; **2008**: 352–57
on territorial asylum (1967), **1989-90**: 52; **2007**: 51, 64
on Universal Declaration of Human Rights (1948), **2007**: 286–89
on victims of crime and abuse of power, **2001**: 39–40

General Assembly, UN (continued)
Resolutions:
10/14 (ES), **2003**: 949–51
16/1653, **1991-99**: 2175
34/180, **1989-90**: 168–69
35/98D, **2004**: 1063–64
39/46, **1989-90**: 176–77
39/708, **2005**: 1015
42/210, **2005**: 539
44/25, **1989-90**: 176
44/26, **1989-90**: 425–27
44/29, **1991-99**: 500
44/225, **1991-99**: 1729, 1731
45/158, **1989-90**: 194
45/197, **1991-99**: 1731
46/215, **1991-99**: 1729, 1731–32, 1737
47/33, **1991-99**: 609
48/37, **2001**: 356
48/102, **1991-99**: 61
49/53, **1991-99**: 609
49/75, **1991-99**: 2170
50/46, **1991-99**: 609
50/48, **1991-99**: 1812
50/245, **1991-99**: 2272
51/162, **1991-99**: 1809
52/160, **1991-99**: 626
52/250, **1991-99**: 1027–29
54/38, **1991-99**: 1026–27
54/175, **2007**: 360
55/2, **2005**: 335–36
55/23, **2000**: 562
56/83, **2005**: 408*n*; **2007**: 413
56/139, **2001**: 275
56/168, **2001**: 272–73; **2003**: 300
57/178, **2002**: 280
57/189, **2002**: 304
57/190, **2002**: 302–3, 304
57/194, **2002**: 274–75
57/195, **2002**: 274–75
57/199, **2002**: 314–15
57/214, **2002**: 318–20
57/215, **2002**: 320
57/219, **2002**: 387–88
57/226, **2002**: 311

General Assembly, UN (continued)
57/228, **2003**: 222
57/233, **2002**: 320
57/299, **2002**: 283–85
58/111, **2003**: 408–9
58/140, **2003**: 342–43
58/142, **2003**: 293
58/147, **2003**: 293
58/156, **2003**: 279, 309, 311
58/159, **2003**: 298
58/160, **2003**: 298
58/165, **2003**: 279, 311, 326
58/172, **2003**: 314–15
58/173, **2003**: 317–19
58/179, **2003**: 319–20
58/183, **2003**: 280
58/196, **2003**: 336–37
58/318, **2004**: 175–76; **2005**: 198
58/874, **2004**: 176
59/24, **2004**: 762
59/25, **2004**: 762
59/35, **2007**: 413
59/49, **2004**: 804*n*
59/111, **2004**: 291–92
59/115, **2004**: 735
59/147, **2004**: 291–92
59/174, **2004**: 385
59/189, **2004**: 331
59/197, **2004**: 183
59/200, **2004**: 183
59/211, **2004**: 183, 409
59/280, **2005**: 771–72
59/290, **2005**: 106–8, 960, 1123–24
59/492, **2004**: 291–92
60/1, **2005**: 451–55; **2008**: 857
60/7, **2005**: 318–19
60/12, **2005**: 889–91
60/21, **2005**: 799–802
60/29, **2005**: 197–98
60/30, **2005**: 731–32
60/31, **2005**: 749–50
60/146, **2005**: 919
60/147, **2007**: 281
60/167, **2005**: 780–81

General Assembly, UN (continued)
60/180, **2005**: 919
60/210, **2005**: 335–36
60/251, **2006**: 328, 341; **2007**: 285
60/288, **2008**: 85, 92
61/21, **2007**: 286
61/28, **2006**: 1060
61/35, **2007**: 415
61/89, **2008**: 1019
61/105, **2006**: 881; **2007**: 710, 713, 714; **2008**: 712
61/106, **2006**: 383
61/135, **2006**: 1031
61/143, **2006**: 375
61/146, **2006**: 385–87
61/222, **2006**: 805
61/255, **2007**: 378
61/261, **2008**: 385
61/295, **2008**: 352–57, 352*n*
61/1221, **2006**: 379
61/1295, **2007**: 368
62/12, **2007**: 180
62/20, **2007**: 662
62/66, **2008**: 71
62/98, **2007**: 735
62/101, **2007**: 661
62/134, **2007**: 318, 320, 906
62/137, **2007**: 321
62/141, **2007**: 358
62/149, **2007**: 383
62/154, **2008**: 289
62/156, **2007**: 365
62/161, **2007**: 367
62/177, **2007**: 714
62/206, **2007**: 323
62/220, **2007**: 315
62/243, **2008**: 830–32
62/288, **2008**: 289
63/3, **2008**: 439
63/21, **2008**: 144
63/122, **2008**: 743
63/162, **2008**: 286
63/167, **2008**: 273
63/168, **2008**: 375
63/178, **2008**: 332

General Assembly, UN (continued)
63/182, **2008:** 376
63/184, **2008:** 338–39
63/186, **2008:** 379
63/187, **2008:** 337
63/241, **2008:** 317–18
63/242, **2008:** 284–86
63/253, **2008:** 387
63/278, **2008:** 335
63/365, **2008:** 289
89/1, **1989-90:** 354, 356
174, **1991-99:** 1106–7
181, **1991-99:** 1025
194, **1991-99:** 1025
217, **1991-99:** 864–65
2205(XXI), **2007:** 760
3068, **2004:** 355
3188, **2006:** 656*n*
3199, **2006:** 656*n*
3314, **2000:** 288
Rules of Procedure of, **2007:** 758, 762; **2008:** 205
General Convention of UN. *See* Privileges and Immunities of the United Nations (General Convention)
General Settlement Fund (GSF) Agreement, 2005: 473, 474, 486, 489–90
Genetic issues
plant genetic resources, treaty on, **2002:** 810–11; **2004:** 789–90; **2008:** 725–27
testing for visa purposes, **1989-90:** 1–3; **1991-99:** 128–31
use of genetic data, UNESCO declaration on, **2003:** 818–19
Geneva Convention I: on Wounded and Sick in Armed Forces in the Field (1949), 1991-99: 2058, 2062, 2072; **2003:** 998–99, 1014–15; **2004:** 331. *See also* Geneva Conventions on law of war (1949)
Geneva Convention II: on Wounded and Sick Armed Forces at Sea (1949), 1991-99: 2058, 2062, 2072. *See also* Geneva Conventions on law of war (1949)
Geneva Convention III: on Prisoners of War (1949), 1989-90: 563; **1991-99:** 2024, 2058, 2061–62; **2002:** 992–93, 1015; **2004:** 1014, 1018, 1019, 1020–25; **2005:** 954, 979. *See also* Geneva Conventions on law of war (1949)
Afghanistan and, **2002:** 976–80, 1003–8; **2003:** 1016–27; **2004:** 1039–41; **2005:** 961–62, 994, 995, 1006–8, 1011, 1015, 1024–29; **2006:** 1134
combatant's privilege, lawful combatants only, **2007:** 912, 979–81
Additional Protocol I and, **2007:** 915

Geneva Convention III: on Prisoners of War (1949) (continued)
criminal charges, continued detention to face, **2007:** 113
extradition and, **2007:** 112–13; **2008:** 69–70
FOIA requests for Abu Ghraib photos, **2005:** 1024–25, 1026–29; **2006:** 1216
Gulf War and, **1991-99:** 2066–70, 2072, 2089–94, 2100
Iraq war (2003) and, **2003:** 997–1015; **2004:** 1039–41; **2005:** 979, 1023–29; **2006:** 1133
juvenile death penalty, **1991-99:** 976; **2008:** 303
lawful combatant immunity, **2002:** 1002–8
limited to international armed conflict, **2007:** 912, 920–21
military commissions and, **2002:** 974; **2004:** 981, 1018–25; **2005:** 969; **2006:** 1153–54, 1170
Panama conflict and, **1989-90:** 561–64
POW status for terrorists contrary to provisions on, **2006:** 1117
release and repatriation, **1991-99:** 2094; **2004:** 1005; **2006:** 1184–94; **2007:** 112, 892
supporters of hostile forces, detention of, **2007:** 941–42
Taliban and al Qaeda, applicability to armed conflict with, **2006:** 1113, 1134; **2007:** 913–14
World War II and, **2002:** 438–39
Geneva Convention IV: on Civilians (1949), 1991-99: 517, 976, 1024–25, 2058, 2062, 2067, 2072, 2074–79, 2083–85, 2089; **2001:** 311–12*n*; **2003:** 974–75; **2004:** 1041; **2005:** 953, 957, 959, 979, 994, 1006–7, 1023–29, 1042; **2008:** 430. *See also* Geneva Conventions on law of war (1949)
FOIA requests for Abu Ghraib photos, **2005:** 1024, 1026–29; **2006:** 1216
military commissions and, **2006:** 1154
rules for internments, **2007:** 889–90, 891
security internment of protected persons, **2007:** 888
Geneva Convention on law of war (1929), 2000: 517*n*; **2006:** 1150–51
Geneva Conventions on law of the sea (1958)
on Continental Shelf, **2000:** 699; **2004:** 675; **2005:** 678, 759–60
on High Seas (1958), **1989-90:** 48, 112, 292, 455, 456
on Territorial Sea and the Contiguous Zone, **1989-90:** 292, 466; **1991-99:** 183*n*, 714–31, 1563, 1597, 1599; **2000:** 703; **2002:** 738, 742, 747–50, 753–54; **2003:** 734, 746; **2004:** 687; **2005:** 677, 683, 699, 703–5
UN Convention on the Law of the Sea (1982) and, **1991-99:** 1562–63, 1588; **2004:** 672, 674, 675, 678, 682, 687, 691
U.S. abiding by, **2007:** 199

Geneva Conventions on law of war (1949), 1991-99: 516, 2058, 2061–63, 2071, 2073, 2090, 2097, 2157, 2189; **2004:** 301; **2005:** 378, 950–51. *See also specific Geneva Conventions*
additional protocols to, **2004:** 332; **2006:** 1075
Additional Protocol I (international conflicts, 1977), **1991-99:** 509, 579, 1025, 2059–60, 2062, 2064–66, 2073–74, 2190; **2004:** 331; **2005:** 381, 955; **2006:** 470–71, 1138; **2007:** 876, 884, 888; **2008:** 876, 879
civilian combatant under, **2007:** 915–16
issues in Gulf War, **1991-99:** 2084, 2088, 2095, 2101–2
nuclear weapons and, **1991-99:** 2177–80; **2006:** 1078–84
U.S. objection to, **2007:** 915
wars of national liberation, **1991-99:** 2189–91
Additional Protocol II (non-international conflicts, 1977), **1991-99:** 497, 509, 513–14, 517, 579, 2062–63, 2073, 2197–98, 2202–3; **2006:** 1084; **2007:** 884, 885; **2008:** 303
Additional Protocol III (additional distinctive emblem, 2005), **2005:** 1042–43; **2006:** 1100–1104; **2007:** 983–84
applicability to conflict with al Qaeda and Taliban, **2002:** 976–80; **2003:** 1016–27; **2004:** 990, 1016, 1038–41; **2005:** 215; **2006:** 1112, 1115, 1152–55, 1162, 1175. *See also specific Geneva conventions*
applicability to non-state actors, **2007:** 876, 884–93
common articles:
Article 1, **1991-99:** 2097
Article 2, **1991-99:** 2190; **2005:** 1026–27; **2006:** 1113; **2007:** 883; **2008:** 169
Article 3, **1991-99:** 511, 513–14, 2190; **2002:** 921; **2007:** 883–85, 917–21, 921–25, 972; **2008:** 169
applicable to conflict with Al Qaeda and Taliban, **2006:** 1112, 1115, 1152–55, 1162, 1175
grave breaches of, **2006:** 1171–73, 1176
military commission as regularly constituted court under, **2007:** 981–82
military commissions as violating, **2006:** 1138–55. *See also* Military commissions for trial of certain non-U.S. enemy combatants[9]
revised legislation and procedures to correct violations of, **2006:** 1115, 1163–77

[9] Editor's note: The Military Commissions Act of 2009, Pub. L. 111-84, uses the term "enemy belligerents" rather than "enemy combatants."

Geneva Conventions on law of war (1949) (continued)
U.S. interpretation of, **2007:** 917–21
Executive Order on implementation of by CIA, **2007:** 921–25
War Crimes Act amendment, **2007:** 884, 919
Crimes Against the Peace and Security of Mankind, Draft Code of and, **1991-99:** 579
differences from ICCPR and Optional Protocol, **2008:** 263
duration of detention, **2008:** 309
enforcement of obligations by U.S., **2007:** 216
grave breaches and other violations of, **1989-90:** 563; **1991-99:** 1106, 2068, 2074–75, 2093, 2094, 2097, 2098, 2101; **2003:** 350–51, 998, 1000–1001, 1004, 1010; **2006:** 1171–73, 1176; **2008:** 377, 430
Gulf War and, **1991-99:** 2057–2108. *See also specific Geneva conventions*
International Committee of the Red Cross and other relief organizations and, **1991-99:** 2061–62, 2066, 2078, 2090, 2177–78; **2002:** 1016
International Criminal Tribunal for former Yugoslavia and, **1991-99:** 514
Iraq war (2003) and, **2003:** 997–1015; **2004:** 1038–41, 1045; **2005:** 977–79, 995, 1023–29, 1037; **2006:** 1133. *See also specific Geneva conventions*
judicial enforceability of in U.S., **2006:** 1150–51, 1162, 1170
outside competence of IACHR, **2004:** 978, 994
prosecution of juveniles for violation of laws of armed conflict, **2008:** 303
self-executing, whether, **1989-90:** 563; **2002:** 992–94, 1004; **2004:** 1024–25
traditional armed conflicts and, **2007:** 883
treatment of detainees and, **2004:** 301, 978, 980, 981, 990, 994, 1004, 1005, 1014, 1016, 1018, 1019, 1020–25, 1038, 1039, 1040–41, 1043, 1044, 1045; **2006:** 1216–18; **2007:** 888–90, 921–25; **2008:** 377
treaty obligations of successor states, **1991-99:** 746
unlawful combatant status implicit in, **2006:** 1132
war crimes legislation, implementing in U.S., **1991-99:** 509–15; **2006:** 1171–73, 1176
Genocide. *See also* Crimes against humanity
Alien Tort Statute, claims under, **2001:** 319, 322, 323–25; **2005:** 395–97, 412–13, 493
Bosnia, **1991-99:** 528, 980–81; **2008:** 139
Cambodia, **1991-99:** 608
charges against Milosevic, **2001:** 167–68, 171, 172

Genocide (continued)
claims
against China, **2004**: 528
against Democratic Republic of the Congo, **1991-99**: 2012, 2013
against Georgia, **2008**: 865
against Papua New Guinea, **2006**: 442–43
against South Africa, **2004**: 355, 356, 359
against Sudan, **2006**: 460–63
against United States, **2004**: 364
Convention on Prevention and Punishment of, **1989-90**: 119–28, 143–50, 184, 355–56, 360–61; **1991-99**: 516, 529, 587, 597*n*, 735, 2071, 2076, 2152; **2001**: 118, 306; **2004**: 129–33, 179, 239, 240, 241, 359, 971
advisory opinion on reservations to (ICJ), **1989-90**: 355–56, 360–61
definition of genocide, **1989-90**: 119–20
ICJ jurisdiction under, **1989-90**: 121–23, 144; **1991-99**: 2152–54; **2006**: 1023
U.S. reservations, **1989-90**: 143–50, 184
criminal tribunals to hear crimes of. *See* Criminal tribunals, international, hybrid, and other
Darfur, **2008**: 844
Canadian policy, **2005**: 824–25
U.S. conclusion re occurrence in, **2004**: 239–43; **2005**: 194, 197; **2006**: 422–23, 1048
definition, **1991-99**: 529, 2076; **2004**: 241, 351*n*
rape as, **1991-99**: 584, 852; **2000**: 242, 252–55
deportation and, **1991-99**: 953
Genocide Accountability Act (2007), **2007**: 377–78
Holocaust and. *See* Holocaust
ICC and, **1991-99**: 611, 615, 616, 621, 623, 631, 639; **2004**: 178, 180, 186; **2006**: 258, 277
ICTY and, **1991-99**: 580–81, 587, 595; **2008**: 141, 147
Iraq, **1991-99**: 532, 534, 538*n*, 2076, 2099, 2119; **2006**: 269
as *jus cogens* violation, **1991-99**: 976–77, 1115
Khmer Rouge
determination as to actions of, **1989-90**: 119–28
possible prosecution of members of, **1989-90**: 121–28. *See also* Criminal tribunals, international, hybrid, and other
prosecution in U.S. for acts committed by foreign nationals in foreign countries, **1989-90**: 125–26
responsibility to protect populations from, **2005**: 375–76, 458–59
Rwanda, **1991-99**: 529–32, 2012; **2004**: 128–29, 131–32; **2007**: 862
ICTR and, **1991-99**: 581, 598, 604, 858; **2008**: 141, 147–49
UNCHR Resolutions on, **2001**: 118–19; **2005**: 199–200, 376–77

Genocide (continued)
universal jurisdiction over, **1991-99:** 503, 637
U.S. policies to hold perpetrators answerable for, **2005:** 12–13, 189, 192, 194, 197, 825; **2007:** 181, 184, 185, 197, 390
World Summit Outcome Document, **2008:** 857
World War II, **1991-99:** 1793–94
Gentlemen's agreement, 1991-99: 683, 684
Geographic Names, U.S. Board on, 2008: 644–45
Georgia
Air Transport Agreement (2007), **2007:** 531
arms control and security, **1991-99:** 2242
beluga sturgeon, management plan for, **2005:** 754–55
conflict with Russia, **2008:** 863–70
diplomatic relations, **1991-99:** 1174
domestic violence laws, lack of, **2005:** 313
immunity of diplomat in civil case, **1991-99:** 1292–95
Millennium Challenge Corporation (MCC), threshold agreement with, **2005:** 672
Open Skies (aerial observation) treaty, **1991-99:** 2239; **2002:** 1029
peace process in, **2003:** 952–53
preservation of American heritage in, **2008:** 736
religious freedom violation, **2003:** 296; **2004:** 270
Russian military presence, **1991-99:** 2236–37, 2238
successor state issues, **1991-99:** 742
Torture, National Action Plan Against, **2005:** 374–75
trade and investment issues, **1991-99:** 1455, 1466
UN Observer Mission in Georgia (UNOMIG), **2008:** 844–45
UN Security Council action on, **2008:** 844–45, 866–70
women, urged by U.S. to improve treatment of, **2005:** 313
Geostationary orbit (GSO), legal issues related to, 2005: 713–15. *See also* Space
Germany
aircraft subsidies and, **2004:** 603; **2005:** 622
Antarctica, claims to, **2004:** 732
consular notification, claims against U.S. for failure of, **1991-99:** 258, 320; **2000:** 33*n*, 41, 43–93; **2001:** 21–24, 26; **2003:** 41, 77, 78–79, 100–102; **2005:** 270; **2006:** 70–72. *See also* Consular notification and access
Democratic Republic of, **1991-99:** 31
lifting of sanctions against, **1989-90:** 521
OPIC agreement with, **1991-99:** 1484
property claims against, **1989-90:** 238–40
relief from immigration requirements for certain resident nationals of, **1991-99:** 250

Germany (continued)
reunification, **1991-99**: 761–64
settlement of expropriation claims against, **1991-99**: 1074–75
Soviet missiles in, **1989-90**: 572
U.S. treaty on World War II final settlement, **1989-90**: 138–42, 274, 395
World War II era compensation and restitution program, **1991-99**: 1047
discovery in, for use in U.S. court, **2003**: 876–80; **2004**: 857–63, 872
drug trade (methamphetamines), **2007**: 164–66
extradition and mutual legal assistance, **1991-99**: 394; **2000**: 178, 186*n*; **2004**: 93–95, 1089; **2005**: 69, 72, 77–78; **2006**: 121–22, 137, 146, 148
Federal Republic of
Convention on Relations between the Three Powers and the Federal Republic of Germany, **1989-90**: 140
international child abduction cases, **1991-99**: 350–53, 354, 357–60, 363–65, 367–70
Missile Technology Control Regime, **1991-99**: 2222, 2356–59
reunification, **1991-99**: 761–64
World War II era claims
compensation and restitution programs, **1991-99**: 1046–53
against corporation as state actor, **1991-99**: 989–90
forced and slave labor claims, **1991-99**: 989–90, 992–93, 1048–49, 1070–71, 1133, 1260–63
insurance claims, **1991-99**: 1049–50, 1066–67, 1069–70, 1071
jus cogens violation as claimed waiver of immunity, **1991-99**: 1191–93
Nazi persecution claims, **1991-99**: 1053–56, 1061–62
restitution of looted gold, **1991-99**: 1043–46, 1056–61
retroactive application of FSIA to, **1991-99**: 1260–63
stolen art, **1991-99**: 1050–51, 1062–66, 1067–69
hoasca abuse, arrests for, **2005**: 144
Holocaust-era archives agreement, **2007**: 380–82
human rights in, **2004**: 235
immunity of foreign official for official acts, **2006**: 641
interpretation of U.S. reservations to Genocide Convention, **1989-90**: 144–45
jurisdictional issues under post World War II occupation, **2005**: 298
Kosovo peace process, role in, **2005**: 935
missile defense and nonproliferation. *See* Nonproliferation, *subheading*: country-specific issues
money laundering, **2004**: 135
nonimmigrant visa waiver pilot program, **1989-90**: 27
occupied territories of, **2007**: 273

Germany (continued)
as occupied territory, **2006**: 348, 1150, 1178, 1208
Open Skies (aerial observation) treaty, **2002**: 1029
parental child abduction
habitual residence on U.S. military base in, **2004**: 62–65
Hague Child Abduction Convention, compliance with, **2003**: 127, 129; **2008**: 50
International Parental Kidnapping Crime Act (1993), **2002**: 56–58
prisoners and U.S. Constitution, **2005**: 998
service by mail in, **2005**: 851
sunken government property, **2004**: 716, 717–18, 722
transition agreement for Berlin air service, **1989-90**: 395–96
Treaty on the Final Settlement with Respect to Germany, **1989-90**: 138–42, 274, 395
trials by military commissions after World War II, **2005**: 969
Underwater Cultural Heritage, Convention on Protection of, position on, **2005**: 766
U.S. anti-subsidy law involving steel products, **2002**: 670–72
warnings of hazardous navigation by vessels registered in, **1989-90**: 459
World War II-era claims against, **2000**: 445–85; **2001**: 386–93, 415–16; **2004**: 431–41. *See also* Federal Republic of, *this heading*
California Holocaust Victim Insurance Relief Act, **2000**: 460–73; **2008**: 419, 422, 424
Foundation "Remembrance, Responsibility, and Future" funds, **2005**: 490–91, 821; **2006**: 507–17; **2007**: 421–27; **2008**: 428
FSIA jurisdiction, **2004**: 472–75
Holocaust victims' compensation agreement, insurance, **2002**: 417, 418, 427, 428, 431–34; **2008**: 419, 422, 424
role in Hungarian Gold Train, **2004**: 446, 448
settlement from fund precluding litigation, **2006**: 517–21
sovereign immunity issues, **2000**: 473–85
Ghana
American Servicemembers' Protection Act waiver and, **2003**: 238
extradition and mutual legal assistance, **2000**: 185*n*
female genital mutilation, consideration in asylum cases, **1991-99**: 211–14
new passport for U.S. citizen escaped from custody in, **2002**: 17–19
sovereign immunity and, **1991-99**: 1198–99
Ghent, Treaty of (1814)
duty exemption for cigarettes from Canada and application to U.S. states' tobacco settlement, **2008**: 170–74
claims alleging violation of, NAFTA Chapter 11 dispute, **2008**: 170–74
Global Anti-Semitism Review Act (2004), **2004**: 276–77

Global Child Survival Partnership, 2004: 280
Global Partnership Initiative Against Spread of Weapons and Materials of Mass Destruction, 2005: 1095; **2008:** 1000
Global warming. *See* Climate change
Globalization, 2004: 290–91. *See also* Trade
Gold Reserve Act (1934), 1991-99: 1495–96, 1498
Gold Train Property (Hungary), 2005: 485–89
Good Friday Agreement (1998), 2006: 122–27
Government in the Sunshine Act (1976), 2002: 234
Great Britain. *See* United Kingdom
Great Lakes
  Charter Annex of, **2001:** 198–200
  Great Lakes–St. Lawrence River Basin Sustainable Water Resources Agreement and Compact, **2005:** 206–7
  Marine Navigation Services Fee levied by Canada, **2005:** 688
  Persistent toxic substances in, U.S.-Canada agreement on, **1991-99:** 1669–71
Greece
  citizenship determinations, **1989-90:** 1–2
  copyright protection, **2008:** 607–8
  extradition and mutual legal assistance, **2000:** 166, 185*n*, 186*n*; **2006:** 137, 146
  Hague Child Abduction Convention, compliance with, **2006:** 102; **2008:** 50
  intellectual property rights Watch List, **2008:** 607–8
  international child abduction issues, **2000:** 93–105; **2001:** 40–47; **2004:** 54
  money laundering in, **2004:** 135
  objections to U.S. reservations to Genocide Convention, **1989-90:** 144
  Open Skies (aerial observation) treaty, **2002:** 1029
  territorial application of International Covenant on Civil and Political Rights, position on, **2005:** 299*n*
  trade issues, **1991-99:** 1407–8, 1506
Grenada
  extradition and mutual legal assistance, **1991-99:** 396, 453; **2000:** 186*n*; **2001:** 92*n*
  longshore work prohibition on alien crewmen from, **2002:** 757; **2003:** 764
  maritime drug interdiction agreements, **1991-99:** 1606
Guam
  political status, **1991-99:** 178, 808–11, 1570
  sovereignty of U.S. and, **2003:** 485
  submerged lands adjacent to, **2002:** 250
Guano Island Act (1856), 1991-99: 842–46

Guantanamo detainees. *See* Detainees, military
Guarantees
assurances and guarantees of nonrepetition. *See* Remedies
Direct Guarantees and Standby Letters of Credit, Convention on (UN), **1991-99**: 1812–14
Limitations, Sales of Goods, Negotiable Instruments, and Guarantees, Conventions on, **2002**: 836
medallion stamp guarantees, **2001**: 59
Guatemala
consular notification, claim against U.S. for failure of, **1991-99**: 258–59
Cooperating Nation Information Exchange System (CNIES), agreement with U.S. concerning, **2005**: 146
cultural property protection agreement, **2002**: 813
drug trade, **2001**: 120; **2002**: 124; **2003**: 181, 183; **2004**: 133–34; **2005**: 135; **2006**: 213; **2007**: 163; **2008**: 113
environmental issues
Environmental Cooperation Agreement with U.S., **2005**: 756–57
forest conservation agreement, **2006**: 886–88, **2008**: 722
European Union–U.S. banana trade dispute, **2001**: 649–50
extradition and mutual legal assistance, **1991-99**: 391; **2000**: 185*n*; **2002**: 68
free trade agreement, **2004**: 617–19
immigration issues
asylum request by national of, **1991-99**: 194–97, 232–39
relief from immigration requirements for certain resident nationals of, **1991-99**: 250
sanctuary movement to protect asylum seekers from, **1989-90**: 40–42
intellectual property rights Watch List, **2006**: 768; **2007**: 610
Inter-American Convention Against Corruption, party to, **2006**: 238
money laundering, **2006**: 243
stolen vehicle treaty, **2000**: 169–70
trade negotiations with U.S., **2003**: 683–86
Tropical Forest Conservation Act agreement, **2006**: 886–88; **2008**: 722
truth commission in, **1991-99**: 962
Guatemala City Protocol (1971), **2000**: 671
Guernsey
money laundering, **2004**: 135
Guinea
U.S. assistance tied to agreement not to enforce Rome Statute against U.S personnel, **2004**: 187
Guinea-Bissau
maritime counterterrorism measures, conditions for failure to take, **2008**: 112
temporary protected status for nationals of, **1991-99**: 246

Gulf War. *See also* Hague Conventions, *subheading*: on law of war; Law of war; *specific Geneva conventions*
applicability of law of war
collateral damage, **1991-99**: 2079–89
conduct of neutral nations, **1991-99**: 2102–7
customary international law applicable to, **1991-99**: 2072–73
Department of Defense report to Congress on, **1991-99**: 2070–2108
environmental damage, **1991-99**: 2101–2
ICRC memorandum on, **1991-99**: 2057–66
Iraqi war crimes, **1991-99**: 2096–2102
surrendering forces, **1991-99**: 2108
taking of hostages in, **1991-99**: 2074–75
targeting, collateral damage and civilian casualties, **1991-99**: 2081–84, 2085–87, 2088–89
treaties applicable to, **1991-99**: 2071–74
treatment of civilians in occupied territory, **1991-99**: 2075–79
treatment of prisoners of war, **1991-99**: 2066–70, 2089–94, 2100
repatriation of, **1991-99**: 2094
U.S. intervention, **1991-99**: 2056–57
United Nations, **1991-99**: 2052–53
U.S. authorization for, **1991-99**: 2053–57
cease-fire, **1991-99**: 2108–11
disarming of Iraq, **1991-99**: 2110–11
events following end of war, **1991-99**: 2112–24
enforcement of no-fly zones, **1991-99**: 2116–17, 2123
response to attempted assassination of President George H. W. Bush, **1991-99**: 2124–25
response to failure to comply with weapons inspections, **1991-99**: 2125–32
law of the sea and, **1991-99**: 1567
sanctions on Iraq, **1991-99**: 1924–31, 2051
Guns and firearms
Firearms, Ammunition, Explosives, and Other Related Materials, Inter-American Convention Against Illicit Manufacturing of and Trafficking in, **1991-99**: 554–58, 2262–63
Gun Control Act (1968), **1991-99**: 558, 2258
National Firearms Act, **1991-99**: 558
nonimmigrant visas, possession of firearms and, **2004**: 53
Second Amendment rights, U.S. Constitution, **2005**: 290
use of force and firearms in law enforcement and human rights, **2004**: 339
Guyana
Article 98 agreement (nonsurrender of Americans to ICC), **2004**: 187
contractual waiver of FSIA immunity claim, **2003**: 523–24

Guyana (continued)
extradition and mutual legal assistance, **2000:** 185*n*
government efforts regarding trafficking in persons, **2004:** 164
money laundering, **2006:** 243
sanctions on, **2003:** 929–30; **2005:** 889
suspension of entry for certain persons from, **2002:** 22–24
visa sanctions for nonacceptance of return of nationals, **2001:** 18–20

H

Habeas corpus
actions before U.S. courts, **2004:** 995–1015, 1017–29, 1030–31
All Writs Act (1911), **2004:** 1030, 1031
common law, **2007:** 889, 940, 955–56; **2008:** 893, 894
criminal convictions, **2005:** 283
enemy combatant detainees.[10] *See* Detainees, military
extradition cases. *See* Extradition
failure to inform foreign national of right to consular notification. *See* Consular notification and access
forcible abduction of alien defendant from Pakistan, **2002:** 77–78
immigration removal cases. *See* Immigration and visas; Removal of aliens from U.S.
jurisdiction over U.S. citizen held in Saudi Arabia, **2004:** 203–6
jurisdiction over U.S. citizen held at Guantanamo Bay, **2002:** 989–90, 996–97; **2003:** 1027–28; **2004:** 978, 979–82, 983, 984, 994, 995–1001, 1017–29; **2005:** 948, 994, 996–97, 1009–16. *See also* Detainees, military
Multinational Force-Iraq detainees, **2006:** 1206
Hague Abduction Convention. *See* Children
Hague Conference on Private International Law (HCCH), 1991-99: 1826–33, 1862–63, 1871; **2000:** 736–41; **2001:** 776, 780, 789; **2002:** 817–18, 826, 829; **2003:** 110, 834, 841–42, 856, 859–60, 865; **2005:** 210–14, 787; **2006:** 105–6. *See also* Hague Conventions
Hague Conventions
Aircraft, Hague Convention for the Unlawful Seizure of (1970), **1989-90:** 34. *See also* Aviation issues
Hague Code of Conduct against proliferation of ballistic missiles, **2005:** 1094

---

[10] Editor's note: On March 13, 2009, in conjunction with a filing in Guantanamo habeas litigation, the U.S. Justice Department declared that it would cease to employ the term "enemy combatant" for detainees in custody of the Defense Department at the Guantanamo Bay Detention Facility.

Hague Conventions (continued)
Hague Conference on Private International Law, conventions adopted by, **1991-99**: 381, 1858, 1862, 1863, 1871. *See also* Children; Evidence
abduction of children. *See* Children, *subheading*: international abduction
adoption. *See* Adoption
judicial assistance, generally, **2003**: 859–63
jurisdiction and recognition of judgments (2005), **1991-99**: 1826; **2000**: 736, 737–40, 741; **2001**: 786, 789; **2004**: 829
legalization. *See* Authentication
maintenance obligations. *See* Maintenance obligations
protection of adults (2000), **1991-99**: 1861–62; **2004**: 830
service of process abroad. *See* Service of process abroad
wills, **1991-99**: 1878
Hague-Visby Rules (International Convention for the Unification of Certain Rules of Law Relating to Bills of Lading), **2005**: 794–95, 798
Industrial Designs, Hague Agreement Concerning the International Deposit of, **2000**: 300; **2006**: 786–90
International Recovery of Child Support and Other Forms of Family Maintenance, Convention for. *See* Maintenance obligations
on law of war. *See also* Law of war
Hague Convention for the Protection of Cultural Property in the Event of Armed Conflict (1954), **1991-99**: 2072, 2075–76, 2079–80, 2086, 2096, 2197–2207; **2007**: 896; **2008**: 888–89
Hague Convention of 1899
Declaration on Expanding Bullets (III), **1991-99**: 2060, 2189
Laws and Customs of War on Land (II), **1991-99**: 511, 514, 1126–28, 2059–60, 2067, 2071–72, 2075–76, 2078–80, 2095–97, 2099, 2101, 2108, 2189; **2005**: 495, 954
Hague Convention of 1907
Bombardment by Naval forces in Time of War (IX), **1991-99**: 2071–72
Laws and Customs of War on Land (IV) (Hague Regulations), **2002**: 1005–6; **2003**: 997–98; **2005**: 495, 951, 954, 957–58; **2008**: 428, 430
Laying of Automatic Submarine Contact Mines (VIII), **1991-99**: 2071–72
Rights and Duties of Neutral Powers and Persons (V), **1991-99**: 2071–72, 2102, 2105

Hague Conventions (continued)
violations in Gulf War, **1991-99:** 2071, 2075–76, 2079, 2080, 2095, 2096–97, 2099, 2101
Hague Regulations of 1899 and 1907, **2007:** 912, 980
Securities Intermediaries, Hague Conference Convention on, **2004:** 801, 829; **2006:** 936–38
Hague Protocol. *See* Aviation issues
Hague Regulations. *See* Hague Conventions, *subheading*: on law of war
Haiti
arms embargo, **2004:** 1070
assertion of contiguous zone authority, **1989-90:** 467
conflict resolution efforts, **2003:** 938, 942–43; **2004:** 937–42
coup, **1991-99:** 1021, 1152–53, 1882–83, 2045–46
diplomatic relations, **1991-99:** 1152–53
drug trade, **2001:** 120; **2002:** 123, 124; **2003:** 181, 182; **2004:** 133–34; **2005:** 135; **2006:** 213, 215; **2007:** 163; **2008:** 113
maritime counter-drug trade agreement, **1991-99:** 1606
extradition and mutual legal assistance, **2000:** 185*n*
Haitian Hemispheric Opportunity through Partnership Encouragement Act (2008), **2008:** 582
head-of-state immunity, **1991-99:** 1266–81
human rights in, **2004:** 398–401, 938
immigration issues
denial of U.S. visa to individuals involved in certain killings in, **1991-99:** 110–12
deportation of paramilitary leader from U.S., **1991-99:** 118–21
deterring illegal migration from, **2003:** 24–25
high-seas interdiction of migrants from, **1991-99:** 150–72, 176–77, 187–94
indefinite detention of criminal deportees and substandard prison conditions not constituting torture, **2005:** 350
national of, in U.S., accused of torture, **2000:** 383
refugees, **1989-90:** 47–54; **2002:** 25–31
relief from immigration requirements for certain resident nationals of, **1991-99:** 250–51
rights of migrants from, in safe haven in Guantanamo, **1991-99:** 188–94
suspension of entry of certain aliens of, **1991-99:** 137–40
U.S. migration policy, **2004:** 34–35
visa denials to certain persons from, **2003:** 23–24
money laundering in, **2004:** 135
multinational humanitarian and peacekeeping mission, **1991-99:** 856, 2045–47; **2008:** 838
President's authority to commit troops to, **1991-99:** 804, 2162–68

Haiti (continued)
naturalization treaty, **2002**: 203
Organization of American States stabilization efforts, **2002**: 926–31
orphan adoption program, **2003**: 123
prohibitions on passage through territorial waters, **1989-90**: 445–46, 465
regime change, **1991-99**: 857–58
sanctions on, **1991-99**: 1882–98
UN peacekeeping mission, **2004**: 188; **2008**: 838
UN personal conduct unit in, **2005**: 946
Haitian Refugee Immigration Fairness Act (1998), **1991-99**: 250–51
Hamas
abduction of Israeli soldier, **2006**: 1233–35
Holy Land Foundation of Relief and Development providing material support to, **2008**: 98–99
Palestinian Authority government, **2006**: 990–95; **2008**: 824
terrorism and, **2006**: 337, 990–95, 1227; **2008**: 97–98, 410, 822
Hariri, Rafik. *See* Lebanon
Hawaii
Northwestern Hawaiian Islands Marine National Monument, **2006**: 872–75
Papahanaumokuakea Marine National Monument, **2008**: 702–3
tax exemptions for diplomatic and consular personnel and missions in, **2000**: 594–99; **2001**: 539–40
Hazardous Chemicals in International Trade, Convention on the Prior Informed Consent Procedure for Certain, **1991-99**: 1683–87
Hazardous waste. *See* Basel Convention on the Control of Transboundary Movements of Hazardous Wastes and their Disposal; Environmental issues
Head of state. *See also* Head-of-state immunity
citizenship of child of, born in U.S., **2004**: 4–5
crime against, as political offense exception to extradition, **2004**: 75–76
Head-of-state immunity
banking fraud claims, **1991-99**: 1285–89
comity and, **1991-99**: 1268, 1284
considerations in deposition, **2005**: 563–66
common law, **1991-99**: 1267–73
to criminal jurisdiction, **2007**: 449–50, 516
customary international law, **2005**: 561–62; **2006**: 678; **2007**: 522–24
discovery process, limitations on, **1989-90**: 320–23
in divorce action, **1989-90**: 314–19
exception for private acts considered, **2001**: 521–22; **2003**: 566

Head-of-state immunity (continued)
Executive branch authority to determine, **1989-90**: 316–19; **1991-99**: 1268–69, 1282, 1284–85; **2001**: 511–26; **2002**: 547–52; **2003**: 570–72; **2004**: 527–31, 547, 548–53; **2005**: 560–67; **2007**: 447, 524–25
determination in absence of Executive branch support for, **1991-99**: 1282–85; **2003**: 569–70
extradition of Pinochet, **1991-99**: 518–19
extrajudicial killing, Haiti, **1991-99**: 1266–81
Falun Gong suit against Chinese president, **2002**: 547–52
former heads of state, **1989-90**: 319; **1991-99**: 1270–71; **2003**: 563; **2007**: 526–27
FSIA not applicable, **1991-99**: 1273–77, 1287–88; **2001**: 516–21; **2004**: 529–30; **2005**: 561–62; **2007**: 523–24
for human rights violations, **2001**: 320–23
for *jus cogens* violations, **2003**: 563–64
of Pope, **1991-99**: 1290–91
service of process, immunity/inviolability, **2002**: 550–52; **2003**: 558; **2004**: 547–53; **2005**: 563, 565–67
where directed at third party entity, **2001**: 531–36; **2002**: 324–25; **2003**: 564–66; **2004**: 553–58
suit by Libya against UK prime minister, **1989-90**: 311–14
Torture Victim Protection Act and, **1991-99**: 1277–81; **2001**: 522–23
waiver of by state, **1991-99**: 1270–71
Head-of-state inviolability. *See* Inviolability
Headquarters Agreement, U.S.–UN. *See* United Nations
Health issues. *See also* Public health; *specific diseases*
children and Health Act of 2001, **2005**: 276
cloning, human, prohibition of (UN General Assembly Resolution 59/280), U.S. approval, **2005**: 771–72
Declaration on Bioethics and Human Rights, **2005**: 784–85
of detainees. *See* Detainees, military
disabilities. *See* Disabilities, persons with
health standards, physical and mental, U.S. vote against UN Commission on Human Rights (UNCHR) Resolution 2004/24 concerning, **2005**: 332–33
International Health Regulations, **2005**: 768–71; **2006**: 891–92; **2007**: 738; **2008**: 1007
medical experimentation on humans, nonconsensual, **2005**: 276–77
nutrition. *See* Food
pandemic influenza preparedness, **2007**: 736–38
patents for pharmaceuticals. *See* Patent law
reproductive rights, **2002**: 308–9; **2003**: 321–22

Health issues (continued)
U.S. comments regarding 2005 World Summit Outcome Document, **2005**: 454
U.S. comments regarding 2008 Fact Sheet No. 31 on Right to Health, produced by OHCHR and WHO, **2008**: 324
U.S. comments regarding UN disabilities convention (draft), **2005**: 321
U.S. comments to UN Commission on Status of Women (CSW), **2005**: 308–9
TRIPS Agreement. *See* Trade Related Aspects of Intellectual Property Rights (TRIPS Agreement), *subheading*: public health and
U.S. comments regarding 2008 Fact Sheet No. 31 on Right to Health, produced by OHCHR and WHO, **2008**: 320–26
World Health Assembly, **2005**: 768
World Health Organization. *See* World Health Organization (WHO)
Helms Amendment on Expropriation, 2003: 480–82. *See also* Expropriation
Helms-Burton Act. *See* Cuban Liberty and Democratic Solidarity (LIBERTAD) Act (1996)
Helsinki Accords, 2001: 142
Helsinki Conference Final Acts (1975), **1989-90**: 271, 273–74, 397
Helsinki Declaration, 2002: 345–46
Herzegovina. *See* Bosnia and Herzegovina
High Seas Convention (1958), **1989-90**: 48, 292, 455; **1991-99**: 716, 1563; **2003**: 735; **2004**: 1088
Highly enriched uranium. *See* Nonproliferation, *subheading*: highly enriched uranium, disposition of
Hijacking. *See* Hostage-taking and hijacking
Himalaya Clause, 2006: 921, 923
Historical heritage. *See also* Cultural issues
International Council on Monuments and Sites (ICOMOS Charter), **2005**: 764, 765
Native Hawaiian culture and history, Northwestern Hawaiian Islands Marine National Monument, **2006**: 872–75
Underwater Cultural Heritage, Convention on the Protection of. *See* Underwater cultural heritage
HIV. *See* AIDS/HIV
Hmong
U.S. entry restriction exemptions and, **2007**: 70–72; **2008**: 29–30
Hoasca. *See* Drug issues
Holocaust
agreement with Italy on preservation of American heritage, **2008**: 736–37
archives agreement, **2007**: 380–82
claims

Holocaust (continued)
American Council for Equal Compensation of Nazi Victims from Austria, **2005**: 470
Foundation Remembrance, Responsibility and the Future Agreement between U.S. and Federal Republic of Germany, **2005**: 490, 821; **2006**: 507–21
General Settlement Fund (GSF) Agreement (Austria), **2005**: 473, 474, 486, 489–90
International Commission on Holocaust Era Insurance Claims (ICHEIC), **2005**: 490–91; **2008**: 418–24
Nazi era property confiscation. *See* World War II
Presidential Advisory Commission on Holocaust Assets in U.S., **2005**: 486
Vatican Bank, **2005**: 481–84
denial of
UN General Assembly resolution condemning, **2007**: 378–80
U.S. law on, **2007**: 326
Holocaust Assets Commission Act (1998), **2000**: 468
Holocaust Victim Insurance Claim Registry and Relief Act (New Jersey 2001), **2001**: 413–17
Holocaust Victims Insurance Relief Act (California 1999), **2000**: 460–73; **2002**: 415–34; **2003**: 462–68; **2008**: 419, 422, 424
International Commission on Holocaust Era Insurance Claims, **2000**: 449; **2001**: 415, 416–17; **2002**: 417–19, 430–34; **2003**: 463, 465, 467; **2008**: 418–24
Remembrance Resolution, UN (A/RES/60/66), **2005**: 318–19
Task Force for International Cooperation on Holocaust Education, Remembrance and Research, **2005**: 319
Holy See. *See* Vatican
Homeland Security, Department of (DHS), **2008**: 6–8, 17–20, 20–25, 33–34, 80–83, 103–12, 280–81, 366, 372–73, 512–13, 730–32
airline passenger name record data for flights between U.S. and EU, **2006**: 168–72
Appropriations Act of 2007, **2006**: 9
cultural property import restrictions, **2003**: 821–25; **2005**: 775; **2006**: 899–901; **2008**: 730–32. *See also* Trade, *subheading*: cultural property, restrictions on
detention standard, **2005**: 363. *See also* Detention of aliens, nonmilitary
due to serious adverse foreign policy consequences, **2005**: 11–12
Maritime Transportation Security Act of 2002, **2005**: 693
National Strategy for Homeland Security, **2005**: 689*n*

Homeland Security, Department of (DHS) (continued)
Office for Civil Rights and Civil Liberties, **2005**: 260
removal of aliens. *See* Removal of aliens from U.S.
Soviet Scientists Immigration Act of 1992 (SSIA) amendments, implementation of, **2005**: 9
trafficking victims, processing of, **2005**: 271–72
verification of travel documents, **2006**: 208–10
Western Hemisphere Travel Initiative, **2005**: 1–5; **2008**: 6–8
Homeland Security Act (2002), **2003**: 34
Homicide
felony murder doctrine, restriction of use in Canada, **2005**: 386
police to videotape or audiotape questioning of suspects in homicide cases, **2005**: 360
torture acts prosecuted as, **2005**: 345
Honduras
American Servicemembers' Protection Act waiver and, **2003**: 238
Cooperating Nation Information Exchange System (CNIES), agreement with U.S. concerning, **2005**: 146
cultural property, **2004**: 791–92
Environmental Cooperation Agreement with U.S., **2005**: 756–57
European Union–U.S. banana trade dispute, **2001**: 649–50
extradition and mutual legal assistance, **2000**: 185*n*; **2002**: 68
free trade agreement, **2004**: 617–19
Hague Child Abduction Convention, compliance with, **2003**: 127, 129; **2004**: 54; **2006**: 101; **2008**: 50
Inter-American Convention Against Corruption, party to, **2006**: 238
law enforcement cooperation relationship, **2002**: 67, 68
maritime boundaries and rights of navigation, **2004**: 705–10
naturalization convention, **2002**: 203
orphan adoption program, **2003**: 123
settlement of expropriation claims against, **1989-90**: 219–20
shrimp import restrictions, **2003**: 791–92
sovereign immunity and, **1991-99**: 1216–18
stolen vehicle treaty, **2002**: 61, 62, 64–65
temporary protected status, **2003**: 36; **2004**: 33
threshold agreement with Millennium Challenge Corporation (MCC), **2005**: 672
trade and investment agreements, **1991-99**: 1466
trade negotiations with U.S., **2003**: 683–86
Hong Kong
alienage diversity jurisdiction, **1991-99**: 769–75, 1251; **2001**: 228–29, 232, 233
extradition and mutual legal assistance, **1991-99**: 403–9, 412–13, 453, 689–93; **2000**: 179, 186*n*
status of Hong Kong as sub-sovereign government, **2000**: 190–203

Hong Kong (continued)
foreign affairs, conduct of, **1991-99**: 404, 405, 689, 690, 1177
Hong Kong Economic and Trade Offices, **1991-99**: 1314
Hong Kong Policy Act (1992), **1991-99**: 764–67, 773, 1178, 1179; **2000**: 191, 197–98; **2002**: 384–85
human rights in, **1991-99**: 868–70; **2002**: 278, 282, 384–85; **2004**: 260–61, 270, 272, 363–64, 395, 405, 528
International Covenant on Civil and Political Rights applicable to, **1991-99**: 405
money laundering in, **2004**: 135
prisoner transfer agreement with U.S., **1991-99**: 382–83, 413, 693
status of U.S. Consulate General, **1991-99**: 1176
transfer of sovereignty to China, **1991-99**: 382, 405, 413, 764, 773–75
Basic Law, PRC (1990), **1991-99**: 405, 693, 1176, 1177
challenge to extradition and, **1991-99**: 411–17
continuation in force of treaties, **1991-99**: 764–67, 1175
United Kingdom-People's Republic of China Joint Declaration on the Question of Hong Kong, **1991-99**: 405, 408, 690, 691, 693, 765, 1175, 1176, 1177–78, 1180
U.S. policy, **1991-99**: 1179–80
treaties and. *See* Treaties, generally
U.S. consular office in, **1991-99**: 1176, 1180–81
visa processing and, **1991-99**: 113–14
Horn of Africa Recovery and Food Security Act (1992), **1991-99**: 937–38, 2044
Hostage-taking and hijacking
Anti-Hijacking Act (1994), U.S. jurisdiction under (1984), **1991-99**: 501–8
Antiterrorism and Effective Death Penalty Act of 1996 (AEDPA), **2005**: 506
aviation hijacking, prosecutions for, **1991-99**: 501–8
Gulf war, taking of hostages in, **1991-99**: 2074–75
Hostage-Taking Act (1984), jurisdiction under, **1991-99**: 501–8
International Convention Against Hostage-taking, **1989-90**: 34; **1991-99**: 501, 503; **2000**: 218; **2001**: 357, 914; **2006**: 585–87; **2007**: 132
Iran and
claims against Iran arising from hostage taking, **2001**: 459–75; **2002**: 523–27; **2003**: 547–49
suit by former Iran Embassy hostages barred by Algiers Accords, **2003**: 547–49
private right of action against Iraq for U.S. hostages held under Hussein, **2006**: 584–92

Hostage-taking and hijacking (continued)
U visas for victims of, **2005**: 271
UN Commission on Human Rights Resolution 2005/31 concerning, **2005**: 184–85
Howard Island
sovereignty of U.S. and, **2003**: 485
Howland Island
U.S. claim to exclusive economic zone surrounding, **2007**: 643–46; **2008**: 642–44
Human cloning
prohibition of (UN General Assembly Resolution 59/280), U.S. approval, **2005**: 771–72
Reproductive Cloning of Human Beings, International Convention Against, **2002**: 807–9; **2003**: 817–18; **2004**: 787–89
Human Genetic Data, UNESCO International Declaration on, 2003: 818–19
Human rights. *See also specific country headings*
Abu Ghraib. *See* Detainees, military, *subheading*: Iraq, prisoners held in
abuse of alien domestic workers employed by diplomatic missions. *See* Diplomatic missions and personnel, *subheading*: employees
Alien Tort Statute (ATS). *See* Alien Tort Statute (ATS)
American Convention on Human Rights. *See* American Convention on Human Rights (1969)
American Declaration of the Rights and Duties of Man. *See* American Declaration of the Rights and Duties of Man
antidiscrimination efforts. *See* Discrimination
in armed conflict, **2004**: 331
assembly, promotion of right of, **2005**: 434–35
right to associate and organize, **2003**: 375–77, 386
asylum and. *See* Asylum
Bioethics and Human Rights, UNESCO Universal Declaration on, **2005**: 784–85
capital punishment. *See* Capital punishment
of children. *See* Children, *subheading*: human rights of; Children, *subheading*: Rights of the Child, Convention on
Civil and Political Rights, International Covenant on. *See* International Covenant on Civil and Political Rights (ICCPR)
civil and political rights, mechanisms for protection of, **2004**: 386–88
civil rights, U.S. *See* Civil Rights, U.S.
claims of violations and foreign policy interests, **2002**: 357–63
climate change and, **2008**: 326–32

Human rights (continued)
command responsibility as basis for liability for violations of, **2002**: 348–51
conscientious objection to military service, **2004**: 394–95
consular notification and. *See* Consular notification and access
corporate responsibility, **2000**: 364–68; **2004**: 299; **2007**: 364
corruption as incompatible with full enjoyment of, **2005**: 432–34
Country Reports on Human Rights Practices, **1991-99**: 847–48, 916, 924–27, 941, 961–62; **2000**: 347; **2001**: 74, 247; **2002**: 261; **2003**: 277; **2004**: 221–22; **2005**: 257; **2006**: 327; **2008**: 249
authority as evidence, **2001**: 63–65*n*, 85–86
crimes against humanity. *See* Crimes against humanity
customary international law and. *See* Customary international law
Darfur Peace and Accountability Act (2006), **2006**: 978–83
democracy and, **1991-99**: 849, 851–52, 1011–14; **2003**: 281–83, 311, 403–4, 414–16; **2004**: 389; **2005**: 427–36
Human Rights and Democracy, Supporting: U.S. Record 2004-2005 (report), **2005**: 257–58
detainees, treatment of. *See* Detainees, military
detention. *See also* Detainees, military; Detention of aliens, nonmilitary
of aliens in U.S. custody, **2003**: 322–34
arbitrary, **2000**: 411–12; **2004**: 339, 352–54, 363–64, 374; **2006**: 429–30
of Cuban nationals (“Mariel Cubans”), **2001**: 341–46; **2005**: 18–23
indefinite, **1991-99**: 93; **2001**: 17–19
development, right to, **1991-99**: 934–38, 1649–55; **2001**: 275–78; **2002**: 304–7; **2003**: 312–16; **2004**: 290, 297–98; **2005**: 326–29, 335–36; **2007**: 367; **2008**: 332–33
disappearances, enforced or involuntary, **2001**: 317–18; **2004**: 333–34; **2006**: 415, 424–30
convention on, **2002**: 320; **2005**: 378–80; **2008**: 379
human rights of families of missing persons, **2004**: 331–33
Protection of All Persons from Enforced Disappearances, draft International Convention for, **2006**: 424–28
UN General Assembly resolution on, **2002**: 320; **2008**: 379
discrimination. *See* Discrimination
economic, social and cultural rights
development, right to. *See* development, right to, *this heading*
International Covenant on, **2000**: 371; **2001**: 279; **2003**: 279, 310, 312, 320, 373; **2004**: 262–63, 294, 295, 299–300; **2005**: 324–33; **2007**: 290–91, 360, 370; **2008**: 319, 321, 322, 328, 334
Optional Protocol, **2008**: 318–20

Human rights (continued)
International Organization for Standardization (ISO) draft guidelines on social responsibility, **2008:** 347–50
right to education, **2003:** 322; **2005:** 333–34
right to food, **2008:** 333–37
right to food and housing, **2000:** 370–72; **2001:** 279–81; **2002:** 310–11; **2003:** 316–17; **2004:** 285–88; **2008:** 333–35
right to health, **1991-99:** 907–8; **2001:** 281–83; **2003:** 317–22, 371–74; **2004:** 292–96; **2005:** 332–33; **2008:** 267–69, 320–26
right to standard of living, **2000:** 371; **2004:** 287
UN Committee on, **2007:** 289–93, 360*n*; **2008:** 267–69
water and, **2007:** 360–64
emigration, freedom of, **1991-99:** 1453–56
in employment, **1989-90:** 194–95; **2000:** 369–70
environmental harms as violation of, **2002:** 333–34, 339–40, 344–45, 357
European Convention for the Protection of Human Rights and Fundamental Freedoms. *See* European Convention on Human Rights
European Court of Human Rights. *See* European Court of Human Rights
evaluation of impartiality of foreign court, **2000:** 412–14
Executive Order 13107 (implementing human rights treaties), **2000:** 376; **2005:** 287
extradition and, **1989-90:** 81, 87; **2004:** 87
extrajudicial killing, **1991-99:** 1266–81; **2000:** 397–98; **2001:** 316–17, 392–93; **2003:** 344–47; **2004:** 362–36387; **2005:** 392; **2006:** 465–76, 479–82; **2008:** 376–78. *See also* Capital punishment
in foreign occupation, **2000:** 353–54
Foreign Sovereign Immunities Act issues. *See* Foreign Sovereign Immunities Act (FSIA) (1976)
forum non conveniens motion and, **2003:** 386–87
free flow of information (TV Marti), **2001:** 353–54; **2004:** 643
freedom of information and ideas, **1989-90:** 397; **2001:** 353–54; **2004:** 643; **2005:** 378
no "right to truth" *per se*, **2005:** 378
Right to the Truth Resolution, **2005:** 379–81
fundamental human rights, no consensus as to, **2001:** 366
gender issues. *See* Gender issues
genocide. *See* Genocide
Global Internet Freedom Task Force, **2006:** 769–70
globalization and, **2004:** 290–91

Human rights (continued)
government responsibility to prevent persecution, **2000**: 397–98
High Commissioner for. *See* United Nations, *subheading*: High Commissioner for Human Rights
human genetic data and, **2003**: 818–19
Human Rights and Measures of Implementation, Draft International Convention on, **2005**: 300
Human Rights Committee. *See* UN Committee on Human Rights
Human Rights Council. *See* UN Human Rights Council
of illegal aliens, **2001**: 343, 344, 346
immunity
head-of-state immunity for violations of, **2001**: 320–23
of UN special rapporteur on, **1989-90**: 353–70
of indigenous people. *See* Indigenous people
of institutionalized persons, **2000**: 378–79, 383–85. *See also* Civil Rights of Institutionalized Persons Act (CRIPA) (1980)
Inter-American Commission on Human Rights. *See* Inter-American Commission on Human Rights
Inter-American Court of Human Rights. *See* Inter-American Court of Human Rights
International Covenant on Civil and Political Rights (ICCPR). *See* International Covenant on Civil and Political Rights (ICCPR)
International Criminal Court. *See* International Criminal Court (ICC)
International Organization for Standardization (ISO) draft guidelines on social responsibility, **2008**: 347–50
International Religious Freedom Act (1998). *See* Religion and religious freedom
jus cogens. *See Jus cogens*
labor issues, **1991-99**: 994–1003
law of
distinct from humanitarian law/law of war, **2003**: 277–78, 344–47, 349–51, 1019–21; **2004**: 334–35; **2005**: 302–4, 391, 393; **2006**: 347, 384, 1121–22
federalism issues in international agreements, **2002**: 191, 290–91
laws of armed conflict and, **2002**: 1009–11, 1013–17
municipal law vs. international law, **2002**: 329–31
migrant workers, **1989-90**: 194–95; **2008**: 347
migrants, protection of, **2005**: 336–41; **2007**: 364–67; **2008**: 338–47
military justice and, **2003**: 343–44
persecution, U.S. immigration law, **2000**: 128–31
of persons with disabilities. *See* Disabilities, persons with
prisoners. *See* Prisoners and prisons
Prisoners of Conscience Declaration, **2008**: 378
race discrimination. *See* Racial discrimination

Human rights (continued)
refugees. *See* Refugees
religion. *See* Religion and religious freedom
remedies for violation of, **2003**: 347–54; **2004**: 334–35; **2005**: 390–91
repression of Falun Gong movement in China. *See* Religion and religious freedom
reproductive rights. *See* Reproductive rights
respect for private family life, **2003**: 124–25
Right to a Remedy and Reparation for Victims of Gross Violations of International Human Rights Law and Serious Violations of International Humanitarian Law, Basic Principles and Guidelines on, **2007**: 281–83
rule of law issues, **1991-99**: 1011–14
self-determination, **2003**: 244; **2004**: 5, 385–86, 392–94
sexual orientation nondiscrimination, **2000**: 353
terrorism and, **2000**: 238–39; **2001**: 117–18; **2003**: 409–12; **2004**: 106–7, 197, 972
counterterrorism actions and, **2002**: 358, 360, 387–88; **2004**: 128, 399–400; **2005**: 436–40; **2006**: 487–88; **2007**: 394–98; **2008**: 105–6
detention and trial of suspected terrorists by U.S. military and, **2001**: 880–81
Inter-American Convention Against Terrorism, **2002**: 116–17
torture and. *See* Torture
trafficking in persons. *See* Trafficking in persons
transborder arrest, **2000**: 407–12; **2004**: 352
treaty-monitoring bodies, role of, **2008**: 249–73
composition of, **2008**: 273–74
UN Commission on Human Rights. *See* UN Commission on Human Rights
UN Committee on. *See* UN Committee on Human Rights
UN Convention on the Rights of the Child. *See* Children, *subheading*: Rights of the Child, Convention on
UN High Commissioner for. *See* United Nations, *subheading*: High Commissioner for Human Rights
UN Secretary General's report on, **2005**: 445–48
Universal Declaration on Human Rights, **1989-90**: 174, 191, 397, 400; **1991-99**: 605, 848, 850, 855, 864–70, 899, 960–61, 1099, 1196, 1456, 1458, 1651; **2000**: 366, 370–71, 391, 408, 409; **2001**: 140, 141, 142, 270–71, 279, 291; **2003**: 20, 300, 320, 345, 364, 373, 1016; **2004**: 259, 260, 292, 294, 297, 389, 393, 405, 643, 919; **2005**: 245, 250, 310, 314, 327, 657, 781, 785, 989; **2007**: 286, 289, 361, 379; **2008**: 320–21, 328, 345–46, 378
legal status of, **2000**: 409; **2001**: 291; **2005**: 245

Human rights (continued)
U.S. border control policy and, **2004**: 232–39; **2006**: 210
U.S. foreign assistance and violations of, **1989-90**: 157, 540, 545; **1991-99**: 860–61
U.S. programs and policies, **1991-99**: 847–66; **2006**: 327
U.S. trade policy consideration, **1991-99**: 851, 1453–60
use of force and firearms in law enforcement and, **2004**: 339
Voluntary Principles of Human Rights and Security, **2007**: 231–35
war crimes tribunals' role in protecting, **1991-99**: 858–59
women. *See* Gender issues; Women's issues
Working Group on, **2006**: 428–29
World Conference on Human Rights, **1991-99**: 848–49
World War II era claims, compensation and restitution. *See* Holocaust; World War II
Humanitarian law. *See also* Armed conflict; Geneva Conventions on law of war (1949); Hague Conventions, *subheading*: on law of war; Law of war; War crimes
human rights law and, **2007**: 280–81
ICRC study on, **2006**: 1069–85
humanitarian relief personnel, treatment of, **2006**: 1076–77
opinio juris, **2006**: 1073–75
state practice, **2006**: 1071–73
"law of war," defined by U.S. as meaning in international instruments, **2007**: 985–87
as *lex specialis* governing armed conflict, **2007**: 209, 280, 886, 926; **2008**: 169, 921
Right to a Remedy and Reparation for Victims of Gross Violations of International Human Rights Law and Serious Violations of International Humanitarian Law, Basic Principles and Guidelines on, **2007**: 281–83
Hungary
Child Abduction Convention, compliance with, **2004**: 54; **2006**: 102
child support enforcement, reciprocity in, **1991-99**: 1866; **2005**: 809–10; **2008**: 759
conventional armed forces deployment in, **1991-99**: 2227
economic assistance programs, **1989-90**: 542–43
EU accession and trade agreements, **2006**: 754–56
extradition and mutual legal assistance, **1991-99**: 390, 395, 398, 399, 450, 456; **2000**: 186*n*; **2006**: 137, 147
Gabcikovo-Nagymaros Project case, **2000**: 664–65
Hungarian Gold Train, **2004**: 445–49
settlement of claims related to, **2005**: 485–89
intellectual property rights Watch List, **2006**: 768; **2007**: 610
judicial system in, **2004**: 339

Hungary (continued)
lifting of sanctions against, **1989-90**: 517–18
missile defense cooperation, **2004**: 1066
money laundering, **2004**: 135
NATO accession, **1991-99**: 738–39, 1030–40, 2243
nuclear fuel return program, **2004**: 1139
Open Skies (aerial observation) treaty, **2002**: 1029
peacekeeping missions to, **1991-99**: 2029–30
preservation of American heritage in, **2004**: 797
relief from immigration requirements for certain resident nationals of, **1991-99**: 250
tourism agreement, **1989-90**: 499
trade issues, **1991-99**: 1384, 1408, 1455
treaty issues, **1991-99**: 744
visa waiver program, **2008**: 81–83
Wallenberg case and, **1989-90**: 277–78

I

IAEA. *See* Atomic Energy Agency, International (IAEA)
ICAO (International Civil Aviation Organization). *See* Aviation issues
ICBMs. *See* Arms control
ICC. *See* International Criminal Court (ICC)
ICCPR. *See* International Covenant on Civil and Political Rights (ICCPR)
Iceland
Arctic environment protection agreement, **1991-99**: 1777–80
arms control and nuclear nonproliferation and, **1991-99**: 2232
consular immunity, **2004**: 537
extradition and mutual legal assistance, **2000**: 185*n*
fisheries negotiations with U.S., **2005**: 613
nonimmigrant visa waiver pilot program, **1991-99**: 76
Open Skies (aerial observation) treaty, **2002**: 1029
peacekeeping and, **1991-99**: 2167
treaty succession, **1991-99**: 705
whaling convention, reservations to, **2001**: 214–18; **2002**: 206–12; **2003**: 243–44, 803; **2006**: 878–80
whaling violations, **2004**: 755–57; **2006**: 878–80
ICJ. *See* International Court of Justice (ICJ)
ICPD (International Conference on Population and Development), **2005**: 309, 454
ICRC. *See* Red Cross, International Committee of (ICRC)
ICTY. *See* International Criminal Tribunal for Former Yugoslavia (ICTY)
IEEPA. *See* Emergency Economic Powers Act, International (IEEPA)
IHO. *See* International Hydrographic Organization (IHO)

IIRIRA. *See* Illegal Immigration Reform and Immigrant Responsibility Act (1996)
ILC. *See* International Law Commission (ILC)
Illegal Immigration Reform and Immigrant Responsibility Act (1996), **1991-99**: 70–71, 76, 79, 80, 82, 83–93, 114–15, 182, 203, 213, 232, 240–41, 249–50; **2000**: 387–88; **2001**: 918; **2004**: 15–16, 17; **2006**: 29–33, 36–39, 153; **2007**: 106
Illicit enrichment, **2000**: 238. *See also* Corruption
IMF. *See* International Monetary Fund (IMF)
Immigration Act (1990), **1991-99**: 73, 75, 76; **2003**: 763. *See also* Asylum; Deportation; Immigration and visas; Refugees; Removal of aliens from U.S.
  amending Immigration Act (1952), **1989-90**: 30–40
  exclusion of aliens under, **1989-90**: 32
    antiterrorism provisions, **1989-90**: 33–34
    foreign policy grounds, **1989-90**: 34–37
    health-related grounds, **1989-90**: 20
    membership in totalitarian party, **1989-90**: 37–39
    requirements to review exclusion lists, **1989-90**: 39
    technology transfer provisions, **1989-90**: 33
  presidential signing statement, **1989-90**: 30–32
  temporary protected status under, **1989-90**: 32, 39–40, 41
Immigration and Nationality Act (INA) (1952), **1989-90**: 4, 331; **1991-99**: 482; **2001**: 262–73; **2002**: 8, 9, 19, 23, 29, 32, 413, 756; **2003**: 2–5, 13–15, 16, 17–18, 27, 173, 274, 328; **2005**: 259–60. *See also* Asylum; Deportation; Immigration and visas; Refugees; Removal of aliens from U.S.
  admissibility, determination of, **2006**: 1191–93
  adoption. *See* Adoption
  as amended by Immigration Act (1990), **1989-90**: 30–40
  antiterrorism provisions, **2001**: 896, 898, 904, 918, 921, 922, 925; **2003**: 155; **2008**: 280
  exemptions from certain terrorism-related provisions
    amendment to (2007), **2007**: 70–71; **2008**: 29–30, 307–8
    discretionary exemptions, **2007**: 71–72; **2008**: 20, 30–31, 307–8
  "arrest" defined under, **1991-99**: 186–87
  child, changes (2007) to definition of, **2007**: 89
  on citizenship claims of "immediate relatives," **1989-90**: 10, 11–12
  Convention on the Rights of the Child and, **2002**: 292–93
  criminal grounds for removal, **2008**: 341
  definition of "aggravated felony," **2006**: 34–35
  definition of "entry," **1991-99**: 175, 182–83
  definition of "United States," **1991-99**: 184*n*

Immigration and Nationality Act (INA) (1952) (continued)
designation of terrorist organizations. *See* Immigration and visas, *subheading*: terrorism and; Terrorism, *subheading*: designation of foreign terrorist organizations (FTOs) by U.S.
detention. *See* Immigration and visas
exclusion of aliens, INA provisions regarding, **1989-90**: 32–39. *See also* Immigration and visas
gender discrimination claim under, **1991-99**: 1–9
inspection by immigration officials, **2005**: 19
interdiction in internal waters, status of aliens, **1991-99**: 183–86
jurisdiction, **1991-99**: 190–91
law enforcement powers, **2004**: 1108
lawful permanent residents (LPRs), **2005**: 259–60
longshore work by aliens, **2002**: 756
nonlawful permanent residents (non-LPRs), **2005**: 259–60
persecutor definition, **2005**: 10
person definition, **2005**: 11–12
Presidential Proclamations suspending entry by aliens, **1991-99**: 136
(7359) (concerning Sierra Leone), **2000**: 19–21
(7452) (concerning the Balkans), **2001**: 15–17
(8015) (concerning Belarus), **2006**: 42–44
Burmese nationals (6925), **1991-99**: 142–44; **2003**: 27–29; **2007**: 41
engaged in corruption (7750), **2004**: 24–25
Haitian nationals (6569) (6685), **1991-99**: 137–40
Lebanon/Syria (8158), **2007**: 39–41
Liberian nationals (6730), **1991-99**: 142
Nigerian nationals (6636), **1991-99**: 141–42
Serbian nationals (7249), **1991-99**: 147–49
Sierra Leonean nationals (7062), **1991-99**: 146–47
Sudanese nationals (6958), **1991-99**: 144–45
UNITA officials (7060), **1991-99**: 146; **2003**: 27
Yugoslavian nationals (7249), **1991-99**: 147–49
Zairean nationals (6574), **1991-99**: 140–41
Zimbabwe, **2002**: 22–24
temporary protected status. *See* Immigration and visas; Temporary protected status
visas. *See* Immigration and visas
Sections:
101, **1991-99**: 74, 77, 78, 202, 209, 228; **2003**: 119, 120; **2004**: 30, 125, 171; **2005**: 272, 349, 1036; **2006**: 33–36, *55*, *56*, 1191–94; **2007**: 31–32, 85, 87, 89; **2008**: 15
106, **1991-99**: 82, 91
201, **1991-99**: 73; **2000**: 3, 4, *5*
202, **1991-99**: 114

Immigration and Nationality Act (INA) (1952) (continued)
203, **1991-99**: 71–72, 73, 75; **2005**: 9
204, **1991-99**: 73, 75
205, **2000**: 3–4, 6
207, **2006**: 55, 56
208, **1991-99**: 195, 198; **2000**: 123, 126, 127, 128–31, 133–34, 136–37, 138–40; **2005**: 10; **2008**: 20
211, **2005**: 2*n*; **2007**: 9*n*
212, **1991-99**: 69–70, 79, 80, 81, 85, 86, 87, 88, 89, 90, 92, 131–36, 137, 139, 172; **2000**: 19–21; **2001**: 15; **2003**: 14, 18, 19, 27–29; **2004**: 24, 122; **2005**: 5*n*, 115; **2006**: 7, 18–29, 36–40, 42–43, 52, 55; **2007**: 9, 10, 20–21, 27–30, 39–41, 71–72, 107; **2008**: 17, 18–19, 30, 31, 307. *See also* Presidential Proclamations suspending entry by aliens, *this heading*
214, **1991-99**: 74, 78; **2003**: 16
215, **1991-99**: 139, 172; **2003**: 16, 17; **2006**: 6*n*, 7, 10*n*; **2007**: 10
217, **1991-99**: 76; **2003**: 18; **2006**: 14; **2007**: 29; **2008**: 21
219, **1991-99**: 78–79; **2003**: 155, 173; **2005**: 113, 115; **2008**: 101, 102
221, **2003**: 27
222, **1991-99**: 131
231, **2003**: 18
235, **1991-99**: 80, 82, 85, 86, 91, 92, 173–74, 182, 183–85; **2003**: 16, 18
235(c), **2005**: 347
236, **1991-99**: 174
237, **1991-99**: 79, 87, 89, 90, 91, 92, 118; **2003**: 1
237(a)(4)(C), **2005**: 10, 11, 12
240, **1991-99**: 84, 87, 185; **2008**: 281
241, **1991-99**: 79, 81–82, 87, 93, 119, 124, 952–53, 955; **2003**: 29–33; **2004**: 12, 13, 14–15, 18, 19–20; **2005**: 347, 351; **2006**: 29–33
242, **1991-99**: 82–83, 91, 92, 944; **2005**: 85, 86
243, **1991-99**: 80–81, 157, 159, 163, 166–68, 177, 198, 232; **2001**: 18, 19–20
244, **1991-99**: 240–48, 250; **2003**: 34–35, 37; **2004**: 31–32
258, **2003**: 763
276, **1991-99**: 80
284, **2005**: 2*n*; **2007**: 9*n*
286, **2003**: 18
287, **1991-99**: 186
301, **2004**: 5
309, **1991-99**: 1–9; **2000**: 1, 6–9; **2001**: 7

Immigration and Nationality Act (INA) (1952) (continued)
312, **1991-99**: 15–16
316, **2003**: 4
320, **2000**: 16*n*; **2001**: 4, 5–6; **2003**: 1, 3–4
321, **2001**: 5
322, **2001**: 4–5, 6; **2003**: 2–4
337, **1991-99**: 14; **2003**: 4–5
340, **1991-99**: 29
349, **1991-99**: 20–21, 22, 24; **2001**: 2; **2007**: 4–7; **2008**: 2, 3–4
358, **2008**: 5–6
360, **2007**: 1–2, 3; **2008**: 6
Immigration and Naturalization Service Data Management Improvement Act (2000), **2003**: 16, 17
Immigration and visas, **2004**: 232–39; **2006**: 18–52. *See also* Aliens; Citizenship; Illegal Immigration Reform and Immigrant Responsibility Act (1996); Immigration Act (1990); Immigration and Nationality Act (INA) (1952); Nationality
adoption. *See* Adoption
Afghans, special immigrant visas for, **2008**: 16–16*n*
AIDS/HIV and, **1989-90**: 18–20; **2007**: 26–30; **2008**: 17–20
alien departure confirmation, **2004**: 28–29
alien guardian for helpless alien, **1991-99**: 88
allotment of, **2005**: 9
Angola, restrictions on certain persons from, **2003**: 27
Asia-Pacific Economic Cooperation Business Travel Card (ABTC), **2007**: 36–37
asylum. *See* Asylum
authority to control, **1991-99**: 8–9, 192–93
Belarus restrictions, **2003**: 25–27
biometric data collection, **2004**: 27–29, 30; **2008**: 24–25
bilateral agreements as part of visa waiver program, **2008**: 81–83
Germany, sharing information with, **2008**: 80–81
Burma, restrictions on certain persons from, **2003**: 27–29; **2007**: 41; **2008**: 28–29, 793–95
child custody claim from foreign father and application for child's asylum, **2000**: 115–41
China, **2005**: 641
deferred enforced departure of Chinese nationals, **1989-90**: 54–57
citizen sponsor of alien, **1991-99**: 117–18
concealment of participation in Nazi atrocities on visa application, **2002**: 5–8
congressional authority in U.S., **2000**: 9–11
consular access for detained immigrants and foreign nationals, **2007**: 203–5

Immigration and visas (continued)
consular non-reviewability doctrine
defined, **2007**: 21
First Amendment claims and, **2007**: 21–22
retroactivity and, **2007**: 24–26
consular relations. *See* Consular Relations, Vienna Convention on (VCCR)
Cuba
Mariel Cubans, **2001**: 341–46; **2005**: 18–23
Migration Accords, **1991-99**: 59–68; **2002**: 20–22; **2003**: 20–21; **2004**: 30
policy on immigration from Cuba, **2003**: 23
travel rights of Cuban nationals, **2003**: 20–21
visa denials, **2004**: 906
denaturalization based on visa misrepresentations, **2004**: 3–4
denial of visas. *See also* Deportation, *subheading*: grounds for; exclusion of aliens, *this heading*
AIDS/HIV and, **2007**: 26–30; **2008**: 17–20
beneficiaries of Cuban expropriation, **1991-99**: 94–102, 1445, 1905–6
under Chemical Weapons Convention Implementation Act, **1991-99**: 2347
child abduction, **1991-99**: 109–10; **2002**: 52–54
confiscators of real property of U.S. nationals, **1991-99**: 103–9
and consular non-reviewability doctrine, **2007**: 21–26
engaged in abortion or sterilization policy, **1991-99**: 112–13
for foreign policy reasons, **1991-99**: 131–36
individuals involved in certain killings in Haiti, **1991-99**: 110–12; **2003**: 23–24
individuals that threaten Lebanon's sovereignty and democracy, **2007**: 38–39
material support to terrorist organization, **2006**: 18–29
to traffickers in confiscated property, **2004**: 31
deportation. *See* Deportation
detention
after removal period, **1991-99**: 86–87, 93; **2001**: 17–19; **2005**: 18
of "Mariel Cubans," **2001**: 341–46; **2005**: 18–23
pending removal. *See* Detention of aliens, nonmilitary
and removal, **1991-99**: 86–87; **2008**: 281, 346–47
deterring illegal migration from Haiti, **2003**: 24–25
driver's license, recognition of foreign driver's license of alien, **2002**: 18–20
drug traffickers, restrictions on, **2003**: 187
economic needs of U.S., **1989-90**: 30–31

Immigration and visas (continued)
employment-based immigrants, classification of certain former Soviet and Baltic State scientists as, **2005**: 9
entry requirements into U.S.
Canadian Border Boat Landing Program, **2007**: 12
entry documents for sea or land ports-of-entry. *See also* immigrant visas, *this heading*; nonimmigrant visas, *this heading*; Passports, U.S.
Department of Defense civilian employees, **2007**: 13
non-passport, **2007**: 15–16
Border Crossing Cards (BCC), **2007**: 14–15
other, **2007**: 15–16
pilot programs to develop additional, **2007**: 15
Trusted Traveler Program documents, **2007**: 13–14, 15
waiver of on basis of reciprocity no longer available, **2007**: 9; **2008**: 7–8
illegal reentry of alien under retroactive application of Illegal Immigration Reform and Immigrant Responsibility Act, **2006**: 29–33
lawful permanent residents, **2005**: 2*n*
nonimmigrant aliens, **2005**: 3
Outlying Area Reporting System (OARS), **2007**: 14
temporary admission to U.S. for aliens with AIDS/HIV, **2007**: 26–30; **2008**: 17–20
US-VISIT, **2008**: 24–25
U.S. citizens, **2005**: 3; **2008**: 8–9
evidentiary standards in visa determinations, **1989-90**: 23–24, 25–26
exclusion of aliens. *See also* denial of visas, *this heading*; terrorism and, *this heading*
consolidation of proceedings with removal, **1991-99**: 84
expedited procedures, **1991-99**: 86
grounds for, **1991-99**: 87–89. *See also* denial of visas, *this heading*
AIDS/HIV, **1989-90**: 18–20
contagious diseases, **1989-90**: 18, 20; **2008**: 17–20
detrimental to the interests of the United States, **2007**: 39–41
disclosure of confidential business information, denial of visas to, **1991-99**: 102–3
foreign policy, **1989-90**: 35–37
membership in totalitarian party, **1989-90**: 37–39
religious freedom violations, **1991-99**: 93–94; **2005**: 316
terrorism. *See* terrorism and, *this heading*
unlawfully admitted, **1991-99**: 84–85
hearing requirement for undocumented aliens interdicted in territorial waters, **1991-99**: 172–81

Immigration and visas (continued)
pursuant to Presidential proclamation. *See* Immigration and Nationality Act (INA) (1952), *subheading*: Presidential Proclamations suspending entry by aliens
false or fraudulent, **2005**: 156; **2006**: 207–10
document fraud in smuggling of migrants, **2004**: 160–61, 162
family reunification visas, **1989-90**: 30
Cuban migrants, **2006**: 40–41
processing of Liberian refugees, **2006**: 59–60
foreign emigration practices, U.S. trade policy and, **1991-99**: 1453–56
General Agreement on Trade in Services provisions, **1991-99**: 77
genetic testing of applicants, **1989-90**: 1–3; **1991-99**: 128–31
Haitian migration policy, **2004**: 34–35
high-speed flight from immigration checkpoint, **1991-99**: 91
immigrant visas
Afghan, special immigrant visas for, **2008**: 16, 16*n*
certain military immigrants, **1991-99**: 72–73
diversity visa program, **1991-99**: 73
Iraqis, special immigrant visas for, **2008**: 15–16
scientists from the former Soviet Union, **1991-99**: 71–72
T visas, **2005**: 272–73; **2007**: 342
Immigration Fraud Conference, **2006**: 209–10
information collection from foreign visitors and immigrants, **2003**: 15–19
interdiction of aliens
on high seas, **1991-99**: 150–72, 176–77, 187–94
in internal waters, **1991-99**: 182–87
in territorial sea, **1991-99**: 172–81
Iraqis, special immigrant visas for, **2008**: 15–16
Libya, student visas, **2004**: 929
Mauritania, restrictions on certain persons from, **2008**: 806
migrant workers
Convention on the Protection of the Rights of, **1989-90**: 194–95
Inter-American Program for the Promotion and Protection of, **2005**: 337–41
rights of, **1989-90**: 194–95
undocumented migrant workers, **2001**: 262–64
migrants
Belarus, suspension of entry from, **2006**: 42–44
human rights of, **2008**: 339–47
Inter-American Program for Promotion and Protection of Human Rights of Migrants, OAS Resolution on, **2005**: 337–41
UN General Assembly resolution governing protection of, **2007**: 364; **2008**: 338–39

Immigration and visas (continued)
in safe haven in Guantanamo, **1991-99**: 188–94
smuggling of, **2005**: 153–56
U.S. views on UN Commission on Human Rights (UNCHR) Resolution 2005/47 concerning, **2005**: 336–37
National Security Entry and Exit Registration System (NSEERS), **2008**: 280–81
nonimmigrant visas
abused spouses and children, **1991-99**: 75
A/G visa holders
revocation of visa, **1989-90**: 328–29, 331
status of, **1989-90**: 28–30
visa classification and diplomatic status, **2004**: 538–39
business visas, **1991-99**: 73–75
crew list visas, **2004**: 30
discontinuation of reissuance, **2004**: 29
entry requirements, **2006**: 6–7
under GATS, **1991-99**: 77
HIV, aliens with, **2008**: 17–20
Irish peace process training program admissions, **1991-99**: 78
possession of firearms and, **2004**: 534
S visas, **1991-99**: 77–78
technology transfers and, **2004**: 1114
treaty-investor, **2007**: 30–32
visa waiver. *See* visa waiver program (VWP), *this heading*
parentage blood testing to establish entitlement to immigrant status, **1989-90**: 2–3
parole
no authority for court to order Executive to parole alien into U.S., **2006**: 1191–94
status of Cuban medical personnel, **2006**: 41–42
passports. *See* Passports, U.S.
pending asylum decision, **2004**: 361
Presidential Proclamations suspending entry. *See* Immigration and Nationality Act (INA) (1952)
protection for victims of trafficking, **2000**: 225–30
refugees. *See* Refugees
removal. *See* Removal of aliens from U.S.
repatriation of Mexican illegal aliens to interior, **2004**: 26–27
requirements for aliens proceeding in transit through U.S., **2003**: 13–15
retroactivity of immigration laws, **1991-99**: 115; **2006**: 29–33, 36–39
right to free association and, **1989-90**: 21, 25

Immigration and visas (continued)
role of civil service employees in performance of consular functions, **1991-99**: 348–49
sanctions for nonacceptance of return of nationals, **2001**: 17–20
Secure Fence Act of 2006, **2006**: 50–52
Soviet Scientists Immigration Act of 1992 (SSIA), **1991-99**: 71–72; **2005**: 9
state law preempted by federal authority, **1991-99**: 786–89
statutory relief for certain resident nationals, **1991-99**: 248–51
student visa abusers, **1991-99**: 89
suspension of entry. *See* Immigration and Nationality Act (INA) (1952), *subheading*: Presidential Proclamations suspending entry by aliens
temporary admission and visas for nonimmigrants with HIV, **2008**: 17–20
temporary protected status. *See* Temporary protected status
terrorism and
agreements concerning exchange of terrorist screening information, **2008**: 110–11
antiterrorism measures, **1991-99**: 78–82
exclusion of terrorists, **1989-90**: 21–26, 33–34; **1991-99**: 79; **2003**: 158–59; **2004**: 122–23. *See also* Deportation, *subheading*: grounds for; Removal of aliens from U.S., *subheading*: based on terrorism
incitement to commit terrorist acts, **2006**: 206–10
material support to terrorist organization, **2006**: 18–29; **2007**: 19–26
exemptions, **2007**: 70–72; **2008**: 20, 29–31
prevention of terrorist activities in U.S., **2001**: 903–4, 908–11, 915–17, 918, 921–22, 925, 932
Terrorist Exclusion List, **2002**: 102–4; **2004**: 122–23
trafficking in persons. *See* Trafficking in persons
transsexual individuals petitions and applications, **2004**: 8–11
treaty obligations of successor states, **1991-99**: 746
U.S. antidiscrimination efforts, **2001**: 251, 254, 262–63
visa waiver program (VWP), **2006**: 207, 209; **2008**: 20–22. *See also* *specific countries*
amendments under Secure Travel and Counterterrorism Partnership Act of 2007, **2007**: 32–36
departure verifications, **2007**: 34–35
Electronic System for Travel Authorization (ESTA), **2007**: 33; **2008**: 22, 23–24
lost and stolen passports, **2007**: 33
passenger information exchange, **2007**: 34

Immigration and visas (continued)
repatriation, **2007**: 34
visa refusal rates; new waiver authority, **2007**: 34, 35–36
arrangements concerning exchange of terrorist screening information, **2008**: 110–11
bilateral agreements to combat serious crime, **2008**: 81–83
Visa Waiver Permanent Program Act (2000), **2003**: 16
waiver pilot program, **1989-90**: 26–27; **1991-99**: 75–76; **2004**: 29
visas
A/G visas, **1989-90**: 28–30, 328–29, 331; **2004** 538–39
allotment, **2005**: 9
G-2 visas, **2006**: 657
lottery, **1989-90**: 40
nonreviewability of consular decisions on, **1989-90**: 22–23, 25; **1991-99**: 68–71, 116
overstaying of, **2005**: 83
place of visa processing as discriminatory, **1991-99**: 113–18
special immigrant visas, **2008**: 15–16, 16*n*
student visas, **1991-99**: 89; **2004**: 929
student visa abusers, **1991-99**: 89
T visas, **2005**: 272–73; **2007**: 342
U visas, **2005**: 271–72
Visitor and Immigrant Status Indicator Technology Program, **2003**: 13–19
Western Hemisphere Travel Initiative (WHTI) of 2007, **2007**: 8–15; **2008**: 6–11
Immigration Reform and Control Act (IRCA) (1986), **1989-90**: 26–27, 31, 385; **1991-99**: 75–76; **2001**: 251
A/G visa holders, **1989-90**: 28–30, 385–87
Immunity. *See also* Consular offices and personnel; Diplomatic missions and personnel; Diplomatic Relations, Vienna Convention on; Foreign Sovereign Immunities Act (FSIA) (1976); Head-of-state immunity; Sovereign immunity
air crew's immunity under Tokyo Convention, **2008**: 519–25
of American Institute in Taiwan and the Coordination Council for North American Affairs. *See* Taiwan
apostille not providing, **2004**: 69
for arms control delegations in Switzerland, **2004**: 1057–59
of culturally significant objects imported under 22 U.S.C. § 2459, **2003**: 825–30; **2004**: 792–96; **2005**: 776–77, **2007**: 742–44; **2008**: 732–34
foreign policy interests and, **2007**: 476–77
of government officials, **2006**: 630–43
based on common law predating FSIA, **2007**: 504, 509–16

Immunity (continued)
criminal jurisdiction, **2008:** 491–92
involved in interdiction of aircraft involved in drug trafficking, **1991-99:** 545–46
special diplomatic missions, **2008:** 490–91
for insurers under U.S. antitrust laws, **1991-99:** 1529–33
of international organizations. *See* International organizations; *specific organizations*
International Organizations Immunities Act (IOIA), **2007:** 448, 527–28
of lawful enemy combatants, **2002:** 1002–5
of military vehicles from taxes under Status of Forces Agreement and UK law, **2005:** 570–74
sovereign. *See* Foreign Sovereign Immunities Act (FSIA) (1976); Sovereign immunity
special missions immunity, **2006:** 662–81; **2007:** 447–48; **2008:** 490–91
of states of U.S. from suits by foreign states, **1991-99:** 316–17
Torture Victim Protection Act and, **2006:** 629, 650–52, 681*n*
UN personnel. *See* Privileges and Immunities of the United Nations (General Convention)
of U.S. military officer serving as member of international peacekeeping force from subpoena by ICTY, **2000:** 268–71
IMO (International Maritime Organization). *See* Maritime issues
Implementing Recommendations of the 9/11 Commission Act of 2007, 2007: 32–36; **2008:** 20–22
Imports. *See* Trade
Impunity, 2001: 318; **2005:** 189, 198, 363
criminal tribunals for Rwanda and former Yugoslavia and, **2005:** 199; **2008:** 147, 149
Darfur situation and, **2005:** 194, 377; **2008:** 836, 842, 843, 844, 873
Somali pirates and, **2008:** 850, 931
UN Commission on Human Rights (UNCHR), U.S. comments on, **2005:** 200–201, 390–92
IMSO (International Mobile Satellite Organization), 2006: 494–97
***In vitro* conception**
citizenship of child conceived *in vitro*, **2002:** 10–11; **2006:** 2–3
INA. *See* Immigration and Nationality Act (INA) (1952)
India
agreements and initiatives with U.S.
for Cooperation Concerning Peaceful Uses of Nuclear Energy (2007), **2005:** 1077–82; **2007:** 1014–18; **2008:** 986–93
defense relationship, **1989-90:** 151, 153
Disaster Relief Initiative, **2005:** 1080

India (continued)
double taxation, avoidance of, **1989-90**: 411–14
Global Democracy Initiative, **2005**: 1079
Global Issues Forum, **2005**: 1083
High-Technology Cooperation Group (HTCG), **2005**: 1080, 1083
Investment Incentive Agreement between U.S. and India, use of arbitration procedure, **2004**: 425, 428, 430; **2005**: 469, 652
Knowledge Initiative on Agriculture, **2005**: 1079
open skies agreement, **2005**: 588; **2008**: 509
political offense exception in extradition treaty, **2005**: 94–97
Science and Technology Framework Agreement between U.S. and India, **2005**: 773, 1080
strategic partnership, **2005**: 1082–89
Antarctica environment agreement, **2002**: 798–800
Bhopal toxic gas disaster, **2001**: 335–36
child abduction to, **2002**: 58–59
Commerce Department nonproliferation control lists, removal from, **2005**: 1089
conduct during Gulf War, **1991-99**: 2104, 2107
crew list exemption, **2007**: 657
Dabhol arbitration, **2005**: 469, 652–53
drug trade, **2001**: 120; **2002**: 124; **2003**: 181; **2004**: 133–34; **2005**: 135; **2006**: 213; **2007**: 163–66; **2008**: 113
excessive air space claims, **2007**: 635
extradition and mutual legal assistance, **1991-99**: 396; **2001**: 92*n*; **2002**: 61, 62, 66–67; **2004**: 80
felony murder doctrine, abolition of, **2005**: 386
forum non conveniens, **2005**: 841–43
hazardous waste disposal agreement, **2002**: 783–85
human rights in, **2004**: 399
intellectual property Watch List, **2006**: 768; **2007**: 608, 610; **2008**: 605*n*
ITER International Fusion Energy Organization, **2006**: 893
Kyoto regime issues, **2005**: 219
marine scientific research claim against U.S., **2007**: 648–50
missile defense cooperation, **2004**: 1066, 1067–68
mission to UN, litigation concerning claimed immunity to tax liens on, **2006**: 592–603; **2007**: 455–63; **2008**: 456–57, 495–98
money laundering in, **2004**: 135
nonproliferation. *See* Nonproliferation, *subheading*: country-specific issues
Overseas Private Investment Corporation arbitration, **2004**: 424–30
religious freedom
actions promoting protection of, **2005**: 315
religious persecution in, **2002**: 282

India (continued)
Somali piracy, cooperation with Transitional Federal Government of Somalia (TFG) in fight against, **2008**: 927
terrorism, countering, **2004**: 399
trade issues, **1991-99**: 1410, 1412–14, 1717
Continued Dumping and Subsidy Offset Act of 2000 (CDSOA), WTO action concerning, **2006**: 707
trafficking in women and children in, **1991-99**: 912
treaty issues, **1991-99**: 744
Vienna Convention on Consular Protection, enforcement of in U.S. courts by Indian national, **2005**: 60
Indian Claims Commission Act (1946), 2002: 371, 378, 379
Indigenous people. *See also* Native Americans
claims against U.S. by, Inter-American Commission on Human Rights report on, **2002**: 367–82
claims against U.S. re removal from Chagos Archipelago, **2004**: 364; **2005**: 415–17
collective tribal claims vs. aggregated individual claims, **2002**: 370–73
internal self-determination, **2004**: 385–86
removal of indigenous persons from Chagos Archipelago to allow establishment of U.S. military facility in Indian Ocean, **2006**: 455–59
rights of, **2007**: 368–73
culture and cultural artifacts, **2004**: 791
customary international law, **2008**: 352–57
development rights, **2003**: 314
internal self-determination, **2002**: 363; **2004**: 385–86
NAFTA claims relating to, **2008**: 351–57
OAS draft declaration on, **1991-99**: 1003–6; **2002**: 364–67, 379–81; **2003**: 402–3
UN Declaration on, **1991-99**: 1006–10; **2002**: 363; **2004**: 383–85; **2006**: 394–401; **2007**: 368–73; **2008**: 352–57
Second International Decade, **2004**: 385
U.S. lands of, issues concerning, **2001**: 260–61
U.S. treaties with, legal status of, **2001**: 254–55, 260–61
use of term "indigenous peoples," **2001**: 353; **2003**: 314
Indigenous plants, 2005: 139
Individuals with Disabilities in Education Act (1968), 2001: 251
Indonesia
act of state doctrine and, **2002**: 575; **2003**: 580–82
Alien Tort Statue and Torture Victim Protection Act, actions brought under relating to, **2003**: 396; **2005**: 411–15; **2008**: 222–27
anti-suit injunction, **2008**: 760–64
antiterrorism cooperation, **2002**: 118, 890

Indonesia (continued)
arbitration of disputes and, **2004**: 821
as archipelagic state, **2003**: 760–62
aviation agreement, **2004**: 567–68
citizens' claims against U.S. corporation for human rights violations, **2002**: 357–63
claimed implicit waiver of FSIA immunity, **2003**: 524–26
claims for archipelagic waters, **1989-90**: 472–75
crimes against humanity in, **2000**: 245–46
drug trade (methamphetamines), **2007**: 164–66
East Timor
atrocities, **1991-99**: 519–20
environmental harm in, claims under Alien Tort Statute, **1991-99**: 990–91
trade claims against, **1991-99**: 1410
immunities, issues concerning, **2004**: 460–63; **2008**: 245
intellectual property rights Watch List, **2006**: 768, 769; **2007**: 610
logging initiative, **2006**: 801–3
maritime counterterrorism measures, conditions for failure to take, **2008**: 112
money laundering, **2004**: 135
religious freedom violation, **2003**: 296
sovereign immunity, **2008**: 245
Straits of Malacca and Singapore, **2006**: 806–10
WTO dispute. *See* World Trade Organization (WTO)
Industrial designs. *See* Hague Conventions
Influenza
avian, **2005**: 756
international partnership to combat, **2005**: 772–73
pandemic influenza, national strategy for, **2006**: 889–90
Information collection and management
airline passenger data
passenger name record data, **2004**: 108–16; **2005**: 586–87
Secure Flight program, **2008**: 103–9
Switzerland agreement, **2008**: 109–10
U.S.–EU agreement on (2007), **2006**: 168–72; **2007**: 158–59; **2008**: 109–10
alien departure confirmation, **2004**: 28–29
bank account data, **2003**: 137
biometric data, **2003**: 16–19; **2004**: 27–29; **2006**: 14, 209; **2007**: 11, 14, 34, 35, 659; **2008**: 24–25
bilateral agreements as part of visa waiver program, **2008**: 81–83
Germany, sharing with, **2008**: 80–82

Information collection and management (continued)
classified information, U.S.–EU agreement on sharing of, **2007:** 128–29; **2008:** 80
in enforcement of competition laws, **1991-99:** 1543, 1546, 1547, 1549
European Union–U.S. mutual legal assistance agreement, **2003:** 137–38
Executive Branch authority over certain, **2004:** 216–17
from foreign visitors at arrival and departure, **2003:** 15–19; **2008:** 24–25
genetic data, use of, **2003:** 818–19
global marine assessment and audit, **2003:** 781–82
Internet restrictions, **2004:** 264
passports, reporting of data on lost or stolen, **2004:** 6–7
registration of space objects, **2004:** 735–38; **2007:** 661
scope of testimony by U.S. witness before ICTR, conditions on, **2007:** 185–90
state secrets privilege in U.S. litigation, **2007:** 238–54
telecommunications surveillance in mutual legal assistance, **2004:** 94
terrorism screening, exchange of information, **2008:** 110–11
Terrorist Finance Tracking Program (TFTP), **2007:** 160–61
Terrorist Surveillance Program (TSP), **2007:** 247–51
visa lookout database, **2003:** 159
Information Society, World Summit on (WSIS), **2003:** 312–14; **2005:** 654–63
data protection and privacy, **2005:** 660
freedom of expression, **2005:** 657
intellectual property rights, **2005:** 658–59
interconnection costs, **2005:** 658
Internet
domain name and addressing systems, **2005:** 654–55, 658, 661–62
stability, **2005:** 657
multilingualism, **2005:** 658
Outcome Document (A/RES/60/1), **2005:** 451–55
spam, **2005:** 659
Tunis Agenda for the Information Society, **2005:** 661–63
Injunctions, **2005:** 124*n*
Americans with Disabilities Act of 1990 (ADA), Title III, **2005:** 709
anti-suit injunctions, **2002:** 864–73; **2004:** 840–50; **2005:** 829–32; **2006:** 953–63; **2008:** 760–77
Anti-Terrorism Act of 1987 (ATA), **2005:** 541
detainee transfers to countries where they could face torture or indefinite imprisonment, **2005:** 1016–18
Foreign Sovereign Immunities Act and, **2005:** 522–31
IIC information, protection of, **2005:** 876–78

Injunctions (continued)
importation of psychotropic substances, **2005**: 137
Marcos estate, injunction against transferring assets, **2005**: 575
Prison Litigation Reform Act of 1996 (PLRA), **2005**: 367
textile and apparel safeguard actions on imports from China, **2005**: 642–44
trademark infringement
comity-based abstention, **2005**: 826–27
litigation in U.S., **2005**: 663–65, 667–69, 671; **2008**: 771–76
Institutionalization, Civil Rights of Institutionalized Persons Act. *See* Civil Rights of Institutionalized Persons Act (CRIPA) (1980)
Insurance, terrorism risk. *See* Terrorism
Insurance industry
claims of Nazi era victims and victims' heirs, **2000**: 449, 460–73
federal and state regulation, **2000**: 468–70
preemption of state action by Convention on the Recognition and Enforcement of Foreign Arbitral Awards (New York Convention), **2008**: 777–82
stolen vehicles treaties, **2000**: 170
Intellectual property rights, 1991-99: 1369, 1463; **2001**: 635, 646–47, 648, 745, 764–67, 785, 794. *See also* Copyright law; Patent law; Trade Related Aspects of Intellectual Property Rights (TRIPS Agreement); Trademark law
applicability of copyright law to Taiwan, **1991-99**: 702–5
Audiovisual Works, Treaty on the International Registration of (1990), **1989-90**: 415–18
bilateral investment treaties, **1991-99**: 1464, 1468
challenges to U.S. copyright law, **2003**: 661–63
China–U.S. agreements, **1991-99**: 1517–23
Convention for the Protection of, **2002**: 518
Convention on the Protection and Promotion of the Diversity of Cultural Expressions, **2005**: 208
crimes, **1991-99**: 406
cybercrime, **2003**: 194, 199–200
drug research and development, **2002**: 718; **2008**: 608
environmental protection and, **1991-99**: 1390, 1653–54, 1759, 1761–62
Fairness in Music Licensing Act, **2003**: 661
industrial designs, Hague Convention, **2000**: 300; **2006**: 786–90
International Bureau of the World Intellectual Property Organization, **1989-90**: 419; **2000**: 298, 299; **2006**: 786
international comity doctrine and, **2005**: 826
International Space Station Partners Agreement, **1991-99**: 1643, 1645–46

Intellectual property rights (continued)
Internet issues, **2000**: 740; **2005**: 659
Madrid Agreement Concerning the International Registration of Marks, Protocol to, **1991-99**: 695–99, 2192, 2247; **2000**: 297–301; **2003**: 699–701
NAFTA provisions, **1991-99**: 1424
Paris Convention, **2005**: 667–70
Performances and Phonograms Treaty, **1991-99**: 1509–17
plant genetic resources, **2002**: 810–11; **2004**: 789–90; **2008**: 725–27
protection in Cuba, **1991-99**: 1908
protection in Japan, **1991-99**: 1394
protection in Vietnam, **1991-99**: 1159; **2008**: 606
public health issues, **1991-99**: 1506–7
registration of audio-visual works, **1989-90**: 415–18
rules of private judicial settlement, **2000**: 740–41
Science and Technology (S&T) Agreements, **2005**: 773
Singapore Treaty on the Law of Trademarks, **2008**: 609–10
Special 301 program (Watch List), **2006**: 766–69; **2007**: 605–11; **2008**: 604–8
Trademark Law Treaty, **1991-99**: 1508–9
trademark registration, **2000**: 298, 300
World Intellectual Property Organization (WIPO), **1989-90**: 416; **1991-99**: 699, 1469–70, 1507–17, 1645; **2000**: 298, 740; **2001**: 791, 794; **2002**: 518; **2003**: 200, 702, 703, 831; **2005**: 689; **2006**: 399; **2007**: 608, 786; **208**: 606, 609
World Summit on Information Society (WSIS), **2005**: 658–59
WTO dispute settlements, **1991-99**: 1407–9, 1410

Intelligence and surveillance
aircraft shootdown accident in Peru, **2001**: 121–28
Terrorist Surveillance Program, **2006**: 363–65
U.S. role in drug interdiction, **2001**: 121–28

Intelligence Reform and Terrorism Prevention Act of 2004 (IRTPA), **2004**: 123–26; **2005**: 2–5, 114, 125, 126–28; **2008**: 7, 102, 103, 104, 105
citizenship and identity, other documents for, **2007**: 15
constitutional challenge to material support for terrorism provisions, **2007**: 143–50
enactment of, **2005**: 2
entry requirements
  nonimmigrant aliens, **2005**: 3
  U.S. citizens, **2005**: 3
Foreign Terrorist Organization designations. *See* Terrorism, *subheading*: designation of foreign terrorist organizations (FTOs) by U.S.

Intelligence Reform & Terrorism Prevention Act (continued)
information sharing, **2006**: 171
material support for terrorism, **2005**: 125–28
passport requirements
passport cards, and § 7209 of IRTPA, **2007**: 11–12; **2008**: 7–9
U.S. citizens, **2007**: 10
President's authority to waive requirements, **2007**: 10
Secure Flight program, **2008**: 103–5
travel document requirements, **2005**: 4–5; **2006**: 4, 7–9
travel to the U.S. and, **2007**: 9–10
treaty issues, **2006**: 297
Western Hemisphere Travel Initiative and, **2006**: 4–11; **2008**: 7–8
statutory and regulatory history, **2006**: 9–11; **2008**: 7–8
Inter-American Commission on Human Rights, **1989-90**: 167; **1991-99**: 864; **2000**: 389–96; **2002**: 73, 315, 369; **2003**: 277–78, 409–11; **2004**: 223–39, 906, 976–94; **2007**: 53, 383–89, 394–97. *See also* American Convention on Human Rights (1969); American Declaration of the Rights and Duties of Man
admissibility of petitions, **2004**: 223–32
alleged violation of American Declaration of the Rights and Duties of Man in death penalty case, **2000**: 389–96
border controls, **2004**: 232–39
authority to issue precautionary measures, **2002**: 261–69, 1008–17
capital punishment, **2001**: 294–302
of juvenile offenders, **1991-99**: 973*n*, 974*n*; **2001**: 303–15
on claims against U.S. by indigenous people, **2002**: 367–82
claims of "Mariel Cubans" detained in U.S., **2001**: 341–46; **2005**: 22–23
consular notification cases, **1991-99**: 281, 289–91; **2002**: 48–52
Declaration on the Rights of Indigenous Peoples, **1991-99**: 1003–6
detention of enemy combatants by U.S., **2004**: 976–94
effect of duplicate petition, **2001**: 314, 343–44
indigenous people, **1991-99**: 1003–6
jurisdiction, **2001**: 314, 342–44; **2002**: 369; **2003**: 410
limitations on, **2002**: 1008–17
precautionary measures authority, **2002**: 261–69, 1008–17; **2003**: 277–78
legal status of determinations, **2001**: 296, 299–302
mandate, **2002**: 262–64
on statehood of District of Columbia, **2001**: 352–53
statute of, **2002**: 381
WWII internment, **2004**: 223–32

Inter-American Convention Against Corruption (1996), 1991-99: *563–71*; **2000:** 231–38; **2001:** *159–63*; **2004:** 139–40; **2006:** 236, 237–38
Inter-American Convention on International Commercial Arbitration (1990), 1989-90: *501–2*
Inter-American Convention on Mutual Assistance in Criminal Matters with Related Optional Protocol, 2000: 166, *167–69*
Inter-American Convention on Serving Criminal Sentences Abroad. *See* Prisoner transfer
Inter-American Court of Human Rights, 1991-99: 320–40; **2000:** 26, 27, 32, 35, 41, 42; **2001:** 299; **2002:** 50, 73, 263, 265, 268; **2003:** 69; **2004:** 234; **2006:** 434, 645*n*
consular notification cases, **1991-99:** 320–40; **2000:** 26–27, 32, 35, 41, 42
interpretation of American Declaration of the Rights and Duties of Man, **1989-90:** 165–68
jurisdiction, **1989-90:** 165–68; **1991-99:** 322–23; **2000:** 32*n*
Inter-American Democratic Charter, 2001: 346–51; **2003:** 406; **2005:** 245, 251
Inter-American Development Bank, 1991-99: 1440; **2003:** *575–76*; **2004:** 802
Enterprise for the Americas Initiative, **1991-99:** 1462
immunities, **1991-99:** 1315, 1317–19
Inter-American Drug Abuse Control Commission (CICAD), 2006: 220
Inter-American Juridical Committee, 2000: 403*n*
Inter-American Treaty of Reciprocal Assistance (1948), 2001: 863–64; **2003:** 346
Inter-American Tropical Tuna Commission (Antigua Convention), Convention for Strengthening. *See* Fish and marine mammals
Inter-carrier Agreement on Passenger Liability. *See* Aviation issues
Intercontinental ballistic missiles (ICBMs). *See* Arms control
Intercountry adoption. *See* Adoption
Intercountry Adoption Act (2000). *See* Adoption
International Agreement Claims Act (1954), 2004: 482
International Air Transportation Fair Competitive Practices Act (1994), 2004: *569, 570*
International Antitrust Enforcement Assistance Act (1994), 1991-99: 1545–50
International Atomic Energy Agency. *See* Atomic Energy Agency, International (IAEA)
International Broadcasting Act (1994), 2001: 293
International Child Abduction Remedies Act (1988), 1991-99: 372; **2001:** 40–47; **2002:** *55, 56*; **2004:** *55–56*

International Civil Aviation, Convention on (Chicago Convention). *See* Aviation issues, *subheading*: Convention on International Civil Aviation (Chicago Convention, 1944)
International Civil Aviation Organization (ICAO). *See* Aviation issues
International Claims Settlement Act (1976), 1989-90: 238, 525
International Claims Settlement Act (1980), 1991-99: 1083
International Claims Settlement Act (1989), 1991-99: 673
International Code of Conduct against Ballistic Missile Proliferation, 2002: 1062–65
International Coffee Organization, 2004: 412–14; **2005:** 467–68; **2006:** 493–94
International Contracts, Inter-American Convention on the Law Applicable to, 1991-99: 1841–43
International Convention on Elimination of All Forms of Racial Discrimination, 1991-99: 861, 883–97, 906; **2000:** 347–50; **2001:** 247–67, 354; **2002:** 274; **2004:** 294; **2005:** 305–6; **2006:** 371–72, 400; **2007:** 326, 329–30; **2008:** 275–84, 920–22
International Convention on Road Traffic (1949), 2000: 295; **2002:** 20–22
International Court of Justice (ICJ), 2000: 290, 553; **2001:** 369, 593, 598, 635; **2002:** 902, 909; **2004:** 421–22, 1023–24; **2005:** 29–31, 32–58, 155, 175, 216–17, 223, 270, 337, 539–40, 651, 952; **2006:** 1021–26
  baselines, drawing of maritime, **2007:** 638
  case against U.S.
    for attack on Iranian oil platforms, **1991-99:** 2182–86; **2003:** 1036–66; **2004:** 974–76; **2006:** 1025
    concerning consular notification. *See* Consular notification and access
    for downing of Iran Air Flight 655, **1989-90:** 212, 214–15; **1991-99:** 544, 1091–94
  case by U.S. against Italy for interference with foreign investment, **1989-90:** 418
  case concerning bridge across the Great Belt, **1991-99:** 1585–86
  cases by Federal Republic of Yugoslavia against NATO member states, **1991-99:** 2151–54
  claim of immunity for UN Special Rapporteur, **1989-90:** 353–70
  conflict resolution and, **2007:** 835–36
  customary international law and, **2002:** 637, 658, 659, 661; **2007:** 59–60, 68, 543
  decisions by not binding in U.S. courts, **2006:** 71–72
  decisions by not preempting contrary law of U.S. states, **2008:** 35, 153, 175–93

International Court of Justice (ICJ) (continued)
decisions by not privately enforceable in U.S. courts, **2007**: 75–77
Genocide Convention violations, **1989-90**: 121, 122–23
implementation of decision by President not upheld in U.S. courts, **2007**: 73–77, 836
initiative by U.S. for greater use of, **1989-90**: 207–9
Inter-American Court of Human Rights and, **1991-99**: 322–23
International Criminal Court and, **2000**: 290
in International Law Commission draft articles on state responsibility, **1991-99**: 1112, 1120
Israel's construction of security barrier, **2004**: 944–49; **2006**: 1023
request for advisory opinion on, **2003**: 949–51
issuance of precautionary measures, **2002**: 265
jurisdiction, **1989-90**: 114, 122–23, 143–44, 147–48, 183, 207–9, 243, 250–51, 354–61; **1991-99**: 157–58, 293, 304–5, 315, 322–23, 464–65, 466–68, 685–86, 894, 2152–54, 2183–85; **2000**: 32*n*, 66–68, 82–85, 87–88; **2001**: 361, 608–11; **2003**: 45, 102–3, 1039, 1049; **2004**: 37, 944–46; **2008**: 213–15
advisory opinions, **1989-90**: 147–48
reservations by U.S. to provisions in treaties providing for, **1991-99**: 890, 894, 909–10, 2153–54; **2007**: 139, 628
U.S. reservation to transnational organized crime convention, **2004**: 148
U.S. reservations to Genocide Convention and, **1989-90**: 143–44
U.S. reservations to Torture Convention and, **1989-90**: 183
U.S. withdrawal from compulsory jurisdiction and consular optional protocol, **2006**: 1026
Kosovo, declaration of independence, UN General Assembly resolution requesting advisory opinion on, **2008**: 439
Libyan claims against U.S. and U.K., **2001**: 98; **2003**: 160, 166
in connection with explosion of Pan Am Flight 103 over Scotland, **1991-99**: 458–59, 460–77
nuclear weapons advisory opinion, **1991-99**: 2170–82; **2006**: 1079, 1081, 1255–57
open to public, **2002**: 712
property rights in U.S., request regarding, **1989-90**: 243, 250–51, 254, 264
protection of diplomatic property when relations severed, **2000**: 553
Provisional Measures order to stop execution, **2001**: 21, 22, 23
on remedies involving violations of Article 36 of Vienna Convention on Consular Relations. *See* Consular notification and access

International Court of Justice (ICJ) (continued)
role in relation to crime of aggression, **2001**: 176–77
on state practice, **2006**: 1072*n*
statute of, Article 38, **2002**: 653, 654
timeliness of requests for action to, **2000**: 88–91
treaty interpretation, **2007**: 555
on treaty law and state responsibility, **1991-99**: 1109
in treaty reference for dispute resolution, **2003**: 264–65
on treaty reservations, **2001**: 306
U.S. boundary case, **2007**: 640, 835
U.S. support for, **2006**: 1021–26
on use of force, **2004**: 972–76
International Covenant on Civil and Political Rights (ICCPR). *See also* Human rights; UN Commission on Human Rights; UN Committee on Human Rights
applicable to Hong Kong, **1991-99**: 405
arbitrary detention, **2004**: 352. *See also* Detainees, military
authority to interpret, **1991-99**: 879–80
capital punishment and, **1991-99**: 58–59, 340, 739, 870, 876–77, 881, 964, 965–70; **2000**: 397; **2002**: 317–18; **2003**: 337, 341; **2005**: 269–70, 289, 384, 390
juvenile offenders, **2001**: 304, 305–7, 310; **2003**: 341; **2005**: 384, 387
Protocol, **2000**: 391
child labor and, **2003**: 305
China's accession to, **1991-99**: 868–70
criminal justice and, **1991-99**: 311, 330, 337, 338, 339, 574*n*, 605, 871–72, 876–78
democracy and, **2004**: 389
derogation, **1991-99**: 574*n*; **2001**: 880–81; **2006**: 412; **2008**: 364
disabilities and, **2003**: 300
due process and, **2008**: 376
erga omnes obligations under, **2007**: 283–84
Executive Order 13107 (implementing human rights treaties), **2005**: 287
extrajudicial killing, **2003**: 345
fair trial, right to, **2000**: 394. *See also* Detainees, military
federalism and, **1991-99**: 872, 875, 906; **2002**: 194–95
free speech rights and, **1991-99**: 870, 874, 876; **2006**: 200–2
freedom of information and ideas, **1989-90**: 397; **2001**: 353–54; **2004**: 643; **2005**: 378
no "right to truth" *per se*, **2005**: 378
Right to the Truth Resolution, **2005**: 379–81
freedom of movement, **2001**: 344; **2008**: 105–6

International Covenant on Civil and Political Rights (ICCPR) (continued)
freedom of religion. *See* Religion and religious freedom
grave breaches, **2008**: 261
Hurricane Katrina response, **2007**: 267–70
indigenous people and, **1991-99**: 1005
international humanitarian law and, **2007**: 280–81
military detainees and, **2005**: 265–66; **2006**: 1122. *See also* Detainees, military
no non-refoulement obligation, **2007**: 266–67, 278–80
no private right of action under, **2001**: 421*n*; **2002**: 461–62; **2003**: 363–64
no retroactive application of, **2004**: 226
nonderogability of certain provisions, **2001**: 307; **2006**: 1122; **2008**: 364
non-self-executing nature of, **1991-99**: 873, 875, 895; **2000**: 408–9; **2001**: 290, 421*n*; **2002**: 461–62; **2003**: 363–64, 377; **2004**: 349; **2005**: 245–46
privacy, **2008**: 442
private conduct, **2007**: 275–78
remedies under, **2007**: 281–83; **2008**: 265–66
removal of aliens, **2008**: 341–42, 345
reservations to, **1991-99**: 878–83
right to religion. *See* Religion and religious freedom
right to return to one's own country, **2001**: 17–20, 344; **2005**: 937
right to vote, **2005**: 249
territorial scope of, **2002**: 388; **2005**: 296–300; **2006**: 346–50; **2007**: 271–75
extraterritorial application of, U.S. disagreement with ICJ on, **2006**: 1024, 1121
torture, freedom from, **2005**: 273–74
trafficking in persons, **1991-99**: 912
travel restrictions, **1991-99**: 250
treatment of detainees held by U.S., **2007**: 267; **2008**: 345
trial issues, **2005**: 277–84
tribal self-determination, **2006**: 351–54
U.K.–U.S. extradition treaty and, **2004**: 81–83
UN resolutions, references to treaties in, **2003**: 278–80; **2004**: 262–63
U.S. ratification and implementation of, **1991-99**: 861, 869, 870–78, 961; **2005**: 258–300; **2006**: 210, 284–87, 346–71
International Covenant on Economic, Social and Cultural Rights. *See* Human rights
International Crime Control Act (proposed), 2000: 188–90
extradition provisions, **2000**: 188–90

International Criminal Court (ICC), 1989-90: 133–36; **1991-99:** 535, 584, 608–41, 739–41; **2000:** 249–50, 274, 275–86; **2001:** 118–19, 165, 173–78, 372, 524–25; **2002:** 61–62, 148–65, 295, 908–9; **2003:** 222–33; **2004:** 175–88; **2005:** 191–203, 215–17, 376, 391–92, 409–10
administrative issues, **1991-99:** 614, 622, 629
aiding and abetting liability, **2004:** 375–76
alternative fora, **2003:** 229, 339–40
American Servicemembers' Protection Act and, **2003:** 237–40; **2006:** 278
arrest and surrender procedures, **1991-99:** 625
Article 98 agreement (nonsurrender of Americans to ICC), **2002:** 68–69, 165–68, 169; **2003:** 224–27, 234–40; **2004:** 179, 184–86, 187, 188; **2005:** 201–2; **2006:** 279
complementarity issues, **1991-99:** 612–13, 622–26, 628, 635
crimes of sexual violence, **2000:** 253
Darfur, referral to, **2005:** 194, 196, 198; **2006:** 258; **2007:** 182–84, 197; **2008:** 144, 842
definition of crime of aggression, **2000:** 286–90
European Union–U.S. extradition agreement and, **2003:** 137
evidence and procedure, **1991-99:** 614, 620–22, 636
evidence exclusion rules, **2003:** 76, 96
head of state immunity and, **2001:** 524–25
initiation of cases in, **1991-99:** 613, 615–19, 623–25, 630, 631–32
role of Security Council, **1991-99:** 613, 615–19, 621, 626, 628, 630, 631–32
International Court of Justice and, **2000:** 290
judicial independence, **1991-99:** 613, 615, 621–22, 628
jurisdiction, **2006:** 257–58
Organization of American States and, **2002:** 321–23; **2004:** 179–81
preparatory work by International Law Commission, **1991-99:** 608–26
prohibition against surrender of extradited persons to, in extradition treaty, **2004:** 80
prosecution of Saddam Hussein and, **1991-99:** 535–36
protection of U.S. military personnel, **2004:** 176, 179
purpose, **1991-99:** 613, 619, 623, 626–27
restrictions on foreign assistance to parties to, **2004:** 186–88
Rome Conference, **1991-99:** 626–27, 635–39, 739–41
Rome Statute, U.S. views on, **2006:** 257, 277; **2008:** 142–44
signing by U.S., **2000:** 292–93
UN General Assembly resolution on report of, U.S. disassociation from consensus, **2005:** 197–98; **2007:** 180–82; **2008:** 144–45

International Criminal Court (ICC) (continued)
UN peacekeeping and, **2003:** 227–29, 231–34
UN Security Council and, **2002:** 150, 151–52, 159–61, 322, 907–9; **2006:** 258; **2008:** 145–46
UN Security Council Resolution 1422, **2002:** 157, 161–65
UN-ICC agreement, **2004:** 175–77
United Nations and, **2000:** 274, 275, 285–86; **2004:** 178–79, 181–83, 188, 409; **2007:** 182
U.S. armed forces subject to, **2000:** 249–50, 278
U.S. objections to references to in resolutions, **2002:** 302, 318–23; **2003:** 336–40; **2008:** 145–46
U.S. policy, **1991-99:** 608–40; **2000:** 272–79; **2002:** 148–61, 162–65, 303, 321–23; **2003:** 222–30; **2004:** 176–88; **2006:** 257–58, 277–79; **2007:** 180–84, 196–97; **2008:** 142–44
U.S. prohibition on cooperation with, **1991-99:** 640–41; **2000:** 172–73; **2002:** 168–75
witness and victim protection, **1991-99:** 586–87
International Criminal Police Organization, 1991-99: 1314
International Criminal Tribunal for Former Yugoslavia (ICTY), 2006: 259–69; **2007:** 188
Ante Gotovina, issues relating to prosecution by, **2005:** 192; **2008:** 147–48
authority to compel evidence from SFOR, **2000:** 255–71
Common Article 3 and decisions of, **2007:** 884, 918–19, 921–22
completion strategy, **2003:** 219–21, 229; **2008:** 139
crimes, **1991-99:** 514, 580–81, 912; **2000:** 241, 252, 287, 756; **2004:** 312*n*, 375–76, 723; **2005:** 395, 410–11
establishment of, **1991-99:** 580–81
Security Council authority for, **1991-99:** 472, 587–97; **2006:** 255
evidence exclusion rules, **2003:** 76, 96
executive agreement and implementing legislation, U.S., **1991-99:** 582
head of state immunity, **2001:** 524–25
independence of, **1991-99:** 594
legal effect of rulings, **2000:** 83; **2004:** 357; **2005:** 395, 410–11
national jurisdiction and, **1991-99:** 511–13; **2008:** 139–40, 147
NATO and, **1991-99:** 2147
procedural equality, **2000:** 393
purpose, **1991-99:** 858–60
request for production of information by U.S., **2003:** 214–19; **2008:** 138–39; **2006:** 259–69
U.S. sanctions and, **1991-99:** 148, 583; **2003:** 930. *See also* Emergency Economic Powers Act, International (IEEPA)
witness and victim protection issues, **1991-99:** 583–87

International Criminal Tribunal for Former Yugoslavia (continued)
U.S. views on and support for, **1991-99**: 148, 962; **2001**: 167, 169–72, 372; **2003**: 229, 930; **2004**: 172–75; **2005**: 188–93, 199, 217, 430, 939; **2006**: 255–56; **2007**: 184–85; **2008**: 138–40, 146–48, 222
International Criminal Tribunal for Rwanda (ICTR), 2007: 186–90
completion strategy, **2003**: 219–20; **2008**: 139, 147
convictions, **2008**: 150
crimes, **2000**: 203–16, 242, 252–53, 287; **2004**: 357, 372, 375–76
establishment of, **1991-99**: 580–81, 591, 593, 596, 598, 599, 603–4, 608
Security Council authority for, **1991-99**: 604–7; **2006**: 255
extradition of indictee from U.S. to, **1991-99**: 388, 597–603; **2000**: 203–16; **2005**: 358
legal effect of rulings, **2000**: 83; **2004**: 357; **2005**: 395, 410–11
national jurisdiction and, **1991-99**: 511–12; **2008**: 139–40, 147
obligations to, **2000**: 193; **2008**: 147
performance assessment, UN, **1991-99**: 606–7, 615
purpose, **1991-99**: 530–31, 858–60
scope of testimony by U.S. witness, conditions on, **2007**: 185–90
Security Council resolution on, **2003**: 219–20
as tool for beginning process of peace and reconciliation, **2005**: 199–200
U.S. rewards program for, **2002**: 137–42; **2008**: 138–40, 148–50
U.S. views on and support for, **1991-99**: 962; **2001**: 167–68, 372; **2003**: 229; **2004**: 128–29, 131–32, 175, 178, 180; **2005**: 188–93, 217, 430; **2006**: 255–56; **2007**: 184–85; **2008**: 139, 146–50, 222
witness and victim protection issues, **1991-99**: 583–87; **2002**: 975
International criminal tribunals, generally. *See* Criminal tribunals, international, hybrid, and other
International Development Law Institute, 1991-99: 1314
International Economic Emergency Protection Act (1977), 1991-99: 486, 487
International Education Act (1966), 1991-99: 891
International Emergency Economic Powers Act. *See* Emergency Economic Powers Act, International (IEEPA)
International Financial Institutions Act (1977), 1989-90: 515–16
International Financing of Mobile Equipment, Cape Town Convention on. *See* Mobile Equipment, Cape Town Convention on International Interests in (2001)
International Frequency Registration Board
Cuba objection to U.S. broadcasts, **1989-90**: 400–9
scope of essential duties, **1989-90**: 403–4, 405–6, 407–8
International Fusion Energy Organization, 2006: 893–95; **2007**: 527–28

International Hydrographic Organization (IHO), 2007: 407–10; **2008:** 397, 628
International Institute for the Unification of Private Law (UNIDROIT), 2001: 775–76; **2002:** 818, 820–23, 825, 827, 828–29; **2004:** 802, 804, 806, 822, 826, 829
on commercial finance, **2001:** 778–79, 790–91
dispute resolution, **2001:** 790
draft space assets protocol to the Cape Town Convention, **2008:** 747–51
Draft Convention on Transactional Law on Cross-border Securities Transactions, **2005:** 808
on electronic commerce, **2001:** 786, 792, 793
on interests in mobile equipment (Cape Town Convention), **2001:** 722–25, 790–91; **2005:** 713, 802; **2006:** 930–34; **2008:** 747–51
on international franchising, **2001:** 786–87
on leasing
International Financial Leasing, UNIDROIT Convention on (Ottawa Convention), **2008:** 745–46
model law, **2008:** 745–47
on secured transactions, **2005:** 808
International Labor Organization (ILO), 1989-90: 194–95; **1991-99:** 1392–93; **2001:** 672; **2003:** 249–50, 376–77; **2004:** 748–49, 906
child protection convention, **2002:** 286–89
Convention 182, **2001:** 151
Convention Concerning the Abolition of Forced Labor, **1991-99:** 996–98
Convention Concerning Discrimination (Employment and Occupation), **1991-99:** 994–95
Convention Concerning Indigenous and Tribal Peoples in Independent Countries, **2008:** 352, 352*n*, 357
Convention Concerning Safety and Health in Mines, **1991-99:** 998–1000
Convention on the Elimination of the Worst Forms of Child Labor, **1991-99:** 929–30, 932–34; **2001:** 151; **2002:** 286–89
Declaration on Fundamental Principles and Rights at Work, **1991-99:** 1000
on forced labor, **2006:** 227
instrument for amendment of Constitution of, **2002:** 192–93
Jordan Free Trade Agreement and, **2001:** 672
on maritime labor, **2006:** 821–25
fair treatment of seafarers in event of maritime accident, **2006:** 825–28
U.S. International Trade Agenda, **2001:** 667
U.S. state law and, **2002:** 192–93

International Law Commission (ILC), 1989-90: 127–28, 133–36; **2000:** 416–20, 610, 611; **2002:** 393–96; **2003:** 71–72, 73, 433–41
draft articles
on diplomatic protection, **2006:** 499–502; **2007:** 415–21
on effect of armed conflict on treaties, **2007:** 208–9; **2008:** 168–70
on expulsion of aliens, **2007:** 38–39; **2008:** 25–28
on jurisdictional immunities of states and their properties, **2006:** 608
on responsibility of international organizations, **2008:** 381–82
on state responsibility. *See* State responsibility
on transboundary aquifers, **2008:** 716–21
on extradite or prosecute, **2006:** 159–60; **2008:** 70–72
immunity of foreign officials from criminal jurisdiction, **2007:** 516; **2008:** 491–92
on *jus cogens*, **2000:** 483–84; **2006:** 647*n*
mandate, **2000:** 64–65
most-favored-nation clause, **2007:** 590–91
protection of persons in disasters, **2007:** 285, **2008:** 274–75
on reservations to treaties and objections to reservations, **1989-90:** 147, 148; **2006:** 294
on responsibility of international organizations, **2006:** 491–92; **2007:** 399–401; **2008:** 381–82
rule of law, **2007:** 390–93
on transboundary harm arising from hazardous activities, **2006:** 861–62; **2007:** 685–86
treaties
effect of armed conflict on, **2007:** 208–9; **2008:** 168–70
on interpretive declarations, **2008:** 164–66
Vienna Convention on Law of, **2007:** 425
on UN Headquarters Agreement, **2000:** 609–10
International Maritime Organization (IMO). *See* Maritime issues
International Military Tribunal at Nuremberg, 2004: 178, 357, 372, 374, 530; **2006:** 649
International Mobile Satellite Organization (IMSO), 2006: 494–97
International Monetary Fund (IMF), 1991-99: 1012, 1495, 1496–97, 1499–1500; **2003:** 837–38
Czechoslovakia and, **1989-90:** 520
immunity of personnel, **2001:** 538–39
Poland and, **1989-90:** 518–19
Special Drawing Rights, **2000:** 671
U.S. opposition to IMF assistance for countries subject to U.S. sanctions for trafficking in persons, **2008:** 117
International Organization for Standardization (ISO)
draft guidelines on social responsibility, **2008:** 347–50

International organizations, 1991-99: 1015–41; **2001:** 355–80; **2004:** 176, 912, 946; **2005:** 441–68. *See also specific organizations*
accountability in, **2003:** 418–19
active in private international law, **2001:** 775–76
adherence to outer space treaties, **2003:** 767–68
biological weapons investigation and, **2004:** 1062
bribery of officials of, **2005:** 170, 172
definition, **2000:** 415–16
employment of dependents of personnel of, **1989-90:** 385–87
European Community as member in, **2000:** 297, 300–1; **2004:** 191, 413
humanitarian activities exceptions to sanctions programs, **2003:** 907–9
immunity. *See also specific organizations*
of African Union, **2006:** 684
of Holy See, **2006:** 684
International Organizations Immunities Act (1945), **2006:** 683–84
child and spousal support claims, **1991-99:** 1315–16
designated organizations, **1991-99:** 1314–15
of employees of International Atomic Energy Agency, **2002:** 572–73
of the European Central Bank, **2003:** 575
garnishment proceedings, **1991-99:** 1317–19
of Inter-American Development Bank, **2003:** 575–76
of Inter-American Tuna Commission, **2005:** 748–49
OPEC not qualifying as, **2003:** 557–58
of Radio Regulations Board, **2006:** 682–84
of United Nations. *See* Privileges and Immunities of the United Nations (General Convention)
of World Bank under Bretton Woods Agreements Act (1945), **1991-99:** 1332
Internet governance, role in, **2004:** 627
legal personality, **2000:** 415
Libya working with, **2004:** 928, 933, 1159
membership, **2003:** 415–17
outer space activities of, **2001:** 719–20; **2003:** 767–68
participation of Puerto Rico in, **2001:** 242–43, 244–45
in private international law, **2003:** 833–34
in promoting democracy, **2003:** 413–14, 419–21
radio regulations and, **2004:** 637; **2006:** 682–84
regional economic intergovernmental organizations, **2004:** 801–2
registration of space objects by, **2004:** 735–36; **2005:** 713
removal of aliens, responsibility of, **2005:** 23
reservations to treaties creating, **1989-90:** 149

International organizations (continued)
response to September 11 terrorist attacks, **2001:** 860–64, 910–13, 935–41
responsibility of, **2004:** 410–11; **2006:** 491–92; **2007:** 399–401; **2008:** 381–82
sovereignty of state over own nationals employed by, **1989-90:** 363–64
succession of Federal Republic of Yugoslavia to membership in, **2000:** 561
terrorism and, **2004:** 105
trafficking in persons and, **2004:** 166
transparency in proceedings of, **2003:** 417–18
as treaty participants, **2000:** 296–308
UN relations with other organizations, **2004:** 177, 407
International Organizations Immunities Act (IOIA) (1945), 1991-99: 1313–19; **2000:** 608*n*, 609, 625; **2001:** 539; **2002:** 536, 555–56*n*, 572–73; **2003:** 558, 575; **2006:** 683–84; **2007:** 448, 527–28; **2008:** 502
International Parental Kidnapping Crime Act (1993), 1991-99: 377–80, 409; **2002:** 56–59
International Plant Protection Convention, 1991-99: 1784–90
International Red Cross and Crescent. *See* Red Cross, International Committee of (ICRC)
International Refugee Organization, 1991-99: 29–30; **2002:** 7; **2003:** 6, 7; **2004:** 2
International Religious Freedom Act of 1998. *See* Religion and religious freedom
International Responsibility of States for Injuries to Aliens, Convention on, 2004: 587*n*
International Security and Development Cooperation Act (1981), 1989-90: 540
International Telecommunication Union (ITU), 1989-90: 399–409; **2001:** 722; **2003:** 426–31; **2005:** 658, 663, 714
amendments to Constitution and Convention, **2006:** 770–74; **2008:** 388–96, 593
radio regulations, **1989-90:** 398–99, 400, 401, 402–3, 408–9; **2004:** 634–39; **2006:** 682–84, 772–73; **2008:** 158–60, 593
U.S. broadcasts to Cuba and, **2004:** 640–44; **2008:** 391–92
World Radiocommunication Conference (2007), **2007:** 598
International Telecommunications Convention, 1989-90: 398–99, 401, 403–4; **2004:** 636, 638; **2008:** 388–96,
International Thermonuclear Experimental Reactor Consortium (ITER), 2005: 1080, 1086
International Fusion Energy Organization, **2006:** 893–95

International Traffic in Arms Regulations (ITAR), 1989-90: 109; **1991-99:** 2253–55; **2004:** 1069–70; **2005:** 1044; **2007:** 1002–7; **2008:** 89, 1021. *See also* Arms Control; Arms Export Control Act (AECA)
International Transportation by Air, Convention for the Unification of Certain Rules Relating to (Warsaw Convention 1929). *See* Aviation issues
International Tribunal for the Law of the Sea, 2004: 422, 676, 684
International Union for Conservation of Nature and Natural Resources, 1991-99: 1314
Internet. *See also* Electronic commerce
  broadband communications, **2004:** 631–34
  domain name registration
    Paris Convention for the Protection of Industrial Property and, **2002:** 389–91
    using name of sovereign country, **2002:** 518–19
  email
    communication of treaty reservation by email, U.S. objection to, **2002:** 394
    service of process by, **2004:** 873–74; **2005:** 861–67
    spam, **2005:** 659, 801
  Global Internet Freedom Task Force, **2006:** 769–70
  governance, **2004:** 627–31
  transactions as basis for personal jurisdiction, **2003:** 901–5
  website designated as foreign terrorist organization, **2006:** 191–99
Interparliamentary Union, 1991-99: 1314
Interpol, 2004: 6–7, 1075; **2006:** 209
Interpreters, courtroom, 2003: 82
Interstate Commerce Commission Termination Act (1995), 2002: 666
Investment, 1991-99: 322, 1179, 1439, 1441, 1454, 1761, 1926, 2313. *See also* Development; North American Free Trade Agreement (NAFTA)
  air carriers, U.S., investment and control by non-U.S. entities, **2005:** 586, 588–92; **2008:** 508–10
  ATS litigation and, **2005:** 407, 423, 822–26
  Australian Securities and Investments Commission (ASIC), mutual recognition arrangement with SEC, **2008:** 603–4
  bilateral investment treaties, **1991-99:** 1463–82, 1489; **2000:** 683; **2003:** 265–66; **2004:** 619–24, 651, 821; **2005:** 646–47, 653; **2007:** 544, 547, 552–53; **2008:** 600–3
  bipartisan agreement on trade issues and, **2007:** 582
  in environment and conservation, **1991-99:** 1676, 1679, 1723
  EU law, understanding concerning compatibility with and related protocols, **2003:** 687–97

Investment (continued)
foreign direct investment, **1991-99**: 1461–63
foreign direct investment in U.S.
Committee on Investment in U.S. (CFIUS)
statutorily established by Foreign Direct Investment and National Security Act (FINSA) (2007), **2006**: 774–80; **2007**: 601–5; **2008**: 593–600
President's open economies statement (2007), **2007**: 599–600, 602
Hague Convention on law applicable to intermediated securities, **2007**: 763–64
Multilateral Agreement on Investment, **1991-99**: 1447, 1486–93
North American Development Bank (NADBank), Protocol concerning Border Environmental Cooperation Commission and North American Development Bank, **2005**: 606
Overseas Private Investment Corporation, U.S., **1991-99**: 1083, 1460
Investment Incentive Agreements, **1991-99**: 1482–86, 2040–41; **2005**: 469, 647–53
private international law and, **1991-99**: 1813, 1853, 1854
securities transactions, **2004**: 803–4
with specific countries, **1991-99**: 122, 1012–13, 1132, 1179, 1449, 1451, 1460, 1635–36; **2005**: 469, 892–94, 1079
Sudan, sanctions concerning investment by state and local governments, **2007**: 816–17
trade, investment, and development cooperation agreements, **2008**: 576–77
trade and investment cooperation agreements, **2008**: 575–76
trade and investment framework agreements, **2005**: 646; **2008**: 573–75
trade benefits and, **2004**: 657–58, 923–24*n*
UN Security Council and, **1991-99**: 470
UNIDROIT Draft Convention on Transactional Law on Cross-border Securities Transactions, **2005**: 808; **2007**: 763–65
U.S.-EU air transport agreement and, **2007**: 530–31; **2008**: 508–10
visas and, **1991-99**: 75; **2007**: 30–32
WTO, **1991-99**: 1372, 1374, 1379–81, 1403, 1407, 1409; **2008**: 533–34
Investment Disputes Act, Convention on the Settlement of (1966), **1991-99**: 1473
Inviolability. *See also* Consular offices and personnel; Diplomatic missions and personnel; Foreign Sovereign Immunities Act (FSIA) (1976); Head-of-state immunity; Immunity
of diplomatic personnel and property, **1989-90**: 351; **2002**: 37, 550–52; **2003**: 564–65, 573
of foreign dignitaries attending UN conference, **2006**: 681–82

Inviolability (continued)
of heads of state to service of process, **2001**: 511, 531–36; **2002**: 550–52; **2003**: 558–69; **2004**: 549, 550, 554–55, 556–57; **2006**: 681–82
of representatives of foreign government to UN Millennium Summit to service of process, **2001**: 511, 531–36
of UN missions, **1991-99**: 1319–31
Iran. *See also* Algiers Accords
access to U.S. courts by, **1991-99**: 1140, 1186
act of state doctrine, **2005**: 579
China–U.S. relations and, **1991-99**: 2317, 2319, 2359
claimed neutral status during Gulf War, **1991-99**: 2102, 2104, 2105–6, 2107
claims against U.S. related to downing of Iran Air Flight 655, **1989-90**: 211–17; **1991-99**: 544, 1091–94
claims against in U.S. court by Tehran hostages, **2001**: 459–75; **2002**: 523–27; **2003**: 547–49
claims arising from bombing of U.S. military base in Saudi Arabia, **2006**: 581–84
claims at ICJ arising from destruction of oil platforms, **1991-99**: 2182–86; **2003**: 1036–66; **2004**: 974–76; **2006**: 1025
claims at U.S.–Iran Claims Tribunal. *See* Iran–United States Claims Tribunal
declaration regarding Convention Against the Taking of Hostages, U.S. response to, **2007**: 132
denial of U.S. visa to national of, for foreign policy reasons, **1991-99**: 132–33
detention of removable Iranian national for foreign policy reasons, **2005**: 10–14
diplomatic relations, **1989-90**: 241; **2003**: 485; **2005**: 13, 545–46, 548
educational exchange program, **2006**: 989–90
efforts to enforce U.S. judgments against in U.S., **2008**: 410–18, 484–89
enforcement of national court judgments in U.S., **1991-99**: 1833–36
excessive air space claims, **2007**: 637–38
financial transactions and assets
Bank Melli, **2007**: 1042–43, 1045, 1049
Bank Saderat, **2006**: 986–90; **2007**: 157, 486, 1042–43, 1046–47, 1049; **2008**: 970
liability of Iranian Bank in U.S. for government actions, **2002**: 545–47
foreign tax credit, **2004**: 659
FSIA immunity. *See* Foreign Sovereign Immunities Act (FSIA) (1976)

Iran (continued)
Hizbollah support in 1983 bombing of U.S. embassy in Beirut, **2005:** 508–16
human rights violations, **2005:** 12–14
religious freedom violations, **1991-99:** 925; **2001:** 272; **2002:** 282; **2003:** 295, 296; **2004:** 270, 272, 273; **2005:** 314, 316; **2006:** 377
torture of returned nationals, **2005:** 349–50
U.S. policy on support of Iranian people, **2006:** 989–90
import ban on Caspian Sea beluga sturgeon products, **2005:** 754
Iraq
support for attacks on American forces in, **2007:** 989, 1046, 1048; **2008:** 805
war with, **2003:** 1000
Israel, statement on, **2005:** 319
U.S. response to, **2007:** 379–80, 995
juvenile offenders, execution of, **2005:** 387
Lebanon
arms embargo and, **2007:** 870
bombing of U.S. embassy in Beirut, claim against Iran concerning, **2005:** 508–16
maritime issues, **1991-99:** 1578, 1583, 1599–1600; **2008:** 862–63; *See also* Straits of Hormuz
nuclear program and other nonproliferation issues. *See* Nonproliferation
private right of action to recover compensation for expropriation, *see* Treaty of Amity, *this heading*
property at issue in U.S. litigation, **2006:** 564–72; 612–21; **2007:** 477–89; **2008:** 484–89
publishing, application of sanctions on, **2004:** 924–25
sanctions against, **1991-99:** 1094–95, 1448, 1971, 1974, 1976, 1977; **2001:** 817–19
arms embargoes on, **2007:** 1003, 1007
under Executive Orders. *See* Executive Orders, *subheading*: Iran
humanitarian activities exceptions, **2003:** 908–9
for earthquake in Bam, Iran, **2003:** 908–9
foodstuffs and carpets, **2000:** 743–44
Iran and Libya Sanctions Act (1996), **1991-99:** 1911–15, 1977; **2001:** 817–19; **2003:** 445
Iranian Transactions Regulations, **2004:** 924–25; **2006:** 986–90; **2008:** 980–84
proliferation. *See* Nonproliferation
terrorism. *See* terrorism and, *this heading*
trafficking in persons, **2006:** 228; **2007:** 169; **2008:** 118

Iran (continued)
Straits of Hormuz, Iranian boats and U.S. Navy warships in, **2008**: 862–63
terrorism and, **1991-99**: 1094, 1227–28, 1263–65. *See also* Terrorism
collection of judgments under Terrorism Risk Insurance Act, **2006**: 612–21; **2007**: 477–89; **2008**: 484–89
designation as state sponsor of terrorism, **1991-99**: 508–9, 1223; **2001**: 464–65, 820; **2004**: 103, 659; **2005**: 506; **2006**: 173, 577; **2007**: 235–36; **2008**: 89, 472
Hizbollah support in 1983 bombing of U.S. embassy in Beirut, **2005**: 508–16
not cooperating fully with antiterrorism efforts, **1991-99**: 508; **2003**: 167; **2004**: 107–8; **2006**: 172; **2007**: 132; **2008**: 88–89
sanctions on persons who commit or support, **2007**: 1042–43, 1046–50
support for in Lebanon, **2006**: 1037, 1039–41, 1226–30, 1233–34
Treaty of Amity, Economic Relations, and Consular Rights Between U.S. and Iran (1957), **2002**: 219–26; **2003**: 258–67, 1036, 1040–66; **2006**: 1023, 1025; **2008**: 155–58
Wassenaar Arrangement and, **1991-99**: 2266
women and asylum, **1991-99**: 218, 221–23
Iran and Libya Sanctions Act (1996), **1991-99**: 1448, 1911–15, 1976, 1977; **2001**: 817–19; **2003**: 445; **2004**: 928–29, 930; **2008**: 770
Iran–Iraq Arms Non-Proliferation Act (1992), **1991-99**: 2362; **2002**: 1070–71; **2003**: 1123–24
Iran–United States Claims Tribunal, **1991-99**: 673, 1086–99, 1119, 1228; **2000**: 429–44, 545, 551; **2001**: 381–85, 580–81, 599–600; **2002**: 632; **2003**: 433–56; **2004**: 415–23, 577*n*
claims against Iran
case A/17, **2000**: 432*n*, 433
case A/28, **2003**: 450–51; **2004**: 416–20; **2008**: 417
case A/33 (maintenance of Security Account balances), **2003**: 450–51; **2004**: 416–20
case B/1 (counterclaim), **2003**: 448–50; **2004**: 420–24
case 298 (dual nationality issues), **1991-99**: 1096
claims against U.S., **2003**: 441–54; **2005**: 546
cases A/4, A/7, A/5 (1:F & III) (1997), **2000**: 556*n*
case A/11, **2000**: 429–44
case A/15 (I:G) (1986), **2000**: 432*n*
case A/15 (II:A), **1991-99**: 1089; **2003**: 441–45; **2008**: 410–11*n*, 489
case A/15 (II:B), **1991-99**: 1089

Iran–United States Claims Tribunal (continued)
case A/15 (IV)/A/24 (compensation for Iranian litigation expenses), **2003:** 446–48
case A/15 (Claim C) (bank claims), **1991-99:** 1091–94
case A/18 (dual nationality issues), **1991-99:** 1095–96; **2000:** 432*n*; **2001:** 644–46
case A/27 (nonenforcement of partial award), **1991-99:** 1090–91; **2008:** 417
case A/30 (interference in Iran's internal affairs), **1991-99:** 1094–95; **2003:** 445–46
case B/1 (Foreign Military Sales), **1989-90:** 223–28, 236
case B/1 (claims 2 & 3), **1991–99:** 1089, **2008:** 410–11*n*, 489
case B/1 (claim 4), **1991–99:** 1087–90; **2000:** 432n
case B/1 (claim 6) **1991–99:** 1089
case B/7, **2008:** 410-11*n*
case B/61, **1991–99:** 1089; **2003:** 441–45; **2006:** 617–18, **2008:** 485, 485*n*, 486–89
efforts of U.S. claimants to attach property at issue in claims against U.S.
before tribunal, **2008:** 484–89
U.S. litigation seeking assignment of claims against U.S. to satisfy private judgment, **2008:** 410–18
failure to revoke sanctions, **1991-99:** 1094–95
nonenforcement of partial award, **1991-99:** 1090–91
return of military equipment to Iran, **1991-99:** 1087–90; **2003:** 441–45
sovereign immunity, **2008:** 410–18
establishment, **1991-99:** 1086–87; **2004:** 415
government-to-government claims, **1989-90:** 222–23
valuation of Iranian properties in U.S., **1989-90:** 224–26, 227–28
jurisdiction, **2003:** 448–50; **2004:** 415, 417, 420–24
Security Account claims, **1989-90:** 228–29
maintenance of Security Account balances (Case A33), **2004:** 416–20
small claims settlement, **1989-90:** 230–37; **1991-99:** 1096–98
status of claims, **1989-90:** 220–23
Terrorism Risk Insurance Act (TRIA) provisions concerning, **2008:** 411, 484–90
U.S. view of Iranian claims, **1989-90:** 229–30
Iraq. *See also* Gulf War; Nonproliferation, *subheading*: country-specific issues
Abu Ghraib. *See* Detainees, military
American Gulf War prisoners of war, claims against, **2003:** 543–47; **2005:** 507–8, 1028
attacks on humanitarian workers in, **2003:** 993–96

Iraq (continued)
authority to prevent Iranian- or Syrian-supported attacks against U.S. forces in, **2007**: 989–90
availability of consular services, **2003**: 106–7
capture of Saddam Hussein, **2003**: 992
claims against, arising from Kuwait invasion, **1991-99**: 1099–1106, 1119, 2111; **2000**: 444; **2002**: 407–8; **2003**: 454–56; **2004**: 430
hostage taking by Hussein government, **2006**: 584–92
claims against former officials of, **2004**: 558–59
Coalition Provisional Authority (CPA), occupying, **2003**: 983–91; **2004**: 451, 558, 883–84, 893–94, 898; **2005**: 871, 951, 957–60, 976
case concerning false claims submitted to, **2005**: 225–34; **2006**: 301–5
whether instrumentality of U.S. for purposes of False Claims Act, **2005**: 227–34; **2006**: 301–5
crimes of Saddam Hussein administration, **1991-99**: 532–38, 607, 851, 962, 2112–16, 2118–19; **2000**: 247; **2003**: 1002
cultural property, **2004**: 886; **2008**: 730–32
Declaration of Principles for a Long-term Relationship of Cooperation and Friendship Between the Republic of Iraq and the United States of America (2007), **2007**: 990–95; **2008**: 462
denial of U.S. visa to nationals of, for foreign policy reasons, **1991-99**: 131–32, 133–34
detainees. *See* Detainees, military
Development Fund for, protection of, **2003**: 914–23; **2004**: 883–84, 887–89, 902–3; **2005**: 869; **2006**: 1235–38; **2008**: 461
Diego Garcia base supplying support services to forces in, **2005**: 417
diplomatic relations, **2003**: 485
economic development, **2004**: 647–51
Executive Order 13303, **2005**: 896
extradition and mutual legal assistance, **2000**: 185*n*; **2008**: 73–78
Foreign Claims Act, **2005**: 982–83
FSIA, cases brought under terrorism exception, **2004**: 489–93, 507–8; **2008**: 463–71
Geneva Conventions. *See* Geneva Conventions on law of war (1949)
Gulf war. *See* Gulf war
human rights in, **2002**: 282, 945
religious freedom in, **1991-99**: 925; **2001**: 272; **2003**: 295; **2004**: 272
immigrant visas (special immigrant visas) for Iraqis, **2008**: 15–16
immunity of UN personnel, **2003**: 572

Iraq (continued)
International Atomic Energy Agency (IAEA), actions in, **2004:** 1119, 1121–22; **2005:** 1115
Investment Incentive Agreement with U.S. Overseas Private Investment Corporation, **2005:** 647–48, 652
Iran–Iraq Arms Non-Proliferation Act. *See* Iran–Iraq Arms Non-Proliferation Act (1992)
Iraq and Afghanistan, Emergency Supplemental Appropriations Act for Defense and for the Reconstruction of 2004, **2005:** 229, 229*n*, 231
Iraqi High Tribunal, **2005:** 191; **2006:** 259, 269–72
Iraq–Kuwait Boundary Demarcation Commission, **1991-99:** 590*n*, 1928
juvenile combatants in, **2008:** 302–4, 308–9
Liberation Act (1998), **1991-99:** 538; **2002:** 934; **2003:** 983
Military Claims Act (MCA), **2005:** 982–83
military interventions in
assassination attempt on President George H.W. Bush, response to, **1991-99:** 2124–25
enforcing UN Security Council resolutions (2003), **2005:** 101, 454
authorization for use of force in, **2002:** 933–37
legal basis, **2003:** 961–74; **2005:** 215, 949–51
post-war governance and programs, **2003:** 974–93
UN resolutions and, **2002:** 937–47, 956–57
failure to comply with weapons inspections, response to, **1991-99:** 2125–32
Gulf war. *See* Gulf war
mistreatment of prisoners of war by, **2003:** 1000–1001
Multinational Force in. *See* Multinational Force in Iraq
occupation, **2005:** 951, 957–60. *See also* Coalition Provisional Authority (CPA), occupying, *this heading*
oil-for-food program, **1991-99:** 1101, 1928–36; **2000:** 444, 617, 619–22, 624; **2001:** 815, 816; **2002:** 894–97; **2003:** 974–75, 984, 991-992; **2004:** 884, 893–900; **2005:** 870–73
Independent Inquiry Committee (IIC)
2005 reports, **2005:** 873–76
information, protection of, **2005:** 876–78
transparency and investigations, **2005:** 871–72
radiological material, removal from, **2004:** 1163–64
Refugee Crisis in Iraq Act of 2007, **2008:** 31–34
refugees from, exemption from certain bars to admission to U.S., **2007:** 70; **2008:** 29

Iraq (continued)
response by U.S. to attempted assassination of U.S. president by, **1991-99**: 2124–25
response to humanitarian crisis, **1991-99**: 2112–13
sanctions on or relating to, **1991-99**: 856–57, 2132; **2000**: 617–21, 623–24; **2001**: 18, 815–17; **2004**: 430, 491–92, 883–93, 895–99
after invasion of Kuwait, **1991-99**: 1924–31, 1935, 1975, 2051
arms embargo, modifications to U.S., **2004**: 884, 890–93
arms embargo, UN, **2007**: 1007
blocked assets in U.S., **2000**: 617–18, 623–24; **2003**: 460, 545–46, 554–55, 909–11, 916–23
blocking assets of persons threatening stabilization of (No. 13438), **2007**: 818, 989; **2008**: 805–6
economic, **2004**: 883–89
humanitarian activities exceptions, **2003**: 907–8
Iraq Sanctions Act (1990), **2000**: 618; **2003**: 555, 909, 912–14; **2004**: 491–92, 890–91; **2008**: 459, 465
suspension of, **2008**: 459
national emergencies, **2003**: 916–18; **2004**: 884, 885, 889; **2005**: 869
oil-for-food program. *See* oil-for-food program, *this heading*
stabilization efforts, individuals threatening (Executive Order 13438), **2007**: 818–20; **2008**: 805–6
suspension of, **2003**: 912–18, 919–20; **2008**: 459
on Syria, undermining stabilization of Iraq (Executive Order No. 13338, 13460), **2008**: 799–800
travel-related, **2004**: 887; **2006**: 1015–19
vesting of blocked assets, **2003**: 909–12, 920–23
sovereign authority, **2004**: 883, 884, 1046
Strategic Framework Agreement for a Relationship of Friendship and Cooperation between U.S. and Iraq (2008), **2008**: 859–62
Syrian support for, **2004**: 902–3; **2005**: 133, 886–88
terrorism and, **1991-99**: 2111, 2123; **2004**: 106, 1046–51
collection of judgments under Terrorism Risk Insurance Act, **2003**: 554–57
designation as state sponsor of terrorism, **1991-99**: 508–9, 1223; **2003**: 168; **2005**: 580
rescinded, **2004**: 103–4; **2005**: 506; **2006**: 177, 179–80
Iraqi government actions against, **2008**: 462, 872
National Defense Authorization Act (2008), Presidential waiver of terrorism-related exceptions to immunity with respect to, **2008**: 457–63

Iraq (continued)
not cooperating fully with U.S. antiterrorism activities, **1991-99**: 508
September 11 terrorist attacks, claims for damages by victims of, **2003**: 458, 551–52
U.S. litigation against under FSIA terrorism exception, **2008**: 463–71
Trade and Investment Framework Agreement (TIFA) with U.S., **2005**: 646
travel to, restrictions on, **1991-99**: 49–51; **2001**: 13–14; **2003**: 11–12
exceptions to, **2000**: 118–19
UN Compensation Commission, claims against Iraq, **1991-99**: 1099–1106; **2000**: 444; **2004**: 430
UN Security Council Resolutions related to, **2006**: 1235–38; **2008**: 460, 731
U.S. diplomatic offices in, **2004**: 451–52
U.S. presence in, **2008**: 857–62
U.S. tax policy, **2004**: 659–60
U.S.S. Stark, claims related to attack on, **1989-90**: 217–19
war crimes liability, **2003**: 229–30, 1000–1004, 1005–8
weapons, **1991-99**: 2100, 2110–11, 2116, 2120, 2266, 2362
international inspections of, **1991-99**: 2125–32
weapons of mass destruction program, **2004**: 891, 1076, 1093, 1164
Withdrawal of United States Forces from Iraq and the Organization of Their Activities during Their Temporary Presence in Iraq, Agreement on (2008) (Security Agreement), **2008**: 859–62
IRCA. *See* Immigration Reform and Control Act (IRCA) (1986)
Ireland
aviation preclearance agreement with, **2008**: 512–13
child and family support enforcement, reciprocity in, **1991-99**: 1871; **2001**: 51; **2008**: 759
electronic commerce policy, **1991-99**: 1527–28
extradition and mutual legal assistance, **2000**: 180, 186*n*; **2002**: 61, 62, 67; **2006**: 137, 147
Hague Child Abduction Convention, compliance with, **2003**: 127
immunity of organ of government under FSIA, **2003**: 510–12
Irish Peace Process Cultural and Training Program Act (1998), **1991-99**: 78
Lusitania (sunken ocean liner), salvage of, **2005**: 760
nonimmigrant visa waiver pilot program, **1991-99**: 76
objections to U.S. reservations to Genocide Convention, **1989-90**: 144
UK Supplementary extradition treaty and, **1991-99**: 428–35
U.S. defense relationship, **1989-90**: 151, 152
U.S. judicial assistance in, **2007**: 97–99

Ireland, Northern
extradition treaty with U.S. by Great Britain and, **2005**: 69–71, 75–77; **2006**: 117–18
IRF Act (International Religious Freedom Act of 1998). *See* Religion and religious freedom
Irish Peace Process Cultural and Training Program Act (**1998**), **1991-99**: 78
IRTPA. *See* Intelligence Reform and Terrorism Prevention Act of 2004 (IRTPA)
Isle of Man
money laundering, **2004**: 135
Israel. *See also* Middle East Conflict, Israeli-Palestinian
abduction of Israeli soldier, U.S. position on, **2006**: 1233–35
anti-Semitism and, **2004**: 275, 277
antitrust assistance agreement, **1991-99**: 1550
child abduction issues, **1991-99**: 354, 355, 366–67, 370–71; **2004**: 54, 60
Hague Child Abduction Convention, compliance with, **2003**: 127
citizenship laws, **1991-99**: 24–25
conflict with Palestinians. *See also* Middle East Conflict, Israeli-Palestinian
claims against in U.S. courts
claim by Palestinian against Israel dismissed on head of state, act of state grounds, **2005**: 566–67, 581–83
Palestine Liberation Organization (PLO), action against arising from death of Israeli national, **2005**: 503–4, 531
Palestinian claims against Israel under ATS, **2005**: 566–67, 581–83
deportation for foreign policy reasons, **1991-99**: 126–28
destruction of, Iranian threat, **2005**: 319; **2007**: 379–80, 995
Eichmann extradition from Argentina to, **1989-90**: 95
extradition and mutual legal assistance, **1991-99**: 391, 452; **2000**: 178, 179, 186*n*; **2005**: 69, 71, 74–75
extradition request to U.S.
exception for political crimes, **1989-90**: 79–80
rule of noninquiry in, **1989-90**: 80–88
free trade agreement, **2004**: 618
head-of-state immunity, **2003**: 571
Holocaust archives agreement, **2007**: 380–82
Holocaust-related compensation and retribution, **1991-99**: 517, 572, 576, 1050, 1053
compensation plan for Nazi era victims and victims' heirs, **2000**: 454–55; **2007**: 421–26
General Settlement Fund (GSF) agreement (Nazi-era claims), effect on relations with U.S., **2005**: 474

Israel (continued)
Human Rights Council, focus on, **2007:** 287
intellectual property rights Watch List, **2006:** 768; **2007:** 608, 610; **2008:** 605*n*
Jerusalem. *See* U.S. policy on status of Jerusalem, *this heading*
Lebanon, conflict with Hezbollah in, **2006:** 1034–42, 1225–33
Lebanon Ceasefire Understanding (1996), **2006:** 1035*n*
liability of companies formerly owned by, **2003:** 512–14
Libyan vessel denied entry to Gaza, **2008:** 647–48
Magen David Adom, **2005:** 1043; **2006:** 1101, 1103–4
missile defense cooperation, **2004:** 1066
money laundering, **2004:** 135
non-legally binding documents and, **1991-99:** 686
non-North Atlantic Treaty Organization (NATO) ally, designation as, **2005:** 1044
nonproliferation issues, **2005:** 1089
organizations designated under IOIA, **1991-99:** 1314
preemptive military action, **2002:** 955–56
record of place of birth for U.S. passport, **2003:** 485–501; **2004:** 452–54; **2006:** 530–47; **2007:** 437–39; **2008:** 447–54
red crystal, adoption of as distinctive emblem, in addition to Red Cross/Red Crescent under Geneva Conventions, **2005:** 1042–43
service of process by international mail, **2005:** 850–52
sovereign immunity for private company indirectly owned by, **2002:** 481, 488
Syria and, **2004:** 902
trade and investment issues, **1991-99:** 658, 1484–86
Treaty and Protocol with Egypt, **1989-90:** 206–7
United Nations and, **1991-99:** 1022–27
U.S. defense relationship, **1989-90:** 151, 152
U.S. passports valid only for travel to, **1991-99:** 41–49, 807
U.S. policy on status of Jerusalem, **1989-90:** 264–68; **1991-99:** 1135–38; **2002:** 243; **2003:** 489–91; **2004:** 452–54; **2006:** 530–47; **2007:** 437–39; **2008:** 447–54
Warsaw Convention litigation and, **1991-99:** 1350
Israel–United States Binational Industrial Research and Development Foundation, 1991-99: 1314
Italy
arms control and nonproliferation. *See* Nonproliferation, *subheading*: country-specific issues
asylum and refugee status, **1991-99:** 153
cultural property
in armed conflict, **1991-99:** 2199

Italy (continued)
memorandum of understanding on protection of, **2001**: 769–72; **2006**: 897, 901
preservation of American heritage in, **2008:** 736–37
driftnet fishing, **1991-99**: 1732–36
eminent domain and, **2003**: 262
evidence gathering abroad, **2005**: 843–46
execution against property of foreign state, **1989-90**: 296–302
extradition and mutual legal assistance, **1991-99**: 391, 400, 421; **2000**: 180, 186*n*; **2006**: 137, 147
hoasca, arrests for use of, **2005**: 144
intellectual property rights Watch List, **2006**: 768; **2007:** 610
International Court of Justice case against, for interference with foreign investment, **1989-90**: 418
International Space Station Partners Agreement, **1991-99**: 1642
Kosovo peace process, role in, **2005**: 935
Middle East peace process and, **1991-99**: 134, 2031, 2039
money laundering, **2004**: 135
nonimmigrant visa waiver pilot program, **1989-90**: 27
objections to U.S. reservations to Genocide Convention, **1989-90**: 144
Open Skies (aerial observation) treaty, **2002**: 1029
peacekeeping missions by, **1991-99**: 2029
service of process in, **2002**: 877–79
terrorism and
cooperation in antiterrorism actions, **2002**: 890
Nuclear Terrorism, Global Initiative to Combat, **2006**: 1295–96
request for transfer of terrorist prisoner, **1989-90**: 72–76
World War II-era restitution and claims, **1991-99**: 1044, 1053
ITAR. *See* International Traffic in Arms Regulations (ITAR)
ITER. *See* International Thermonuclear Experimental Reactor Consortium (ITER)
ITU. *See* International Telecommunication Union (ITU)

J

Jackson-Vanik Amendment, 2006: 746–47*n*
Jamaica
aviation agreement, **2002**: 597; **2008**: 512
consular notification, **1991-99**: 262
Cooperating Nation Information Exchange System (CNIES), agreement with U.S. concerning, **2005**: 146
coral reef protection, **1991-99**: 1755
drug trade, **2001**: 120; **2002**: 124; **2003**: 181; **2004**: 133–34; **2005**: 135; **2006**: 213; **2007**: 163; **2008**: 113
maritime counter-drug trade agreements, **1991-99**: 499, 1606

Jamaica (continued)
extradition and mutual legal assistance, **1991-99**: 447–50; **2000**: 186*n*
family support enforcement, **1991-99**: 1866
forest conservation agreement, **2004**: 745; **2008**: 722
intellectual property rights Watch List, **2006**: 768; **2007**: 610
Inter-American Convention Against Corruption, party to, **2006**: 238
real property tax exemptions, **2001**: 545
trade and investment agreements, **1991-99**: 1466
trafficking in persons actions, **2005**: 162
Tropical Forest Conservation Act agreement, **2004**: 745; **2008**: 722

Japan
act of state doctrine, legal decision related to, **2005**: 535
air transport agreement with U.S., **1991-99**: 1359–61
Antarctica, claims to, **2004**: 732
anti-suit injunction, **2006**: 958–63; **2008**: 764–71
antitrust issues, **1991-99**: 1534–36, 1551
Apartheid Convention and, **2004**: 358
arms control and nonproliferation. *See* Nonproliferation, *subheading*: country-specific issues
aviation relations discussions (2007), **2007**: 532
bill of lading agreement, **1991-99**: 1846
Burma, sanctions on, **1991-99**: 1881
citizenship of dual national who served in Japanese military, **1991-99**: 21–23
comfort women, claims against Japan, **2001**: 430–57; **2002**: 494–503; **2003**: 522–23; **2004**: 472, 475–76, 483
  Alien Tort Statute (ATS) action initiated against Japan, **2005**: 475–81
  nonjusticiable political questions in, **2001**: 445–57
  retroactive application of FSIA to claims by Korean "comfort women," **2002**: 494–503
  sovereign immunity, **2001**: 430–45
consular notification, **1991-99**: 310
cultural objects protection, **1991-99**: 1804
customs agreement, **2004**: 626
extradition and mutual legal assistance, **2000**: 179, 186*n*; **2003**: 143–45; **2005**: 69, 72–73, 78–79; **2006**: 148
fisheries, regulation of, **1991-99**: 1703–7, 1726, 1738; **2005**: 736–37
Food Aid Convention, **1991-99**: 936
global positioning system technology, **1991-99**: 1635–37; **2004**: 740–41

Japan (continued)
health care abroad, **2004:** 49, 50
Inter-American Tropical Tuna Commission, **2000:** 307
International Coffee Organization and, **2004:** 413
ITER International Fusion Energy Organization, **2006:** 893
jus cogens violation as claimed waiver of immunity under FSIA, **2003:** 514–15
Kyoto Protocol, **1991-99:** 1677–78
Marianas Islands, administration of, **1991-99:** 838
maritime issues, **1991-99:** 1562, 1590, 1755
salvage of Japanese minisubmarine sunk off Pearl Harbor, **1991-99:** 1619–20
migratory bird and animal protection agreement, **1991-99:** 1773, 1775
military commissions used for Japanese war crimes in World War II, **2005:** 969
money laundering, **2004:** 135
most-favored-nation status, **2006:** 755
nonimmigrant visa waiver pilot program, **1989-90:** 27
non-North Atlantic Treaty Organization (NATO) ally, designation as, **2005:** 1044
North Korea and, **2002:** 1050–51
outer space agreements, **1991-99:** 1640–47
Peace Treaty with (1951), **2000:** 501–3, 505, 506–12, 515–31; **2001:** 431–32, 446–53, 455–57; **2004:** 442–43; **2005:** 476–78
claims of nonparty nations preempted by, **2000:** 533–35, 536–39
post-World War II occupation, **2005:** 298
prohibition of service of process by Federal Express, **2005:** 847–52
sea transport of radioactive materials, **2001:** 700, 701–3
Security Council and, **2005:** 457; **2007:** 402; **2008:** 383
service of process in, **2004:** 869
shark protection, **2004:** 766
Space Station Intergovernmental Agreement, **1989-90:** 482
Special Measures Law Concerning U.S. Antidumping Act of 1916, **2006:** 959; **2008:** 764–71
sunken government property, **2004:** 718, 722, 723–24
trade agreements with U.S.
autos and auto parts, **1991-99:** 1451–52
Enterprise for the Americas Initiative and, **1991-99:** 1462
investment initiatives, **1991-99:** 1463
Japan–U.S. Framework for a New Economic Partnership, **1991-99:** 1448–51
trade claims, **1991-99:** 1408, 1410, 1411, 1504, 1505

Japan (continued)
trafficking in women and children in, **1991-99:** 912
Treaty of 1965 (Japan–Korea), **2005:** 481
U.S. apples, import restrictions on, **2005:** 622–23
U.S. request for extradition of Nicaraguan diplomat from, **1989-90:** 77–78
war claims by Asian nationals against, **2000:** 532–40
whaling activities, **2003:** 803; **2004:** 755; **2007:** 720–21
whaling research program, **2001:** 684–85
World War II-era claims, **1991-99:** 1134; **2001:** 197*n*; **2003:** 468
allegations of sexual slavery, **2003:** 394, 396, 522–23
"comfort women" cases. *See* comfort women, claims against Japan, *this heading*
prisoners' claims, **2002:** 434–61
slave and forced labor of prisoners claims against Japanese corporations, **2000:** 500–5; **2001:** 197*n*, 339–40*n*, 447–48*n*; **2004:** 441–45
claims of allied prisoners, **2000:** 505–31
claims of nonallied prisoners, **2000:** 531–40
against U.S. for Japanese actions, **2003:** 475–76
WTO dispute. *See* World Trade Organization (WTO)
Jarvis Island
sovereignty of U.S. and, **2003:** 485
Jay Treaty (1794)
duty exemption for cigarettes from Canada and application to U.S. states' tobacco settlement, **2008:** 170–74
claims alleging violation of, NAFTA Chapter 11, **2008:** 170–74
JCIC Agreements (Joint Compliance and Inspection Commission), 2005: 1045–48
Jersey
money laundering, **2004:** 135
Jerusalem, status of, 1989-90: 264–68; **1991-99:** 1135–38; **2002:** 243; **2003:** 489–91; **2004:** 452–54; **2006:** 530–47; **2008:** 447–54
Johnson (Gambling Devices) Act, 1991-99: 1625–29
Johnston Atoll
sovereignty of U.S. and, **2003:** 485
Joint and several liability, 2001: 379–80
Joint Compliance and Inspection Commission (JCIC Agreements), 2005: 1045–48
Joint declarations, generally, 1991-99: 683, 688
Jordan
agreement with U.S. on Free Trade Area, **2001:** 213–14, 665, 670–74
bilateral investment treaty, **1991-99:** 1466

Jordan (continued)
chancery in U.S., **2004:** 559–60
claimed neutral status during Gulf War, **1991-99:** 1207, 2102–6
deportation and, **1991-99:** 126
Economic Support Fund (U.S.), assistance from, **2005:** 202
extradition and mutual legal assistance, **1991-99:** 401–3; **2000:** 184, 186*n*
free trade agreement, **2004:** 618; **2005:** 757
head-of-state immunity, **2001:** 536
immunity of government officials in employment actions, **1991-99:** 1188–89, 1296
Israeli-Palestinian conflict, King Abdullah involved in mediation of, **2005:** 905, 907
Middle East peace process, participation in, **1991-99:** 1986–88, 1991, 1995–97, 2003; **2004:** 951
non-North Atlantic Treaty Organization (NATO) ally, designation as, **2005:** 1044
parental access to children, MOU on cooperation with U.S., **2006:** 103
reservations to terrorism financing convention, **2004:** 197–98
Judgment debtor, immunity as, 2000: 590–93
Judicial assistance. *See also* Evidence; Service of process abroad
in antiterrorism effort, **2001:** 103–4, 105, 106, 896, 901–2, 907–8, 911–13, 935–41
antitrust case and gathering of evidence, **2006:** 969–70
apostille. *See* Authentication
authentication of documents. *See* Authentication
in criminal matter in China, **2000:** 160–62
discovery abroad. *See* Evidence
electronic records, **2004:** 66, 69
extradition and mutual legal assistance. *See* Extradition
to foreign and international tribunals, **1991-99:** 383–84, 573
in Ireland, **2007:** 97–99
letters rogatory, **1991-99:** 453–54, 455
P.R.C. rules, **2000:** 161, 162
Vienna Convention on Consular Relations on, **2000:** 161
medallion stamp guarantees, **2001:** 59
prior to initiation of judicial proceeding, **1991-99:** 385
request for, **2000:** 161, 162
at International Criminal tribunal for Former Yugoslavia, **2000:** 255–71; **2003:** 214–19
responsible U.S. agencies, **2001:** 55–56
service of process, **2003:** 865–68. *See also* Service of process abroad
in foreign countries, **2000:** 150–52, **2004:** 866–75
role of private attorneys in U.S., **2004:** 70–71, 839–40

Judicial assistance (continued)
travel of foreign officials in matters of, **2000**: 158
U.S.–Russia agreements, **2006**: 107–10
U.S.–USSR memorandum of understanding on Nazi war criminals, **1989-90**: 99–100
Judicial procedure, 1991-99: 1090. *See also* Evidence; Judicial assistance; Service of process abroad
access of foreign nationals to U.S. courts, **1989-90**: 242–43, 247–48; **1991-99**: 1138–42
access of unlawful combatant detainees to counsel or court, **2003**: 1024. *See also* Detainees, military
access of U.S. citizens to Cuban courts, **2002**: 237–42
capital punishment cases. *See also* Capital punishment
human rights and sentencing in, **2001**: 294–302
right to fair trial and due process in, **2000**: 389–90, 392–96; **2008**: 376, 377
courtroom interpreters, **2003**: 82
deposition abroad. *See* Evidence
detention and trial of suspected terrorists by U.S. military. *See* Detainees, military
doctrine of international comity. *See* Comity
equality of arms in, **2000**: 392–96
evaluation of impartiality of foreign court, **2000**: 412–14. *See also* Comity; Jurisdiction
execution against property of foreign state. *See* Foreign Sovereign Immunities Act (FSIA) (1976)
extradition process. *See* Extradition
Fifth Amendment invoked based on fear of foreign prosecution, **1991-99**: 571–76
forum shopping, **2004**: 819–24
gatekeeping requirement of U.S. Code, **2001**: 298–99
Hague Conventions on judicial assistance, **2003**: 859–63. *See also* Evidence; Service of process abroad
human rights protections, **1991-99**: 853
injunction against concurrent proceeding in foreign court. *See* Anti-suit injunctions
international prisoner transfer, **2001**: 52–55
local standards, **2001**: 36–37
procedural default. *See* Consular notification and access, *subheading*: U.S. litigation concerning
prolonged detention. *See* Human Rights, *subheading*: detention; Removal of aliens from U.S., *subheading*: detention and
protection of civil and political rights. *See* Human rights; International Covenant on Civil and Political Rights (ICCPR)

Judicial procedure (continued)
racial discrimination in, **2001**: 258, 259–60
rule of noninquiry in extradition request. *See* Extradition, *subheading*: non-inquiry, rule of
trial in absentia, **2001**: 87–89
UN resolution on integrity of judicial system, **2004**: 338–39
Judiciary Act (1789), **2001**: 230; **2003**: 358, 359, 371; **2004**: 343, 367, 997
Jurisdiction. *See also* Foreign Sovereign Immunities Act (FSIA) (1976); *specific tribunals and subjects*
Act of Mar. 3, 1875 as conferring, **2006**: 84
admiralty, **2004**: 485, 830, 832
agency or instrumentality of foreign state, **2002**: 488–90
antitrust law
civil claims, **1991-99**: 1529–33
criminal prosecution, **1991-99**: 1533–39
European Union–U.S. agreements, **1991-99**: 1540–45
international enforcement guidelines, **1991-99**: 1552
arbitration vs. court, **2004**: 809–14. *See also* Arbitration
in child custody cases, **2004**: 61. *See also* Children, *subheading*: international abduction
Uniform Child Custody Jurisdiction Act (1988), **1991-99**: 372, 378
Uniform Child Custody Jurisdiction and Enforcement Act (1997), **1991-99**: 378
civilians living abroad with military, **2004**: 168–71
claims by former U.S. employees in Vietnam, **2002**: 413
claims growing out of treaties, **1991-99**: 660–66
comity principle and, **1991-99**: 1529, 1530, 1532–33, 1537–39; **2004**: 432, 436, 437; **2006**: 945–46
commercial law. *See* Commercial law
conventions on
Brussels Convention on Jurisdiction and Enforcement of Judgments in Civil and Commercial Matters, **2005**: 789
Choice of Court Convention, **2005**: 213, 787–89, 791
Hague Convention on Jurisdiction and Recognition of Judgments (2005), **1991-99**: 1826; **2000**: 736, 737–40, 741; **2001**: 786, 789; **2004**: 829
Crimes Against the Peace and Security of Mankind, Draft Code of, **1991-99**: 578–79
cultural issues. *See* Cultural issues
cybercrime, **2003**: 193, 202–6
delegation of, to ICC, **2000**: 283–84. *See also* International Criminal Court (ICC)
diplomatic missions, claims related to employment by, **1989-90**: 389

Jurisdiction (continued)
electronic commerce issues, **2000**: 740–41; **2001**: 794–95; **2003**: 901–5
enforcement of judgments, **1991-99**: 1826–41; **2003**: 840–42
Brussels Convention on Jurisdiction and Enforcement of Judgments in Civil and Commercial Matters, **2005**: 789
in enforcement of maintenance obligations and family support, **1991-99**: 1862, 1871–78
Hague Convention on Jurisdiction and Recognition of Judgments (2005), **1991-99**: 1826; **2000**: 736, 737–40, 741; **2001**: 786, 789; **2003**: 840–42; **2004**: 829
in U.S. courts, **1991-99**: 1833–41
exclusion hearing requirement for undocumented aliens interdicted in territorial waters, **1991-99**: 172–81
in exclusive economic zone, **1989-90**: 463–64, **2008**: 643, 644
exhaustion of domestic remedies. *See* Remedies, *subheading*: exhaustion of remedies, requirement for
extradition. *See* Extradition
extraterritorial criminal offenses, **2002**: 131–37, 421, 422–23, 454; **2008**: 120, 123–30
extraterritorial jurisdiction and conflicts of jurisdiction, **1989-90**: 100–7, 109; **1991-99**: 1810, 1857; **2004**: 124–25, 168–72; **2005**: 789–91; **2008**: 232, 237
aircraft sabotage, **1991-99**: 541–43
ATS, **2008**: 218, 219, 228
Constitution, U.S., **2008**: 892, 894, 897
deference to foreign courts in concurrent civil litigation, **2002**: 859–64
extradition, U.S.–UK treaty on, **2006**: 119–20
flag-state jurisdiction, **1991-99**: 1600–8
gambling on American flag vessels, **1991-99**: 1621
in Guantanamo, **1991-99**: 190–91; **2008**: 897–98
hostage taking and airline hijacking, **1991-99**: 501–8
on space station, **1991-99**: 1643, 1646–47
in territorial sea, **1991-99**: 1623–24
terrorism, **1991-99**: 482, 484–95
torture, **2004**: 172
failure to contest in court as waiver of immunity, **1989-90**: 281–83
of foreign tax claims, **2002**: 837–41
forum shopping, **2004**: 819–24
habeas corpus proceedings. *See* Habeas corpus
immunity. *See also* Consular offices and personnel, *subheading*: immunity and inviolability; Diplomatic missions and personnel, *subheadings*: immunity *and* inviolability; Head-of-state immunity; Immunity

Jurisdiction (continued)
of agents and instrumentalities of U.S. government, **2002**: 245–46
of artwork and cultural objects, **2004**: 792–96
criminal jurisdiction and foreign officials, **2008**: 491–92
Indian Claims Commission Act, **2002**: 378
individuals detained by the Department of Defense at Guantanamo Bay, **2004**: 978, 979
International Civil Aviation Organization, **2000**: 663–67
international civil litigation, U.S., **2004**: 840–82
International Covenant on Civil and Political Rights, **2002**: 461–62
International Criminal Court. *See* International Criminal Court (ICC)
international criminal tribunals, **1991-99**: 581, 587, 595–96; **2001**: 166–67; **2004**: 375
International Frequency Registration Board, **1989-90**: 403–4, 405–6
international intellectual property rights, **2000**: 740
International Seabed Authority, **2004**: 685
Internet transactions as basis for personal jurisdiction, **2003**: 901–5
Iran–U.S. claims tribunal, **2003**: 448–50; **2004**: 415, 417, 420–24
Iraqi war crimes, prosecution of, **2003**: 1005–7
location and construction of diplomatic missions in U.S., **1989-90**: 377–81
loss of citizenship, review of determinations relating to, **2008**: 4–6
maritime accidents in international waters, investigation of, **2006**: 825–28
military. *See* Military activities
nexus with forum, **2008**: 755
nonjusticiable political issues, **2004**: 206–14, 351–52*n*, 431–32, 434–36, 439–41, 443–44, 453–54; **2006**: 322–24; **2008**: 444, 445, 447–54
nonreviewability of alien removal order, **1991-99**: 91–92
nonreviewability of consular decisions, **1991-99**: 70–71
Organization of American States Headquarters Agreement, **1991-99**: 1016–17
passive personality, **1991-99**: 503–4; **2002**: 132–33
personal jurisdiction, general and specific, **2003**: 567–69
protection of children, Hague convention on (1996), **1991-99**: 1859–61, 1876; **2000**: 121; **2004**: 63, 830
piracy, **2008**: 125–30
proposed reservation to Hague Convention on the International Recovery and Maintenance of Child Support re certain, **2008**: 755–56

Jurisdiction (continued)
reservations to transnational organized crime convention and protocols re certain, **2004**: 145, 146–48, 150, 158
right of private action in U.S. courts for acts of torture in foreign countries, **1989-90**: 191–94
rights of coastal states, **2001**: 713; **2008**: 136, 652
rules of private international law, **2000**: 736, 737–39
scientific research rules, **1989-90**: 478–80
service and, **2000**: 435. *See also* Service of process abroad
ships and vessels, **1989-90**: 454–55; **2003**: 733–34
cargo claims, fora for litigation of, **2003**: 845–47
detained vessels under PSI, **2004**: 1084–85, 1088–89
flagged vessels, **1989-90**: 454–55
foreign ship, **2003**: 733–34
maritime accidents in international waters, investigation of, **1989-90**: 447–48
maritime interdiction in international waters, **1989-90**: 448–49
offenses committed aboard, **2000**: 363–64; **2008**: 125–30, 135–36, 924, 926–28
stateless, treaty implementation in U.S., **2004**: 678
U.S. warship in territorial waters of Brazil, **1989-90**: 476–77
in state succession cases, **2000**: 569–70, 574
tax disputes, international, **2001**: 485–88
torture, **2004**: 172; **2008**: 123–25
trafficking in persons, **2008**: 120
UN International Tribunal, **2000**: 213–15
universal, **1991-99**: 503, 637–39, 1265; **2003**: 297, 396; **2008**: 128–29
U.S. Coast Guard, **2004**: 1109
U.S. War Crimes Act, **1991-99**: 509–15
in U.S. courts
alien for torture committed abroad, **2000**: 382
Alien Tort Statute. *See* Alien Tort Statute (ATS)
alienage diversity statute, **1991-99**: 35–36, 769–75, 1141–42; **2001**: 227–35; **2002**: 227–31
bombing of U.S. embassy in Kenya, claims against U.S. arising from, **2001**: 417, 418
civil tort actions by alien, **2000**: 399–400
Constitutional provisions, **2000**: 738
criminal, **2001**: 103–4, 105, 106, 361, 905, 924; **2008**: 120, 123–25, 125–36
extradition to Hong Kong, **2000**: 190–203
extradition-related, **2001**: 72–87, 484–85
Federal Tort Claims Act, **2001**: 418

Jurisdiction (continued)
Foreign Sovereign Immunities Act, **2000**: 476, 477, 478, 578–79, 592–93; **2001**: 429, 463–64
head-of-state immunity and, **2001**: 510–31, 536–37
Mexico, legality of U.S. arrest in, **2001**: 326–34
military commissions, **2001**: 877–79
offenses committed aboard ship or aircraft, **2000**: 363–64; **2008**: 125–36
procedural default, **2000**: 44, 62–63
regardless of manner of bringing to U.S., **2004**: 341
special maritime and territorial jurisdiction, **2004**: 171–72
torture, **2008**: 125–30
Torture Victim Protection Act. *See* Torture
trafficking in persons, **2008**: 120
WW II claims. *See* World War II
Vienna Convention on Consular Relations, disputes arising under, **2000**: 32*n*
Jus cogens, **2000**: 419, 473–74, 478, 479–80, 481–85; **2001**: 396, 430–32, 436, 437, 438–43; **2005**: 395–96, 581, 583
Alien Tort Statute claims, **2001**: 327; **2006**: 436, 442, 445. *See also* Alien Tort Statute (ATS)
capital punishment and, **1991-99**: 739, 965–67, 974*n*, 976–78; **2001**: 312–15
customary international law and, **1991-99**: 976; **2003**: 381–82; **2004**: 530–31
definition, **1991-99**: 976, 1190–91; **2003**: 514; **2004**: 530; **2006**: 647*n*
International Convention for the Suppression of Terrorist Bombings and, **2003**: 244
International Law Commission on, **2000**: 483–84
nonderogable provisions of ICCPR as distinct from, **2006**: 1122
right of self-determination, **2003**: 244
Vienna Convention on the Law of Treaties and, **2003**: 244
violation of
cause of action based on violation of, **2003**: 363, 381–82
corporate liability for violations of *jus cogens* and other norms, **2005**: 396, 823
extrajudicial killings as, **2007**: 507
Foreign Sovereign Immunities Act (FSIA), no implied waiver of immunity for, **2007**: 507
genocide as *jus cogens* violation, **1991-99**: 976–77, 1115
immunity and, **1991-99**: 1190–91; **2003**: 510, 514–15, 522, 563–64

Jus cogens (continued)
Foreign Sovereign Immunities Act, no exception to immunity under, **1991-99**: 1133, 1190–95, 1260; **2000**: 479–80, 481–85; **2001**: 396, 430–32, 436, 437, 438–43, 481; **2002**: 467, 491–94, 501; **2003**: 514–15, 522, 523, 563–64; **2006**: 646–50, 678, 680–81. *See also* Foreign Sovereign Immunities Act (FSIA) (1976), *subheading*: exceptions to immunity
head-of-state immunity and, **2004**: 529, 530–31
sovereign immunity, **2000**: 479–80, 481–85
violation as claimed waiver of immunity, **1991-99**: 1191–93; **2003**: 514–15
official torture and cruel, inhuman, degrading punishment as, **2007**: 178
refoulement to danger of torture not, **2007**: 65–66
sex trade as *jus cogens* violation, **2003**: 514
torture as *jus cogens* violation, **1991-99**: 1115, 1190–91, 1196, 1208; **2004**: 304*n*; **2006**: 1122; **2007**: 178–79; **2008**: 270
Justice for United States Prisoners of War Act (proposed), **2002**: 456–60

K
Kazakhstan
act of state doctrine and, **2002**: 574
asylum seekers returned to Uzbekistan by, **2006**: 60–61
diplomatic relations, **1991-99**: 1173
domestic violence laws, lack of, **2005**: 313
import ban on Caspian Sea beluga sturgeon products, **2005**: 754
intellectual property rights, **2006**: 769
Lisbon Protocol to the Strategic Arms Reduction Treaty (START), party to, **2005**: 1045*n*
longshore work prohibition on alien crewmen from, **2002**: 757; **2003**: 764
nuclear-related issues. *See* Nonproliferation, *subheading*: country-specific issues
strategic offensive arms agreements, **1991-99**: 2210–17, 2218, 2221, 2222; **2004**: 1053–55; **2006**: 1252
succession issues, **1991-99**: 742, 750–61, 1170
trade and investment issues, **1991-99**: 1455, 1466
Kenya
aviation agreement, **2008**: 511
bombing of U.S. embassy in, **1991-99**: 2133; **2001**: 417–21; **2002**: 461–62; **2005**: 372, 517–21, 578–80
claims related to, **2005**: 517–21, 578–80; **2006**: 578–81
extradition and mutual legal assistance, **2000**: 185*n*

Kenya (continued)
International Criminal Tribunal for Rwanda (ICTR), obligations to, **2005:** 193; **2008:** 147
U.S. defense relationship, **1989-90:** 151; **2006:** 278
waiver of Article 98 agreement with U.S. (nonsurrender of Americans to ICC), **2006:** 279
women's justice program, U.S. assistance for, **2005:** 307–8
Khan, A.Q., 2004: 1073, 1074, 1094, 1095, 1130, 1146, 1158, 1160
Kidnapping. *See* Children, *subheading*: international abduction; Crime, *subheading*: transborder arrest
Kingman Reef
sovereignty of U.S. and, **2003:** 485
Kiribati
environmental protection agreement, **2002:** 791
extradition and mutual legal assistance, **2000:** 185*n*
maritime interdiction agreement, **2008:** 650
Kleptocracy, 2006: 234–36
Knowledge requirement in U.S. law
material support for terrorist organization and, **2007:** 24–26
Korea, North (Democratic People's Republic of Korea (DPRK))
arms control, **2002:** 282; **2004:** 1070; **2007:** 1003. *See also* Nonproliferation, *subheadings*: country-specific issues, sanctions, U.S., *and* UN Security Council and
denial of consular access to U.S. citizen in, **2001:** 1–3
diplomatic relations, absence of, **1989-90:** 241; **2003:** 485
liaison offices, **1991-99:** 2325–26
drug trade, **2003:** 183–84; **2005:** 135; **2006:** 215
Export Administration Regulations, **2000:** 746–48
foreign tax credit restrictions, **2004:** 659
human rights violations, **2004:** 261; **2005:** 302
North Korean Human Rights Act of 2004, **2006:** 57–59
religious freedom violations, **1991-99:** 925; **2001:** 272; **2003:** 295, 296; **2004:** 270, 272; **2005:** 314–16; **2006:** 377
immigration issues
agreement with U.S. addressing dual nationals, **2001:** 34
refugees from, **2002:** 35–38; **2006:** 56–59
maritime vessels and, **2007:** 1084
money laundering, **2005:** 181–83
nonproliferation. *See* Nonproliferation, *subheading*: country-specific issues
North Korea Export Administration Regulations, **2000:** 746–48
territorial sea limits, **1989-90:** 462, 469
terrorism and, **2004:** 1153–55; **2008:** 89–94, 960–66

Korea, North (Democratic People's Republic of Korea (DPRK)) (continued)
not cooperating fully with antiterrorism with antiterrorism efforts, **1991-99**: 508; **2003**: 167; **2004**: 108; **2006**: 172; **2008**: 88–89
state sponsor of, **1991-99**: 508–9, 1223; **2001**: 819; **2003**: 168; **2004**: 103, 659; **2005**: 506; **2006**: 173, 577; **2007**: 235–36
rescission of designation as, **2008**: 89–94, 960–66
trade restrictions and embargo, **1991-99**: 1974; **2000**: 745–48; **2006**: 1269–70, 1299–1300; **2008**: 960–66
trafficking in persons, **2003**: 188; **2004**: 164; **2005**: 161–62; **2006**: 228; **2007**: 169; **2008**: 118
U.S. national security policy, **2001**: 850–53
U.S. non-recognition of, **1989-90**: 462, 469
weapons of mass destruction and. *See* Nonproliferation, *subheading*: country-specific issues
Korea, South (Republic of Korea (ROK)), **2004**: 261, 389, 607
"comfort women" suit against Japan. *See* Japan
democracy promotion and, **2004**: 389
disposition of unidentified remains of aviation disaster victims, **1991-99**: 347–48
drug trade (methamphetamines), **2007**: 164–66
extradition and mutual legal assistance, **1991-99**: 401, 450; **2000**: 179, 186*n*
fisheries, regulation of, **1991-99**: 1705–7; **2005**: 736–37
free trade agreement, **2007**: 585; **2008**: 571*n*
intellectual property rights Watch List, **2006**: 768; **2007**: 610
ITER International Fusion Energy Organization, **2006**: 893
judicial assistance in obtaining evidence, **2000**: 152–60
landmines in, **1991-99**: 2249–50
non-North Atlantic Treaty Organization (NATO) ally, designation as, **2005**: 1044
nonproliferation. *See* Nonproliferation, *subheading*: country-specific issues
post-World War II war claims against Japan, **2000**: 534, 535–36; **2001**: 450; **2002**: 444–46, 456; **2005**: 481
trade issues, **1991-99**: 1385, 1408, 1410, 1411, 1414, 1441–45; **2003**: 588; **2004**: 607; **2006**: 766
treaty relations with U.S. under Hague Protocol and Warsaw Convention, **2001**: 555–65; **2003**: 588
U.S. air services agreements, **2002**: 601, 603–4
U.S. military survey operation in coastal waters of, **2001**: 698–99
U.S.–Korea Consular Convention, **2000**: 156–57

Korea, South (Republic of Korea (ROK)) (continued)
visa waiver program, **2008:** 81–83
WTO complaint related to Continued Dumping and Subsidy Offset Act of 2000 (CDSOA), **2006:** 707
Korean Peninsula Energy Development Organization (**KEDO**), **1991-99:** 1314, 2323–29; **2003:** 1102
Kosovo
declaration of independence, **2008:** 815–16
Belgrade embassy of U.S., attack on following, **2008:** 493–95
European Union Rule of Law Mission in Kosovo (EULEX), **2008:** 439–43
human rights violations in, **1991-99:** 135, 147–48, 867, 962
military intervention in, **1991-99:** 248, 2138–62; **2004:** 971–72
peace process, **2005:** 934–35
Kosovo Albanian role, **2005:** 937–38
peace settlement elements, **2005:** 936–37
Serbian role, **2005:** 938
UN role, **2005:** 454, 935–36
U.S. role, **2005:** 934–35, 938–40; **2008:** 815–16
peacekeeping efforts in, **1991-99:** 524, 1168, 1958, 2026, 2031–43
sanctions with respect to, **1991-99:** 1958–62
status
declaration of independence, UN General Assembly request for ICJ advisory opinion, **2008:** 439
efforts to resolve, **2007:** 429–33
recognition of, **2008:** 433–39
temporary protected status for nationals of Province of, **1991-99:** 247–48
UN interim administration for, **1991-99:** 2036–37; **2008:** 845–47
violence control in, **2002:** 903
Ku Klux Klan Act of 1871, 2006: 82–83
Kurdistan Workers' Party (PKK), 2008: 102, 871–72
Kuwait. *See also* Gulf War
claims arising from Iraq invasion and occupation of, **1991-99:** 1099–1106; **2002:** 407–8, 944, 945; **2003:** 454–56, 985; **2004:** 430, 884, 895; **2006:** 584–92
immunity of UN envoy and wife, **2004:** 531–34
intellectual property rights Watch List, **2006:** 768, 769; **2007:** 610
Kuwaiti detainees at Guantanamo, **2003:** 1028; **2005:** 967
non-North Atlantic Treaty Organization (NATO) ally, designation as, **2005:** 1044
reflagging of merchant vessels during Iran–Iraq war, **2003:** 1038
trafficking in persons, **2005:** 159, 162; **2007:** 169; **2008:** 118
travel restrictions, **1991-99:** 49–50
war crimes charges against Iraq, **2003:** 1003, 1013

Kyoto Protocol, 1991-99: 1673–81; **2000**: 711–25; **2001**: 730–32, 733, 738; **2004**: 743–44; **2005**: 727–30; **2008**: 681–82, 689
Adaptation Fund, **2008**: 679
aviation emissions and, **2007**: 696–97
determining whether issues fall under Framework Convention or the Protocol, **2005**: 728
meeting of parties, **2005**: 728
U.S. proposal for new framework, **2007**: 673–78
U.S. refusal to ratify, **2005**: 215–17, 219; **2007**: 198; **2008**: 681
Kyrgyzstan
asylum seekers returned to Uzbekistan by, **2006**: 60–61
cooperation in antiterrorism actions, **2002**: 890
diplomatic relations, **1991-99**: 1173
Open Skies (aerial observation) treaty, **2002**: 1029
trade and investment issues, **1991-99**: 1455, 1466
women, U.S. calls to improve treatment of, **2005**: 313

L

Labor Cooperation, Commission for, 1991-99: 1314
Labor issues. *See also* Employment
abuse of alien domestic workers employed by diplomatic missions, **1989-90**: 389
alien crewmen performing longshore work, prohibition on, **2003**: 763–64
antidiscrimination convention, **1991-99**: 994–95
applicability of U.S. labor laws to foreign missions in U.S., **1989-90**: 388–90
bilateral investment treaties, **2008**: 600–3
Burma, **2008**: 796*n*
child labor. *See* Children
claims under U.S. law
denial of right to organize, **2003**: 374–78, 386
forced labor in Burma, **2003**: 355–71
World War II-era forced labor, **2003**: 468–74
comparable worth doctrine, **1991-99**: 903–4, 995
under Comprehensive Anti-Apartheid Act, **1989-90**: 523
discrimination against women of childbearing years, **1989-90**: 171
employment of dependents of diplomatic personnel, **1989-90**: 385–87
employment of foreign nationals by U.S. diplomatic missions, **1989-90**: 390
employment of U.S. citizens by foreign diplomatic missions, **1989-90**: 388–89
forced. *See* Slavery and forced labor
free trade agreements and, **2007**: 579, 581–82, 584–85; **2008**: 572

Labor issues (continued)
gender issues, **1991-99:** 903–5
Guidelines for Fair Treatment of Seafarers, **2006:** 825–28
household servants of foreign diplomats in U.S., **1989-90:** 389–90
ILO conventions and declarations, **1991-99:** 994–1000; **2008:** 352*n*
immunity of diplomatic personnel, **1991-99:** 1296–97
international aviation issues, **2008:** 510
International Covenant on Civil and Political Rights (ICCPR), **2008:** 345
International Organization for Standardization (ISO), **2008:** 347–48
international labor standards, **1991-99:** 998–1000, 1392–93, 1399, 1426, 1487, 1490–91
international maritime crew issues
crew list exemption, **2007:** 657
identification credential, **2007:** 658–59
Marine Casualty Code, **2007:** 660
internationally recognized worker rights, **2004:** 658–59
in Jordan–U.S. agreement, **2001:** 672–73
laborers and others supporting hostile forces, detention of during armed conflict, **2007:** 888, 941
Maritime Labor Convention (2006), **2006:** 821–25
Multilateral Agreement on Investment and, **1991-99:** 1487, 1490–91, 1492
NAFTA supplemental agreement on, **1991-99:** 1425–26
Protection of the Rights of All Migrant Workers and Members of Their Families (1990), **1989-90:** 194–95
right to organize, **2005:** 432
trade and, **2007:** 581–82, 584–85
unfair practices, **2004:** 360, 906
unions, **2004:** 387, 394, 396, 906
U.S. International Trade Agenda, **2001:** 666–67
U.S.–Central America Free Trade Agreement, **2003:** 685–86
U.S.–Oman Free Trade Agreement, **2008:** 572
U.S.–Ukraine Trade Investment Cooperation Agreement, **2008:** 575–76
William Wilberforce Trafficking Victims Protection Act (2008), **2008:** 119–20
workers' compensation plans, applicability to employees of consulates, **1989-90:** 390–93
World War II era claims, **1991-99:** 989–90, 992–93, 1048–49, 1070–71, 1133, 1134, 1260–63
Labor Management Relations Act (1947), 1991-99: 1308
Lacey Act (1981), 2003: 580
Landmines. *See* Arms control
Lanham Act (1946), 2005: 664, 667–71; **2008:** 775

Lansing–Ishii exchange of notes, 1991-99: 683
Laos
antiterrorism cooperation, **2002:** 118
aviation agreement, **2008:** 511
drug trade, **2001:** 120; **2002:** 124; **2003:** 181; **2004:** 133–34; **2005:** 135; **2006:** 213; **2007:** 163; **2008:** 113
money laundering, **2006:** 243
prisoners of war, **1991-99:** 1161, 1970
trafficking in persons, **2006:** 229
U.S. trade agreement with, **2001:** 665
visa application processing, **1991-99:** 113–18
Latin America. *See also* Organization of American States (OAS); *specific countries*
Economic Commission on, **2005:** 890
Latvia
Anti-Corruption Bureau (ACB), **2005:** 179
Australia Group member, **2004:** 1130
bilateral investment treaty, **2003:** 687, 695; **2004:** 623
diplomatic relations with U.S., **1989-90:** 242
EU accession and trade agreements, **2006:** 754–56
extradition and mutual legal assistance, **1991-99:** 453; **2000:** 185*n*; **2006:** 127, 137, 138–39, 147; **2008:** 54
fisheries agreements, **2003:** 731
intellectual property rights, **2006:** 768, 769; **2007:** 609
longshore work prohibition on alien crewmen from, **2002:** 757; **2003:** 764
money laundering, **2004:** 135
Financial Crimes Enforcement Network (FinCEN) action concerning Multibanka (Latvian commercial bank), **2005:** 176–80; **2006:** 253
Financial Crimes Enforcement Network (FinCEN) action concerning VEF Banka (Latvian commercial bank), **2006:** 249–52
NATO membership, **2003:** 424–26; **2004:** 411–12
nonrecognition of incorporation by USSR, **1989-90:** 272, 274; **1991-99:** 1169*n*
nuclear fuel return program, **2004:** 1139
relief from immigration requirements for certain resident nationals of, **1991-99:** 250
trade and investment issues, **1991-99:** 1455, 1466; **2003:** 695
visa waiver program, **2008:** 81–83
Law enforcement, 1991-99: 77–78, 746; **2004:** 169–70. *See also* Crime; Extradition; Jurisdiction; Mutual legal assistance
actions under color of law, **2000:** 377

Law enforcement (continued)
Antarctica, visitors to, **2004**: 782
anti-Semitism, combating, **2005**: 318–19. *See also* Anti-Semitism
antitrust law, **1991-99**: 1534–53
applicability of U.S. law to actions taken abroad, **1989-90**: 100–7, 109. *See also* Jurisdiction, *subheading*: extraterritorial jurisdiction and conflicts of jurisdiction
arbitrary detention, **2004**: 339, 352–54, 363, 364, 374; **2006**: 429–30
archeological and cultural artifacts. *See* Cultural issues
assistance to developing countries, **2003**: 212
attack on civil aircraft in course of. *See* Aviation issues, *subheading*: interdiction
certification of drug-producing and drug-transit countries. *See* Drug trade, *subheading*: U.S. narcotics report and certification
child support enforcement, international reciprocity in. *See* Maintenance obligations
consular notification and. *See* Consular notification and access
corporate social responsibility, **2000**: 368
counternarcotics cooperation in, **2005**: 136, 141, 143*n*, 144; **2006**: 212. *See also* Drug trade
criminally accused, rights of, **2005**: 282. *See also* Constitution, U.S.; Due Process; Human rights; International Covenant on Civil and Political Rights (ICCPR)
cybercrime. *See* Crime
damage claims against personnel, **2005**: 60–64
denial of passport for purposes of, **2002**: 18
drug trafficking. *See* Drug trade
European Union–U.S. agreement, **2003**: 135, 137
Europol–U.S. agreement on transfer of personal data, **2002**: 80–84, 467–69; **2006**: 164
excessive force complaints against, **2005**: 346, 361, 363, 368–70, 375
executions, extrajudicial, summary, and arbitrary. *See* Human rights
extradition, **2005**: 71–72, 77, 80, 100–1. *See also* Extradition
firearms and use of force, **2004**: 339. *See also* Guns and firearms
G-8 recommendations, **2002**: 121–22
hostage taking. *See* Hostage-taking and Hijacking
human rights and, **1991-99**: 853. *See also* Human rights
investigation and prosecution in U.S., **2000**: 377–79
prolonged detention, **2000**: 411–12
use of excessive force, **2000**: 374, 377
immunity. *See* Immunity
international cooperation, **2000**: 224; **2002**: 62–63; **2004**: 141, 662. *See also* Mutual legal assistance

Law enforcement (continued)
Convention against Corruption; **2008**: 122–23
Convention against Transnational Organized Crime, **2000**: 221–25; **2008**: 122–23
Convention for the Suppression of Unlawful Acts Against the Safety of Civil Aviation, **2000**: 218
Convention for the Suppression of Unlawful Acts Against the Safety of Maritime Navigation and its fixed platforms protocol, **2000**: 218; **2002**: 105–6; **2004**: 1110; **2008**: 926–29, 930–32
2005 protocols to, **2007**: 140
Convention on Combating Bribery of Foreign Public Officials in International Business Transactions. *See* Corruption
Europol–U.S. agreement on transfer of personal data in law enforcement, **2002**: 80–84
extradition treaties, **2000**: 163, 164–66. *See also* Extradition
Inter-American Convention Against Corruption, **2000**: 231–38; **2001**: 159–63. *See also* Corruption
Inter-American Convention on Mutual Assistance in Criminal Matters with Related Optional Protocol, **2000**: 166, 167–69
International Convention for the Suppression of the Financing of Terrorism, **2000**: 216–21
mutual legal assistance treaties, **2000**: 166–69; **2002**: 69–70
Organization of American States agreements, **2002**: 117
stolen vehicle treaties, **2000**: 169–70
Tax Matters, Convention on Mutual Administrative Assistance in, **1989-90**: 410–11
treaties for, **2000**: 164; **2005**: 69–79
juveniles, questioning and detention of, **2000**: 383–84
law enforcement information
defendant's access to information, **1991-99**: 451–52
evidence, use of information by requesting state as, **2000**: 169
information used in, **2004**: 113, 114
protection of, **2005**: 104, 1025; **2008**: 80–82
maritime, **2005**: 689. *See also* Jurisdiction, *subheading*: ships and vessels; Maritime issues, *subheading*: interdiction
maritime interdiction rules, **1989-90**: 448–56
in territorial sea contiguous zone, **1989-90**: 465–66
U.S. Coast Guard, **2004**: 1090, 1109
U.S.–Canada fisheries enforcement agreement, **1989-90**: 488–89
military use of force vs., against terrorists, **2006**: 1105, 1111–12
money laundering concerns, **2002**: 126–31. *See also* Money laundering

Law enforcement (continued)
nonproliferation initiatives, **2004**: 1075, 1080–81, 1091, 1098, 1108–9, 1110. *See also* Nonproliferation
Oil-for-Food Program and. *See* Corruption
organized crime and corruption. *See* Corruption; Crime, *subheading*: organized crime
prisoner rights. *See* Prisoners and prisons
racial discrimination in, **2001**: 257–58. *See also* Constitution, U.S.; Discrimination
investigation and prosecution in U.S., **2003**: 285–89
return of stolen vehicles or aircraft, **2002**: 61, 62, 64–65
spam, combating, **2005**: 659
terrorism and, **2001**: 100–1, 103–4, 105, 106–9, 896, 901–6, 907–8, 911–13, 935–41; **2004**: 1092; **2005**: 439, 896. *See also* Terrorism
military action vs., **2002**: 904, 906
OAS terrorism convention and, **2005**: 111
prevention of terrorist activities in U.S., **2001**: 897–913, 915–17, 923–27
torture and, **1989-90**: 181–82. *See also* Torture
trafficking in persons. *See* Crime
transborder arrest. *See* Crime
UN crime prevention activities, **2003**: 342–43
Violence Against Women Act of 2000, **2005**: 264
Violent Crime Control and Law Enforcement Act (1994), **1991-99**: 75, 77–78; **2005**: 264
WMD interdiction and, **2005**: 1098, 1103, 1104, 1118
Law of the Sea, UN Convention on (UNCLOS) (1982), **2001**: 218; **2003**: 436. *See also* Maritime issues
accession to, executive branch efforts to obtain Senate advice and consent to, **1991-99**: 1555–64, 1709; **2002**: 731–32; **2003**: 715–54; **2004**: 671–96; **2005**: 675–82; **2007**: 613–30; **2008**: 619–21
Agreement for the Implementation of the Provisions of UNCLOS relating to the Conservation and Management of Straddling Fish Stocks and Highly Migratory Fish Stocks (UN Fish Stocks Agreement, 1995), **1991-99**: 734, 1708–11; **2001**: 685–87; **2002**: 786, 797; **2004**: 762–64; **2005**: 735, 744, 746, 748, 749–50; **2007**: 714–16; **2008**: 704, 709, 713
Agreement Relating to the Implementation of Part XI of (1994), **1991-99**: 700; **2002**: 732; **2007**: 613–14, 615, 621, 625; **2008**: 619

Law of the Sea, UN Convention on (UNCLOS) (1982) (continued)
ratification of, executive branch efforts to obtain Senate advice and consent to, **1991-99**: 1555–56, 1557, 1559, 1560–62; **2003**: 715, 718, 720–22, 750–52; **2004**: 671, 673–74, 676, 678, 680, 682–84, 689, 691; **2005**: 675–76, 678, 682; **2008**: 619
Alien Tort Statute jurisdiction, **2002**: 334, 339
archipelagic states, **1989-90**: 451, 472; **1991-99**: 1598; **2002**: 257*n*, 258*n*; **2004**: 700, 703; **2007**: 641–42
artificial islands/platforms, **2004**: 698
contiguous zone, **1989-90**: 466–70; **1991-99**: 716, 1570; **2003**: 716, 734, 748; **2004**: 678, 687, 691, 696, 702, 704, 1084, 1088
Continental Shelf. *See* Annex II, *this heading*; Continental Shelf
Convention on the Removal of Wrecks and, **2007**: 654*n*
criminal jurisdiction provisions, **2003**: 733–34
customary international law and, **1989-90**: 48, 164, 292, 427, 439, 440–41, 442, 444, 445, 455, 457, 459–76; **1991-99**: 1566–69, 1579–80, 1586, 1587–88, 1597–98, 1599, 1627, 1703, 1708; **2000**: 703–4, 706–7; **2001**: 698–99; **2003**: 723–24, 727, 746; **2004**: 678, 679, 680, 682, 689, 691, 697, 703, 713, 1079; **2005**: 80–681, 683–84; **2007**: 617, 626–27, 635, 638–39, 647, 649
deep seabed mining provisions, **1989-90**: 425–27; **1991-99**: 1566, 1568–69; **2004**: 672; **2005**: 678, 681–82; **2007**: 615, 621–22; **2008**: 621, 629. *See also* Agreement Relating to the Implementation of Part XI of (1994), *this heading*
deep water ports, **2005**: 694–95
dispute settlement provisions, **1991-99**: 1560, 1563–64, 1711; **2000**: 84; **2003**: 718–20, 744; **2004**: 422, 672, 676–77, 679, 684, 688, 694
dumping restrictions, **2003**: 741–42; **2008**: 135–36
environmental protections under, **1991-99**: 1559, 1567–68; **2003**: 718, 731, 733, 737–38, 740, 741–42, 744, 747, 748–50, 752–54, 786; **2004**: 675, 681–82; **2005**: 684
exclusive economic zone, **1989-90**: 445, 451, 463–65, 478–79; **1991-99**: 716, 1558, 1583, 1710, 1727–28; **2001**: 698, 700, 704; **2003**: 716–17, 737–41, 753–54, 801; **2004**: 675, 681–82, 686, 687–88, 689, 691, 696, 698, 700, 702, 704–5, 713; **2006**: 817–18; **2007**: 619, 626, 643; **2008**: 135, 136, 623, 628, 642–44, 649, 693, 694, 702, 998
litigation concerning existence of U.S. EEZ around small islands, **2007**: 643–46; **2008**: 642–44

Law of the Sea, UN Convention on (UNCLOS) (1982) (continued)
fish and marine mammals. *See* Fish and marine mammals
flag state responsibility for safety of vessels, **1989-90**: 456–58, 459
funding of, **1989-90**: 426; **2003**: 722
Geneva Conventions on the Law of the Sea (1958) and, **1991-99**: 1562–63, 1588; **2004**: 672, 674, 675, 678, 682, 687, 691; **2005**: 678–80. *See also* Geneva Conventions on law of the sea (1958)
global rules and standards, **2003**: 742–43
high seas, **1991-99**: 1703, 1710
freedoms, **2007**: 625, 626
interdiction on, **1989-90**: 47–48, 448–50, 451–56, 468–70
historic bay claim and, **1991-99**: 1579–80
immunity of sunken government property, **2004**: 717–18
implementing legislation, **2003**: 743–44; **2004**: 672–73
intelligence activities, **2007**: 615, 627–28
International Oceanographic Commission, **2008**: 653
International Seabed Authority (ISA), **2007**: 623, 627–29
military activities not subject to, **2007**: 628
International Tribunal for, **2004**: 422, 676, 679, 684
marine scientific research, **1989-90**: 478–79; **1991-99**: 1559–60, 1564, 1567; **2003**: 718, 727, 732; **2005**: 684, 694; **2008**: 624, 637, 652–56
military activities and, **1991-99**: 1559, 1565–69; **2003**: 719–20, 726–29, 737–38; **2004**: 674–75, 677, 688, 689–90, 693–94; **2005**: 679–81; **2007**: 617, 626, 628, 647–50
national security and, **1991-99**: 1565–66, 1567; **2003**: 736–37; **2004**: 677–79, 681–82, 690–91, 692–96; **2005**: 676
navigational freedom, **2001**: 700; **2004**: 674–75, 680, 687–713; **2006**: 805–15; **2007**: 619, 625. *See also* contiguous zone, *this heading*; Continental shelf; exclusive economic zone, *this heading*; territorial sea and baselines, *this heading*
archipelagic sea lane passage, **1989-90**: 472–73, 474; **2000**: 706–7; **2003**: 760–62; **2004**: 699–700, 703; **2007**: 617, 626, 642–43
Arctic, **2006**: 814–15; **2008**: 623–24
Australian compulsory pilotage scheme for Torres Strait, **2006**: 810–12
foreign-flagged gambling ships in U.S. territorial waters, **1991-99**: 1627–29
innocent passage, **1991-99**: 1587–89, 1597, 1599–1600, 1628; **2007**: 617, 625–26, 638–41
overflight rules, **2001**: 704–6, 713; **2004**: 700–702; **2007**: 617, 634–38

Law of the Sea, UN Convention on (UNCLOS) (1982) (continued)
shipping restrictions of coastal state, **2001:** 711–14
straits, **1991-99:** 1585–90; **2006:** 806–12; **2007:** 617, 626, 638–41
Straits of Malacca and Singapore, **2006:** 806–10
Swedish territorial waters, innocent right of passage, **2006:** 812–14
no private right of action to enforce in U.S. courts, **2003:** 745, 747; **2004:** 672–73, **2007:** 644–45
non self-executing even if U.S. were party to, **2007:** 629, 645
Ocean Policy Statement (1983), **2007:** 615, 616, 626
ocean sustainability and, **2007:** 619–20
piracy and, **1989-90:** 112; **2007:** 631 ?
Proliferation Security Initiative, **2004:** 677–78, 691, 693, 1079, 1087
search and rescue, **2008:** 625
self-executing provisions, **2003:** 745–46
ship boarding, **1989-90:** 454–55; **2003:** 735–36; **2004:** 681–82, 691–92, 693
slave trade and, **2003:** 735–36
sovereign immunity of government vessels, **1989-90:** 292–94, 476–77; **1991-99:** 1568; **2004:** 717–18; **2005:** 763–64
sovereignty issues, **2004:** 676, 684–85, 726–27; **2007:** 617–18, 623. *See also* Sovereignty
state law and, **2003:** 746
technology transfer and, **2004:** 681, 685
territorial sea and baselines, **1989-90:** 445, 459, 460, 461, 462, 463–65; **1991-99:** 1558, 1568–69, 1579, 1580–81, 1583, 1587, 1597–98; **2000:** 703–4; **2003:** 716, 752; **2004:** 674–75, 698, 702–10
contiguous zone authority, **1989-90:** 466–70
innocent passage, right of in, **1989-90:** 437–47, 468, 471; **1991-99:** 1586–89, 1597, 1599–1600, 1628; **2000:** 706–7; **2003:** 717, 719–20, 736–37, 753, 759, 762; **2004:** 703; **2006:** 812–14
Underwater Cultural Heritage Convention and, **2001:** 694; **2005:** 759–64, 766
U.S. accession issues, **2004:** 671–96; **2005:** 675–82; **2008:** 619–23
U.S. concerns, **2003:** 722–25, 726, 744–45
U.S. nonparty observer status, **2001:** 676–81
U.S. nonparty status, **2001:** 675–76, 682–83, 684
U.S. Ocean Policy Statement (1983), **2004:** 674
U.S. security and, **2007:** 616–17, 627–29
Proliferation Security Initiative, **2007:** 615, 617, 626–27, 628
violation of, as basis for ATS claim, **2006:** 433, 436, 442
Annexes:, **2004:** 676–77, 731, 732–33

Law of the Sea, UN Convention on (UNCLOS) (1982) (continued)
II, **2004**: 731–32
VI, **1991-99**: 1563; **2003**: 744–45
VI, *VII*, *VIII*, **1991-99**: 1563–64, 1711
VII, **1991-99**: 1563; **2003**: 719
VIII, **1991-99**: 1563–64, 1711; **2003**: 676–77, 719
Articles:
4, **2004**: 732
5, **1991-99**: 1580, 1597
7, **1991-99**: 1580, 1597–98
9, **2005**: 684
12, **2005**: 695
14, **2004**: 687
17, **2007**: 639
17–21, **2004**: 703
18, **1991-99**: 1627; **2004**: 703
19, **1991-99**: 1587; **2003**: 734–37; **2004**: 687, 695, 703; **2007**: 648
20, **2004**: 687, 695, 703
21, **1991-99**: 1587–88, 1627–28; **2003**: 747, 753; **2004**: 703; **2007**: 648; **2008**: 700
22, **2001**: 712; **2005**: 694
24, **2001**: 700; **2003**: 748
25, **1991-99**: 1599; **2004**: 704
26, **2004**: 703
27, **2003**: 733–34
31, **1991-99**: 1588
32, **2004**: 717; **2007**: 1075*n*
33, **1991-99**: 716; **2003**: 748; **2004**: 704; **2005**: 759
34, **2007**: 640
36, **2004**: 717
37–44, **1991-99**: 1589
38, **1991-99**: 1588
39, **2003**: 745, 747
40, **2007**: 68
42, **2001**: 700; **2007**: 1075*n*
44, **2001**: 700
45, **1991-99**: 1588; **2007**: 639
46, **2007**: 642
47, **2001**: 714; **2007**: 642
50, **2003**: 737–38
52, **2001**: 712; **2003**: 762; **2004**: 703, 717
53, **2007**: 642
54, **2001**: 700; **2007**: 648

Law of the Sea, UN Convention on (UNCLOS) (1982) (continued)
56, **1991-99**: 61, 62, 63, 64, 67, 116–19, 1710; **2001**: 704, 706; **2003**: 738; **2004**: 704, 726; **2005**: 759; **2007**: 649
58, **2001**: 704–6; **2003**: 738; **2005**: 759; **2007**: 648, 649; **2008**: 700
59, **2005**: 759
60, **2004**: 698; **2005**: 694, 695, 759, 763
60(7), **2005**: 695
61, **2003**: 730, 739–40
62, **2003**: 730, 741
66, **1991-99**: 1703, 1710
76, **2000**: 699; **2003**: 732; **2004**: 730, 732
77, **2004**: 732
81, **2005**: 759
86, **2005**: 759
87, **2001**: 706; **2005**: 759; **2008**: 700
91, **2007**: 1068
92, **1989-90**: 48, 455; **2004**: 1088; **2007**: 1068
92 & 94, **2004**: 1088
94, **2004**: 1088
95, **2003**: 738; **2007**: 1075*n*
96, **2003**: 738; **2007**: 1075*n*
99, **2003**: 735
100, **2007**: 631*n*
101, **2007**: 631*n*
110, **1989-90**: 452; **2003**: 735–36; **2004**: 1088; **2007**: 1075*n*
121, **2007**: 644, 645, 646
149, **2005**: 759
187, **2003**: 746
194, **1991-99**: 1627–28
210, **2003**: 741–42; **2007**: 702
211, **2003**: 733, 742, 752–53; **2005**: 694
216, **2007**: 702; **2008**: 135–36
218, **2008**: 135
220, **2008**: 135
221, **2007**: 656
230, **2003**: 748–50; **2008**: 135–36
236, **2003**: 738; **2004**: 717; **2005**: 759, 761; **2007**: 1075*n*
246, **2007**: 648
287, **1991-99**: 1564
290, **2000**: 84
292, **2003**: 747
297, **2003**: 730, 740
298, **1991-99**: 1564; **2003**: 738
301, **2001**: 704–5

Law of the Sea, UN Convention on (UNCLOS) (1982) (continued)
302, **2004**: 681
303, **2005**: 759, 760
311, **1991-99**: 1562; **2005**: 759; **2007**: 655
Law of the sea conventions (1958). *See* Geneva Conventions on law of the sea (1958)
Law of war. *See also* Al-Qaida/Qaeda; Conventional weapons; Geneva Conventions on law of war (1949); Hague Conventions; Humanitarian law; War crimes; War on Terror; *specific Geneva conventions*
allocation of war powers in U.S. Constitution, **2002**: 987–89, 990–91; **2004**: 206–14. *See also* President, U.S., *subheading*: war powers
arms control. *See* Arms control
authority to prevent Iranian- or Syrian-supported attacks against U.S. forces in Iraq, **2007**: 989–90
Brussels Declaration of 1874, **2002**: 1005*n*
civilians, protection of, **1991-99**: 2060–61, 2063, 2064, 2065; **2005**: 303, 372, 393, 823, 953–56, 1006. *See also* Geneva Convention IV: on Civilians (1949)
collateral damage, **1991-99**: 2079–89
military advantage, **1991-99**: 2082
responsibilities of defender, **1991-99**: 2084–87
use of civilian persons and objects as shields, **1991-99**: 2083
command responsibility for violations of, **1991-99**: 2100–2101; **2002**: 348–51
conventional weapons convention. *See* Conventional weapons
cultural property, **1991-99**: 514, 2072, 2075–76, 2079–80, 2086, 2096, 2197–2207. *See also* Hague Conventions
customary international law, **1991-99**: 517, 2073, 2080, 2083, 2088, 2097, 2171, 2172, 2173, 2175, 2176, 2183, 2204–5, 2227; **2006**: 1069–85
International Committee of the Red Cross study on, **2006**: 1069–85
opinio juris, **2006**: 1073–75
state practice, **2006**: 1071–73
dangerous forces, release of, **1991-99**: 2065
deficiencies in existing framework for conflicts with terrorists, **2007**: 873–74, 876–77, 880, 882–93, 910, 917
authorized detentions, **2007**: 887–89
procedures for determining, **2007**: 889–90
criminal law versus, in antiterrorism efforts, **2007**: 878–79
customary international law, **2007**: 885–86
release of detainees, **2007**: 890

Law of war (continued)
defined, **1991-99**: 2071
Department of Defense report to Congress, in context of Gulf War, **1991-99**: 2070–2108
detention of enemy combatants and, **2004**: 984–91. *See also* Detainees, military
developments in, **2006**: 1105
due process and, **2004**: 1009
end of the conflict, **2007**: 879–80, 899–91
enemy property doctrine, **2004**: 206–14
environment, protection of, **1991-99**: 2065, 2101–2, 2177; **2006**: 1105
European and U.S. approaches to, **2005**: 949–53
exploding bullets, use of, **2006**: 1085
Gulf War. *See* Gulf War
herbicides, use of during Vietnam war not violation of, **2005**: 493, 591–97
hostage-taking, **1991-99**: 2074–75
human rights law distinct from, **2002**: 1009–11, 1013–17; **2003**: 277–78, 344–47, 349–51, 1019–21; **2004**: 334–35; **2005**: 302–4, 390–91, 393; **2006**: 347, 384, 1121–22; **2007**: 280–81, 886, 925–30
IACHR not competent to apply, **2002**: 1008–17; **2004**: 978–79
humanitarian workers, protection in, **2003**: 993–96; **2006**: 1076–77
illegitimate combatancy, **2005**: 954–55
International Committee of the Red Cross memorandum on, **1991-99**: 2057–62
U.S. views on, **1991-99**: 2062–66
international humanitarian law as meaning, in international instruments, **2007**: 985–87
international organizations and right of self-defense, **2006**: 492
law enforcement vs., against terrorists, **2006**: 1105, 1111–12
as *lex specialis*, **2002**: 1009–10; **2003**: 1020; **2004**: 331, 978–79; **2005**: 223; **2007**: 209, 280, 886, 926
Lieber Code, **2003**: 997
military activities covered by, exempted from coverage of other international instruments, **2007**: 985–87
military necessity, **1991-99**: 2088–89; **2004**: 972
neutral nations, **1991-99**: 2102–7, 2180
occupation
of Iraq (2003). *See* Iraq, *subheading*: Coalition Provisional Authority (CPA), occupying
by Israel in Occupied Palestinian Territory, ICJ opinion on wall in, **2004**: 972–76

Law of war (continued)
role of UN Security resolutions, **2005**: 957–60
by U.S. in Panama, **1991-99**: 1126–28
perfidy, acts of, **1991-99**: 2095–96; **2003**: 1000–1, 1004, 1010
preemptive action in self-defense, **2002**: 947–57; **2004**: 970–72; **2005**: 444, 448
protected persons, **2005**: 953–55
protection of medical transport, **1991-99**: 2061, 2065–66
red crystal, adoption of additional distinctive emblem under Geneva Conventions, **2005**: 1042–43
release of detainees, **2007**: 890, 892–93
reprisals, **1991-99**: 596, 2074, 2177, 2179–80
riot-control agents, **1991-99**: 2345–46; **2003**: 1013–14; **2006**: 1223–25
role of ICRC, **1991-99**: 2061–62, 2066
Security Council, role of, **1991-99**: 596
self-defense, **2002**: 951, 953–56; **2004**: 971–72, 974–76; **2007**: 876–78, 880–81; **2008**: 671. *See also* preemptive action in self-defense, *this heading*; United Nations, *subheading*: Charter of (1945); use of force, *this heading*
proportionality, **1991-99**: 2080–81; **2004**: 248, 971, 975
U.S. disagreements with ICJ language concerning
in advisory opinion on wall in Occupied Palestinian Territory, **2004**: 972–74
in Oil Platforms case, **2004**: 974–76
surrender, **1991-99**: 2107–8
torture and, **2007**: 927–28
training and penalizing U.S. military personnel concerning violations, **1991-99**: 2061, 2066, 2097–98; **2004**: 991, 993–94, 1038
treatment of prisoners of war. *See* Detainees, military; Geneva Convention III: on Prisoners of War (1949); Prisoners of War
UN Charter. *See* United Nations, *subheading*: Charter of (1945)
U.S. congressional authorization for military operations
Authorization for Use of Military Force (AUMF) (2001)
authority to detain enemy combatants, **2007**: 941–43, 971–74; **2008**: 917–18
authority to issue Executive Order on implementation of Common Article 3, **2007**: 922
Authorization for Use of Military Force (AUMF) (2002)
authority for military operations in Iraq, **2007**: 889, 990–91
authority to transfer detainees to Iraqi authorities, **2007**: 962*n*
use of force, **2004**: 969–72, 985–86; **2005**: 215, 372, 949–51, 957; **2008**: 853–77. *See also* self-defense, *this heading*; September 11 terrorist attacks

Law of war (continued)
in Bosnia, **1991-99**: 2168–70
executive branch statements concerning, **2008**: 853–56
in Gulf War. *See* Gulf War
in Haiti, **1991-99**: 2162–68
humanitarian intervention, **2004**: 971–72; **2008**: 856–57
in Iraq
agreements with Iraq, **2008**: 859–62
constitutional authority, **2008**: 857–59
UN resolutions and Iraqi violations of (2003), **2002**: 937–47, 956–57; **2003**: 961–74
U.S. congressional authorization for, **2002**: 933–37
in Kosovo, **1991-99**: 2154–62; **2004**: 971–72
legal rationale, **1989-90**: 561–64
in Panama, **1989-90**: 552–64
in response to September 11, 2001 attacks
against al Qaeda in states harboring, **2006**: 1109–10
announcement of War Against Terrorism, **2001**: 856–60
assassination and, **2001**: 867
right of self-defense, international recognition of, **2001**: 860–64; **2006**: 1106–7, 1108–10, 1121
U.S. congressional authorization for, **2001**: 864–66
war powers. *See* President, U.S.; War Powers Resolution (U.S.)
weapons, certain, whether allowed under, **1991-99**: 514, 2060, 2071, 2195–97. *See also* Conventional weapons
lasers, **1989-90**: 550
nuclear weapons, ICJ advisory opinion on, **1991-99**: 2170–82
Lawful Permanent Residents (LPRs). *See also* Immigration and Nationality Act (INA) (1952); Immigration and visas
Cuban Refugee Adjustment Act, **2005**: 19
entry requirements, **2005**: 2*n*
equal protection rights, **2005**: 259
INA treatment of, **2005**: 259
Soviet Scientists Immigration Act of 1992 (SSIA) not applicable to, **2005**: 9
Lebanon
bombing of U.S. embassy in Beirut, claim against Iran concerning, **2005**: 508–16
Doha Agreement (2008), **2008**: 827–30
elections, inability to hold (2008), **2008**: 824–27
FSIA and, **1991-99**: 1218; **2004**: 484, 511
Gebran Tueni, murder of, **2005**: 884–86
Gemayel assassination, **2006**: 1041
Hariri murder

Lebanon (continued)
Fitzgerald report, **2005**: 878–79
independent investigation commission, **2005**: 878–80, 883, 885–86; **2006**: 272, 985–86; **2008**: 142
presidential statement, **2005**: 878
Special Tribunal for, establishment of, **2006**: 272–75, 1041; **2007**: 190–93; **2008**: 141–42
UN Security Council Resolutions related to
1559, calling for withdrawal of all foreign forces from Lebanon, **2005**: 881; **2006**: 1037–38, 1041, 1226–30; **2008**: 824–27, 830
1595, establishing investigation commission, **2005**: 878–79
1636, sanctions under Chapter VII, **2005**: 880–84; **2006**: 985
1644, extending commission mandate, **2005**: 885–86
1664, requesting Secretary-General to negotiate agreement with Lebanon aimed at establishing Hariri tribunal, **2006**: 272–75; **2007**: 192
1757, to bring to justice those responsible for murder of, **2007**: 190–93; **2008**: 141
intellectual property rights Watch List, **2006**: 768; **2007**: 608, 610; **2008**: 607
Interim Force in Lebanon (UNIFIL), **2005**: 917–18; **2006**: 1035, 1037, 1039, 1060–61; **2007**: 869–71
Israeli firing on observers with, **2006**: 1230
Israel vs. Hezbollah conflict in, **2006**: 1034–42, 1225–33
ceasefire and subsequent peacekeeping efforts, **2006**: 1039–42
Human Rights Council special session on, **2006**: 338–41
Syria and Iran, roles in, **2006**: 1040–42, 1227
UN Security Council Resolution 1701 calling for ceasefire, **2006**: 1034–41, 1233; **2008**: 830
embargo under, **2006**: 1035, 1037, 1039–40; **2008**: 826
use of force issues, **2006**: 103, 1226, 1230–33
Israel-Lebanon Ceasefire Understanding (1996), **2006**: 1035*n*
longshore work prohibition on alien crewmen from, **2002**: 757; **2003**: 764
Middle East peace process and, **1991-99**: 1985, 1986–87
money laundering, **2004**: 135
passports, **1991-99**: 45
Relief and Works Agency (UNWRA), **2005**: 918
request for U.S. protection of Lebanese embassy in U.S., **1989-90**: 243–64
Rome Conference, **2006**: 1228–29
sanctions on persons undermining the sovereignty of, **2007**: 805–7
blocking assets, **2007**: 805–7
restrictions on entry into U.S., **2007**: 39–41

Lebanon (continued)
sovereignty issues, **2005**: 878–79, 881; **2007**: 39–41; **2008**: 824–27
Special Tribunal for, **2007**: 190–93; **2008**: 141–42
Syria Accountability and Lebanese Sovereignty Restoration Act (2003), **2003**: 1084–86; **2007**: 40–41, 805–7
Syria and, **2004**: 900, 902, 945; **2007**: 39–40, 805, 870
closure of border with, **2005**: 933
Hariri murder, **2005**: 882–84; **2006**: 984–86, 1041
occupation of Lebanon, **2005**: 133–34, 880–87
withdrawal of forces from, **2005**: 931–32
temporary protected status for nationals of, **1991-99**: 241–43
travel restrictions, **1991-99**: 51
U.S. views on situation in, **2005**: 932–33
Legal Assistance Treaties, Mutual (MLATs). *See* Mutual legal assistance
Legalization. *See* Authentication
Lesotho
Article 98 agreement and, **2006**: 278
extradition and mutual legal assistance, **2000**: 185*n*
waivers to prohibition on assistance, **2006**: 278
Letters rogatory. *See* Evidence, *subheading*: discovery; Judicial assistance
Liberia
access to U.S. courts by government not officially recognized, **1991-99**: 1138–41
Air Transport Agreement (2007), **2007**: 532
Article 98 agreement (nonsurrender of Americans to ICC), **2004**: 187
child soldiers, **2003**: 308; **2004**: 281, 282
civil war, **1991-99**: 2016, 2018
consular bank accounts, **2005**: 558
extradition and mutual legal assistance, **2000**: 185*n*
former President Charles Taylor, **2004**: 130, 282, 919, 920, 921, 935; **2006**: 256–57, 275–77, 422; **2008**: 123–25, 140
immigration issues
refugee admissions for family reunification, **2006**: 59–60
suspension of entry of certain nationals of, **1991-99**: 141–42; **2000**: 19
temporary protected status for nationals of, **1991-99**: 243–44; **2003**: 36
jurisdiction over investigation of maritime accidents in international waters, **1989-90**: 447–48
maritime counterterrorism measures, conditions for failure to take, **2008**: 112
peacekeeping operations in, **2003**: 233–34, 955–57; **2008**: 838

Liberia (continued)
Proliferation Security Initiative (PSI), **2004**: 691–92, 1078, 1079–91
ship boarding agreement with U.S., **2005**: 1100, 1102*n*, 1106
sanctions on, **2004**: 919–22
arms embargo, **2007**: 1003, 1007
Blocking Property of Certain Persons and Prohibiting the Importation of Certain Goods from Liberia (Executive Order No. 13348), **2007**: 820–22
diamond trade, **2001**: 799–801; **2003**: 708, 709
logging, **2003**: 776–77
Special Court for, **2004**: 130, 180
termination of national emergency, **2004**: 934–35
torture indictment and, **2007**: 173–80
trafficking in persons in, **2003**: 188
Libya
bombing of Pan Am Flight 103 and UTA 772, **1989-90**: 95; **1991-99**: 457–60, 470, 480, 489, 857, 1256–57, 1921; **2003**: 160–61
cases in U.S. courts, **1991-99**: 1194–95, 1197–98, 1234–52, 1256–57
Libyan offers of compensation to victims, **2003**: 162–65
claims before International Court of Justice, **1991-99**: 460–77; **2003**: 166
Montreal Convention claims by Libya, **1991-99**: 460, 466, 467–69, 477
dismantlement of WMD program. *See* WMD, elimination of, *this heading*
prosecution of named terrorists in Scottish court, **1991-99**: 457–60, 462, 465, 467–69, 477–80, 542; **2001**: 98–99; **2002**: 111–12
renunciation of terrorism, **2003**: 161–63; **2004**: 927–28; *see also* terrorism, *this heading*
role of Security Council, **1991-99**: 462–64, 465–67, 468, 469–77
sanctions on, U.S., **1991-99**: 857, 1922–24, 1971, 1974, 2260
easing of in light of subsequent Libyan actions, **2004**: 927–34
Iran and Libya Sanctions Act, **1991-99**: 1265, 1446, 1448, 1911–15, 1976; **2001**: 817–19
UN Security Council resolutions, **1991-99**: 458–60, 1029–30, 1921–22
lifting of sanctions imposed by, **2003**: 161–63
claims settlement
Claims Settlement Agreement (2008), **2008**: 402–6
Executive Order 13477, **2008**: 408–10
Libyan Claims Resolution Act (2008), **2008**: 399–402, 406–8

Libya (continued)
diplomatic relations with U.S., **1989-90:** 242; **2004:** 451
diplomatic liaison offices, **2005:** 499
embassy opening, **2006:** 527–28
Israel's denial of entry to Libyan vessel to Gaza, **2008:** 647–48
Overseas Private Investment Corporation (OPIC) agreement, **2005:** 648
passport restrictions, revocation of, **1991-99:** 52; **2004:** 6
as president of UNCHR, **2003:** 283
suit in U.S. courts against U.S. and UK officials for 1985 air strikes on, **1989-90:** 311–14
tax lien against property of in U.S., **2002:** 576–79
termination of national emergency regarding, **2004:** 930, 931–34, 1158
terrorism and. *See also* bombing of Pan Am Flight 103 and UTA 772, *this heading*
designation as state sponsor of terrorism, **1991-99:** 509; **2001:** 820; **2003:** 168; **2004:** 103, 659, 932, 934
de-listing as state sponsor of terrorism, **2005:** 506; **2006:** 173
Export Administration Regulations to implement, **2006:** 177–79
Presidential Determination (2006-14), **2006:** 173–77
legislation restoring Libya's immunity for acts prior to June 30, 2006, **2008:** 399–402, 462–63
not cooperating fully with antiterrorism efforts, **1991-99:** 508; **2003:** 167; **2004:** 107–8
decision not to include Libya on list of countries not cooperating fully with antiterrorism efforts, **2006:** 172, 175
International Traffic in Arms Regulations amendment to implement, **2007:** 1005
travel restrictions on, **2001:** 15; **2003:** 12–13 check passport restrictions
exceptions to, **2000:** 118–19
U.S. relations with, **1991-99:** 1029–30; **2006:** 527–28
U.S. response to 1986 terrorist attack by, **1989-90:** 95
U.S. tax policy, **2004:** 659, 660–61, 933
weapons of mass destruction issues. *See* Nonproliferation, *subheading*: country-specific issues
Lieber Code, 2003: 997. *See also* Law of war
Liechtenstein
extradition and mutual legal assistance, **2000:** 185*n*; **2002:** 61, 62, 67
money laundering, **2004:** 135
nonimmigrant visa waiver pilot program, **1991-99:** 76
Liens
sovereign immunity, **2008:** 413–14

Limitation Period in the International Sale of Goods, Convention on (UN), 1991-99: 1817–20
Limitations, Sales of Goods, Negotiable Instruments, and Guarantees, Conventions on, 2002: 836
Limited Test Ban Treaty (1963) (U.S.–USSR), 1989-90: 567, 571, 574
Lithuania
bilateral investment treaty, **2003:** 695; **2004:** 623
border shared with Latvia, **2005:** 178
diplomatic relations with U.S., **1989-90:** 242
domestic violence laws, lack of, **2005:** 313
EU accession and trade agreements, **2006:** 754–56
extradition and mutual legal assistance, **1991-99:** 453, 572–76; **2000:** 185*n*; **2002:** 61, 62, 63–64, 69, 175; **2006:** 137, 147
fisheries agreements, **2003:** 730–31
intellectual property rights Watch List, **2006:** 768; **2007:** 610
removal from intellectual property rights Watch List, **2008:** 607
NATO membership, **2003:** 424–26; **2004:** 411–12
naturalization treaty, **2002:** 203
nonrecognition of incorporation by USSR, **1989-90:** 271–75
relief from immigration requirements for certain resident nationals of, **1991-99:** 250
Soviet Union incorporation of, **1991-99:** 1169*n*
trade and investment issues, **1991-99:** 1455, 1466
visa waiver program, **2008:** 81–83
weapons of mass destruction nonproliferation, **2004:** 1130
Local government. *See also* States, U.S.; *specific states*
NAFTA coverage of action of, **2000:** 679–81
status of Hong Kong as sub-sovereign government, **2000:** 190–203
Local remedies rule. *See* Remedies, *subheading*: exhaustion of remedies, requirement for
London Debt Agreement, 1991-99: 992; **2004:** 432
Long Range Transboundary Air Pollution, Convention on, 1991-99: 1666, 1668–69; **2004:** 744–45
Longshore and Harbor Workers Compensation Act (1927), 1991-99: 179*n*
Loss of citizenship. *See* Citizenship
Lost passports. *See* Passports, U.S.
Louisiana
insurance law, preemption of Convention on the Recognition and Enforcement of Foreign Arbitral Awards (New York Convention), **2008:** 777–82

Lumber
Indonesia logging initiative, **2006**: 801–3
softwood. *See* Canada; North American Free Trade Agreement (NAFTA), *subheading*: Softwood Lumber Agreement (SLA)
Lusaka Peace Accords, 1991-99: 145, 1142
Luxembourg
arms control and nuclear nonproliferation and, **1991-99**: 2232
extradition and mutual legal assistance, **1991-99**: 396, 453; **2000**: 180, 185*n*; **2001**: 92*n*; **2006**: 137, 147
money laundering, **2004**: 135
nonimmigrant visa waiver pilot program, **1991-99**: 76
Open Skies (aerial observation) treaty, **2002**: 1029
World War II-era restitution and claims, **1991-99**: 1044

M
Macau Special Administrative Region, China
continuity and succession issues, **1991-99**: 1180–81
longshore work prohibition on alien crewmen from, **2002**: 757; **2003**: 764
money laundering, **2004**: 135; **2005**: 180–84
North Korean involvement, **2005**: 181–82, 1073
Macedonia
Adriatic Charter, **2003**: 939
American Servicemembers' Protection Act waiver, **2003**: 238
domestic violence laws, **2005**: 313
extradition and mutual legal assistance, **2000**: 185*n*
nonproliferation sanctions, **2004**: 1135
peace process after breakup of Yugoslavia, **1991-99**: 1147, 1167, 1945, 1952, 1979–82, 2140; **2008**: 815–16
Framework Agreement, **2001**: 825–27
peacekeeping operations, **1991-99**: 2022, 2024–31, 2144, 2169
UN membership and U.S. recognition of, **1991-99**: 1167, 1979
Machias Seal Island, maritime boundary dispute, 2005: 707
Madagascar
threshold agreement with Millennium Challenge Corporation (MCC), **2005**: 672
Madrid Agreement Concerning the International Registration of Marks, Protocol Relating to, 1991-99: 695–99, 2192, 2247; **2000**: 297–301; **2003**: 699–701
Madrid Protocol Implementation Act (2002), 2003: 702–4
Magen David Adom (Israeli aid society), 2005: 1043; **2006**: 1101, 1103–4

Maintenance obligations
child support and other maintenance obligations, **2003**: 856–59; **2007**: 769–70
denial of passport for nonpayment of, **1991-99**: 49, 1866; **2001**: 9–13; **2002**: 13–15; **2006**: 15–16
family support obligations, **1991-99**: 1862–78; **2002**: 841–58; **2004**: 836–39; **2008**: 759–60
international enforcement of obligations, **1991-99**: 1862–78; **2002**: 841–58
international organizations and, **1991-99**: 1315–16
International Recovery of Child Support and Other Forms of Family Maintenance, Convention for, **2004**: 837–39; **2006**: 938–42; **2007**: 769–70; **2008**: 751–59
proposed instrument for recovery of, **1991-99**: 1862–78; **2002**: 842–58
reciprocal arrangements for enforcement of, **1991-99**: 1865–68; **2001**: 49–51; **2002**: 841–42; **2004**: 826; **2005**: 809–10; **2006**: 942–44; **2007**: 770–72; **2008**: 759–60
U.S. system for enforcement, **1991-99**: 1864–71; **2008**: 752–59
enforcement of judgments, jurisdiction and, **1991-99**: 1862, 1871–78
Recognition and Enforcement of Decisions Relating to, Hague Conventions on (1958 and 1973), **1991-99**: 1868, 1872, 1874–75; **2002**: 842
Recovery Abroad of Maintenance, New York Convention on (1956), **2002**: 842
Uniform Interstate Family Support Act (1992), **1991-99**: 1864, 1869–71, 1875–76; **2008**: 753, 758–59

Malawi
extradition and mutual legal assistance, **2000**: 185*n*

Malaysia
antiterrorism cooperation, **2002**: 118
challenge of U.S. ban on shrimp imports, **2001**: 752–56
extradition and mutual legal assistance, **1991-99**: 395, 398, 399, 405; **2000**: 179, 186*n*; **2006**: 147–48; **2008**: 79
intellectual property rights Watch List, **2006**: 768; **2007**: 610; **2008**: 606
Iran and Libya Sanctions Act (1996) and, **1991-99**: 1915
Straits of Malacca and Singapore, **2006**: 806–10
trade claims against U.S., **1991-99**: 1412–13, 1717–19
trade issues, **2006**: 766

Maldives
maritime claims, **2001**: 711–14; **2005**: 683–84
open skies agreement with U.S., **2005**: 588
U.S. diplomatic relations with, **1989-90**: 241

Mali
cultural property protection agreement, **1991-99**: 1799–1800; **2002**: 813
open skies agreement with U.S., **2005**: 588
U.S. military assistance, **2006**: 278
waiver of Article 98 agreement with U.S. (nonsurrender of Americans to ICC), **2006**: 279
Malicious prosecution, 2001: 477–80, 483–85
Malta
Australia Group member, **2004**: 1130
EU accession and trade agreements, **2006**: 754–56
extradition and mutual legal assistance, **2000**: 185*n*; **2006**: 127, 137, 138–39, 147; **2008**: 54
Maritime Drug Law Enforcement Act jurisdiction and, **2002**: 134–37
U.S. military assistance, **2006**: 278
visa waiver program, **2008**: 81–83
MAMCO Manufacturing case, 1989-90: 418–24
Man-portable air defense systems (MANPADS), 2005: 1066; **2006**: 210–11
Mariana Islands, Northern. *See* Northern Mariana Islands, Commonwealth of (CNMI)
Marianas Marine Sovereignty Act (1980), 1991-99: 840–41
Marianas Submerged Lands Act (1988), 1991-99: 839–40
Mariel boat people, detention of, 2001: 341–46; **2005**: 18–23
Marine conservation. *See also* Environmental issues; Fish and marine mammals; Law of the Sea, UN Convention on (UNCLOS) (1982)
Antarctic Marine Living Resources, Convention on the Conservation of (CCAMLR), **2005**: 738; **2007**: 709–12; **2008**: 712
ballast water controls, **2001**: 683
convention on, **2004**: 747; **2007**: 704–5
Bering and Chukchi Seas pollution, agreement with USSR on, **1989-90**: 489–90
Caribbean region, **1991-99**: 1766–69; **2003**: 789–90
Control of Harmful Anti-Fouling Systems on Ships, Convention on, **2008**: 695–98
coral reef protection, **1991-99**: 1755–57
customary international law and, **1991-99**: 1567
global marine assessment, **2003**: 781–82
hazardous materials, maritime transport of, **1989-90**: 445–46, 492–93, 494, 495–96
Basel Convention on, **1989-90**: 445; **1991-99**: 1687–93; **2002**: 775, 783–85; **2004**: 747–49; **2006**: 863–65
shipment of nuclear materials through Arctic, **2001**: 701–2

Marine conservation (continued)
International Oceanographic Commission, **2008:** 653
law of the sea and. *See* Law of the Sea, UN Convention on (UNCLOS)
Marine Environment of the Wider Caribbean Region, Convention for the Protection and Development of (Cartagena Convention) (1983), **1991-99:** 1766–69; **2007:** 724–28;
protocol concerning pollution from land-based sources and activities, **2007:** 724–28; **2008:** 715–16
protocol on specially protected areas and wildlife (1990), **2002:** 792–94; **2003:** 789–90
Marine Protection, Research, and Sanctuaries Act (MPRSA), **2007:** 700–703
Marine Sovereignty Act (1980), **2003:** 276
oceans
and law of the sea, **2005:** 731–32
Northwestern Hawaiian Islands Marine National Monument, **2006:** 872–75
Ocean Dumping Act (1972), **2003:** 741–42
Oceans Policy, U.S. Commission on, **2001:** 681–84
Pacific islands, agreement on fishing rights, **2002:** 189–90
pollution, **1989-90:** 489–90, 491–96
Marine Pollution, Washington Conference on Land-Based Sources of, **2005:** 726
Marine Pollution By Dumping of Wastes and Other Matter, Convention on, **1989-90:** 492, 495, 496; **2003:** 742; **2007:** 580, 699–703
Oil Pollution Act (1990), **1991-99:** 775, 779–80; **2003:** 733, 752
Oil Pollution Preparedness, Response and Cooperation, International Convention on, **1991-99:** 1681–83; **2003:** 752
persistent toxic substances in the Great Lakes, U.S.-Canada agreement on, **1991-99:** 1669–71
Protection and Development of the Marine Environment of the Wider Caribbean Region, Convention for the, Protocol Concerning Pollution from Land-based Sources and Activities (1999), **2007:** 724–28; **2008:** 715–16
from ships. *See also* Pollution from Ships, International Convention for Prevention of (MARPOL) (1973)
ballast water management, convention on, **2004:** 747; **2007:** 704–5
Control of Harmful Anti-Fouling Systems on Ships, Convention on, **2008:** 695–98
removal of wrecks, convention on, **2006:** 815–21; **2007:** 653–57
ship dismantling, **2004:** 747–49

Marine conservation (continued)
transboundary water pollution, **2006**: 855–59
transfer of oil cargo between oil tankers at sea, **2008**: 698–702
undersea noise pollution, **2004**: 746–47
responsibility for environmental contamination from sunken state-owned vessel, **1991-99**: 1620–21
South Pacific Regional Environment Agreement and Programme, **1989-90**: 491–97; **1991-99**: 1754–55
specially protected areas, **2007**: 705–6; **2008**: 702–3
trade agreements and, **2007**: 580–81
transboundary aquifers, **2008**: 716–21
Marine mammals. *See* Fish and marine mammals
Maritime issues. *See also* Environmental issues; Fish and marine mammals; Law of the Sea, UN Convention on (UNCLOS) (1982); Marine conservation
accidents in international waters, guidelines for fair treatment of seafarers in, **2006**: 825–28
archipelagic states, **1989-90**: 451, 460–61, 472–76; **1991-99**: 840, 1558, 1567, 1568, 1598; **2002**: 258, 747–56; **2004**: 700
waters of, innocent passage through, **2001**: 713–14; **2004**: 700, 703
Arctic continental shelf, **2007**: 617–19, 630
bills of lading. *See* Bills of lading
boundaries
archipelagic states. *See* archipelagic states, *this heading*
Arctic, Canadian claims in, **2006**: 814–15
Beaufort Sea, **2004**: 734–35, 1081, 1082, 1084, 1090; **2005**: 705–7; **2008**: 640–42
Canada–U.S. Boundary Waters Treaty 1958, **2005**: 688, 718
contiguous zone. *See* contiguous zone, *this heading*
continental shelf. *See* Continental shelf
exclusive economic zone. *See* exclusive economic zone, *this heading*
high seas. *See* high seas, *this heading*
interdiction. *See* interdiction, *this heading*
Law of the Sea, UN Convention on and. *See* Law of the Sea, UN Convention on (UNCLOS)
Machias Seal Island, **2005**: 707
Mexico–U.S. treaties, **1991-99**: 1571–73; **2000**: 697–700
Niue–U.S. treaty, **1991-99**: 1576–78
offshore platforms and, **2004**: 696–99, 974–76
straits. *See* straits, *this heading*
territorial sea. *See* territorial sea, *this heading*
UK–U.S. treaties concerning Caribbean, **1991-99**: 1574–76
U.S.–USSR maritime boundary agreement, **1989-90**: 434–37

Maritime issues (continued)
Canada claims against Panama Canal Commission, **2001**: 219–24
Carriage of Goods by Sea Act (COGSA). *See* Carriage of goods by sea
contiguous zone, **1989-90**: 465–70; **1991-99**: 840, 1569–70, 1578, 1597; **2000**: 697–700
Convention on. *See* Geneva Conventions on law of the sea (1958)
high seas freedom of navigation in, **1991-99**: 1570
Presidential Proclamation extending for U.S. to 24 miles by, **1991-99**: 714–31, 1569–70
continental shelf. *See also* Continental Shelf
Convention on. *See* Geneva Conventions on law of the sea (1958)
fixed platforms on continental shelf, safety of. *See* Suppression of Unlawful Acts Against the Safety of Maritime Navigation, Convention for (1988) and fixed platforms protocol, *this heading*
U.S.–Mexico Treaty on Delimitation of the Continental Shelf in the Western Gulf of Mexico Beyond 2000 Nautical Miles, **2000**: 697–700
counternarcotics law enforcement agreements. *See* Drug trade
crew issues, **2007**: 657–59
cruise ships, foreign-flag, applicability of U.S. law to, **1989-90**: 447–48; **1991-99**: 1621–29; **2002**: 131–33; **2005**: 707–11
customary international law. *See* Customary international law
Deep Seabed Hard Mineral Resources Act (1980), **2007**: 622
Deepwater Port Act of 1974 (DWPA), liquefied natural gas facility approval, **2005**: 693–95
diplomatic protection of foreign crew members of flagged ship, **2003**: 433–36
Dubai Ports World proposal to acquire U.S. ports, **2006**: 774–80
entry into ports under *force majeure*, **2007**: 650–53
exclusive economic zone, **1989-90**: 162–64, 445, 451, 463–65, 478–79; **1991-99**: 716, 840–41, 1558, 1574–75, 1576–77, 1583, 1588–89, 1710, 1727–28; **2000**: 698; **2001**: 694–95, 698, 699, 700, 704, 708–9; **2003**: 716–17, 737–41, 753–54, 801; **2004**: 675, 681–82, 686, 687–88, 689, 691, 696, 698, 700, 702, 704–5, 713; **2005**: 677–78, 683–84; **2006**: 817–18; **2007**: 619, 626, 643; **2008**: 135, 136, 623, 628, 642–44, 649, 693, 694, 702, 998
fishing rights, **1991-99**: 1707–11, 1726–34; **2004**: 675
no compensable property right to, **2004**: 724–30
high seas freedom of navigation in, **1989-90**: 445, 451; **1991-99**: 1690; **2001**: 698–99, 703–7, 710, 711–14; **2004**: 687–88, 696
Presidential Proclamation establishing, **2004**: 726

Maritime issues (continued)
fixed platforms on continental shelf, safety of. *See* Suppression of Unlawful Acts Against the Safety of Maritime Navigation, Convention for (1988) and fixed platform protocol, *this heading*
flag state responsibility for safety of vessels, **1989-90**: 456–59
Global Maritime Distress and Safety System, **2006**: 496–97
guano islands, U.S. sovereignty over, **1991-99**: 842–46
Gulf of Maine boundary case, **2007**: 640
hazardous materials, transport of, **1989-90**: 445–46, 492–93, 494, 495–96
Basel convention on, **1989-90**: 445; **1991-99**: 1687–93; **2002**: 775, 783–85; **2004**: 747–49; **2006**: 863–65
Head Harbor Passage, **2007**: 638–40
high seas, **1989-90**: 451, 452–59, 468–69, 492; **1991-99**: 1250, 1586, 1588–90, 1621, 1625, 1703–5, 1707–11, 1726–44, 1746, 1927; **2008**: 699. *See also* interdiction, *this heading*
Convention on. *See* Geneva Conventions on law of the sea (1958)
internal/inland waters, **1991-99**: 183; **2000**: 703–6; **2002**: 257–58, 738–47, 753–54; **2005**: 698–703. *See also* interdiction, *this heading*
interceptions during armed conflict pursuant to Security Council resolution, **1991-99**: 2107
interdiction
of aliens by U.S., rights of
asylum applications by migrants in safe haven, **1991-99**: 187–94
on high seas, **1991-99**: 150–72, 176–77
in U.S. internal waters, **1991-99**: 182–87
in U.S. territorial sea, **1991-99**: 172–80
for law enforcement purposes, **1989-90**: 448–56, 468–70; **1991-99**: 1600–1608; **2006**: 836–40; **2008**: 649–50
Mexico–U.S. letter of intent on maritime safety and security, **2008**: 651
UK–U.S. memorandum of understanding on suppression of illicit maritime traffic, **2008**: 650–51
International Maritime Organization (IMO), **1989-90**: 427; **1991-99**: 1040–41, 1590–92, 1637, 1639, 1681–82; **2001**: 683–84, 712, 940; **2002**: 104–5; **2004**: 748, 749, 1110; **2005**: 112, 685–86, 694, 732, 1117; **2008**: 621, 624, 626, 637, 706
Arctic region, **2008**: 633, 637
assembly (2007), **2007**: 634
Athens Protocol (2002), **2006**: 292–94
Control and Management of Ships' Ballast Water and Sediments, Convention for, **2004**: 747; **2007**: 704–5

Maritime issues (continued)
Control of Harmful Anti-Fouling Systems on Ships, Convention on, **2008**: 695–98
Convention on (1948), **1991-99**: 1040–41
ice-covered waters, ships in (Polar Code), **2008**: 624, 626
International Ship & Port Facility Security (ISPS) Code, **2008**: 112
long range identification and tracking of ships. *See* Long Range Identification and Tracking of Ships, *this heading*
Maritime Safety Committee, **2006**: 496–97, 835
piracy, **2007**: 634; **2008**: 622, 645–47
protection of particularly sensitive sea areas, **2002**: 788–90; **2008**: 702–3
recycling of ships, **2006**: 864
traffic separation scheme, **1989-90**: 470–71
Wrecks, Convention on Removal of, **2006**: 815–21; **2007**: 653–57
Iran–Iraq war, threats to shipping in Persian Gulf during, **2003**: 1037–39, 1040, 1043–46
jurisdiction, U.S. *See also* territorial sea, *this heading*
investigation of maritime accidents in international waters, **1989-90**: 447–48
over crimes committed aboard ships, **2000**: 363–64; **2002**: 133–37; **2008**: 125–36
reservation to transnational crime convention and protocols, **2004**: 146–47, 150, 158
labor sector, Maritime Labor Convention (2006), **2006**: 821–25
Long Range Identification and Tracking of Ships, **2006**: 494–96, 835–38
Maritime Drug Law Enforcement Act (2002), **2002**: 134–37; **2008**: 128, 129
Maritime Security, National Strategy for, **2005**: 688–89*n*, 691
Maritime Transportation Security Act of 2002 (MTSA), **2005**: 693; **2008**: 111–12
MARPOL. *See* Pollution from Ships, International Convention for Prevention of (MARPOL) (1973)
military survey activities: marine scientific research
China and, **2007**: 647–48
India and, **2007**: 648–50
navigation rights, **2006**: 806
archipelagic states. *See* archipelagic states, *this heading*
Canada, Marine Navigation Services Fee, **2005**: 688
contiguous zone. *See* contiguous zone, *this heading*
continental shelf. *See* Continental shelf
customary international law and freedom of navigation, **2008**: 700
exclusive economic zone. *See* exclusive economic zone, *this heading*

Maritime issues (continued)
fixed platforms and. *See* Suppression of Unlawful Acts Against the Safety of Maritime Navigation, Convention for (1988) and fixed platform protocol, *this heading*
high seas. *See* high seas, *this heading*
interdiction. *See* interdiction, *this heading*
International Commercial Navigation Treaty, **1989-90**: 292
interstate navigation, U.S. federal legislation controlling, **1991-99**: 775–82
marine scientific research, right to perform, **1989-90**: 477–80; **1991-99**: 1559–60, 1564, 1567; **2000**: 708; **2001**: 698–99, 713; **2003**: 718; **2005**: 684; **2008**: 624, 652
military survey, **2001**: 698–99
shipment of radioactive materials, **2001**: 699–703
stop and search of unflagged vessel, **2002**: 1052–54, 1056
straits. *See* straits, *this heading*
surveillance and emergency landing, **2001**: 703–11
territorial sea. *See* territorial sea, *this heading*
UN Convention on the Law of the Sea, **2006**: 806
U.S. transit through Dixon entrance, **1991-99**: 1593–96
of warships, **2000**: 707, 708
passport cards for sea travel to enter and depart U.S., **2006**: 11–13; **2008**: 8–9
patrimonial sea concept, **1989-90**: 451
piracy, **2007**: 630–34. *See also* Somalia, *subheading*: piracy
pollution from ships. *See* Pollution from Ships, International Convention for Prevention of (MARPOL) (1973)
preemption of state law by federal U.S. authority, **2006**: 904
paramountcy doctrine, **2002**: 251–55
statutes and treaties, **1991-99**: 775–82
protection of particularly sensitive sea areas, **2002**: 788–90; **2007**: 705–6; **2008**: 702–3
Protocol against the Smuggling of Migrants by Land, Sea and Air, **2007**: 1067
Public Vessels Act (1925), **1989-90**: 215–17
reflagging of Kuwaiti merchant vessels during Iran–Iraq war, **2003**: 1038
research. *See* Research
right to control submerged lands. *See* Submerged lands
rights of coastal states, **2000**: 708–9; **2001**: 713
Safety of Life at Sea Convention (SOLAS), **1991-99**: 784–85; **2003**: 752; **2005**: 694, 710; **2006**: 497, 835–38; **2007**: 660; **2008**: 634–35. *See also* Long Range Identification and Tracking of Ships, *this heading*

Maritime issues (continued)
salvage at sea, **1989-90**: 427–29; **2004**: 714; **2006**: 828–35
captured World War II German submarines, **1991-99**: 1617–18
determination of abandonment, **1991-99**: 1611–17
environmental issues, **1989-90**: 427–28
government rejection of salvage services, **2004**: 714–15
International Convention for the Unification of Certain Rules with Respect to Assistance and Salvage at Sea (1910), **1989-90**: 427
International Convention on Salvage (1989), **1989-90**: 427–29
Japanese minisubmarine sunk off Pearl Harbor, **1991-99**: 1619–20
Lusitania (sunken ocean liner), salvage of, **2005**: 760
protection of U.S. sunken government property and grave sites, **2001**: 688–92; **2004**: 716–24
rights of successor states, **1991-99**: 1608–11
Titanic salvage, **2001**: 695–97; **2004**: 715–16; **2005**: 762; **2006**: 828–35; **2008**: 657–65
U.S. claims to sunken ship in territorial waters of France, **1989-90**: 429–34
wrecks, authority over, **2006**: 818–19
search and rescue operations
Arctic region, **2008**: 634–35
Mexico, **1989-90**: 480
U.S.–Costa Rica Memorandum of Understanding between Ministry of Public Security and Coast Guard, **2008**: 656–57
Security and Accountability for Every Port Act (2006), **2006**: 305
shipping-related sanctions on entities of former Yugoslavia, **1991-99**: 1950, 1951
shrimp harvested in manner endangering sea turtles. *See* Fish and marine mammals, *subheading*: sea turtle protection
sovereign status of state-owned or operated vessels, **1989-90**: 477–80; **1991-99**: 1601, 1689, 1765–66
nuclear submarine, as sovereign representative in port visit, **1989-90**: 476–77
specially protected areas, **2007**: 705–6
straits
bridges across, **1991-99**: 1585–92
compulsory pilotage scheme for Torres Strait, **2006**: 810–12; **2007**: 640–41
Hormuz, **2008**: 862–63
Malacca and Singapore Straits, security of, **2006**: 806–10
Northwest Passage, **2006**: 814–15; **2008**: 631–32
right of transit passage, **1989-90**: 470–73; **1991-99**: 1586–90; **2005**: 684–87; **2008**: 620, 682–83

Maritime issues (continued)
submerged lands. *See* Submerged lands
Suppression of Unlawful Acts Against the Safety of Maritime Navigation, Convention for (1988) and fixed platform protocol, **1989-90**: 34, 110, 111–14; **2000**: 218; **2002**: 104–10, 133–34; **2008**: 125–30
2005 protocols, **2004**: 1110; **2005**: 112–13, 715, 1117–20, 1119*n*; **2006**: 211–12; **2007**: 140–42, 985–88, 1062–71; **2008**: 94–97, 889–90, 926–28, 930–32; 941–44
combating Somali piracy and, **2008**: 926–28, 930–32
Tank Vessel Act (1936), **1991-99**: 778, 784
territorial sea. *See also* interdiction, *this heading*
Convention on. *See* Geneva Conventions on law of the sea (1958)
Cuban, regulations concerning entry of U.S. vessels into, **2004**: 915–17
innocent passage through, right of, **1989-90**: 443–47; **1991-99**: 1586–88, 1596–1600, 1628, 1690, 1732; **2000**: 706–8; **2001**: 700, 711–12; **2002**: 739, 753; **2003**: 758–59; **2004**: 687, 701, 702, 713; **2006**: 812–14; **2008**: 620
exceptions to, **1991-99**: 1599–1600; **2004**: 687
Law of the Sea, UN Convention on (UNCLOS), **1989-90**: 459–62; **1991-99**: 1558, 1568–69, 1579–83, 1587, 1597–98; **2003**: 716; **2004**: 674–75, 698, 705–10; **2005**: 676, 679–80
limits of, **1989-90**: 445, 450; **1991-99**: 716, 725, 838, 840, 1574–75, 1577, 1579, 1583–84; **2002**: 257*n*; **2004**: 674–75, 698, 701, 702, 711, 725; **2005**: 676, 680; **2008**: 128, 623
baselines, **1989-90**: 459–62; **1991-99**: 179, 1580–83; **2000**: 703–4; **2002**: 732–33; **2004**: 705–10
Presidential proclamation extending for U.S. from 3 to 12 miles, **1991-99**: 173, 179; **2002**: 258*n*
ship-to-ship transfers, **2008**: 698–701
U.S. legislation relating to
in definition of "United States," **1991-99**: 179*n*
federal criminal jurisdiction, **1991-99**: 481, 485
state and federal gambling law, **1991-99**: 1621–29
state jurisdiction, **1991-99**: 1626–29; **2004**: 734; **2005**: 697–98
wrecks, authority over, **2006**: 818–19
terrorism and, **2001**: 683–84; **2008**: 111–12
transport of decommissioned nuclear reactor vessel, **2004**: 711–13
underwater cultural heritage. *See* Underwater cultural heritage
U.S. Commission on Ocean Policy, **2001**: 681–84

Maritime issues (continued)
U.S.–Mexico Treaty Relating to Utilization of Waters of the Colorado and Tijuana Rivers of the Rio Grande (1944), **2001**: 714–16
weapons of mass destruction nonproliferation initiatives, **2003**: 1095–99; **2004**: 1072–91, 1109. *See also* Nonproliferation
whaling. *See* Fish and marine mammals
Wreck Removal, Convention on, **2006**: 815–21; **2007**: 653–57
MARPOL. *See* Pollution from Ships, International Convention for Prevention of (MARPOL) (1973)
Marshall Islands
administration of, **1991-99**: 829
Compact of Free Association, **1991-99**: 814, 816, 817, 818; **2003**: 271–73; **2004**: 219; **2007**: 257–59; **2008**: 245–47
diplomatic relations with U.S., **1989-90**: 268–71
environmental protection agreement, **2002**: 791
maritime interdiction agreement, **2008**: 650
Nuclear Claims Tribunal award, litigation against U.S. concerning, **2006**: 316–25; **2007**: 256–63; **2008**: 245–47
Proliferation Security Initiative, **2004**: 1078, 1091
South Pacific regional environmental convention, **1989-90**: 491
trusteeship termination, **1989-90**: 161; **1991-99**: 817
Massachusetts
Massachusetts-Burma law regulating state procurement, **2000**: 319–40, 342; **2001**: 193, 194
Material witness warrants, 2003: 334
Mauritania
Alien Tort Statute litigation alleging trafficking of children from to UAE, **2008**: 227–36
maritime counterterrorism measures, conditions for failure to take, **2008**: 112
military coup in, **2008**: 806, 873
territorial sea baselines, **1989-90**: 461
travel restrictions, **2008**: 29, 806
Mauritius
American Servicemembers' Protection Act waiver, **2003**: 238
exclusive economic zone, intelligence operations in, **2004**: 688
extradition and mutual legal assistance, **2000**: 185*n*
Hague Child Abduction Convention, compliance with, **2003**: 127, 129; **2004**: 54; **2006**: 101
navigation hazards near, **2002**: 737–38
trade and investment issues, **2006**: 759–60
McCarran–Ferguson Act (1945), **1991-99**: 1529, 1530–33; **2000**: 468–70; **2003**: 467–68

Medallion stamp guarantees, 2001: 59
Mediation Act, Uniform (UMA), 2005: 805–7
Medical experimentation. *See also* Cloning
nonconsensual experimentation on humans, **2005:** 276–77
Memoranda of understanding, 2004: 1045. *See also* Agreements, generally; Treaties, generally
Anti-Ballistic Missile Systems Treaty, **1991-99:** 750–61
cultural property, **1991-99:** 1795–97, 1798–1800; **2001:** 769–74; **2002:** 813–15; **2004:** 791–92; **2006:** 901; **2007:** 739–40, 741–42; **2008:** 729–30
diplomatic parking program, **2004:** 541–42
Egypt–U.S. agreement concerning parental access, **2003:** 129–31
Fisheries and Aquaculture cooperation, **2002:** 796–98
Jordan–U.S. cooperation on parental access to children, **2006:** 103
legal status of, **2004:** 194–95
lost or stolen passports, U.S.–New Zealand MOU, **2006:** 17
missile defense, **2004:** 1066, 1068
piracy, International Maritime Organization, **2008:** 646
provisional application of treaty amendments through, **2002:** 186–90
related to START, **2004:** 1055
repatriation of Mexicans, **2004:** 238–39
search and rescue operations, **2008:** 656–57
stock exchanges and broker-dealers, mutual recognition, **2008:** 604–5
suppression of illicit maritime traffic, **2008:** 650–51
tax treaty arbitration, **2008:** 616
Memorandum of Agreement Regarding International Trade in Commercial Launch Services (1989) (U.S.–China), 1989-90: 481
***Mens rea*, 2004:** 327, 375
Methamphetamine. *See* Drug trade
Methyl bromide
amendment of EPA regulations to allow production for critical uses, **2005:** 719–25; **2006:** 866–71
Mexico. *See also* North American Free Trade Agreement (NAFTA)
admissibility of evidence obtained in, in U.S. court, **1989-90:** 100–7
adoption law, **2003:** 121
aviation, overflights, **2008:** 108
border issues
air travel and passport requirements, **2006:** 4–9
border control issues at IACHR, **2004:** 232–39
counterterrorism recommendations, **2006:** 210
cross-border broadcasting services, **2004:** 641
cross-border fiber optic installation, **2001:** 566–68
cross-border motor carriers, regulation of, **2002:** 666–70
new document requirement for U.S. entry by citizens of, **2007:** 8–10, 14–15; **2008:** 7–8

Mexico (continued)
Border Crossing Card (BCC). *See* passport cards, *this subheading*
Trusted Traveler Program and, **2007:** 15
visa requirement, **2007:** 14
passport cards (Border Crossing Cards (BCC)), **2006:** 11–13; **2007:** 14
passport cards for pedestrian, vehicular traffic, and sea travel by U.S. citizens to and from, **2008:** 8–9
presidential permits for construction and maintenance of U.S. border facilities, **2002:** 607
protocol on establishment of Border Environmental Cooperation Commission, **2005:** 606–7
Secure Fence Act of 2006, **2006:** 50–52
smart-border plan, **2002:** 121
transborder abduction from, **1991-99:** 435–45; **2000:** 398–412
trucking, U.S.-Mexico cross-border obligations under NAFTA, **2007:** 556–63
California Proposition 187 and, **1991-99:** 798
capital punishment
claims in ICJ against U.S. for failure of consular notification in capital punishment cases involving Mexican nationals, **2007:** 73–74; **2008:** 175–215. *See also* Consular notification and access
protest, **2005:** 270
cement trade, **2006:** 758–59
Chamizal, Convention between U.S. and Mexico for Solution of Problem of, **2000:** 294
child support enforcement, **1991-99:** 1866
citizenship laws, **1991-99:** 25–27
coercive measures against foreign states, comments on, **2005:** 528
consular notification. *See* Consular notification and access
consular privileges and immunities, **1991-99:** 1309–11
cultural objects protection, **1991-99:** 1803
deep water port approval, **2005:** 695
deportation of former government official from U.S., **1991-99:** 121–26
drug trade, **2001:** 120; **2002:** 124; **2003:** 181; **2004:** 133–34; **2005:** 135; **2006:** 213, 218; **2007:** 163–66; **2008:** 113
environmental issues
hazardous wastes, **1991-99:** 1686, 1689, 1692
migratory bird and animal protection agreement, **1991-99:** 1770–71, 1774–77
European Union–U.S. banana trade dispute, **1991-99:** 1415; **2001:** 649–50
Exchange Stabilization Fund, **1991-99:** 1494–1500

Mexico (continued)
extradition and mutual legal assistance, **1991-99**: 392–93, 396, 436, 437–41, 444–45, 959; **2000**: 178, 179, 186*n*, 394*n*; **2001**: 93*n*; **2003**: 140, 141
extradition request, **2001**: 70–87; **2005**: 353
extradition, life imprisonment assurances request, **2002**: 73–74
extradition, temporary surrender under extradition agreement, **2008**: 72–73
extraterritorial arrest and detention by U.S. law enforcement officials in, **2001**: 326–34; **2002**: 346; **2003**: 380–83; **2004**: 340–54
fish and marine mammals
sea turtle protection, **1991-99**: 1713, 1720
shark protection, **2004**: 766
Foreign Trade Act, **2005**: 624
Hague Child Abduction Convention, compliance with, **1991-99**: 355–56, 366; **2002**: 54–56; **2003**: 127, 129; **2004**: 54; **2006**: 102; **2008**: 50
immigration issues, U.S. immigration policy, **2001**: 254, 263
immunity, **2005**: 562, 569
indigenous peoples, views concerning UN declaration on, **2008**: 353–54, 354*n*
intellectual property rights Watch List, **2006**: 768; **2007**: 610
Inter-American Convention Against Corruption, party to, **2006**: 238
Inter-American Convention Against Terrorism (OAS Terrorism Convention), party to, **2004**: 97; **2005**: 111
international civil litigation, **2004**: 850
maritime boundaries, **1991-99**: 699, 1571–73
maritime safety and security, Mexico–U.S. letter of intent on, **2008**: 651
Maritime Search and Rescue, Agreement on, **1989-90**: 480
money laundering in, **2004**: 135
NAFTA, **2004**: 616, 622
Chapter 11 disputes, **1991-99**: 1436; **2001**: 568–70, 574, 606, 624, 641–46; **2003**: 642–48; **2004**: 576*n*, 583–84*n*, 586*n*, 596–601
removal of remaining tariffs and quotas with U.S., **2008**: 542
NAFTA Consolidation Tribunal, **2005**: 600
objections to U.S. reservations to Genocide Convention, **1989-90**: 144
prisoner transfer agreement, **2000**: 37; **2001**: 51; **2003**: 69–70, 131–33; **2008**: 51–52
property takings claims against Mexico, request for U.S. espousal of, **1991-99**: 1075–76
recognition of judgment from, **1991-99**: 1838–41

Mexico (continued)
requests to U.S. embassy for notarial service for parental consent to adoption, **2003**: 118–22
satellite regulation and, **2008**: 392
search and seizure of property owned by nonresident alien conducted in, **1991-99**: 194
stolen vehicle treaty, **2000**: 170
tax treaties, **2008**: 612
telecommunications issues under General Agreement on Trade in Services (GATS), **2005**: 624
tequila trade, **2006**: 757–58
trade agreements, **2005**: 639
trafficking in persons, **2008**: 296
transborder arrest. *See* Crime
tuna
Inter-American Tropical Tuna Commission, **2000**: 307
U.S. embargo on tuna from, **2001**: 750–52
U.S. claims convention with, **2001**: 582
U.S. jurisdiction in crime committed in Mexican territorial waters, **2002**: 131–33
U.S. military assistance, **2006**: 278
U.S. water allocation agreement, **2001**: 714–16; **2002**: 757–59
U.S.–Mexico Treaty on Delimitation of the Continental Shelf in the Western Gulf of Mexico Beyond 2000 Nautical Miles, **2000**: 697–700
voluntary repatriation to, **2004**: 26–27
waiver of Article 98 agreement with U.S. (nonsurrender of Americans to ICC), **2006**: 279
Western Hemisphere Travel Initiative, **2005**: 1–5; **2006**: 4–5, 7, 9, 10; **2007**: 8–12, 14–15; **2008**: 6–8
WTO and. *See* World Trade Organization (WTO)
Mexico City policy, 2001: 283–93
Micronesia. *See also* Marshall Islands; Northern Mariana Islands, Commonwealth of (CNMI); Palau
Compact of Free Association between U.S. and (1986), **1991-99**: 826, 829, 830; **2003**: 271–73; **2006**: 318–20
diplomatic relations with U.S., **1989-90**: 268–71
environmental protection agreement, **2002**: 791
longshore work by alien crewmen from, **2002**: 757; **2003**: 764
maritime interdiction agreement, **2008**: 650
Micronesian Claims Act (1971), **2002**: 985
satellite regulation and, **2003**: 699
South Pacific regional environmental convention, **1989-90**: 491
trusteeship termination, **1989-90**: 161; **2006**: 318

Middle East Conflict, Israeli-Palestinian, 2002: 910–19; 2004: 944–45, 947, 950–56
abduction of Israeli soldier, U.S. position on, **2006**: 1233–35
agreement on access and movement (2005), **2005**: 915–17
Agreement on the Gaza Strip and the Jericho Area (1994), **1991-99**: 1994–95
Annapolis conference, **2007**: 850–54
Arab League Beirut Summit Initiative, **2002**: 915, 917
Arab Peace Initiative, **2007**: 846–47, 856; **2008**: 819, 823
Gulf Cooperation States, Egypt, Jordan, and U.S., joint statement, 2007: 855–59
Hebron redeployment protocol (1997), **1991-99**: 1997–98
Human Rights Council special sessions on, **2006**: 335–38
Interim Agreement on the West Bank and Gaza Strip (1995), **1991-99**: 1995, 1999; **2003**: 943–51; **2004**: 947
Israeli disengagement from captured territories, **2004**: 287, 950–54
ICJ advisory opinion on Israel's construction of wall in Palestinian Territory (2004), **2003**: 949–51; **2004**: 944–49, 972–74; **2006**: 1023–24
Jordan and, **1991-99**: 1986, 1991
Israel–Jordan Common Agenda (1993), **1991-99**: 1995–96
Treaty of Peace, Israel–Jordan (1994), **1991-99**: 1997
Washington Declaration (1994), **1991-99**: 1996
Madrid Conference (1991), **1991-99**: 1983–88; **2002**: 915, 919
Mecca agreement, **2007**: 844
Middle East Peace Facilitation Act (1993), **1991-99**: 1992–94
Occupied Territory. *See* Law of war
Oslo Accords (1993), **1991-99**: 1989–92, 2001–2
Palestinian Anti-Terrorism Act (2006), **2006**: 306, 993–95
Palestinian government
death of Yasser Arafat, U.S.–UK joint statement, **2004**: 957
election of Palestinian President Abbas and subsequent developments (U.S. views), **2005**: 905–10
national unity government (2007), **2007**: 845
break-up and establishment of government without Hamas, **2007**: 847–48
Quartet (U.S., EU, Russia and UN) statements, **2005**: 905–6, 907–10, 913–15; **2006**: 1028–32; **2007**: 844–48; **2008**: 816–19
U.S. sanctions removal, **2007**: 825–27
Palestinian refugees, **2005**: 918
Quartet (EU, Russia, UN, U.S.) peace efforts, **2002**: 915, 916–19; **2004**: 953–54, 956; **2005**: 905–6, 908–10, 913–15; **2007**: 844–50; **2008**: 816–19. *See also* Palestinian government, *this heading*

Middle East Conflict, Israeli-Palestinian (continued)
Roadmap to two-state solution, **2002**: 915; **2003**: 943–48; **2004**: 945, 947, 949, 955; **2005**: 537–38, 906, 910–15; **2006**: 1027
special envoy for Gaza disengagement, **2005**: 907–10, 915
Security Council resolutions, **2008**: 819–24
Sharm el-Sheikh Fact-Finding Committee report (2001), **2001**: 823–25
Sharm el-Sheikh Memorandum (1999), **1991-99**: 2003–4
"State of Palestine," **1989-90**: 203–5
two-state solution, statements by President Bush on, **2002**: 910–14; **2005**: 910–13; **2006**: 1026–28
UN role, **2004**: 287, 955–56; **2005**: 917–19. *See also* Quartet (EU, Russia, UN, U.S.) peace efforts, *this heading*
U.S. role in, **2005**: 906–7; **2007**: 441–43, 838–39
Wye River Memorandum (1998), **1991-99**: 1998–2001
Middle East Peace Facilitation Act (1993), 1991-99: 1992–94
Midway Islands
sovereignty of U.S. and, **2003**: 485
Migrants. *See* Immigration and visas
Migration Accords, U.S.–Cuba, 2002: 20–22
Migration and Refugee Assistance Act of 1962, 2006: 55, 56
Migratory birds
Albatrosses and Petrels, Agreement on the Conservation of, **2008**: 153–54, 166–68, 722–25
Migratory Bird Treaty Act (1948), **1991-99**: 1769
Migratory Birds and Game Mammals, Convention for the Protection of (Mexico–U.S.), **1991-99**: 1770, 1776–77
Migratory Birds in Canada and U.S., Convention for Protection of, **1991-99**: 1770–76
Military activities. *See also* Armed conflict; Arms control; Detainees, military; Gulf War; Law of war; Military personnel; Peacekeeping missions; Prisoners of war
accidental conflict, U.S.–USSR agreement on prevention of, **1989-90**: 549–51
Army Act of 1955, **2005**: 573
Army Field Manual, **2006**: 1164–68
attacks on civil aircraft, **1991-99**: 544
authorization for U.S. use of force. *See* Law of war, *subheading*: use of force
collision and emergency landing of U.S. military aircraft in China, **2001**: 703–11
compensation for bombing of Chinese Embassy in Belgrade, **2000**: 421–29

Military activities (continued)
Conference on Security and Cooperation in Europe, **1991-99:** 2241–43
conscientious objection, **2004:** 394–95
conscription and recruitment, **2000:** 357–58, 359–60
conventional armed forces in Europe, **1991-99:** 2222–38
Conventional Weapons Convention. *See* Conventional weapons
disproportionate use of military force, **2006:** 465–76
downing of Iran Air Flight 655, **1989-90:** 212–17
as exception to extradition, **2000:** 182; **2004:** 75–77
exceptions for in certain conventions
Convention for the Physical Protection of Nuclear Material, amendment to, **2007:** 1076–78; **2008:** 890
International Convention for the Suppression of Acts of Nuclear Terrorism, **2007:** 133–35; **2008:** 890
MARPOL Convention, **2003:** 785
Protocols of 2005 to the Convention for the Suppression of Unlawful Acts Against the Safety of Maritime Navigation and to the Protocol Concerning Safety of Fixed Platforms on the Continental Shelf, **2007:** 140–41, 985–88; **2008:** 890
terrorist bombings convention, **1991-99:** 497–98
Foreign Military Sales, **2004:** 420
GPS and, **2004:** 739
head-of-state immunity and, **1989-90:** 311–14
humanitarian protection treaties, **2000:** 756
as infringement on freedom of commerce, **2003:** 1062–64, 1065–66
military abduction by U.S. military forces in Peru claim, **2004:** 226
military assistance, **2004:** 185, 187, 251–54; **2006:** 278–79
Military Claims Act (MCA), **2005:** 982–83
military commissions. *See* Military commissions for trial of certain non-U.S. enemy combatants[11]
Military Extraterritorial Jurisdiction Act. *See* Military Extraterritorial Jurisdiction Act (2000)
military training by terrorist organization, criminalization of receipt of, **2004:** 125
missile attack on U.S.S. Stark, **1989-90:** 217–19
Open Skies Treaty, **1991-99:** 2238–41
radioactive waste management, **1991-99:** 1698–99
right of maritime navigation and overflight, **1989-90:** 439–40, 444–45, 451–52, 468–69, 476–77; **1991-99:** 1559, 1565–69, 1596–1600; **2000:** 707, 708; **2004:** 674–75, 681, 693–94, 699–702, 710–11

---

[11] Editor's note: The Military Commissions Act of 2009, Pub. L. 111-84, uses the term "enemy belligerents" rather than "enemy combatants."

Military activities (continued)
sunken vessels, protection of, **2004**: 716–24
survey operation in coastal waters of South Korea, **2001**: 698–99
Takings Clause and, **2004**: 206–14
terrorist acts as distinct from, **2001**: 104, 106
UN Law of the Sea and, **2003**: 719–20, 726–29, 737–38; **2004**: 674–75, 681, 682, 683, 689–90, 693–96
dispute settlement procedures, **2004**: 677, 687, 688, 694
Uniform Code of Military Justice. *See* Uniform Code of Military Justice (UCMJ)
use of force issues. *See* Law of war, *subheading*: use of force
use of lasers, **2006**: 1093–94
use of outer space, **2001**: 717
U.S.–USSR agreement on advance notification of strategic exercises, **1989-90**: 566
War Claims Act (1948), **2000**: 503, 505, 511, 512–14, 528–31
war crimes. *See* War crimes
war powers. *See* President, U.S.
Military commissions for trial of certain non-U.S. enemy combatants,[12] **2002**: 972–76; **2005**: 187, 965; **2006**: 1115, 1138–77
appellate procedure, **2006**: 1169–70, 1175
Court of Military Commission Review, **2007**: 977–82
Detainee Treatment Act (2005), **2005**: 1030, 1035, 1036
litigation in U.S. courts concerning, **2004**: 981, 998, 1018–29; **2005**: 994
Military Commissions Act (MCA) (2006), **2006**: 1104, 1156, 1160–63, 1168–77, 1179–83; **2007**: 111, 917, 919, 922, 939, 944, 945, 950–51, 968, 970, 977–79, 981; **2008**: 891–92
presidential authority to convene, **2006**: 1144–54
presidential military order establishing, **2001**: 872–81; **2006**: 1139–40
determinations of individuals subject to, **2003**: 1032–33; **2005**: 969
procedures, instructions and appointments for, **2002**: 957–72; **2003**: 1030–36; **2007**: 976
military courts martial and, **2006**: 1146–50
Supreme Court decision invalidating for violations of UCMJ and Geneva Conventions, **2006**: 1144–51
establishment of new procedures in response to. *See* Military Commissions Act (MCA) (2006), *this heading*
proceedings by, in individual cases

[12] Editor's note: The Military Commissions Act of 2009, Pub. L. 111-84, uses the term "enemy belligerents" rather than "enemy combatants."

Military commissions for trial of certain non-U.S. enemy combatants (continued)
conviction for material support to terrorism by, **2007:** 976; **2008:** 917
determination of status as "alien unlawful enemy combatant,"[13] **2007:** 976–82; **2008:** 916–17
report to UN Committee on Torture, **2005:** 969
response to UN human rights rapporteurs, **2005:** 992–93
war crimes, jurisdiction over, **2006:** 1115, 1160, 1162, 1169, 1171–74, 1176, 1182
Military Extraterritorial Jurisdiction Act (2000), **2004:** 168–71, 172, 306*n*; **2005:** 185–88
Military Extraterritorial Justice Act, 2007: 929–30
Military personnel
American Servicemembers' Protection Act, **2002:** 168–75; **2003:** 226–27, 228–29, 234, 237–39; **2004:** 176, 185; **2005:** 202
bringing to justice, **2003:** 343–44; **2004:** 400, 991, 993, 1025–28, 1037, 1038
child soldiers. *See also* Children, *subheading*: Rights of the Child, Convention on
Child Soldiers Accountability Act (2008), **2008:** 312–14
Child Soldiers Prevention Act (2008), **2008:** 314–15
citizenship of dual national who served in foreign army, **1991-99:** 21–23
employment of American citizen in foreign military, **2000:** 586*n*
extraterritorial jurisdiction. *See* Military Extraterritorial Jurisdiction Act (2000)
International Criminal Court jurisdiction, **1991-99:** 629–31, 636, 639; **2000:** 249–50, 278, 280*n*; **2002:** 152–53, 157–61, 162, 323, 908–9; **2003:** 222–30, 231–40; **2004:** 176, 179, 184, 185, 188
in Multinational Force and Observers, **1989-90:** 206–7
in NATO forces, jurisdiction over, **2004:** 481–82
in peacekeeping operations, **2004:** 188
Persian Gulf Conflict Supplemental Authorization and Personnel Benefits Act, **1991-99:** 2070
POW/MIA issues, **1991-99:** 348, 1155, 1159–61, 1493
recruitment age, **2002:** 287–88, 295, 296; **2003:** 307; **2008:** 301, 302
role of women, **1989-90:** 170; **1991-99:** 902–3
safety of UN peacekeeping forces. *See* Peacekeeping missions
Selective Service Act (1948), **2001:** 473
War Crimes Act, **1991-99:** 509–10, 512–13

[13] Editor's note: The Military Commissions Act of 2009, Pub. L. 111-84, uses the term "enemy belligerents" rather than "enemy combatants."

Military property
immunity from attachment or execution, **1989-90**: 299
Military tribunals, 1991-99: 513. *See also* Military commissions for trial of certain non-U.S. enemy combatants[14]
Millennium Challenge Act (2003), **2004**: 187, 280, 298; **2005**: 671–73
Millennium Challenge Corporation, 2005: 429, 671–72
compacts, **2005**: 673–74
Threshold Country Program, **2005**: 673
Millennium Declaration, 2005: 334, 445
Millennium Development Goals, U.S. views on, 2005: 333–35, 453
Mines and landmines. *See* Arms control
laying of mines. *See* Hague Conventions, *subheading*: on law of war
Mining
gold mining and NAFTA Chapter 11 disputes, **2006**: 709–26
Mineral Lands Leasing Act (1920), **1991-99**: 1476
Safety and Health in Mines, Convention Concerning, **1991-99**: 998–1000
Minnesota. *See also* Great Lakes
Devils Lake flooding and ecological protection, **2005**: 717
police to videotape or audiotape questioning of suspects in homicide cases, **2005**: 360
Minors. *See* Children
Missile Technology Control Act (1990), **1991-99**: 2359
Missile Technology Control Regime (MTCR). *See* Nonproliferation
Missiles. *See* Arms control; Ballistic missiles; Nonproliferation
ABM Treaty. *See* Anti-Ballistic Missile (ABM) Treaty (1972) (U.S.–USSR)
Missing persons, 2004: 331–36
Mississippi, NAFTA Chapter Eleven claims arising out of litigation in, 2001: 623–42
Missouri, Memorandum of Understanding between Province of Manitoba and, 2001: 179–98
MLATs (Mutual Legal Assistance Treaties). *See* Mutual legal assistance
Mobile Equipment, Cape Town Convention on International Interests in (2001), 1991-99: 1822; **2001**: 722–25, 778–79, 790–91; **2002**: 759, 818, 823, 825–26, 827; **2003**: 768–69, 834–35, 848–54; **2004**: 801, 802, 834; **2005**: 802, 803
Aircraft Protocol, **2004**: 742, 834–36; **2008**: 746, 748, 749, 750
draft protocol on space assets, **2004**: 802; **2005**: 802–5; **2006**: 931–34; **2008**: 747–51

[14] Editor's note: The Military Commissions Act of 2009, Pub. L. 111-84, uses the term "enemy belligerents" rather than "enemy combatants."

Moldova
commercial activities exception to FSIA immunity in sale of military aircraft, **1991-99**: 1220–23
diplomatic relations, **1991-99**: 1174
domestic violence laws, lack of, **2005**: 313
foreign military presence, **1991-99**: 2236–38
sanctions, **2002**: 1069; **2003**: 1119–20
succession issues, **1991-99**: 742
trade and investment issues, **1991-99**: 1455, 1466
trafficking in persons, **2008**: 118
Monaco
diplomatic relations, **2006**: 528
extradition and mutual legal assistance, **2000**: 185*n*
nonimmigrant visa waiver pilot program, **1991-99**: 76
Money laundering, **2006**: 241–54; **2008**: 120–21. *See also specific countries*
Banco Delta Asia, fifth special measure against, **2007**: 172–73
Corruption Convention (UN, 2003), **2005**: 170, 172, 173–74
designation of countries and financial institutions involved in, **2002**: 126–31; **2003**: 208–12; **2004**: 135, 136–38; **2005**: 176–84; **2006**: 241–49
Egmont Group combating, **2001**: 911; **2002**: 892–93; **2005**: 1105
extradition and, **2003**: 136
Financial Action Task Force (FATF) to combat, **2001**: 108, 893, 911; **2002**: 115, 891–92; **2003**: 154, 157, 210–11; **2004**: 117, 122, 138; **2005**: 442–43, 898, 902; **2006**: 999; **2007**: 1043, 1047–50; **2008**: 984
Financial Crimes Enforcement Network (FinCEN), **2002**: 892–93; **2003**: 208–11; **2004**: 136–37, 138; **2005**: 176–84, 896, 1073; **2006**: 141, 243–53; **2008**: 120–21, 981
International Narcotics Control Strategy report on, **2004**: 135; **2005**: 136
OAS Inter-American Convention Against Terrorism, **2005**: 111
Security Council 1267 sanctions committee, statements to, **2005**: 895, 898
Transnational Organized Crime Convention, **2004**: 145, 150–51, 159; **2005**: 155, 156
Yugraneft takeover, **2005**: 833
Mongolia
Article 98 agreement, **2003**: 238
most-favored-nation status, **1991-99**: 1455
sanctions on, **1991-99**: 1945–62
succession issues and UN membership, **1991-99**: 1163–69
trade and investment agreements, **1991-99**: 1466

Mongolia (continued)
UN mission's liability for local property taxes, dispute concerning, **2006:** 592–603; **2007:** 455–62; **2008:** 456–57, 495–98
Montagnards
entry restriction exemptions and, **2007:** 70–72; **2008:** 29–31
Montenegro. *See also* Serbia and Montenegro
diplomatic relations, **2006:** 529
peace process after breakup of Yugoslavia, **1991-99:** 147–48, 1147, 1979–82; **2008:** 815–16
preservation of American heritage in, **2008:** 735–36
status of, **2005:** 499, 939–40; **2006:** 528–29
unblocking of blocked assets of, **2002:** 897–900
Yugoslavia sanctions program, **2001:** 803–6
Montreal Convention. *See* Aviation issues
Montreal Protocol on Substances that Deplete the Ozone Layer. *See* Air pollution, *subheading*: ozone protection
Montreal Protocols (1975). *See* Aviation issues
Montserrat
temporary protected status for nationals of, **1991-99:** 246–47; **2003:** 36; **2004:** 32–33
Moral damages, state responsibility for, 2001: 378–79
Morocco
environmental cooperation, **2004:** 776
free trade agreement, **2002:** 722–23; **2003:** 682; **2004:** 616, 618, 776; **2005:** 640, 757; **2006:** 766
Guantanamo detainees, **2004:** 987; **2005:** 967
non-North Atlantic Treaty Organization (NATO) ally, designation as, **2005:** 1044
Nuclear Terrorism, Global Initiative to Combat, **2006:** 1295–96
Western Sahara conflict resolution, **2008:** 851–52
Moscow Treaty on Strategic Offensive Reductions, 2002: 1017–23; **2003:** 1068; **2004:** 1056–59; **2005:** 1054, 1110; **2008:** 950
Most-favored-nation status. *See* Trade
Motor vehicles
recognition of foreign driver's license, **2002:** 18–20
stolen vehicle treaties, **2000:** 169–70; **2002:** 61, 64–65, 68
Mozambique
conflict resolution in, **1991-99:** 2010
trade and investment agreements, **1991-99:** 1466
MTCR (Missile Technology Control Regime). *See* Nonproliferation
Multilateral Agreement on Investment (OECD), 1991-99: 1447, 1486–93

Multinational Force in Iraq, 2004: 1046–50; **2005:** 975–78, 1039–41; **2006:** 1235–38
civilian security detainees, authority to hold, **2007:** 959–60, 962*n*
described, **2007:** 959; **2008:** 919
detention by, whether constitutes detention in U.S. custody, **2006:** 1194–1202, 1207–13; **2008:** 918–20. *See also* Detainees, military
effect of extension of authority in Iraq, **2008:** 858
establishment of, **2007:** 959
participation of U.S. troops, **2008:** 461
U.S. prisoners held by, challenges to transfer to Iraqi government in U.S. court, **2006:** 1194–1213; **2007:** 956–68; **2008:** 73–78, 916, 918–20
Mutual Administrative Assistance in Tax Matters (1988) (Council of Europe-OECD), 1989-90: 410–11
Mutual Educational and Cultural Exchange Act (1961), 1991-99: 891, 1807–8
Mutual legal assistance, 2004: 1065. *See also* Evidence; Judicial assistance; Law enforcement
assistance benefits of, **2002:** 65–66, 74
bank secrecy and, **1989-90:** 131
basis for denial of requests for, **2000:** 167, 168
compulsory process and, **1991-99:** 451–52
in criminal matters, **2006:** 108
cybercrime, **2003:** 204–5; **2004:** 96, 97–99
in death penalty cases, **2002:** 69–70
defendant's access to information, **1991-99:** 451–52
enforcement of competition laws, **1991-99:** 1540–50
evidence, use of information by requesting state as, **2000:** 169; **2006:** 144–45
forfeiture of assets, **1991-99:** 449–50; **2000:** 168
goals, **2000:** 166–67
illicit arms trafficking, **1991-99:** 555–56
International Crime Control Strategy, **1991-99:** 396–97
International Criminal Court and, **1991-99:** 640–41; **2000:** 173; **2002:** 168–71, 174
investigation of human rights abuses in Argentina, **2002:** 270–71
joint investigative teams, **2006:** 142–44
letters rogatory and, **1991-99:** 453–55
litigation concerning implementation of treaty with Canada, **2003:** 145–49
political offense exceptions, **2002:** 109
as potential threat to ongoing investigation, **1989-90:** 132
reporting lost or stolen passports, **2004:** 6–7

Mutual legal assistance (continued)
Summit of the Americas declaration, **2004:** 1065
in tax matters, **1989-90:** 410–11; **2000:** 168
treaties (MLATs), **1991-99:** 447–56; **2000:** 163, 164, 166–69; **2002:** 61, 62–63, 65, 66–67, 69–70, 74–76, 79; **2003:** 145; **2005:** 174–75; **2008:** 11
Canada–U.S., litigation concerning implementation of, **2003:** 145–49
European Union–U.S., **2003:** 135–38, 241–43; **2004:** 73; **2005:** 78; **2006:** 139–47; **2008:** 78
bilateral implementing instruments with EU member states, **2004:** 74; **2006:** 146–47; **2008:** 78
territorial application, **2006:** 145–46
Germany–U.S., **2004:** 93–95; **2005:** 69, 72, 77–78; **2006:** 148
Japan–U.S., **2003:** 143–45; **2005:** 69, 72–73, 78–79; **2006:** 148
Malaysia–U.S., **2006:** 147–48; **2008:** 79
Mexico–U.S., **2000:** 394*n*
Sweden–U.S., **2004:** 74; **2006:** 147; **2008:** 89
treaties (non-MLAT), provisions in
Convention Against Illicit Traffic in Narcotic Drugs and Psychotropic Substances, **1989-90:** 129, 130–31
Inter-American Convention against Corruption, **1991-99:** 563–71; **2001:** 160
Inter-American Convention Against Terrorism, **2002:** 115–16
Nuclear Terrorism Convention, **2005:** 107
OECD bribery convention, **1991-99:** 561
Transnational Organized Crime Convention and protocols, **2004:** 96, 100, 153*n*
UN Corruption Convention, **2003:** 208; **2005:** 165, 174–75
U.S.–USSR memorandum of understanding on Nazi war criminals, **1989-90:** 99–100
video-conferencing, **2006:** 144
Myanmar. *See* Burma

N

NADBank. *See* North American Development Bank (NADBank)
NAFTA. *See* North American Free Trade Agreement (NAFTA)
NAFTA Implementation Act (1993), 2002: 694–95
Nagorno-Karabakh conflict, 2008: 830–32
Namibia
control over exclusive economic zone, **1989-90:** 470
crash of U.S. Air Force C-141 in, **2001:** 691–93
lifting of sanctions, **1989-90:** 522–24
longshore work prohibition on alien crewmen from, **2002:** 757; **2003:** 764

Namibia (continued)
UN impartiality package, **1989-90:** 200–1
UN plan for independence for, **1989-90:** 197–200
U.S. military assistance, **2006:** 278
U.S. support of UN peacekeeping action, **1989-90:** 201–3
waiver of Article 98 agreement with U.S. (nonsurrender of Americans to ICC), **2006:** 279
Narcotrafficking. *See* Drug trade
National Counterterrorism Center (NCTC), 2006: 167
National Emergencies Act (1976), 1989-90: 512; **1991-99:** 547, 1366, 1889, 1917, 1925, 1950, 1956, 1964, 2363; **2000:** 618; **2001:** 143, 797, 804, 806, 848, 866, 883, 889; **2002:** 883, 884, 1039; **2003:** 909, 917, 923, 929, 931, 1117; **2004:** 888, 915, 920, 1133; **2005:** 265, 889, 1126; **2006:** 975, 984; **2008:** 792, 799, 801
National Environmental Policy Act (1969), 2001: 750; **2002:** 670
National Firearms Act (1954), 1991-99: 558
National Foundation on the Arts and Humanities Act (1965), 1991-99: 891
National Historic Preservation Act (1966), 1989-90: 377–79; **2001:** 691; **2003:** 757
National Industrial Transportation League, 2002: 831
National Nuclear Security Administration Act (1999), 2004: 1104
National Public Safety Commission (Japan), 2005: 73, 78–79
National security, U.S., 1991-99: 37, 154, 745, 850, 1241, 1323, 1578, 1633, 1811, 1882, 1957, 2082, 2303. *See also* Antiterrorism and Effective Death Penalty Act (AEDPA) (1996); Homeland Security, Department of (DHS); Intelligence and surveillance; PATRIOT Act, USA (2001); Terrorism
access to airline passenger name record data, **2004:** 108–16; **2005:** 586–87
AIDS/HIV and, **2003:** 816–17
aliens. *See also* Deportation; Immigration and visas, *subheading*: exclusion of aliens; Removal of aliens from U.S.
collection of information from foreign visitors and immigrants, **2003:** 15–19
detention based on, **2003:** 29–33; **2005:** 22*n*, 291–92, 1001, 1008–9. *See also* Detainees, military
exclusion of aliens for danger to national security, **1989-90:** 33, 40, 46, 52
fingerprinting of arriving aliens, **2004:** 27–29
removal. *See* Detainees, military; Detention of aliens, nonmilitary; Removal of aliens from U.S.

National security, U.S. (continued)
allocation of responsibilities in U.S. Constitution, **2002**: 987–89
Anti-Terrorism Act of 1987 (ATA), **2005**: 539–42
Anti-Terrorism and Effective Death Penalty Act of 1996 (AEDPA). *See* Anti-Terrorism and Effective Death Penalty Act of 1996 (AEDPA)
attorney–client privilege and, **2004**: 1033–34
Burma as threat to, **2005**: 891–92
Chagos Archipelago litigation and, **2005**: 417
claims to submerged lands by U.S. state and, **2002**: 740–41, 754–56
Committee on Foreign Investment in U.S. (CFIUS), **2006**: 774–80; **2008**: 593–600
congressional authorization for U.S. military action against Iraq, **2002**: 933–37
congressional authorization for U.S. military action in response to 9/11, **2001**: 864–66, 871–72
Cuba and, **1991-99**: 55, 57–59, 65, 1445
Defense Department investigations and, **2005**: 231
drug trafficking, **1991-99**: 545, 547, 551, 553; **2005**: 145; **2007**: 166–67
Executive Branch waiver based on, **1991-99**: 2294, 2353, 2360, 2361
executive order on biochemical weapons, **1989-90**: 512–13. *See also* Executive Orders, Presidential
Export Administration license requirements, **2005**: 1044–45
financial areas targeted by Treasury Department, **2005**: 1130. *See also* Money laundering
FISA court and, **2005**: 1001
foreign control of U.S. company, prohibition on, **1989-90**: 418–24
foreign investment and, **1991-99**: 1461
Foreign Investment and National Security Act of 2007 (FINSA), **2007**: 601–5; **2008**: 593–600
Foreign Missions Act (FMA), **2005**: 532, 533, 535–39
freedom of navigation and, **2005**: 690
human rights and, **2005**: 439
India, strategic partnership with U.S. and, **2005**: 1082–83
International Criminal Court and, **2002**: 908
International Health Regulations (IHRs), application to U.S. armed forces, **2005**: 770
Iraq, national emergency concerning, **2005**: 869
judicial deference to Executive on matters of, **2005**: 535
Law of the Sea and, **1991-99**: 1557, 1565–66, 1567, 1568; **2004**: 677–79, 681–82, 690–91, 692–96
importance of U.S. accession to, **2005**: 675–77, 679; **2007**: 613, 615, 616–17, 624–29; **2008**: 620

National security, U.S. (continued)
Libya, chemical weapon (CW) destruction in, **2005**: 1065–66
military considerations and, **1991-99**: 626, 2160, 2163, 2166, 2194, 2220, 2222, 2239, 2247, 2275, 2313–14, 2334, 2342, 2344, 2347, 2349, 2354, 2364
missile technology, **2005**: 1132. *See also* Arms control
national emergency based on threat to, **1991-99**: 1886, 1924, 1937, 1946, 1953, 1958, 1964, 2363. *See also* Emergency Economic Powers Act, International (IEEPA)
National Security Decision Directive 187, **2005**: 405
National Security Letters, use of, **2006**: 362–63
National Security Presidential Directive on reconstruction and stabilization (NSPD-44), **2005**: 947
National Security Presidential Directive on Trafficking in Persons (NSPD-22), **2005**: 164
National Security Strategy, **2005**: 689*n*
NATO expansion and, **1991-99**: 1031, 1033–34, 1036
passports
reporting on lost or stolen passports, **2004**: 6–7
revocation of passport for reasons of, **1989-90**: 13–17
protection of information based on, **1991-99**: 131, 344, 628, 636, 663, 680, 681, 789–801, 804, 1645, 1698. *See also* President, U.S., *subheading*: protection of information
refusal to produce requested information to International Criminal Tribunal for reasons of, **2003**: 217–19
requirements for aliens proceeding in transit through U.S., **2003**: 13–15
scientists, codes of conduct for, **2005**: 1057
Soviet violations of arms control agreements, **1989-90**: 575–76
space assets protocol (draft), **2005**: 803–4
state secrets, litigation concerning, **2007**: 338–53
territorial sea limits, **1989-90**: 465–70
terrorism. *See* Terrorism
trade agreements and, **2005**: 636
travel and border security. *See also* aliens, *this heading*; Immigration and visas; passports, *this heading*; Passports, U.S.
NEXUS program, **2005**: 4–5
smart-border plan, **2002**: 121
travel restrictions and, **1991-99**: 58–59
waiver of funding prohibitions, based on, **2005**: 202
weapons of mass destruction. *See* Weapons of mass destruction (WMDs)
wiretaps, **2006**: 363–65

National Strategy for Maritime Security, 2005: 688–92
Nationality. *See also* Citizenship; Immigration and visas
access by Vietnamese national to U.S. courts, **1989-90:** 242–43
and citizens of outlying possessions of the U.S., **2007:** 3
citizenship and, **2001:** 2, 645
citizenship versus, **2007:** 3
continuous nationality requirement for claims, **2001:** 385–86; **2002:** 395, 626–33; **2003:** 437–41, 610–13; **2007:** 417–19
dominant and effective nationality, Iran–United States Claims Tribunal (Case A/18; Case 298), **1991-99:** 1095–96
equitable vs. nominal ownership of claims, **2002:** 634–36
in NAFTA Chapter 11 disputes, **2002:** 624–41; **2003:** 610–12
loss of continuous nationality after corporate reorganization, **2002:** 624–41; **2003:** 613–15
transfer of international claims to corporate entity, **2002:** 636–40
U.S. espousal of property takings claims against Mexico, **1991-99:** 1075–76
diplomatic protection and, ILC on, **2007:** 417–20
diplomatic protection and nationality, ILC on, **2000:** 419
dual, **1989-90:** 6; **1991-99:** 19–23, 26–27, 34–41; **2000:** 344–45; **2001:** 645, 646; **2002:** 1–4
child custody case involving, **2001:** 40–47
claims, continuous nationality requirement. *See* continuous nationality requirement for claims, *this heading*
conscription into foreign military of person with, **2003:** 10–11
consular notification in detention of citizen with, **2001:** 33–35
consular protection for, **2001:** 31–36
diplomatic immunity and, **2002:** 4
dual U.S. and "Puerto Rican" nationality, **2000:** 344–45
and employment in U.S. consular and diplomatic missions, **2002:** 1–4
Iran–United States Claims Tribunal (Case A/18; Case 298), **1991-99:** 1095–96
naturalization in second state and, **1989-90:** 6
taxation, **2008:** 499
use of U.S. passport required for, **2001:** 34–35
duty to accept by state of, **2001:** 17–20, 344
enemy combatants and detainees. *See* Detainees, military
extradition and, **2005:** 71, 76, 85–86, 173. *See also* Extradition
nationals of requested state, **2000:** 165–66, 177–80, 185–86
jurisdiction of International Criminal Court, **2000:** 281–82
loss of U.S. *See* Citizenship, *subheading*: loss of; Citizenship, *subheading*: revocation

Nationality (continued)
maritime law and, **2005:** 150–53, 1098, 1101–2
NAFTA and
investor discrimination, **2005:** 595–96
Nationality Act (1940), **2003:** 10, 275
standing to bring Chapter 11 claims, **2001:** 642–46
non-citizen nationals
defined, **2007:** 2
Taiwan claimants, **2008:** 1
Philippine independence and U.S., **1991-99:** 12
statelessness, **2006:** 1–2
Torture Victim Protection Act and, **2005:** 393–94
U.S. jurisdiction and, **2005:** 791, 814
U.S. legislative authority in matters of, **2001:** 2
USG to determine U.S. citizenship, not DPRK, **2001:** 2–3
Nationality Act (1940), 2003: 10, 275
Native Americans, 2001: 129, 130–31, 136–39, 254–55, 260–61. *See also* Indigenous people
California Sacred Sites Act (1976), **2006:** 714; **2007:** 537, 538, 539–40
cigarette sales on reservations, **2008:** 539
construction of treaties with, **2008:** 283
economic development programs, **2008:** 275
equal protection, **2008:** 282
funding, training, and services for, **2005:** 295
Jay Treaty, **2008:** 172
Makah tribe subsistence whaling, **2007:** 722–24; **2008:** 714–15
OAS Inter-American Program for the Promotion and Protection of the Human Rights of Migrants, **2005:** 340
Persistent Organic Pollutants' effect on reliance on fish, marine mammal, and wildlife species, **2005:** 726
peyote, use of, **2005:** 139, 142–43*n*
recognition of rights of, **2005:** 295; **2008:** 282–83
tribal recognition, **2005:** 295; **2007:** 369
tribal self-determination, **2006:** 351–54
U.S. treaties with, congressional abrogation of, **2008:** 282–84
Natural disasters. *See* Disaster relief
Natural resources. *See* Environmental issues; Fish and marine mammals; Marine conservation; Water use agreements
Naturalization. *See* Citizenship; Immigration and visas
Nauru
environmental protection agreement, **2002:** 791
extradition treaty, **2000:** 185*n*
money laundering in, **2002:** 127, 130; **2003:** 208–11; **2004:** 135; **2006:** 243; **2008:** 121

Navassa
sovereignty of U.S. and, **2003:** 485
sovereignty status of, **1991-99:** 854–58
Navigation. *See* Maritime issues, *subheading*: navigation rights
Nazi era property confiscation claims. *See* Holocaust; World War II
NCTC (National Counterterrorism Center), 2006: 167
Netherlands
aviation agreement, **2002:** 1029; **2008:** 512–13
on claims to Antarctica, **2004:** 732
discovery in, for use in U.S. litigation, **2003:** 881–85
drug trade, **2003:** 182; **2005:** 135
ayahuasca abuse in, **2005:** 144
extradition and mutual legal assistance, **2000:** 180, 186*n*; **2004:** 73, 1089; **2005:** 75; **2006:** 136, 137, 147
Immigration Advisory Program at airports, **2006:** 209
missile defense and nonproliferation cooperation, **2004:** 1066, 1074
money laundering, **2004:** 135
nonimmigrant visa waiver pilot program, **1989-90:** 27
nuclear fuel, assurances of reliable access to, **2006:** 1292–93
objections to U.S. reservations to Genocide Convention, **1989-90:** 144
Proliferation Security Initiative (PSI), involvement in, **2005:** 1099
reciprocity in recovery of family support obligations, **2002:** 841–42; **2008:** 759
tax treaties, **2008:** 612
undersea technology, **2005:** 766
warnings of hazardous navigation by Dutch registered vessels, **1989-90:** 456–58
Netherlands Antilles, 2002: 204
Neutral Powers and Persons, Hague Convention Respecting. *See* Hague Conventions, *subheading*: on law of war
Neutrality Act (1984), 1991-99: 543
New Caledonia
fisheries regulation, **2005:** 736, 742–43
New Mexico
protection from illegal trafficking in persons, **2008:** 296
New York City
property taxes on UN missions, **2006:** 592–603; **2008:** 495–98
New Zealand
ANZUS Treaty, **2001:** 862; **2004:** 985; **2005:** 372
arms control and nonproliferation, **1991-99:** 2271
driftnet convention, **1989-90:** 137–38
environmental protection agreement, **2002:** 791
extradition and mutual legal assistance, **2000:** 186*n*
fisheries negotiations with U.S., **2005:** 613

New Zealand (continued)
Highly Migratory Fish Stocks in the Western and Central Pacific Ocean, Convention for the Conservation and Management of (WCPF Convention)
ratification of, **2005:** 737
territorial discrimination issues, **2005:** 742–43
indigenous peoples, views concerning UN declaration on, **2006:** 394–401; **2008:** 353–54
maritime boundary, **1991-99:** 1577–78
nonimmigrant visa waiver pilot program, **1991-99:** 76
non-North Atlantic Treaty Organization (NATO) ally, designation as, **2005:** 1044
Open Skies agreements, **2001:** 565–66
Regional Movement Alert List pilot, **2006:** 209
South Pacific regional environmental convention, **1989-90:** 491
stolen and lost passport data exchange agreement with U.S., **2006:** 17
Tokelau, **2005:** 743
Nicaragua
cultural property protection in, **1991-99:** 1800–1801; **2005:** 775–76
customary international law, alleged breaches of by U.S., **2005:** 38–39*n*, 56–57
eminent domain and, **2003:** 262
Environmental Cooperation Agreement with U.S., **2005:** 756–57
free trade agreement, **2004:** 617–19
freedom of navigation program and, **2004:** 709
humanitarian assistance commitments, **1989-90:** 156–60
Inter-American Convention Against Corruption, party to, **2006:** 238
Inter-American Tropical Tuna Commission, **2000:** 307
Millennium Challenge Corporation (MCC), threshold agreement with, **2005:** 672
murder of American by Nicaraguan Contras, **2005:** 484
naturalization convention, **2002:** 204
Nicaraguan Adjustment and Central American Relief Act (1997), **1991-99:** 249
property loss claims against, **1989-90:** 237–38
relief from immigration requirements for certain resident nationals of, **1991-99:** 249–50
restrictions on U.S. aid resulting from expropriation by, **2003:** 709–12
temporary protected status for nationals of, **1991-99:** 247; **2003:** 36; **2004:** 33
trade and investment agreements, **1991-99:** 1466
trade negotiations with U.S., **2003:** 683–86
treaty affairs, **2002:** 202
U.S. request for extradition of Nicaraguan diplomat from Japan, **1989-90:** 77–78

Niger
coup, **1991-99**: 1962, 1963
sanctions on, **1991-99**: 1962–64
U.S. military assistance, **2006**: 278
waiver of Article 98 agreement with U.S. (nonsurrender of Americans to ICC), **2006**: 279
Nigeria
act of state doctrine, **2005**: 580–81
American Servicemembers' Protection Act waiver, **2003**: 238
anti-suit injunctions, **2005**: 831–32
consular notification, claim against U.S. for failure of, **2008**: 44–47
drug trade, **2001**: 120; **2002**: 124; **2003**: 181; **2004**: 133–34; **2005**: 135; **2006**: 213, 215; **2007**: 163; **2008**: 113
experimental drug, claim against U.S. drug manufacturer for, **2003**: 386–87
extradition and mutual legal assistance, **1991-99**: 450; **2000**: 164, 166, 185*n*
FSIA issues, **2005**: 504–5, 561–62
human rights violations
citizens' claim against European corporations for, **2002**: 352–55; **2003**: 569–70
judicial adequacy, **2006**: 483–84
intellectual property rights, **2008**: 606
international child abduction, **1991-99**: 355
juvenile offenders, execution of, **2005**: 387
longshore work prohibition on alien crewmen from, **2002**: 757; **2003**: 764
money laundering, **2004**: 135
religious freedom violations, **2003**: 296
shrimp import restrictions, **2004**: 765
suspension of entry of certain aliens of, **1991-99**: 141–42
TVPA claims, exhaustion requirement, **2006**: 482–84
war crimes in Africa and, **2004**: 130
Niue
environmental protection agreement, **2002**: 791
maritime boundaries, **1991-99**: 1576–78; **2004**: 733–34
Noise regulation
aviation issues, **2000**: 641–43, 646–51, 661; **2008**: 507–8
undersea noise pollution, **2004**: 746–47
Non-Detention Act (1948), 2005: 266, 1018
Noninquiry, rule of, 2006: 1203. *See also* Extradition

Nonproliferation, 1991-99: 72, 500, 805, 821, 1220, 1478, 1595, 2361; **2001**: 499; **2004**: 914, 1054–55; **2005**: 1093–97; **2006**: 1255–1301. *See also* Arms control; Atomic Energy Agency, International (IAEA); Biological weapons; Chemical weapons; Nuclear Non-Proliferation Treaty (NPT) (1968); Nuclear weapons, use of; Strategic Arms Reduction Treaty (START)
Agreement Between U.S. and International Atomic Agency for Application of Safeguards in U.S., **2004**: 1118–28
Additional Protocol to, **2008**: 944–48
Australia Group, **1991-99**: 2351; **2004**: 89, 1094, 1117, 1130–32; **2005**: 1086, 1133, 1135–36
chemical/biological weapons nonproliferation activities, **2003**: 1124–25; **2004**: 1100–1; **2005**: 1054–66; **2006**: 1238–43, 1246–50, 1267, 1270; **2008**: 1006–8
Comprehensive Test Ban Treaty (CTBT), **1991-99**: 2271–79, 2280–81, 2295, 2297
country-specific issues. *See also specific countries*
Armenia, **2002**: 1069
Austria, **2005**: 1134
Belarus
nuclear nonproliferation, **2005**: 1107
nuclear materials in, **1991-99**: 2245, 2307, 2314; **2004**: 1139
Treaty on Non-Proliferation of Nuclear Weapons (NPT), compliance with, **2005**: 1107
U.S. sanctions against Belarusian entity for transfers to Iran, **2004**: 1135, 1136
Bulgaria
nuclear fuel return program, **2004**: 1139, 141
Soviet missiles in, **1989-90**: 572
China
cooperation with U.S., **1991-99**: 2298, 2316–22, 2361; **2008**: 946
espionage and intelligence gathering, **1991-99**: 2320–22
India–Pakistan nuclear tests, **1991-99**: 2298
Iran nuclear program, **2006**: 1276–79, **2008**: 975–77
nonproliferation issues, **2004**: 1129–30, 1135, 1136, 1149
Nuclear Terrorism, Global Initiative to Combat, **2006**: 1295–96
nuclear test by, **1991-99**: 2271
NPT, support for, **2008**: 938–41
nuclear-free zones, **1991-99**: 2315–16
party to NPT, **1991-99**: 2286; **2008**: 938–41
sanctions, U.S., **1991-99**: 1458, 1459–60, 2317, 2318–19, 2320–22, 2359–61; **2002**: 1067–71; **2003**: 1116–18, 1120–22; **2004**: 1134–36; **2005**: 1132–34. *See also* sanctions, U.S., *this heading*

Nonproliferation (continued)
Six-Party talks with North Korea, **2005:** 1067–73; **2006:** 1271–72; **2007:** 1018; **2008:** 961–63, 965, 967–68
Taiwan retransfer agreements, **1991-99:** 2334–35
Cuba, **2006:** 1298–99
France, **1991-99:** 2232; **2004:** 1074, 1144, 1146, 1149; **2008:** 946
Iran nuclear program, **2004:** 1146, 1149; **2005:** 1110, 1113; **2006:** 1274, 1277–78; **2007:** 1032–33, 1036–38; **2008:** 975–77
Missile Technology Control Regime, **1991-99:** 2222, 2356–59
NPT, support for, **2008:** 938–41
Nuclear Terrorism, Global Initiative to Combat, **2006:** 1295–96
nuclear weapons, position concerning use and testing of, **1991-99:** 2174, 2175, 2178, 2272, 2286, 2295, 2315–16
Proliferation Security Initiative (PSI), involvement in, **2005:** 1099
nuclear fuel, assurances of reliable access to, **2006:** 1292–93
Germany, **2004:** 1066, 1068, 1074, 1123, 1146, 1149
German ship searched for uranium centrifuge parts, **2005:** 1102
Iran nuclear program, **2004:** 1146, 1149; **2005:** 1110, 1113; **2006:** 1274–78; **2007:** 1032–33, 1036–38; **2008:** 975–77
nuclear fuel, assurances of reliable access to, **2006:** 1292–93
nuclear fuel return program, **2004:** 1139
Nuclear Terrorism, Global Initiative to Combat, **2006:** 1295–96
Proliferation Security Initiative (PSI), involvement in, **2005:** 1099
India, **1991-99:** 2289; **2006:** 1284–87, 1298–99
Henry J. Hyde United States and India Nuclear Cooperation Promotion Act (2006), **2006:** 1284–87
IAEA Additional Protocol to safeguards agreement, **2005:** 1081, 1084
joint statement with U.S. (2004), **2004:** 1067–68
joint statement with U.S. (2005), on new relationship, **2005:** 1077–89
sanctions, U.S. *See also* sanctions, U.S., *this heading*
nuclear tests by and sanctions imposed in response to, **1991-99:** 2287, 2289, 2294–2303; **2001:** 808–13
sanctions against Indian companies trading with Iran, **2002:** 1070–71; **2003:** 1123–24; **2004:** 1136; **2005:** 1133–34; **2006:** 1298–99
U.S. export controls against, **1991-99:** 2301
removal from Commerce Department control lists, **2001:** 811–13; **2005:** 1089
U.S.–India Agreement for cooperation concerning peaceful uses of nuclear energy (2007), **2005:** 1077–82; **2007:** 1014–18; **2008:** 986–93

Nonproliferation (continued)
Iran, **2003**: 1087, 1088–89, 1092, 1105–10; **2004**: 1077, 1122–23, 1142–49
biological warfare agents and, **2002**: 1065; **2006**: 1240
chemical weapons program, **2003**: 1074
IAEA and, **2003**: 1088–89, 1105–10; **2004**: 1142–49; **2005**: 1073–77, 1097, 1108; **2006**: 1272–84; **2007**: 839, 857, 1016, 1033; 1031–36; **2008**: 951, 971, 972
IAEA Safeguards Agreement, **2005**: 1073
National Intelligence Estimate on nuclear weapons program of, **2007**: 1050–52
nonproliferation sanctions, **1991-99**: 2362; **2003**: 1116–18, 1122–24; **2004**: 1135–36, 1161; **2005**: 1130–32; **2006**: 1298–99; **2007**: 1041–45, 1047–50, 1082–85, 2042–50; **2008**: 971, 978–84; 1025–27. *See also* sanctions, U.S., *this heading*; Security Council and, *this subheading*
Nuclear Non-Proliferation Treaty (NPT) and, **2007**: 379, 837, 1033; **2008**: 951, 975
nuclear weapons program, **2003**: 1087, 1088–89, 1092, 1105–10; **2004**: 1076, 1077, 1093, 1122–23, 1129, 1142–49; **2005**: 1113; **2008**: 1001
Paris Agreement, **2005**: 1076–77
P5 + 1 diplomatic effort, **2006**: 1276; **2007**: 1038–41; **2008**: 972–73, 975–77
Proliferation Security Initiative and, **2005**: 1099, 1100, 1105
Security Council and, **2007**: 837, 857; **2008**: 939, 969–75, 1001
Resolution 1696, **2006**: 1278–84; 1031, 1033–34, 1037, 1074
Resolution 1737, **2007**: 857, 1031–34, 1037–38, 1040, 1042-45, 1074; **2008**: 970–71, 973–74, 979
Resolution 1747, **2007**: 857, 1031–47, 1074; **2008**: 971, 973, 979
Resolution 1803, **2008**: 939, 969–75, 979
Resolution 1835, **2008**: 974–75
Iraq, **1991-99**: 2054, 2111, 2125; **2004**: 1163–64
basis for military intervention in, **2003**: 961–74; **2005**: 949–50, 957
biological warfare agents, **2002**: 1065; **2004**: 891, 1164
sanctions, U.S., **2002**: 894–96; **2002**: 1070; **2003**: 1123–24; **2003**: 1123–25. *See also* sanctions, U.S., *this heading*
UN resolutions on Iraqi weapons proliferation (678, 707, 1441), **2002**: 934, 937–47; **2004**: 891

Nonproliferation (continued)
Italy
missile defense and nonproliferation cooperation, **2004:** 1066, 1068, 1074
Missile Technology Control Regime, **1991-99:** 2222, 2356–59
nuclear weapons, **1991-99:** 2178
Proliferation Security Initiative (PSI), involvement in, **2005:** 1099
Japan, **1991-99:** 2268, 2271, 2325, 2327, 2329, 2338
denuclearization of Korean Peninsula, participation in joint statement regarding, **2005:** 1067–73
missile defense and nonproliferation cooperation, **2004:** 1066, 1074, 1123
Missile Technology Control Regime, **1991-99:** 2222, 2356–59
North Korean nuclear program, **2004:** 1149, 1152, 1155
Nuclear Terrorism, Global Initiative to Combat, **2006:** 1295–96
peaceful nuclear cooperation, agreement with U.S. on, **2001:** 701
Proliferation Security Initiative (PSI), involvement in, **2005:** 1099
Six-Party talks with North Korea, **2007:** 839, 1018–27
Kazakhstan, **2005:** 1107
nuclear materials in, **1991-99:** 2245, 2307, 2314; **2004:** 1139
Nuclear Terrorism, Global Initiative to Combat, **2006:** 1295–96
Treaty on Non-Proliferation of Nuclear Weapons (NPT), compliance with, **2005:** 1107
Libya
biological warfare agents, **2002:** 1065; **2004:** 1074
chemical weapons, **2003:** 1068–69, 1074; **2004:** 1059; **2005:** 1059, 1065–66
fuel return program, **2004:** 1141
nuclear-related sanctions, waiver of, **2004:** 1162
shipment of nuclear equipment to, **2004:** 692, 1074
weapons program, **1991-99:** 1030, 2266
WMD, elimination of, **2003:** 166–67, 1068–69; **2004:** 927–32, 1059–60, 1073–74, 1143–44, 1154–55, 1158–63; **2005:** 1059, 1065–66, 1102–3, 1107
Macedonia, **2004:** 1135
North Korea, **1991-99:** 2266, 2289, 2323–29; **2001:** 822, 850; **2002:** 1044–52, 1065; **2003:** 1087–88, 1089, 1092, 1100–5, 1114; **2004:** 1076, 1093, 1122, 1149–55, 1161; **2005:** 1067–73, 1085, 1099–1100, 1105, 1108, 1110, 1112–13, 1130–31; **2006:** 1265–72; **2008:** 961–63, 1025–27
Agreed Framework, **1991-99:** 2323–29
ballistic missiles, launch of, **2006:** 1265–68
biological weapons, **2002:** 1065; **2006:** 1240

Nonproliferation (continued)
chemical weapons, **2003**: 1074
nuclear detonation, **2006**: 1268–71
Nuclear Non-Proliferation Treaty, withdrawal from, **1991-99**: 2323; **2003**: 1100–1103; **2008**: 949, 961
sanctions, U.S., **2002**: 1066–67; **2003**: 1118–19, 1122–23; **2004**: 1135, 1136; **2005**: 1130–31, **2006**: 1265–71, **2006**: 1271, 1298–1300; **2007**: 1027–31, 1083–84; **2008**: 1025–27. *See also* UN Security Council and, *this subheading*; sanctions, U.S., *this heading*
shipment of missiles to Yemen, **2002**: 1052–57
Six-Party talks, **2003**: 1104; **2004**: 1156–58; **2006**: 1271–72; **2007**: 839, 1018–27; **2008**: 939–40, 961
UN Security Council and
Resolution 1695, **2006**: 1265–69; **2007**: 1073
Resolution 1718, **2006**: 1965–72; **2007**: 1027–31, 1073–74
verification, **2008**: 964–65, 966–69
Pakistan, **1991-99**: 2289. *See also* Khan, A.Q., *this heading*
missile-related sanctions, **2001**: 813–15
nuclear tests by and sanctions imposed in response to, **1991-99**: 2294–2303; **2001**: 808–13
U.S. export controls against, **1991-99**: 2301
removal of Pakistani entities from Commerce Department control lists, **2001**: 811–13, 820
Russia, **1991-99**: 2244–47, 2330–31, 2339–40; **2006**: 1298–99; **2008**: 946–47. *See also* Arms control
arsenal and threat reduction, disposition of nuclear materials, **1991-99**: 2303–8, 2310–14, 2330–31; **2001**: 832–35, 847–48; **2002**: 1039–42; **2003**: 1110–12; **2004**: 1137–41, 1161; **2005**: 1090–91, 1109
cooperative threat reduction program, **1991-99**: 2312–14
debt forgiveness for Russian spending on nonproliferation, **2002**: 1042–44
disposition of fissile materials, **1991-99**: 2303–8, 2311–14
highly enriched uranium, disposition of, **1991-99**: 2303–7; **2001**: 847–48; **2002**: 1039–42; **2003**: 1110–12; **2004**: 1137–38; **2005**: 1090–91; **2008**: 954–60
plutonium, joint statement concerning, **1991-99**: 2307–8
chemical and biological weapons, **1991-99**: 2330–31; **2005**: 1054–55, 1061, 1064–65
Global Initiative to Combat Nuclear Terrorism, **2006**: 1293–96
Gore–Chernomyrdin Commission, **1991-99**: 2308–12

Nonproliferation (continued)
Intermediate Range Nuclear Forces Treaty (INF) (1987), **1989-90:** 567, 569–70, 572–74; **1991-99:** 757, 933, 937, 2306, 2311
Iran nuclear program, **2005:** 1076; **2007:** 1032–33, 1036–38; **2008:** 975–77
Korean Peninsula, **2004:** 1149; **2005:** 1067–68, 1070
missile defense and nonproliferation, **1991-99:** 2355–56; **2002:** 1064–65; **2004:** 483–84, 1066
NPT assurances, **1991-99:** 2174, 2286
NPT, support for, **2008:** 938–41
nuclear energy, peaceful use of (123 agreement), **2008:** 986–89
nuclear fuel, assurances of reliable access to, **2006:** 1292–93
nuclear security cooperation with U.S., **2005:** 1091–93
Nuclear Terrorism Convention, proposal for, **2005:** 108
protection of nuclear material, **2001:** 843–45; **2002:** 1039–41
research reactor fuel return program, **2004:** 1138–41
sanctions, U.S., on Russian entities, **2004:** 1132–36
sea transport of radioactive materials, **2001:** 699–703
Soviet Union
visas for scientists from the former Soviet Union, **1991-99:** 71–72,
position on use of nuclear weapons, **1991-99:** 2174, 2178, 2285–86
arsenal of former Soviet Union and threat reduction, **1991-99:** 2306, 2312–13, 2330–31
Protocol to the Treaty Between U.S. and USSR on nuclear weapon tests, **2002:** 181
Soviet Nuclear Threat Reduction Act (1991), **1991-99:** 2312–14
START, **1991-99:** 2215–17, **2002:** 1027
spent fuel repatriation, **2004:** 1137–41, 1161
START, **1991-99:** 2210–12, 2214–17, 2221–22; **2002:** 1027; **2006:** 1253–54; **2007:** 1008–12
Trilateral Initiative, **1991-99:** 2339–40
U.S.–Russia joint statement, **2007:** 1012–14
South Africa, **2005:** 1107
South Korea
North Korean nuclear program and Agreed Framework, **1991-99:** 2323–29. *See also* Korean Peninsula Energy Development Organization (KEDO)
nuclear technology activities, **2004:** 1156–58
Six-Party talks, **2003:** 1104; **2004:** 1156–58; **2006:** 1271–72; **2007:** 1018–19
trilateral statement, **2002:** 1050

Nonproliferation (continued)
Syria
biological weapons, **2006:** 1240
chemical weapons, **2003:** 1074
Missile Technology Control Regime (MTCR) issues, **2005:** 1136
nonproliferation concerns, **2004:** 1161; **2007:** 1025; **2008:** 984–86, 1025–27
nuclear reactor, IAEA investigation of clandestine construction, **2008:** 984–86
Proliferation Security Initiative (PSI), issues, **2005:** 1100, 1105; **2008:** 1001
sanctions, U.S., **2005:** 1130–32; **2007:** 1083–84; **2008:** 1025–27
U.S. export controls against Syrian entities, **2005:** 1136
Ukraine, **2005:** 1107
nuclear fuel return program, **2004:** 1139
nuclear materials in, **1991-99:** 2307, 2314
Treaty on Non-Proliferation of Nuclear Weapons (NPT), compliance with, **2005:** 1107
U.S. sanctions against Ukrainian entity, **2004:** 1136
United Arab Emirates, **2004:** 1135
United Kingdom, **2008:** 947
Biological Weapons Convention (BWC), support for, **2005:** 1054–55
intelligence concerning uranium centrifuge parts, **2005:** 1102
Iran nuclear program, **2004:** 1144, 1146, 1149; **2006:** 1276–78; **2007:** 1032–33, 1036–38; **2008:** 975–77
Libyan weapons program, **2004:** 928, 933, 1074, 1159, 1162
missile defense cooperation, **2004:** 1066–67
Missile Technology Control Regime, **1991-99:** 2222, 2356–59
NPT, support for, **2008:** 938–41
nuclear fuel, assurances of reliable access to, **2006:** 1292–93
position on use and testing of nuclear weapons, **1991-99:** 2174, 2175, 2178, 2274, 2285, 2286, 2295, 2315–16
Nuclear Terrorism, Global Initiative to Combat, **2006:** 1295–96
Proliferation Security Initiative (PSI), involvement in, **2005:** 1099
Uzbekistan, **2001:** 848–50
Yemen, **2002:** 1054–55
dismantling or disarming of existing weapons stocks by U.S., **2003:** 1090–91
dual-use technology, **1991-99:** 2263–66, 2287–88; **2004:** 1111, 1113–14
European Atomic Energy Community agreement, **1991-99:** 2336–39; **2005:** 109, 1121
European Union, **2005:** 1093–97
Executive Order 12938, 13094 (proliferation of weapons of mass destruction (WMD)), **1991-99:** 2363–66; **2003:** 1116–18; **2005:** 1126, 1129; **2007:** 1082–83

Nonproliferation (continued)
Executive Order 13382 (weapons of mass destruction (WMD)), **2005**: 1125–31; **2006**: 1297; **2007**: 1041–45, 1083–84; **2008**: 977–80, 983
Fissile Material Cut Off Treaty (FMCT), **2003**: 1070–72; **2005**: 1081, 1084, 1088, 1111; **2006**: 1289–91; **2007**: 1060, 1079
freedom of navigation and, **1991-99**: 1595–96, 1598; **2004**: 703, 711–13
nuclear weapons free zone
Africa, **1991-99**: 2314–15
South Pacific, **1991-99**: 2315–16
Global Threat Reduction Initiative, **2004**: 1137–38, 1141; **2005**: 1095
highly enriched uranium, disposition of, **1999-91**: 2303–7; **2001**: 847–48; **2004**: 1137–38; **2008**: 954–60
Agreement between U.S. and Russian Federation concerning, **2005**: 1090–91; **2008**: 954–60
transfer of Russian-origin stocks to Russian Federation, **2003**: 1110–12
transfer of Serbian uranium stocks to Russia, **2002**: 1041–42
International Atomic Energy Agency. *See* Atomic Energy Agency, International (IAEA)
International Code of Conduct against Ballistic Missile Proliferation, **2002**: 1062–65
Khan, A.Q., **2004**: 1073, 1074, 1094, 1095, 1130, 1146, 1158, 1160
Latin America, Treaty for the Prohibition of Nuclear Weapons in, **2002**: 185–86
low-enriched uranium, antidumping law applicable to, **2008**: 953–60
Maritime Navigation, 2005 protocols to UN Convention for the Suppression of Unlawful Acts against the Safety of (SUA) and Fixed Platforms Protocol, **2005**: 112–13, 1117–20; **2007**: 140–42, 1062–71; **2008**: 94–97, 941–44
Missile Technology Control Regime (MTCR), **1989-90**: 503–8; **1991-99**: 2356–61; **2001**: 845–46; **2003**: 1115–16; **2005**: 1136; **2006**: 1063–64; **2008**: 989
missile technology. *See also* Missile Technology Control Regime (MTCR), *this heading*
ballistic missile defense radar site in Czech Republic, **2008**: 1008–9
control of, **2001**: 845–46
interdiction of, **2003**: 1095–99
nonproliferation sanctions. *See* sanctions, U.S., *this heading*
NATO, **1991-99**: 1035
Nonproliferation and Disarmament Fund, **1991-99**: 2330–31

Nonproliferation (continued)
nuclear fuel, assurances of reliable access to, **2005**: 1124–25; **2006**: 1292–93
nuclear materials
control and protection of, **2001**: 844–45; **2003**: 1092–93, 1095, 1112–16; **2004**: 1103–4, 1106–7, 1126
Convention on the Physical Protection of (CPPNM), **1991-99**: 501, 746; **2001**: 107–8; **2002**: 1072; **2004**: 1100
amendment to, **2005**: 109–10, 960, 1092, 1095, 1121, 1122, 1123; **2007**: 142–43, 1076–78; **2008**: 94–97, 889–90
disposition of fissile and radioactive materials, **1991-99**: 1013, 1032, 2214–15, 2216–17, 2221–22, 2244, 2303–8, 2311–14, 2330–31, 2333–34; **2001**: 847–48; **2002**: 1039–42; **2003**: 1110–12; **2004**: 1137–38; **2005**: 1090–91; **2008**: 954–60
safety of stockpiles, **1991-99**: 2215–17, 2276, 2277
Fissile Material Cut Off Treaty. *See* Fissile Material Cut Off Treaty (FMCT), *this heading*
interdiction of, **2003**: 1095–99
International Convention for the Suppression of Nuclear Terrorism, **2005**: 11, 18, 106–10, 960, 1092, 1123–24; **2007**: 132–39; **2008**: 94–97, 889–90
nuclear terrorism, protection against, **2001**: 842–43
sea transport of, **2001**: 699–703, 711–14
as weapon of mass destruction, **2004**: 1080, 1089*n*
Nuclear Safety, Convention on, **1991-99**: 1693–99
Nuclear Weapons Treaty on Non-Proliferation of. *See* Nuclear Non-Proliferation Treaty (NPT) (1968)
Proliferation Security Initiative (PSI), **2003**: 1095–99; **2004**: 691–92, 1074–75, 1077–91; **2005**: 442, 447, 1073, 1086, 1095, 1097–1106, 1109; **2006**: 1288–89; **2007**: 1071–75; **2008**: 1001–4
sanctions, U.S., **1991-99**: 2289–94, 2298–2303; **2004**: 1099–1100, 1101–2, 1103–4, 1105–7, 1111, 1112–13, 1115. *See also* specific countries, *this heading*; UN Security Council, *this heading*
chemical and biological weapons, **1989-90**: 513–15; **1991-99**: 2352–55
Executive Order 12735, **1989-90**: 509–10, 512–16
imposition of sanctions, **2002**: 1070; **2003**: 1124–25
termination of sanctions, **2004**: 1136–37
veto of legislation concerning, **1989-90**: 508–9
nonproliferation sanctions generally

Nonproliferation (continued)
Executive Orders (12938, 13094, 13382), **1991-99**: 2363–66; **2003**: 1116–18; **2005**: 1125–31; **2006**: 1297; **2007**: 1041–45, 1082–84; **2008**: 977–80, 983
Foreign Assistance Act prohibition on assistance for states not complying with nonproliferation agreements, **1991-99:** 2289
Iran Nonproliferation Act of 2000, **2002:** 1067–69; **2003:** 1122–23; **2004:** 1135–36; **2005:** 1132–35
Iran and Syria Nonproliferation Act; **2005:** 1131–32
Iran, North Korea, and Syria Nonproliferation Act, **2008:** 1025–27
Iran-Iraq Arms Nonproliferation Act (1992), **1991-99**: 2362; **2002**: 1070–71; **2003**: 1123–24
missile-related sanctions, **1989-90**: 503–5; **2003**: 1116–23; **2004**: 1132–35; **2005**: 1127, 1129, 1130–36; **2007**: 1028, 1030, 1031–32, 1033, 1044–45; **2008**: 970, 1298
for transfers of missile technology (Arms Export Control Act)
on China or Chinese entities for transfers of, **1991-99:** 2359–61; **2003:** 1116–18, 1120–22; **2004:** 1134–35
waiver of, **1991-99:** 2361; **2005:** 1132
on Iranian entities for transfers of, **2003:** 1117–18
on Moldovan entities for transfers of, **2003:** 1119–20
on North Korean entities or government, **2002:** 1066–67; **2003:** 1118–19
on Pakistani entities for transfers of, **1991-99:** 2359–61; **2001:** 813–15; **2003:** 1117–18
on Russian entities for transfers of, **2004:** 1132–33
nuclear-related sanctions
imposition on India and Pakistan, **1991-99:** 2298–2303
imposition on North Korea, **2006:** 1271
lifting from India and Pakistan, **2001:** 808–13
Nuclear Proliferation Prevention Act (1994), **1991-99**: 2290–94
waiver for Libya, **2004:** 1162
terrorism and. *See* Terrorism
UN Security Council, **2007**: 837, 857, 1007; **2008**: 939, 969–75, 1001. *See also* Security Council, UN
Nuclear Non-Proliferation Treaty, role in responding to withdrawals from; **2008:** 937
Resolution 1540, **2004:** 107, 1060, 1092–1118, 1130; **2005:** 447, 900–901, 1059, 1092, 1094, 1103, 1104–23; **2006:** 1073, 1241, 1242, 1267, 1294; **2007:** 1063, 1072; **2008:** 952, 999–1001, 1007–8
1540 Committee, **2004**: 1095; 1096–1118; **2005**: 900–1, 1094; **2008**: 999–1001

Nonproliferation (continued)
Resolution 1695, **2006**: 1265–69; **2007**: 1073
Resolution 1673, 2006, 1073
Resolution 1696, **2006:** 1278–80; **2007:** 1031, 1033, 1034, 1037, 1074
Resolution 1718, **2006:** 1965–72; **2007**: 1027–31, 1073–74
Resolution 1737, **2007:** 857, 1031–34, 1037–38, 1040, 1042–45, 1074; **2008:** 970–71, 973–74, 979
Resolution 1747, **2007:** 857, 1031–47, 1074; **2008:** 971, 973, 979
Resolution 1803, **2008:** 939, 969–75, 979
Resolution 1835, **2008:** 974–75
U.S. views and priorities, **2004**: 1072–77, 1092–1118; **2006**: 1255–65
Wassenaar Arrangement, **1991-99**: 2251, 2265–66; **2001**: 912; **2003**: 1122; **2004**: 893, 1093, 1132; **2005**: 1086, 1133, 1137; **2006**: 1300–1301; **2007**: 1030; **2008**: 1024–25, 1026
weapons of mass destruction, **1991-99**: 2362–66; **2005**: 1125–31. *See also* Weapons of mass destruction (WMDs)
Zangger Committee, **1991-99**: 2317, 2319; **2003**: 1092, 1114–15; **2004**: 1094, 1113, 1129
Nonsurrender agreements protecting American citizens from International Criminal Court (ICC) (Article 98 agreements). *See* International Criminal Court (ICC)
North American Development Bank (NADBank), 1991-99: 1314
Agreement Between U.S. and Mexico on Establishment of, **2005**: 606
North American Free Trade Agreement (NAFTA), 1991-99: 101, 1368, 1370–71, 1470, 1489; **2004**: 618, 622, 821
allocation of costs, **2007**: 525–26
architecture, Mutual Recognition Agreement and, **2007**: 535
binational panel review provisions, constitutional challenge to, **2006**: 726–37
Border Environmental Cooperation Commission, **2005**: 606
business visa provisions, **1991-99**: 73–74
Chapter 10 provisions, **2001**: 613–16
Chapter 11 disputes, **1991-99**: 1433–34; **2000**: 685–88, 692–95; **2001**: 568–646; **2004**: 572–601; **2005**: 593–607; **2006**: 688–726; **2007**: 535–48; **2008**, 170–74, 351–57, 525–42
actions of U.S. state governments and, **2000**: 679–81; **2006**: 688–93
allocation of costs, **2007**: 549–51; **2008**: 525–26
alternative dispute resolution of commercial disputes, **1991-99**: 1848–52
anti-competitive practice claims against Canada, **2002**: 661–65

North American Free Trade Agreement (NAFTA) (continued)
antidumping and countervailing duties, Chapter 19 and, **2003**: 636–42; **2004**: 594–96; **2006**: 702–9, 727, 734
arbitration rules, **2000**: 685–88, 692–95
claims against U.S., **1991-99**: 1434–36; **2001**: 574–642; **2002**: 607–61; **2003**: 607–42; **2004**: 573–96; **2005**: 593–602; **2006**: 688–701; **2007**: 535–51, 553–56, **2008**: 170–74, 351–57, 527–42
claims by U.S. investors against Canada, **2000**: 674–94; **2002**: 661–65
claims by U.S. investors against Mexico, **1991-99**: 1436; **2000**: 694–95; **2001**: 642–46; **2003**: 642–48; **2004**: 596–601; **2007**: 551–53
claims for possible future breaches, **2002**: 648
consolidation of claims, **2005**: 596–602
continuous nationality requirements, **2002**: 624–41; **2003**: 610–15
customary international law, Article 1105(1) as incorporating, **2001**: 570; **2006**: 710, 721–26; **2007**: 536, 542–49; **2008**: 532–33
denial of justice claims, **2001**: 627–41
due process, **2004**: 599–600
exclusion of evidence, **2004**: 589
expatriation and minimum standard of treatment, **2007**: 535–49
expropriation, **1991-99**: 1434–36; **2000**: 679, 681–83, 685; **2001**: 574–601, 623, 642; **2002**: 617, 623–24, 649; **2003**: 615, 616, 630–36, 637, 642–43; **2004**: 575, 586–89, 597–98, 600–601; **2005**: 596, 598, 601; **2006**: 695, 709–26; **2008**: 538–42
measures tantamount to, **2000**: 679, 681–83, 685
failure to pursue domestic remedies, **1991-99**: 1434–35; **2003**: 611, 614–15
fair and equitable treatment rules, **2000**: 688–91, 693–94; **2008**: 532–33, 537
immunity of U.S. municipal agency from claims of tortious interference, **2002**: 607–9, 614–16
indigenous people's claims, **2008**: 170–74, 351–57, 528–42
investment in own state, **2007**: 551–56; **2008**: 527–28
investment issues, **2004**: 572–610; **2005**: 593–605; **2008**: 525–28
investor right of action, **2004**: 598–601
investors and preexisting limitations, **2007**: 536–48
jurisdiction, **2001**: 575, 576, 599, 602, 608–11; **2003**: 608, 613, 614, 615, 638, 639, 640–42; **2004**: 574, 575, 596
admissibility, no power to rule on objections relating to, **2002**: 618–19

North American Free Trade Agreement (NAFTA) (continued)
Canadian investors' claims where all investments are in Canada, **2006**: 693–701; **2007**: 553–56; **2008**: 527–30
consent to arbitrate, **2003**: 637–39; **2006**: 694
four considerations in determining, **2006**: 703–4
standing, **2001**: 602–5, 642–46; **2003**: 643–44. *See also* continuous nationality requirements, *this subheading*
time bar, when triggered, **2006**: 688–93; **2008**: 526–27, 527–30
minimum standard of treatment principles, **2000**: 688–93; **2001**: 568–74, 589–90, 592, 594–95, 627–41; **2002**: 611–16, 623–24, 642, 648–59; **2003**: 615, 616, 621–30; **2005**: 596; **2006**: 724; **2008**: 531, 532–38
national treatment requirements, **2000**: 676–78, 684–85; **2001**: 611, 618–27; **2002**: 621–24, 642, 643–44, 645, 646–48; **2003**: 607–10, 617–22, 625, 637, 642–43; **2004**: 578–86, 594; **2005**: 595–96; **2006**: 693, 695, 698–701
nondisputing parties, participation of, **2003**: 604–7; **2004**: 592–94
performance requirements, **2000**: 678; **2002**: 642, 645
pre-NAFTA events, relevance of, **2002**: 609–11
private international law and, **2003**: 612–13
procurement
Buy America procurement requirement, **2001**: 611–22; **2002**: 642, 647, 661
by state of United States as procurement by a party, **2001**: 612–18; **2002**: 641–48
proximate cause standards, **2004**: 575–78
public health, **2004**: 575, 586–89
reconsideration of partial awards, **2004**: 589–92
state of U.S. ban on gasoline additive MTBE, **2001**: 574–611; **2002**: 616–23; **2003**: 615–36; **2004**: 574–89; **2005**: 593–96
state of U.S. judicial process, **2001**: 623–42; **2002**: 623–41; **2003**: 610–15; **2004**: 573
Tobacco Master Settlement Agreement and, **2006**: 688–93; **2008**: 170, 351, 528–42
transparency obligations, **2001**: 595–96
Chapter 15 claim, **2002**: 662–65
Chapter 19 disputes, **1991-99**: 1432–33; **2003**: 637–42; **2004**: 594–96; **2005**: 602–7; **2006**: 702
rules of procedure, **2007**: 535
Chapter 20 arbitration, **1991-99**: 1370, 1431–32; **2002**: 651, 663, 666–70; **2003**: 639–40, 641
Chapter 20 dispute, **2007**: 557–58

North American Free Trade Agreement (NAFTA) (continued)
constitutionality of in U.S., **2001**: 200–211; **2005**: 605
Cuban Liberty and Democratic Solidarity Act and, **1991-99**: 101
Environmental Cooperation, Supplemental Agreement on, **1991-99**: 1426–28, 1429
as executive-legislative agreement for U.S., **1991-99**: 657–58
challenge to validity of for failure to ratify under Treaty Clause of U.S. Constitution, **2001**: 200–211
Extraordinary Challenge Committee (ECC), **2005**: 603–4; **2006**: 728
Free Trade Commission
alternative dispute resolution of commercial disputes, role in, **1991-99**: 1848–52
establishment under Article 2001, **1991-99**: 1849
interpretations of Chapter 11, **2002**: 651–52, 660–61; **2008**: 532
access to documents in Chapter 11 arbitration, **2001**: 569–70
minimum standard of treatment under section 1105(1), **2001**: 568–74; **2002**: 611–14
Joint Statement, **2006**: 686–88; **2007**: 532–35
statements on transparency measures in Chapter 11 disputes, **2003**: 603–4
nondisputing party participation, **2003**: 604–7
open hearings, **2003**: 607
Harmonized Commodity Description and Coding System (2007) and, **2007**: 534
Implementation Act (1993), **1991-99**: 74, 1421; **2002**: 694–95; **2004**: 597*n*; **2005**: 607; **2006**: 708, 726, 727; **2008**: 8
Import Surges, Supplemental Agreement on, **1991-99**: 1428–30
challenge to validity of, **2001**: 200–211
intellectual property provisions, **1991-99**: 1424
investment disputes. *See* Chapter 11 disputes, *this heading*
key provisions, **1991-99**: 1421–24
Labor Cooperation, Supplemental Agreement on, **1991-99**: 1425–26, 1429
Mexico, removal of remaining tariffs and quotas with U.S., **2008**: 542
Multilateral Agreement on Investment and, **1991-99**: 1489–90
negotiation and entry into force, **1991-99**: 1420–21
North American Development Bank, **2005**: 606
responsibility under prior to entry into force, **2002**: 609–11
rules of origin, **2007**: 534–35
Presidential Proclamation 8067 modifying, **2006**: 688
Softwood Lumber Agreement (SLA), **2007**: 549
arbitration concerning, **2007**: 591–97; **2008**: 582–93
supplemental agreements, **1991-99**: 1426–30
taxation, **2001**: 642–46

North American Free Trade Agreement (NAFTA) (continued)
tobacco settlement
Chapter 11 disputes, **2006**: *688–93*; **2008**: 170, 351, *528–42*
as alleged violation of Jay Treaty and Treaty of Ghent, **2008**: 170–74
trucking, U.S.-Mexico cross-border obligations, **2007**: *556–62*
Working Group on Rules of Origin, **2006**: *688*
Articles:
4, **2006**: *689n*
5, **2006**: *689n*
102, **2001**: *585*, *595–96*; **2003**: *642*; **2006**: *696*; **2007**: *553*
201, **2001**: 644, 646
1003, **2002**: 646
1024, **2002**: *645–46*
1101, **2001**: *573–74*, 606, 607–8, 610–11; **2002**: *619–23*, 647; **2003**: 634; **2005**: *594*, *597*; **2006**: *694–96*, *698–99*, 701, 704; **2007**: *546*, *552*, *554*; **2008**: *529–30*
1102, **1991-99**: 1434, 1435, 1436; **2001**: *575*, *590–91*, *593–94*, 610, 611–17, 618–23, *625–27*; **2002**: 611, 617, 624, 642, 643, 646–48, 662, 665; **2003**: 607, 608–9, 615, 617–21, 622–23, 637, 638, 643; **2004**: *578–86*, *595*, *597*; **2005**: *594*, *598*; **2006**: 693, *695*, *699–700*, 709; **2008**: *532*
1103, **2001**: 612; **2003**: 608, 609, 637, 638; **2004**: *595*, *597*; **2005**: *598*; **2008**: *529*, *532*
1104, **2004**: *597*
1105, **1991-99**: 1435; **2001**: *570–74*, *575*, *588–93*, *594–95*, 606–8, 610, 611, 623–24, 627–41; **2002**: 609, 611–16, 617, 624, 642, 648–59, 660, 662; **2003**: 608, 609–10, 615, 616, 621–25, 630, 637, 638, 643; **2004**: *585–86*, *595*, *597*, *599–600*; **2005**: *594*, *598*; **2006**: *695*, 710, 720–26; **2007**: *536*, *542–46*, *547*; **2008**: 170, 171, 172, 351, 352, *529*, *531*, *532–33*, *534*, *536*, *537*, *538*
1106, **2001**: 611–17, 618; **2002**: 642; **2003**: 609
1107, **2001**: 612
1108, **2001**: 612–17; **2002**: 642, 644, 645; **2003**: 608, 609, 623–24
1110, **1991-99**: 1435, 1436; **2001**: *575*, *584–88*, *590*, 601, 610, 623, 642; **2002**: 611, 617, 624; **2003**: 615, 616, 628–29, 630–31, 636, 637, 638; **2004**: *585–86*, *595*, *597*, *599–600*; **2005**: *594*; **2006**: *695*, 710, 717, 721–22; **2007**: *536*, *546*; **2008**: *529*, *534*, *538–39*, 541
1111, **2005**: *598*
1112, **2003**: 640
1114, **2003**: 634

North American Free Trade Agreement (NAFTA) (continued)
1115, **2003:** 641
1116, **2001:** *576–83, 595, 598–605*, 612–13, 644; **2002:** 611, 631, 648, 651, 654, 660, 662–63; **2003:** 611, 644–48; **2004:** *573, 575, 576, 577, 596, 597*, 600, 601; **2006:** 689, 692–93, 704; **2008:** *526–27*
1117, **2001:** *580–82, 595*, 602, 604–5, 610–11, 613, 643–46; **2002:** 611, 630, 631, 640–41, 648, 654; **2003:** 611, 644–48; **2004:** *575, 576, 577, 597–601*; **2006:** 688–89, 690, 692–93, 704; **2008:** *526*
1118, **2006:** 704
1119, **2003:** 604; **2006:** 704
1120, **2002:** 648; **2003:** 613; **2005:** *599*, 600, 601; **2006:** 704; **2007:** *549, 550, 551*
1121, **2003:** 613; **2004:** *596*; **2005:** *598*; **2006:** *699*, 704
1126, **2005:** *596n, 599*, 600; **2007:** *549, 550, 551*; **2008:** *525*
1128, **1991-99:** 1436; **2001:** 641–42, 643; **2003:** 606, 643; **2004:** *576, 579, 583, 584, 586–87n, 597*; **2006:** *697n*; **2007:** *552*; **2008:** *526*
1131, **2001:** 645; **2002:** *626–27*; **2003:** 613; **2008:** *533*
1135, **2001:** *605*; **2003:** 646–47
1136, **2002:** 631, 651
1139, **2001:** *584–87*, 644; **2002:** 630, 631; **2003:** 631; **2004:** 600; **2006:** *699*
1222, **2002:** 620–21
1502, **2002:** 654, 662–65
1901, **2003:** 642; **2004:** *595*; **2005:** *597*; **2006:** 702, 704–6, 709
1902, **2006:** 705, 707, 708, 709
1903, **2006:** 705, 707
1904, **1991-99:** 1432–33; **2005:** 603–4; **2006:** 728
1911, **2006:** 709
2001, **1991-99:** 1849
2021, **2003:** 613
2022, **1991-99:** 1848–49; **2003:** 613
2101, **2004:** *585*
2203, **2003:** 638; **2004:** *595*
North American Regional Broadcasting Agreement, 1989-90: 400
North Atlantic Treaty Organization (NATO), 1991-99: 1593, 2155, 2156, 2231, 2242, 2271; **2001:** 825, 860, 861–62; **2003:** 424–26, 939; **2004:** 971, 985; **2008:** 874–76
accession to, **2008:** 874*n*, 875–76
Bulgaria, Estonia, Latvia, Lithuania, Romania, Slovak Republic, Slovenia, Protocol on Accession, **2003:** 424–26; **2004:** 411–12

North Atlantic Treaty Organization (NATO) (continued)
Poland, Hungary and Czech Republic, **1991-99**: 738–39, 1030–40, 2243
Article 5 invocation, **2008**: 874
ballistic missile defense (BMD) interceptor facility in Poland, **2008**: 1010
ballistic missile defense radar site in Czech Republic, **2008**: 1008
Conventional Armed Forces in Europe Treaty, **1989-90**: 578–79; **2007**: 1001–2; **2008**: 1011–17
entry into U.S., alternative documents for armed forces of, **2007**: 16
former Yugoslavia, **1991-99**: 248, 1981, 2033–34, 2136–48
Bosnia–Herzegovina Stabilization Force, **2004**: 967
case in ICJ against NATO countries, **1991-99**: 2151–54
peace keeping efforts in former Yugoslavia, **1991-99**: 1981, 2025–31, 2034–35, 2148–51
FSIA immunity and NATO-SOFA, **2004**: 478–82
Georgia, **2008**: 865–66
initiative to combat trafficking in persons, **2004**: 165–66
International Traffic in Arms Regulations and Export Administration Regulations and new NATO members, **2005**: 1044
intervention in, **2004**: 971–72
Kosovo, **2005**: 935–39; **2008**: 433, 436, 438
meeting on nonproliferation of WMD, **2005**: 111
missile defense efforts, **2007**: 1076
Missile Technology Control Regime, **2005**: 1136
North Atlantic Treaty and UK Congestion Charge, **2005**: 573
participation in Multi-National Force in Iraq, **2005**: 975
Partnership for Peace, **2004**: 173
peacekeeping operations, **1991-99**: 2033, 2034–35, 2138–57
response to attacks of 9/11, **2005**: 372
Russia, **1991-99**: 1031–40; **2008**: 875–76
Somali pirates, **2008**: 927
special immigration benefits, **1991-99**: 72–73
Status of Forces Agreement (SOFA), **1991-99**: 1539, 1595; **2005**: 573
Czech Republic, **2008**: 1009
Russian understanding, **2008**: 160–64
Treaty on Open Skies, **1991-99**: 2238–41
U.S. participation in, **1991-99**: 2022, 2025–31, 2034, 2140–45, 2168–70, 2228
visas, **2004**: 29
waiver of restriction on assistance for member country of, **2004**: 187
North Dakota
flood control negotiations between U.S. and Canada concerning Devils Lake, **2005**: 717–19

North Korea. *See* Korea, North (Democratic People's Republic of Korea (DPRK))
North Pacific Anadromous Fish Commission, 1991-99: 1315
North Pacific Marine Science Organization, 1991-99: 1315
Northeastern Interstate Forest Fire Protection Compact, 2000: 296
Northern Mariana Islands, Commonwealth of (CNMI)
citizenship status of residents, **1989-90:** 9–12; **2003:** 273–75; **2004:** 218
control of submerged lands, **1991-99:** 831–41; **2002:** 246–59; **2003:** 275–76; **2005:** 251–55; **2006:** 315–16
Covenant to Establish a Commonwealth of the Northern Mariana Islands in Political Union with the United States (1976), **1989-90:** 9–12, 162–64; **1991-99:** 832–41; **2002:** 246–59; **2003:** 273–75
entry into force of provisions (Article X), **2005:** 252–53
legal foundations of government (Article I), **2005:** 252
local self-government under U.S. sovereignty (Article I), **2005:** 252
property distribution (Article VIII), **2005:** 252–53
selective applicability of U.S. Constitution and laws to Commonwealth (Article V), **2005:** 252
U.S. responsibility for foreign affairs and defense (Article I), **2005:** 252
fisheries issues, **2005:** 736, 742–44
government description, **2005:** 252
political status, **1989-90:** 161–64; **1991-99:** 808–11, 814, 816, 817, 819, 1570
sovereignty of U.S., **2003:** 485
North-South peace accord (Sudan). *See* Sudan
Norway
Arctic environment protection agreement, **1991-99:** 1777–80
Arctic region, **2008:** 623, 624, 628
arms control, **1991-99:** 2232, 2252–53, 2338
boundary dispute with United Kingdom, **2005:** 702
coastline definition, **2002:** 751–52
discovery in U.S. for use in, **2003:** 880–81
extradition and mutual legal assistance, **2000:** 186*n*
family support enforcement, **1991-99:** 1866
Food Aid Convention, **1991-99:** 936
Ilulissat Declaration, **2008:** 636–38
initiative to combat trafficking in persons, **2004:** 165–66
intellectual property Watch List, **2008:** 608
International Space Station Partners Agreement, **1991-99:** 1642
Kosovo peace process, role in, **2005:** 935
Middle East peace process, **1991-99:** 1027, 1993, 1995
naturalization convention, **2002:** 205

Norway (continued)
nonimmigrant visa waiver pilot program, **1991-99**: 76
objections to U.S. reservations to Genocide Convention, **1989-90**: 144
Open Skies (aerial observation) treaty, **2002**: 1029
parental abduction case, **2004**: 54–62
patent protection for pharmaceutical products, **2008**: 608
Proliferation Security Initiative, **2004**: 1074
reciprocity in recovery of family support obligations, **2002**: 841–42; **2008**: 759
Sudan peace negotiations, support of, **2005**: 920, 926
trade issues, **1991-99**: 1385
treaty succession, **1991-99**: 744
Underwater Cultural Heritage, Convention on Protection of, position on, **2005**: 766
whaling and, **2002**: 210
NPT. *See* Nuclear Non-Proliferation Treaty (NPT) (1968)
NSG (Nuclear Suppliers Group). *See* Atomic Energy Agency, International (IAEA); Nonproliferation, *subheading*: country-specific issues
Nuclear Claims Tribunal, 2006: 316–25
Nuclear energy, 2001: 734
Agreed Framework, Korean peninsula, **1991-99**: 2323–29
agreements for cooperation on peaceful uses of nuclear energy with India, Russia, and Turkey (123 agreements), **2008**: 986–93
Convention on Supplementary Compensation for Nuclear Damage (CSC), **2008**: 993–99
dual-use technology, **1991-99**: 2287–88
International Thermonuclear Experimental Reactor Consortium (ITER), **2005**: 1080, 1086
ITER International Fusion Energy Organization, **2006**: 893–95
NPT and, **2008**: 940–41
nuclear fuel, assurances of reliable access to, **2005**: 1124–25; **2006**: 1292–93
outer space, **1991-99**: 1629, 1631, 1633; **2005**: 712
reactor safety, **1991-99**: 2309–10
transport by sea of civil nuclear materials, **2001**: 699–703, 712; **2004**: 711–13
U.S. views on proliferation risks associated with, **2008**: 951
Nuclear nonproliferation. *See* Nonproliferation
Nuclear Non-Proliferation Treaty (NPT) (1968), 1991-99: 1170, 2111; **2002**: 1032–33, 1034; **2005**: 447, 1094, 1118–19, 1125, 1136; **2008**: 932–33. *See also* Nonproliferation
compliance and implementation, **2003**: 1086–94; **2006**: 1262–65
disarmament obligations, **1991-99**: 2216; **2006**: 1257–60; **2007**: 1052–62

Nuclear Non-Proliferation Treaty (NPT) (1968) (continued)
export control provisions, **2003**: 1114–15
extension and security assurances, **1991-99**: 2279–87
former Soviet republics and, **1991-99**: 2211–12, 2214, 2216
India as non-party, **1991-99**: 2296–97; **2005**: 1087
Iran and, **2007**: 379, 837, 1033; **2008**: 939, 951, 973, 975
Iraq and, **1991-99**: 2111; **2002**: 945
Kazakhstan and, **2005**: 1107
Libya and, **2003**: 1069
Middle East free of nuclear weapons, **2008**: 940
North Korea and, **1991-99**: 2323; **2002**: 1045–46, 1047, 1052; **2003**: 1100–1105; **2005**: 1067–73; **2006**: 1266, 1268; **2008**: 939–40
Pakistan as non-party, **1991-99**: 2296–97
review conferences, **1991-99**: 2271–72, 2279–81; **2002**: 1071–73; **2003**: 1086–94; **2005**: 1091, 1106–14; **2006**: 1260–61; **2007**: 1053, 1959
2010 Review Conference, preparatory committee for, **2008**: 933–41
strategies for strengthening, **2003**: 1094–95
Taiwan not a party following recognition of PRC, **1991-99**: 2334
U.S. pledge concerning use of nuclear weapons against parties to, **1991-99**: 2173–74, 2283–87
pledges by China, France, Russia, U.K. concerning use of nuclear weapons against parties to, **1991-99**: 2286
withdrawal by treaty violators, **2007**: 1052–59; **2008**: 936–37, 949
Nuclear Safety, Convention on, 1991-99: 1693–96, 2331–32; **2008**: 997, 998
Nuclear weapons, use of. *See also* Nonproliferation; Nuclear Non-Proliferation Treaty (NPT) (1968)
ICJ advisory opinion on legality of use of, **1991-99**: 2170–82; **2006**: 1079–80
customary international law on, **1991-99**: 2171, 2172, 2173, 2175, 2176, 2181–82
no ban on use or deterrence, **2006**: 1255–57, 1263
Geneva Convention Additional Protocol I not applicable to, **2006**: 1079–80
Nuclear Posture Review, **2008**: 949–50
U.S. response to nuclear threat, **2008**: 948–53

O

OAS. *See* Organization of American States (OAS)
Ocean Dumping Act (1972), 2003: 741–42
Oceans. *See* Fish and marine mammals; Law of the Sea, UN Convention on (UNCLOS); Marine conservation; Maritime issues

Oceans Act (2000), 2001: 681
OECD. *See* Organization for Economic Cooperation and Development (OECD)
OFAC. *See* Office of Foreign Assets Control (OFAC)
Office of Federal Contract Compliance Programs (OFCCP), 2005: 288
Office of Foreign Assets Control (OFAC), 2000: 438, 618–19, 621, 623–24, 743–46, 748, 749; **2008:** 99–100, 114–15
  Cuban litigation against over trademark denial, **2006:** 1006–15
  educational travel to Cuba, **2008:** 810–13
  Iranian Transactions Regulations, **2006:** 986–90; **2008:** 983–84
  Iraqi Sanctions Regulations, **2006:** 1016–17
  Palestinian Authority government under Hamas, **2006:** 990–95
Oil. *See also* Marine conservation, *subheading*: pollution
  antidumping duty order on tubular goods from Mexico, **2005:** 634
  anti-suit injunction
    contaminated oil, **2005:** 831–32
    foreign litigation to overturn U.S. courts' enforcement of arbitral award, **2008:** 760–64
  division of oil revenues in Sudan, **2005:** 921
  ethnic cleansing of civilian populations in southern Sudan in order to facilitate oil exploration, claims of, **2005:** 394–400
  industry support for accession by U.S. to the LOS Convention, **2005:** 677
  MARPOL record book requirement, **2008:** 131–36
  oil tankers
    regulations implementing double hull requirements for, **2005:** 732–33
    transfer of oil cargo between oil tankers at sea, **2008:** 698–702
  Oil-for-Food Program. *See* Iraq
  Russian petroleum company, case involving U.S. banks, *forum non conveniens*, **2005:** 833–39
  security personnel killed while protecting Colombian oil production facility and pipeline, claims for, **2005:** 418–24
Oman
  contiguous zone authority, **1989-90:** 468–69
  free trade agreement with U.S., **2005:** 637; **2006:** 765–66; **2008:** 572
  longshore work prohibition on alien crewmen from, **2002:** 757; **2003:** 764
  maritime issues, **1991-99:** 1583, 1596, 1598–99
    Strait of Hormuz, alleged international law violation by transiting U.S. ships, **2005:** 684–86
  trafficking in persons, **2008:** 118
Omnibus consolidated appropriations acts. *See* Appropriations Acts
Open Skies Agreements. *See* Aviation issues
Open Skies Treaty (aerial observation), 1991-99: 2238; **2002:** 1029; **2004:** 1068–69

OPIC Agreements. *See* Investment
Orbit, geostationary (GSO), legal issues related to, 2005: 713–15. *See also* Space
Orderly Departure Program. *See* Vietnam
Oregon
foreign heirs under probate law of, **2000:** 472
role in international agreements, **2000:** 294, 295
Organ harvesting, 2000: 362
Organic Act of Guam (1950), 2003: 275
Organic Act of Puerto Rico (1917), 2003: 275
Organization for African Unity, 1991-99: 479, 1937, 1963, 2011–13, 2017, 2018, 2314
Organization for Economic Cooperation and Development (OECD), 1991-99: 1032, 1541, 1811, 1927; **2002:** 307
agreement on mutual assistance in tax matters, **1989-90:** 410–11
anti-bribery convention. *See* Corruption
development of guidance and standards, **2008:** 1007
Draft Convention on the Protection of Foreign Property, **2000:** 688–89
guidelines for multinational enterprises, **2002:** 727–28
Multilateral Agreement on Investment, **1991-99:** 1463, 1464, 1486–93
tax systems, **2002:** 685–87
Organization for Security and Cooperation in Europe (OSCE), 1991-99: 47, 686, 764, 1032, 1148, 1952, 2141, 2228, 2241–43; **2001:** 880–81, 912, 941; **2002:** 316, 1030; **2003:** 26, 154; **2004:** 1072
arms control, **2004:** 1071
Human Dimension Implementation meetings
Article 98 agreement, U.S. statement on, **2004:** 184
death penalty, U.S. statements on use of, **2003:** 340–42; **2004:** 335–37; **2005:** 389–90
human rights commitments to, **2005:** 439–40
Belarus failure to honor, **2005:** 435–36
preventing torture in fight against terrorism, U.S. statements on, **2004:** 371–75; **2005:** 371–75
measures to eliminate racial and religious hatred, **2004:** 263–69; **2005:** 319
anti-Semitism conference, **2003:** 297–98; **2004:** 274–76
Minsk Group efforts to settle Nagarno-Karabakh conflict, **2008:** 830–32
national emergencies and executive power, **2005:** 265
terrorism and, **2003:** 154
U.S. presidential election in 2004, observation by, **2005:** 285–86
women's rights, **2005:** 311–13

Organization for the Prohibition of Chemical Weapons, 1991-99: 1315, 2344; **2002:** 1033–35; **2004:** 928, 933, 1059, 1074, 1107, 1115–16, 1159, 1160–62; **2008:** 1006
Organization of American States (OAS), 1991-99: 852; **2001:** 291; **2004:** 226, 804, 827, 985. *See also* Inter-American Commission on Human Rights; Inter-American Court of Human Rights; Prisoner transfer
American Declaration of the Rights and Duties of Man. *See* American Declaration of the Rights and Duties of Man
Charter, **1991-99:** 330, 438, 1438; **2000:** 406–7; **2002:** 192, 263, 369; **2005:** 467
Protocols amending, **1991-99:** 1018–22
U.S. federalism reservation, **2002:** 192
violations in capital punishment sentencing, **2001:** 297–98
citizens and voting rights, **2005:** 250
commercial finance regulation, **2001:** 779
extradition and mutual legal assistance, **2000:** 163, 167–68; **2002:** 117
General Assembly meeting, **2005:** 466
Haiti and, **1991-99:** 857, 862, 863, 1883–84, 2047; **2003:** 938, 942–43; **2004:** 399, 937, 938, 940
Headquarters Agreement, **1991-99:** 1015–18
human rights, **1991-99:** 852
democracy and, **2003:** 406–7
violations by U.S., complaints alleging, **2005:** 287
immunity of diplomatic personnel, **1991-99:** 1017, 1297–1305; **2000:** 382–83
Inter-American arms trade convention, **1991-99:** 554–58, 2262–63
Inter-American Convention Against Corruption, **1991-99:** 563–71; **2000:** 231–38; **2001:** 159–63; **2004:** 139–40; **2006:** 236, 237–38
Inter-American Convention Against Terrorism. *See* Terrorism
Inter-American Convention Against the Illicit Manufacturing of and Trafficking in Firearms, Ammunition, Explosives, and Other Related Materials, **1991-99:** 554–58, 2262–63
Inter-American Convention on International Commercial Arbitration, **1989-90:** 501–2
Inter-American Convention on Serving Criminal Sentences Abroad, **1991-99:** 381–82; **2000:** 171–72; **2001:** 51–55; **2006:** 104; **2008:** 51, 52
Inter-American Declaration on the Rights of Indigenous Peoples, **1991-99:** 1003–6; **2002:** 364–67, 379–81
Inter-American Democratic Charter, **2001:** 346–51; **2003:** 406; **2005:** 245, 251

Organization of American States (OAS) (continued)
claim of privately enforceable rights, **2001**: 298
on rights of indigenous peoples, **2001**: 353; **2003**: 402
Inter-American Juridical Committee, **1991-99**: 442; **2000**: 403*n*
Inter-American Program for Promotion and Protection of Human Rights of Migrants, OAS Resolution on, **2005**: 337–41
Inter-American Treaty of Reciprocal Assistance, **2001**: 863–64
International Criminal Court and, **2002**: 321–23; **2003**: 338–40; **2004**: 179–81
in maintenance of regional stability, **2002**: 926–31; **2003**: 937–38
Permanent Council meeting, **2005**: 245*n*
poverty reduction goals, **1991-99**: 1020–21
private international law, **1991-99**: 1841–43, 1852–53; **2001**: 723, 776, 779, 787–88, 789, 794
Inter-American Specialized Conference on Private International Law (CIDIP)
CIVIP V (Mexico City Convention), **2007**: 751–52
CIDIP VI
Model Inter-American Law on Secured Finance, **2002**: 823, 833–34; **2004**: 803
transboundary pollution, conflict of laws relating to, **2002**: 833, 834
CIDIP VII
cross-border consumer protection proposals, **2007**: 745–51
electronic arbitration of cross-border e-Commerce disputes, **2007**: 752–54
OAS Panama Convention on Commercial Arbitration, **2007**: 753
transportation of goods, **2001**: 787–88; **2002**: 819–20, 834
racism, resolution on prevention of, U.S. reservations, **2005**: 305–6
response to coup in member country, **1991-99**: 1019–20, 1021–22
response to September 11 attacks, **2001**: 862–63; **2005**: 372
Rio Treaty, **2001**: 863–64; **2005**: 372
service of process agreements, **2003**: 867–68
trade negotiations and, **1991-99**: 1480
U.S. military action in Panama and, **1989-90**: 554, 555, 556
Organization of Petroleum Exporting Countries, 2003: 557–58
Organized crime. *See* Crime
Orphan First program, 2003: 122–23
OSCE. *See* Organization for Security and Cooperation in Europe (OSCE)
Outer space. *See* Space
Overseas Private Investment Corporation, U.S. (OPIC), 1991-99: 1482–83; **2005**: 469, 647–53
Ozone protection. *See* Air pollution

P

Pacta sunt servanda principle, **1991-99**: 721, 772, 882; **2001**: 131–32, 592; **2002**: 661; **2008**: 326

Pakistan

advanced mine detection equipment, **2005**: 1042

Alien Tort Statute litigation alleging trafficking of children from to UAE, **2008**: 227–36

alleged failure of consular notification, **1991-99**: 263

Anti-Hijacking Act, extraterritorial jurisdiction over national of, **1991-99**: 506

China–U.S. relations and, **1991-99**: 2359

drug trade, **2001**: 120; **2002**: 124; **2003**: 181; **2004**: 133–34; **2006**: 213; **2007**: 163; **2008**: 113

extradition and mutual legal assistance, **2000**: 185*n*; **2008**: 64–69

foreign sovereign immunity laws, **2005**: 529

Guantanamo detainees transferred to, **2005**: 967

human rights in, **2002**: 282

immunity, Pakistan State Immunity Ordinance, **2006**: 609

India aviation dispute, **2000**: 663–64

individual rendered to U.S. by, **2002**: 77–78

intellectual property rights Watch List, **2006**: 768, 769; **2007**: 610; **2008**: 605

juvenile offenders, execution of, **2005**: 387

money laundering, **2004**: 135

non-North Atlantic Treaty Organization (NATO) ally, designation as, **2005**: 1044

nonproliferation issues. *See* Nonproliferation

religious freedom, measures promoting, **2005**: 315

service of process, **2003**: 891; **2005**: 856–59, 862*n*; **2006**: 970–73

shrimp imports, challenge of U.S. ban on, **2001**: 752–56

terrorism and

cooperation of Pakistan with U.S., **2008**: 870–71

reservation to International Convention for the Suppression of Terrorist Bombings, **2003**: 244–45

terrorist acts in, **2004**: 106; **2008**: 870–71

trade and investment agreements, **2004**: 651–52

trade issues, **1991-99**: 744, 1408, 1504, 1717–19

Palau

free association compact with U.S., **1991-99**: 815, 816–23

diplomatic relations, **1991-99**: 824–25, 1152

Trusteeship Agreement

status under for U.S. domestic law purposes, **1991-99**: 811–16

termination of, **1991-99**: 823–25

maritime interdiction agreement, **2008**: 650

Palestine Red Crescent Society, 2005: 1043; **2006:** 1104
Palestinian issues. *See also* Middle East Conflict, Israeli-Palestinian
legal actions against Israel by Palestinian nationals, **2005:** 566–67, 581–83
Overseas Private Investment Corporation investment incentives, **1991-99:** 1484–86
Palestine Liberation Organization (PLO), **1989-90:** 203–5; **1991-99:** 1185–86, 1339, 1448, 1989, 1993, 1994, 1997, 1999, 2003; **2005:** 503–4, 531
Palestinian Anti-Terrorism Act (2006), **2006:** 306, 993–95
Palestinian Authority, **1991-99:** 1484–86, 1994, 1995, 2002
Jerusalem, attachment of properties, **2005:** 531–42
Legislative Council elections, Quartet comments on, **2006:** 1028–32
no foreign state status under FSIA, **2005:** 503–4
sanctions against, **2006:** 990–95
sanctions removal, **2007:** 825–27
Quartet Statement. *See* Middle East Conflict, Israeli-Palestinian
self-determination and, **2004:** 392, 393
terrorism and, **2004:** 902, 947, 949, 951, 953, 957, 973
UN issues, **1991-99:** 1024–25; **2006:** 1032–42
observer mission, **1991-99:** 1027–29, 1243; **2005:** 538
Palmyra Atoll
sovereignty of U.S. and, **2003:** 485
Panama
American Servicemembers' Protection Act waiver, **2003:** 238
claimed head-of-state immunity of General Noriega, **1991-99:** 1269, 1281–85
compliance with international child abduction convention, **2003:** 127, 129; **2004:** 54
conservation initiatives, **2003:** 776
consular privileges and immunities, **1991-99:** 1311–12
Convention on Protection of Underwater Cultural Heritage, party to, **2005:** 766
Cooperating Nation Information Exchange System (CNIES), agreement with U.S. concerning, **2005:** 146
drug trade, **2001:** 120; **2002:** 124; **2003:** 181; **2004:** 133–34; **2005:** 135; **2006:** 213; **2007:** 163; **2008:** 113
maritime counter-drug trade agreement, **1991-99:** 1606–7
extradition and mutual legal assistance, **1991-99:** 450, 455–56; **2000:** 185*n*; **2001:** 90–96
forest conservation agreement, **2004:** 745; **2008:** 722
free trade agreement, **2004:** 618, 622; **2006:** 765; **2008:** 571*n*
Hague Child Abduction Convention, compliance with, **2006:** 102
human rights in, **1989-90:** 561

Panama (continued)
immigration and, **1991-99**: 60, 69
Inter-American Convention Against Corruption, party to, **2006**: 238
Inter-American Convention Against Terrorism (OAS Terrorism Convention), party to, **2005**: 111
Inter-American Tropical Tuna Commission, **2000**: 307
interdiction of Panamanian-flagged ship in international waters, **1989-90**: 452–56
marine conservation, **1991-99**: 1702, 1713
Panama Declaration, **1991-99**: 1748–49
money laundering, **2004**: 135
Panama Canal Commission, **2001**: 219–24; **2004**: 198–201
Panama Canal Treaty. *See* Panama Canal Treaty (1977)
Panama Canal Zone, **1991-99**: 69*n*
Panama Convention, **2005**: 807
prisoner transfer treaty, **2001**: 51
private claims against U.S. by nationals of, **1991-99**: 1126–28
Proliferation Security Initiative (PSI) ship boarding agreement with U.S., **2005**: 1100
request for U.S. protection of Panamanian embassy in U.S., **1989-90**: 370–74
shark protection, **2004**: 766
stolen vehicle treaty, **2000**: 169–70; **2002**: 68
trade and investment issues, **1991-99**: 1385; **2003**: 682–83
Tropical Forest Conservation Act agreement, **2004**: 745; **2008**: 722
U.S. military action in
authorization, **1989-90**: 552–54, 556–59
claims against U.S. by Panamanian businesses, **1991-99**: 1126–11128
cooperation of Panamanian government in, **1989-90**: 559–61
justification, **1989-90**: 552, 554–56
Panama Canal Commission, 2001: 219–24
Panama Canal Treaty (1977), **1989-90**: 553, 554, 556–59; **1991-99**: 190*n*, 650, 744; **2000**: 312–17; **2004**: 198–201
rights of U.S. under, **1989-90**: 556–59
Pandemic influenza, national strategy for, 2006: 889–90
Papua New Guinea
act of state doctrine and, **2002**: 574–75
citizens' claim against international corporation under Alien Tort Statute, **2002**: 333–43, 357; **2003**: 396; **2006**: 431–36; **2008**: 238–44
environmental protection agreement, **2002**: 791
extradition and mutual legal assistance, **2000**: 185*n*
human rights in, **2001**: 338–39; **2006**: 946–50
pilotage agreement with Australia concerning Torres Strait, **2005**: 687

Papua New Guinea (continued)
political question doctrine, **2005:** 420
trafficking in persons, **2008:** 118
U.S. prosecution of alleged human rights violations, **2007:** 227–28; **2008:** 239
Par Value Modification Act (1973), 2001: 472–73
Paraguay
arms exports, **1991-99:** 2252
consular notification, case against U.S. for failure of. *See* Consular notification and access
cultural objects protection, **1991-99:** 1803
drug trade, **2001:** 120; **2002:** 124; **2003:** 181; **2004:** 133–34; **2005:** 135; **2006:** 213; **2007:** 163; **2008:** 113
extradition and mutual legal assistance, **1991-99:** 392; **2000:** 165–66, 179, 186*n*; **2001:** 92*n*
forest conservation agreement, **2006:** 886–88; **2008:** 722
intellectual property rights, **2006:** 769; **2007:** 610
Inter-American Convention Against Corruption, party to, **2006:** 238
Inter-American Convention Against Terrorism (OAS Terrorism Convention), party to, **2005:** 111
money laundering, **2004:** 135
open skies agreement with U.S., **2005:** 588
prisoner transfer treaty, **2000:** 171; **2001:** 51
Tropical Forest Conservation Act agreement, **2006:** 886–87; **2008:** 722
U.S. military assistance, **2006:** 278
waiver of Article 98 agreement with U.S. (nonsurrender of Americans to ICC), **2006:** 279
Paramountcy doctrine, federal, 2002: 248–55; **2005:** 251, 253–54
Parental Responsibility and Measures for the Protection of Children, Convention on Jurisdiction, Applicable Law, Recognition, Enforcement and Co-operation in Respect of, 1991-99: 1859–61, 1876; **2000:** 121; **2004:** 63, 830
Paris Act (1971), 2003: 200
Paris Convention for the Protection of Industrial Property, 2002: 389–91; **2005:** 667–71
Passenger Information Exchange, 2007: 34
Passports, U.S., 1991-99: 23, 40, 348, 1156; **2004:** 12, 23, 30, 69; **2006:** 4–17; **2008:** 6–15. *See also* Children, *subheading*: international abduction; Immigration and visas
authority to issue, **1991-99:** 56
biometrics in, **2004:** 29; **2006:** 14, 209; **2007:** 11, 34
book format, **2007:** 11
card format passports, **2006:** 11–13; **2007:** 16; **2008:** 8–9
for child, **2004:** 7–8; **2008:** 9–11

Passports, U.S. (continued)
age to sign for passport application, **2008:** 10
foreign-born adopted child of U.S. parents, **2001:** 6
two-parent consent for, **2001:** 8–9; **2002:** 11–13; **2008:** 10
citizenship and, **2004:** 4–5, 218
claimed entitlement to, **2007:** 18–19; **2008:** 11–15
denial or revocation of, **2007:** 17–18
escaped prisoner in foreign country, denial to, **2002:** 16–17
for foreign criminal charges, **2006:** 16–17
for foreign warrant of arrest for felony, **2008:** 10–11
grounds for, **2002:** 16, 17–18
for law enforcement purposes, **2002:** 18
lost or stolen passports. *See* lost or stolen, *this heading*
for national security concerns, **1989-90:** 13–17
for nonpayment of child support, **1991-99:** 49, 1866; **2001:** 9–13; **2002:** 13–15; **2006:** 15–16
to persons with mental illness, **2002:** 18
revocation hearing requirement, **1991-99:** 52–53
subject of federal arrest warrant, **1991-99:** 52–53
diplomatic and official passports, constitutional powers of President with respect to, **1991-99:** 41–49, 807, 1136–37
dual nationals, use of U.S. passport required for, **2001:** 34–35
electronic (e-passports), **2005:** 8–10; **2006:** 13–15, 208; **2007:** 11
Executive Branch authority for issuance, **1991-99:** 47; **2003:** 486, 495–97, 498; **2007:** 437–43; **2008:** 11–15
false or fraudulent, related to trafficking or smuggling of persons, **2004:** 160–61, 162; **2005:** 156
issued for purpose of compliance with citizenship retention requirements, **1989-90:** 8–9
limited, **2004:** 51
lost or stolen
invalidation of, **2004:** 6
reporting on, **2004:** 6–7; **2007:** 33
stolen and lost passport data exchange agreement with U.S., **2005:** 5–6
U.S.–Australia agreement on data exchange, **2005:** 5–6
U.S.–New Zealand memorandum of understanding, **2006:** 17
Passport Act (1926), **1991-99:** 56
place of birth, designation of, **2006:** 530–47; **2007:** 437–39; **2008:** 15, 447–54
Regional Movement Alert List pilot, **2006:** 209
regulations, new global, **2007:** 16–18; **2008:** 9–11
requirements for aliens proceeding in transit through U.S., **2003:** 13–15

Passports, U.S. (continued)
restriction on use of, **1991-99**: 49–52, 56; **2001**: 13–15. *See also* Travel restrictions
restrictions on travel to Iraq, **2003**: 11–12
restrictions on travel to Lebanon, **1991-99**: 51–52
restrictions on travel to Libya, **2003**: 12–13; **2004**: 6
sovereign immunity and, **2006**: 307
U.S. policy regarding Jerusalem as place of birth for, **2003**: 485–501; **2004**: 452–54; **2006**: 530–47; **2008**: 447–54
Western Hemisphere Travel Initiative, **2005**: 1–5; **2006**: 4–13; **2007**: 8–12; **2008**: 6–8
alternative documents
Free and Secure Trade (FAST), **2007**: 12, 15
Merchant Mariner document, **2007**: 11
NEXUS, **2007**: 12
pilot programs to develop additional, **2007**: 15
Secure Electronic Network for Travelers Rapid Inspection (SENTRI), **2007**: 12
Trusted Traveler Program documents, **2007**: 12, 15
U.S. military identification card, **2007**: 13
Outlying Area Reporting System, **2007**: 12
reporting by telephone, **2007**: 12
spouses and dependents of U.S. citizen members of Armed Forces and other non-military contractors and employees, **2007**: 13
waiver by President, **2007**: 10
Patent law. *See also* Intellectual property rights
applicability to outer space activities, **1989-90**: 481–83
biological diversity and, **1991-99**: 1762
drug research and development, **2002**: 718; **2003**: 815–16
International Space Station Partners Agreement on, **1991-99**: 1645, 1646
Internet issues, **2000**: 740
parallel judicial proceedings, **2002**: 862–63, 872–73
Patent Cooperation Treaty, **2006**: 783
Patent Law Treaty, **2006**: 780–86
patentability of plants and animals, **1991-99**: 1505
pharmaceuticals, protections for, **1991-99**: 1386, 1506–7; **2001**: 646–48, 764–67; **2003**: 673–79; **2004**: 785; **2008**: 607, 608
protection in China, **1991-99**: 1517, 1520, 1521
rules of private international law, **2000**: 740
trade cases by U.S. concerning, **1991-99**: 1408–9, 1410, 1504, 1506
TRIPS agreements, **1991-99**: 1501–3, 1505
drug patents and, **1991-99**: 1506

PATRIOT Act, USA (2001), 2001: 821, 896, 897, 899, 918, 921, 922, 923–28; **2002:** 86–89, 102, 126–27, 128; **2003:** 17, 19, 137, 155–56, 158–59, 208, 910–11; **2004:** 136–38, 139, 171–72, 901, 1102; **2005:** 22*n*, 176, 180, 344, 355, 356, 362, 896, 1073; **2006:** 206, 243, 361–63; **2008:** 120
exclusion of aliens and terrorist activity, **2007:** 20–21
provisions concerning immigration and terrorism, **2008:** 279–80
PATRIOT Improvement and Reauthorization Act, USA (2006), 2007: 162
methamphetamine production and trafficking, **2006:** 216
search warrants, **2006:** 362
Peace process. *See* Conflict resolution
Peacebuilding Commission, 2005: 443, 446, 449, 454–57, 946–47
Peacekeeping missions. *See also* African Union; Conflict resolution; United Nations, *subheading*: peacekeeping role
Afghanistan, **2003:** 958–59
Angola, **1991-99:** 145
appropriate use of forces, **2007:** 866–67
Chad (MINURCAT), **2008:** 839
children, protection of by, **2003:** 307
criminal accountability in, **2007:** 864–66; **2008:** 387–88
Darfur (UNAMID), **2006:** 1043–54; **2007:** 867–69; **2008:** 837, 839, 841–44
Democratic Republic of Congo, **2007:** 862; **2008:** 838
East Timor, **1991-99:** 2047–48
former Yugoslavia, **1991-99:** 2024, 2031–43, 2168–70
gender-based violence and, **2004:** 166–68
Georgia (UNOMIG), **2008:** 837, 844–45
Haiti, **1991-99:** 856, 2045–47, 2162–68; **2004:** 34–35, 188, 940–42; **2008:** 838
International Criminal Court jurisdiction and, **1991-99:** 626, 629–30, 2019–24; **2002:** 152–53, 157–68; **2003:** 227–29, 231–34; **2004:** 188. *See also* International Criminal Court (ICC), *subheading*: Article 98 agreement (nonsurrender of Americans to ICC)
Japan, peace treaty with allied powers (1951), **2005:** 476–78
Lebanon, **2006:** 1035, 1037, 1039, 1060–61
extension of mandate of the UN Interim Force in, **2007:** 869–71
Liberia, **2003:** 233–34, 955–57; **2008:** 838
Peru and Ecuador, **1991-99:** 2005
protection of peacekeeping personnel, **2003:** 993–96; **2004:** 409
reconstruction and stabilization assistance for troubled areas, **2005:** 947–48
riot control agents and. *See* Armed conflict
Rwanda, **1991-99:** 531

Peacekeeping missions (continued)
sexual exploitation and abuse at hands of UN peacekeepers, **2005**: 449, 945–46; **2006**: 1065–68; **2007**: 319–21; **2008**: 286, 288, 840–41
Sierra Leone, **1991-99**: 2017
Somalia (AMISOM), **2008**: 847–50
Somalia humanitarian relief operation, **1991-99**: 2043–45; **2006**: 1061–64
Sudan (UNMIS), **2006**: 1047–54; **2008**: 839
UN. *See* United Nations, *subheading*: peacekeeping role
U.S. participation in, American Servicemembers' Protection Act provisions, **2002**: 171–73; **2003**: 228–29
Western Sahara, **2003**: 958; **2006**: 1064–65; **2008**: 850–52
Penalties. *See* Sanctions
Persecution, 2004: 272, 278, 395
asylum denied due to participation in, **1989-90**: 46; **2008**: 308
asylum request based on well-founded fear of, **1989-90**: 41–42, 45–46; **1991-99**: 85, 86, 154–56, 251; **2000**: 128–31, 141; **2002**: 26–28
Canada–U.S. agreement on examination of, **2004**: 33–34, 35
child claimants, **1991-99**: 226–32; **2008**: 306, 307
claim against Zimbabwean political party for under Torture Victim Protection Act, **2002**: 324–33
consular notification and fear of, **1991-99**: 268
deferred forced departure of Chinese nationals based on possibility of, **1989-90**: 54–57
definition of, **1991-99**: 200, 201–2; **2002**: 26
female genital mutilation as basis for, **1991-99**: 207–15
forced behavior contrary to beliefs as, **1991-99**: 218–19
gender guidelines, **1991-99**: 215–26
intent to harm not required, **1991-99**: 197–202
for membership in particular group, **1991-99**: 207–15; **2008**: 32
children as group, **1991-99**: 230–32
family as group, **1991-99**: 223–24
gender as group, **1991-99**: 221–23, 230–31
for political opinion, **1991-99**: 197–207, 219–21, 230, 232–39
family planning policy as, **1991-99**: 202–7
"on account of," **1991-99**: 194–97
by private actor, **1991-99**: 224–25
proof of, **1991-99**: 195, 197, 205–7, 213–14
psychiatric intervention as, **1991-99**: 197–99
punishment vs., **1991-99**: 201–2
sexual violence or harassment as, **1991-99**: 218, 225
denial of visa based on participation in, **2002**: 5–8

Persecution (continued)
government responsibility to prevent, **2000**: 397–98
Nazi, **1991-99**: 571–76, 953
restitution and claims based on, **1991-99**: 1045, 1048, 1053–56, 1061–62, 1070, 1192
revocation of U.S. citizenship for participation in, **1991-99**: 27–34; **2004**: 1–4
nonrefoulement obligation and, **1991-99**: 150–94
religious, **1991-99**: 919, 923, 926; **2002**: 280–82
as basis for inadmissibility, **1991-99**: 93–94
Falun Gong practitioners' claims against Chinese government officials, **2002**: 469–76. *See also* Religion and religious freedom
of returned asylum-seekers, **2002**: 29
withholding of deportation based on possibility of, **1991-99**: 232–39, 434
Persistent Organic Pollutants (POPs)
Stockholm Convention on, **1991-99**: 1667–69; **2001**: 727–30; **2002**: 771–77; **2004**: 769, 771, 772
U.S. comments on, **2005**: 725–27
UN Economic Commission for Europe regional agreement on, **1991-99**: 1668, 1669
Personal Responsibility and Work Opportunity Reconciliation Act (1996), **1991-99**: 49, 788–89, 1870; **2001**: 9–10, 49; **2002**: 13–15
Peru
aircraft shootdown incident, **1991-99**: 538, 539; **2001**: 121, 127–28
Alien Tort Statute claims involving, **2001**: 336–37; **2002**: 344–45; **2003**: 251–52, 371–74
Andean Trade Promotion and Drug Eradication Act (2002), **2008**: 577–79
asset sharing agreement with U.S., **2004**: 140–41
border dispute with Ecuador, **1991-99**: 2004–10
claim of invalidity of consent to treaty, **2003**: 251–52
Cooperating Nation Information Exchange System (CNIES), agreement with U.S. concerning, **2005**: 146
cultural property protection, **1991-99**: 1798–99; **2002**: 813; **2007**: 741–42
drug trade, **2001**: 120; **2002**: 124; **2003**: 181; **2004**: 133–34; **2005**: 135; **2006**: 213; **2007**: 163; **2008**: 113
mistaken interdiction of civilian aircraft in counternarcotics effort, **2001**: 121–28; **2003**: 187

Peru (continued)
U.S. counternarcotics assistance to, **1991-99**: 538–44, 546; **2001**: 121–27; **2003**: 187
environmental and conservation issues, **1991-99**: 1782
extradition and mutual legal assistance, **2000**: 185*n*; **2001**: 90–96; **2002**: 61, 62, 63, 69, 175
fisheries negotiations with U.S., **2005**: 613
forest conservation, **2008**: 721–22
free trade agreement, **2003**: 682–83; **2004**: 618; **2005**: 637; **2007**: 584–85; **2008**: 571*n*
head-of-state immunity, **1991-99**: 1284
intellectual property rights Watch List, **2006**: 768; **2007**: 610
Inter-American Commission on Human Rights, **2004**: 223, 226, 234
immunity of delegation to, **2000**: 382–83
Inter-American Convention Against Corruption, party to, **2006**: 238
Inter-American Convention Against Terrorism (OAS Terrorism Convention), party to, **2004**: 97; **2005**: 111
judiciary system, **2000**: 412–14; **2002**: 72–73
marine conservation, **1991-99**: 1749
maritime issues, **2004**: 710–11; **2005**: 42*n*
naturalization convention, **2002**: 205
Tropical Forest Conservation Act agreement, **2008**: 722
UN Commission on Human Rights, **2004**: 390–91
UN High Commissioner for Refugees (UNHCR), **2005**: 435
U.S. military assistance, **2006**: 278
waiver of Article 98 agreement with U.S. (nonsurrender of Americans to ICC), **2006**: 279
Peyote, 2001: 136–39; **2005**: 139, 142–43*n*
Philippines
act of state doctrine, case concerning Marcos asset seizure, **2005**: 575–78
antiterrorism cooperation, **2002**: 118
comfort women from, Alien Tort Statute action brought against Japan, **2005**: 475–81
coral reef protection, **1991-99**: 1755
diplomatic relations, **1991-99**: 1152
extradition and mutual legal assistance, **1991-99**: 395, 398, 399, 405, 450, 456; **2000**: 179, 186*n*; **2008**: 57–64
freedom of navigation, **1991-99**: 1596; **2004**: 686, 699–700
immunities in U.S. courts
head-of-state immunity, depositions, **1989-90**: 320–23
effect of dismissal on immunities grounds, case to settle ownership of assets, **2008**: 475–81

Philippines (continued)
residual head-of-state immunity waived by sitting head of state, **1991-99**: 1270, 1272, 1277
sovereign, **1989-90**: 302–11; **1991-99**: 1265–66, 1274
intellectual property rights Watch List, **2006**: 768, 769; **2007**: 610
money laundering, **2004**: 135
naturalization of World War II veterans, **1989-90**: 12–13
orphan adoption program, **2003**: 123
Philippine Autonomy Act (1916), **1991-99**: 10
Philippine Government Act (1902), **1991-99**: 10
Philippine Independence Act (1934), **1991-99**: 10–11
Philippine Presidential Commission on Good Government, **1989-90**: 302, 305
reciprocity in consular relations, **1989-90**: 344
restrictions on departure from U.S.
on transport of remains of former president Marcos to, **1989-90**: 57–59
of wife of former president Marcos from U.S. to, **1989-90**: 60–62
territorial application of International Covenant on Civil and Political Rights, position on, **2005**: 299*n*
during territorial period, citizenship of persons born in, **1991-99**: 9–13
trade issues, **1991-99**: 1384, 1408, 1412–13
trafficking in women and children in, **1991-99**: 912
Tropical Forest Conservation Act agreement, **2008**: 722
U.S. defense relationship, **1989-90**: 151, 152
non-North Atlantic Treaty Organization (NATO) ally, designation as, **2005**: 1044
U.S. military assistance at request of, **1991-99**: 2167
Physical Protection of Nuclear Material, Convention on. *See* Atomic Energy, International Agency for (IAEA); Nonproliferation
Piracy, 1989-90: 112
International Maritime Organization, **2007**: 634; **2008**: 622, 645–47
Law of the Sea, UN Convention on (UNCLOS), **2008**: 622–23
Libyan vessel denied entry to Gaza, not piracy, **2008**: 647–48
Somali pirates. *See* Somalia
U.S. policy on, **2007**: 630–34
U.S. prosecution under legislation implementing Convention for the Suppression of Unlawful Acts Against the Safety of Maritime Navigation, **2002**: 133–34; **2008**: 125–30
PKI (Public Key Infrastructure) for digital signatures, 2005: 7, 801–2
Plant Genetic Resources for Food and Agriculture, International Treaty on, 2002: 810–11; **2004**: 789–90; **2008**: 725–27
Plant Quarantine Act (1912), 1991-99: 1790

Plastic Explosives for the Purpose of Detection, Convention on Marking of, 1991-99: 481, 489–93
Poland
American Aid to Poland Act (1988), **1989-90:** 546
bilateral investment treaty, **2003:** 687, 695; **2004:** 623–24
citizenship issues, **2004:** 2
agreement with U.S. addressing dual nationals, **2001:** 34
claims arising from post-World War II Nazi persecution
restitution processes, **1991-99:** 1044, 1047, 1053, 1069–70
in U.S. court, **2002:** 492–94, 513–16
of U.S. nationals settled by agreement (1960), **2004:** 499–500
democracy promotion and, **2004:** 389
economic assistance programs, **1989-90:** 542–43, 546–47
environmental and conservation issues, **1991-99:** 1782
EU accession and trade agreements, **2006:** 754–56
extradition and mutual legal assistance, **1991-99:** 396, 400; **2000:** 186*n*; **2001:** 92*n*; **2004:** 80; **2006:** 137, 147
family support enforcement, **1991-99:** 1866, 1871; **2001:** 51
fish and marine mammals, **1991-99:** 1705–7
sustainable fisheries resolution, sponsor of, **2004:** 763
Hague Child Abduction Convention, compliance with, **1991-99:** 353; **2003:** 127, 129; **2004:** 54; **2006:** 102; **2008:** 50
Immigration Advisory Program at airports, **2006:** 209
intellectual property rights Watch List, **2006:** 768; **2007:** 610
Kosovo Diplomatic Observer Mission, **1991-99:** 2042
lifting of sanctions against, **1989-90:** 518–19
Ministry of Treasury, takings exception to FSIA, **2006:** 558–61, 572–77
missile defense and nonproliferation cooperation, **2004:** 1066, 1074, 1139
nuclear fuel return program, **2004:** 1139
Proliferation Security Initiative (PSI), **2005:** 1099
chemical weapons shipments drill, **2005:** 1104–5
U.S. ground-based ballistic missile defense interceptors, **2008:** 1009–11
NATO accession, **1991-99:** 738–39, 1030–40, 2243
Open Skies (aerial observation) treaty, **2002:** 1029
orphan adoption program, **2003:** 123
preservation of American heritage in, **2004:** 797
reciprocity in child support enforcement, **2008:** 759
relief from immigration requirements for certain resident nationals of, **1991-99:** 250
trade and investment issues, **1991-99:** 1385, 1466, 1480–81; **2003:** 695
treaty succession, **1991-99:** 744
World War II-era restitution and claims, **1991-99:** 1044, 1047, 1053, 1069–70

Political offense, 1991-99: 144. *See also* Extradition
criminalization of hate speech on Internet and, **2004:** 263–64
evaluation of, in withholding of deportation, **1991-99:** 232–39, 953
exception to extradition for, **1989-90:** 79–80; **1991-99:** 412, 428–35; **2000:** 182; **2002:** 109; **2004:** 75–77; **2005:** 75–76, 95
extradition and mutual legal assistance, **2004:** 75–77, 96
terrorist acts and, **2002:** 109, 114–15
Pollution. *See* Air pollution; Environmental issues; Marine conservation, *subheading*: pollution
Pollution from Ships, International Convention for Prevention of (MARPOL) (1973), 1991-99: 784–85; **2003:** 750, 752
air pollution protocol to and new Annex VI (1997), **2003:** 745, 783–88; **2008:** 691–95
Arctic region, **2008:** 636
double-hull revisions to Annex I, **2005:** 732–33
oil cargo transfer between oil tankers at sea, **2008:** 698–702
oil record book requirement, **2008:** 131–36
protocol modifying (1978), **1991-99:** 784–85; **2002:** 184–85; **2008:** 131–36
shipboard response provision, **1991-99:** 1683
POPs. *See* Persistent Organic Pollutants (POPs)
Population and Development, International Conference on (ICPD), 2005: 309, 454
Ports. *See* Maritime issues
Ports and Waterways Safety Act (1972), 1991-99: 778–83
Portugal
arms control and nuclear nonproliferation and, **1991-99:** 2232
Proliferation Security Initiative (PSI), involvement in, **2005:** 1099
Enterprise for the Americas Initiative and, **1991-99:** 1462
extradition and mutual legal assistance, **1991-99:** 391; **2000:** 185*n*; **2006:** 137, 147
naturalization convention, **2002:** 205
nonimmigrant visa waiver pilot program, **1991-99:** 76
Open Skies (aerial observation) treaty, **2002:** 1029
peacekeeping missions, **1991-99:** 145
reciprocity in child support enforcement, **2001:** 51; **2008:** 759
trade issues, **1991-99:** 1408–9, 1504
transfer of sovereignty over Macau, **1991-99:** 1180
World War II issues, **1991-99:** 1058–59
Pregnancy Discrimination Act of 1978 (PDA), 1991-99: 904; **2005:** 262
President, U.S. *See also* Executive Branch; Executive Orders, Presidential; Foreign affairs; Presidential Declarations, Determinations, Memoranda, Proclamations, and Directives

President, U.S. (continued)
authority to act inconsistently with international law, **1989-90**: 92
authority to decline to execute unconstitutional statutes, **1991-99**: 802–8. *See also* separation of powers, *this heading*
authority to receive foreign emissaries, **2006**: 668
special missions immunity and, **2006**: 678–80
commander in chief authority. *See* war powers, *this heading*
constitutional responsibility for issues concerning
consular immunity, **2005**: 569
customary international law applicability, **2005**: 496–97
disposition of foreign missions, **2005**: 533, 534–35
enforcement of treaty rights and obligations, **2005**: 53, 246. *See* Agreements, generally; Treaties, generally
extradition, **2005**: 81–82, 90, 92; **2007**: 122
faithful execution of laws, **2007**: 215, 391
foreign affairs
signing statements to legislation on, **2007**: 438–39, 442–43, 708–9, 817. *See also* separation of powers signing statements, *this heading*
head-of-state immunity, **2005**: 561–62
interpreting statutes having effect on, **2005**: 162, 231*n*
removal decisions, **2005**: 17
U.S. response to ICJ decision, **2005**: 38–39, 41–43, 45, 53
diplomatic relations, constitutional authority with respect to, **2002**: 244; **2003**: 270
election of, **2005**: 243–51
emergency powers. *See* Emergency Economic Powers Act, International (IEEPA); Trading with the Enemy Act (1917)
foreign affairs authority, **1989-90**: 243–64; **1991-99**: 656, 1250, 2167; **2003**: 497–98, 541; **2004**: 511–12; **2005**: 38–39, 42, 52; **2006**: 540–42; **2007**: 122, 170, 214, 221, 242, 245, 262, 435, 438–40, 954; **2008**: 39–40, 66, 119, 192, 217, 224–25, 246, 446, 451–52, 467–68, 473
authority to issue passports as necessary for official USG travel, **1991-99**: 41–49. *See also* recognition, exclusive presidential authority, *this heading*
maritime boundaries, determination of, **1991-99**: 725, 730–31, 1572
power to determine compliance with ICJ decision, **2005**: 37–48; **2007**: 76–77
power to preempt customary international law, **2005**: 494, 496–97
power to regulate foreign assets, **2007**: 482
power to settle claims. *See* Executive Branch, *subheading*: claims
protection of information

President, U.S. (continued)
classified information for national security purposes, **1991-99**: 791–801, 804; **2006**: 1222
confidential diplomatic communications, **1991-99**: 791–92, 795–801, 923
intelligence and foreign relations information, **2002**: 231–36, 242–45, 994
recognition, exclusive presidential authority, **1989-90**: 243–64; **1991-99**: 758–59, 1135–38, 1239, 1250–51, 1270; **2000**: 201–2; **2003**: 488–501; **2004**: 452–54; **2006**: 540–42; **2007**: 437–43
and passports, **2003**: 485–501; **2004**: 452–54; **2008**: 447–54
and U.S. custody of foreign mission property, **1989-90**: 370–71
recommendations for foreign policy legislation, unfettered power to make, **2002**: 243. *See also* separation of powers, *this heading*
separation of powers. *See also* Executive Branch, *subheading*: deference to; Separation of powers
nonjusticiable question. *See* Foreign affairs; World War II, *subheading*: claims
signing statements, **1989-90**: 508–12; **1991-99**: 801–8, 922–24; **2002**: 242–45; **2003**: 269–71; **2004**: 214–18; **2005**: 2, 242, 607, 1037–39; **2006**: 305–7, 402, 536–37, 1286–87; **2007**: 438–39, 442–43, 708–9, 817
veto of biological and chemical weapons control legislation, **1989-90**: 508–12
state secrets privilege and, **2007**: 241–42
war powers, **1991-99**: 2162–70; **2000**: 758–65; **2002**: 987–89; **2004**: 209, 210–11, 1012–13; **2005**: 1010–11, 1016; **2008**: 902. *See also* War Powers Resolution (U.S.)
authority with respect to enemy combatants, **2002**: 990–91, 996, 997, 998–1001, 1006; **2004**: 997–98, 1001, 1003, 1009–11, 1012–13; **2005**: 1004–5, 1008, 1011–12, 1018. *See also* Detainees, military
commander-in-chief, **2004**: 215, 216, 941; **2006**: 522–26
congressional authorization for military operations, **1991-99**: 2056
in Bosnia, **1991-99**: 2168–70
in Haiti, **1991-99**: 804, 2162–68
in Iraq, **2002**: 933–37
in Kosovo, **1991-99**: 2155–62
in response to 9/11, **2001**: 864–66, 871–72
use of force, **2005**: 962, 1001–4, 1009, 1014, 1037; **2008**: 853–56

Presidential Declarations, Determinations, Memoranda, Proclamations, and Directives. *See also* Executive Orders, Presidential
Presidential Declarations
long-term relationship of cooperation and friendship with Iraq, **2007**: 990–95
security assurances on use of nuclear weapons, **1991-99**: 2283, 2285–87
Presidential Determinations
aerial counternarcotics efforts involving lethal force (2005-32), **2005**: 145
cooperation with Vietnam (97-10), **1991-99**: 1161
designation of drug-transit and drug-producing countries
(2004-47), **2004**: 133–34
(2005-36), **2005**: 135
(2006-24), **2006**: 212–13
(2007-33), **2007**: 163
(2008-28), **2008**: 113
identification and certification of countries re methamphetamines (2007-14), **2007**: 164
implementing *Avena* decision, **2005**: 30, 34, 37–47, 217, 952; **2006**: 87, 1026
Iraq sanctions (2003–23), **2004**: 489, 490, 492, 493, 890; **2008**: 464, 467
waiver (2008-9), **2008**: 460, 470
Libya sanctions (2004-30), **2004**: 44, 660–61, 930, 1162–63
none to allow torture, **2004**: 303
North Korea sanctions (2007-7), **2006**: 1271; **2007**: 1028
nuclear cooperation with China (98-10), **1991-99**: 2318
nuclear cooperation with EURATOM (96-4), **1991-99**: 2336
nuclear energy cooperation with Russia (2008-19), **2008**: 986, 987
nuclear-related sanctions on India–Pakistan (98-22), **1991-99**: 2298–2302
refugee admission numbers and authorizations for fiscal 2007 (2007-1), **2006**: 55–56
rescission of Iraq as state sponsor of terrorism (2004-52), **2004**: 103
rescission of Libya as state sponsor of terrorism (2006-14), **2006**: 173–77; **2008**: 400
resumption of certain counternarcotics assistance (95-7), **1991-99**: 546–47
on Sudan negotiations (2004-29), **2004**: 958*n*
suspension of sanctions (96-7), **1991-99**: 1953–56
suspension or waiver of provisions of U.S. law (92-21, 94-130, 99-1), **1991-99**: 1226, 1455–56, 1994
trafficking in persons

Presidential Declarations, Determinations, Memoranda, Proclamations, and Directives (continued)
(2004-46), **2004**: 163–65
(2005-37), **2005**: 161–62
(2006-25), **2006**: 228–29
(2008-4), **2007**: 168–70
(2009-5), **2008**: 117–19
waiver of prohibition on assistance to Lesotho and St. Kitts and Nevis, **2006**: 278
waiver of prohibition on military assistance, **2006**: 278
Presidential Directives, Homeland Security
HSPD-6, **2008**: 110–11
Presidential Directives, National Security
National Security Decision Directive 187, **2005**: 405
National Security Strategy, **2005**: 689*n*
Reconstruction and Stabilization, **2005**: 947–48
Trafficking in Persons, **2005**: 163–64
Presidential Executive Orders. *See* Executive Orders, Presidential
Presidential Memoranda
to implement ICJ *Avena* decision, **2005**: 29–59; **2006**: 87, 1026; **2007**: 73–74, 836; **2008**: 175–93
rescission of North Korea's designation as a state sponsor of terrorism, **2008**: 89–90
Presidential Proclamations
Bahrain free trade agreement (8039), **2006**: 765–66
Bolivia counternarcotics (8323), **2008**: 581
China trade policy (7516), **1991-99**: 1460
Compact of Free Association Between United States and Palau (6726), **1991-99**: 817–19
contiguous zone (7219), **1991-99**: 714–31, 1569–70
Cote d'Ivoire trade status (7858), **2004**: 923
establishing U.S. exclusive economic zone (5030), **2004**: 726
Haiti trade benefits (8296), **2008**: 582
implementation of Uruguay Round agreements (6763), **1991-99**: 1372–73
interdiction of illegal aliens (4865), **1991-99**: 164, 172
jurisdiction over foreign flag vessels (7219), **2004**: 1088
maritime contiguous zone (7219), **2003**: 745
national emergency relating to Cuba (6867), **2004**: 912–17
North Korea trade relations, termination of exercise of authorities under Trading with the Enemies Act, **2008**: 954, 960–66
Northwestern Hawaiian Islands Marine National Monument (8031), **2006**: 872–75
regulation of anchorage and movement of vessels (6867), **1991-99**: 1365–67

Presidential Declarations, Determinations, Memoranda, Proclamations, and Directives (continued)
sanctions on entities of former Yugoslavia (6389), **1991-99:** 1945
steel import safeguard measures (7529; 7741), **2003:** 657–60
suspension of entry by aliens. *See* Immigration and Nationality Act (INA) (1952)
suspension of GSP benefits for Yugoslavia in 1991 (6389), **2004:** 655
territorial sea (5928), **1991-99:** 173, 179–81, 725, 1623–24
treaty compliance and, **1991-99:** 714–31
Ukraine trade relations (7995), **2006:** 748
Vietnam trade relations (8096), **2006:** 749–50
signing statements. *See* Separation of powers
Prevention and Punishment of Crimes Against Internationally Protected Persons, Including Diplomatic Agents (1973), 1989-90: 34, 283; **2000:** 218; **2001:** 357
Prevention and Punishment of the Crime of Genocide. *See* Genocide
Prisoner transfer, 2000: 37; **2006:** 104–5. *See also* Extradition
consent of parties to, **2000:** 172
Mexico, treaty with, **2001:** 51; **2003:** 69–70, 131–33; **2008:** 51–52
prisoner consent, **2001:** 54
prisoner mental competency and, **2003:** 131–33
request for transfer of terrorist, **1989-90:** 72–76
temporary, for mutual legal assistance, **2002:** 64, 110, 116
temporary surrender for trial in requesting state, **1991-99:** 394–95
torture concerns, **2003:** 325
translation of documentation for, **2000:** 172
treaties for serving of sentence abroad, **2000:** 37, 171–72
Council of Europe Convention on Transfer of Sentenced Persons, **1989-90:** 72; **1991-99:** 381–83; **2000:** 295; **2001:** 52; **2006:** 104–5; **2008:** 51–52
Inter-American Convention on Serving Criminal Sentences Abroad, **1991-99:** 381–82; **2000:** 171–72; **2001:** 51–55; **2006:** 104; **2008:** 51–52
Prisoners and prisons. *See also* Prisoner transfer
in foreign custody. *See also* Prisoner transfer
international standards of care, **2001:** 37
U.S. consular assistance to Americans abroad, **2001:** 36–38
human rights of, **2005:** 274–77, 292, 366–71, 393
Prison Litigation Reform Act of 1996 (PLRA), **2005:** 367
Prison Rape Elimination Act of 2003 (PREA), **2005:** 275
Prisoners of Conscience Declaration, **2008:** 378
in U.S., rights of, **2000:** 378–79, 383–85, 387; **2005:** 618–19
juveniles, **2006:** 366–69
monitoring mechanisms for protecting, **2000:** 385

Prisoners and prisons (continued)
questioning and detention of juveniles, **2000**: 383–84
restraint procedures, **2000**: 384–85
Prisoners of war. *See also* Detainees, military; Geneva Convention III: on Prisoners of War (1949)
blindfolds or hoods, **2003**: 1013
charged with violation of U.S. law, **1989-90**: 564
claims by U.S. POWs against Iraq, **2003**: 543–49; **2005**: 507–8, 1028
detainees of Iraq conflict (2003), **2003**: 997–1015; **2004**: 300, 301
determination of status as, **1991-99**: 2091–92; **2003**: 1004–5, 1007–11, 1021–23; **2004**: 981, 1014, 1018, 1022, 1023
determination as, **2007**: 886, 889
Geneva Convention Relative to the Treatment of. *See* Geneva Convention III: on Prisoners of War (1949)
from Gulf War. *See* Gulf war
habeas corpus and, **2004**: 998, 1020, 1021
humiliation or degradation of, **1991-99**: 2091; **2003**: 1000, 1008, 1009
immunity of lawful enemy combatants, **2002**: 1002–5
Iraq's violations of laws of war, **2003**: 1000–4
media portrayals, **2003**: 1000, 1008–9
medical personnel and chaplains as, **2003**: 1014–15
military justice, **2003**: 343–44
Panama, taken in U.S. military action in, **1989-90**: 561–64
protection from against insults and public curiosity, applicability to photographs of, **2005**: 1024–25, 1026–29; **2006**: 1216–18
release after cessation of hostilities, **2004**: 1005
repatriation, **1991-99**: 2092, 2094; **2007**: 112, 115, 892–93, 981
separation of officers, **2003**: 1011–12
surrender, **1991-99**: 2107–8
unlawful enemy combatants distinguished from, **2007**: 912–15, 979–82
U.S. military training concerning, **2007**: 917
World War II-era forced labor claims, **2003**: 468–72
in World War II-era Japan, **2002**: 434–61
Privacy rights, 1991-99: 885, 900–2, 1394, 1526
airline passenger name record data, **2004**: 112–13; **2008**: 108–9, 110
asylum application process, confidentiality in, **1989-90**: 46–47
constitutionality of California law requiring disclosure of European insurance information, **2002**: 423–25
consular notification and, **1991-99**: 268, 326, 329–30
cybercrime violations of, **2001**: 154
deposition in Argentina and, **2004**: 865
of embassy data, **2002**: 567–70

Privacy rights (continued)
Eurojust–U.S. agreement on transfer of personal data in criminal prosecution, **2006**: 165–67
Europol–U.S. agreement on transfer of personal data in law enforcement, **2002**: 80–84
ICCPR provisions, **2008**: 342
international agreement to prosecute narcotrafficking and, **1989-90**: 131–32
monitoring of enemy combatant detainee's communications with counsel, **2004**: 1031–35
of passport holder, **2004**: 7
passport cards, **2008**: 9
Privacy Act (1974), **2002**: 234
of trafficking victims, **2004**: 102, 156
Private international law. *See also* Comity; Hague Conference on Private International Law (HCCH); International Institute for the Unification of Private Law (UNIDROIT)
abstentions, comity-based, **2002**: 859–64; **2005**: 815–29. *See also* Comity
adoption. *See* Adoption
arbitration. *See also* Arbitration
commercial, **2005**: 807–8
enforceability of foreign arbitration clauses, **1991-99**: 1843–48
enforcement of foreign arbitral awards, **2002**: 873–75
Federal Arbitration Act, **2005**: 602
Inter-American arbitration convention, **1989-90**: 501
power of arbitral tribunals to grant *ex parte* interim relief, **2004**: 806–14
UN Convention on the Recognition and Enforcement of Foreign Arbitral Awards, **2005**: 788, 789; **2008**: 187, 760–64, 777–82
attorney's fees, award of for nonappearance of defendant at deposition, **2005**: 813–15
bankruptcy, **1991-99**: 1814–17
cross-border insolvency, **2002**: 821–22, 828
insolvency, **1991-99**: 1814–17; **2001**: 781–83; **2003**: 837–38; **2004**: 804
children. *See* Children
civil litigation
concurrent proceedings, **2003**: 868–72
personal jurisdiction over foreign entities, **2004**: 878–82
service of process, **2002**: 877–79; **2003**: 887–95; **2004**: 866–75. *See also* Service of process abroad
comity principles, **2004**: 825–26. *See also* Comity

Private international law (continued)
commercial law. *See also* Commercial Law; Contracts; Electronic Commerce; UNCITRAL (UN Commission on International Trade Law)
bills of lading, **2002**: 819, 833–34
Carriage of Goods by Sea. *See* Carriage of goods by sea
Choice of Court Convention, **2005**: 213, 787–89, 791
commercial dispute resolution, **2001**: 789–90
commercial finance, **2001**: 777–81, 790–91, 792
consumer protection, **2007**: 745–54
contracts, **1991-99**: 1825
contracts for the international sale of goods, UN Convention on, **1991-99**: 1817, 1824; **2002**: 824; **2003**: 838–39; **2004**: 805, 823
electronic commerce. *See* Electronic commerce
enforcement of foreign judgments. *See* Jurisdiction
environmental law, **1991-99**: 1856
equipment financing, mobile, **2003**: 848–54; **2004**: 834–36
space equipment, draft protocol to the Cape Town Convention (2001), **2005**: 713, 802–5; **2006**: 930–34; **2008**: 747–51
European Union as party to certain instruments. *See* Treaties, generally, *subheading*: capacity to enter into
extraterritoriality and conflicts of jurisdiction. *See* Jurisdiction
finance standards, **2002**: 818–19
financing of international projects, **2002**: 821
franchising, **1991-99**: 1825–26; **2001**: 786–87; **2002**: 820–21
fraud, **2004**: 805–6
infrastructure project development, **1991-99**: 1852–53
international organizations in, **2003**: 833–34. *See also* Hague Conference on Private International Law (HCCH); International Institute for the Unification of Private Law (UNIDROIT); UNCITRAL (UN Commission on International Trade Law)
investment securities, **2004**: 803–4; **2007**: 762–64
jurisdiction and enforcement. *See* Jurisdiction, *subheading*: enforcement of judgments
Mediation Act, Uniform (UMA), **2005**: 805–7
model law on leasing, UNIDROIT, **2008**: 745–47
model law on public procurement, **1991-99**: 1820–22
Organization of American States conference on, **1991-99**: 1841–43
payment guarantees and credit, **1991-99**: 1812–14
railway rolling stock, Cape Town Convention on rolling stock finance (2001) and Luxembourg Protocol (2007), **2007**: 765–69

Private international law (continued)
receivables financing, **1991-99**: 1822–24; **2003**: 854–55
Receivables in International Trade, Convention on the Assignment of, **1991-99**: 1822
secured transactions, **1991-99**: 1853–56; **2002**: 818–19, 822–29; **2003**: 836–37; **2004**: 803
stolen or illegally exported cultural objects, **1991-99**: 1803–7
torts, **1991-99**: 1831, 1856, 1857, 1873
travel and tourism-related disputes, **1991-99**: 1857
uniform international rules, **2004**: 806
cooperation among national bar associations, **2002**: 822
discovery for use in foreign tribunal. *See* Evidence
enforcement of judgments. *See* Jurisdiction, *subheading*: enforcement of judgments
enjoining foreign litigation. *See* Anti-suit injunctions
family law, **2003**: 856–59; **2004**: 828; **2007**: 769–72. *See also* Children
family support enforcement. *See* Maintenance obligations
family support obligations, international enforcement of, **2007**: 769–72
intercountry adoption. *See* Adoption
parental child abduction. *See* Children, *subheading*: international abduction
protection of adults, Hague Convention on (1999), **1991-99**: 1861–62; **2004**: 830
protection of children, Hague Convention on (1996), **1991-99**: 1859–61, 1876; **2000**: 121; **2004**: 63, 830
Uniform International Wills Act (1991), **1991-99**: 1878
fora for litigation of cargo claims, **2003**: 845–47
forum non conveniens doctrine, **2003**: 895–901; **2004**: 875–78; **2005**: 833–43; **2007**: 795–800; **2008**: 513–19
forum shopping, **2004**: 819–24
Hague-Visby Rules. *See* Hague Conventions
harmonization efforts, **2004**: 822–30; **2006**: 903–4
identification of parallel judicial proceedings, **2002**: 860–61
insolvency law reform, **2001**: 781–83
intellectual property issues, **2000**: 740–41
Inter-American Specialized Conference on Private International Law, **2007**: 745–54
intercountry adoption. *See* Adoption
international child abduction. *See* Children
international civil litigation, **2007**: 772–95
concurrent proceedings, **2007**: 772–95; **2008**: 760–76
foreign arbitral award, enforcement of, **2007**: 792–95

Private international law (continued)
foreign judgment of assets forfeiture, enforcement of, **2007**: 474–76
forum non conveniens, **2007**: 795–800
judicial assistance for foreign court, **2007**: 800–804
judicial assistance. *See* Authentication; Evidence; Judicial assistance; Service of Process abroad
jurisdiction. *See* Jurisdiction
NAFTA and, **2003**: 612–13
recent multilateral developments, **2001**: 775–90
Rotterdam Rules. *See* Carriage of goods by sea
scope, **2001**: 776–77
service of process abroad. *See* Service of process abroad
space equipment finance, **2005**: 802–5; **2006**: 930–34; **2008**: 747–51
statute of limitations
convention on, in international sale of goods, **1991-99**: 1817–20
Limitation Period in the International Sale of Goods, Convention on (UN), **1991-99**: 1817–20
Limitations, Sales of Goods, Negotiable Instruments, and Guarantees, Conventions on, **2002**: 836
stolen or illegally exported cultural objects convention and, **1991-99**: 1805
transportation issues, **2002**: 819–20, 829–33, 834
transportation of goods, **2001**: 787–89. *See also* Carriage of goods by sea
UN Commission on International Trade Law, **2007**: 754–64
UNIDROIT, **2007**: 764, 766–77
Draft Convention on Transactional Law on Cross-border Securities Transactions, **2005**: 808
Draft Protocol on Space Assets, **2005**: 713, 802–5; **2006**: 930–34; **2008**: 747–51
model law on leasing, UNIDROIT, **2008**: 745–47
U.S. approach to, **2006**: 905–9
Private rights of action under international instruments. *See also* Standing; Treaties, generally
American Declaration of the Rights and Duties of Man, **2001**: 298
Brown Commitment (U.S. letter to ROK (1966)), **2000**: 491–95
Climate Change, UN Framework Convention on, and other international climate change, **2008**: 328
Convention on Chemical Weapons Protocol III, **2008**: 886
Elimination of All Forms of Racial Discrimination, Convention on, **2008**: 279
Inter-American Democratic Charter, **2001**: 298

Private rights of action under international instruments (continued)
International Covenant on Civil and Political Rights. *See* International Covenant on Civil and Political Rights (ICCPR)
Law of the Sea, UN Convention on, **2007:** 644–45
Libyan Claims Resolution agreement, **2008:** 401
Nuclear Terrorism, Convention for the Suppression of Acts of, **2008:** 95
Panama Canal Treaty, **2000:** 312–17, 401
Physical Protection of Nuclear Material, Convention for, amendment to, **2008:** 95, 97
Protection of Cultural Property in the Event of Armed Conflict, Hague Convention for, **2008:** 889
Suppression of Unlawful Acts Against the Safety of Maritime Navigation, Convention on, and fixed platforms protocol, 2005 protocols to, **2008:** 95
UN Charter, **2001:** 290; **2005:** 56
U.S.–Iran Treaty of Amity, **2002:** 219–24; **2003:** 258–67; **2008:** 154–58
U.S.–Mexico agreements on workers, **2002:** 212–18
U.S.–Mexico extradition agreement, **1991-99:** 438
U.S.–Republic of China agreement on foreign assistance, **2000:** 491–95
Vienna Convention on Consular Relations, **2006:** 76, 84–85; **2007:** 74, 78–81; **2008:** 35–47
Privileges and Immunities of the United Nations (General Convention), **1989-90:** 353, 354; **1991-99:** 1305, 1321–22; **2000:** 578, 589–90, 603, 604–5, 607, 610–11, 612, 613, 614, 624, 625; **2001:** 320, 511, 527–31; **2002:** 554, 555, 557–61, 564–65, 571; **2003:** 572, 573; **2004:** 532, 539, 554–56, 557–58
applicability to state's own nationals, **1989-90:** 363–66, 368
dispute resolution mechanisms, **1989-90:** 355–57, 358–59, 360–61
experts on UN missions, **1989-90:** 361–63, 368–70
ICJ case concerning immunity for Special Rapporteur, **1989-90:** 353–70
sex discrimination and sexual harassment claims, **2008:** 501–4
U.S. ratification, **2000:** 604–5
visiting foreign officials, **2006:** 653, 655–57, 682
Procedural default doctrine, **2003:** 44, 63–64, 82–83; **2005:** 29, 33, 34, 47, 54, 503; **2006:** 64, 70
Process, service of abroad. *See* Service of process abroad
Procurement
Millennium Challenge Compacts, **2005:** 673
UN Commission on International Trade Law (UNCITRAL) model laws relating to, **2005:** 808
UN contractors in Iraq, **2005:** 873–74
U.S. Federal Acquisition Regulations (FAR) on, **2005:** 232

Proliferation Security Initiative (PSI). *See* Nonproliferation
Property confiscation claims relating to Nazi era. *See* World War II
Property rights, 1991-99: 835, 1008, 1802. *See also* Consular offices and personnel; Cultural issues; Diplomatic missions and personnel; Expropriation; Intellectual property rights
belligerent occupation, **1989-90:** 267–68
business conditions and investments as property interests, **2001:** 584–88
claims based on, **1991-99:** 1051, 1077, 1128
definition and scope, **1991-99:** 1098
FSIA provisions. *See* Foreign Sovereign Immunities Act (FSIA) (1976)
of Native American tribes, **2001:** 260–61
outer space, **2004:** 741–42
protection of Russian property related to highly enriched uranium agreements, **2001:** 847
seizure of property subject to civil forfeiture, **2001:** 113–14
of state vs. government, **1989-90:** 255–57
tax exemptions for diplomatic missions, **2006:** 592–603, 659*n*
women's rights, **2001:** 270–71
PROTECT Act (2003), 2003: 189–90
Protection of adults. *See* Hague Conventions
Protection of Literary and Artistic Works, Berne Convention for (1971), 1989-90: 417; **1991-99:** 1512, 1513, 1518–19; **2003:** 200
Protocols. *See specific topics and countries*
Prussian and German Confederation Treaty, 1991-99: 649
PSI (Proliferation Security Initiative). *See* Nonproliferation
Psychotropic substances. *See* Drug trade
Public health, 1991-99: 1569; **2004:** 713
abortion policies, **2000:** 353; **2002:** 770; **2008:** 324. *See also* Abortion
access to medication as human right, **2001:** 281–83; **2003:** 319–20
avian influenza, **2005:** 756, 772–73
biological agents and toxins and, **2004:** 1062, 1105
child mortality, **2004:** 280
children's access issues, **1991-99:** 930
cloning. *See* Cloning
disease prevention initiatives, **2002:** 715–18, 805–7; **2006:** 891–92
HIV/AIDS, **1989-90:** 18–20; **2001:** 648, 763, 764–67; **2004:** 784–86; **2008:** 17, 19
human rights and, **2003:** 309, 310, 317–22; **2008:** 282, 323
institutionalized populations. *See* Civil Rights of Institutionalized Persons Act (CRIPA) (1980)

Public health (continued)
intellectual property issues for pharmaceuticals, **1991-99**: 1386, 1506–7; **2001**: 646–48, 764–67; **2003**: 673–79; **2004**: 785; **2008**: 607, 608
amendment to TRIPS regarding access to medicines, **2005**: 618–19
international border crossings and, **2004**: 572
International Health Regulations, **2005**: 768–71; **2006**: 891–92; **2007**: 738; **2008**: 1007
malaria, **2004**: 784–86
nondiscriminatory measures to protect and NAFTA, **2004**: 575, 586–89
nuclear regulations and, **2004**: 1104
pandemic influenza, national strategy for, **2006**: 889–90
passport restrictions and, **1991-99**: 50–51
Public Health Security and Bioterrorism Response Act (2002), **2004**: 1105
Public Health Service Act (1946), **2001**: 764
right to adequate standard of living, **2000**: 371; **2004**: 287
right to food, **2001**: 280; **2004**: 285–88; **2005**: 325–26; **2008**: 333–37
right to health. *See* Human rights, *subheading*: economic, social and cultural rights
tobacco control measures, **2003**: 813–15; **2004**: 786–87
trafficking in persons as threat to, **2004**: 167
transboundary air pollution and, **2004**: 744
women's access issues, **1991-99**: 907–8
workplace discrimination and, **1989-90**: 171
WTO agreements and, **1991-99**: 1386, 1506–7; **2001**: 646–48, 764–67; **2003**: 673–79; **2005**: 618–19
Public Key Infrastructure (PKI) for digital signatures, 2005: 7
Puerto Rico
citizenship issues, **2000**: 340–41, 344–45
claim by Puerto Rican resident of constitutional right to vote for U.S. President, **2005**: 242–51
foreign relations issues, **1991-99**: 830–31; **2000**: 340–44, 345–46
legislation regarding referendum, **1991-99**: 825–28
maritime boundaries, **1991-99**: 1574–76
political status, **1991-99**: 12, 178, 808–11; **2000**: 340–45; **2001**: 242–45; **2003**: 485; **2006**: 311–15
presidential memorandum, **1991-99**: 828–30
Punishment
capital. *See* Capital punishment
cruel and unusual. *See* Cruel and unusual punishment
sentencing. *See* Sentencing and sentences
Pyongyang Declaration, 2005: 1068, 1072

Q

Qatar
Doha Declaration on TRIPS Agreement and Public Health (Doha Declaration), **2005**: 618–19
enforcement of arbitral awards, **1991-99**: 1258–59
trafficking in persons, **2005**: 159, 162; **2008**: 118

Quiet Title Act (1972), 1991-99: 844

R

Racial discrimination, 1991-99: 883–97; **2000**: 347–51; **2001**: 247–69; **2003**: 290; **2004**: 263–69, 355; **2005**: 304–6; **2006**: 371–72; **2008**: 276–86. *See also* Discrimination
Alien Tort Statute jurisdiction, **2002**: 338–39; **2006**: 946–50
antidiscrimination efforts, **1991-99**: 883–97; **2002**: 271–75; **2003**: 285–89
capital punishment and, **2007**: 303–5
claims concerning Muslim and Arab people, **2003**: 285–89, 298, 299; **2008**: 519–20
claims in U.S. courts, **2004**: 355, 364
disenfranchisement of convicted criminals, **2007**: 307–8
draft convention on, OAS, **2005**: 305–6
Elimination of All Forms of Racial Discrimination, International Convention on, **1991-99**: 861, 883–97, 906; **2000**: 347–50; **2001**: 247–67, 354; **2002**: 274; **2004**: 294; **2005**: 305–6; **2006**: 371–72, 400; **2007**: 326, 329–30; **2008**: 276–84, 920–22
periodic U.S. report on implementation to UN Committee on, **2007**: 293–315; **2008**: 275–84
U.S. state law and, **2002**: 195
free speech rights and, **2001**: 248–49, 256, 264–65; **2007**: 302, 310–11, 329–30; **2008**: 286
hate crimes, **2007**: 302–3, 330–31
in law enforcement, **2000**: 378
racial profiling, **2007**: 297–98
against migrants, **2005**: 340–41; **2008**: 347
obligations of state and local governments, **2007**: 309–10
Organization of American States (OAS), resolution on prevention of racism, U.S. reservations, **2005**: 305–6
Protocol to the Convention on Cybercrime on Criminalisation of Acts of a Racist or Xenophobic Nature, **2001**: 267–69
"special and concrete measures," **2007**: 298–2300
UN resolutions against, **2002**: 271–75; **2005**: 304–5; **2007**: 315–17; **2008**: 284–86

Racial discrimination (continued)
U.S. policies, **2001**: 247–67; **2002**: 271–75; **2007**: 295–97, 300–305, 327, 329–31
voting rights, **2007**: 305–8
World Conference Against Racism, **2001**: 267–68; **2002**: 271–76; **2003**: 290, 298, 299; **2008**: 284–85
Racketeer Influenced and Corrupt Organizations (RICO) Act (1970), 1989-90: 73; **1991-99**: 1286; **2002**: 837–38, 839–40, 841; **2003**: 355, 855, 895; **2004**: 361, 820, 1102; **2005**: 514
Radio Broadcasting to Cuba Act (1983), 1989-90: 396
Radio regulations. *See* International Telecommunication Union (ITU)
Radioactive Waste Management, Joint Convention on the Safety of Spent Fuel and, 1991-99: 1696–99
Radiological materials, accidental or intentional release of, 2005: 769–70, 1095, 1122
Rape
to achieve military or political objectives, **2007**: 289, 317–21, 355–56, 841, 843, 906, 918; **2008**: 287–88
definition, **2000**: 252, 253–54
Security Council resolutions on, **2008**: 286–88
as war crime, crime against humanity, genocide, **1991-99**: 584, 852; **2000**: 241–42, 251–55
Ratification, Protocol on Exchange of Instruments of, 2002: 79
***Ratione temporis* competence of Inter-American Commission on Human Rights, 2004**: 223–30
RCRA (Resource Conservation and Recovery Act) (1976), 2002: 775
REAL ID Act, 2006: 155, 206, 1194; **2007**: 15, 24–26
Receivables in International Trade, Convention on the Assignment of, 1991-99: 1822
Reciprocity, 2004: 830, 844, 854, 985. *See also* Comity
access to U.S. courts by foreign national, **1989-90**: 215–16; **2002**: 237–42
attachment of assets, **1989-90**: 296, 299–300, 302; **2005**: 554, 568
bilateral investment treaties, **2004**: 623–24
child abduction cases, **2000**: 119, 137; **2001**: 43–47; **2005**: 66
consular and diplomatic relations, **1989-90**: 340, 383; **1991-99**: 1330; **2000**: 58, 75–76, 119, 554; **2005**: 64
in diplomatic immunity practices, **2002**: 566–67
discovery from heads of state, **2005**: 563
enforcement of judgments, **1991-99**: 1830; **2004**: 826
in extradition, **2001**: 63; **2005**: 98
family support enforcement. *See* Maintenance obligations
foreign sovereign immunity, **2005**: 527
implications of unconsented extraterritorial arrest and, **1989-90**: 98

Reciprocity (continued)
implications of U.S. civil cause of action against foreign states for terrorist acts, **1989-90**: 116
India, nuclear nonproliferation, **2005**: 1081, 1086
International Criminal Court (ICC), **2005**: 198
investment in air carriers, **2005**: 592
maritime matters, **2005**: 700
in Middle East conflict resolution, **2004**: 949
monetary contempt sanctions, **2005**: 522
most-favored-nation treatment, **1989-90**: 340, 341, 342, 343–46; **2008**: 498, 499
Palau and, **1991-99**: 824
permission for aliens to perform longshore work, **2002**: 756–57
protection of diplomatic missions, **1989-90**: 249, 250, 254
service of process on visiting foreign officials and, **2002**: 592–93
ship boarding agreements, **2005**: 1101
sunken military craft, treatment of, **2004**: 719
treaties and, **1991-99**: 415–516, 705, 1109, 1478, 1514, 2204; **2001**: 131–32; **2004**: 545
reservations, **1989-90**: 185
unfair competition, **2005**: 670
visa waiver pilot program, **1989-90**: 27
work agreements, **2004**: 561
Recognition and Enforcement of Foreign Judgments in Civil and Commercial Matters and its Supplementary Protocol. *See* Hague Conventions
Recognition of foreign states. *See* Diplomatic relations and recognition
Reconstruction and stabilization assistance for troubled areas, 2005: 947–48. *See also* Foreign assistance
Red Cross, International Committee of (ICRC), 2003: 334–36, 351, 999, 1000, 1005, 1007, 1009, 1012, 1026, 1066; **2005**: 378, 380–81. *See also* Geneva Conventions on law of war (1949); Hague conventions, *subheading*: on law of war; Humanitarian law, *subheading*: ICRC study on; Law of war
access to military detainees, **2005**: 965, 971, 977–78; **2006**: 1125, 1127, 1161
additional distinctive emblem under Geneva Conventions, Protocol III, **2005**: 1042–43; **2006**: 1100–4; **2007**: 982–84
Israeli and Palestinian organizations admitted to Red Cross and Red Crescent movement, **2006**: 1103–4
communications, confidentiality of, **2005**: 971, 1020–22; **2006**: 1127, 1219–20
Conference (2007), **2007**: 894–95, 984

Red Cross, International Committee of (ICRC) (continued)
Holocaust era archives, role in, **2007**: 380–81
humanitarian law, customary law of, study, **2006**: 1069–85
prisoners of war, photography of, **2005**: 1025, 1029
Refugees, 2004: 446, 447, 943, 1065; **2006**: 52–60. *See also* Deportation; Removal of aliens from U.S.
admission numbers and authorizations for fiscal 2007 (Presidential Determination 2007–1), **2006**: 55–56
Agreement for Cooperation in the Examination of Refugee Status Claims from Nationals of Third Countries, **2002**: 31–35; **2004**: 33–34
asylum applicants. *See* Asylum
Burma and, **2006**: 52–55; **2007**: 842
Cartagena Declaration on Refugees (1984), **2007**: 51
children as, **1991-99**: 228; **2004**: 282
child soldiers, **2008**: 306–8
Comprehensive Plan of Action (1989) (Southeast Asia), **1991-99**: 113
Convention Relating to Status of Refugees (1951), **1989-90**: 49–51, 49*n*; **1991-99**: 81, 150–72, 177–78, 190, 952–53; **2000**: 381; **2001**: 916; **2002**: 185, 193, 198, 289; **2004**: 82–83, 157; **2005**: 983
applicability of non-refoulement protections to individuals convicted of particularly serious crimes, **2008**: 344
on expulsion of aliens, **2008**: 25–28
extraterritorial application of, U.S. objections to opinion on, **2007**: 41–70
Protocol (1967), **1989-90**: 47, 49*n*; **1991-99**: 81, 150, 157–58, 160–61, 162, 163–64, 168–70, 188, 190, 232, 237; **2002**: 32, 37, 185, 289; **2004**: 82; **2005**: 347, 349; **2007**: 41–42, 49–52, 55–65, 69, 279
U.S. state law and, **2002**: 193–94
from Cuba, **2003**: 23
Cuban Refugee Adjustment Act, **2005**: 19
Cuba–U.S. migration agreements, **1991-99**: 59–68
customary international law, **1989-90**: 47–48, 49*n*
definition under draft articles on diplomatic protection, **2007**: 415*n*
detention of, **2002**: 29–30
eligibility for treatment as, **2000**: 128–31; **2004**: 2
exemptions from terrorism-related entry restrictions for certain refugees, **2007**: 70–72; **2008**: 29–31
Haitian, **1989-90**: 47–54; **2002**: 25–31; **2003**: 25
identification and protection, **2002**: 26–28
International Refugee Organization, **2004**: 2
Iraqi, **2008**: 31–34

Refugees (continued)
Liberian family reunification processing, **2006**: 59–60
minors, **2007**: 342–43
in naturalization case, **2003**: 6, 7
nonrefoulement obligations, **1989-90**: 49–53
extradition and, **2004**: 82–83, **2008**: 367–72
military activity and, **2007**: 60
policy and custom vs. legal obligation under international law, **2007**: 65, 68*n*; **2008**: 368–69
principle of, **2007**: 57–60
under Refugee Convention, **1991-99**: 232, **2008**: 27, 344, 367–68
on high seas, **1991-99**: 150–72, 176–77, 187–94
in internal waters, **1991-99**: 182–87
in territorial sea, **1991-99**: 172–81
victims of trafficking, **2004**: 156–57
North Korean, **2002**: 35–38; **2006**: 56–59
OAU Convention Concerning Specific Aspects of Refugee Problems in Africa, **2007**: 51
Palestinian, **2004**: 952; **2005**: 918
Refugee Act (1980), **1989-90**: 42–43; **1991-99**: 159, 176, 177, 190, 201, 209, 232
Refugee Crisis in Iraq Act of 2007, **2008**: 15
Refugee Relief Act (1953), **1991-99**: 28
refugees who are a danger to the country in which present, **2007**: 45–47
right to return, **2005**: 937
seafarers, **2007**: 986
Sudanese, **2004**: 132, 239, 244–45, 248, 959; **2007**: 817, 906
temporary refuge for, **1989-90**: 53
UN High Commissioner for. *See* United Nations, *subheading*: High Commissioner for Refugees
U.S. antiterrorist efforts and, **2001**: 915–17
Vietnamese Montagnards in Cambodia, **2002**: 24–25
World War II, **2004**: 446, 447; **2005**: 485–88
Region 2 MF Broadcasting Agreement, 1989-90: 400
Regional Economic Integration Organisations, 1991-99: 693–99; **2000**: 303, 304, 307, 308; **2005**: 211, 212–13, 214, 746
Registration of Objects Launched into Outer Space. *See* Space
Rehabilitation Act (1973), 1991-99: 17–18; **2003**: 4; **2005**: 292
Religion and religious freedom
annual report on, **1991-99**: 918–20, 924–27; **2000**: 355; **2001**: 271; **2002**: 280–82; **2003**: 295–97; **2004**: 270–74; **2005**: 314–16; **2006**: 376–77; **2007**: 324; **2008**: 288
anti-Semitism, **2003**: 297–99; **2004**: 274–77, 955–56; **2005**: 305, 317–19

Religion and religious freedom (continued)
conscientious objection to military service, **2004:** 395
Convention on the Rights of the Child on, **1989-90:** 173–74
in Cuba, **1991-99:** 1908
cultural property of religious significance, return of Iraqi, **2004:** 886
Declaration on the Elimination of All Forms of Intolerance and Discrimination Based on Religion or Belief, **2001:** 142; **2005:** 989
defamation of, U.S. comments on, **2005:** 320; **2008:** 288–90
denial of visa to religious persecutors, **1991-99:** 93–94
detainees, **2005:** 978–83
discrimination or persecution, **2004:** 4, 76, 105, 106, 157, 263, 301, 363, 389, 394, 448, 498, 527–31; **2006:** 198–99
freedom of speech and, **2007:** 324–26, 329–30, 332
hate crimes and, **2007:** 328, 330
Hate Crime Sentencing Enhancement Act (1994), **2007:** 330, 331
importance of, **1991-99:** 866; **2001:** 140; **2002:** 280–82; **2004:** 278–79, 390
in relation to creation of Palestinian state, **2004:** 907
International Covenant on Civil and Political Rights (ICCPR) and, **2006:** 380; **2007:** 326
International Religious Freedom Act of 1998 (IRF Act), **1991-99:** 93–94, 918–24, 925, 926; **2000:** 355; **2001:** 141–42, 271, 272; **2002:** 280–82; **2003:** 294–95; **2004:** 271–72; **2005:** 13, 314, 315, 317; **2008:** 288
definition of "violations of religious freedom," **2001:** 141–42
designation of countries of particular concern, **1991-99:** 920–21, 925; **2001:** 271; **2003:** 294–95; **2004:** 272–74; **2005:** 314; **2006:** 377
severe violations of, U.S. response to, **1991-99:** 920–24
1969 law, **2007:** 330–31
Religious Freedom Restoration Act of 1993 (RFRA), **2001:** 129, 131, 132–33; **2002:** 98, 99; **2003:** 184–85; **2005:** 137, 139–40, 143–44; **2006:** 222; **2007:** 325; **2008:** 914
Religious Land Use and Institutionalized Persons Act (2000), **2007:** 327–28
religious use of controlled substances, **2001:** 128–43; **2003:** 184–86; **2006:** 221–25
repression of Falun Gong movement in China, **2002:** 469–76; **2003:** 394, 396, 397, 398–99, 558–69; **2004:** 380–82; **2006:** 663, 664
in Sudan, **1991-99:** 925, 1937; **2005:** 314, 316
genocide and, **2004:** 241
terrorism and, **2004:** 106, 198; **2005:** 439

Religion and religious freedom (continued)
UN Commission on Human Rights resolution, **2004**: 278–79
UN General Assembly resolution, **2006**: 379–80; **2008**: 288–89
UN Human Rights Council, **2006**: 380–81
U.S. Commission on, **2005**: 311
U.S. Report on International Religious Freedom, **1991-99**: 918, 919–22, 924–27; **2000**: 355; **2001**: 271; **2002**: 280–82; **2003**: 294–97; **2004**: 270–74; **2005**: 314–16; **2006**: 376–78; **2007**: 324–32; **2008**: 288
U.S.–Vietnam Religious Freedom Agreement, **2005**: 316–17
Remedies, **1991-99**: 8–9, 432, 636, 776, 961, 981, 982, 1010, 1081, 1407, 1476, 1502, 1510–11, 1541, 1545, 2182; **2004**: 205, 419, 428, 429, 669–70, 806. *See also* Espousal of claims; State responsibility
apology
for bombing by U.S. of Chinese Embassy in Belgrade, **2000**: 425
for failure to provide consular notification, **2000**: 58, 65
assurances and guarantees of nonrepetition, **2000**: 65–73; **2001**: 22, 23–24, 377–78; **2003**: 77, 99–100
availability of, in comity and *forum non conveniens* cases, **2005**: 822, 829, 841
claims. *See also* Expropriation; Iran–United States Claims Tribunal; North American Free Trade Agreement (NAFTA)
attack on U.S.S. Stark, **1989-90**: 217–19
injuries to members of Multinational Force and Observers, **1989-90**: 206–7
to Kuwait by Iraq for invasion and occupation, **1991-99**: 1099–1106
Nazi and World War II-era claims. *See* World War II
U.S./Cambodia property settlement, **1991-99**: 1081
compensation. *See also* damages, *this heading*; victim compensation, *this heading*; World War II, *subheading*: claims
Iraq compensation to Kuwait for damages resulting from invasion and occupation, **1991-99**: 1099–1106
consular notification, for failure of. *See* Consular notification and access
in Convention on Jurisdictional Immunities of States and Their Properties, **2004**: 456–57; **2006**: 599–600, 603, 607–9
countermeasures, **1991-99**: 1107–15, 1120, 1122, 1414; **2000**: 417, 665; **2001**: 365–71
damages, **1991-99**: 1115–19; **2001**: 8–79, 373–74. *See also* claims, *this heading*
under Alien Tort Statute, **2002**: 325
Convention on Supplementary Compensation for Nuclear Damage (CSC), **2008**: 993–99

Remedies (continued)
Gulf War damages, **1991-99**: 1099, 1102, 1104, 2101–2
for mental/emotional injury, **2003**: 597–602
moral damages, **2001**: 378–79
punitive damages, **2001**: 373–74; **2008**: 457–58
transboundary damage, **2000**: 420
violations of Vienna Convention on Consular Relations, Article 36, **2008**: 36–42
diplomatic intercession, **2005**: 526. *See also* Espousal of claims
equitable, **1991-99**: 1265–66
ex gratia payment, **1989-90**: 333–35; **1991-99**: 333, 335, 538–39, 541
for bombing by U.S. of Chinese Embassy in Belgrade, **2000**: 428–29
for murder of former Chilean ambassador in U.S. (Letelier case), **1989-90**: 97–98, 537–41; **1991-99**: 1072–73; **2000**: 656–62; **2005**: 523, 558–59
exhaustion of remedies, requirement for, **1991-99**: 124, 289, 991, 1075–76, 1110, 1278, 1434–35, 1481; **2001**: 379; **2004**: 223, 230–32, 351, 374*n*, 474–75*n*, 494–95, 977–81, 984, 994; **2005**: 569–70
administrative, **2005**: 367, 412–13
under Alien Tort Statute, **1991-99**: 991; **2002**: 336–37; **2008**: 238–44. *See also* Alien Tort Statute (ATS)
criminal, **2005**: 283
for filing foreign claims with European Commission, **2004**: 351*n*
under FSIA, **2004**: 494–95; **2005**: 777. *See also* Foreign Sovereign Immunities Act (FSIA) (1976)
local, **2006**: 501–2
under Torture Victim Protection Act, **1991-99**: 991; **2003**: 379, 385; **2005**: 427; **2006**: 482–84
Flatow Amendment. *See* Foreign Sovereign Immunities Act (FSIA) (1976)
against foreign states, absence of, **2005**: 402, 504, 883–84
against foreign states and instrumentalities. *See* Foreign Sovereign Immunities Act (FSIA) (1976); Immunity
guarantee of nonrepetition. *See* assurances and guarantees of nonrepetition, *this heading*
injunctive relief. *See* Injunctions
International Law Commission on, **1991-99**: 1108, 1115–19; **2000**: 416–20, 666–67; **2001**: 364–71, 377–80
local remedies rule. *See* exhaustion of remedies, requirement for, *this heading*
for Nazi and World War II-related claims. *See* World War II
reparations. *See* damages, *this heading*; World War II, *subheading*: claims

Remedies (continued)
restitution, **1991-99**: 1117–18; **2001**: 395–401, 411. *See also* World War II, *subheading*: claims
Softwood Lumber Agreement, arbitration between Canada and U.S., **2008**: 585–89
victim compensation, **2001**: 39, 40
crime committed by diplomatic personnel, **1989-90**: 332–37
victims of human rights violations, **2004**: 315, 334–35
for violation of human rights and laws of war. *See* Alien Tort Statute (ATS); Criminal tribunals, international, hybrid, and other; Human rights
wrecks at sea, under customary international law, **2006**: 819–21
Removal of aliens from U.S. *See also* Extradition; Rendition; Torture, *subheading*: transfers to other countries and likelihood of
based on terrorism, **2002**: 102–4; **2003**: 155–59; **2004**: 122–28; **2005**: 100–105, 116, 119. *See also* Deportation, *subheading*: grounds for; Immigration and visas, *subheading*: terrorism and; Torture, *subheading*: transfers to other countries and likelihood of
Canada–U.S. understanding, **2004**: 21–23
criminal aliens, **2005**: 63–64; **2006**: 33–36; **2008**: 314*n*, 341–44
criteria for, **1991-99**: 86–87, 93–94, 109–10; **2005**: 20–21; **2008**: 313–14
detention and, **1991-99**: 86–87; **2008**: 281, 341–42, 345, 347
after removal period, **1991-99**: 86–87, 93; **2001**: 17–19; **2005**: 18
continued detention of unadmitted alien while awaiting removal, **2006**: 45–50
determination of country removed to, **2005**: 15–17
acceptance by foreign country, **2004**: 11–21
country of citizenship, **2005**: 15, 17
country without functioning government, **2004**: 12, 13–14, 16, 20; **2005**: 14–18
implementation of non-*refoulement* obligations under Torture Convention, **1991-99**: 239–40, 944, 952–59; **2003**: 32, 38; **2005**: 347–51, 983, 993–94; **2008**: 366–75
sanctions on for nonacceptance of nationals, **2001**: 17–20
DHS role, **2005**: 84*n*, 290–91
diplomatic assurances and, **1991-99**: 958–59; **2008**: 366–75
illegal reentry after, **2006**: 29–33
International Law Commission, report on, **2005**: 23–24; **2007**: 38–39; **2008**: 25–28
procedure, **2005**: 15–17, 496
appeals, **2006**: 414
beyond 90 days, **2005**: 18, 21
review of final order, **2004**: 88; **2005**: 85
timely, **2003**: 29–33

Removal of aliens from U.S. (continued)
protection of aliens in, **2005**: 17–18
rendition. *See* Rendition
right to return to country of nationality, **2001**: 17–20, 344; **2005**: 937
torture allegations in proceedings for, **2005**: 347–51, 993–94, 1012–14; **2006**: 413–14
withholding and suspension of, **1991-99**: 952–56, 957–58
wrongful, in child abduction cases. *See* Children, *subheading*: international abduction
Rendition, 1991-99: 435–45; **2003**: 323–25; **2004**: 340–54, 992–93; **2005**: 100–105, 1017; **2006**: 160–63, 414–15
of alien defendant from Pakistan, **2002**: 77–78
disclosure of state secrets, **2006**: 163
effects of irregular rendition, **1991-99**: 435–41, 504–5, 506
of Guantanamo detainees, **2006**: 1123
state secrets claim in case concerning, **2007**: 238–46
Repatriation. *See also* Detainees, military, *subheading*: enemy combatants, unlawful; Prisoners of war; Removal of aliens from U.S.; Rendition; Torture, *subheading*: transfers to other countries and likelihood of
of assets, **2007**: 476, 485, 742
Cuba, agreement with, **2005**: 22
of detainees, **2004**: 992, 1005
of Haitians, **2004**: 35, 941
of Mexicans, **2004**: 26–27, 238–39
of smuggled migrants, **2004**: 162–63
of spent fuel, **2004**: 1138–41
travel documents and, **2004**: 13
of victims of trafficking, **2004**: 156
of income, **2005**: 804
indigenous people, **2007**: 373
migrants, **2003**: 25; **2007**: 365*n*
persons held by U.S. forces, **2005**: 979, 993, 1017–18
refugees, post World War II, **2005**: 487
UN peacekeepers accountable for crimes, **2008**: 387
United Arab Emirates and trafficked children, **2008**: 229
of Vietnamese Montagnards in Cambodia, **2002**: 24–25
Visa Waiver Program and, **2007**: 34; **2008**: 21
Reproductive rights, **2002**: 308–9; **2003**: 321–22; **2008**: 324. *See also* Human cloning
2005 World Summit Outcome Document, **2005**: 454
UN Commission on Status of Women (CSW), **2005**: 308–9
UN disabilities convention (draft), **2005**: 321
Republic of Korea. *See* Korea, South (Republic of Korea (ROK))

Res judicata, **1991-99**: 53; **2001**: 43*n*; **2004**: 591, 848; **2005**: 818; **2008**: 525
Rescue operations. *See* Maritime issues, *subheading*: search and rescue operations
Research
Antarctic Treaty, **2005**: 755
biomedical, **2005**: 785
Controlled Substances Act (CSA), **2005**: 138
drug research and development, **2002**: 718
human cloning. *See* Cloning
marine, **1989-90**: 478–79; **2003**: 718, 727, 732; **2005**: 684, 694; **2008**: 652–56
whaling, **2001**: 684–85
medical experimentation on humans, **2005**: 276–77, 294
nuclear, **2003**: 1085, 1105, 1117; **2008**: 940, 975
outer space, **2003**: 766
reactors, **2005**: 1092; **2008**: 971
Joint Statement on Cooperation to Transfer Russian-origin High-enriched Uranium Research Reactor Fuel to the Russian Federation, **2003**: 1110–12
science and technology agreements, **2005**: 773–74
scientific research rules and codes of conduct, **1989-90**: 478–80; **2005**: 1055–56
use of genetic data, **2003**: 818–19
weapons of mass destruction, **2003**: 1085, 1105; **2008**: 1007
Resource Conservation and Recovery Act (RCRA) (1976), **2002**: 775
Restatement (Second) of Conflict of Laws, **2005**: 512
Restatement (Second) of Foreign Relations, **2004**: 497; **2005**: 576; **2006**: 595
Restatement (Third) of Foreign Relations, **2000**: 157–58, 400*n*, 403, 405, 409, 412, 484, 493–94, 571–72, 666; **2003**: 148, 259, 260*n*, 363, 376, 564; **2004**: 231, 304*n*, 353, 487*n*, 497–98, 845; **2005**: 504, 512; **2006**: 66, 676, 948–49; **2008**: 43, 135, 156, 179*n*, 232, 233, 239, 240, 241, 243, 244, 893, 894
Retroactivity
antidumping, **2008**: 769
of FSIA. *See* Foreign Sovereign Immunities Act (FSIA) (1976)
of immigration law. *See* Immigration and visas
of international norms and treaty provisions, **2004**: 81, 225, 226
Softwood Lumber Agreement, retroactive compensation, **2008**: 586, 587–88
of U.S. law, **1991-99**: 115, 259, 332, 2202; **2004**: 47, 81, 463–78, 496, 511, 796*n*

Revenue Act (1916), 2004: 612
Revenue rule, 2004: 825–26
common-law, and relationship to U.S. criminal law, **2005:** 235–41
Revised Statutes of 1874, 2006: 82–83
RFRA (Religious Freedom Restoration Act of 1993). *See* Religion and religious freedom
Rights of the Child. *See* Children
Rio Declaration on Environment and Development, 1991-99: 1649–55; **2002:** 768–69; **2003:** 373
Risk insurance, terrorism. *See* Terrorism
Road Traffic, Convention on (1949), 2000: 295; **2002:** 20–22
ROK. *See* Korea, South (Republic of Korea (ROK))
Romania
Article 98 agreement (nonsurrender of Americans to ICC), **2002:** 166; **2003:** 238
Chemical Weapons Convention, Implementation Assistance Program, **2005:** 1059
child abduction convention compliance, **2004:** 54; **2006:** 102
domestic violence laws, lack of, **2005:** 313
educational exchange program, **1991-99:** 1807–8
enforcement of court judgments in U.S., **1991-99:** 1836–38
extradition and mutual legal assistance, **2000:** 166, 185*n*; **2004:** 91–93; **2006:** 148–55
immigration requirements, relief for certain resident nationals, **1991-99:** 250
immunity for UN Special Rapporteur, **1989-90:** 353–70
intellectual property rights Watch List, **2006:** 768; **2007:** 610
maritime issues, **1989-90:** 445, 464–65
import ban on Caspian Sea beluga sturgeon products, **2005:** 754–55
NATO membership, **2003:** 424–26; **2004:** 411–12
nuclear fuel return program, **2004:** 1139, 1141
Open Skies (aerial observation) treaty, **2002:** 1029
preservation of American heritage in, **1991-99:** 1793–94
rule of law and democracy, coordination of UN programs promoting, **2005:** 435
trade and investment agreements, **1991-99:** 1455, 1466; **2004:** 624
Protocol Between U.S. and Romania to Treaty Concerning Reciprocal Encouragement and Protection of Investment, **2003:** 694–97
Understanding Concerning Certain U.S. Bilateral Investment Treaties, **2003:** 687–94
UN Commission on Human Rights and, **2004:** 390–91
Rome Statute of the International Criminal Court, Rome Treaty. *See* International Criminal Court (ICC)

Rotterdam Convention on the Prior Informed Consent Procedure for Certain Hazardous Chemicals and Pesticides in International Trade (1999), 2002: 776

Russia
accession process to WTO, **2006:** 751–52
adopting orphans in, Hague Apostille Convention and, **2007:** 95–97
Arctic region, **2008:** 623, 624, 628
boundaries, **2008:** 630, 638–39
environment protection agreements, **1991-99:** 1777–80
arms control, **1991-99:** 2243–47. *See also* Nonproliferation, *subheading*: country-specific issues; Strategic Arms Reduction Treaty (START)
agreements with U.S., **1991-99:** 2210, 2213, 2216, 2222, 2242–47, 2253–55, 2263–65, 2303–14, 2339–40, 2355–56
Anti-Ballistic Missile (ABM) Treaty (1972). *See* Anti-Ballistic Missile (ABM) Treaty (1972) (U.S.–USSR)
Cooperative Threat Reduction Umbrella Agreement, **2006:** 1287–88
Open Skies (aerial observation), treaty on, **1991-99:** 2238–41; **2002:** 1029; **2004:** 1068
Strategic Offensive Reductions, treaty with U.S. on ("Moscow Treaty") (2002), **2002:** 1017–23; **2003:** 1068; **2004:** 1056–59; **2005:** 1054, 1110; **2008:** 950
Draft Protocol on Prohibitions or Restrictions on the Use and Transfer of Mines Other than Anti-Personnel Mines (MOTAPM), **2005:** 1042
export controls, **1991-99:** 2253–55, 2263–65
Joint Declaration on New Strategic Relationship, **2002:** 1023–27
Man-Portable Air Defense Systems (MANPADS), Arrangement on, **2005:** 1066
asylum request by citizen of, **1991-99:** 194–202
aviation agreement, **2005:** 588; **2008:** 510
chemical and biological weapons. *See* Nonproliferation, *subheading*: country-specific issues
copyright law, **2008:** 606
domestic violence laws, lack of, **2005:** 313
environmental and conservation issues, **1991-99:** 1669, 1677, 1681
Arctic environment protection agreements, **1991-99:** 1777–80
polar bears, agreement on protection of, **2002:** 800–805; **2007:** 728
extradition limitation, **2001:** 69–70
fisheries agreements and management, **1991-99:** 1703–7, 1731–32, 1738, 1744–45; **2003:** 730–31; **2005:** 557; **2008:** 711
Foreign Sovereign Immunities Act (FSIA) (1976) litigation, **2001:** 501–2, 505–10; **2005:** 557

Russia (continued)
forum non conveniens, **2005**: 833–39
Georgia, military presence in, **1991-99**: 2236–37; **2008**: 863–70
Guantanamo detainee transferred to, **2005**: 967
Holocaust-era claims, **1991-99**: 1047, 1068, 1258
human rights and, **1991-99**: 927; **2004**: 338–39; **2005**: 313
democracy promotion programs, **1991-99**: 853, 1011–14
religious freedom, **2003**: 297; **2005**: 315
Ilulissat Declaration, **2008**: 636–38
immunity for diplomatic agent, **2006**: 653–57
immunity for U.S. foreign service officer in, **2006**: 308–11
indigenous peoples, views concerning UN declaration on, **2008**: 353–54, 354*n*
intellectual property rights Watch List, **2006**: 768; **2007**: 607, 610; **2008**: 605–6, 605*n*
International Space Station (ISS), **2005**: 1132
investment and trade
import ban on Caspian Sea beluga sturgeon products, **2005**: 754
most-favored-nation treatment, **1991-99**: 1377*n*, 1455
treaties and agreements, **1991-99**: 1466, 1483–84; **2005**: 650
U.S.–Russia market access agreement, **2006**: 751–52
Iraq no-fly zones, enforcement of, **1991-99**: 2116
ITER International Fusion Energy Organization, **2006**: 893
judicial system, **2004**: 338–39
law of the sea
Alexander Archipelago, passage, **2005**: 699–701
Antarctica and, **2004**: 732
continental shelf, **2002**: 732–37; **2003**: 731–32; **2008**: 638–39
maritime boundaries, **1991-99**: 1583
underwater cultural heritage, **2005**: 761, 766
legal assistance, **2002**: 79; **2004**: 68
letters rogatory on judicial assistance, **2006**: 107–10
longshore work prohibition on alien crewmen from, **2002**: 757
money laundering, **2004**: 135; **2005**: 177–78
Moscow Embassy arbitration, **1991-99**: 1124
NATO and, **1991-99**: 1031–40
Status of Forces Agreement (SOFA), Russian understanding, **2008**: 160–64
nuclear energy, peaceful use of (123 agreement), **2008**: 986–87
nuclear weapons and material and nonproliferation. *See* Nonproliferation, *subheading*: country-specific issues
outer space agreements, **1991-99**: 1641–47, 2309
outer space, voluntary transparency and confidence-building measures concerning, **2008**: 672

Russia (continued)
peace process
former Yugoslavia, **1991-99**: 1980, 2139, 2142, 2147
Israeli-Palestinian conflict, **1991-99**: 1027, 1989–90, 1995; **2002**: 916–19; **2003**: 943–47; **2004**: 945–53; **2005**: 905, 918; **2007**: 838, 844–48; **2008**: 816–19
Kosovo, **1991-99**: 2031, 2042, 2147; **2005**: 935
Nagorno-Karabakh, OSCE Minsk Group co-chair, **2008**: 830–32
relations with U.S., **1991-99**: 746, 750–61, 2243–47, 2263–65, 2303–14, 2330–31; **2001**: 832
agreement concerning documentation of, **2002**: 227
Investment Incentive Agreement, **2005**: 650
Russian–Chechen conflict, **1991-99**: 516–17
service of process in, **2005**: 810–13
Somali piracy, cooperation with Transitional Federal Government of Somalia (TFG) in fight against, **2008**: 927
succession issues, **1991-99**: 742–61, 1170–73
sunken government property and, **1991-99**: 1618; **2004**: 717, 718, 722
suspension of Treaty on Conventional Armed Forces in Europe, **2007**: 1001–2; **2008**: 1011–17
terrorism and, **2004**: 105–7; **2005**: 108
U.S.-Russia Interoperability Work Plan, **2007**: 670
Rwanda. *See also* International Criminal Tribunal for Rwanda (ICTR)
arms embargo, **2003**: 1081–82; **2007**: 1007
bilateral investment treaty, **2008**: 600–3
democracy promotion programs, **1991-99**: 1011
genocide in, **1991-99**: 529–32, 858–59, 2012; **2004**: 128–29, 130–32, 247, 258
participation in peace process in Ethiopia/Eritrea, **1991-99**: 2011
peacekeeping operations, **1991-99**: 589, 2347
regional peace agreement, **2004**: 942–43
temporary protected status for nationals of, **1991-99**: 245
World Summit Outcome Document, **2005**: 376

S

Safety and Health in Mines, Convention Concerning, 1991-99: 998–1000
Safety of Life at Sea, International Convention on. *See* Maritime issues
Safety of Maritime Navigation, Convention for the Suppression of Unlawful Acts Against (SUA) (1988). *See* Maritime issues; Piracy; Terrorism
St. Christopher and Nevis
longshore work prohibition on alien crewmen from, **2002**: 757; **2003**: 764

St. Kitts and Nevis
Article 98 agreement and, **2006**: 278
extradition and mutual legal assistance, **1991-99**: 396, 453; **2000**: 179, 186*n*; **2001**: 92*n*
human rights in, **2004**: 398
Inter-American Convention Against Corruption, party to, **2006**: 238
maritime counter-drug trade agreement, **1991-99**: 1607
money laundering, **2006**: 243
St. Lucia
extradition and mutual legal assistance, **1991-99**: 452; **2000**: 179, 186*n*; **2001**: 92*n*
maritime counter-drug trade agreement, **1991-99**: 1607
St. Vincent and the Grenadines, 1991-99: 1602–4
extradition and mutual legal assistance, **1991-99**: 396, 452–55; **2000**: 179, 186*n*; **2001**: 92*n*
Inter-American Convention Against Corruption, party to, **2006**: 238
maritime counter-drug trade agreement, **1991-99**: 1607
U.S. military assistance, **2006**: 278
Sales Convention, Vienna, 2002: 820
SALT II treaty, 2001: 213
Salvage at sea. *See* Maritime issues
Samoa
U.S. military assistance, **2006**: 278
waiver of Article 98 agreement with U.S. (nonsurrender of Americans to ICC), **2006**: 279
Samoa, American, 2005: 736, 742–44
San Marino
diplomatic relations, **2006**: 529–30
extradition and mutual legal assistance, **2000**: 185*n*
nonimmigrant visa waiver pilot program, **1991-99**: 76
Sanctions. *See also* Emergency Economic Powers Act, International (IEEPA); Executive Orders, Presidential; Nonproliferation, *subheadings*: sanctions, U.S., and Security Council and; Security Council, UN; Terrorism, *subheading*: sanctions related to; *specific countries*
Al-Qaida/Qaeda. *See* Al-Qaida/Qaeda
arms control. *See also* Arms control; Nonproliferation, *subheading*: sanctions, U.S.
arms embargoes, **2001**: 801–2; **2002**: 881–82, 884–85, 894; **2003**: 152, 1081–86; **2004**: 884, 890–93, 901, 922–23, 929, 932, 934, 962, 1069–70, 1110–11; **2005**: 894, 899, 903, 929–30; **2006**: 1047, 1269; **2007**: 1003–7, 1048; **2008**: 87–88, 1021–23
MANPADS transfer to state-sponsors of terrorism, **2006**: 210–11

Sanctions (continued)
contempt sanctions against foreign state under FSIA, **2005**: 522–31; **2006**: 603–11
on countries providing sanctuary to indictees of international criminal tribunals, **1991-99**: 583
cybercrime, **2003**: 202
development of international law and targeted UN sanctions, **2007**: 391
diamonds, prohibition on import of. *See* Trade, *subheading*: diamonds
drug trafficking. *See also* Drug trade
against countries, **1991-99**: 547–54; **2001**: 143, 144–45, 822; **2002**: 122–26; **2003**: 186–87; **2006**: 217
against foreign drug traffickers (Executive Order 12978), **1991-99**: 547–50; **2001**: 144, 822
Emergency Economic Powers Act, International. *See* Emergency Economic Powers Act, International (IEEPA)
enforcement, **2007**: 827–28
Executive Branch authority, **2000**: 749–50; **2002**: 244; **2003**: 541; **2006**: 796–801, 1006–19
extradition treaty noncompliance, **2000**: 187–88; **2008**: 72
foreign policy and, **1991-99**: 1973–78; **2003**: 459–60
for frivolous filings against foreign government, **1989-90**: 313–14
humanitarian exceptions, **1991-99**: 1907–11, 1971–73; **2003**: 907–9; **2005**: 132–33
Iran and Libya Sanctions Act (1996), **1991-99**: 1448, 1911–15, 1976, 1977; **2001**: 817–19; **2003**: 445; **2004**: 928–29, 930; **2008**: 770. *See also* Iran and Libya
Iraq Sanctions Act (1990), **2000**: 618; **2003**: 555, 909, 912–14; **2004**: 491–92, 890–91; **2008**: 459, 465
for nonacceptance of return of nationals, **2001**: 18–20
nonproliferation. *See* Nonproliferation, *subheadings*: sanctions, U.S., *and* Security Council and
related to entities of former Yugoslavia, **1991-99**: 1168, 1945–62, 1950, 1951, 1980, 2027–28, 2031
related to World War II era insurance claims, **1991-99**: 1071
religious freedom, for severe violations of, **1991-99**: 922–23
role of U.S. states, **2002**: 446
Sanctions Policy Reform Act (1999), **1991-99**: 1974
on Taliban. *See* Taliban
targeted sanctions to implement UN Security Council resolutions, **1991-99**: 1967; **2001**: 15–17, 797–801, 802–3, 803–6, 895–96, 900–1; **2002**: 882–85, 889–90; **2003**: 174–75, 916–23, 1081–84; **2004**: 883–93, 922–24, 927–34, 1069–70, 1109–15; **2005**: 894–97, 899; **2006**: 975–78, 984–88, 995–98, 1269; **2007**: 821–23, 1004, 1006–7, 1041–50; **2008**: 98–101

Sanctions (continued)
termination of, **2003**: 934–35; **2004**: 884
terrorism-related. *See* Terrorism, *subheading*: sanctions related to
third-state consequences, **2002**: 391–92; **2007**: 824–25
Trade Sanctions Reform and Export Enhancement Act (2000), **2000**: 749–50; **2001**: 807, 819–22, 886, 926; **2003**: 924, 932; **2005**: 132–33; **2008**: 792
trademark renewal for Cuban company, denial of license related to, **2007**: 828–30
trafficking in persons. *See* Trafficking in persons
Satellites. *See* Space
Saudi Arabia
FSIA immunity, **1991-99**: 1183, 1199, 1208–15, 1257–58; **2000**: 577–90
Guantanamo detainees transferred to, **2005**: 967
Gulf War and, **1991-99**: 2057, 2072, 2078, 2089–92, 2094, 2096, 2099, 2104
habeas corpus jurisdiction over U.S. citizen held in, **2004**: 203–6
head-of-state immunity, **1991-99**: 1289–90; **2003**: 571–72
human rights in, **2002**: 282
intellectual property rights Watch List, **2006**: 768, 769; **2007**: 610
inviolability of embassy documents, **2002**: 567–70
inviolability of UN missions, **2003**: 573
Iraq sanctions and, **1991-99**: 1930
juvenile offenders, execution of, **2005**: 387
religious freedom violations, **1991-99**: 925; **2003**: 296; **2004**: 270, 272, 273; **2005**: 314, 316; **2006**: 377
service of process by e-mail in, **2005**: 865–67
temporary refuge for U.S. citizens in U.S. diplomatic posts, **2003**: 104–6
terrorism and
cooperation in antiterrorism actions, **2002**: 889
liability of government officials for September 11 terrorist attacks, **2003**: 508–9, 533–36
terrorist attack on U.S. personnel in, **1991-99**: 494, 496
claims in U.S. court against Iran for, **2006**: 581–84
trafficking in persons, **2005**: 159; **2006**: 229; **2007**: 169; **2008**: 118
forced labor trafficking, **2005**: 159, 162
Science and technology agreements, 2005: 773–74
Scientific research. *See* Research
Scotland. *See* United Kingdom
Pan Am Flight 103 terrorist case. *See* Libya
Sea. *See* Fish and marine mammals; Maritime issues
Carriage of Goods by Sea Act (COGSA). *See* Carriage of goods by sea
Continental Shelf. *See* Continental Shelf

Sea (continued)
UN Convention on Law of. *See* Law of the Sea, UN Convention on (UNCLOS)
underwater cultural heritage. *See* Underwater cultural heritage
Sea turtle protection. *See* Fish and marine mammals
Seafarers, International Convention on Standards of Training, Certification and Watchkeeping for, 1991-99: 784–85
Searches
Chemical Weapons Convention inspections and, **1991-99:** 2349–50
constitutional rights outside U.S., **1989-90:** 100–107; **1991-99:** 194
Law of the Sea and, **2004:** 681–82, 691–92, 693
PATRIOT Act, USA (2005) and, **2006:** 361–63
unflagged vessels, **2002:** 1052–54, 1056
unreasonable, prohibitions on, **2005:** 294
Section 1983 actions
Vienna Convention on Consular Relations and, **2006:** 82–85; **2008:** 36, 42–44
Secure Electronic Network for Travelers Rapid Inspection (SENTRI), 2005: 4
Secure Fence Act of 2006, 2006: 50–52
Securities intermediaries. *See* Hague Conventions
Security Council, UN. *See also* Law of war; Nonproliferation, *subheading*: UN Security Council; Nuclear Non-Proliferation Treaty (NPT) (1968); Sanctions; United Nations, *subheading*: Charter of (1945); *specific countries*
arms embargoes, **2001:** 801–2; **2002:** 881–82, 885, 894, 923; **2003:** 152, 1081–84; **2004:** 884, 890–92, 922–23, 962, 1069–70; **2005:** 894, 899, 903, 929–30; **2006:** 1047, 1269; **2007:** 1004, 1006–7, 1048; **2008:** 87–88, 1021–23
authority to create ad hoc tribunals, **1991-99:** 603–7; **2000:** 213–15; **2007:** 184–85, 190–92, 835
corporate liability, **2005:** 395
genocide protection, **2005:** 458–60
Georgia. *See* Georgia
human rights issues, **2005:** 461
International Court of Justice (ICJ) and, **1991-99:** 473–77; **2000:** 290
enforcement of judgments by, **2005:** 35–36, 38–39, 55–56, 197–99; **2008:** 181–82
International Criminal Court (ICC) and, **1991-99:** 613, 615–19, 621, 624–25, 627, 628–30, 631–32, 636, 638, 639; **2005:** 391; **2008:** 145–46
determination of act of aggression, responsibility for, **2001:** 176–78
lack of oversight over, **2005:** 191, 197, 199

Security Council, UN (continued)
referrals to, **2000:** 275, 285–86; **2008:** 145–46
referral of Darfur to, **2005:** 192, 193–96
relationship with, **2007:** 181–82
Kosovo, **2008:** 433–38, 845–47
UN interim administration for, **1991-99:** 2036–37
obligation of members to comply with resolutions, **1991-99:** 463, 469, 471, 476, 593, 603, 605–6, 627, 1121–22, 1197, 2103; **2000:** 406*n*
Open-Ended Working Group, **2008:** 383–84
Palestinian-Israeli conflict, **2006:** 1032–33; **2008:** 819–24
Peacebuilding Commission answerable to, **2005:** 446, 946
peacekeeping mandates, **2008:** 838–39
peacekeeper conduct, **2005:** 940–42, 945–46
Presidential Statements
on Burma, **2007:** 842–43
on Darfur, **2006:** 1053–54
on Iranian nuclear situation, **2006:** 1274–76
on Israeli use of force in Lebanon, **2006:** 1230–32
on Lebanon, **2007:** 870
on Somalia, **2008:** 848, 925
on terrorism sanctions, **2006:** 1000–3
reform of, **2005:** 444–45, 448, 457–58; **2006:** 489–90; **2007:** 401–2; **2008:** 383–85
Repertoire of Practice of, **2007:** 407
responsibility to protect, role in, **2005:** 458–60; **2008:** 856–57
Russia, succession to permanent membership of USSR in, **1991-99:** 1169–71
specialized bodies of law, creation of, **2005:** 956–60
Sudan Sanctions Committee, **2008:** 836–37
targeted sanctions to implement resolutions, **1991-99:** 1943–35; **2001:** 801–3, 806–8, 895–96; **2002:** 883–84, 889–90; **2003:** 930–34; **2004:** 935; **2006:** 995–98; **2008:** 98–101
terrorism sanctions and other counterterrorism efforts, review of 1267, 1373 and 1540 Committees, **2005:** 900–2; **2006:** 1002–3; **2008:** 87–88. *See also* Terrorism; Nonproliferation, *subheading*: sanctions, U.S.
Transitional Administration in East Timor for, **2000:** 308–10; **2001:** 426–27
women and international peace and security, **2008:** 286–88, 841
Zimbabwe, draft resolution for sanctions on, **2008:** 803–5
Resolutions:
242, **1991-99:** 1025, 1983–84, 1987, 1988, 1990; **2003:** 945, 950; **2004:** 952, 953; **2005:** 911; **2007:** 855; **2008:** 819

Security Council, UN (continued)
255, **1991-99**: 2286; **2006**: 1262
338, **1991-99**: 1025, 1983–84, 1987, 1988, 1990; **2003**: 945, 950; **2004**: 952, 953; **2005**: 911; **2007**: 855
418, **2004**: 355, 891, 1164
425, **2006**: 1038, 1226, 1228
435, **1989-90**: 161, 197–200, 198, 535
479, **2003**: 1044
552, **1991-99**: 2185; **2003**: 1044
598, **2003**: 1037, 1044
649, **2002**: 934
660, **1991-99**: 2051–53, 2054; **2000**: 618; **2002**: 934, 956–57; **2003**: 962, 972
661, **1991-99**: 1925, 1926, 1932, 2051, 2052, 2054, 2104, 2107; **2000**: 618, 620; **2002**: 934; **2005**: 870; **2006**: 1016; **2007**: 991, 994
662, **1991-99**: 2052; **2002**: 934
664, **1991-99**: 2052, 2054, 2074; **2002**: 934
665, **1991-99**: 2052, 2054, 2107; **2002**: 934
666, **1991-99**: 1926, 2052, 2054, 2062; **2002**: 934; **2006**: 1016
667, **1991-99**: 2054, 2098; **2002**: 934
669, **1991-99**: 2052, 2054; **2002**: 934
670, **1991-99**: 2052, 2054, 2062, 2067; **2002**: 934
674, **1991-99**: 2052, 2054, 2062, 2067, 2098; **2002**: 934
677, **1991-99**: 2052, 2054; **2002**: 934
678, **1991-99**: 2052, 2053, 2054, 2056, 2103, 2104, 2106, 2109, 2110, 2116–17; **2002**: 934, 937, 938, 944, 956–57; **2003**: 962, 968, 969, 970, 971–72; **2005**: 950
686, **1991-99**: 2109, 2110; **2002**: 944
687, **1991-99**: 1099, 1100, 1102–3, 1104, 2109, 2114, 2118, 2125, 2128–29, 2130; **2002**: 407–8, 934, 944–45, 957; **2003**: 454, 968, 969–70, 971, 972; **2004**: 891, 1164; **2005**: 950
688, **1991-99**: 2112, 2114, 2118; **2002**: 934, 945; **2006**: 1059
692, **1991-99**: 1100, 1103; **2002**: 407–8; **2003**: 454, 468; **2004**: 430
705, **1991-99**: 1101
706, **1991-99**: 1101, 1928–29
707, **1991-99**: 2129; **2004**: 891
713, **1991-99**: 1949
715, **1991-99**: 2129
731, **1991-99**: 458–59, 469, 1914, 1921; **2003**: 160; **2004**: 930
733, **1991-99**: 2043; **2006**: 1064; **2007**: 1004
748, **1991-99**: 459–60, 462–63, 469, 473, 476, 480, 1197, 1914, 1921–22; **2003**: 160–61, 162, 163; **2004**: 375, 930

Security Council, UN (continued)
751, **2008**: 926
757, **1991-99**: 1164, 1946, 1949, 1951, 1952
760, **1991-99**: 1952
771, **1991-99**: 591–92
777, **1991-99**: 1166
778, **1991-99**: 1101, 1929
781, **1991-99**: 2136
787, **1991-99**: 1947, 1948, 1949, 1951
794, **1991-99**: 2043–44
795, **1991-99**: 2024–25
816, **1991-99**: 2136
820, **1991-99**: 149, 1947, 1949, 1980
824, **1991-99**: 2136
827, **1991-99**: 580, 592, 593, 594; **2001**: 16, 166–67, 804; **2004**: 375; **2006**: 263
836, **1991-99**: 2136–37
837, **1991-99**: 2045
841, **1991-99**: 1887–88, 1889, 1895
842, **1991-99**: 2025
861, **1991-99**: 1887–88
864, **1991-99**: 1939–40
867, **1991-99**: 2045–46
873, **1991-99**: 1888, 1889, 1895
875, **1991-99**: 1889
883, **1991-99**: 460, 469, 473, 480, 1922, 1923; **2003**: 160–61, 162, 163; **2004**: 930
917, **1991-99**: 138–40, 1884, 1885, 1890, 1891, 1894, 1895
918, **2003**: 1081
940, **1991-99**: 1153, 1885, 2045, 2046
942, **1991-99**: 149, 1953
944, **1991-99**: 1885–86, 1895
949, **1991-99**: 2119, 2120, 2121, 2122–23; **2002**: 934
955, **1991-99**: 581, 591*n*, 606; **2000**: 204–5; **2001**: 166–67
956, **1991-99**: 823–24
984, **1991-99**: 2174, 2281–83
986, **1991-99**: 1101, 1931–36; **2000**: 619, 620–21, 625–26; **2005**: 870–73
1011, **2003**: 1081, 1082
1021, **1991-99**: 1956
1022, **1991-99**: 1955
1031, **1991-99**: 2029; **2000**: 259; **2001**: 16
1044, **1991-99**: 144, 145, 1936–37
1054, **1991-99**: 144, 1937

Security Council, UN (continued)
1070, **1991-99**: 1937
1074, **1991-99**: 1957
1088, **2000**: 259
1127, **1991-99**: 145, 146, 1941–43
1130, **1991-99**: 145, 146
1132, **1991-99**: 147
1135, **1991-99**: 145, 146
1153, **1991-99**: 1934, 1936
1154, **1991-99**: 2126–27, 2129
1160, **1991-99**: 1958, 2032–33, 2151
1172, **1991-99**: 2294, 2297, 2300
1173, **1991-99**: 1943
1177, **2006**: 1056
1192, **1991-99**: 480; **2003**: 149, 160–61, 162
1194, **1991-99**: 2129
1199, **1991-99**: 2138–39, 2140–41
1203, **1991-99**: 2138–39, 2140–41
1205, **1991-99**: 2129
1214, **2001**: 883
1244, **1991-99**: 2033–37, 2038–39, 2041, 2149; **2001**: 16, 806, 807; **2003**: 930, 931, 932; **2005**: 936; **2007**: 429–31, 433; **2008**: 433, 435–36, 437, 438, 846, 847
1264, **1991-99**: 2047–48
1267, **1991-99**: 1966–67; **2001**: 803, 883; **2002**: 101, 119, 881, 885, 886–87, 888, 889; **2003**: 152, 154, 156, 168, 169, 170–71, 1083; **2004**: 117, 121–22, 650; **2005**: 894, 899, 900; **2006**: 206, 999, 1000–1003; **2007**: 1049; **2008**: 87–88, 92, 99
1269, **2001**: 883, 915
1272, **2000**: 308–10; **2001**: 426
1306, **2001**: 797, 800
1308, **2003**: 816–17; **2006**: 1066
1315, **2000**: 243
1325, **2002**: 276; **2003**: 291–92; **2007**: 320
1333, **2001**: 801–2; **2002**: 881, 885, 889; **2003**: 152, 168, 1083; **2006**: 1003; **2008**: 87
1343, **2001**: 800
1363, **2001**: 883
1368, **2001**: 855–56, 883, 915; **2002**: 906; **2003**: 346, 1017; **2004**: 970, 973, 974, 985
1372, **1991-99**: 1937
1373, **2001**: 860–61, 893–94; **2002**: 119; **2003**: 152, 154, 169, 175, 949; **2004**: 97, 117, 118–19, 123, 970, 973, 974, 985, 1095; **2005**: 111, 442, 900, 902; **2006**: 999, 1295; **2008**: 99

Security Council, UN (continued)
1377, **2007**: 858
1382, **2001**: 815
1386, **2001**: 424
1390, **2002**: 119, 885, 889; **2003**: 152, 168, 175, 240, 1082–83; **2006**: 1003; **2008**: 87
1397, **2003**: 945; **2007**: 855; **2008**: 819
1402, **2008**: 819
1409, **2002**: 894–95, 896–97
1422, **2002**: 157, 161–65; **2003**: 228, 231–32; **2004**: 179, 184–88
1430, **2006**: 1056
1441, **2002**: 937–40, 957; **2003**: 961–65, 968, 969, 970, 971–73
1448, **2003**: 934, 935
1452, **2002**: 887–88; **2003**: 152, 157, 174; **2006**: 1001, 1005
1454, **2002**: 895–97
1455, **2003**: 152, 168, 169–70, 175, 240, 1082–83; **2004**: 122
1466, **2006**: 1056
1472, **2003**: 974
1483, **2003**: 454–55, 545, 546, 914–15, 920, 983, 985, 988, 989, 991, 992; **2004**: 430, 883–84, 886, 887, 888, 891–92, 902–3, 1049; **2005**: 228–29, 870, 958; **2008**: 730–32
1487, **2003**: 231–33; **2004**: 179, 188
1495, **2003**: 958
1497, **2003**: 233–34, 240, 955–57
1500, **2003**: 985–86
1502, **2003**: 994–95
1503, **2003**: 219–21
1506, **1991-99**: 1923–24; **2003**: 161, 163–64, 166; **2004**: 927
1509, **2003**: 234, 957
1510, **2003**: 959
1511, **2003**: 986–91; **2005**: 958; **2007**: 855, 856
1515, **2003**: 948, 950; **2004**: 955; **2007**: 855; **2008**: 819
1518, **2004**: 883–84
1521, **2004**: 920, 935; **2007**: 821, 822*n*
1526, **2004**: 121; **2005**: 898, 902; **2006**: 1004
1529, **2004**: 35, 940–41
1532, **2004**: 919, 920
1533, **2007**: 823
1538, **2004**: 893–94
1539, **2004**: 281
1540, **2004**: 107, 1060, 1092–1118, 1130; **2005**: 447, 900–901, 1059, 1092, 1094, 1103, 1104–23; **2006**: 1241, 1242, 1267, 1294; **2007**: 1063, 1072, 1073; **2008**: 952, 999, 1000–1, 1007–8

Security Council, UN (continued)
1546, **2004**: 883–84, 887, 888, 890, 891, 1046, 1048–50; **2005**: 958, 959, 975–76, 978, 1039–40; **2006**: 1194, 1199, 1200, 1235, 1236; **2007**: 856, 956, 959, 962*n*
1547, **2004**: 960
1556, **2004**: 245, 962, 963; **2005**: 929; **2006**: 1047
1558, **2006**: 1064
1559, **2005**: 880–82, 884, 885, 931–33; **2006**: 1037, 1038, 1041, 1226, 1228–29, 1230; **2007**: 858, 870; **2008**: 824–27, 830
1564, **2004**: 240, 963
1566, **2004**: 104–7, 119–21; **2005**: 902
1572, **2004**: 922–23; **2006**: 995
1574, **2004**: 964–66
1583, **2006**: 1226
1590, **2005**: 928, 931, 940–41; **2006**: 1047
1591, **2005**: 929, 931; **2006**: 975, 976
1593, **2005**: 192, 193–96, 931, 952; **2007**: 183; **2008**: 842
1595, **2005**: 878–79, 881, 884, 932
1596, **2006**: 997
1603, **2005**: 934
1612, **2007**: 354
1617, **2005**: 903–4; **2006**: 1004, 1005
1618, **2007**: 855, 856
1624, **2006**: 199–210, 999
1627, **2005**: 941–42
1636, **2005**: 880, 884; **2006**: 985
1637, **2005**: 1039; **2007**: 855, 856, 956, 962*n*
1638, **2006**: 276
1644, **2005**: 885–86
1645, **2005**: 455–57
1649, **2006**: 997
1655, **2006**: 1226
1661, **2006**: 1057
1664, **2006**: 272–75; **2007**: 192
1672, **2006**: 975–76, 1054
1673, **2007**: 1063
1679, **2006**: 1043
1680, **2006**: 1037, 1038, 1226, 1228; **2007**: 858, 870
1686, **2006**: 272
1688, **2006**: 275–77
1689, **2007**: 821, 822*n*
1695, **2006**: 1265, 1266, 1269; **2007**: 1073
1696, **2006**: 1278–80; **2007**: 1031, 1033, 1034, 1037, 1074
1697, **2006**: 1060

Security Council, UN (continued)
1698, **2006:** 997
1701, **2006:** 1034–42, 1060–61, 1233; **2007:** 858, 869, 870, 871; **2008:** 826*n*, 830
1706, **2006:** 423, 1047–54
1709, **2006:** 1048
1718, **2006:** 1268, 1271; **2007:** 1027–31, 1073–74
1720, **2006:** 1064
1723, **2006:** 1235, 1236; **2007:** 856, 951
1724, **2006:** 1063–64
1725, **2006:** 1061–63
1730, **2006:** 1003; **2007:** 391, 825
1735, **2006:** 1003, 1004
1737, **2006:** 1281–82; **2007:** 857, 1031, 1032, 1034, 1035, 1037, 1038, 1040, 1042–45; **2008:** 969*n*, 971, 973, 979
1744, **2007:** 1004
1747, **2007:** 857, 1031, 1032, 1033, 1034, 1037, 1038, 1042–45, 1048; **2008:** 971, 973, 979
1757, **2007:** 190, 192, 835, 858; **2008:** 141
1763, **2008:** 999
1769, **2007:** 817, 860, 867; **2008:** 838, 842
1772, **2008:** 847–48
1773, **2007:** 869
1790, **2008:** 858
1801, **2008:** 847
1803, **2008:** 939, 969–75, 969*n*, 971, 973, 974, 979, 984
1808, **2008:** 869
1810, **2008:** 999–1001
1811, **2008:** 1023
1813, **2008:** 850, 851
1816, **2008:** 646, 922–32
1820, **2008:** 286–88
1822, **2008:** 87
1828, **2008:** 841–43
1831, **2008:** 848
1835, **2008:** 969–75
1838, **2008:** 646, 848, 922–32
1839, **2008:** 845
1844, **2008:** 926, 1022, 1023
1846, **2008:** 848, 922–32
1850, **2008:** 819–24
1851, **2008:** 848, 922–32
1853, **2008:** 1022–23
1859, **2008:** 460*n*

Security Treaty between Australia, New Zealand, and the U.S. (ANZUS treaty, 1952), 2001: 862; **2004:** 985; **2005:** 372
Seizure of assets. *See also* Expropriation; Iran–United States Claims Tribunal; Terrorism; *specific countries*
in connection with extradition, **2000:** 185*n*; **2004:** 78–79
constitutionality, **2002:** 97–101
Convention Against Illicit Traffic in Narcotic Drugs and Psychotropic Substances and, **1989-90:** 129
of designated terrorist organization chartered in U.S., **2002:** 94–98. *See also* Terrorism
diplomatic property, immunity to. *See* Diplomatic missions and personnel
Foreign Narcotics Kingpin Designation Act, **2008:** 114–15
Foreign Narcotics Kingpins Sanctions Regulations, **2000:** 744–45. *See also* Drug trade
foreign state assets, immunity to. *See* Foreign Sovereign Immunities Act (FSIA) (1976)
forfeited assets, sharing of, **2004:** 140–41
freezing or blocking, **2004:** 21, 123, 173, 527, 577–78*n*, 650, 883–89, 901–3, 919–22, 929, 930, 933–34, 975, 1110–12. *See also* Terrorism
international agreement to prosecute narcotrafficking, **1989-90:** 129
International Criminal Tribunal for the Former Yugoslavia and, **2004:** 173
International Emergency Economic Powers Act. *See* Emergency Economic Powers Act, International (IEEPA)
provisions of Treaty of Peace with Japan, **2000:** 510–12, 524–25, 526, 538
United Nations
Missions to UN, property of, immunity to. *See* United Nations, *subheading*: immunity
UN property, immunity to. *See* United Nations, *subheading*: immunity
Senegal
Article 98 agreement (nonsurrender of Americans to ICC), **2003:** 238
Sentencing and sentences
capital punishment. *See* Capital punishment
cruel and unusual punishment. *See* Cruel and unusual punishment
life imprisonment
assurances in extradition treaties. *See* Extradition, *subheading*: denial of, possible bases for
juveniles, **2006:** 366–69

Sentencing and sentences (continued)
Sentenced Persons, Council of Europe Convention on transfer of (COE Convention), **1989-90**: 72; **1991-99**: 381–83; **2001**: 52; **2005**: 71, 74–75; **2008**: 51. *See also* Prisoner transfer
Serving Criminal Sentences Abroad, Inter-American Convention on. *See* Prisoner transfer
SENTRI (Secure Electronic Network for Travelers Rapid Inspection), 2005: 4
Separation of powers, **1991-99**: 709, 985, 992; **2004**: 1012; **2008**: 157, 224–26, 471–75, 892, 894, 902, 907, 911–14. *See also* President, U.S., *subheadings*: foreign affairs authority *and* separation of powers
constitutional challenges
to extradition, **1991-99**: 413, 416, 417–19, 421, 430
to FSIA § 1605, **1991-99**: 1234–40, 1248–52
Guantanamo detainees and, **2008**: 902, 907, 911–14
international anti-suit injunctions and, **2004**: 842
jurisdiction over U.S. citizen held abroad, **2004**: 203, 204–5
Military Commissions and, **2004**: 1019
nonjusticiable question. *See* Foreign affairs; World War II, *subheading*: claims
presidential reservation of constitutional prerogatives in signing legislation; signing statements, **1989-90**: 508–12; **1991-99**: 801–8, 922–24; **2002**: 242–45; **2003**: 269–71; **2004**: 214–18; **2005**: 2, 242, 607, 1037–39; **2006**: 305–7, 402, 536–37, 1286–87
recommendations for foreign policy legislation, unfettered power to make, **2002**: 243
veto of biological and chemical weapons control legislation, **1989-90**: 508–12
service of process on foreign official by federal security officers. *See* Service of process abroad
treaty power and, **1991-99**: 67, 661, 757, 967, 977. *See also* Treaties, generally
use of force, **2005**: 962, 1001–4, 1009, 1014, 1037
war powers, **1991-99**: 2162–70; **2000**: 758–65; **2004**: 209, 210–11; **2005**: 1010–11, 1012–13, 1016; **2008**: 902
authority with respect to enemy combatants, **2002**: 990–91, 996, 997, 998–1001, 1006; **2004**: 997–98, 1001, 1003, 1009–11, 1012–13; **2005**: 1004–5, 1008, 1011–12, 1018. *See also* Detainees, military
commander-in-chief, **2004**: 215, 216, 941
congressional authorization for military operations, **1991-99**: 2056

Separation of powers (continued)
in Bosnia, **1991-99**: 2168–70
in Haiti, **1991-99**: 804, 2162–68
in Iraq, **2002**: 933–37
in Kosovo, **1991-99**: 2155–62
in response to 9/11, **2001**: 864–66, 871–72
September 11 terrorist attacks, 2001: 855–941; **2002**: 106, 112–13, 902, 904, 935, 937, 951, 953, 973, 1011–12, 1025; **2003**: 136, 153, 170, 172, 254, 285, 286, 287, 289, 323, 324, 327, 328–29, 346–47, 385–86, 411, 508–9, 533–36, 551–52, 555–57, 974, 1017, 1019, 1089, 1090; **2004**: 96, 114, 116, 969, 970, 972, 984–85, 995, 1003. *See also* Detainees, military; Geneva Conventions on law of war (1949); Hague Conventions, *subheading*: on law of war; Law of war
victim compensation fund, **2002**: 408, 409
Serbia. *See also* International Criminal Tribunal for Former Yugoslavia (ICTY); Serbia and Montenegro
Alien Tort Statute and, **1991-99**: 982, 983, 988
Belgrade embassy of U.S., attack on, **2008**: 493–95
Defining the Rights, Immunities and Privileges of Consular Offices (1881) (U.S.–Serbia), **1989-90**: 339–40, 342, 346, 347–48
head-of-state immunity, **1991-99**: 1281–82
immigration issues, **1991-99**: 133, 134–35, 147–49
peace process after breakup of Yugoslavia, **1991-99**: 1147, 1975, 1979–82
prosecution for human rights violations in, **1991-99**: 522–28, 583, 867
religious freedom in, **1991-99**: 925
sanctions on, **1991-99**: 1168, 1945–62, 2027–28; **2001**: 803–6
Serbia-Montenegro as successor state, **1991-99**: 1162–69
transfer of uranium stocks to Russia, **2002**: 1041–42
UN membership, **1991-99**: 1163–67
unblocking of blocked assets of, **2002**: 897–900
U.S. military assistance, **2006**: 278
Serbia and Montenegro, 2004: 173, 174. *See also* Montenegro
Constitutional Charter, **2005**: 939
International Criminal Tribunal for Former Yugoslavia (ICTY), **2004**: 173, 174; **2005**: 188–93, 199, 217, 395, 410–11, 430, 939. *See also* International Criminal Tribunal for Former Yugoslavia (ICTY)
Kosovo peace process, role in, **2005**: 935–36, 938
Montenegro, status of, **2005**: 499, 939–40
sturgeon, beluga, ban on importation of caviar from, **2005**: 754–55
U.S. trade policy, **2004**: 655–56

Service of process abroad
Convention parties objecting to, **2000:** 150–52
service by U.S. private attorney, **2004:** 70–71, 839–40
service on U.S. private attorney, **2005:** 856–59
untimely service by Central Authority, **2004:** 870–72
on diplomatic and consular personnel. *See* Consular Relations, Vienna Convention on (VCCR); Diplomatic missions and personnel, *subheading*: immunity; Diplomatic Relations, Vienna Convention on; Foreign Sovereign Immunities Act (FSIA) (1976)
Foreign Sovereign Immunities Act, under. *See* Foreign Sovereign Immunities Act (FSIA) (1976)
Hague Convention on (1965), **2000:** 152; **2002:** 877–79; **2003:** 859–63, 866–67, 887–92; **2004:** 70–71, 827, 829, 839–40, 861–62, 866–74, 879; **2005:** 810–13, 839, 853–56; **2008:** 83*n*
by email, **2004:** 873–74
by mail or delivery service, **2000:** 152; **2002:** 877–79; **2003:** 887–92; **2004:** 866–70; **2005:** 847–52
unknown address of party to be served, **2006:** 971, 972
indirect service
service on U.S. Coalition Provisional Authority as agent for Iraqi defendants, **2004:** 558–59
service on U.S. private attorney, **2005:** 856–59
service on U.S. protective detail for visiting foreign dignitary, **1991-99:** 1335–36; **2001:** 549–53; **2002:** 581–95; **2004:** 550–53
service on visiting foreign officials as agents for foreign defendant, **2001:** 319–20, 531–36; **2004:** 547–50, 553–58; **2006:** 681–82
inviolability and. *See* Diplomatic missions and personnel; Head-of-state immunity; Immunity; Inviolability
by mail or delivery service, **2002:** 877–79; **2003:** 887–925; **2004:** 866–70, 874–75; **2005:** 859–61
foreign governments objecting to service by mail by foreign government, **2000:** 150–52
by publication in newspaper, **2006:** 970–73
in Russian Federation, **2000:** 150–52; **2005:** 810–13
service in violation of local law, **2000:** 152; **2003:** 892–95
service of foreign process in U.S., procedures for, **2003:** 865–68; **2004:** 70–71, 839–40; **2005:** 856–59
service on foreign state, time requirement under customary international law, **1989-90:** 295; **2004:** 457–58

Service of process abroad (continued)
service on visiting foreign government officials, **2001**: 319–20, 531–36, 549–53; **2002**: 581–95; **2003**: 399; **2004**: 547–58. *See also* Foreign Sovereign Immunities Act (FSIA) (1976); Head-of-state immunity; Immunity
Settlement of disputes. *See* Arbitration
Settlement of Investment Disputes, Convention for, 2004: 657
Sex trade, 2003: 189–90. *See also* Trafficking in persons
of children, **2003**: 198–99; **2007**: 334–35, 337–38, 339–40, 344; **2008**: 291–95, 297–99
child sex tourism, **2008**: 293
criminalization of trafficking in persons for, **2004**: 154–55; **2008**: 292
Eliminating Demand for Trafficked Women and Girls for All Forms of Exploitation (Resolution 49/2, UN Commission on Status of Women), **2005**: 162–64
and HIV/AIDS control programs, **2007**: 254–55
as *jus cogens* violation, **2003**: 514
PROTECT Act (2003), **2003**: 189–90
standards of behavior for UN peacekeepers, **2004**: 168
trafficking of persons and, **2007**: 167–68; **2008**: 291–92, 295–96
World War II "comfort women" cases, **2004**: 475–76, 483
Sexual abuse and violence. *See also* Rape; Trafficking in persons
sale of children protocol, **2000**: 360–61, 362; **2008**: 290–300, 317
Security Council resolutions on, **2008**: 286–88
UN peacekeepers committing, **2005**: 449, 945–46; **2006**: 1065–68; **2007**: 319–21; **2008**: 286, 288, 840–41
Sexual harassment
immunity of UN officials, **2008**: 501–4
immunity under FSIA from claims of, **2002**: 477–78
Title VII actions, **2005**: 263–64
Sexual orientation, 2000: 353
persecution based on, **2000**: 398
Seychelles, 2002: 133
extradition and mutual legal assistance, **2000**: 185*n*
maritime issues, **2000**: 706–9; **2008**: 125
Shanghai Communique (1972), **1991-99**: 687
Shark Finning Prohibition Act (2000), **2003**: 798; **2008**: 706, 707
Sherman Act (1890), **1991-99**: 1529, 1530–36; **2003**: 557–58
Shrimp imports. *See* Fish and marine mammals, *subheading*: sea turtle protection
Sierra Leone
Armed Servicemembers' Protection Act waiver, **2003**: 238
arms embargo, **2007**: 1007
child soldiers, **2008**: 304

Sierra Leone (continued)
conflict resolution efforts in, **1991-99**: 2015–18
crimes against humanity in, **2000**: 243–44
diamond trade, **1991-99**: 522; **2001**: 797–801; **2003**: 706, 708–9
extradition and mutual legal assistance, **2000**: 185*n*
government efforts regarding trafficking in persons, **2004**: 164
immigration issues
suspension of entry of certain aliens of, **1991-99**: 146–47; **2000**: 19–21
temporary protected status for nationals of, **1991-99**: 245; **2003**: 38
orphan adoption program, **2003**: 123
Special Court for, **2001**: 168; **2002**: 147–48, 322–23; **2003**: 339–40; **2004**: 130, 180–81; **2005**: 190–91, 217, 430; **2006**: 256–57, 275–77; **2008**: 140–41
termination of national emergency, **2004**: 934–35
war crimes in, **2004**: 130–31; **2008**: 140
Singapore
act of state doctrine, **2005**: 577–78
antiterrorism cooperation, **2002**: 118, 890
drug trade (methamphetamines), **2007**: 164–66
extradition and mutual legal assistance, **2000**: 185*n*
extradition to, allegation of torture risk in, **1991-99**: 942–43
free trade agreement, **2002**: 723; **2004**: 618; **2005**: 640, 757; **2006**: 766*n*
immunity, Singapore State Immunity Act, **2005**: 529; **2006**: 609
longshore work prohibition on alien crewmen from, **2002**: 757; **2003**: 764
money laundering in, **2004**: 135
nonimmigrant visa waiver pilot program, **1991-99**: 76
Open Skies agreement, **2001**: 565–66
Proliferation Security Initiative, **2004**: 1074
Regional Emerging Diseases Intervention Center, **2004**: 785–86
Straits of Malacca and Singapore, **2006**: 806–10
trade agreement with U.S., **2003**: 679–80
U.S.–Singapore environmental cooperation agreement, **2003**: 811–12
Warsaw Convention and, **2001**: 560–61*n*
Slavery and forced labor, **2004**: 152–54, 156, 281, 374, 447, 499, 528, 659, 924*n*
Abolition of Slavery, the Slave Trade and Institutions and Practices Similar to Slavery, Convention on (1956), **1991-99**: 996–98; **2003**: 735; **2004**: 153, 154
Alien Tort Statute litigation alleging trafficking in persons to the UAE for forced labor, **2008**: 227–36
in Burma, **2007**: 317; **2008**: 796, 796*n*

Slavery and forced labor (continued)
in China prisons, **1991-99**: 1000–1003, 1456, 1458
forced labor trafficking, **2005**: 156–57, 159, 162, 164; **2008**: 115, 227–36
as human rights violation, **2007**: 275–77; **2008**: 325
Slave Trade and Slavery, Convention to Suppress (1926), **2003**: 735
South African apartheid-era claims, **2004**: 354–61
trafficking as modern-day, **2004**: 280
trafficking in persons and, **2007**: 167–68; **2008**: 115
U.S. constitutional and statutory prohibitions, **2007**: 312, 337, 340; **2008**: 297
World War II-era claims for forced labor, **1991-99**: 989, 992, 1048–49, 1070–71; **2003**: 468–74; **2004**: 441–45; **2005**: 482, 484, 489, 490; **2007**: 423

Slovak Republic
EU accession and trade agreements, **2006**: 754–56
extradition and mutual legal assistance, **2006**: 137, 147
intellectual property rights, **2006**: 769
reciprocating country designation for child support, **2008**: 759
visa waiver program, **2008**: 81–83

Slovakia
diplomatic relations, **1991-99**: 764, 1148–49, 1174–75
educational exchange program, **1991-99**: 1807
extradition and mutual legal assistance, **2000**: 185*n*
Gabcikovo-Nagymaros Project case, **2000**: 664–65
NATO membership, **2003**: 424–26; **2004**: 411–12
naturalization treaty, **2002**: 203
Open Skies (aerial observation) treaty, **1991-99**: 2238; **2002**: 1029
preservation of American heritage in, **1991-99**: 1794
reciprocating country designation for child support, **2001**: 51
trade and investment agreements, **1991-99**: 1466, 1480–82
  bilateral investment treaty, **2003**: 687–94; **2004**: 624

Slovenia
EU accession and trade agreements, **2006**: 754–56
extradition and mutual legal assistance, **2000**: 185*n*; **2006**: 137, 147
NATO membership, **2003**: 424–26; **2004**: 411–12
nonimmigrant visa waiver pilot program, **1991-99**: 76
peace process after breakup of Yugoslavia, **1991-99**: 1979–82
preservation of American heritage in, **1991-99**: 1793–94
Treaty on Open Skies (aerial observation), **2004**: 1068–69
UN membership, **1991-99**: 1163
U.S. recognition and diplomatic relations, **1991-99**: 1146–48, 1945, 1979
Wassenaar member countries, added to list of, **2005**: 1137
weapons of mass destruction nonproliferation, **2004**: 1130

Smuggling. *See also* Trafficking in persons
of goods. *See* Crime
of persons. *See also* Trafficking in persons
Smuggling of Migrants by Land, Sea and Air, Protocol against the (Smuggling Protocol), **2000:** 24, 221–23; **2003:** 142, 213, 736; **2004:** 95–96, 99–101, 102–3, 141–42, 149–63, 201–2; **2005:** 153–56; **2006:** 838–40; **2007:** 1067
Social rights. *See* Cultural issues; Human rights, *subheading*: economic, social and cultural rights
Social Security Act (1935), 2001: 49, 50; **2005:** 144
Social Security payments
bilateral totalization agreements, **2007:** 81
Softwood lumber disputes. *See* Canada; North American Free Trade Agreement (NAFTA), *subheading*: Chapter 11 disputes
Solomon Islands
environmental protection agreement, **2002:** 791
extradition and mutual legal assistance, **2000:** 185*n*
fish and marine mammals, **2002:** 190
South Pacific regional environmental convention, **1989-90:** 491
Somalia
arms embargo, **2004:** 1070; **2007:** 1007; **2008:** 1022–23
child soldiers, **2003:** 308
extension of temporary protected status of refugees from, **2003:** 36
Horn of Africa Recovery and Food Security Act, **1991-99:** 938
lack of functioning government, **2004:** 16
removal of alien to, **2005:** 14–18
peace and stability, promotion of, **2007:** 863–64; **2008:** 832–33, 847–50, 922–32
piracy, **2008:** 645–47, 847–50, 922–32, 1022–23
cooperation with Transitional Federal Government of Somalia (TFG) against. *See specific countries*
Convention for the Suppression of Unlawful Acts Against the Safety of Maritime Navigation and efforts to combat, **2008:** 126–29, 926–28, 930–32
Security Council resolutions, **2006:** 1061–64; **2008:** 622–23, 645–47, 847–50, 922–32, 1022–23
temporary protected status for nationals of, **1991-99:** 245
UN Convention on Rights of the Child, nonratification of, **2005:** 387
UN humanitarian relief operations, **1991-99:** 2043–45
World Food Programme deliveries to, **2008:** 925, 927
South Africa
apartheid-era claims against multinational corporations, **2003:** 387–90, 399; **2004:** 351*n*, 354–61; **2005:** 400–411; **2008:** 236–38
child support enforcement, **2006:** 943–44

South Africa (continued)
Comprehensive Anti-Apartheid Act (1986), **1989-90**: 522–23; **2004**: 360
consular notification cooperation with U.S., **2006**: 88–89
Cote d'Ivoire peace process, involvement in, **2005**: 933–34
domain name ownership case, **2002**: 518–19
drug trade (methamphetamines), **2007**: 164–66
educational exchange program, **1991-99**: 1807–8
extradition and mutual legal assistance, **2000**: 166, 185*n*; **2001**: 92*n*
fish and marine mammals, **2004**: 766
Namibian Independence and, **1989-90**: 197, 198, 199
parental child abduction, **2004**: 60
Hague Child Abduction Convention, compliance with, **2003**: 127
private international law and, **2004**: 835
Treaty on Non-Proliferation of Nuclear Weapons (NPT), compliance with, **2005**: 1107
Truth Commissions in, **1991-99**: 962
U.S. military assistance, **2006**: 278
waiver of Article 98 agreement with U.S. (nonsurrender of Americans to ICC), **2006**: 279
women's justice program, U.S. assistance for, **2005**: 307
South Korea. *See* Korea, South (Republic of Korea (ROK))
South Ossetia
Georgia–Russia conflict over, **2008**: 863–70
Southeast Europe Trade Preference Act (2000), **2001**: 666
Southern African Customs Union (SACU), **2002**: 721–23
Trade, Investment, and Development Cooperation Agreement (TIDCA), **2008**: 576–77
Sovereign immunity. *See also* Foreign Sovereign Immunities Act (FSIA) (1976); Immunity; Sovereignty
absolute sovereign immunity doctrine
China and, **2003**: 397
Japan and, **2001**: 432–33
USSR claims of, **1989-90**: 277–91
before adoption of Foreign Sovereign Immunities Act in U.S., **2000**: 474–75; **2001**: 429, 432–33, 457; **2002**: 503–11. *See also* absolute sovereign immunity doctrine, *this heading*; restrictive theory, *this heading*
attachment, garnishment, and liens, **2008**: 410–18
Australian Foreign States Immunities Act of 1985, **2005**: 529
of Canadian power utility, **2006**: 550–58
Canadian State Immunity Act, **2005**: 529; **2006**: 609
deference to U.S. foreign policy concerns in cases where no immunity, **2005**: 469–84

Sovereign immunity (continued)
European Convention on State Immunity, **2001**: 509; **2005**: 527–28; **2006**: 599, 603, 607
government-owned vessels, **1989-90**: 291–94. *See also* sunken government property, U.S. and foreign provisions, *this heading*
International Convention for the Unification of Certain Rules Regarding Immunity of State Owned Vessels, **1989-90**: 292
Protocol to Convention on the Prevention of Marine Pollution by Dumping of Wastes and Other Matter and, **2007**: 703
of individuals sued in their official capacity under federal common law, **1989-90**: 302; **2006**: 629–52
Iran–United States Claims Tribunal, claims against U.S. and, **2008**: 410–18
Italian law on execution against property of foreign state, **1989-90**: 296–302
Libyan Claims Resolution Act (2008), **2008**: 399–402, 406–8
New York Passport Agency, **2006**: 307
Pakistan State Immunity Ordinance, **2005**: 529
passport-related, **2006**: 307
restrictive theory, **1991-99**: 1200–1204; **2000**: 475; **2003**: 503–4; **2004**: 455, 459, 463, 464, 466–67, 470
Singapore State Immunity Act, **2005**: 529; **2006**: 609
sunken government property, U.S. and foreign provisions, **2004**: 716–19. *See also* government-owned vessels, *this heading*
Tate letter U.S., **2001**: 457; **2002**: 465–66, 505–9
UK State Immunity Act, **2005**: 529; **2006**: 609
UN Convention on Jurisdictional Immunities of States and Their Properties, **2002**: 571–72; **2004**: 455–58; **2005**: 528–29; **2006**: 599–600, 603, 607–9
of United States
Algiers Accords, no sovereign immunity to certain claims by Iran in U.S. courts, **2000**: 439–40; **2008**: 414, 416
Alien Tort Statute, no waiver under, **1991-99**: 1126–28; **2004**: 364–65
American Institute in Taiwan, no waiver for, **2001**: 239–41; **2002**: 245–46
claims against U.S. by private Korean national, no waiver for, **2000**: 489–90, 498–99
claims related to downing of Iran Air Flight 655, no waiver, **1989-90**: 212
foreign country exception to waiver of under Federal Tort Claims Act, **2004**: 342

Sovereign immunity (continued)
in foreign relations, **2008:** 245
Hague Convention on law of war (1907), no waiver to claims by Panamanian businesses, **1991-99:** 1126–28
international agreements, accession to not constituting waiver, **1989-90:** 311–12
U.S. policy not to assert as defendant in litigation abroad where not available in U.S., **1989-90:** 294–95
World War II-era claims, U.S. undertakings to oppose challenge to sovereign immunity in certain cases, **2000:** 450, 489
Sovereignty, 1991-99: 18, 1147, 1158, 1256, 1365, 1802; **2004:** 913. *See also* Foreign Sovereign Immunities Act (FSIA) (1976); Sovereign immunity
act of state and, **2005:** 582
Alien Tort Statute litigation as intruding on, **2003:** 401; **2005:** 398, 402, 412, 414; **2008:** 220
ambassadors and (historically), **1991-99:** 1326–27; **2004:** 345
Arctic, **1991-99:** 1777; **2008:** 623
areas of special sovereignty of U.S., **2003:** 485
arms control and nuclear nonproliferation and, **1991-99:** 2210, 2232, 2245
arrest of individual within state's territory who had voluntarily traveled there, **2007:** 964
authentication or notarization of documents related to, **2004:** 70
border controls and, **2005:** 336; **2008:** 343
Cambodia, during political transition in, **1989-90:** 529, 530–31, 535
claims to in Antarctica, **2004:** 733; **2008:** 625
Convention on Rights of the Child impinging on U.S., **2005:** 323
country code top level domains (ccTLD), **2005:** 655, 658
Cuban Liberty and Democratic Solidarity Act and, **1991-99:** 101
Diego Garcia and Chagos Archipelago under British, **2005:** 417
dual nationality and, **2000:** 344–45
equality of nations, **2004:** 143, 367, 545–47
exclusive economic zone rights, **1989-90:** 463–64; **2004:** 734
maritime jurisdiction and, **1991-99:** 540, 725, 1558, 1568, 1623–24; **2004:** 675–76, 684–85, 725–29, 730
maritime rights of coastal states, **2000:** 708–9
force, threat or use of and, **1991-99:** 461, 2109, 2151, 2246
state consent to foreign military presence, **1991-99:** 2234–38
U.S. military action in Panama and, **1989-90:** 560, 561
FSIA and, **2005:** 523–25, 550
Guantanamo Bay, Cuba, **2002:** 983–86; **2004:** 996, 998; **2005:** 1012; **2008:** 892–94, 914–15

Sovereignty (continued)
Hong Kong, transfer of, **1991-99**: 382–83, 404–5, 689–90, 764, 772–74, 1175–78
ICC as violating, **2002**: 150, 152, 322; **2005**: 194
international broadcast rights and, **1989-90**: 407
international criminal tribunals and, **1991-99**: 594–96
Iraq, **2004**: 1046
judicial assistance and, **2000**: 156, 157, 158; **2001**: 57; **2004**: 858, 860–63, 865
Kosovo, **2008**: 442–43
law enforcement and, **1991-99**: 443–44, 445–46, 1604; **2008**: 74–76, 78, 134–35
law of the sea and, **2003**: 716–17; **2004**: 676, 684–85, 726–27; **2005**: 678–82, 691, 699–700, 759; **2008**: 623
Lebanon, **2005**: 878–79, 881; **2007**: 39–41; **2008**: 142, 824–27
Macau, **1991-99**: 1180–81
mutual legal assistance, refusal of based on prejudice to, **2005**: 175
and nations' interest in controlling admission and departure of aliens from their territories, **2008**: 343
non-recognition of any state sovereignty over Jerusalem, **2008**: 448, 451
of Native American tribes, **2001**: 255, 260; **2006**: 353*n*
as nonjusticiable question, **2004**: 453–54
OAS Charter, **2005**: 467
of other countries, respect for, **2005**: 947, 1068
outer space, in uses of, **2001**: 722; **2005**: 714
Palau, U.S. and, **1991-99**: 811–25
Palestinian, **2005**: 912
renditions and, **1989-90**: 93–95; **2005**: 103–4
rights of state not vested in particular government, **1989-90**: 255–57
sovereign state, definition of, **1991-99**: 813, 983, 1187
standing of individual to seek remedy for violation of, **2000**: 400–2, 406–7
state over own nationals employed by international organizations, **1989-90**: 363–64
state's exclusive jurisdiction to punish offenses committed within its borders, **2007**: 961–63
submerged lands. *See* Submerged lands
sunken government property, **1991-99**: 1608–20; **2004**: 716–19
Taiwan, **2007**: 1–3; **2008**: 1–3, 443–47
transborder arrest as violation of, **2000**: 398–411; **2001**: 326–34; **2003**: 380–83; **2004**: 352
UN interim administration for Kosovo, **1991-99**: 2036–43
U.S. Bureau of Geographic Names geographic database as not reflecting U.S. views on sovereignty, **2008**: 645

Sovereignty (continued)
of United States
Alaska, claims over submerged lands. *See* Submerged lands
Beaufort sea, **2005**: 705–6; **2008**: 641
Machias Seal Island, **2005**: 707
military bases outside U.S., **1991-99**: 187–90, 353. *See also* Detainees, military, *subheading*: Guantanamo, enemy combatants[15] held in
over constituent entities, **1991-99**: 11, 13, 808–16, 817, 825–31, 835; **2008**: 206
Commonwealth of Northern Mariana Islands (CMNI) under U.S., **1989-90**: 162–64
Puerto Rico, **2000**: 340–45; **2003**: 485
over guano island, **1991-99**: 842–46
trade and, **1991-99**: 1404, 1429, 1492; **2001**: 665
treaty power and state sovereignty, **1991-99**: 652–57, 678; **2005**: 217–18
unincorporated territories and, **2002**: 249–50
Soviet Scientists Immigration Act of 1992 (SSIA), **1991-99**: 71–72; **2005**: 9
Soviet Union
agreement on trial verification and stability measures, **1989-90**: 565–66
aircraft subsidies and, **1991-99**: 2239
arms control, **1991-99**: 2242
ABM treaty, **2002**: 198–202, 205
agreement on advance notification of strategic exercises, **1989-90**: 566
agreement on prevention of accidental conflict, **1989-90**: 549–51
Anti-Ballistic Missile Treaty. *See* Anti-Ballistic Missile (ABM) Treaty (1972) (U.S.–USSR)
compliance with arms control agreements, **1989-90**: 566–76
Interim Agreement between U.S. and [former] USSR on Certain Measures with Respect to Limitation of Strategic Offensive Arms, **2002**: 181
strategic offensive arms treaty, **1991-99**: 2210, 2213
Treaty on the Reduction and Limitation of Strategic Offensive Weapons (1989) (U.S.–USSR), **1989-90**: 565, 566
assignment to U.S. of claims against U.S. nationals, **1991-99**: 672, 1269

[15] Editor's note: On March 13, 2009, in conjunction with a filing in Guantanamo habeas litigation, the U.S. Justice Department declared that it would cease to employ the term "enemy combatant" for detainees in custody of the Defense Department at the Guantanamo Bay Detention Facility.

Soviet Union (continued)
conventional armed forces in Europe treaty, **1991-99**: 2222–38
democracy promotion, **1991-99**: 1011–13
diplomatic recognition of successor states, **1991-99**: 1169–74
environmental and conservation issues, **1991-99**: 1669, 1704–5, 1782
agreement on pollution in Bering and Chukchi Seas, **1989-90**: 489–90
Bering Sea fisheries conservation agreement, **1989-90**: 487–88
FSIA claims and, **2002**: 498, 504, 507, 513
judicial assistance, **2006**: 108
maritime issues
maritime boundary agreement, **1989-90**: 434–37
navigation, bridge across international straits and, **1991-99**: 1592
U.S.–USSR agreement on rights of innocent passage, **1989-90**: 437–40, 446
memorandum of understanding on Nazi war criminals with U.S., **1989-90**: 99–100
nonproliferation. *See* Nonproliferation, *subheading*: country-specific issues
peacekeeping efforts, **1991-99**: 1142–43, 1985–86, 2021
relief from immigration requirements for certain resident nationals of, **1991-99**: 250
shootdown of Korean Airlines flight, **1991-99**: 539–40, 1351
status before 1933, **1989-90**: 247
status of Baltic states, **1989-90**: 272–73, 274, 275
treaty obligations of successor states, **1991-99**: 742–61
U.S.–Russia agreement concerning documentation of U.S.–Soviet relations, **2002**: 227
Wallenberg case and, **1989-90**: 247
sovereign immunity claims in, **1989-90**: 277–91
Warsaw Convention, damages under, **1991-99**: 1354
World War II issues, **1991-99**: 28, 1048, 1068, 1123–24
Space, **2001**: 716; **2002**: 759–60, 828–29
activities of international organizations, **2001**: 719–20; **2003**: 767–68
advertising regulation, **2001**: 718
Agreements on the Rescue of Astronauts and the Return of Astronauts and the Return of Objects Launched into Outer Space, **2003**: 765, 767
arms control, **2001**: 717; **2007**: 664–70; **2008**: 669–71
Chinese anti-satellite weapon test, **2007**: 665–67
Prevention of an Arms Race in Outer Space (PAROS), **2007**: 664–68
Assets Protocol to the UNIDROIT Convention on International Interests in Mobile Equipment (draft). *See* Mobile Equipment, Cape Town Convention on International Interests in (2001)

Space (continued)
bilateral agreements for cooperation in, **1991-99**: 1640–41
commercial launch service agreement, U.S.–China, **1989-90**: 481
commercial uses of, **1991-99**: 1647–48
Committee on the Peaceful Uses of Outer Space (COPUOS),
communications satellite regulation, **2004**: 637–39
conceptual evolution, **2003**: 764–66
debris management, **1991-99**: 1633; **2007**: 664, 665–66
destruction of decaying U.S. satellite, **2008**: 665–69
Inter-Agency Space Debris Coordination Committee (IADC) Space Debris Mitigation Guidelines, **2005**: 712
Space Debris Mitigation Guidelines, **2007**: 662–64
definition/delimitation of space, **2001**: 720–21; **2003**: 766–67
financing issues, **2001**: 722–25, 790–91; **2003**: 768–69, 834–36; **2004**: 802; **2005**: 802–5; **2008**: 747–51. *See also* Mobile Equipment, Cape Town Convention on International Interests in (2001)
geostationary orbit issues, **2001**: 721–22; **2003**: 430, 698–99
global positioning system, **1991-99**: 1632, 1635–39; **2004**: 738–41
international cooperation, **2005**: 711–13; **2006**: 845–47
declaration on, **1991-99**: 1633–34
U.S.–India cooperation in, **2005**: 1078, 1080, 1083, 1089
International Mobile Satellite Organization (IMSO), **2006**: 494–97, 838
International Space Station Partners Agreement, **1991-99**: 1641–47
"launching state" concept, **2002**: 762–63
Liability for Damage Caused by Space Objects, Convention on International, **1991-99**: 1641; **2004**: 737, 738; **2008**: 667
nuclear power, **1991-99**: 1629, 1631, 1633; **2002**: 761
Outer Space Arms Control Treaty (proposed), **2007**: 668; **2008**: 669–71
private property rights, **2004**: 741–42
registration of outer space objects, **2002**: 760–61, 762–63; **2005**: 713; **2006**: 849–51; **2007**: 661
Convention on (1975), **2003**: 770–71; **2004**: 735–36
remote sensing principles, **2001**: 717–18
salvage of sunken state spacecraft, **2001**: 688–93
status of international treaties, **2001**: 719; **2002**: 760–61
threats to U.S. space assets, **2006**: 843–45; **2007**: 665–66
transparency and confidence-building measures, **2008**: 671–72
UN Committee on Peaceful Uses of Outer Space (COPUOS), **1991-99**: 1629–35; **2001**: 716–19; **2003**: 835–36; **2005**: 711–13; **2006**: 847–51; **2007**: 661–64
UN General Assembly, Outer Space (Disarmament Aspects), **2007**: 668–70

Space (continued)
UN Outer Space Treaty, **1989-90:** 482–83; **2001:** 718, 719, 720, 722; **2002:** 759; **2003:** 765, 766, 835; **2005:** 714, 803; **2006:** 932–34; **2007:** 665, 667
U.S. space policy, **2007:** 664–65, 666, 668–69
consistent with international law, **2007:** 660–61, 667–68
U.S. National Space Policy, **2006:** 840–47; **2007:** 666, 668
U.S. patent law and, **1989-90:** 481–83
U.S. space program activities, **2006:** 847–49
U.S.–France Framework Agreement for Cooperative Activities in the Exploration and Use of Outer Space for Peaceful Purposes, **2007:** 670–72
U.S.–Russia Interoperability Work Plan, **2007:** 670
Space Station Intergovernmental Agreement, 1989-90: 482
Spacecraft. *See* Space
Spain
agreement concerning taxation exemption for certain consular employees, **2008:** 498–501
Airbus subsidies, **2004:** 603; **2005:** 622
Andorra independence and, **1991-99:** 1151
arms control and nuclear nonproliferation and, **1991-99:** 2232
missile defense cooperation, **2004:** 1066
nonproliferation sanctions, **2004:** 1136
Proliferation Security Initiative (PSI), involvement in, **2005:** 1099
consular agent, **1989-90:** 63–64
Enterprise for the Americas Initiative and, **1991-99:** 1462
environmental and conservation issues, **1991-99:** 1782
extradition and mutual legal assistance, **1991-99:** 394, 396, 443, 447, 449, 518–19; **2000:** 186*n*; **2004:** 73; **2006:** 138, 147
fish and marine mammals, **2004:** 763
Friendship and General Relations, Treaty on (Friendship Treaty), **2008:** 498–501
Guantanamo detainee transferred to, **2005:** 967
Hague Child Abduction Convention, compliance with, **2003:** 127, 129; **2006:** 102
intellectual property rights Watch List, **2008:** 608
Inter-American Tropical Tuna Commission, **2000:** 307
International Court of Justice, **1991-99:** 2152
International Space Station Partners Agreement, **1991-99:** 1642
Internet piracy, **2008:** 608
maritime counter-drug trade agreement, **1991-99:** 1607
money laundering in, **2004:** 135
NATO expansion and, **1991-99:** 1036
nonimmigrant visa waiver pilot program, **1991-99:** 76

Spain (continued)
Open Skies (aerial observation) treaty, **2002**: 1029
Philippines and, **1991-99**: 10
salvage of government-owned vessel in U.S. waters, **1991-99**: 1611–17
Somali piracy, cooperation with Transitional Federal Government of Somalia (TFG) in fight against, **2008**: 925, 927
Spanish-American War, **2005**: 243
sunken government property, **2004**: 718–19
tax agreement with U.S., **1989-90**: 415
World War II issues, **1991-99**: 1058–59
Spam, 2005: 659, 801
Special Drawing Rights, 2000: 671
Special Missions, Convention on, 2004: 1059; **2006**: 676–77
Special missions immunity, 2006: 675–80; **2007**: 447–48; **2008**: 490–91
Spent Fuel Management and the Safety of Radioactive Waste Management, Joint Convention on the Safety of, 1991-99: 2333–34
Sports. *See also* Doping in sports
detainees at Guantanamo, **2005**: 971
Sri Lanka
bilateral investment treaty, **1991-99**: 1466
extradition and mutual legal assistance, **2000**: 166, 179, 185*n*; **2001**: 92*n*
passport, request for replacement when U.S. citizen arrested for alleged involvement with terrorist group in, **2006**: 16–17
Srpska, Republika, 2004: 173, 174, 1072; **2008**: 815–16
Standards Organization, International (ISO)
specifications 7816 and 14443 for computer chips used in electronic passports, **2005**: 7–8
draft document on social responsibility, **2008**: 347–50
Standing, 2001: 207–8; **2004**: 1033
act of state doctrine, **2004**: 470
Alien Tort Statute jurisdiction, **2000**: 400–2
of domestic organization claiming harm from U.S. foreign assistance policy, **2001**: 283–93
of individual to complain of state-sponsored transborder arrest, **2000**: 410–11
of individual to enforce ICJ decisions, **2005**: 56
of individual to seek remedy for violation of national sovereignty, **2000**: 400–2, 406–7
of injured state, **1991-99**: 1108
Iranian claims against U.S. for damages arising from 1953 coup d'etat, **2003**: 451–54

Standing (continued)
lawsuit by members of Congress against Executive Branch, **1989-90**: 156–60
for violation of war powers in Kosovo, **2000**: 760–61, 762–64, 765
Marshall Islands, nonresident aliens, **2008**: 247
NAFTA Chapter 11 arbitration, **2001**: 602–5, 642–46; **2003**: 643–44
for objection to passport rules, **2003**: 491; **2004**: 452–53
OFAC not allowing educational travel to Cuba, **2008**: 810–13
for President's termination of treaty, **2002**: 198–99
private Korean national claim against U.S., **2000**: 490
private right of enforcement of international instruments. *See* Private rights of action under international instruments
of shareholders and corporations, **2001**: 602–5; **2003**: 644–48; **2004**: 598–600; **2006**: 501
of U.S. in case concerning foreign officials, **2004**: 553–54
START treaty. *See* Strategic Arms Reduction Treaty (START)
State Department Authorities Act (2006), 2006: 210–11
State Department Basic Authorities Act (1956), amendments to, 1989-90: 64, 66; **1991-99**: 345–46
State laws, U.S. *See* States, U.S.; *specific states*
State responsibility. *See also* Alien Tort Statute (ATS); Espousal of claims; Expropriation; Foreign Sovereign Immunities Act (FSIA) (1976); North American Free Trade Agreement (NAFTA)
assurance and guarantees of nonrepetition. *See* Remedies
bombing of Chinese Embassy in Belgrade, compensation for, **2000**: 421–29
bombing of U.S. embassy in Kenya, no action against U.S. arising from, **2001**: 417–21
codification, **2000**: 418–19; **2001**: 364–80
composite acts as breaches of, **2001**: 375–76
countermeasures, **1991-99**: 1107–15; **2000**: 417; **2001**: 365–71. *See also* Remedies, *subheading*: countermeasures
definition of "injured state," **2000**: 418; **2001**: 374–75
definition of international crimes, **1991-99**: 1108
dispute settlement, **1991-99**: 1108, 1110–12, 1119–21
exhaustion of local remedies, **2001**: 379. *See also* Remedies, *subheading*: exhaustion of remedies, requirement for
final version, **2001**: 380
international claims and, **2001**: 381–423
joint and several liability, **2001**: 379–80
moral damages, **2001**: 378–79
punitive damages of, **2001**: 373–77

State responsibility (continued)
reparations and compensation, **1991-99**: 1108, 1115–19; **2000**: 417–18
responsibility for acts of another state, **2001**: 376–77
responsibility for conduct of private parties, **2001**: 375
serious breaches of essential obligations, **2001**: 372–74
standing and injury, **1991-99**: 1108
treaty law and, **1991-99**: 1109
unilateral acts of state, **2000**: 419–20
for conduct of organ of the state, **2001**: 629
customary international law and, **2007**: 536, 546
damages. *See* International Law Commission draft articles on, *this heading*
ex gratia payments. *See* Remedies
International Law Commission draft articles on, **1991-99**: 1106–23; **2000**: 64–66, 68, 70–71, 416–20, 666–67; **2001**: 364–80; **2002**: 393–96; **2006**: 645*n*; **2007**: 413–14
responsibility of international organizations distinguished, **2007**: 399–401; **2008**: 381–82
International Responsibility of States for Injuries to Aliens, Convention on, **2004**: 587*n*
marine pollution, **1991-99**: 1567
military activities, **1991-99**: 498
minimum standard of treatment of aliens, **1991-99**: 1436, 1467, 1470; **2001**: 568–74, 589–90, 594–95, 627–41; **2002**: 611–16, 623–24, 642, 648–59
police protection and security, obligation to provide, **2001**: 628, 633–36
protection and security, humanitarian intervention for, **2008**: 856–57
terrorists, preventing from launching attacks outside own territory, **2006**: 1109–10
World War II claims. *See* World War II
wrongful act of state officials, **2008**: 193–215
State secrets
discussion and legal analysis of doctrine, **2007**: 241–43, 245
litigation in U.S., **2007**: 238–54
Statelessness
Convention on Reduction of (1961), **2006**: 1–2
Country Reports on Human Rights Practices (2007), **2008**: 249
Stateless Persons, Convention on (1954), **2006**: 1–2; **2008**: 28
States, U.S.
aliens and access to consular assistance, **2007**: 73–77
apostille form and affixation. *See* Authentication

States, U.S. (continued)
capital punishment, **2000:** 63, 396–97; **2001:** 313*n*; **2004:** 335, 336. *See also* Capital punishment
of juvenile offenders in, **2001:** 311
policy and practice, **2002:** 316–18
Compact Clause provisions. *See* Treaties, generally, *subheading*: U.S. law and
diplomatic and consular posts and personnel. *See also* Consular offices and personnel, *subheading*: immunity and inviolability; Diplomatic missions and personnel, *subheading*: immunity
claims related to employment by missions, **1989-90:** 389, 390–93
compensation for victims of crime committed by diplomats, **1989-90:** 332–38
tax exemption, **1989-90:** 384; **2000:** 594–99; **2001:** 538–40, 546, 548–49
Enhanced Border Security and Visa Entry Reform Act (2002), **2003:** 17
federal authority to waive states' claims, **1991-99:** 676–79
foreign policy interests, request in state court inconsistent with, **2007:** 231–35
jurisdiction and powers
extraterritorial regulation, prohibition on, **2002:** 421–25, 436, 453–56
FSIA immunity and, **2004:** 508
maritime jurisdiction, **2004:** 734–35
salvage of foreign-owned vessel, **1991-99:** 1611–17
submerged lands, claims to. *See* Submerged lands
laws of states taken into account in private international law, **2004:** 815, 824, 826, 840, 846, 859, 861, 866
legal authority. *See* Local government
NAFTA cases involving state and local governments, **2002:** 607–16
expropriation claims under NAFTA for regulatory actions of, **2001:** 574–611; **2002:** 616–23; **2003:** 615–36; **2004:** 574–89; **2005:** 593–96; **2006:** 688–93; **2007:** 535–49
Mississippi state court judicial process, **2001:** 623–42; **2002:** 623–41; **2003:** 610–15; **2004:** 573
procurement requirements, **2001:** 611, 612–18; **2002:** 641–46
nonrecognition of foreign monetary judgment, **1991-99:** 1836–41
preemption of state action by federal foreign affairs authority, **1991-99:** 775–89; **2002:** 447–52, 453; **2003:** 462–74; **2004:** 441–45, 512, 831–32; **2007:** 235–38
air crew and captain's actions under Warsaw Convention, **2008:** 524–25

States, U.S. (continued)
authority to impose sanctions against foreign government, **2002**: 446
California attachment law, **2008**: 416–18
California immigration law, **1991-99**: 786–89
federal interest in compensation plan for Nazi era victims and victims' heirs, **2000**: 460–73; **2001**: 413–17
immigration regulation, **1991-99**: 785–89
insurance industry regulation, **2000**: 416–17, 420–21, 422, 426–29, 468–70; **2008**: 777–82
international maritime commerce, **1991-99**: 775–85
MOU between Missouri and Canadian province, **2001**: 193–98
trade with Burma, **1991-99**: 785–86; **2000**: 319–40
treaties and. *See also* Treaties, generally, *subheading*: U.S. law and
agreements entered into by States. *See* Compact Clause; Treaties, generally, *subheading*: U.S. law and
effect on state law as relevant to whether U.S. agreement should be treaty, **2002**: 182
federal treaty authority and sovereignty of, **1991-99**: 652–57, 678–79, 905–6
federalism issues in, **2000**: 190–202
Corruption Convention, UN, **2005**: 168
Cybercrime Convention, **2001**: 157–59; **2003**: 193, 205–6. *See also* Crime, *subheading*: cybercrime
International Adoption Convention, **2003**: 117–18
International Health Regulations, **2007**: 211–12
prisoner transfer treaty and, **2000**: 295; **2001**: 52–53
Racial Discrimination, Convention on the Elimination of All Forms of and, **2001**: 261–62, 266, 267
reservations to transnational organized crime convention, **2004**: 143–44, 145–47, 156
Rights of the Child convention, **2000**: 290–91; **2003**: 305; **2005**: 323
UN Convention on the Law of the Sea and, **2003**: 746
U.S. extradition treaties and, **2001**: 61–62
Vienna Convention on Consular Rights, **2007**: 74–77, 200–6
national treaty obligations and, **1989-90**: 169–70; **2000**: 40–41, 295, 341–42, 386, 528–31, 536–39, 680; **2002**: 642–46
role of states in U.S. treaty practice, **2000**: 293–96, 341–43
World War II era restitution and compensation claims, **1991-99**: 1071, 1133–34
dismissal of claims against Japan by World War II-era prisoners, **2002**: 434–56

Status of forces agreements, 1991-99: 1539, 1595; **2005:** 187–88, 573
Czech Republic, **2008:** 1008–9
Iraq, Security Agreement with, **2008:** 859–62
London congestion charge, imposed on military vehicles, as contrary to, **2005:** 573–74
NATO, **2008:** 76*n*
as pre-existing international agreement under FSIA, **2004:** 479–79
Russian understanding, **2008:** 160–64
Status of refugees, convention on. *See* Refugees
Statute of limitations, 1991-99: 823, 859, 979, 1334, 1817–20; **2004:** 57*n*, 806
Alien Tort Statute, **1991-99:** 992; **2001:** 339–40; **2004:** 382
Carriage of Goods by Sea Act, **2006:** 918–28
completion of service of process, **2004:** 870–72
Convention on Nonapplicability of (1968), **2001:** 119
disappearances, draft convention on, **2006:** 427
extradition requests, **2000:** 180–81; **2004:** 77–78, 83–84
Limitation Period in the International Sale of Goods, Convention on (UN), **1991-99:** 1817–20
Limitations, Sales of Goods, Negotiable Instruments, and Guarantees, Conventions on, **2002:** 836
NAFTA Chapter 11 disputes, **2008:** 526–27
national security issues in foreign investment in U.S., none, **2006:** 778
in Torture Victim Protection Act, **2004:** 340, 382–83; **2006:** 431
treaty rights suits against U.S. by Native Americans, **2006:** 352
in U.S. Court of Claims, **2002:** 460–61; **2006:** 324
Statute of Rome. *See* International Criminal Court (ICC)
Stockholm Convention on Persistent Organic Pollutants. *See* Persistent Organic Pollutants (POPs)
Stolen aircraft. *See* Aviation issues
Stolen or Illegally Exported Cultural Objects, Convention on, 1991-99: 1803–7
Stolen passports. *See* Passports, U.S.
Stolen vehicle treaties, 2000: 169–70; **2002:** 68
Straits of Hormuz
alleged international law violation by transiting U.S. ships, **2005:** 684–86
Iranian boats; U.S. Navy warships, **2008:** 862–63
Strategic Arms Reduction Treaty (START), 1991-99: 688; **2002:** 1017, 1019; **2005:** 1045–46, 1050, 1053, 1110; **2006:** 1251–55. *See also* Arms control; Nonproliferation
expiration, **2007:** 1061
extension meeting (2008), **2008:** 1017–18

Strategic Arms Reduction Treaty (START) (continued)
Joint Compliance and Inspection Commission, **2005**: 1047–52; **2007**: 1007–12; **2008**: 1017
noncompliance report, U.S., **2005**: 1053
parties to, **2005**: 1045*n*
Protocol on Inspections and Monitoring, **2004**: 1055; **2005**: 1047–48, 1050; **2007**: 1011
Protocol on Notifications, **2005**: 1049–50
Protocol on Procedures Governing the Conversion or Elimination, **2007**: 1011
Protocol on Ratification, **2005**: 1049–50
site diagram change for inspectable facility, **2006**: 1251–55
Trident II SLBM warheads, **2006**: 1251, 1254–55
key features, **1991-99**: 2207–10
Lisbon Protocol, **1991-99**: 2210–12; **2005**: 1045
Memorandum of Understanding, **2005**: 1047
ratification by U.S., **1991-99**: 2207–17
START II Treaty (1993), **1991-99**: 2217–22; **2002**: 1021–22, 1027–28; **2005**: 216
U.S compliance, **2006**: 1263
Sturgeon, beluga, ban on importation of caviar from, 2005: 753–55
SUA (Convention for Suppression of Unlawful Acts against Safety of Maritime Navigation). *See* Maritime issues; Nonproliferation; Piracy; Terrorism
Submarine-launched ballistic missiles (SLBMs), 2005: 1045–47
Submerged lands
Arctic region, **2008**: 627
disputes as to sovereignty over
Alaska, **2002**: 738–47; **2005**: 696–705
Northern Mariana Islands, Commonwealth of (CNMI), **1991-99**: 831–41; **2002**: 246–59; **2003**: 275–76; **2005**: 251–55; **2006**: 315–16
Submerged Lands Act (1953), **1991-99**: 839–40; **2003**: 276; **2005**: 697–98
Succession of states. *See also* Treaties, generally; *specific countries*
Czechoslovakia succeeded by Czech Republic and Slovak Republic, **1991-99**: 1174–75
diplomatic relations, **2000**: 563–64. *See also* Diplomatic relations and recognition
Hong Kong, **1991-99**: 1175–80
Macau, **1991-99**: 1180–81
Pakistan, **2008**: 65
Soviet Union, successor states, **1991-99**: 1172–74
Russia as continuation of USSR in UN Security Council, **1991-99**: 1169–71

Succession of states (continued)
to treaties. *See* Treaties, generally
Yugoslavia, successor states to
Bosnia-Herzegovina, **1991-99**: 1163–64
Croatia, **1991-99**: 1163–64
Federal Republic of Yugoslavia (Serbia and Montenegro)
attempt to claim sole successor status, **1991-99**: 1162–67; **2000**: 561–75
membership in international organizations, **2000**: 561–63
Macedonia, **1991-99**: 1167
as political question in U.S. litigation, **2000**: 565–75
protection of assets for the five successor states, U.S., **1991-99**: 1167–69
Slovenia, **1991-99**: 1163–64
successor state liability, **2000**: 566–67, 568, 569–73
Sudan. *See also* Darfur
accountability in, **2005**: 952
African Union Mission, **2006**: 1043, 1044, 1046
Alien Tort Statute (ATS) issues, **2003**: 383–86, 505; **2005**: 394–400, 411, 413, 502–3, 581; **2006**: 460–65; **2008**: 227–36
atrocities in, **2004**: 128, 132, 239–50; **2005**: 192, 376–77, 952
membership in UN Commission on Human Rights, **2004**: 257–59; **2005**: 453
referral of war crimes to International Criminal Court (ICC), **2005**: 193–96
exemption of nonparty state persons in Sudan from ICC prosecution, **2005**: 196
child soldiers, **2006**: 387, 388; **2008**: 304
comity-based abstentions, **2005**: 822–26
Comprehensive Peace Agreement, **2006**: 978–79; **2007**: 860; **2008**: 833–35
conflict resolution efforts, **2002**: 919–25; **2004**: 957–61; **2005**: 192, 194, 952; **2008**: 833–37, 872–73
Comprehensive Peace Agreement, **2005**: 920–31, 940–41
constitution, **2005**: 925–28
N'djamena Ceasefire Agreement, **2005**: 929
North–South issues
conflict, comments on, **2005**: 920–21
peace accord, **2005**: 940–42
protocols, **2004**: 958–59, 960
Norwegian support of peace negotiations, **2005**: 920, 926
peacekeeping efforts, **2003**: 940–42; **2006**: 1043–54
Sudan Peace Act, U.S. (2002), **2002**: 922–25; **2003**: 940–41
Sudan Peace Act, U.S. (2004), **2004**: 217–18, 958*n*
UN extraordinary session, **2004**: 964–66

Sudan (continued)
Darfur. *See* Darfur
Darfur Peace Agreement, signing of, **2006**: 1042–54
foreign tax credit, **2004**: 657
Horn of Africa Recovery and Food Security Act, **1991-99**: 938
impunity, climate of, **2005**: 194
Islamic African Relief Agency (IARA) based in, **2005**: 128*n*
maritime issues
longshore work prohibition on alien crewmen from, **2002**: 757; **2003**: 764
territorial sea claims, **1989-90**: 442, 460–61, 465–66
refugees, **2007**: 817, 906
religious freedom violations, **1991-99**: 925; **2001**: 272; **2002**: 282; **2003**: 295, 296; **2004**: 270, 272, 273; **2005**: 314, 316; **2006**: 377
sanctions against, **1991-99**: 1936–39, 1971, 1974; **2004**: 924–25; **2005**: 930; **2006**: 975–83; **2007**: 816–17; **2008**: 807–8. *See also* terrorism and, *this heading*; United Nations, *this heading*
arms embargo, **2004**: 1070; **2005**: 929–30; **2007**: 1003, 1007
new economic sanctions (2007), **2007**: 811–12
provision of non-lethal military assistance, **2007**: 827
trade restrictions, **2000**: 749
Sudan Accountability and Divestment Act of 2007, **2007**: 816–17
suspension of entry of certain aliens of, **1991-99**: 144–45
temporary protected status for nationals of, **1991-99**: 245, 246; **2003**: 36
terrorism and, **1991-99**: 144, 1936–37, 2134–35; **2008**: 90, 471–75
Al-Qaida/Qaeda, protection of, **2005**: 521
not cooperating fully with U.S. antiterrorism efforts, **1991-99**: 508; **2003**: 167
not determined to be not fully cooperating, **2004**: 108
litigation under FSIA terrorism exception, **2008**: 471–75
private suit against for support of terrorist bombings of African embassies, **2006**: 578–81
state sponsor of, **1991-99**: 508–9, 1223; **2001**: 820; **2004**: 103, 108, 659; **2005**: 506; **2006**: 173, 577; **2007**: 236; **2008**: 89, 472
terrorist rendition, **2005**: 102
U.S. strikes against, **1991-99**: 2133–35
destruction of extraterritorial enemy property in, **2004**: 206–14
torture and extrajudicial murder in, **2005**: 581
trafficking in persons, **2003**: 188; **2004**: 164, 165; **2005**: 162; **2006**: 229; **2008**: 118

Sudan (continued)
United Nations, **2004:** 964–65
peacekeeping mission in (UNMIS), **2005:** 940–42
Security Council referral to ICC, **2007:** 197; **2008:** 144, 836–37
Security Council Resolutions
1556, **2004:** 245, 962, 963; **2005:** 929; **2006:** 1047
1564, **2004:** 240, 963
1590, **2005:** 928, 931, 940–41; **2006:** 1047
1591, **2005:** 929, 931, **2006:** 975, 976
1593, **2005:** 192, 193–96, 931, 952; **2007:** 183; **2008:** 842
1627, **2005:** 941–42
1706, **2006:** 423, 1047–48
violence against women in, **2004:** 258; **2006:** 976; **2008:** 287
Supersedeas bonds, 2001: 624, 632–33
Support for East European Democracy Act (1989), 1989-90: 541–44
Suppression of financing of terrorism. *See* Terrorism
Suppression of terrorist bombings. *See* Terrorism, *subheading*: conventions against
Supranational organizations, 2000: 296–308. *See also* International organizations
Supremacy Clause. *See* Constitution, U.S.
Surface Transportation Assistance Act (1982), 2001: 611
Suriname
extradition and mutual legal assistance, **2000:** 185*n*
maritime counter-drug trade agreement, **1991-99:** 1607
Surrogate parentage
citizenship claims and, **1989-90:** 13
Suspension Clause, 2005: 995; **2006:** 1177, 1180–82
Sustainable development. *See* Environmental issues
Sustainable Fisheries Act (1996), 1991-99: 1745; **2003:** 740
Swaziland
extradition and mutual legal assistance, **2000:** 185*n*
Sweden
Arctic region, **2008:** 625, 628, 633
asylum and refugee status, interpretation, **1991-99:** 153
environmental and conservation issues, **1991-99:** 1782
Arctic environment protection agreement, **1991-99:** 1777–80
coral reef protection, **1991-99:** 1755
EU accession and trade agreements, **2006:** 755–56
extradition and mutual legal assistance, **2000:** 186*n*; **2002:** 61, 62, 67, 74–76; **2004:** 73; **2006:** 138, 147; **2008:** 78
family support enforcement, **1991-99:** 1866
Hague Child Abduction Convention compliance, **2002:** 75–76; **2003:** 129

Sweden (continued)
International Space Station Partners Agreement, **1991-99**: 1642
naturalization convention, **2002**: 205
nonimmigrant visa waiver pilot program, **1989-90**: 27
objections to U.S. reservations to Genocide Convention, **1989-90**: 144
proposed purchase of property in U.S., **1989-90**: 377–79
Protocol Amending Tax Convention with U.S., **2005**: 671
real property tax exemptions, **2001**: 545–47
reciprocity in consular relations, **1989-90**: 346
trade issues, **1991-99**: 1409, 1504
transfer of detainees to, **2004**: 987; **2005**: 967
Underwater Cultural Heritage, Convention on Protection of, position on, **2005**: 766
Union with Norway, dissolution of, **1991-99**: 744
U.S. vessels not violating Swedish territorial waters, **2006**: 812–14
warnings of hazardous navigation by vessels registered in, **1989-90**: 458–59
Warsaw Convention, damages under, **1991-99**: 1354
women, role of in conflict prevention and crisis management, **2005**: 312
World War II issues, **1991-99**: 1053, 1058, 1059, 1061, 2105
Switzerland
airline passenger name record data, **2008**: 109–10
Antarctica, environmental protection of, **1991-99**: 1783
asset freeze order by Swiss government, **2005**: 577–78
aviation agreement, **2008**: 511
Congestion Charge in London, **2005**: 572
cooperation in antiterrorism actions, **2002**: 893
drug trade (methamphetamines), **2007**: 164–66
extradition and mutual legal assistance, **1991-99**: 390, 395, 398, 399, 447; **2000**: 180; **2001**: 62–70
family support enforcement, **2004**: 836–37
Food Aid Convention, **1991-99**: 936
Gulf War and, **1991-99**: 2102, 2104–7
Hague Child Abduction Convention, compliance with, **1991-99**: 355; **2003**: 129; **2004**: 54; **2006**: 102
immigration issues
asylum and refugee status, interpretation, **1991-99**: 153
nonimmigrant visa waiver pilot program, **1989-90**: 27
injuries sustained on embassy grounds, **2002**: 522
International Space Station Partners Agreement, **1991-99**: 1642
Middle East peace process and, **1991-99**: 1024, 1025
money laundering, **2004**: 135
most-favored-nation status, **1989-90**: 341–42

Switzerland (continued)
privileges and immunities for arms control delegations in, **2004**: 1057–59
reciprocity in recovery of family support obligations, **2008**: 759
trade and investment issues, **1991-99**: 1384; **2006**: 761
World War II issues, **1991-99**: 1047, 1051–52, 1059–60
claims of Nazi era victims and victims' heirs against Swiss banks, **2000**: 445–46, 458, 466–67
Holocaust victims' compensation agreements, **2002**: 417, 427, 428
Syria
arms control. *See also* Nonproliferation, *subheading*: country-specific issues
arms embargo non-licensing policy, **2004**: 1070; **2007**: 1003
UN Register of Conventional Arms and, **1991-99**: 2267
violations of arms embargoes. *See* Lebanon and Iraq and, *this heading*
Lebanon and, **2004**: 945; **2006**: 1036*n*
closure of border with, **2005**: 933
control and interference in, **2007**: 39–40, 805, 870
sanctions on Syria because of, **2007**: 40–41, 805–7
Hariri murder and, **2005**: 882–84; **2006**: 984–85, 1041
occupation by Syria, **2005**: 133–34, 880–87
withdrawal of forces from, **2005**: 931–32
sovereignty of Lebanon, **2008**: 825–26
Syria Accountability and Lebanese Sovereignty Restoration Act (2003), **2003**: 269–70, 1084–86
sanctions imposed under, **2004**: 900–3; **2005**: 886–88
terrorism support in, **2006**: 1037, 1039–41, 1226–30, 1233–34
violations of UN Security Council Resolution 1701 (2006) concerning, **2008**: 826
longshore work prohibition on alien crewmen from, **2002**: 757; **2003**: 764
maritime issues
boundaries and rights of navigation, **1989-90**: 467; **2004**: 702–5
counterterrorism measures, conditions for failure to take, **2008**: 112
Middle East peace process, **1991-99**: 1024, 1026–27, 1986–87, 1988; **2004**: 945; **2005**: 917
Palestinian refugees in, **2005**: 918
money laundering in, **2004**: 139
nonproliferation. *See* Nonproliferation, *subheading*: country-specific issues
removal to for purpose of interrogation under torture, **2006**: 484–85
reservations to Vienna Convention on the Law of Treaties, **1989-90**: 149

Syria (continued)
sanctions on, **2003**: 269–70; **2004**: 900–3; **2005**: 133–34, 886–88, 914; **2006**: 243–49, 984–86; **2008**: 112, 798–800, 1025–27. *See also* arms control, *this heading*; terrorism, *this heading*; Nonproliferation, *subheading*: country-specific issues
denial of foreign tax credit, **2004**: 659
support for attacks on American forces in Iraq, **2007**: 989
support for terrorist groups, pursuit of weapons of mass destruction, destabilization of Iraq, and other actions, **2004**: 900–3
terrorism and
maritime counterterrorism measures, conditions for failure to take, 112
not cooperating fully with with antiterrorism efforts, **1991-99**: 508; **2003**: 167; **2004**: 107–8; **2006**: 172; **2007**: 131–32; **2008**: 88–89
as state sponsor of terrorism, **1991-99**: 508–9, 1223; **2001**: 819; **2003**: 168; **2004**: 103, 659, 902; **2005**: 506; **2006**: 173, 577; **2007**: 236; **2008**: 89, 472
support of international terrorism, **2005**: 133–34
threats to stabilization of Iraq. *See* sanctions on, *this heading*
trafficking in persons, **2006**: 228; **2007**: 169; **2008**: 118
UN Commission on Human Rights and, **2004**: 405
United Arab Republic, dissolution of, **1991-99**: 744
U.S. interviews of Iraqi refugees in Syria, **2008**: 34

T

TADA (Terrorist and Disruptive Activities Act), 2005: 96
Taipei Economic and Cultural Representative Office, 1991-99: 658–66; **2000**: 599–602; **2002**: 79, 535–45, 796–98
immunity of bank accounts under AIT-TECRO Agreement, **2002**: 536–37, 543–45
Taiwan
accession to WTO, **2001**: 649, 651–53
American Institute in Taiwan (AIT), **2007**: 437
Agreement on Privileges, Exemptions and Immunities Between Coordination Council for North American Affairs and, **1991-99**: 658–66; **2000**: 600–602; **2002**: 79, 245–46
immunity from suit as U.S. government instrumentality, **2001**: 235–41
status of agreement between AIT and TECRO, **1991-99**: 658–66
applicability of copyright law to, **1991-99**: 702–7705
claimants of U.S. non-citizenship national status, **2007**: 1–3; **2008**: 1
comfort women from, Alien Tort Statute action brought against Japan, **2005**: 475–81

Taiwan (continued)
derecognition of, **1991-99**: 702, 703
no longer party to NPT, **1991-99**: 2334
drug trade (methamphetamine), **2007**: 164–66
fish and marine mammals, **2005**: 734, 736–37, 740, 746–47
Convention on the Conservation and Management of Highly Migratory Fish Stocks in the Western and Central Pacific Ocean, **2000**: 701–2
drift-net fishing, **1991-99**: 1726
intellectual property rights, **2007**: 608, 610
enforcement agreement, **1991-99**: 1522
Watch List, **2006**: 768; **2007**: 610; **2008**: 606
maritime claims, **2005**: 683–84
missile defense cooperation, **2004**: 1066
money laundering in, **2004**: 135
nonproliferation sanctions against company of, **2004**: 1135
nuclear retransfer agreements, **1991-99**: 2334–35
passport giving as place of birth, **2006**: 545, 546
post-World War II claims, **2000**: 533–34, 535; **2001**: 449–50
PRC treaties not applicable to, **1991-99**: 706–9
service of process in, **2004**: 874–75
Taipei Economic and Cultural Representative Office
status of agreement between AIT and TECRO, **1991-99**: 658–66
status of TECRO and employees in U.S., **2000**: 599–602; **2002**: 536–39
UN participation, **2002**: 405
U.S.–Taiwan relations, **1991-99**: 662, 702–5; **2000**: 533–34, 600; **2001**: 237, 238–39; **2004**: 187
history of, **2007**: 434–37
non-North Atlantic Treaty Organization (NATO) ally, designation as, **2005**: 1044
sovereignty issues, **2008**: 443–47
Taiwan Relations Act (1979), **1991-99**: 662–64, 701–2, 703, 705, 708; **2000**: 600, 601; **2001**: 237–39; **2002**: 79, 536; **2006**: 545–46; **2007**: 434, 436; **2008**: 446
Tajikistan
Article 98 agreement (nonsurrender of Americans to ICC), **2003**: 238
diplomatic relations, **1991-99**: 1174
intellectual property rights Watch List, **2006**: 768; **2007**: 610
trade and investment issues, **1991-99**: 1455
women, need to improve treatment of, **2005**: 313
Taking evidence abroad. *See* Evidence

Takings of property. *See also* Expropriation
claim against U.S. government for settlement of espoused claims against Iran, **1991-99**: 1097–98
Cuban litigation over denial of trademark, **2006**: 1007, 1013–15
destruction of extraterritorial enemy property and, **2004**: 206–7, 208–9, 210, 211
espousal of claims. *See* Espousal of claims
exception to sovereign immunity. *See* Foreign Sovereign Immunities Act (FSIA) (1976), *subheading*: exceptions to immunity
fishing rights in EEZ, no compensable right to, **2004**: 724–30
nuclear testing by U.S. in Marshall Islands, **2006**: 324
preemption of claims by federal foreign affairs authority and, **2004**: 444–45
Treaty of Peace with Japan as, **2003**: 476

Taliban. *See also* Detainees, military; Detainees, military, *subheading*: enemy combatants, unlawful
armed conflict with, **2004**: 985, 995–96, 1002–3, 1006; **2005**: 372; **2006**: 1106–10, 1111, 1121, 1139, 1152; **2007**: 267, 875–76, 922, 926–27, 935, 937, 946, 953, 973; **2008**: 309
counter-interrogation techniques, **2005**: 967
in definition of enemy combatant, **2006**: 1040*n*
designation as terrorist organization under INA, **2007**: 71
Geneva Conventions applying to, **2002**: 977; **2004**: 1021, 1039–40; **2006**: 1134. *See also* Afghanistan, *subheading*: Geneva Conventions, applicability to conflict in
mistreatment of women in Afghanistan, **2002**: 277–78, 280
sanctions against, **1991-99**: 1964–67; **2001**: 801–3, 822; **2002**: 101–2, 881–88; **2004**: 121–22; **2005**: 894–900, 902–3; **2006**: 1000, 1002–3, 1005; **2007**: 1043, 1046–49; **2008**: 87–88, 99

Tanzania
Al Qaeda attack on U.S. embassy in, **1991-99**: 2133; **2005**: 372
legal action related to, **2005**: 517–21, 578–80; **2006**: 578–81
consular bank accounts, **2005**: 559
extradition and mutual legal assistance, **2000**: 185*n*
FSIA claims and, **2003**: 507–8
U.S. military assistance, **2006**: 278
waiver of Article 98 agreement with U.S. (nonsurrender of Americans to ICC), **2006**: 279

Tariffs
agriculture, **2002**: 704–5; **2007**: 570; **2008**: 336
GATT. *See* General Agreement on Tariffs and Trade (GATT)
NAFTA, removal of remaining tariffs and quotas with U.S., **2008**: 542

Tariffs (continued)
non-agricultural market access, **2007:** 571
preferential tariff treatment programs, **2008:** 580, 582
steel, **2002:** 693–97
Tariff Act (1930), **2004:** 595, 606, 612, 1108; **2005:** 626
telecommunications services and equipment, **1991-99:** 1368, 1375, 1378–81, 1393–94, 1396, 1475, 1526, 1810–11, 1829, 1899–1901, 1902, 1968
U.S. proposal to eliminate, **2002:** 698–701
U.S. and EU proposal to eliminate tariffs on clean energy technologies and services, **2007:** 577–79, 677, 682; **2008:** 676, 682
Tate letter, **2005:** 400, 501, 822–23
Taxation
agreements for the avoidance of double taxation, **1989-90:** 411–15; **2005:** 671; **2008:** 610–16
Belgium, **2008:** 610–16
Canada, **2008:** 610–16
Finland, **1989-90:** 415
Germany, **2008:** 610–16
Indonesia, **1989-90:** 472, 474–75; **2003:** 761
Spain, **1989-90:** 415
Tunisia, **1989-90:** 415
claims against U.S., **1991-99:** 659–66
common law revenue rule, **2003:** 855–56; **2004:** 825–26
consular and diplomatic personnel and properties and. *See* Consular offices and personnel; Diplomatic missions and personnel
Convention on Mutual Administrative Assistance in Tax Matters, OECD, **1989-90:** 410–11
diplomatic immunity from claims related to. *See* Diplomatic missions and personnel, *subheading*: immunity
discrimination against foreign commerce, **2000:** 322, 322*n*, 323–24*n*, 326, 326*n*
evasion, **2005:** 234–36; **2008:** 610–16
exemptions for international organizations. *See* International organizations
expropriation and, **2000:** 685
foreign tax credit restrictions, **2004:** 659–61
indigenous people, **2004:** 384–85
International Seabed Authority, **2005:** 681
jurisdiction to resolve international tax disputes, **2001:** 485–88
Law of the Sea and, **2004:** 683–84; **2005:** 681
mandatory arbitration provision in bilateral agreements, **2008:** 610–16
mutual assistance treaties, **1989-90:** 410–11; **2000:** 168
NAFTA Chapter 11 claims against Mexico, **2001:** 642–46

Taxation (continued)
OPIC and its operations not subject to, **2005:** 650–52
Puerto Rico income taxes, **2005:** 248
Puerto Rico political status and, **1991-99:** 827–28
renunciation of citizenship to avoid, **1991-99:** 90
royalties income, **1989-90:** 412–13
sovereign immunity from claims related to. *See* Foreign Sovereign Immunities Act (FSIA) (1976)
territorial systems, **2002:** 685–87
treaty shopping, **1989-90:** 414
Uniformity Clause, applicability to U.S. possessions, **1991-99:** 810–11
wire fraud statute and, **2005:** 235–42
WTO disputes. *See* World Trade Organization (WTO)
Technology transfer. *See* Arms control
TEDs (turtle excluder devices). *See* Fish and marine mammals, *subheading*: sea turtle protection
Telecommunications, 1991-99: 915, 1013, 1375, 1461, 1829; **2001:** 795–96. *See also* Electronic commerce
Agreement on Basic Telecommunications Services, WTO, **1991-99:** 1368, 1378–81, 1396, 1475
broadcast interference, **1989-90:** 398–99, 400–401, 402–3, 405, 406–7
criminalization of hate speech, **2004:** 263–69
cross-border fiber optic installation, **2001:** 566–68
Cuba
complaint alleging U.S. interference with communications services, **2005:** 663
gifts of mobile phones to, **2008:** 808–9
cybercrime, **2001:** 152–59; **2004:** 97–99
developing nations, **2005:** 714
disaster mitigation and relief operations, **1991-99:** 1791
extradition and mutual legal assistance, **2004:** 94–95
with Germany, **2005:** 72
geostationary orbit issues, **2001:** 721–22; **2003:** 430, 698–99
Hong Kong Ministerial Declaration, **2005:** 616
implications of draft space assets protocol, **2003:** 769–70
International Contracts, Convention on Use of Electronic Communications in. *See* Electronic commerce
International Telecommunication Union. *See* International Telecommunication Union (ITU)
Internet. *See* Internet
multilateral law enforcement, **2004:** 96
NAFTA and, **1991-99:** 1423
protection of, **2001:** 930, 931, 939

Telecommunications (continued)
racially threatening communication, **2001**: 264–65, 267–68
radio regulations. *See* International Telecommunication Union (ITU)
rights to geostationary satellite orbit, **2003**: 430, 698–99
sanctions and, **1991-99**: 1894, 1899–1902, 1968
satellite launch service agreement, **1989-90**: 481
Telecommunications Act (1996), **2002**: 284
U.S. broadcasts to Cuba, **1989-90**: 396–99, 409; **2003**: 429–30, 698; **2004**: 639–44; **2008**: 391–92
Cuban objections to, **1989-90**: 399–409; **2008**: 391–92
U.S. consultations with Mexico, **2005**: 624
U.S. Telecommunications Training Institute (USTTI), **2005**: 661
World Radiocommunication Conference (2007), **2007**: 598–99
World Summit on the Information Society. *See* Information Society, World Summit on (WSIS)
WTO disputes. *See* World Trade Organization (WTO)
Television Broadcasting to Cuba Act (1990), 1989-90: 396–99
Temporary protected status, 1989-90: 32, 39–40, 41; **1991-99**: 240–48
Bosnia and Herzegovina nationals, **1991-99**: 245
Burundi nationals, **1991-99**: 245; **2003**: 36
El Salvador nationals, extension of status for, **2003**: 33–36
Guinea-Bissau nationals, **1991-99**: 246
Honduran nationals, **2003**: 36; **2004**: 33
Kosovo nationals, **1991-99**: 247–48
Lebanon nationals, **1991-99**: 241–43
Liberia nationals, **1991-99**: 243–44; **2003**: 36
Montserrat nationals, **1991-99**: 246–47; **2003**: 36; **2004**: 32–33
Nicaragua nationals, **1991-99**: 247; **2003**: 36; **2004**: 33
Rwanda nationals, **1991-99**: 245
Sierra Leone nationals, **1991-99**: 245; **2003**: 38
Somalia nationals, **1991-99**: 245
Sudan nationals, **1991-99**: 245, 246; **2003**: 36
termination of, **2003**: 36–38
Territorial sea. *See* Maritime issues
Terrorism, 1991-99: 577, 2202. *See also* Al-Qaida/Qaeda; Detainees, military; September 11 terrorist attacks; Taliban
airline passengers
name record data, access to, **2004**: 108–16; **2006**: 168–72; **2007**: 158–59; **2008**: 109–10
Secure Flight program, **2008**: 103–9
alien detention and inadmissibility of on terrorism-related grounds. *See* Detention of aliens, nonmilitary; Removal of aliens from U.S.

Terrorism (continued)
Anti-Terrorism and Arms Export Amendments Act (1989), **1989-90**: 108–9
Antiterrorism and Effective Death Penalty Act. *See* Antiterrorism and Effective Death Penalty Act (AEDPA) (1996)
arms control and, **1989-90**: 108–9; **1991-99**: 555–56, 2330, 2346, 2352, 2357; **2001**: 801–2, 901; **2003**: 1082–84; **2005**: 894, 899, 903; **2008**: 87–88
Asia Pacific Economic Cooperation forum statement, **2002**: 119–21
boarding of ship suspected of involvement in, authority for nonconsensual, **2003**: 735–36
Bombings Convention. *See* conventions against, *this heading*
bombings of U.S. embassies in Africa, **1991-99**: 494, 1967, 2133–35; **2001**: 417–21; **2002**: 461–62; **2005**: 517–21, 578–80; **2006**: 578–81
border controls, **2002**: 121; **2003**: 158–59
civil cause of action for terrorist acts abroad against U.S. nationals, **1989-90**: 115–19; **2007**: 150–54
condemnation of in 2005 World Summit Outcome Document, **2005**: 110
constitutionality of U.S. antiterrorism statutes. *See* Constitution, U.S.
conventions against, **2001**: 100–9, 357, 914–15
Airports, Protocol for the Suppression of Unlawful Acts of Violence at, **1989-90**: 34, 110–11
Comprehensive Convention on International Terrorism (proposed), **2005**: 108, 110, 447, 450, 1078; **2007**: 131
Inter-American Convention Against Terrorism (OAS Terrorism Convention), **2002**: 112–17; **2003**: 153–54, 938; **2004**: 95–97, 1065; **2005**: 111
Marking of Plastic Explosives for the Purpose of Detection, Convention on the, **1991-99**: 489–93
Nuclear Terrorism, International Convention for Suppression of. *See* nuclear terrorism, protection against, *this heading*
Offenses and Certain Other Acts Committed on Board Aircraft, Convention on, **2008**: 519–24
Physical Protection of Nuclear Material, Convention on. *See* nuclear terrorism, protection against, *this heading*
Prevention and Punishment of Crimes Against Internationally Protected Persons Including Diplomatic Agents, Convention on the **1989-90**: 34, 283; **2000**: 218; **2001**: 357
Suppression of Financing of Terrorism, International Convention for the, **2000**: 216–21; **2001**: 100–2, 104–9, 915; **2002**: 106, 108, 113–14, 116–17, 891; **2003**: 142, 153; **2004**: 97, 197–98; **2007**: 985–88

Terrorism (continued)
Suppression of Unlawful Acts Against the Safety of Civil Aviation, Convention for the, **1989-90**: 34
Suppression of Unlawful Acts Against the Safety of Maritime Navigation, Convention for the, and fixed platforms Protocol, **1989-90**: 34, 111–14; **2000**: 218; **2002**: 104–10, 133–34; **2004**: 1110; **2008**: 125–30
2005 protocols to, **2005**: 112–13, 1117–20; **2006**: 211–12; **2007**: 140–42, 985–88, 1062–71; **2008**: 94–97, 889–90, 926–28, 930–32, 941–44
Terrorist Bombings Convention, **1991-99**: 493–99; **2000**: 218–19; **2001**: 100–104, 106–9, 915; **2002**: 106, 109–10, 116–17; **2003**: 142, 153, 244–45; **2005**: 107; **2006**: 288–91; **2007**: 985–88, 1078
military activity as exception to, **1991-99**: 497–98
reservations to, **2006**: 288–91
Unlawful Seizure of Aircraft, Convention for the, **1989-90**: 34; **1991-99**: 501, 504, 507–8; **2001**: 357
country-specific issues
Afghanistan and. *See* Afghanistan. *See also* Taliban
Algeria and, **1991-99:** 867–68
Bulgaria and, **2004:** 1137
Colombia and, **2004:** 188, 376–79
Cuba and. *See* Cuba, *subheading*: terrorism and
Eritrea, not cooperating fully with U.S. antiterrorism activities, **2008:** 88–89
Iran and. *See* Iran, *subheading*: terrorism and
Iraq and. *See also* Iraq, *subheading*: terrorism and
Libya and. *See* Libya, *subheading*: terrorism and
North Korea and. *See* Korea, North (Democratic People's Republic of (DPRK)), *subheading*: terrorism
Pakistan and, **2004:** 651–52
International Court of Justice claims, **1991-99**: 458–59, 460–77; **2003**: 166
Russia
Chechnya and, **1991-99:** 516; **2003:** 953–54
Russia–U.S. Joint Declaration on New Strategic Relationship, **2002:** 1025
South Korea and, **2004:** 1156–58
Sudan and. *See* Sudan, *subheading*: terrorism and
Syria and. *See* Syria, *subheading*: terrorism and
UK, UK law and, **2004:** 82
Venezuela, not cooperating fully with U.S. antiterrorism activities, **2006:** 172; **2007:** 132; **2008:** 88

Terrorism (continued)
countries not cooperating fully with antiterrorism efforts, designation of, **1991-99**: 484, 508; **2003**: 167; **2004**: 107–8; **2006**: 172; **2007**: 131–32; **2008**: 88–89
country reports on, Department of State, **1991-99**: 1265; **2001**: 96–97; **2005**: 105; **2006**: 167–68; **2007**: 130; **2008**: 83
criminalization in U.S., **1991-99**: 484–85; **2001**: 904–7
of support for, **1991-99**: 481, 482, 483–84; **2001**: 897–901; **2008**: 97–98
cyber-terrorism, **2001**: 152, 154–55
definition, **1989-90**: 33–34, 113, 117; **2000**: 218, 219–20; **2001**: 97, 105; **2004**: 105; **2006**: 355–56
of "international terrorism" in 22 U.S.C. § 2656d, **2005**: 105
proposed international conference on, **1991-99**: 499–501
of terrorist activity, **1991-99**: 79, 482, 2074*n*; **2002**: 87–88, 102–3, 411–12; **2006**: 356
designation of foreign terrorist organizations (FTOs) by U.S., **1991-99**: 77, 78–79, 89, 127, 481–83, 488, 1922, 1967, 2000; **2001**: 109–17, 822, 899, 918–23, 925; **2002**: 95–96, 412–13; **2003**: 154–58, 174–80; **2004**: 122–23, 124, 127; **2005**: 113–16, 118–23; **2006**: 180–99, 204–6, 1000–1006; **2007**: 71, 144–45; **2008**: 101–3
blocking assets of. *See* sanctions related to, *this heading*
criminal penalties for material support to, **2007**: 144–50; **2008**: 97–98
criteria for, **2002**: 85–89, 102–3
effects of, **2002**: 89–90
legal ramifications, **2002**: 89
litigation concerning, **2002**: 91–92, 93–94, 98–101; **2004**: 126–28; **2005**: 116–34; **2006**: 180–99
reviews of, **2003**: 113–15; **2008**: 101–3
dissemination of government warnings to all Americans, **1989-90**: 64–65
Dromoland Castle Declaration on Combating Terrorism and on the Non-Proliferation of Weapons of Mass Destruction, **2005**: 1096
enemy combatants suspected of. *See* Detainees, military
environmental, **1991-99**: 2101–2
European Union–U.S. summit, **2004**: 114–18
exception to FSIA immunity. *See* Foreign Sovereign Immunities Act (FSIA) (1976), *subheading*: exceptions to immunity

Terrorism (continued)
Executive Branch authority to designate extraterritorial property associated with, **2004**: 206–14
Executive Order 12947, **1991-99**: 127, 485–89; **2001**: 822, 899, 918; **2002**: 98, 100; **2003**: 157, 172, 179; **2005**: 133; **2006**: 991–92
Executive Order 13224, **2001**: 822, 881–93, 895, 896, 899, 918; **2002**: 94–98, 100–101; **2003**: 156–57, 171–75, 180; **2004**: 123; **2005**: 129, 132–33; **2006**: 183–91, 205–6; **2007**: 155–58, 1041–43, 1046, 1049–50; **2008**: 99, 100–1, 806
delisting procedures for persons and entities designated under, **2002**: 101, 886–87, 889; **2006**: 1000–6; **2008**: 88
extradition and, **1991-99**: 389, 395, 396–97, 398, 428–35, 444; **2003**: 142; **2006**: 122–27
extraterritorial jurisdiction, **1991-99**: 504–5, 506; **2001**: 331–32; **2003**: 383; **2004**: 124–26, 1089–90*n*
financing of, **2002**: 89, 95, 115; **2003**: 168–80; **2004**: 97, 117, 118, 122–28, 197–98, 650–51; **2005**: 899. *See also* Executive Order 13224, *this heading*; sanctions related to, *this heading*
International Convention for Suppression of Financing of Terrorism (2000), **2000**: 216–21; **2001**: 100–102, 104–9, 915; **2002**: 106, 108, 113–14, 116–17, 891; **2003**: 142, 153; **2004**: 97, 197–98; **2007**: 985–88
Security Council, UN, 1267 sanctions committee, statements to or concerning, **2005**: 894–99; **2006**: 1000; **2008**: 87–88
Terrorist Finance Tracking Program (TFTP), **2007**: 160–61
foreign tax credit restrictions and, **2004**: 659–60
G-8 counterterrorism recommendations, **2002**: 121–22
General System of Preferences and, **2004**: 658
Geneva Conventions. *See* Geneva Conventions on law of war (1949)
hostage-taking. *See* Hostage-taking and hijacking
human rights, protection of while countering, **2000**: 238–39; **2001**: 117–18; **2002**: 358, 360, 387–88; **2003**: 409–12; **2004**: 399–400; **2005**: 436–40; **2006**: 487–88; **2007**: 394–97
immigration laws of U.S. and, **1991-99**: 77, 78–83, 86, 89
deportation of legal permanent U.S. resident for acts of, **1991-99**: 126–28
exclusion of aliens, **1989-90**: 33–34; **2004**: 122–23; **2006**: 206–10
exemption of African National Congress and related individuals from terrorism-related immigration provisions, **2008**: 20

Terrorism (continued)
exemptions from "material support" grounds for aliens linked to, **2007:** 70–72; **2008:** 29–31, 307–8
immigration exclusion list, **2002:** 102–4
visa denial for terrorist activity, **1989-90:** 21–26; **2006:** 18–29
visa waivers for aliens proceeding in transit through U.S. and risk of, **2003:** 14–15
incitement to commit acts of, **2006:** 200–210
information collection from foreign visitors and immigrants to prevent, **2003:** 15–19; **2004:** 27–28; **2008:** 24–25
information exchange arrangements, **2007:** 157–59; **2008:** 109–11
Intelligence Reform and Terrorism Prevention Act of 2004 (IRTPA), **2005:** 2–5, 114, 125, 126–28; **2008:** 7, 102, 103, 104, 105. *See also* Intelligence Reform and Terrorism Prevention Act of 2004 (IRTPA)
International Covenant on Civil and Political Rights, no derogation from after 9/11, **2005:** 265; **2006:** 412
international convention on civil redress for, **1989-90:** 117–18
International Crime Control Strategy, **1991-99:** 396–97
International Criminal Court jurisdiction and, **1991-99:** 611, 627, 632
International Maritime Convention, Athens Protocol, **2006:** 292–94
International Maritime Organization instruments for protection against, review of, **2002:** 104–5
international norms against, **2003:** 151–54
interrogation of persons in connection with, **2004:** 302–3, 990–91, 992, 1038–39, 1040
Joint Declaration for Cooperation to Combat International Terrorism (U.S.–ASEAN), **2002:** 118–19
killing of suspected terrorists in Yemen, **2003:** 345–47
lack of functioning governments and, **2004:** 16
Law of the Sea and, **2004:** 681, 691
liability of government for actions of its employees or agents, **2002:** 531
liability of government officials for supporting, **2003:** 508–9, 533–36
maritime operations and, **2001:** 683–84
Middle East peace process and, **1991-99:** 126–28, 485–89, 1185, 1990, 1998; **2003:** 944–46, 948–49, 951; **2004:** 951–53, 957; **2008:** 818, 819, 821–24
Israel–Palestinian Liberation Organization agreement, **1991-99:** 2000
Palestinian Anti-Terrorism Act (2006), **2006:** 306, 993–95
National Counterterrorism Center (NCTC), **2006:** 167
National Strategy for Combating Terrorism, **2005:** 689*n*
nuclear terrorism, protection against, **2001:** 842–43; **2008:** 951–53

Terrorism (continued)
Global Initiative to Combat Nuclear Terrorism, **2006**: 1293–96; **2008**: 953
nuclear nonproliferation efforts and, **2003**: 1089–90; **2008**: 854–56
Nuclear Material, Amendment to Convention on Physical Protection of, **2005**: 109–10, 960–61, 1092, 1095, 1121–23; **2007**: 142–43, 1076–79; **2008**: 94–97, 889–90
Nuclear Terrorism, International Convention for Suppression of, **2005**: 11, 18, 106–9, 960, 1092, 1123–24; **2007**: 132–39; **2008**: 94–97, 889–90
Suppression of Unlawful Acts against the Safety of Maritime Navigation and fixed platforms protocol, 2005 protocols to, **2005**: 112–13, 1117–20; **2007**: 140–42, 1062–71; **2008**: 94–97, 889–90, 941–44
reduction of nuclear stockpiles and, **2004**: 1138–40
Omnibus Diplomatic Security and Antiterrorism Act (1986), **1989-90**: 93
Pan Am Flight 103 and French UTA bombing, **1991-99**: 457–80, 857, 1029–30, 1911–15, 1921–24; **2004**: 108, 927, 928, 930, 934, 1160. *See also* Libya
cases in U.S. courts, **1991-99**: 1194–95, 1197–98, 1234–52, 1256–57
International Court of Justice claims, **1991-99**: 458–59, 460–77; **2003**: 166
prosecution of named terrorists in Scottish court, **1991-99**: 457–60, 462, 465, 467–69, 477–80, 542; **2001**: 98–99; **2002**: 111–12
UN Security Council resolutions, **1991-99**: 458–60, 469–77, 1029–30, 1921–22
passport, request for replacement when U.S. citizen arrested for alleged involvement with terrorist group in, **2006**: 16–17
PATRIOT Act. *See* PATRIOT Act, USA (2001)
political offenses and, **2002**: 109, 114–15
procedures of military commissions for trial of non-U.S. citizens suspected of. *See* Military commissions for trial of certain non-U.S. enemy combatants[16]
provision of material support or resources for, **2002**: 89, 93–94, 95, 115, 529, 888–93; **2004**: 484–89, 1101–2; **2007**: 143–50, 154–58, 1041–43, 1046–50
Holy Land Foundation of Relief and Development, **2008**: 97–98
U.S. legislation and litigation concerning, **2004**: 122–28

[16] Editor's note: The Military Commissions Act of 2009, Pub. L. 111-84, uses the term "enemy belligerents" rather than "enemy combatants."

Terrorism (continued)
rewards, **2005**: 134–35
right of self-determination and, **2003**: 244–45
role of international law in prosecuting or preventing, **2002**: 902, 904
sanctions related to. *See also* Afghanistan; Cuba; designation of foreign terrorist organizations (FTOs) by U.S., *this heading*; Iran; Korea, North (Democratic People's Republic of (DPRK)); Libya; Sudan; Syria
against al-Qaida. *See* Al-Qaida/Qaeda
arms trade with, prohibitions on, **2002**: 801–2; 884–85; **2003**: 152, 1082–84; **2005**: 894, 899, 903; **2006**: 1003; **2007**: 1048; **2008**: 87–88
against foreign terrorists that disrupt the Middle East peace process, **1991-99**: 127, 485–89; **2001**: 822, 899, 918; **2002**: 98, 100; **2003**: 157, 172, 179; **2005**: 133; **2006**: 991–92
freezing or blocking assets of designated terrorist organization or supporters, **1991-99**: 127, 485–89; **2001**: 114–15, 881–93, 895, 896, 899, 918, 919, 925–26; **2002**: 94–98, 100–101; **2003**: 152, 153–55, 156–58, 168–80, 552; **2005**: 129, 132–33, 896; **2006**: 183–91, 205–6; **2007**: 154–58, 1041–43, 1046, 1049–50; **2008**: 99, 100–101, 806
against individuals and entities supporting terrorism, **2001**: 881–93; **2005**: 129, 132–33; **2004**: 174–75; **2006**: 183–91, 205–6; **2007**: 19–21, 154–58, 1041–43, 1046–50; **2008**: 99, 100, 101
Iran and Libya Sanctions Act, **1991-99**: 165, 1448, 1911–15, 1977
against foreign governments that transfer MANPADS to state sponsors of terrorism or terrorist organizations, **2006**: 210–11
on Syria. *See* Syria, *subheading*: sanctions on
on Taliban. *See* Taliban
screening information, exchange arrangements, **2008**: 110–11
Secure Travel and Counterterrorism Partnership Act of 2007, **2007**: 32–36
September 11 terrorist attacks, **2002**: 106, 112–13, 902, 904, 935, 937, 951, 953, 973, 1011–12, 1025; **2003**: 136, 153, 170, 172, 254, 285, 286, 287, 289, 323, 324, 327, 328–29, 346–47, 385–86, 411, 508–9, 533–36, 551–52, 555–57, 974, 1017, 1019, 1089, 1090; **2004**: 96, 114, 116, 969, 970, 972, 984–85, 995, 1003
Specially Designated Global Terrorist status, **2002**: 91–92, 97, 98
State Department travel advisory system abroad, **1991-99**: 343

Terrorism (continued)
state sponsors of, **1989-90**: 108, 113; **1991-99**: 144, 483–84, 508–9, 937, 1223, 2352; **2003**: 159; **2004**: 103–4, 108, 485, 487, 489, 492, 501, 502, 505, 507, 510, 890–91, 893, 912, 927, 929, 931–32, 934, 1137, 1153–55; **2006**: 173–80; **2007**: 235–36, 479, 481, 1005, 1019, 1022, 1036, 1049; **2008**: 89–94, 960–66. *See also specific countries*
Summit of the Americas declaration, **2004**: 1065
Taliban. *See* Taliban
Terrorism Risk Insurance Act (TRIA) (2002), **2002**: 410; **2003**: 458, 552–57, 910, 919; **2004**: 518, 519–20, 522–23, 524–25, 526–27; **2005**: 543, 544, 546, 547, 548; **2007**: 477–89; **2008**: 411, 466, 467, 484–90
Terrorist and Disruptive Activities Act (India), **2005**: 96
Terrorist Finance Tracking Program (TFTP), **2007**: 160–61
Terrorist Surveillance Program (TSP), **2007**: 247–51
training from terrorist organization, criminalization of, **2004**: 125
transfer of terrorist prisoner, request for, **1989-90**: 72–76
travel documents and, **2004**: 6–7
UN General Assembly review of Global Counter-Terrorism Strategy, **2008**: 85–87
UN high-level event preparation, **2005**: 449–51
UN role in confronting, **2007**: 130–31; **2008**: 83–87
UN Security Council committees on, **2004**: 118–22; **2005**: 900, 901
Counter-Terrorism Committee (CTC), **2005**: 898, 899, 900, 901; **2006**: 199–210, 999–1000
review of 1267, 1373 and 1540 committees, **2005**: 900–2; **2006**: 1002–3; **2008**: 87–88
1267 sanctions committee, statements to or concerning, **2005**: 894–99; **2006**: 1000; **2008**: 87–88
UN 1267 Committee de-listing procedures, **2002**: 886–87; **2006**: 1000–6; **2008**: 88
UN Security Council Resolutions relating to, **2001**: 801–3, 893–917; **2002**: 885–88; **2003**: 168–71; **2004**: 104–7, 118–22, 985, 1092–96; **2005**: 894–99, 900–904, 1092; **2006**: 1294; **2008**: 1000
Resolution 1373 counterterrorism obligations and U.S. report under, **2001**: 893–920
Resolution 1617, adoption of, **2005**: 903–4
Resolution 1624, U.S. report pursuant to, **2006**: 199–210
Resolution 1822, adoption of, **2008**: 87
Resolution 1540 (nonproliferation of weapons of mass destruction), **2004**: 1096–1118; **2008**: 952–53, 999–1001, 1006

Terrorism (continued)
U.S. civil cause of action for terrorist acts committed abroad, **1989-90**: 114–19
U.S. response to, **2003**: 150–59. *See also* September 11 terrorist attacks, *this heading*
U.S.–ASEAN Joint Declaration for Cooperation to Combat International Terrorism, **2002**: 118–19
use of force
executive branch statements concerning, **2008**: 853–56
military action against, **2001**: 104, 106, 118
preemptive military action in response to imminent threat and, **2002**: 947–57
right of self-defense against, **1989-90**: 94, 95–96
against terrorists responsible for 9/11, joint resolution authorizing, **2005**: 266, 1002, 1004, 1005, 1009, 1010, 1011, 1012, 1018
violent extremists, executive right to use of force against, **2008**: 853–56
war against terrorism, **2001**: 856–57; **2005**: 355
U.S.–VISIT Program and, **2003**: 15–19; **2004**: 27–28; **2008**: 24–25
victims of, **1991-99**: 481, 1234; **2000**: 226, 229, 540–60; **2002**: 244–45, 408–13; **2003**: 456–62; **2005**: 272
weapons of mass destruction and, **2004**: 1092, 1093–1118, 1128, 1138, 1140, 1163; **2008**: 854–56, 933, 952–53, 1000, 1006. *See also* Nonproliferation; nuclear terrorism, protection against, *this heading*
Texas
case concerning Mexican subject to ICJ decision on consular notification, **2005**: 32–59; **2007**: 73–77; **2008**: 35, 175–215
international agreements and, **2000**: 294
Thailand
air transport agreement, **2003**: 602
antiterrorism cooperation, **2002**: 118
debt for nature swaps, **2001**: 737
drug trade, **2001**: 120; **2002**: 124; **2003**: 181; **2004**: 133–34
extradition and mutual legal assistance, **1991-99**: 390; **2000**: 179, 186*n*
intellectual property rights Watch List, **2006**: 769; **2007**: 608, 610 **2008**: 605*n*
maritime boundaries, **1991-99**: 1583; **2000**: 703–6
money laundering, **2004**: 135
non-North Atlantic Treaty Organization (NATO) ally, designation as, **2005**: 1044
open skies agreement with U.S., **2005**: 588
reciprocity in consular relations, **1989-90**: 346

Thailand (continued)
service on Thailand defendant by international registered mail, return receipt requested, **2005**: 859–61
trade issues, **1991-99**: 1385, 1412–13, 1717–19; **2004**: 618
trafficking in women and children in, **1991-99**: 852, 912–16
U.S. ban on shrimp imports, challenge of, **2001**: 752–56
WTO and. *See* World Trade Organization (WTO)
Thermonuclear Experimental Reactor Consortium, International (ITER), 2005: 1080, 1086
Threshold Country Program, 2005: 672–73
Threshold Test Ban Treaty (1974) (U.S.–USSR), 1989-90: 567, 571
Tibet
human rights violations and, **1991-99**: 869, 1457, 1458
U.S. foreign policy authority and, **1991-99**: 818
Tibetan Mustangs
entry restriction exemptions and, **2007**: 70–72; **2008**: 29–30
Timor-Leste
programs promoting rule of law, **2005**: 435
UN Administration for, **2005**: 410
UN Commission on Human Rights and, **2004**: 390–91
UN reform, commitment to, **2004**: 403
Titanic Maritime Memorial Act (1986), 2001: 695–97; **2004**: 716; **2008**: 658, 660
Tobacco. *See also* Cigarettes
Tobacco Control, WHO Framework Convention on, **2003**: 813–15; **2004**: 786–87
Togo
trafficking in persons actions, **2005**: 162
Tokelau, 2005: 743
Tonga
environmental protection agreement, **2002**: 791
extradition and mutual legal assistance, **2000**: 185*n*
longshore work prohibition on alien crewmen from, **2002**: 757; **2003**: 764
Tort claims. *See also* Alien Tort Statute (ATS); Federal Tort Claims Act (1946)
exceptions to sovereign immunity. *See* Foreign Sovereign Immunities Act (FSIA) (1976), *subheading*: exceptions to immunity
failure to notify consul in detention of foreign national, **2001**: 335
price fixing giving rise to, **2001**: 334–35
state claims over actions of flight crew and captain, preempted by Tokyo Convention, **2008**: 524–25

Torture. *See also* Detainees, military
act of state doctrine, applicability of, **1991-99**: 1333; **2005**: 580–81
Alien Tort Statute claims of brought under, **1991-99**: 980–90; **2001**: 323–24; **2004**: 528; **2005**: 411–15, 425–27, 475–81
apprehension abroad for trial in U.S. and, **1991-99**: 505, 506
coerced statements, **2005**: 359–60, 1003–4
Committee against, U.S. reports to, **1991-99**: 960–63; **2000**: 372–88; **2005**: 341–71, 961–87; **2006**: 421, 1119, 1124–37; **2008**: 269–73, 357–66
Committee conclusions and recommendations, U.S. observations on, **2005**: 365–71; **2006**: 403–9
General Comments, U.S. views on, **2008**: 269–73, 357–66
one-year follow up, **2007**: 374–77, 930–38
U.S. view on role of, **2008**: 269–73
Convention against (CAT) (UN 1984), **2007**: 53–54, 65, 66–67
conditions on U.S. ratification, **1989-90**: 176–90; **1991-99**: 894–95; **2002**: 195–96
cruel, inhuman or degrading treatment. *See* cruel, inhuman or degrading treatment, *this heading*
definition, **1989-90**: 179–81, 188; **1991-99**: 946–47, 953, 955, 958; **2000**: 380; **2004**: 305, 306, 308–26, 363; **2005**: 343–45, 350, 973–74, 1015, 1020; **2006**: 409–11, 1132; **2008**: 325*n*, 362
draft optional protocol to, **2002**: 313–15
implementation by U.S., **2006**: 357, 403–21; **2008**: 57–59, 367–75. *See also* Detainees, military; transfers to other countries and likelihood of, *this heading*
criminal prohibition and jurisdiction, **2005**: 343–46, 353–58; **2006**: 416–17, 1159; **2007**: 216, 928, 929; **2008**: 360–61
constitutional challenge to, **2007**: 173–80
definition of torture in, **2007**: 174–77
Detainee Treatment Act, **2005**: 1031–37
diplomatic assurances, **2008**: 371–72, 922
exclusion of evidence obtained by torture, **2007**: 216
executive branch statements, **1991-99**: 861–64; **2004**: 300–303, 329–30; **2005**: 103–4, 342, 371–75, 993–94, 1038
lawful sanctions, **1989-90**: 181–82, 188
legal opinion on, Department of Justice, **2004**: 303–29; **2006**: 409–11, 1132
non-derogability, **2008**: 363–64
not self-executing, **2004**: 88–89; **2005**: 1015–16
private conduct, **2008**: 361–63
prohibition on torture, **2007**: 397, 923, 928, 937

Torture (continued)
reservations, **2006**: 419
specific intent in, **2004**: 308, 309, 326–29
state action requirement, **1991-99**: 980, 982, 984, 989, 1281; **2007**: 277
territorial scope, **2006**: 413, 419–20; **2008**: 364–66
not prohibiting all incommunicado detention, **2006**: 1122
optional protocol to, **2006**: 421
cruel, inhuman or degrading treatment, **1989-90**: 182–83; **2003**: 324; **2005**: 104, 360–61, 1018, 1031; **2006**: 401–22, 1126–27, 1130, 1173–74; **2008**: 358–60
Cuba and, **2004**: 906
Declaration on the Protection of all Persons from Being Subjected to Torture and Other Cruel, Inhuman or Degrading Treatment or Punishment, **2000**: 373
defamation of religions and, **2007**: 327
European Convention for the Prevention of, **2002**: 1015–16
extradition. *See* transfers to other countries and likelihood of, *this heading*
extraterritorial jurisdiction, **2004**: 172; **2008**: 123–25, 368
FSIA claims alleging, **2003**: 549–51; **2004**: 475–76. *See also* Foreign Sovereign Immunities Act (FSIA) (1976)
commercial activity exception not applicable, **2004**: 483, 499
immunity of foreign state under FSIA and, **1991-99**: 1190–91, 1196, 1208–15, 1218–19
antiterrorism exception to, **1991-99**: 1223, 1265; **2004**: 485–89, 490, 502–3; **2005**: 506; **2008**: 457
Georgia National Action Plan Against, **2005**: 374–75
head-of-state immunity and, **1991-99**: 1266–81; **2001**: 522–23
human rights report and, **2004**: 222
ICC jurisdiction and, **1991-99**: 611
International Covenant on Civil and Political Rights and, **1991-99**: 94, 202, 521, 849, 869, 923, 960–61, 2015, 2119; **2001**: 293–94; **2005**: 259, 271, 275; **2007**: 277–83
interrogation and, **2003**: 325; **2004**: 302–3, 992, 1038–39, 1040; **2006**: 1130, 1173–77
as *jus cogens* violation, **1991-99**: 1115, 1190–91, 1196, 1208; **2004**: 304*n*; **2006**: 1122; **2007**: 178–79; **2008**: 270
law of war, prohibition of, **2007**: 889, 927–28
McCain Amendment, **2006**: 402
migrants, protection against, **2004**: 35

Torture (continued)
Military Commissions Act (2006) and, **2006**: 1171–77
no authority to authorize torture, **2006**: 1128–29
offense of, **2008**: 360–61
predicate acts for severe mental pain and suffering, **2004**: 321–26
preventing in war against terrorism, **2005**: 371–75, 438–40
in religious persecution, **2004**: 272–73, 528
Sudan and, **2004**: 132
Torture Victim Protection Act (TVPA), **2006**: 479–85; **2008**: 215–27, 243
Alien Tort Statute and, **2001**: 339; **2002**: 323–24, 352–55; **2004**: 340, 394; **2005**: 425–27; **2008**: 215–45
apartheid litigation and, **2007**: 226–27
color of law, **2006**: 484–85
command responsibility as basis for liability under, **2002**: 348–51, 470
corporate liability, whether applicable to, **2002**: 357–63; **2003**: 378–79; **2005**: 411, 424–25
definition of torture, **2004**: 314–16, 325–26
exhaustion of local remedies and, **1991-99**: 991; **2002**: 336; **2003**: 379, 385; **2005**: 427; **2006**: 482–84
extrajudicial killing, **2006**: 479–82, 485
foreign policy interests of U.S. and, **2002**: 357–63; **2004**: 376–80
and Foreign Sovereign Immunities Act (FSIA), **2007**: 224
forum non conveniens and, **2001**: 336; **2005**: 819
head-of-state immunity and, **1991-99**: 1266, 1277–81; **2001**: 522–23; **2002**: 563
immunity of government official to claims under, **2002**: 470–72, 474–75, 563; **2005**: 515–16; **2006**: 629, 650–52, 681*n*
indirect participation/accomplice liability in violations of, **2002**: 347–48, 351–55
jurisdiction, **2003**: 380; **2004**: 363
legislative history, **2001**: 325–26
purpose, **2002**: 324; **2003**: 354; **2005**: 515–16
scope, **2001**: 319, 325–26; **2004**: 340
state action requirement, **1991-99**: 980, 982; **2002**: 352–55; **2004**: 516; **2005**: 513; **2006**: 485
statute of limitations, **1991-99**: 979, 992; **2001**: 339; **2003**: 354; **2004**: 340, 382–83
U.S. views at time of adoption, **1989-90**: 190–94
transfers to other countries and likelihood of, **2006**: 416; **2007**: 278–80; **2008**: 74–77
to be held by foreign government on behalf of U.S., **2003**: 323, 325; **2004**: 992–93; **2005**: 103–4, 1017

Torture (continued)
diplomatic assurances, **1991-99**: 941, 958–59; **2003**: 323, 325; **2004**: 86–87, 992–93; **2005**: 81–82, 86, 91, 103, 347–48, 352–53, 983–87; **2007**: 933–35; **2008**: 61, 62, 77, 366–75, 922
extradition, **1991-99**: 390, 518–19, 939–52; **2000**: 176, 379, 380–81; **2001**: 70–87; **2003**: 325; **2004**: 86–89, 91–93; **2005**: 79, 81–86, 89–94, 344–45, 348, 351–53, 358; **2006**: 157–59; **2007**: 101–8; **2008**: 57–69, 369–71, 373–75
from Guantanamo, **2003**: 1015; **2004**: 992–93; **2005**: 983–87, 993–94, 1016–18
to Iran, torture of returned nationals, **2005**: 349–50
judicial review, **1991-99**: 944, 948–49, 951–52, 959; **2008**: 67–69, 76–78
"more likely than not" standard, **1991-99**: 940, 945, 947, 948, 949–50, 953–54, 955–56; **2005**: 347; **2006**: 416; **2008**: 58, 60–61, 69, 367–71, 373
nonrefoulement
detainees suspected as terrorists, **2006**: 356–60, 413
role of diplomatic assurances, **2006**: 415–16, 421–22; **2008**: 367–75
procedure, **2008**: 59–64
removal in immigration context, **1991-99**: 239–40, 944, 952–59; **2000**: 380–81, 387–88; **2003**: 32, 38; **2005**: 17, 347–51, 983, 993–94; **2007**: 54, 65–66, 106–8, 932–34; **2008**: 308, 366, 372–73
asylum request based on fear of, Canada–U.S. agreement on examination of, **2004**: 33–34
rendition, **2006**: 358–59, 414–16
victims assistance, **1991-99**: 343–44. *See also* Torture Victims Protection Act (TVPA), *this heading*
Torture Victims Relief Act (1998), **2000**: 375
UN Voluntary Fund, **1991-99**: 858
as war crime, **1991-99**: 512, 513, 520, 526, 2076–77, 2093, 2096, 2099
Tourism
agreement, U.S.–Hungary, **1989-90**: 499
child sex tourism, **2008**: 293
regulation of in Antarctica, **2004**: 779–84
Toxic Substances Control Act (1976), **2002**: 775, 776, 777
TPA Act. *See* Bipartisan Trade Promotion Authority Act of 2002 (TPA Act)

Trade. *See also* North American Free Trade Agreement (NAFTA); Sanctions; UNCITRAL (UN Commission on International Trade Law); World Trade Organization (WTO); *specific countries*
- Agreement on Subsidies and Countervailing Measures (WTO), **2001**: 648; **2003**: 655, 656, 663; **2005**: 622, 625, 628, 631–32, 636; **2008**: 561–62. *See also* World Trade Organization (WTO)
- agreements during 1990s, **1991-99**: 1403. *See also* World Trade Organization (WTO); *specific agreements*
- agricultural. *See also* Agricultural policy and trade
  - exceptions from U.S. sanctions programs, **2000**: 748–50
- Antidumping Agreement (WTO), **2005**: 625, 630–32. *See also* World Trade Organization (WTO)
- antitrust law and. *See* Antitrust law
- APEC Region, Enhancing Secure Trade in, **2002**: 120
- applicability of Uniformity Clause to U.S. constituent entities, **1991-99**: 810–11
- arbitration on Softwood Lumber Agreement, **2007**: 591–97; **2008**: 582–93
- arms embargoes. *See* Arms control
- assignment of receivables in, **2003**: 854–55
- bilateral investment treaties and, **1991-99**: 1465, 1468, 1469–70
- cement trade, U.S.–Mexico agreement, **2006**: 758–59
- China prison labor products, **1991-99**: 1000–1003
- China–U.S. relations, **2001**: 651–53
- claims for losses resulting from export controls, **2003**: 441–45
- coffee. *See* Coffee
- congressional agreement on, **2007**: 579–84
- Convention on the Protection and Promotion of the Diversity of Cultural Expressions, effect on trade, **2005**: 778–80
- Cote d'Ivoire restrictions, **2004**: 922–24
- cultural property, restrictions on, **1991-99**: 1794–1801; **2001**: 769–74; **2002**: 813–15; **2003**: 821–25; **2004**: 791–92, 886; **2005**: 775–76; **2006**: 897–901; **2007**: 739–42; **2008**: 729–30
- customs agreements, **2004**: 95–96, 624–26
- declaration on economic cooperation, U.S.–EU, **2004**: 644–47
- defense trade cooperation treaties, **2007**: 206–7, 996–1000; **2008**: 1020–21
- democracy and, **2001**: 350
- diamonds, **1991-99**: 522, 1943–45, 2252; **2001**: 797–801; **2002**: 728–29; **2003**: 704–9; **2004**: 653–54, 935; **2006**: 1060
  - Clean Diamond Trade Act (2003), **2003**: 704–9; **2004**: 216, 653–54, 935; **2006**: 1060

Trade (continued)
dispute resolution systems, **1991-99:** 1367–71, 1403–20, 1430–36. *See also* North American Free Trade Agreement (NAFTA); World Trade Organization (WTO)
Doha development agenda, **2007:** 569–79
Dominican Republic–Central America–United States Free Trade Agreement. *See* Dominican Republic
drugs. *See* Drug trade
electronic commerce. *See* Electronic commerce
environmental issues, **1991-99:** 1388–90, 1392, 1401, 1412, 1422, 1424, 1425, 1426–28, 1429, 1430, 1437–38, 1441, 1505, 1651–53, 1655–56, 1657–58; **2001:** 663–65, 667–70, 671–72; **2003:** 808–13; **2004:** 767–76; **2007:** 580–81; **2008:** 572, 574–75, 576, 682
hazardous chemicals and pesticides, **1991-99:** 1683–87
Hazardous Waste, Basel Convention on the Control of Transboundary Movements of. *See* Basel Convention on the Control of Transboundary Movements of Hazardous Wastes and their Disposal
shrimp import restrictions to protect sea turtles. *See* Fish and marine mammals, *subheading*: sea turtle protection
Export Administration Act of 1979. *See* Export Administration Act (1979)
Export Administration Regulations (EAR), **2000:** 746–48; **2005:** 1044, 1089, 1135–36, 1137; **2006:** 177–80, 989, 990, 1299, 1300–1301; **2008:** 808, 809, 1024, 1027
Export-Import Bank reauthorization, **2002:** 726–27
"fast track" authority, **1991-99:** 1453. *See also* Bipartisan Trade Promotion Authority Act of 2002 (TPA Act)
federal authority to regulate, **2000:** 465, 466, 468–69
Massachusetts-Burma law regulating state procurement, preempted by, **1991-99:** 785–86; **2000:** 319–40, 342
in financial services, **1991-99:** 1376–78
fish, **2004:** 753
Mexican tuna, U.S. embargo on. *See* Fish and marine mammals, *subheading*: dolphin protection in tuna harvesting
Foreign Commerce Clause, **2000:** 321–22; **2001:** 203–4
Foreign Trade Act, **2003:** 277; **2005:** 624
free trade agreements, **2002:** 722–25; **2004:** 615–19, 646; **2006:** 763–69; **2007:** 584–85
Australia–U.S., **2004:** 615–16, 776; **2005:** 637
Bahrain–U.S., **2004:** 616; **2005:** 757; **2006:** 765
Canada–U.S., **2005:** 605
Central American Free Trade Agreement (CAFTA), **2003:** 683–86; **2004:** 616–19; **2005:** 636–37, 640, 757

Trade (continued)
Chile–U.S., **2003:** 679–82; **2005:** 757
Colombia–U.S., **2004:** 618; **2006:** 764–65; **2007:** 585; **2008:** 571–72
Dominican Republic–Central American Free Trade Agreement (CAFTA–DR), **2005:** 636–37, 640, 757; **2006:** 764; **2008:** 573
Free Trade Agreement of the Americas, **1991-99:** 1437–41, 1491
Jordan–U.S., **2001:** 665, 670–674; **2005:** 757
Morocco–U.S., **2003:** 682; **2004:** 616, 776; **2005:** 757
NAFTA. *See* North American Free Trade Agreement (NAFTA)
Oman–U.S., **2005:** 637; **2006:** 765–66; **2008:** 572
Panama–U.S., **2006:** 765; **2007:** 585; **2008:** 571*n*
Peru–U.S., **2005:** 637, **2007:** 580–81, 584–85; **2008:** 571*n*
Republic of Korea, **2007:** 585; **2008:** 571*n*
Singapore–U.S., **2003:** 679–80; **2005:** 757
Freedom for Russia and Emerging Eurasian Democracies and Open Markets Support Act, **1991-99:** 1011–14, 2330–31
General Agreement on Tariffs and Trade. *See* General Agreement on Tariffs and Trade (GATT)
General Agreement on Trade in Services. *See* General Agreement on Trade in Services (GATS)
Generalized System of Preferences, **2004:** 654–59; **2008:** 581
Haitian Hemispheric Opportunity through Partnership Encouragement Act (2008), **2008:** 582
human rights policy and, **1991-99:** 851, 1453–60
import safety issues, **2007:** 587–90
indirect commerce in petroleum products, **2003:** 1063–64
information technology products, **1991-99:** 1378, 1523–25
in instruments of torture, **2001:** 293–94
intellectual property. *See* Intellectual property rights
International Coffee Agreement, **2005:** 467–68; **2007:** 585–87
International Natural Rubber Agreement, **1991-99:** 1452–53
Internet and, **2004:** 627–34
investment, trade and, instruments, **2004:** 651–52; **2006:** 759–62; **2008:** 573–75
investment and, **2007:** 582
investment law and, **2004:** 584*n*
Iraq, U.S. policy toward, **2006:** 177, 179–80
Japan–U.S. agreements, **1991-99:** 1448–52
Jordan–U.S. Free Trade Area, **2001:** 213–14
Korea–U.S. agreements (1995), **1991-99:** 1441–45
labor issues, **2007:** 581–82, 584–85
labor standards and, **2001:** 663–67, 671, 672–73

Trade (continued)
least-restrictive measures principle, **2001**: 596–98
Libya, easing of restrictions on, **2004**: 660–61, 931–34, 1161; **2006**: 177–79
medical commodities, exceptions from U.S. sanctions programs, **2000**: 748–50
Mexico's Foreign Trade Act, **2005**: 624
military action as infringement on freedom of commerce, **2003**: 1062–64, 1065–66
most-favored-nation status, **1989-90**: 340–48; **1991-99**: 1377*n*, 1453–60; **2006**: 755; **2007**: 590–91; **2008**: 498–501, 529, 531–32, 538
NAFTA. *See* North American Free Trade Agreement (NAFTA)
Non-Agricultural Market Access (NAMA), **2005**: 614–15; **2007**: 569–71; **2008**: 568–70
normal trade relations status, **1991-99**: 1377*n*
Omnibus Export Amendments Act (1990), **1989-90**: 508–12
Omnibus Trade and Competitiveness Act (1988), **1989-90**: 419; **1991-99**: 559, 1372, 1373; **2006**: 767
payment guarantees and credit, **1991-99**: 1812–14
port security, **2007**: 584
promotion of, **2005**: 638–40
Puerto Rican authority to regulate, **2000**: 344
sanctions. *See* Sanctions
in services, **2001**: 670–71
Softwood Lumber Agreement (SLA), **2006**: 762–63; **2007**: 549, 591–97; **2008**: 582–93. *See also* North American Free Trade Agreement (NAFTA)
Southern Africa Customs Union–U.S. negotiations, **2003**: 682. *See also* Trade, Investment, and Development Cooperation Agreement (TIDCA), *this heading*
Soviet Union–U.S., Soviet debt repayment and, **1991-99**: 1123–24
Special 301 program. *See* Intellectual property rights
statute of limitations for transaction-related claims, **1991-99**: 1817–20
tariffs. *See* Tariffs
tax havens, use of, **2001**: 656–57
taxes on. *See* Taxation
tequila trade, U.S.–Mexico agreement, **2006**: 757–58
textiles and clothing, **2004**: 923–24; **2008**: 582
Cambodia–U.S. textile agreement, **2002**: 725–26
Textiles and Clothing, Agreement on (U.S.–China), **2005**: 640–45
tourism agreement, **1989-90**: 499
trade embargoes, **1991-99**: 1974; **2001**: 750–52; **2004**: 286, 918, 927–34; **2005**: 665, 667, 671, 890

Trade (continued)
Trade, Investment, and Development Cooperation Agreement (TIDCA)
Southern African Customs Union (SACU)–U.S., **2008:** 576–77
Trade Act (1974
§ 141 (Office of U.S. Trade Representative), **2001:** 764
§ 151 (approval of agreements), **2002:** 719
§ 182(a) (protection of intellectual property rights), **1991-99:** 1517–18; **2007:** 606; **2008:** 605
§§ 201-204 (injury from import competition), **2002:** 694–96; **2003:** 657, 659–60
§§ 301-310 (unfair trade practices), **1991-99:** 1375, 1406, 1412, 1416–18, 1442–43, 1517–18, 1520; **2001:** 649, 764
Special 301 program (intellectual property), **2006:** 767; **2007:** 606–7
§ 402 (Freedom of emigration), **2001:** 652
§§ 501-507 (GSP), **1991-99:** 847, 941; **2002:** 261; **2004:** 221, 654–56, 923; **2008:** 249, 581
§ 604 (tariff schedules), **2002:** 696; **2003:** 680
U.S. trade policy, **1991-99:** 1455
Trade Act (1988), **1989-90:** 423
Trade Act (2002), **2002:** 719, 722; **2003:** 684; **2004:** 658–59; **2005:** 638; **2008:** 577, 578
Trade and Investment Cooperation Agreements (TICA)
Ukraine–U.S., **2008:** 575–76
Trade and Investment Framework Agreements (TIFA)
Afghanistan–U.S., **2004:** 652
East African Community–U.S., **2008:** 573–74
Iraq–U.S., **2005:** 646
Pakistan–U.S., **2004:** 651–52
Uruguay–U.S., **2008:** 574–75
Trade Promotion Authority. *See* Bipartisan Trade Promotion Authority Act of 2002 (TPA Act)
trade-distorting domestic support, reduction of, **2005:** 611–12
TRIPS Agreement. *See* Trade Related Aspects of Intellectual Property Rights (TRIPS Agreement)
Ukraine, **2006:** 746–48; **2008:** 575–76
UN Commission on International Trade Law (UNCITRAL). *See* UNCITRAL (UN Commission on International Trade Law)
U.S. International Trade Agenda, **2001:** 663–68
U.S. policy toward Colombia and, **2004:** 379
U.S. policy toward Iraq and, **2004:** 492, 647–51
U.S.–Middle East Free Trade Area, **2003:** 686–87
wildlife, restrictions on trade in, **2003:** 579–82; **2004:** 771; **2005:** 756; **2006:** 888; **2007:** 580, 731–32; **2008:** 707, 724–25

Trade (continued)
wine-making practices and labeling, **2006:** 757
WTO and. *See* World Trade Organization (WTO)
Trade Related Aspects of Intellectual Property Rights (TRIPS Agreement), 1991-99: 1372, 1374–75
bilateral investment treaties (BITs), **1991-99:** 1464, 1470
Convention on Cybercrime, **2003:** 194, 200
environment, **1991-99:** 1390
phase-in of commitments, **1991-99:** 1395
public health and, **1991-99:** 1386, 1506–7; **2001:** 646–48, 764–67; **2003:** 673–79; **2005:** 618–19
amendment regarding access to medicines, **2005:** 618–19
technical assistance, **1991-99:** 1368
WIPO Copyright Treaty and, **1991-99:** 1512–13
WIPO Performances and Phonograms Treaty and, **1991-99:** 1514–16
WTO
disputes, **1991-99:** 1408–9; **2002:** 673; **2003:** 651–52, 661–63; **2005:** 621
public health and. *See* public health and, *this heading*
Trademark law, 1991-99: 1508–9; **2004:** 663–70, 873
anti-suit injunction, **2008:** 771–77
comity-based abstention, **2005:** 826–27
Cuban litigation in U.S., **2005:** 663–71; **2006:** 796–801, 1006–15
domain name registration
Paris Convention for the Protection of Industrial Property and, **2002:** 389–91
use of names of sovereign countries, **2002:** 518–19; **2003:** 651–52
European Union–protection of trademarks and geographical indications for agricultural products and foodstuffs, **2005:** 621–22
Lanham Act, **2005:** 664, 667–71; **2008:** 775
Madrid Agreement Concerning the International Registration of Marks, Protocol Relating to, **1991-99:** 695–99, 2192, 2247; **2000:** 297–301; **2003:** 699–701
rules of private international law, **2000:** 740
Singapore Treaty on the Law of Trademarks, **2008:** 609–10
Trademark Act (1946), **2002:** 673, 676
Trademark Law Treaty Implementation Act (1998), **1991-99:** 1508
WTO disputes. *See* World Trade Organization (WTO)
Trading with the Enemy Act (1917), 1991-99: 54, 55, 1225, 1901–2, 1906; **2000:** 229, 513, 543; **2002:** 412, 674; **2004:** 667, 925, 1090*n*, 1109; **2006:** 1013–14; **2007:** 1019, 1022; **2008:** 415, 810, 960, 963, 964, 965–66

Trafficking
in drugs. *See* Drug trade
in persons. *See* Trafficking in persons
in weapons. *See specific types of weapons*
in wildlife, **2005**: 756; **2006**: 888
Trafficking in persons, 1991-99: 61; **2000**: 23–24, 222, 223, 225–30; **2001**: 145–52, 253–54, 264; **2003**: 188–90, 213, 291; **2004**: 101–3, 149–68; **2006**: 226–29; **2008**: 115–20
authority for nonconsensual boarding of ship suspected of involvement in, **2003**: 735–36
Alien Tort Statute litigation concerning, **2008**: 227–36
children as trafficking victims
Agreement between U.S. and Socialist Republic of Vietnam Regarding Cooperation on Adoption of Children, **2005**: 67–68
protection of children, **1991-99**: 911–17, 928–29, 930, 1859; **2006**: 226, 227, 374, 384–85; **2008**: 292
Protocol to Prevent, Suppress and Punish Trafficking in Persons, Especially Women and Children (2000), **2000**: 221–22, 223–24; **2001**: 151; **2003**: 142, 735–36; **2004**: 95–96, 101–2, 141–42, 149–57; **2005**: 153, 155; **2007**: 345
Sale of Children, Child Prostitution and Child Pornography, Protocol on, **2000**: 360–62; **2007**: 167–68; **2008**: 291–300
UN Commission on Human Rights resolutions, **2005**: 162–64
definition, **2001**: 147; **2004**: 151–52; **2007**: 167–68
forced labor and, **2008**: 115, 227
human rights and, **2004**: 388
interim assessment, special watch list, **2005**: 158–60; **2006**: 227
National Security Presidential Directive on Trafficking in Persons (NSPD-22), **2005**: 163, 164
NATO policy, **2004**: 165–66
OAS Inter-American Program for the Promotion and Protection of the Human Rights of Migrants, **2005**: 340
prevalence, **2004**: 280
prevention of, **2001**: 146–52; **2003**: 188–90, 213
sanctions on countries involved in, **2001**: 150; **2003**: 188–89; **2004**: 164–65; **2006**: 228–29; **2007**: 168–70; **2008**: 116–17
scope, **2001**: 146, 147, 148
transfer of organs for profit, **2000**: 362
UN Commission on Human Rights resolutions against trafficking, **2004**: 269; **2005**: 162–64
UN reform and, **2004**: 403

Trafficking in persons (continued)
U.S. report on foreign governments' efforts (TIP report), **2001**: 145–51; **2003**: 402; **2004**: 163–65; **2005**: 156–59; **2006**: 226–27; **2007**: 167–68, 170, 345; **2008**: 115–17, 293
Victims of Crime Act of 1984 (VOCA), **1989-90**: 334; **1991-99**: 481; **2005**: 271, 272
Victims of Trafficking and Violence Protection Act (TVPA) (2000), **2000**: 225–30, 540, 541–42; **2001**: 145, 146–47, 148, 149, 150, 151–52, 264; **2002**: 244–45, 532–33; **2003**: 188–89, 190, 540; **2004**: 101–2, 156; **2005**: 156–57, 159, 160–61, 162, 272–74; **2007**: 167–70, 335, 342, 345; **2008**: 115–20, 292
Discretionary Grant Program, **2005**: 273
Presidential Determination on countries' performance, **2003**: 188–89; **2004**: 164–65; **2005**: 160–62; **2006**: 227–29; **2007**: 168–70; **2008**: 117–19
Special Watch List, **2003**: 190; **2005**: 158–60; **2006**: 227; **2008**: 116
tier classification of countries' efforts, **2001**: 149–50; **2004**: 164; **2005**: 158–59; **2006**: 228–29; **2007**: 169, **2008**: 115–17
Trafficking Victims Protection Reauthorization Act (2003), **2005**: 159–60; **2006**: 227
Trafficking Victims Protection Reauthorization Act (2005), **2006**: 1066
Trafficking Victims Protection Reauthorization Act (2008), **2008**: 119–20
women as trafficking victims, **2000**: 223–24, 225–30, 251; **2004**: 101, 142, 149, 151, 166–68, 475, 483
in conflict/post-conflict situations, **2004**: 166–68
empowerment in Africa, **2005**: 308
prostitution, **2007**: 318
protection of women, **1991-99**: 911–17; **2006**: 374
Protocol to Prevent, Suppress and Punish Trafficking in Persons, Especially Women and Children (2000), **2000**: 221–22, 223–24; **2001**: 151; **2003**: 142, 735–36; **2004**: 95–96, 101–2, 141–42, 149–57; **2005**: 153, 155
sexual exploitation, **2005**: 162–64
Training, Certification and Watchkeeping, International Convention on Standards of, 2003: 752–53
Transactional Law on Cross-border Securities Transactions, UNIDROIT Draft Convention on, 2005: 808
Transboundary Movement of Hazardous Wastes. *See* Basel Convention on the Control of Transboundary Movements of Hazardous Wastes and their Disposal

Transfer of prisoners. *See* Prisoner transfer
Transit of Goods for Trade with Land-locked States, Convention on, 2002: 837
Transnational organized crime. *See* Crime, *subheading*: organized crime
Transport Terminals, Convention on, 2002: 836
Transportation. *See* Aviation issues; Carriage of goods by sea
Transportation, U.S. Department of, 2005: 586, 588–89, 693–94
Travel Initiative, Western Hemisphere, 2005: 1–2; **2006:** 4–11; **2007:** 8–12, 15; **2008:** 6–11
Travel restrictions. *See also* Immigration and visas; Passports, U.S.
authority to impose, **1991-99:** 56–57
in connection with International Criminal Tribunal for the Former Yugoslavia, **2004:** 173
departure restrictions on wife of former President Marcos of Philippines, **1989-90:** 60–62
exceptions for minors, **2000:** 118–19
national security rationale, **1991-99:** 58–59
related to Burma, **2003:** 27–29; **2007:** 41; **2008:** 28–29, 793–95
related to Cuba, **1991-99:** 53–59, 1903, 1907–8, 1909, 1910; **2000:** 749, 750; **2003:** 21–23; **2004:** 906, 907–8, 910–12, 915–17; **2007:** 830–31; **2008:** 810–13
related to Iraq, **1991-99:** 49–51, 1924; **2001:** 13–14; **2004:** 887; **2006:** 1015–19
related to Kuwait, **1991-99:** 49–50
related to Lebanon, **1991-99:** 51
related to Libya, **1991-99:** 52; **2001:** 15; **2004:** 930–31
related to Mauritania, **2008:** 29, 806
related to UNITA officials, **1991-99:** 1941–43
Travel Act (Florida, 2006), **2007:** 235–36
travel of foreign officials in matters of judicial assistance, **2000:** 158
on UN Special Rapporteur by Romanian government, **1989-90:** 366–67
Treaties, generally, 1991-99: 643–44. *See also* Agreements, generally; Memoranda of understanding; Vienna Convention on the Law of Treaties (VCLT) (1969); *specific topics and countries*
acceptance, **1991-99:** 1787*n*; **2003:** 248–50
applicability. *See also* succession, *this heading*
to colonies and constituent entities, **1991-99:** 772
to Taiwan, **1991-99:** 700–9
application prior to entry into force
by MOU, **2002:** 186–90
NAFTA treaty responsibility prior to entry into force, **2002:** 609–11

Treaties, generally (continued)
obligations of signatories before ratification, **2001**: 212–13
provisional application, **1991-99**: 699–700, 1571–72
armed conflict, effect of on, **2005**: 222–24; **2006**: 295–98; **2007**: 208–9; **2008**: 168–70
breach and noncompliance
and countermeasures, **1991-99**: 1109
effect of material breach, **2005**: 1063
independence of judiciary as justification for, **2001**: 256–57
capacity to enter into, **2006**: 281–82
East Timor, prior to independence, **2002**: 177
EU member states, **2002**: 598–600
European Community, **2004**: 191–93
European Union, **1991-99**: 696–99, 1511–12; **2000**: 296–308; **2003**: 241–43, 834; **2004**: 148–49, 191–93, 801–2
Hong Kong. *See* Hong Kong, *this heading*
international organizations, **2000**: 296–308
Puerto Rico, **2000**: 340–44
U.S. states. *See* U.S. law and, *this heading*
Case Act and, **2006**: 295
claims against U.S. arising from in U.S. courts, **1991-99**: 658–61, 664–66, 1128
compliance regime for environmental agreements, **2000**: 711–25
constituent parts of a state, obligations of, **2002**: 643. *See also* U.S. law and, *this heading*
customary international law
interpretation of, **2008**: 250, 360
modification of treaty by subsequent, **1991-99**: 714–31
treaty as evidence of, and, **2002**: 658
depositary practice, **1991-99**: 739–42
enforcement by Attorney General, **2005**: 42
enforcement through political and diplomatic channels, **2005**: 49, 246
entry into force date, **2001**: 213–14
federalism. *See* U.S. law and, *this heading*
FSIA and. *See* Foreign Sovereign Immunities Act (FSIA) (1976)
full powers, **1989-90**: 142–43
good faith in treaty compliance, **2001**: 592
Hong Kong
capacity to enter into treaties, **1991-99**: 382–83, 689–93; **2000**: 190–203
Agreement Between U.S. and Hong Kong for Surrender of Fugitive Offenders, **1991-99**: 403–5, 408, 412–13, 689–93; **2000**: 190–203

Treaties, generally (continued)
Agreement Between U.S. and Hong Kong for Transfer of Sentenced Persons, **1991-99**: 382–83
continuation in force of treaties, **1991-99**: 764–67, 1175
International Covenant on Civil and Political Rights applicable to, **1991-99**: 405
ICJ
on treaty law and state responsibility, **1991-99**: 1109
in treaty reference for dispute resolution, **2003**: 264–65
on treaty reservations, **2001**: 306
implementation
in the absence of diplomatic relations, **2003**: 103–4
in armed conflict, **2005**: 222–24; **2006**: 295–98
governed by procedural law of the forum state, **2005**: 47
interpretation of, **1991-99**: 151, 498–99, 711–12, 1329; **2000**: 516*n*, 518, 519*n*; **2004**: 198–202, 225, 309, 423, 480, 536–37, 544–47, 584*n*, 1041; **2005**: 32–33, 51, 223, 296, 722; **2007**: 43–47
authority to interpret, **2002**: 440, 460, 1001
congressional role, **1991-99**: 756–58
consultation for interpretation, **2003**: 252–56
customary international law and, **2002**: 653; **2004**: 199–202
deference to Executive Branch views, **1991-99**: 712; **2000**: 38–39, 526–28, 597–99; **2002**: 440, 1001; **2004**: 869; **2005**: 52, 54, 56, 64, 143, 480–81, 1024–25; **2008**: 40–41, 66
modification vs., **1991-99**: 718–19, 723
presidential authority regarding, **1991-99**: 756–58
travaux preparatoires, role of, **2003**: 60–61, 235–36; **2004**: 200–202; **2006**: 287–88
weight of Executive Branch views expressed to Senate, **2004**: 312–13
weight of ICJ views on, in U.S. courts, **1991-99**: 315; **2005**: 54
invalidity, claim of defects in consent, **2003**: 251–52
Military Commissions Act (2006) and, **2006**: 1170–74
modification, **1991-99**: 722, 757–58
authority for, **1991-99**: 727
by congressional–executive agreement, **1991-99**: 666–70
by estoppel, **1991-99**: 721
interpretation vs., **1991-99**: 718–19, 723
by judicial or arbitral precedent, **1991-99**: 723–24
by subsequent customary international law, **1991-99**: 714–31
subsequent practice, **1991-99**: 720, 727–28
tacit amendments, **2008**: 158–59, 609, 698, 715–16, 741–42
non-state parties. *See also* applicability, *this heading*; capacity to enter into, *this heading*

Treaties, generally (continued)
with American Indian tribes, **2001:** 254–55
regional economic integration organizations as parties to, **1991-99:** 693–99
role of commonwealths and territories, **1989-90:** 163
supranational organizations as parties to, **2000:** 296–308
object and purpose, **1991-99:** 719, 968–70
obligations of nonparties to, **2005:** 195, 199–200, 391
obligations of U.S. states under, **1989-90:** 169–70; **1991-99:** 1109; **2000:** 293–96, 385–86, 528–31, 536–39, 680; **2001:** 179–200, 202; **2002:** 190–98; **2003:** 40–41, 193
VCCR in absence of consular or diplomatic relations, **2003:** 103–4
outer space law, **2001:** 716–19; **2003:** 765–66; **2004:** 802
pacta sunt servanda principle, **1991-99:** 721–22; **2001:** 131–32, 592; **2002:** 661
president's powers with respect to, **1991-99:** 705, 726–29, 752–61; **2000:** 38–39, 201–2; **2001:** 752; **2002:** 198–208, 242, 1001; **2005:** 42; **2007:** 74–75; **2008:** 207, 518, 911. *See also* Agreements, generally; interpretation of, *this heading*
private right of action under, **2006:** 84–85; **2008:** 35–47, 95, 97, 153–54, 155–58, 179*n*, 279, 328, 401, 886, 889. *See also* Private rights of action under international instruments; Standing
as derivative of right of state party, **1991-99:** 438
as distinct from self-executing, **2002:** 221–22; **2003:** 258–67
presumption against, **1989-90:** 347–48; **1991-99:** 1128; **2000:** 491–95; **2002:** 214–15; **2005:** 49, 53, 58, 62, 83–84, 245–46, 1007, 1015; **2008:** 39–40
provisional application. *See* application prior to entry into force, *this heading*
ratification
versus acceptance, **1991-99:** 1787*n*
conditional ratification, **2000:** 386
process, **1991-99:** 877–78
protocols of convention without ratification of underlying convention, **2002:** 183–86, 288–89
Senate conditions attached to, legal status of, **1991-99:** 738–39, 759–61
when ratification is required under U.S. law, **1991-99:** 599–601, 644–58; **2001:** 200–211; **2002:** 177–83
reciprocity, **1989-90:** 185; **1991-99:** 415–516, 705, 1109, 1478, 1514, 2204; **2001:** 131–32; **2004:** 545

Treaties, generally (continued)
reservations, **1989-90**: 143–50; **1991-99**: 734–38, 880–83; **2000**: 146, 171–72, 217, 221, 385–86, 420, 503, 509–10, 605*n*, 614; **2001**: 214–18, 305–7; **2002**: 206–12, 393–94; **2003**: 243–58; **2004**: 196–98; **2006**: 288–92
collective reservation as substitute for amendment, **2006**: 292–94
conditions on entry into force of NATO protocols, **1991-99**: 738–39
declaration as reservation, **2003**: 244–45
effect of, **2005**: 221–22, 366
human rights treaties, **1991-99**: 878–83
ICJ on, **2001**: 306
International Law Commission on, **2006**: 294–95
no-reservation clauses, **1991-99**: 732–34
objections to treaty reservations, effect of, **1991-99**: 969–70; **2005**: 221–22
retroactive application, presumption against, **1989-90**: 122; **2004**: 81, 225, 226
separation of powers and, **1991-99**: 738–39, 967–68
UN Human Rights Committee General Comment 24 on, **1991-99**: 878–83
in violation of treaty object and purpose, **1991-99**: 968–70; **2005**: 221–22, 366
self-executing and non-self-executing, **1991-99**: 159–62, 873, 875, 882, 886, 895, 908–9, 951–53, 959, 997; **2000**: 38–39; **2001**: 290; **2007**: 206–7, 629, 645; **2008**: 39, 57, 78–79, 95–96, 153–54, 155–56, 158, 179, 180, 184, 186, 189, 190, 191, 278–79, 395, 615, 698, 723, 753, 780, 886, 889. *See also* International Covenant on Civil and Political Rights (ICCPR); private right of action under, *this heading*
deference to Executive Branch views regarding, **2000**: 38–39; **2008**: 153–54
succession, **1991-99**: 705, 742–67; **2000**: 563; **2003**: 245–48. *See also specific countries*
Austria and Hungary, **1991-99**: 744
Bosnia and Herzegovina, **2003**: 245–48
Czech and Slovak Republics, **1991-99**: 764
East Timor, **2002**: 177
Ecuador (Colombian Union), **1991-99**: 744
Egypt and Syria, **1991-99**: 744
Federal Republic of Yugoslavia, **2000**: 561, 563
Finland, **1991-99**: 744
Germany, **1991-99**: 761–64

Treaties, generally (continued)
Hong Kong, **1991-99**: 382–83, 403–5, 408, 412–13, 689–93, 764–67, 773–75, 1175, 1179; **2002**: 384–85
Iceland, **1991-99**: 705
Norway and Sweden, **1991-99**: 744
Pakistan, **1991-99**: 744; **2008**: 64–67
Panama, **1991-99**: 744
Poland, **1991-99**: 744
Soviet Union, **1991-99**: 742–61, 1170–73
Taiwan, **1991-99**: 706–9
Supremacy Clause, **1991-99**: 729–30. *See also* U.S. law and, *this heading*
suspension, **1991-99**: 721; **2007**: 1001
termination
by President, **2002**: 202–6
procedures, **1991-99**: 704, 719, 720, 727–28; **2001**: 205
understandings to, **2000**: 172–73, 217, 220, 235
unilateral acts of states, **2006**: 281–83
U.S. law and, **1991-99**: 709–14, 729–30, 731–32; **2007**: 74–75; **2008**: 183–84
abrogation of obligation by later-enacted statute, **2001**: 132–33; **2008**: 282–84
Compact Clause, **2001**: 179–93, 198; **2005**: 207. *See also* Constitution, U.S.
Constitution, precedence of over treaties, **2005**: 244, 247; **2007**: 105, 211–12
constitutional requirements, **1991-99**: 643–44; **2002**: 178–79; **2004**: 39. *See also* Constitution, U.S.
domestic vs. international law in relation to, **1991-99**: 731–32
Presidential powers with respect to, **2007**: 74–75, 176, 202–3, 215
requiring state and local compliance with, **2007**: 200–5
state law preempted by, **1991-99**: 775–76, 782–85; **2000**: 528–31, 536–39; **2004**: 444
status of unratified instruments, **2003**: 361–68
statutes should be construed consistently with treaty obligations, **1991-99**: 957
treaties as legal basis for actions of U.S., **2005**: 215–19
U.S. states and, **1989-90**: 169–70; **1991-99**: 566–68, 652–57, 676*n*, 678–79, 822, 875, 905–6; **2000**: 293–96, 386, 528–31, 536–39, 680; **2001**: 156–59, 180–93, 198; **2002**: 156–59, 190–98, 290–91; **2003**: 117–18, 206; **2004**: 143–44, 156, 159, 825; **2005**: 154–55, 168–69, 207, 770–71; **2007**: 202, 211–12. *See also* Compact Clause, *this subheading*; Constitution, U.S.; States, U.S., *subheading*: treaties and

Treaties, generally (continued)
U.S. policies on entering into treaties, **2006**: 283–84; **2007**: 195–99; **2008**: 887
U.S. priority list for treaties, **2007**: 200
U.S. Treaty Affairs Regulations, **2006**: 295–97
Vienna Convention on. *See* Vienna Convention on Law of Treaties (VCLT) (1969)
Webpage of Office of Treaty Affairs, **2006**: 298
what constitutes
agreements as, **1991-99**: 659, 661–65, 689–93
definition of, **1991-99**: 645, 661, 683, 783; **2005**: 83
executive agreement vs., **2001**: 200–211
other international agreements vs., **2002**: 177–79
separate adherence by two states to different version of treaty, **2001**: 555–65
when agreement must take the form of a treaty under U.S. law, **1991-99**: 599–601, 644–58; **2001**: 200–211; **2002**: 177–83
state declarations versus, **2001**: 291–92
withdrawal, authority, **2002**: 198–202
Treaty Clause of U.S. Constitution, 1991-99: 645–52, 705; **2001**: 200–211, 563
TRIA (Terrorism Risk Insurance Act). *See* Terrorism
Trinidad and Tobago
bilateral investment treaty, **1991-99**: 1466
extradition and mutual legal assistance, **1991-99**: 396, 453; **2000**: 179, 186*n*; **2001**: 90–96
Inter-American Convention Against Corruption, party to, **2006**: 238
maritime counter-drug trade agreement, **1991-99**: 1607
U.S. military assistance, **2006**: 278
Tripartite Commission for the Restitution of Monetary Gold, 1991-99: 1043–46, 1080–81
TRIPS Agreement. *See* Trade Related Aspects of Intellectual Property Rights (TRIPS Agreement)
Trust Territory of the Pacific Islands, 1989-90: 9, 161
Truth, right to
UN Commission on Human Rights (UNCHR) Resolution 2005/66, **2005**: 380–81; **2006**: 425
Truth in Negotiations Act (TINA), 2005: 232
Tucker Act (1887), 1991-99: 660–61, 664; **2008**: 247
Tueni, Gebran, murder of, 2005: 884–86
Tuna. *See* Fish and marine mammals

Tunisia
reservations to Vienna Convention on the Law of Treaties, **1989-90**: 150
tax agreement with U.S., **1989-90**: 415
trade and investment agreements, **1991-99**: 1466
Tunis Agenda for the Information Society, **2005**: 661–63
Turkey
agricultural trade policy, **1991-99**: 1384
compliance with international child abduction convention, **2004**: 54
extradition and mutual legal assistance, **2000**: 186*n*
Hague Child Abduction Convention, compliance with, **2006**: 102
intellectual property rights Watch List, **2006**: 768; **2007**: 608, 610; **2008**: 607
longshore work prohibition on alien crewmen from, **2002**: 757; **2003**: 764
maritime navigation safety and, **2002**: 105
missile defense cooperation, **2004**: 1066
money laundering in, **2004**: 135
NATO member, **2005**: 1044
NATO Summit and, **2004**: 165
North Korean diplomats, arrest of for narcotrafficking, **2005**: 182
Nuclear Terrorism, Global Initiative to Combat, **2006**: 1295–96
Open Skies (aerial observation) treaty, **2002**: 1029
PKK terrorism in, **2008**: 871–72
religious freedom in, **2004**: 270
service of process rules, **2003**: 891
WTO dispute over rice importation, **2006**: 742
zoning restriction on U.S. chancery, **1989-90**: 379–81
Turkmenistan
diplomatic relations, **1991-99**: 1174
human rights in, **2002**: 282
import ban on Caspian Sea beluga sturgeon products, **2005**: 754
intellectual property rights Watch List, **2006**: 769; **2007**: 610
religious freedom
actions promoting, **2005**: 315
violations, **2003**: 296
trade and investment issues, **1991-99**: 1455
Turks and Caicos Islands
maritime counter-drug trade agreement, **1991-99**: 1608
Tuvalu
extradition and mutual legal assistance, **2000**: 185*n*
longshore work prohibition on alien crewmen from, **2002**: 757; **2003**: 764
TVPA (Torture Victim Protection Act). *See* Torture
TVPA (Trafficking Victim Protection Act). *See* Trafficking in persons

U

UCMJ. *See* Uniform Code of Military Justice (UCMJ)

Uganda
American Servicemembers' Protection Act waiver, **2003**: 238
child soldiers in, **2003**: 308; **2004**: 281, 282–83; **2006**: 387, 389
Open Skies agreement, **2002**: 597
regional peace agreement, **2004**: 942–43; **2005**: 926

Ukraine
accession to WTO, **2006**: 745–46
arbitration of disputes and, **2004**: 821
arms control
Lisbon Protocol to the Strategic Arms Reduction Treaty (START), party to, **2005**: 1045*n*
missile defense cooperation, **2004**: 1066; **2005**: 1136
strategic offensive arms agreements, **1991-99**: 2210–17, 2245–46; **2004**: 1053–55
asylum seekers returned to Uzbekistan by, **2006**: 60–61
Demjanjuk case, **2004**: 1
democracy promotion programs, **1991-99**: 1011–14
diplomatic relations, **1991-99**: 1173
extradition and mutual legal assistance, **2000**: 166
intellectual property rights Watch List, **2006**: 768, 769; **2007**: 610; **2008**: 607
Law of the Sea Convention and, **2004**: 763
money laundering in, **2002**: 127–28, 130; **2003**: 208, 211–12; **2004**: 135
nonproliferation. *See* Nonproliferation, *subheading*: country-specific issues
Open Skies (aerial observation) treaty, **2002**: 1029
preservation of American heritage in, **1991-99**: 1793–94
successor state issues, **1991-99**: 748–50, 751–61, 1171
Trade and Investment Cooperation Agreement (TICA), **2008**: 575–76
trade and investment issues, **1991-99**: 1455, 1466
U.S.–Ukraine trade relations, **2006**: 746–48

UMA (Uniform Mediation Act), **2005**: 805–7

UN Commission on Human Rights, 2007: 272, 286. *See also* Human rights; International Covenant on Civil and Political Rights (ICCPR)
Note: The Commission changed in 2006 into the UN Human Rights Council.
Chechnya, **2003**: 953–54
children, rights of, **2001**: 273; **2003**: 303–6, 342; **2004**: 283
claims of "Mariel Cubans" detained in U.S., **2001**: 343–44
corporate responsibility, **2004**: 299; **2005**: 328–29

UN Commission on Human Rights (continued)
cultural rights and identities, **2004**: 799–800
Darfur, **2004**: 246–50, 257–59
death penalty, **2000**: 392; **2001**: 118–19, 310; **2003**: 342; **2004**: 337–38
democracy promotion, **2004**: 390–92; **2005**: 431–32
development, right to, **2001**: 275–78; **2003**: 315–16; **2005**: 326–28
disappearances, enforced or involuntary, **2001**: 317–18; **2004**: 331–34
discrimination, resolution against, **2004**: 269
Durban Declaration, **2003**: 290, 299
economic, social and cultural rights, **2001**: 279; **2003**: 309–12; **2004**: 299–300, 799–800; **2005**: 324–25
extrajudicial killing, **2000**: 397–98; **2001**: 316–17; **2003**: 344–47; **2005**: 392–93
food, right to, **2000**: 370–72; **2001**: 280–81; **2004**: 285–88; **2005**: 325–26
freedom of expression and opinion, **2001**: 353
genocide, **2001**: 118–19
health, right to, **2003**: 318; **2004**: 292–96; **2005**: 332–33
access to medication, **2001**: 281–83
HIV/AIDS, **2005**: 329–31
hostage-taking, **2005**: 184–85
housing, right to, **2000**: 370–71; **2001**: 279–80
Human Rights Council, replacement of, **2005**: 446, 453–54, 460–62; **2007**: 285–86
immunity of Special Rapporteur, **1989-90**: 353–70
impunity, **2001**: 318; **2003**: 337–38; **2005**: 200–1, 391–92
indigenous peoples, rights of, **2004**: 383–86
International Criminal Court and, **2003**: 337–38; **2004**: 181–83. *See also specific resolutions by subject*
Israel, treatment of, **2004**: 956; **2005**: 918, 919
Israeli–Palestinian conflict, **2003**: 949
judicial system integrity, **2003**: 343–44; **2004**: 338–39
jurisdiction, **2003**: 351
Khmer Rouge, **1989-90**: 124–25
law enforcement use of force, **2004**: 339
mandate is human rights not laws of war, **2003**: 343–47, 351
membership issues
Cuba, **2003**: 403–5
physical attack by representative, **2004**: 261–62
human rights abusers, **2003**: 415–16, 418; **2004**: 405
Libya, **2003**: 283
Sudan, **2004**: 257–59

UN Commission on Human Rights (continued)
migrants, rights of, **2005:** 336–37
military justice, **2003:** 343–44
missing persons, **2004:** 331–33
protections while combating terrorism, **2004:** 399–400
racism, **2000:** 350–51; **2003:** 288–89; **2005:** 304
ratione temporis jurisdiction, **2004:** 225–26
reform of, **2003:** 280–83, 415–18; **2004:** 254–57, 404–5; **2005:** 301, 443–44
religious freedom, **2004:** 278–79
remedy, right to, **2003:** 347–54; **2004:** 334–35; **2005:** 390–91
role of in relation to specific countries, **1991-99:** 866–70; **2004:** 259–62, 388
self-determination, right to, **2004:** 392–94
situations in specific countries, **2005:** 302
terrorism and human rights, **2000:** 238–39; **2001:** 117–18; **2003:** 411–12, 953–54
torture, **1991-99:** 962; **2000:** 375; **2001:** 293–94, 375; **2003:** 326; **2004:** 330
trafficking in persons, resolution against, **2004:** 269
treatment of individual countries, **2003:** 280–83; **2004:** 259–62
truth, right to, **2005:** 380–81; **2006:** 425
women, **2001:** 269–71; **2004:** 269
UN Human Rights Committee, 2006: 284–87, 346–71; **2008:** 251
Committee suggestions and recommendations, **2005:** 286–95; **2006:** 346–50
General Comment 24 on reservations to treaties, **1991-99:** 878–83
General Comment 31 on obligations imposed by, **2007:** 42–44, 53, 66–67, 270–71
U.S. comments on, **2007:** 270–85
General Comment 33 on obligations of state parties, **2008:** 252–66
interpretations of Covenant by not legally binding or authoritative, **2007:** 267
legal status of "views" of, **2008:** 253–59, 262–65
non-binding nature of decisions, **2002:** 265–67
"subsequent practice" of the parties, **2008:** 259–61
suggestions and recommendations to the U.S., **2005:** 286–95
U.S. implementation of ICCPR, follow-up report on, **2007:** 266–85
U.S. periodic report on implementation, **2005:** 258–86
U.S. responses to Committee questions, **2006:** 350–71
UN Human Rights Council, 2006: 328–43; **2007:** 285–86
climate change, resolution on, **2008:** 328
composition of, **2006:** 332

UN Human Rights Council (continued)
Convention on Forced Disappearances, U.S. submission concerning, **2008**: 379
creation of, **2005**: 301, 446–47, 453–54, 460–62; **2006**: 328; **2007**: 285–86
follow up to World Conference on Racism, **2008**: 285
history of, **2006**: 331
human rights and terrorism, report of Special Rapporteur, **2007**: 925–26
membership criteria for, **2006**: 331–32
Peer Review Working Group, **2006**: 341
procedure of, **2006**: 332–33, 341–43
religious freedom, **2006**: 380–81
special rapporteur's report on rights of migrants, **2008**: 339–47
special sessions, **2006**: 335–41. *See also specific countries*
trafficking in children, **2006**: 384–85
universal periodic review, **2006**: 341
U.S. not seeking election to, **2006**: 328
U.S. support for, **2006**: 329–30
use of mercenaries, **2008**: 876
violence against women, **2007**: 317–18
report on, **2006**: 374–75
Unborn Victims of Violence Act (2004), 2005: 267
UNCAC (Convention against Corruption, UN). *See* Corruption, *subheading*: conventions on
UNCITRAL (UN Commission on International Trade Law), **1991-99**: 1473, 1802; **2001**: 775, 778, 780–86, 788–94, 796; **2002**: 818, 819–23, 825–27, 829–37; **2004**: 803, 804–5, 806–18, 822; **2005**: 594, 601, 653, 793, 807, 808
Arbitration Convention, **2002**: 618–19, 620–21
Arbitration Rules, **2000**: 686–87; **2001**: 384, 608–10; **2002**: 618–19, 620–21; **2007**: 550–51; **2008**: 529
assignments financing, convention on, **2007**: 766
cattle cases, **2008**: 527–28
Convention on Carriage of Goods by Sea. *See* Carriage of goods by sea
Convention on the Use of Electronic Communications in International Contracts, **2005**: 214, 799–802
Model Law on Cross-Border Insolvency Procedure, **2005**: 808–9
Model Law on Electronic Commerce, **1991-99**: 1809–12; **2006**: 934–36
Model Law on International Commercial Conciliation, **2005**: 805, 806–7, 809
observers, **2007**: 760

UNCITRAL (UN Commission on International Trade Law) (continued)
rules of procedure and methods of work, **2007**: 756–59
work of, **2007**: 754–56
UNCLOS. *See* Law of the Sea, UN Convention on (UNCLOS)
Underwater cultural heritage
UNESCO Convention on the Protection of Underwater Cultural Heritage (2001), **2001**: 693
clarification of existing coastal State authority, **2005**: 762–63
jurisdictional overlap with UNCLOS, **2005**: 761
scientific management rules and standards, **2005**: 762, 764–65
U.S. concerns, **2001**: 693–95; **2005**: 758, 765–66
warships and other State owned vessels, treatment of, **2005**: 763–64
UNEP. *See* United Nations, *subheading*: Environment Program (UNEP)
UNESCO (Educational, Scientific, and Cultural Organization), **2002**: 403–5; **2003**: 420, 421–23, 830–32; **2004**: 797–99; **2005**: 208–10, 758, 759, 761, 764, 766, 778
Declaration on Bioethics and Human Rights, **2005**: 784–85
Doping in Sport, International Convention against, **2005**: 774, 781–84; **2008**: 737–42
Illicit Import, Export and Transfer of Ownership of Cultural Property, Convention on the Means of Prohibiting and Preventing the. *See* Cultural issues
law of the sea, **2008**: 653–56
Protection and Promotion of Diversity of Cultural Expressions, adoption of Convention on, **2005**: 208–9, 778; **2006**: 284; **2007**: 197–98
Underwater Cultural Heritage, Convention on the Protection of. *See* Cultural issues
UNIDROIT (International Institute for the Unification of Private Law). *See* Mobile Equipment, Cape Town Convention on International Interests in (2001)
Uniform Child Custody Jurisdiction Act (1988), **1991-99**: 372, 378
Uniform Child Custody Jurisdiction and Enforcement Act (1997), **1991-99**: 378
Uniform Code of Military Justice (UCMJ), **2005**: 186–87, 354, 357, 979–80, 994
military commissions as violating, **2006**: 1138–55
penalizing torture and other mistreatment, **2006**: 417, 420
Uniform Commercial Code (UCC)
Article 2A, **2008**: 745
Article 8, **2005**: 808
Uniform Dissolution of Marriage Act (1997), **1991-99**: 362
Uniform Electronic Transactions Act (1999), **2003**: 838; **2004**: 805
Uniform Foreign Monetary Judgments Act (1962), **2000**: 737
Uniform International Wills Act (1991), **1991-99**: 1878

Uniform Interpretation of the Rules for International Law Governing Innocent Passage (1989) (U.S.–USSR), 1989-90: 437–40, 446
Uniform Interstate Family Support Act (1992), 1991-99: 1864, 1869–71, 1875–76; **2008:** 753, 758–59
Uniform Reciprocal Enforcement of Support Act (1992), 1991-99: 1864–66
Unilateral acts
India's unilateral moratorium on nuclear testing, **2005:** 1081, 1084, 1089
of states, International Law Commission report on, **2005:** 205–6; **2006:** 281–82
Union of Soviet Socialist Republics. *See* Soviet Union
United Arab Emirates
comity issues, **2008:** 227–36
abstentions, **2005:** 815–18
Dubai Ports World proposal to acquire U.S. ports, **2006:** 774–80
head-of-state immunity, **1991-99:** 1285–89
longshore work prohibition on alien crewmen from, **2002:** 757; **2003:** 764
money laundering in, **2004:** 135
nonproliferation sanctions, **2004:** 1135
religious freedom, actions promoting protection of, **2005:** 315
status of diplomatic mission employees, **2000:** 583–85
trafficking in persons, **2005:** 159, 162
warships, restrictions on innocent passage of, **1991-99:** 1596
United Arab Republic, 1991-99: 744
United Kingdom
aviation issues
Airbus subsidies, **2004:** 603; **2005:** 622
airport user charges on U.S. airlines, arbitration. *See* Arbitration
emissions, proposed per-plane duty, **2008:** 684–86
citizens of detained by U.S. as enemy combatants,[17] **2003:** 1033; **2005:** 967
citizenship status of corporations in overseas territories, **2001:** 227–35; **2002:** 229–30
civilians' rights of access to a British territory, agreements with U.S. concerning, **2005:** 417
common law tradition, **2005:** 790
consular convention with, **2008:** 498–501

[17] Editor's note: On March 13, 2009, in conjunction with a filing in Guantanamo habeas litigation, the U.S. Justice Department declared that it would cease to employ the term "enemy combatant" for detainees in custody of the Defense Department at the Guantanamo Bay Detention Facility.

United Kingdom (continued)
consular notification, **1991-99**: 310
Convention on Protection and Promotion of Diversity of Cultural Expressions, position on, **2005**: 209–10
counterterrorism recommendations, **2006**: 210
customary international law, law of war, **2006**: 1078–82
death penalty, abolition of, **2005**: 387–88
Declaration of Rights of 1689, **2005**: 388
defamation judgment, enforcement of, **2005**: 865
defense trade cooperation treaty, **2007**: 206–7, 996–1000; **2008**: 1020–21
drug trade
maritime counter-drug trade agreements, **1991-99**: 1607, 1608; **2005**: 147–53
methamphetamines, **2007**: 164–66
environmental and conservation issues, **1991-99**: 1782. *See also* aviation issues, *this heading*
contamination from UK vessel sunk in U.S. waters, **1991-99**: 1620–21
London Congestion Charge, **2005**: 570–74
extradition and mutual legal assistance, **1991-99**: 427, 428–35, 450, 456, 518–19; **2000**: 185*n*; **2004**: 73–83; **2006**: 136, 138, 147
extradition treaties with U.S.
treaty (2003), **2005**: 70–71, 73–77; **2006**: 111–27; **2007**: 126–28
treaty (1931), political offense exception in, **2005**: 94–97
Webster-Ashburton Treaty, **2005**: 50*n*
protection of confidential communication from, in extradition case, **1991-99**: 789–801
territories covered by UK treaties, **2006**: 136, 138, 147
family support enforcement, **1991-99**: 1866
reciprocating country for, **2007**: 771; **2008**: 760
Foreign Extraterritorial Measures Act, **2008**: 770
forum non conveniens, **2004**: 875–78
Gulf War and, **1991-99**: 2057, 2089, 2116
human rights and, **2004**: 234
humanitarian intervention and, **2004**: 971
immunity issues
head-of-state immunity, **1991-99**: 1269
members of the military under NATO-SOFA, **2004**: 479–82
sovereign immunity, **2005**: 528–29
UK State Immunity Act, **2005**: 529; **2006**: 609
special mission immunity, **2006**: 672
Indian Ocean Territory Agreement (U.S.–UK), **2005**: 417

United Kingdom (continued)
International Space Station Partners Agreement, **1991-99**: 1642
Iraq and, **2003**: 980–82; **2005**: 232, 233*n*
Oil-For-Food Program and, **2004**: 897
irregular rendition and, **1991-99**: 441
Kosovo peace process, role in, **2005**: 935
Libya
Pan Am 103 shootdown over Lockerbie, Scotland, **1991-99**: 457–64, 477–80, 857; **2006**: 174–75. *See also* Libya
suit by Libya against U.S. and for 1985 air strikes, **1989-90**: 311–14
London Congestion Charge, **2005**: 570–74
maritime issues
coral reef protection, **1991-99**: 1755
fisheries dispute with Norway, **2005**: 702
maritime boundary treaties concerning the Caribbean, **1991-99**: 1574–76
suppression of illicit maritime traffic, **2008**: 650–51
whaling and, **2001**: 218; **2002**: 210
money laundering, **2004**: 135
most-favored nation status and tax exemption for consular employees, **2008**: 498–501
nonimmigrant visa waiver pilot program, **1989-90**: 27
nonproliferation. *See* Nonproliferation, *subheading*: country-specific issues
objections to U.S. reservations to Genocide Convention, **1989-90**: 145–50
Open Skies (aerial observation) treaty, **2002**: 1029
parallel judicial proceedings, **2002**: 859–62, 868–71
parental child abduction and, **1991-99**: 351–52, 369, 372–77; **2004**: 60
peacekeeping in the former Yugoslavia, **1991-99**: 134, 2031–33, 2057
satellite coordination and, **2004**: 637
security internees, detention of, **2005**: 959
service of process, **2005**: 866
by mail, **2004**: 875
Sierra Leone sanctions and, **1991-99**: 2017
Somali piracy, cooperation with Transitional Federal Government of Somalia in fight against, **2008**: 927
sovereignty over Hong Kong, **1991-99**: 383, 403–6, 411–13, 416, 689–92, 764–67, 769–75, 1175, 1177
strategic partnership between U.S. and India, support of, **2005**: 1082
Subsidies and Countervailing Measures, Agreement on, **2005**: 622, 625, 628, 636

United Kingdom (continued)
Sudan, assistance in, **2005**: 920, 926; **2006**: 1051
sunken government property, **2004**: 717, 719
suppression of illicit maritime traffic, **2008**: 650–51
Taliban and, **2004**: 985
Titanic protection agreement, **2004**: 715–16; **2006**: 828–35
trade claims, **1991-99**: 1415, 1533, 1538
treaty affairs, **1991-99**: 661
views on memoranda of understanding, **2004**: 194–95
Treaty of Paris (U.S.–UK (1783)), **2005**: 479
Warsaw Convention claims, **1991-99**: 1348
World War II restitution and compensation issues, **1991-99**: 1043–46, 1053, 1064, 1081
salvage of captured World War II German submarines, **1991-99**: 1617–18
United Nations. *See also* General Assembly, UN; Human rights; Security Council, UN; *specific countries*
accountability for crimes committed by UN officials and experts on missions, efforts to promote, **2008**: 387–88
ad hoc tribunals. *See* International Criminal Tribunal for Former Yugoslavia (ICTY); International Criminal Tribunal for Rwanda (ICTR)
administration of justice within, **2007**: 403–6; **2008**: 385–87
advisory opinion from International Court of Justice, requests for
concerning construction of a wall in the Occupied Palestinian Territory, by General Assembly, **2004**: 944–49
concerning immunity of special rapporteur, by ECOSOC, **1989-90**: 353–70
concerning legality of use of nuclear weapons
by General Assembly, **1991-99**: 2170–82
by World Health Organization, **1991-99**: 2170, 2180
concerning declaration of independence by Kosovo, **2008**: 439
arms control compliance monitoring, **2002**: 1032–35
Cambodia, conflict resolution and transition management in, **1989-90**: 528–31, 532–33, 535–37
Khmer Rouge tribunal, **1991-99**: 608; **2003**: 221–22. *See also* Criminal tribunals, international, hybrid, and other
Charter Committee, **2007**: 406–7, 823–25
Charter of (1945), **1989-90**: 354, 355, 356, 357, 358, 360–61, 407, 576, 578; **1991-99**: 311, 438, 468–75, 540, 580, 615, 647, 723, 732, 1171, 1196, 1321–22, 1438, 2013, 2071, 2149, 2175, 2183, 2227, 2282, 2285–86, 2347, 2367; **2000**: 406–7, 603–4, 607, 608, 609, 624, 625; **2001**: 142, 176, 290, 366; **2002**: 152, 161, 164, 391–93, 554, 555, 559, 953–54; **2003**: 152, 161, 231, 416, 577, 994;

United Nations (continued)
2004: 121, 177, 250, 963, 970, 973, 974, 975, 1087, 1092; **2007**: 76, 131, 402, 407, 667, 876, 887, 985, 1033, 1056, 1078; **2008**: 180*n*
Article 2, **1991-99**: 578, 594, 2103; **2000**: 289; **2001**: 174–75; **2007**: 1036
Article 9, **2008**: 205
Article 24, **2007**: 824
Article 25, **1991-99**: 463, 471, 606, 1121–22, 1197, 2103
Article 33, **2007**: 834
Article 39, **2000**: 289
Article 41, **2000**: 618–19*n*; **2007**: 1031, 1038; **2008**: 939, 969
Article 49, **1991-99**: 2103
Article 50, **2007**: 824
Article 51, **1991-99**: 2054, 2124, 2133, 2134, 2174, 2181, 2283, 2285; **2000**: 290; **2001**: 856, 863, 869–70; **2002**: 953–54, 1012*n*; **2003**: 971, 1049, 1053; **2004**: 970, 973–76; **2005**: 444, 448, 950; **2006**: 1108–9, 1256; **2007**: 876, 887; **2008**: 403*n*
Article 55, **2005**: 57*n*
Article 56, **2005**: 57*n*
Article 92, **2005**: 35
Article 94, **2001**: 420, 705–6; **2005**: 36, 36*n*, 38, 44, 48, 54–58; **2007**: 76; **2008**: 177, 180–81
Article 103, **2001**: 525
Article 105, **2000**: 625; **2001**: 527–28
Chapter VI, **1991-99**: 463, 2020, 2025, 2347; **2005**: 191
Chapter VII, **1989-90**: 578; **1991-99**: 145, 459, 462–63, 464–76, 580, 588, 589, 590–94, 595, 596, 604–5, 606, 617–18, 1099, 1121–22, 1197, 1814, 1921, 1939, 1958, 1966, 2020–21, 2032, 2033, 2037, 2043, 2045, 2048, 2051–53, 2109, 2112, 2127, 2138, 2141, 2149, 2176, 2227, 2347; **2000**: 83, 204, 259–60, 275–76, 281, 283, 290, 406*n*; **2001**: 356, 359–60, 524–25, 863, 869, 893; **2002**: 161, 164, 887, 889, 938; **2003**: 152–53, 161, 168, 219, 228, 231, 233, 705, 955–56, 970, 974, 983–84, 986; **2004**: 104, 121, 922, 940, 941, 962, 1048–49, 1092, 1096; **2005**: 466, 881–95, 929, 949, 956–60, 1039, 1041; **2006**: 263, 275, 331, 975, 1043, 1047, 1060, 1063–64, 1235, 1268, 1269, 1277–82; **2007**: 822*n*, 990–91, 994, 1027–28, 1031, 1038, 1056, 1058, 1072, 1073; **2008**: 87, 847, 856, 922, 939, 969, 971, 999
Chapter VIII, **2001**: 941
priority over other international agreements, **2005**: 957
Children, Special Session on, **2002**: 300–2; **2004**: 279–84

United Nations (continued)
Children's Fund (UNICEF), **2008:** 229–30, 293, 301
climate change. *See* Climate change; Kyoto Protocol
Commission on Human Rights. *See* UN Commission on Human Rights
Commission on International Trade Law. *See* UNCITRAL (UN Commission on International Trade Law)
Commission on Narcotic Drugs, Resolution 49/3, on methamphetamine, **2006:** 217–20
Commission on Population and Development, **2003:** 321
Committee Against Torture. *See* Torture
Committee on Economic, Social and Cultural Rights, **2007:** 289–93; **2008:** 267, 268, 268*n*, 269*n*
Committee on Human Rights. *See* Human rights
Committee on the Peaceful Uses of Outer Space. *See* Space
Compensation Commission, for claims against Iraq, **1991-99:** 1099–1106; **2000:** 444; **2004:** 430
Conference on Environment and Development, **1991-99:** 1649–55, 1671, 1758
Consumer Protection Guidelines, **2005:** 660
conventions. *See specific topics (e.g., Torture)*
Corruption, Convention against (UNCAC). *See* Corruption, *subheading*: conventions on
Counter-Terrorism Committee (CTC), **2005:** 898, 899, 900, 901; **2006:** 199–210, 999–1000
counterterrorism obligations, U.S. reports on implementation of, **2001:** 893–917; **2006:** 199–210
Cultural Property, Convention on Prohibiting and Preventing the Illicit Import, Export and Transfer of Ownership of. *See* Cultural issues
Declarations. *See specific declarations*
disabilities convention. *See also* Disabilities, persons with
  adoption of, **2006:** 383
  U.S. as nonparty to, **2006:** 284
  U.S. views on draft, **2006:** 382–84
East Timor, **2005:** 410. *See also* peacekeeping role, *this heading*
  Second Transitional Government, **2002:** 177
  Transition Administration, **2001:** 426–27
Economic Commission on Latin America (ECLAC), **2005:** 890
Environment Program (UNEP), **1991-99:** 1658, 1757; **2005:** 462; **2006:** 865; **2007:** 724–25
European Community, role of in conferences, **2004:** 407–8
fish and marine mammals and, **2002:** 786, 797; **2004:** 762–66; **2005:** 735, 744, 746, 748, 749–50

United Nations (continued)
Food and Agriculture Organization. *See* Agricultural policy and trade, *subheading*: UN Food and Agriculture Organization
Framework Convention on Climate Change. *See* Climate change
Freedom of Opinion and Expression, Special Rapporteur on, **2006**: 486–87
funding issues, **2002**: 399–403; **2003**: 423–24
General Assembly powers, **1991-99**: 593, 604; **2001**: 176
General Assembly Resolutions. *See* General Assembly, UN
headquarters, U.S. obligation to ensure safety of and access to, **2003**: 476–579
Headquarters Agreement, **1991-99**: 1321–22, 1336–38; **2000**: 578, 588, 589, 603, 604, 605, 607–12, 613, 614; **2002**: 554, 555–57, 559–60, 561, 577; **2005**: 539–42; **2008**: 211. *See also* immunity, *this heading*
High Commissioner for Human Rights, **2002**: 273; **2008**: 250, 285, 288, 320, 326
High Commissioner for Refugees, **1989-90**: 46–47; **1991-99**: 157–58; **2000**: 135, 138–39; **2001**: 37; **2002**: 24, 29, 31, 36, 37; **2004**: 282; **2005**: 435; **2008**: 34, 502
advisory opinion on extraterritorial application of non-refoulement obligations concerning, **2007**: 41–70
Executive Committee role in treaty interpretation, **2007**: 50–51
HIV/AIDS prevention initiatives, **2001**: 763; **2002**: 805–7
host country relations, U.S., **2003**: 476–579; **2004**: 539–42
human cloning, **2002**: 807–9; **2003**: 817–18; **2004**: 787–89; **2005**: 771–72
Human Genetic Data, International Declaration on, **2003**: 818–19
Human Rights Commission Resolutions. *See* Human rights
Human Rights Committee. *See* International Covenant on Civil and Political Rights (ICCPR)
Human Rights Council. *See* Human rights; UN Human Rights Council
immunity. *See also* inviolability, *this heading*
of conference attendees, **2004**: 539
Convention on Privileges and Immunities of UN (General Convention). *See also* Privileges and Immunities of the United Nations (General Convention)
absolute immunity of United Nations under, **2002**: 570–72
of escrow account, to attachment, **2000**: 616–26
of permanent representative to United Nations, **2003**: 572; **2004**: 261–62
of IMF Principal Resident Representative, **2001**: 538–39

United Nations (continued)
of invitees to, **1991-99**: 987–88, 1335–39
of missions to, **2002**: 576–81; **2003**: 573; **2006**: 592–603
of personnel of, **2000**: 602–16; **2002**: 552–70; **2004**: 531–34
of Special Rapporteur, **1989-90**: 353–70
indigenous people. *See* Indigenous people
International Atomic Energy Agency. *See* Atomic Energy Agency, International (IAEA)
International Court of Justice. *See* International Court of Justice (ICJ)
International Criminal Court and. *See* International Criminal Court (ICC)
International Criminal Tribunal for Former Yugoslavia. *See* International Criminal Tribunal for Former Yugoslavia (ICTY)
International Criminal Tribunal for Rwanda. *See* International Criminal Tribunal for Rwanda (ICTR)
International Independent Investigation Commission, **2005**: 878–80, 883, 885–86; **2006**: 272, 985–86; **2008**: 142
International Law Commission. *See* International Law Commission (ILC)
inviolability. *See also* immunity, *this heading*
of missions to, **1991-99**: 1319–31; **2006**: 681–82
of officials attending UN conference, **2004**: 553–58; **2006**: 681–82
Jurisdictional Immunities of States and Their Properties, Convention on. *See* Immunity
membership in, **2003**: 415–17
of Czech and Slovak Republics, **1991-99**: 1174–75
obligation of members to pay assessed contributions, **1991-99**: 731–32, 806
of Russia, **1991-99**: 1170, 1173
of states of former Yugoslavia, **1991-99**: 1163, 1167
Taiwan's status in, **2002**: 405
Middle East, role in conflict resolution. *See* Middle East Conflict, Israeli-Palestinian, *subheading*: Quartet (EU, Russia, UN, U.S.) peace efforts
Millennium Development Goals, U.S. views on, **2005**: 333–35
nonbinding instruments of, **2003**: 280, 356–57, 360, 364, 374, 393
nongovernmental organizations and, **2004**: 407
Office of Drugs and Crime (UNODC), **2008**: 396–97
peacekeeping role, **1989-90**: 201–3; **1991-99**: 476, 591, 732, 806, 2347; **2001**: 355–63; **2002**: 903, 907, 908–9; **2003**: 232, 233–34, 817, 955–59; **2004**: 940–42; **2008**: 838–39
appropriate use of, **2007**: 866–67
criminal accountability in, **2007**: 864–66; **2008**: 387–88

United Nations (continued)
Darfur, **2006**: 1043–54; **2007**: 867–69; **2008**: 841–43
MINURCAT (Chad), **2008**: 839
MINURSO (Western Sahara), **2008**: 850–52
MINUSTAH (Haiti), **2004**: 34–35, 188, 940–42; **2008**: 838
MONUC (DRC), **2007**: 862; **2008**: 838
protection of personnel, **2004**: 409
protection of women from illegal trafficking, **2004**: 166–68
reform of, **2005**: 443, 942–43
Secretary General comments on, **2005**: 448
sexual exploitation and abuse by UN peacekeepers, **2005**: 449, 945–46; **2006**: 1065–68; **2007**: 319–21; **2008**: 286, 288, 840–41
UNAMID (Darfur), **2007**: 860, 867–69; **2008**: 839, 841–44
UNAVEM (Angola), **1991-99**: 145
UNIFIL (Lebanon), **2006**: 1035, 1037, 1039, 1060–61; **2007**: 869–71
UNMEE (Eritrea-Ethiopia), **2005**: 943–45
UNMIBH (Bosnia-Herzegovina), **2002**: 157–61
UNMIH (Haiti), **1991-99**: 2045–47
UNMIK (Kosovo), **2008**: 845–47
UNMIS (Sudan), **2005**: 940–42; **2008**: 839
UNMISET (East Timor), **2002**: 157–58
UNOMIG (Georgia), **2008**: 844–45
UNOSOM (Somalia), **1991-99**: 2045
UNPREDEP (FYR of Macedonia), **1991-99**: 2030
UNPROFOR (former Yugoslavia), **1991-99**: 1305–6, 1948, 2030
UNTAES (Croatia), **1991-99**: 2047–48
U.S. policy, **1991-99**: 856, 2019–24
personnel, protection of, **2001**: 355–63; **2003**: 993–96; **2004**: 409, 1048
in enforcement actions, **2001**: 359–60
Plan for Namibian Independence, **1989-90**: 197–201
Population Fund, **2002**: 308–9
poverty eradication goals, **2004**: 289–90
reform of, **2004**: 403–7; **2006**: 489–90; **2008**: 383–86
high-level event preparation, **2005**: 449–51
Human Rights Council, **2005**: 446–47, 453–54, 460–62
internal justice system, **2007**: 403–6; **2008**: 385–87
In Larger Freedom: Towards Development, Security and Human Rights for All (report), **2005**: 445–48
More Secure World (report), **2005**: 441–45
Peacebuilding Commission, **2005**: 443, 446, 454–57, 946–47
role of Charter Committee, **2007**: 406–7
Security Council, **2005**: 442, 444–45, 448, 457–58; **2007**: 401–3

United Nations (continued)
Register of Conventional Arms, **1991-99**: 2267–68
Registration of Objects Launched into Outer Space, Convention on. *See* Space
Safety of United Nations and Associated Personnel, Convention on, **1991-99**: 611; **2001**: 355–63; **2003**: 994–95, 996
Security Council. *See* Security Council, UN
September 11 terrorist attacks, response to, **2001**: 855–56, 860–61; **2004**: 935, 970
Sierra Leone Special Court (SCIL), **2002**: 147–48; **2005**: 190–91; **2008**: 140–41
sovereign equality and, **2004**: 143
on state responsibility
Charter provisions, **2001**: 366
draft articles, **1991-99**: 1106–23; **2001**: 364–80
sustainable development activities, **2001**: 743–48
telecommunications and, **2004**: 635, 640
terrorism-related measures. *See* Terrorism
Torture Convention. *See* Torture
transparency in proceedings of, **2003**: 417–18
trust territories, **1991-99**: 814, 815, 816, 817–18, 819–20, 834, 836–38
UN Food and Agriculture Organization. *See* Agricultural policy and trade
UNESCO (Educational, Scientific, and Cultural Organization). *See* UNESCO (Educational, Scientific, and Cultural Organization)
United Nations Participation Act (1945), **1991-99**: 1950; **2000**: 618–19*n*, 619; **2001**: 797–98, 804, 883; **2002**: 412, 883; **2003**: 172, 917; **2004**: 888, 920; **2005**: 38, 44; **2006**: 975, 1017; **2007**: 155–56; **2008**: 99
war crimes tribunals, **1991-99**: 511–12, 514, 530. *See also* International Criminal Tribunal for Former Yugoslavia (ICTY); International Criminal Tribunal for Rwanda (ICTR)
authority to establish, **1991-99**: 587–96, 598, 603–7
women's issues
advancement of women, **2006**: 373–74
antidiscrimination efforts, **2002**: 277–80
Commission on Status of Women, **2003**: 290; **2005**: 162–64, 308–9
Fourth World Conference on Women, Beijing, **1991-99**: 917–18; **2000**: 351–52; **2007**: 321–22
security during armed conflict, **2002**: 275–76; **2008**: 286–88
UN Development Fund for Women (UNIFEM), **2006**: 372–73

United Nations (continued)
World Conference Against Racism, **2001**: 267–68; **2002**: 271–76; **2003**: 290, 298, 299; **2008**: 285
World Health Organization. *See* World Health Organization (WHO)
Uniting and Strengthening America by Providing Appropriate Tools Required to Intercept and Obstruct Terrorism Act of 2001 (PATRIOT Act). *See* PATRIOT Act, USA (2001)
Universal Declaration on Bioethics and Human Rights, **2005**: 784–85
Universal Declaration on Human Rights. *See* Human rights
Uranium. *See* Nonproliferation, *subheading*: highly enriched uranium, disposition of
Uruguay
aviation agreement, **2004**: 568
bilateral investment treaty, **2004**: 621–23; **2005**: 646–47; **2006**: 790–96; **2008**: 574–75
extradition and mutual legal assistance, **1991-99**: 391, 400, 442, 447–50; **2000**: 186*n*
immunity of naval vessel involved in commercial activity, **1989-90**: 291–94
intellectual property rights, **2006**: 769
Inter-American Convention Against Corruption, party to, **2006**: 238
International Covenant on Civil and Political Rights (ICCPR), support for U.S. amendment to, **2005**: 300*n*
money laundering, **2004**: 135
naturalization convention, **2002**: 205
nonimmigrant visa waiver pilot program, **1991-99**: 76
Trade and Investment Framework Agreement, protocols to (2008), **2008**: 574–75
U.S. military assistance, **2006**: 278
Uruguay Round, 1991-99: 77, 644–58, 1368–69, 1371–76, 1378, 1381, 1383–84, 1386, 1391, 1394, 1395–1403, 1404, 1438, 1453, 1462, 1470, 1500, 1786; **2005**: 609; **2006**: 767. *See also* General Agreement on Tariffs and Trade (GATT)
Framework Agreement, **2005**: 609
Uruguay Round Agreements Act (1994), **1991-99**: 1372–73, 1525; **2008**: 552, 605
U.S. Constitution. *See* Constitution, U.S.
U.S. Holocaust Assets Commission Act (1998), 2003: 468
U.S. Telecommunications Training Institute (USTTI), 2005: 661
USA PATRIOT Act. *See* PATRIOT Act, USA (2001)
U.S.–Canada Treaty on Extradition, 1989-90: 78

Use of force. *See* Armed conflict; Conventional weapons; Geneva Conventions on law of war (1949); Hague Conventions, *subheading*: on law of war; Law of war
USSR. *See* Soviet Union
Uzbekistan
Article 98 Agreement (nonsurrender of Americans to ICC), **2002**: 166–68
asylum seekers returned to Uzbekistan by Ukraine, **2006**: 60–61
diplomatic relations, **1991-99**: 1174
domestic violence laws, lack of, **2005**: 313
human rights in, **2002**: 282
intellectual property rights Watch List, **2006**: 769; **2007**: 610
nuclear fuel return program, **2004**: 1139–41
religious freedom in, **1991-99**: 927; **2006**: 377, 378
threat reduction agreement, **2001**: 848–50
trade and investment issues, **1991-99**: 1455, 1466
trafficking in persons, **2006**: 229

V

Vanuatu
Inter-American Tropical Tuna Commission, **2000**: 307
Vatican, 1991-99: 1290–91; **2003**: 494
chancery, **2000**: 633
immunity, **2006**: 684
Vatican Bank, Holocaust-era claims against, **2005**: 481–84
VCCR. *See* Consular Relations, Vienna Convention on (VCCR)
VCLT. *See* Vienna Convention on Law of Treaties (VCLT) (1969)
Venezuela
attempted military coup in, **2002**: 385–87
Child Abduction Convention, compliance with, **2006**: 101; **2008**: 50
drug trade, **2001**: 120; **2002**: 124; **2003**: 181; **2004**: 133–34; **2005**: 135–36; **2006**: 212–13; **2007**: 163; **2008**: 113
sanctions concerning, **2007**: 163–64; **2008**: 113
maritime counter-drug trade agreement and mutual legal assistance treaties, **1991-99**: 453, 1607–8
excessive air space claims, **2007**: 634
extradition and mutual legal assistance, **2000**: 185*n*; **2001**: 90–96
fish and marine mammals
Inter-American Tropical Tuna Commission, **2000**: 307
shrimp import restrictions, **2003**: 791–92
intellectual property rights Watch List, **2006**: 768; **2007**: 608, 610; **2008**: 605*n*
Inter-American Convention Against Corruption, party to, **2006**: 238

Venezuela (continued)
Inter-American Convention Against Terrorism (OAS Terrorism Convention), party to, **2005**: 111
money laundering, **2004**: 135
persona non grata, declarations concerning, **2008**: 492–93
prisoner transfer treaty, **2000**: 171; **2001**: 51
service of process rules, **2003**: 891–92
territorial sea contiguous zone, **1989-90**: 466–67
terrorism and, not cooperating fully with antiterrorism efforts, **2006**: 172; **2007**: 132, 1005; **2008**: 88–89
trade claims against U.S., **1991-99**: 1412
trafficking in persons
Presidential Determination on trafficking in persons, **2007**: 169
sanctions, **2004**: 164, 165; **2005**: 161–62; **2006**: 228
U.S.–Venezuela Extradition Treaty (1922), **2007**: 118
Vessels. *See* Maritime issues
Victim assistance and compensation, **2001**: 38–40
child victims of sexual exploitation, **2002**: 288
claims. *See* Holocaust; World War II
Pan Am Flight 103 victims, **2001**: 99
private Korean national claim against U.S., **2000**: 489–99
provisions of Treaty of Peace with Japan, **2000**: 507–12, 515–31
provisions of War Claims Act (1948), **2000**: 512–14
smuggled migrants, **2004**: 157–59, 162, 163
sovereign immunity and, **2000**: 473–85
victims of crime committed by diplomatic personnel, **1989-90**: 332–37
victims of human rights violations, **2004**: 334–35
victims of terrorism, **2000**: 226, 229, 540–43; **2002**: 244–45, 408–13
victims of torture, **2001**: 319; **2004**: 300–4
victims of trafficking. *See* Crime, *subheading*: victims
Victims of crime. *See* Crime
Victims of trafficking. *See* Crime
Vienna Convention on Consular Relations. *See* Consular Relations, Vienna Convention on (VCCR)
Vienna Convention on Diplomatic Relations. *See* Diplomatic Relations, Vienna Convention on
Vienna Convention on Law of Treaties (VCLT) (1969), **1989-90**: 122; **1991-99**: 683–84, 715, 735–37, 1109; **2001**: 131, 212, 305; **2004**: 530, 544; **2005**: 217, 296, 722, 1063. *See also* Treaties, generally
on applicability of amended treaties, **2001**: *559–60n*
as not binding on nonparties, **2000**: 282

Vienna Convention on Law of Treaties (VCLT) (1969) (continued)
as customary international law, **1989-90**: 122, 145; **1991-99**: 1302*n*; **2001**: 212–13, 678; **2003**: 60; **2004**: 544; **2005**: 217–18, 722; **2006**: 287, 291, 392; **2008**: 360, 1013
definition of "state practice" under, **2007**: 425
"full powers" provisions, **1989-90**: 142
on fundamental change in circumstances, **2006**: 282
on interpretation of treaty, **2000**: 432–33, 434*n*, 501–2, 516*n*, 519*n*; **2002**: 653; **2006**: 348, 695, 816, 1260–61; **2007**: 43–47
travaux préparatoires, **2003**: 60–61, 235–36; **2004**: 200–202; **2006**: 287–88
jus cogens and, **2003**: 244; **2006**: 647*n*
on reservations, **1989-90**: 145, 147, 148–49; **2000**: 386, 420; **2001**: 218, 305–7; **2002**: 208–9, 393–94
retroactivity, **2001**: 215
on suspension, termination, and withdrawal, **2008**: 1013–17
on treaty responsibility prior to entry into force, **2002**: 609–10
Articles:
2, **2001**: 305; **2003**: 249, 250
4, **2001**: 215; **2002**: 208
5, **2002**: 208–9; **2003**: 245
7, **2008**: 204, 205
14, **2003**: 250
18, **2001**: 212
19, **1989-90**: 148–49; **2001**: 307; **2002**: 211–12; **2003**: 245; **2004**: 196, 198; **2005**: 222
20, **1989-90**: 149; **1991-99**: 736, 970; **2000**: 386; **2001**: 306; **2002**: 208–9
21, **2006**: 291
26, **2001**: 592
27, **2000**: 385–86
28, **1989-90**: 122; **2000**: 386; **2004**: 225–26, 227
31, **1991-99**: 151, 153–54, 719; **2000**: 432–33, 434*n*; **2001**: 55, 606–8, 612; **2002**: 268, 619, 621, 656; **2003**: 60–61; **2004**: 421, 423, 424, 576, 584*n*; **2005**: 296, 722; **2006**: 695; **2007**: 43–44, 50–52, 596; **2008**: 38, 43, 259, 531, 1012
32, **1991-99**: 151; **2000**: 434*n*; **2002**: 436–37; **2003**: 60–61; **2004**: 201–2, 421; **2005**: 297; **2006**: 287; **2007**: 43–44, 596; **2008**: 259
34, **2004**: 1091
35, **2004**: 1091
36, **2004**: 1091
37, **2004**: 1091

Vienna Convention on Law of Treaties (VCLT) (1969) (continued)
40, **2001**: 559–60*n*
46, **2003**: 251, 252
53, **2001**: 312; **2003**: 244–45
57, **2008**: 1012
60, **1991-99**: 721
62, **2006**: 282
64, **1991-99**: 719
Vietnam
access by Vietnamese national to U.S. courts, **1989-90**: 242–43
accession process to WTO, **2006**: 748–50
adoption agreement between U.S. and Socialist Republic of Vietnam, **2005**: 67–68
Agent Orange litigation, **2005**: 491–97; **2006**: 522–26; **2008**: 427–30
antiterrorism cooperation, **2002**: 118
authorization of U.S. use of force in, **1991-99**: 2160–61, 2165
aviation agreement, **2003**: 602–3; **2008**: 512
Cambodia issues, **1989-90**: 526, 527, 534
claims by former U.S. employees in, **2002**: 413–15
diplomatic relations, **1989-90**: 241; **1991-99**: 1153–62, 1493
diplomatic property agreement with U.S., **1991-99**: 1083, 1085–86
normalization of relations with U.S., **1989-90**: 526, 527
drug trade, **2001**: 120; **2002**: 124; **2003**: 181; **2004**: 133–34
drug transit and producer list, removal from, **2005**: 136
dual nationals, agreement with U.S. addressing, **2001**: 34
human rights in, **1991-99**: 594, 916; **2002**: 282
humanitarian resettlement initiative with U.S., **2005**: 25–27
processing of refugees from, **1991-99**: 113–18
repatriation of Montagnard refugees, **2002**: 24–25
intellectual property rights Watch List, **2006**: 769; **2007**: 608, 610; **2008**: 606
longshore work prohibition on alien crewmen from, **2002**: 757; **2003**: 764
nuclear fuel return program, **2004**: 1139
POW/MIA accounting, **1991-99**: 1159–61, 1969–70
religious freedom, **1991-99**: 926; **2003**: 296; **2004**: 270, 272, 273; **2005**: 314, 316; **2006**: 377–78
U.S.–Vietnam Religious Freedom Agreement, **2005**: 316–17
rights of citizen arrested in U.S. before consular or diplomatic relations, **2003**: 103–4
sanctions on, **1991-99**: 1493–94, 1968–71
arms embargo, non-licensing policies toward, **2004**: 1070; **2007**: 1005
disposition of blocked assets, **1989-90**: 525–26
state succession cases, **2000**: 570

Vietnam (continued)
trade and investment issues, **1991-99:** 1455
U.S. trade agreement with, **2001:** 665; **2006:** 748–50
trafficking in women and children in, **1991-99:** 916
U.S. refugee policy, **2006:** 56
Violence Against Women Acts. *See* Gender issues
Violent Crime Control and Law Enforcement Act (1994), 1991-99: 75, 77–78; **2005:** 264; **2006:** 418
Virgin Islands, British, 1991-99: 1574–76, 1608
hazardous spills agreement, **2004:** 750–51
Virgin Islands, U.S.
political status, **1991-99:** 808–11
sovereignty of U.S. and, **2003:** 485
Virginia
tax exemptions for diplomatic and consular personnel and missions in, **2001:** 539–40
Visas. *See* Immigration and visas
Volcker Commission, 2005: 452
Voting Rights Act (1965), 2001: 250; **2008:** 277–78
Voting rights in District of Columbia, 2001: 266–67

W
Wake Island
sovereignty of U.S. and, **2003:** 485
Wallis and Futuna, 2005: 743
War. *See* Armed conflict; Geneva Conventions on law of war (1949); Hague Conventions, *subheading*: on law of war; Law of war
War Claims Act (1948), 2000: 503, 505, 511, 512–14, 528–31; **2002:** 458, 461
War crimes. *See also* Customary international law; Detainees, military; Geneva Conventions on law of war (1949); Hague conventions, *subheading*: on law of war; International Criminal Tribunal for Former Yugoslavia (ICTY); International Criminal Tribunal for Rwanda (ICTR); Law of war; Military commissions for trial of certain non-U.S. enemy combatants[18]
accountability for, **1991-99:** 615; **2000:** 239–43; **2004:** 180; **2005:** 12, 189, 192, 197, 377; **2007:** 181, 184, 197, 390, 909; **2008:** 137

[18] Editor's note: On March 13, 2009, in conjunction with a filing in Guantanamo habeas litigation, the U.S. Justice Department declared that it would cease to employ the term "enemy combatant" for detainees in custody of the Defense Department at the Guantanamo Bay Detention Facility.

War crimes (continued)
Agent Orange litigation, **2005**: 491–97; **2006**: 522–26; **2008**: 427–30
aiding and abetting liability, **2004**: 374–75. *See also* Alien Tort Statute (ATS)
availability of habeas corpus for U.S. prosecution overseas, **2004**: 1018
command responsibility, **2002**: 348–51
definition in International Criminal Court statute, **1991-99**: 628, 637
detainees held at Guantanamo Bay. *See* Detainees, military
Draft Code of Crimes Against the Peace and Security of Mankind and, **1991-99**: 579
extradition requests involving, **2005**: 358
extraordinary chambers in Cambodia, **2002**: 148
international and hybrid criminal tribunals for, U.S. policy regarding, **1991-99**: 516, 858–60; **2001**: 164–72; **2004**: 172–75, 178, 180. *See also* Criminal tribunals, international, hybrid, and other; *specific tribunal headings*
International Criminal Court jurisdiction. *See* International Criminal Court (ICC)
international humanitarian law vs. human rights law, **2003**: 277–78, 344–47, 349–51, 1019–21; **2004**: 334–35; **2005**: 302–4, 336–41, 391, 393. *See also* Human rights
juveniles perpetrating, **2008**: 303, 311
Nazi. *See* World War II
Nonapplicability of Statutory Limitations to War Crimes and Crimes Against Humanity, Convention on (1968), **2001**: 119
Papua New Guinea tort litigation, **2001**: 338–39; **2008**: 238–44
rape as, **1991-99**: 584, 637, 918; **2000**: 41–42, 241, 251–55, 287
responsibility to protect from, **2005**: 375–76, 458–59; **2008**: 857
Rewards for Justice campaign, **2008**: 148–50
role of domestic courts, **2005**: 190–93; **2007**: 185; **2008**: 139
specific conflicts and areas
Africa, **2004**: 128–31, 248, 355
Chechnya, **1991-99**: 516–17
Darfur/Sudan, **2002**: 924–25; **2005**: 193, 377; **2008**: 873. *See also* Darfur; Sudan
Eritrean-Ethiopian conflict, **2000**: 247–48
former Yugoslavia, **1991-99**: 1146, 1945–62, 1979–82, 2024–45
Gulf War, prosecutions arising from, **2003**: 1000–4, 1007
Iraq, **1991-99**: 532–38, 2067–70, 2080, 2085, 2096–2102, 2118; **2003**: 229–30, 1000–4, 1005–8, 1012–13; **2005**: 19; **2006**: 269
Liberia, **2008**: 140
Papua New Guinea, **2008**: 239
Sierra Leone, **2006**: 276–77
WWII. *See* World War II

War crimes (continued)
state action requirement, **1991-99**: 981
trials in absentia, **2003**: 1010–11
United Nations and, **1991-99**: 468, 526, 615–16
universal jurisdiction over, **1991-99**: 503; **2006**: 1085
War Crimes Act, **1991-99**: 509–15; **2005**: 1014; **2006**: 474–75, 650, 1162, 1171–74, 1176
amendment on violations of Common Article 3, **2007**: 884, 918–20
War on terror, 2005: 104, 355, 372, 374, 437. *See also* Detainees, military; Geneva Conventions on law of war (1949); Hague conventions, *subheading*: on law of war; Law of war; Terrorism; *specific Geneva conventions*
announcement of "War against Terrorism" by President Bush, **2001**: 856–60
"global war on terrorism," meaning of, **2006**: 1108–9; **2007**: 874–75
human rights and, **2004**: 329–30, 994; **2005**: 372, 374
international cooperation in, **2002**: 1055; **2003**: 1068–69; **2004**: 27–28, 119–21, 400
Law of the Sea, UN Convention on and, **2003**: 726; **2004**: 681, 691
legal standards applicable to, **2001**: 872–78, 893; **2002**: 902–6, 935, 976–77; **2003**: 1030–31, 1033–34; **2004**: 1034–35; **2005**: 104, 355, 372, 374; **2006**: 1104–17
persons covered by executive order on Common Article 3 and, **2007**: 924
War Powers Resolution (U.S.), 1991-99: 2044, 2055–56, 2057, 2144, 2145, 2155, 2156, 2157, 2158–62, 2164–65; **2000**: 758, 759, 765; **2001**: 865, 871; **2002**: 933, 937
Warrants
constitutional requirement for, in search for evidence abroad, **1989-90**: 100–7
Warsaw Convention (1929), 2000: 669, 670, 671, 672; **2001**: 473, 555–56. *See also* Aviation issues
South Korea–U.S. treaty relationship under, **2001**: 555–65
Washington state
role in international agreements, **2000**: 294, 295, 296
Wassenaar Arrangement, 1991-99: 2251, 2265–66; **2001**: 912; **2003**: 1122; **2004**: 893, 1093, 1132; **2005**: 1086, 1133, 1137; **2006**: 1300–1; **2007**: 1030; **2008**: 1024–25, 1026
Waste disposal. *See* Environmental issues
Water
human rights and, **2007**: 360–64
navigation. *See* Maritime issues
pollution. *See* Marine conservation

Water use agreements, 2002: 396. *See also* Great Lakes
Memorandum of Understanding between Province of Manitoba and Missouri, **2001:** 179–98
Mexico–U.S., **2001:** 714–16; **2002:** 757–59
WCPF Convention (Convention for Conservation and Management of Highly Migratory Fish Stocks in Western and Central Pacific Ocean). *See* Fish and marine mammals
Weapons, conventional. *See* Conventional weapons
Weapons of mass destruction (WMDs). *See also* Biological weapons; Chemical weapons; Nonproliferation; Terrorism
in antiterrorism conventions, **2001:** 107–8; **2007:** 140–43, 1062–71; **2008:** 942–44
Executive Order 12938, **2005:** 1126, 1129
Global Partnership Initiative Against, **2005:** 1095; **2008:** 1000
interdiction and law enforcement, **2005:** 1098, 1103, 1104
Iran procuring, **2008:** 979, 980, 1001
maritime interdiction of, **2005:** 679–80, 1101–2*n*, 1118; **2008:** 1001–4
Missile Technology Control Regime (MTCR), **1989-90:** 503–8; **1991-99:** 2356–59; **2001:** 845–46; **2003:** 1115–16; **2005:** 1136; **2006:** 1063–64
National Strategy to Combat Weapons of Mass Destruction, **2005:** 689*n*, 1098, 1098*n*
nonproliferation programs. *See also* Nonproliferation
European Union and, **2005:** 1093–94, 1096
export controls, U.S., **2004:** 1108,–15; **2005:** 1135–37; **2006:** 1300–1; **2007:** 1030, 1084
freezing assets of involved individuals and entities (Executive Order 13382), **2005:** 1125–31; **2006:** 1297; **2007:** 1041–45, 1083–84; **2008:** 977–80, 983
Nonproliferation and Disarmament Fund, **1991-99:** 2330–31
UN Security Council, **2005:** 444, 447, 900–1, 1059, 1092, 1094, 1103, 1104–23
Proliferation Security Initiative and, **2003:** 1095–99; **2004:** 692, 1077–91; **2005:** 447, 1097–1106, 1109; **2006:** 1288–89; **2007:** 1071–75; **2008:** 1001–4
research issues, **2003:** 1085, 1105; **2008:** 1007
U.S. intelligence capabilities and, **2005:** 1126
U.S. strategy to combat, **2005:** 1097–98, 1103, 1109
Western Hemisphere Travel Initiative, 2005: 1–2; **2006:** 4–11; **2007:** 8–12, 15; **2008:** 6–11
Western Sahara
peacekeeping missions and, **2003:** 958; **2006:** 1064–65; **2008:** 850–52

Western Samoa
environmental protection agreement, **2002:** 791
South Pacific regional environmental convention, **1989-90:** 491
Whaling. *See* Fish and marine mammals
WHO. *See* World Health Organization (WHO)
Wildlife
Conservation of Migratory Species of Wild Animals, Convention on (1979), **2008:** 167, 168
illegal trade in wildlife and wildlife parts, **2005:** 756; **2006:** 888; **2007:** 730–32
marine. *See* Fish and marine mammals
persistent organic pollutants and. *See* Persistent Organic Pollutants (POPs)
Protocol Concerning Specially Protected Areas and Wildlife, **2003:** 789–90
Wills
Uniform International Wills Act (1991), **1991-99:** 1878
Wine
EU–U.S. trade agreement on wine-making and labeling, **2006:** 757
WIPO. *See* World Intellectual Property Organization (WIPO)
Wire fraud statute, 2005: 234–39, 241–42, 833
Wisconsin
market-participant exceptions to Commerce Clause, **2000:** 328–29
Witness and victim protection, 1991-99: 583–87; **2000:** 375–76; **2001:** 319; **2002:** 975
Women's issues. *See also* Gender issues
World Bank, 2001: 666; **2003:** 837–38
Czechoslovakia and, **1989-90:** 520
disqualification for corruption, **2008:** 122
Poland and, **1989-90:** 518–19
World Customs Organization
European Community membership, **2007:** 410–12
World Health Assembly, 2001: 282
World Health Organization (WHO), 2002: 405; **2003:** 1080; **2004:** 786–87; **2005:** 768–70
Fact Sheet No. 31 on right to health, U.S. concerns about, **2008:** 249–52, 320–26
International Health Regulations, **2006:** 891–92; **2007:** 209–12, 738; **2008:** 1007
lawsuit against in Indonesia, **2008:** 245
Palestine Liberation Organization, status of, **1989-90:** 203, 204
pandemic influenza, strategy for, **2006:** 889–90; **2007:** 736–38
tobacco control. *See* Tobacco

World Intellectual Property Organization (WIPO), 1989-90: 416; **1991-99:** 699, 1469–70, 1507–17, 1645, 2170, 2180; **2000:** 298, 299, 740; **2001:** 791, 794; **2002:** 518; **2003:** 200, 702, 703, 831; **2005:** 689; **2006:** 399; **2007:** 608, 786; **2008:** 606, 609

World Meteorological Organization
amendments to preamble of convention, **2007:** 207

World Radiocommunication Conference (WRC), 2008: 160

World Shipping Council, 2002: 831

World Summit 2005, 2005: 110, 333, 375, 451, 458

World Summit on the Information Society (WSIS). *See* Information Society, World Summit on (WSIS)

World Trade Organization (WTO), 1991-99: 1453, 1491–92, 1731; **2006:** 737–54
- accession to
  - China, **1991-99:** 1460; **2001:** 649, 651–53; **2004:** 602; **2008:** 544, 545
  - Iraq, **2004:** 648, 650
  - Russia, **2006:** 751–52
  - Taiwan, **2001:** 649, 651–53
  - Ukraine, **2006:** 745–48
  - Vietnam, **2006:** 748–50
- agreements, **1991-99:** 1372–76
  - Agriculture, **2001:** 669, 670
    - Peace Clause, **2004:** 608–9
  - Antidumping, **2005:** 625, 630; **2006:** 743–44; **2008:** 545–46, 550–55
  - Basic Telecommunications Services, **1991-99:** 1378–81, 1475
  - Dispute Settlement Understanding, **2008:** 546, 560, 562–63, 565–67
  - Executive Branch authority to execute trade agreements, **1991-99:** 644–58
  - Financial Services, **1991-99:** 1376–78
  - General Agreement on Tariffs and Trade. *See* General Agreement on Tariffs and Trade (GATT)
  - Sanitary and Phytosanitary Measures (SPS Agreement), **2008:** 562, 564, 566
  - Subsidies and Countervailing Measures, **2005:** 622, 625, 628, 631–32, 636; **2007:** 573–74; **2008:** 561–62
  - Technical Barriers to Trade (TBT), **2007:** 575; **2008:** 350
  - Telecommunications Services, **1991-99:** 1378–81
  - Textiles and Clothing, **2005:** 642–43
  - Trade in Financial Services, **1991-99:** 1376–78

World Trade Organization (WTO) (continued)
Trade Related Aspects of Intellectual Property Rights. *See* Trade Related Aspects of Intellectual Property Rights (TRIPS Agreement)
agricultural policy and trade, **1991-99**: 934–37, 1372–73, 1381–89, 1395–97, 1401, 1403, 1408, 1410, 1414, 1419, 1439, 1443, 1501–5, 1784–90; **2001**: 647–51, 669–70; **2002**: 701–7; **2004**: 602–3, 608–10, 645; **2005**: 609–12, 617–18, 621–22; **2006**: 687, 737–39, 742, 753–54. *See also* dispute resolution, *this heading*
China, textile and apparel safeguards, **2004**: 612–15; **2005**: 642–46
Clean Diamond Trade Act waiver and, **2003**: 705
Cuban Liberty and Democratic Solidarity Act and (EU), **1991-99**: 101, 1445–48
dispute resolution, **1991-99**: 653–54, *655n*, 657–58, 1368–69, 1404–6; **2006**: 737–45; **2008**: 543–67
amicus curiae submissions, **2002**: 714–15; **2003**: 668
brought against U.S., **1991-99**: 1411–15, 1420; **2004**: 605–12; **2006**: 743–61; **2008**: 545–67
Antidumping Act of 1916, **2003**: 636, 655, 656; **2004**: 612; **2008**: 765
antidumping measures, oil country tubular goods (OCTG) (Mexico), **2005**: 634
antidumping measures, "zeroing" in dumping calculations, **2007**: 567–68
antidumping measures, "zeroing" in dumping calculations (EU), **2008**: 557
antidumping measures, "zeroing" in dumping calculations (Japan), **2006**: 743–44; **2008**: 557
antidumping measures, "zeroing" in dumping calculations (Mexico), **2008**: 545–57
Continued Dumping and Subsidy Offset Act of 2000 (CDSOA), **2003**: 655–57; **2004**: 606–7; **2005**: 626–27; **2006**: 707
copyright protection for music (EU), **2003**: 661–63
cotton subsidies (Brazil), **2003**: 663; **2004**: 608–10; **2005**: 633; **2008**: 557–62
cross-border supply of gambling and betting services, **2004**: 606–7; **2005**: 635; **2007**: 566–67
Cuban trademark provision (EU), **2002**: 672–76
Foreign Sales Corporation (FSC) tax provisions (EU), **2001**: 653–63; **2002**: 677–93; **2003**: 660–61; **2004**: 605–6, 645; **2005**: 625–26
gambling and betting service regulation (Antigua and Barbuda), **2003**: 663–64; **2004**: 610–11; **2005**: 635

World Trade Organization (WTO) (continued)
hormones in meat (EU), **2008:** 562–67
Japan, **2007:** 567–69
shrimp and sea turtles, **1991-99:** 1717–19; **2001:** 752–56, 759–60
softwood lumber from Canada, **2005:** 627–32; **2006:** 745. *See also* Canada
steel import policies (EU), **2002:** 670–72, 693–97; **2003:** 657–60
subsidies on large civil aircraft (EU), **2004:** 611; **2005:** 635–36
brought by U.S., **1991-99:** 1406–11, 1415–20; **2006:** 737–42; **2008:** 543–45
China: automobile parts, **2006:** 741–42; **2008:** 544–45
China: financial information services, **2008:** 543–44
China: intellectual property rights, **2007:** 563–64
China: prohibited subsidies, **2007:** 565–66
China: trading rights and distribution services for certain publications and audiovisual entertainment products, **2007:** 564–65
China: value-added tax on integrated circuits, **2004:** 601–2; **2005:** 620
European Union: bananas, **1991-99:** 1415–18; **2001:** 649–51
European Union: beef hormone case (with Canada), **1991-99:** 1418–20; **2004:** 645
European Union: biotech approvals, **2003:** 648–51; **2004:** 645; **2006:** 737–39
European Union: customs administration, **2006:** 739–40
European Union: on restrictions on registration of geographical indicators, **2003:** 651–52; **2005:** 621–22
European Union: steel restrictions, **2002:** 697
European Union: subsidies on large civil aircraft, **2004:** 603–4; **2005:** 622
Japan: apple importation, **2003:** 652–54; **2004:** 602–3; **2005:** 622–23
Mexico: antidumping measures on beef and rice, **2003:** 654–55; **2005:** 624–25
Mexico: antidumping measures on high-fructose corn syrup, **1991-99:** 1415
Mexico: telecommunications services, **2004:** 604–5; **2005:** 624
Turkey: rice imports, **2006:** 742
common law system, **2008:** 548
moratorium on, for HIV/AIDS and other health crises, **2002:** 715–18
procedures, U.S. proposals for, **1991-99:** 1393; **2002:** 711–15; **2003:** 664–73
role of dispute panels and Appellate Body, U.S. views on, **2008:** 547–49, 559–62, 564–67

World Trade Organization (WTO) (continued)
transparency in, **2002**: 711–15; **2003**: 664–68
U.S. policies and interests, **1991-99**: 1403–6
Doha declarations, **2001**: 646–49, 764; **2003**: 673, 808–11; **2005**: 607–19
agricultural policy and trade, **2006**: 753–54
Doha round of negotiations, **2002**: 697–711; **2004**: 618, 645; **2005**: 448, 607–19; **2006**: 687; **2007**: 569–71; **2008**: 567–70
environmental goods and services agreement (EGSA), **2007**: 576–79
fisheries subsidies, **2007**: 571–76
intellectual property rights, **2007**: 563–64
suspension of, **2006**: 753–54
environmental issues, **1991-99**: 1388–90, 1392, 1412–13; **2003**: 808–11; **2004**: 767–76
fisheries subsidies, **2005**: 612–13
establishment, **1991-99**: 1371–73, 1375–76, 1390–94. *See also* General Agreement on Tariffs and Trade (GATT); Uruguay Round
Free Trade Agreement of the Americas and, **1991-99**: 1438–41
GSP, linkage to, **2004**: 656
Millennium Round of negotiations, **1991-99**: 1395–1402
privileges and immunities, **1991-99**: 1314–15
on trade in information technology products, **1991-99**: 1523–26
U.S. policies and interests, **1991-99**: 1367–71, 1390–1402
WTO Committees, U.S. reports to, **1991-99**: 1381–90
World War II. *See also* Germany, *subheading*: World War II-era claims against; Holocaust
admissibility of petition to Inter-American Commission on Human Rights relating to events during, **2004**: 223–32
claims
against Albania, **2006**: 502–3
against Austria and Austrian companies, **1991-99**: 1134; **2000**: 485–89; **2001**: 388, 394–406, 417; **2002**: 417, 503–11; **2004**: 377, 432, 436, 446–48, 463–75, 494–95; **2005**: 397, 423*n*, 469–75, 485–90, 505, 542, 579, 777
compensation and restitution for, **1991-99**: 989–90, 1043–71, 1132–34; **2003**: 468–74; **2004**: 433–34, 438, 476
constitutionality of U.S. state law allowing, **2004**: 441–42
forced and slave labor claims, **1991-99**: 989–90, 1048–49, 1070–71, 1133–34, 1260–63; **2004**: 374, 441–45, 483, 485–87; **2005**: 480, 482, 484, 490
Foundation Agreement, **2004**: 432, 433–34, 435, 436, 437–39, 440–41; **2006**: 507–24; **2008**: 424–27

World War II (continued)
historical development, **2004**: 432–33
Hungarian Gold Train case, **2004**: 445–49
insurance claims, **1991-99**: 1049–50, 1051–52, 1066–67, 1069–70, 1071, 1133; **2001**: 413–17; **2004**: 442
Nazi persecution claims, **1991-99**: 1053–56, 1061–62
property claims, **1991-99**: 1051, 1077
restitution and claims based on, **1991-99**: 1045, 1048, 1053–56, 1061–62, 1070, 1192
restitution of looted gold, **1991-99**: 1043–46, 1047, 1056–61
sterilization claims, **2004**: 439–41
stolen art claims, **1991-99**: 1050–51, 1062–66, 1067–69
Foreign Sovereign Immunities Act and, **1991-99**: 1191–93, 1260–63; **2003**: 515–23; **2004**: 463–78. *See also* Foreign Sovereign Immunities Act (FSIA) (1976)
against France and French companies, **2001**: 406–13; **2004**: 476–78
against French banks, **2006**: 504–7
against Germany and German companies, **2000**: 449–89; **2001**: 386–93, 413–16; **2003**: 474–75; **2004**: 431–39, 474–75; **2006**: 507–17
compensation from Foundation precluding litigation, **2006**: 517–24; **2007**: 426
interest dispute over German company contributions, **2006**: 507–17; **2007**: 421–26
against Japan and Japanese companies, **2001**: 39–40*n*, 197*n*, 339–40*n*, 430–57; **2002**: 434–61
China/Taiwan World War II claims settlement with Japan, **2001**: 449–50
"comfort women," claims against Japan (sexual slavery), **2001**: 430–57; **2002**: 494–503; **2003**: 394, 396, 522–23; **2004**: 472, 475–81, 483; **2005**: 475–81
slave and forced labor of prisoners claims against Japanese corporations, **2000**: 500–40; **2001**: 197*n*, 339–40*n*, 447–48*n*; **2002**: 434–61; **2003**: 468–74; **2004**: 441–45
against the Russian Federation, **1991-99**: 1258
against Swiss banks, **1991-99**: 1051–52, 1134
against United States
for leaving individuals vulnerable on Pacific Islands, **2003**: 475–76
for Treaty of Peace with Japan as wrongful taking, **2003**: 476
U.S. state laws
California statute permitting forced labor claims, **2002**: 434–40; **2003**: 471–74; **2004**: 441–45

World War II (continued)
California's Holocaust victims' insurance legislation and, **2000**: 460–73; **2002**: 415–34; **2003**: 462–68; **2008**: 419, 422, 424
New Jersey's proposed Holocaust victims' insurance legislation and, **2001**: 413–17
preemption of state law by federal foreign affairs authority. *See* States, U.S., *subheading*: preemption of state action by federal foreign affairs authority
congressional declarations of war and, **1991-99**: 2155–56
enemy combatants, prosecution of, **2005**: 969
Holocaust-era archives, **2007**: 380–82
importation of World War II-era weapons, **1991-99**: 2256–62
International Commission on Holocaust Era Insurance Claims. *See* Holocaust
maritime salvage
captured World War II German submarines, **1991-99**: 1617–18
Japanese minisubmarine sunk off Pearl Harbor, **1991-99**: 1619–20
Nazi war crimes and crimes against humanity, **1989-90**: 99–100; **1991-99**: 517–18, 2080; **2000**: 445–89; **2004**: 374, 472–78
Fifth Amendment invoked by resident alien based on fear of prosecution abroad, **1991-99**: 571–76
Nuremberg International Military Tribunal, **2004**: 178, 357, 372, 374, 530
revocation of U.S. citizenship for participant in, **1991-99**: 27–34; **2002**: 5–8; **2003**: 5–11; **2004**: 1–4
U.S.–USSR memorandum of understanding on Nazi war criminals, **1989-90**: 99–100
nonjusticiable political question and, **1991-99**: 992–93; **2004**: 431–32, 434–36, 439–41, 443–44; **2005**: 476–81; **2006**: 507–17. *See also* President, U.S., *subheading*: separation of powers
protection of cultural heritage, including of victims of the Holocaust, bilateral agreements addressing, **1991-99**: 1793–94; **2008**: 734–37
service in Japanese armed forces and loss of U.S. citizenship, **1991-99**: 21–23
service of U.S. troops during, **1991-99**: 2022
Soviet lend-lease debt to U.S., **1991-99**: 1123–24
U.S.–German treaty on final settlement ending Allied occupation, **1989-90**: 138–42
against Vatican Bank, **2005**: 481–84
veterans of Philippines, **1989-90**: 12–13
Wallenberg case, **1989-90**: 277–91
WTO. *See* World Trade Organization (WTO)

Y

Yemen
- chancery offices, **2004**: 559–60
- immunity of diplomatic personnel, **2004**: 534–39
- immunity status of diplomatic staff dependents, **2003**: 574
- juvenile offenders, execution of, **2005**: 387
- killing of terrorists in, **2003**: 344–47
- North Korean missile shipment to, **2002**: 1052–57
- Proliferation Security Initiative (PSI), **2005**: 1098

Yugoslavia, Federal Republic of (Serbia and Montenegro). *See also* Kosovo
- American Servicemembers' Protection Act waiver, **2003**: 238
- Bosnia and Herzegovina peace agreement, **2004**: 1071–72
- claims against NATO member states in International Courts of Justice, **1991-99**: 2151–54; **2000**: 91
- compensation for bombing of Chinese Embassy in Belgrade, **2000**: 421–29
  - creation and claimed succession to Socialist Federal Republic of Yugoslavia, **1991-99**: 1146–48, 1162–69, 1979; **2000**: 561–75
- denial of U.S. visas and suspension of entry to certain nationals of, **1991-99**: 134–35, 147–49
- Draft International Convention on Human Rights and Measures of implementation, position on, **2005**: 300*n*
- human rights violations in, **1991-99**: 867
- military intervention and peacekeeping in Kosovo, **1991-99**: 2031–43, 2135–62
- nuclear fuel return program, **2004**: 1139
- relief from immigration requirements for certain resident nationals of, **1991-99**: 247
- sanctions against, **1991-99**: 1945–62; **2001**: 803–8
  - against Federal Republic of Yugoslavia and certain Serbian-controlled areas, **1991-99**: 1945–62
  - U.S. sanctions, **2003**: 930–34
- sovereign immunity under Foreign Sovereign Immunities Act, **2002**: 466–67, 491–92
- temporary protected status for nationals of Province of Kosovo, **1991-99**: 247–48
- territorial application of International Covenant on Civil and Political Rights, position on, **2005**: 299*n*
- treaties, succession to. *See* Treaties, generally
- unblocking of blocked assets of, **2002**: 897–900
- U.S. military action in Kosovo, **2000**: 758–65
- U.S. trade policy, **2004**: 654–59

Yugoslavia, Socialist Federation Republic of. *See also* International Criminal Tribunal for Former Yugoslavia (ICTY)
advance notice requirements for passage through territorial waters, **1989-90:** 446–47
agreement with U.S. resolving disputes (1964), **2002:** 632
humanitarian and peacekeeping operations after breakup of, **1991-99:** 2024–43, 2168–70
immunity of consular personnel from criminal prosecution, **1989-90:** 339–52
International Criminal Tribunal for. *See* International Criminal Tribunal for Former Yugoslavia (ICTY)
peace process, **1991-99:** 1979–82

Z
Zaire. *See also* Congo, Democratic Republic of
arms trade restrictions, **2004:** 1069–70
suspension of entry of certain aliens of, **1991-99:** 140–41
Zambia
extradition and mutual legal assistance, **2000:** 185*n*
women's justice program, U.S. assistance for, **2005:** 307–8
Zimbabwe
diplomatic immunity, **2004:** 539, 553–58
head-of-state and diplomatic immunity of government officials, **2001:** 510–31; **2006:** 681–82
extradition and mutual legal assistance, **1991-99:** 396; **2000:** 179; **2001:** 92*n*
Hague Child Abduction Convention, compliance with, **2003:** 127
human rights violations, **2001:** 319–26, 510–36; **2004:** 261, 405; **2005:** 453
citizens claim against Zimbabwean political party for, **2002:** 324–33
inviolability of government officials for service of process, **2001:** 531–36; **2006:** 681–82
money laundering, **2006:** 243
sanctions on, **2003:** 929–30; **2005:** 889; **2008:** 800–3
suspension of entry for certain persons from, **2002:** 22–24
UN Security Council, U.S. effort to obtain resolution concerning, **2008:** 803–5
trafficking in persons, **2006:** 228
U.S. embassy staff, protection of, **2008:** 495